Mod paper Design	Ink on Paper
Ch. 1, 2, 3, 4, 9, 5	Ch. 1
6 - div	2
8 - color	7 (proof)
9) makeup	3
10)	4
12	5
13	10
	11) Plates & color
	12)
	13)
	14) Gravure
	15) effect

Modern Newspaper Design

MODERN NEWSPAPER DESIGN

by Edmund C. Arnold

Editor, *Linotype News*
Chairman, Graphic Arts Department,
School of Journalism, Syracuse University

1817

HARPER & ROW, PUBLISHERS • New York, Evanston, and London

To Paul S. Swensson
*whom I admire as a newspaperman
and cherish as a friend*

Contents

Preface

NEWSPAPERMEN AND TEACHERS have much in common. This I have found out since combining the two professions a few years ago. Each is a communicator; each seeks the memorable phrase.

Some of such phrases have been labeled "Arnold's ancient axioms" by my students and some journalistic colleagues have since adopted the term.

This book is a companion to one I wrote a dozen years ago, *Functional Newspaper Design*. Both were written for the student as well as the professional journalist. I hope the latter will bear with some of the basic information conveyed herein, if for no other reason than that even the old pro benefits from reviewing the basics in the tackling pit or the batting cage.

I also hope both young and older readers will keep in mind ancient axiom number one: "Take all axioms with a grain of salt." For there are exceptions to all statements; the more general, the more exceptions.

But I believe that the axiom, the broad statement, the arbitrary premise, is the best way to stimulate the creative mind. When I state my premise, the reader can assess the logic that produced it. He may use my premise to test his own; he may accept or reject mine. But he always has a tangible gauge against which to measure his reaction. He is spared— I fervently hope—any doubt as to just what point of view the author holds.

That point of view has remained constant over these dozen years. It is that underneath the principle of typography is a deeper and far more important principle: The newspaper is a vital tool of democracy and the good life, and as such deserves the best skills, talent, and devotion that we can bring to it.

There have been modifications in the specifics of the point of view regarding typography. I have sometimes changed my mind. Sometimes this has been due to new facts learned from continuing and growing research in this area. Sometimes it has resulted from impeccable logic leveled at me by fellow newspapermen. Sometimes it's been due simply to the highly educative process of growing older. Sometimes it has been because I agree with Emerson, "What's the use of having a mind if you can't change it?"

About one thing I shall never change my mind. The longer I am in journalism, the more impressed I am with people who have ink on their fingers. I salute them for their professional skills and their personal integrity as I extend my thanks to the many, many who have contributed to this book.

My special thanks go to the editors and publishers who have provided me with the living examples of typography shown in this book—pages from their newspapers; to the staff of the American Press Institute, where I have—against some of the keenest minds in journalism—tested and tempered articulation of principles; to my academic colleagues, faculty and student, who have contributed insights as well as research findings; and to my wife, Viola, who did all the fearsome secretarial tasks attendant on the production of this book.

EDMUND C. ARNOLD
Syracuse, New York

Modern Newspaper Design

chapter 1

Functional Typography

THE NEWSPAPER TYPOGRAPHER is a communicator. His sole job is to use type as a tool for quick, accurate transmission of information.

"Designers" who work with type may use the handsome forms of the Latin alphabet as decoration or may arrange the lines and blocks of type as elements of abstract composition. Whether the type is—or even can be—read is immaterial to them. Not to the typographer, though; he considers unread type as a waste of costly materials, equipment, and manpower.

"My job," as the newspaper typographer defines it, "is to induce the buyer of my paper to read the first three paragraphs of a story. After that it's the responsibility of the writer and editor to keep the reader in the story. But until he has sampled the writing, he can't decide whether or not he wants to continue."

That sounds simple, but so does the whole theory of communications. Communication, says the theorist, requires a *sender* or *encoder,* a *message,* a *receiver* or *decoder,* and a *system* in which these three operate. (Italicized words and phrases here and throughout the book are defined in the Glossary.) In homelier terms, communication is football's forward pass. The encoder is the quarterback, the message is the ball, the decoder is the end, and the system is the gridiron. Unless the ball is properly caught, there is no forward pass; it is simply a wasted down. Unless a message is properly received by a reader, a listener, or a viewer, there is no communication; there is just a waste of ink, breath, or paint.

"Properly receiving" a message is more than just seeing type or hearing sounds. The message must be comprehended.

Unfortunately, the analogy of the football pass to newspaper communication is inaccurate in one major detail. The passer and receiver

1

work as a team; the receiver has a responsibility to catch the ball and will even hazard broken bones to accomplish his job. The potential receiver of a newspaper message has no such responsibility. He may read or not read as he well pleases. And even if he does choose to read, he is not obligated to concentrate sufficiently to comprehend the message. The only responsibility is that of the sender. Even in theory, however, that responsibility is overwhelming: Having led a horse to the water, just how *do* you make him drink?

In practice the sender's responsibility is not a bit less; indeed, there are two responsibilities, the economic and the social. Each is vital. The first responsibility of a newspaper as an entity is to make a profit. Without profit a newspaper cannot exist, and a dead newspaper can't serve a community, state, or nation. So the newspaper must live; profit is its lifeblood. The greater the profit, the more independent the newspaper can be against those pressures which might color or control the information the paper transmits. The second, but co-equal, responsibility of the newspaper is to be just that, a *news*paper. Its basic job is to provide its readers with that accurate, complete information without which a viable democracy cannot exist.

Profits are made only in the marketplace. For newspapers this marketplace is a crowded one; never have American papers faced competition as keen and numerous as today's.

At first glance, this statement may seem hyperbole or sheer inaccuracy. Isn't the number of newspapers decreasing slightly each year? Aren't "monopoly towns," with all their newspapers in single ownership, becoming more numerous? Aren't newspaper "groups" or "chains" proliferating? The answer is "yes" to each query. But that doesn't mean that competition is decreasing.

The newspaper competes for money, advertising, and circulation revenues. More important, it competes for the time, attention, and energy of an audience. Without that audience it will have neither advertising nor circulation. Competition for audience today is fierce.

Here newspapers do not basically compete against other newspapers. Their real competition is magazines, newsletters, direct-mail advertising, books, and correspondence, both business and social. More insidious are the nonprint media, radio and television. But there are even more competitors, for anything that a person may do in his leisure—from trout fishing to home-workshopping to attending Chamber of Commerce meetings—is in a sense a competitor to the newspaper.

Take the electronic media, for instance. Radio isn't too bad. You can listen and read a newspaper at the same time. Teenagers even insist that a transistor quivering at top decibels helps them with their homework. But television is an excluding medium; you can't watch and read simultaneously.

The worst effect of the electronic media, though, is the false impression they give, apparently successfully, that "a complete news report" can be given in 15—or even five—minutes. And this with the encroachment of commercials! The news that can be read in the dozen actual minutes of a quarter-hour broadcast is only about a column and a half of a newspaper! Yet the listener is assured that he has been given a complete report.

As a result, he may well wonder, if only subconsciously, why he need devote far more time to get such a complete report from his newspaper. And, he may wonder, why should he forgo the pleasant lethargy of sitting in front of the cathode tube, being spoonfed tiny mouthfuls of news, for the all too real expenditure of physical and mental energy that is required for reading—and thinking.

The editor must, then, reduce to a minimum the effort required to read his paper and reward that effort with enough information and pleasure to hold the reader, not only for the edition of the moment but for succeeding issues as well.

The best way to meet any competition is to offer a product that the consumer needs and wants. For the newspaper, that product is information. It is essential that the staff cover, report, write, and edit the news and attendant feature material at the highest level of quality.

The best typographic materials used by the best typographer will not for long veneer inadequacy of news content. Brilliant *display* may sell occasional readership, but for repeat business—as necessary to a newspaper as to a grocery—the content of the paper is the essential.

Only when the product itself is competitive does the packaging become important. Given two products of comparative excellence, the one that is best packaged will be the best seller. You need only to look at the shelves of a food store—better yet, at cosmetics in a department store—to see that packaging is of the utmost importance in today's marketplace.

That is what *typography* and *layout* are: the packaging of information. But they are more than that; they are also nonverbal communication (a rather pedantic phrase for which there is no workaday synonym). Good typography expands the verbal communication of copy, but it also communicates all by itself.

Typography has several meanings. The dictionary defines it as "the art of printing with types; the work of setting and arranging types and of printing from them; the general character or appearance of printed matter." For the purposes of this book, we shall define typography as "a set of principles for the use of printing elements." (A *printing element* is anything that puts ink on paper; it may be as small as a period in a font of agate type or as large as a full-page halftone.)

Layout is the application of typographic principles to specific problems of news presentation.

Having defined the two terms with which this book is concerned, we must define the special problems of the newspaperman as he uses typographic art and skill.

Newspaper editors have three distinct sets of problems, corresponding to their three distinct jobs. The typical newspaperman probably won't take it as a compliment to be called an artist, a manufacturer, or a merchandiser. Yet he is each of these, and he usually is all three at once.

First, the editor is an artist. He is a communicator, and communicators are artists, creative people, whether their medium is a news story, novel, poem, symphony, or oil painting. We shall often note in this book the striking parallels between communication by printing and by other artistic forms.

As a communicator, the editor has a whole complement of problems. Not the least of these is that the reader would often prefer not to receive the message. As we've already noted, in newspaper communication the responsibility of completing the pass is solely the sender's.

Failure to complete the communications process brings penalties. Incomplete communication may send a friend on a wild goose chase when he fails to receive adequate instructions on how to reach an isolated hunting lodge. It may send a school chemistry lab up in an explosion because a student misunderstood which chemicals to mix in a test tube. It may result in the total demise of Custer's cavalry because Benteen didn't complete the communicative process with his military orders.

But if a newspaperman fails to communicate adequately, the consequences may be even more catastrophic. A free journalist in a free society assumes the responsibility of informing his readers so thoroughly that they can act intelligently and from knowledge when called upon to make the decisions required constantly in a democracy. This knowledge is often distasteful to the reader. Every editor has had a reader tell him, "I'm tired of reading about a new crisis in the Far East, another confrontation in Europe, higher taxes, rising prices, riots and murder. I've

The Clymer Independent.

WAYNE E. MORRISON, SR., PROPRIETOR & EDITOR. TERMS — $3.00 PER YEAR, STRICTLY IN ADVANCE.

An Independent Newspaper - - Devoted to Clymer Home Life and the Family Circle.

VOL. XXI, NO. 36. CLYMER, CHAUTAUQUA CO., N. Y., THURSDAY, SEPTEM'R. 5, 1968. WHOLE NO. 1,082.

THE ELECTION.

CHARTER PROPOSED FOR COUNTY GOVERNMENT.

VOTE SET FOR TUESDAY.

The Towns of Clymer, French Creek, Harmony and a portion of North Harmony will be represented by only one person on the new Chautauqua County Legislature if the electors of the county approve a charter form of government at a special election next Tuesday. The thirty-seven member County Board of Supervisors, in session since the formation of the county in 1811, would be abandoned under the proposition and an elected Legislature of twenty-nine persons would take its place.

The City of Jamestown, with a representation of six, would be given an increase of an additional two, in the effective date of the charter which has been set at January 1, 1970. Should the Charter be approved, an appointed County Manager would head the new form of government, and citizens of the county no longer would have the opportunity to elect the County Treasurer or four Coroners, but would elect an Auditor, a post now held through appointment.

The charter has been drawn, it was explained, to meet the so called "one man—one vote" decision of the Supreme Court, which has been carried down to the county level. The twenty-nine legislators would represent approximately 5,080 residents, and their election would in no way, at present, effect the existing Town Supervisor Office, with the exception that the Supervisor could not represent his town at the county level. The proposal calls for twenty-nine members elected from seventeen single-member districts and six two-member districts.

The local district (District No. 8) would be one of two in the plans, where four townships would be forced into a single district to be represented by one man in the County Legislature.

SOLDIER OF THE MONTH.

Army Specialist Four Donald E. Proctor, son of Mr. and Mrs. Lee E. Proctor, who reside near Corry, Penn'a., was named Soldier Of The Month for Fort Buckner, Okinawa, on Saturday, August 17th. A petroleum lab specialist in the 398th Quartermaster Co., Spec. Proctor was selected for his soldierly appearance, knowledge and performance of duties, and military courtesy.

He entered the United States Army in January of 1967, completed basic training at Fort

CLYMER FIRE ALARMS.

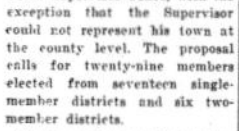

Saturday, October 22, 4:15 p. m.

Barn destroyed on the Jim Samee place near North Clymer.

Tuesday, October 25th, 1:25 p. m.

Pasture grass fire on the Glen Holthouse farm.

The Republican

LIST OF NOMINATIONS.

For The November Election.

— For President —

RICHARD M. NIXON

Of New-York.

: o :

— For Vice-President —

SPIRO T. AGNEW

Of Maryland.

HUNTER INVESTMENT AS'N. CO-SPONSORS REGATTA.

The Buffalo Boat Racing Association and the Chautauqua County Hunter Investment Association, with the cooperation of local Cattaraugus County officials, will co-sponsor the First Annual Cornplanter Regatta at the Onoville Boat Launching Ramp of the Allegany Resevoir of the Kinzua Dam on Sunday afternoon, September 8th, commencing at one o'clock. Along with providing the public with the opportunity of seeing spectacular boat racing filled with thrills and spills, the visitors will be able to see the beautiful boating facilities available in the scenic setting in what is planned to be the first annual affair for the two organizations.

The Schedule of Events calls for twenty heats of racing, ten for hydroplanes and ten for the utility outboard, with the special feature for the day the nine to fourteen year age classes. According to Commodore Chet Polowy, upwards of one hundred entries will be included in the Regatta, featuring some of the best drivers in the eastern United States and Canada. The Junior Classes will feature Glenn Tate of Endwill, the leading J Stock Hydro Driver and Little Beth Ann Chalk of Fishers Landing in the J Utility.

Wayne Pobest of Ottawa, Ontario, will be seen in the B Utility as the current top man in his class and Gordy McGrady of Brockville, Ontario, will flash along in his front running A Utility. Also included will be Doug Nelson of Catskill, who has been leading the boys in the B Stock Hydro, John Stone of Rochester, the leader in regional high points in both the C & D Stock Hydros and a leading contender for the national crown, and Dick Sommerfelt of Toronto, Ontario, high utility man in both C & D Utility and the leader for national honors in his class.

The local police and fire departments will extend their full cooperation to make the event pleasant for all concerned. The Sheriff's Office, with waterway patrols in the area, will also assist.

Mr. and Mrs. Clayton Duink held a family dinner on Monday, August 26th, to celebrate the eighth birthday of their daughter Elaine. Present were Mr. and Mrs. Lewis Duink, Jerrold Duink, Mr. and Mrs. Andrew Hutton, Bruce and Mary Lou, and Mr. and Mrs. Earl Duink, Linda and Larry.

AN ACCIDENT.

TWO MEN INVOLVED IN FINDLEY LAKE CRASH.

ESCAPES SERIOUS INJURY.

Two elderly men were injured in a two car accident on Shadyside Road, Findley Lake, about seven-thirty o'clock last Thursday evening. Deputy William A. Tornstrom of the Chautauqua County Sheriff's Office, who investigated, reported that an automobile operated by Milton B. Chesley, age 83, of Findley Lake, was involved in a collision with an oncoming car driven by Robert H. Kelly, age 71, of Erie, Penn'a., as Mr. Kelly was turning into a driveway.

Mr. Chesley sustained an elbow injury and Mr. Kelly a hand laceration. Both men said that they would see their physician.

Michael F. Baker, age 17, of Troy, Penn'a., was arraigned and fined $35 last Thursday morning before Justice of the Peace Craig Kinney of the Town of Mina, after he pleaded guilty to a charge of leaving the scene of an accident. The youth was taken into custody by Deputies John R. Scorse and Jerome G. Adams of the Chautauqua County Sheriff's Office, after they reported that his car had struck a number of newspaper delivery tubes in the Findley Lake area.

NOMINATED.

Vice President Hubert H. Humphrey of Minnesota received the Democrat nomination for President of the United States of America on the first ballot of the Convention at Chicago, Illinois, last week. Senator Edmund S. Muskie of Maine received the party nomination for Vice President.

CLYMER FIRE ALARMS.

— No Fires This Week —

THE PROJECT

EXPLORATORY MEETING IS HELD ON POND IMPROVEM'T.

DEVELOPMENTS AWAITED.

A group of twenty interested persons met with representatives of the Southwestern New York Resources and Conservation Development Project at the Dutch Village Restaurant last Tuesday evening to discuss cleaning up the pond in this village and the acquesition of State and Federal funds to aid in the work. Supervisor Arthur Goggin, representing the Town Board, conducted the exploratory session.

Robert Wiltsie and Homer Senett of Jamestown, representing the Development Project, explained recreational and conservation usages for the pond, and said that the possibility exists of making a survey by an engineer at no cost to the Town providing it has a clear title to land around the pond, that the dam is sufficient, and that pollution can be haulted.

Further investigation will be made into the matter with the hope that the eyesore can be put back into use, if necessary on a part-at-a-time basis. Other groups represented included the Community Club and Businessmen.

Try An Independent Ad.

THE DEMOCRAT

LIST OF NOMINATIONS.

For The November Election.

— For President —

HUBERT W. HUMPHREY

Of Minnesota.

: o :

— For Vice-President —

EDMUND S. MUSKIE

Of Maine.

3% COUNTY SALES TAX NOW IN EFFECT.

The enactment of a three per cent. County Sales Tax by the Chautauqua County Board of Supervisors took effect on Sunday, September 1st. The legislation, seen as returning a minimum of six million dollars annually for application in lowering real property taxes, calls for fifty per cent. of the receipts to be retained by the County with the remainder divided among the Towns and Cities. The measure was originally approved by the Board of Supervisors on Friday afternoon, May 10th, by a vote of 26 to 9.

Enacted despite widespread citizen criticism, it can be viewed clearly now as another Republican tax scheme, perhaps one of the most regressive yet enacted. Voting against it were Supervisors Arthur Goggin of Clymer, Joseph Lepkowski of French Creek, James Ferris of Mina, Clifford Briggs of Stockton, Perryy Colburn of Charlotte, Donald Crowell of Villenova, Herbert L. Johnson of Arkwright and Newell McCroskey and Chester Tarnowski, both of Dunkirk.

The Finance Committee, which made the proposal, agreed that the County's share of the tax will go "toward reducing the present County Tax." Revenues allocated to the Towns and Cities also has been proposed for use in reducing local taxes. The Finance Committee of the Board, entirely of Republicans, is composed of Daniel F. Lincoln of Jamestown, Leon E. Button of Harmony, Newell McCrosky of Dunkirk, Stewart Dudley of Pomfret, Robert A. Owens of Westfield, Frederick E. Mattison of Ellicott and Hamilton H. Clothier of Hanover. County Treasurer Robert H. Miller is Committee Secretary.

Officials at Jamestown, facing a financial crisis in city government, met last spring with County representatives to discuss the possibility of a Sales Tax, but there was no indication in the Finance Committee action that these sessions influenced their decision to call for the tax. A surprise in the measure came with the omission of a portion for education. It was felt by the committee that schools have a broader tax base and already receive substantial State Aid.

The measure levies the three per cent. sales tax on specifically the same items affected by the present New York State Sales Tax. Collection will be made through the State Tax Division in Albany, with about a one per cent. administrative charge, with revenues remitted quarterly. The two combined taxes are the highest allowed under present New York State Lak, which establishes a maximum Sales Tax of five per cent.

ISSUE REPORT.

LOCAL STUDENTS RESUME CLASSES SEPTEMBER 4TH.

ENROLLMENT INCREASES.

Schools in the Clymer Central School District re-opened on Wednesday, September 4th, with an all day session, except for Kindergarten pupils, who were registered on Wednesday morning and began their first full day session today. According to Hubert W. Brown, Supervising Principal, total enrollment stands at 831 pupils, up from the 813 figure the year before, with 751 at Clymer and 80 at Findley Lake. The report showed 51 in Kindergarten at Clymer and 19 at Findley Lake.

A lunch was served in the Cafeterias at both Clymer and Findley Lake on Wednesday with the prices on all meals increased three cents to cover increased costs of food, labor and milk. The price of white milk remains the same at three cents per half pint, but the price of chocolate milk has been raised to five cents per half pint. A meal ticket will cost $1.50 in advance for grades Kindergarten through Eight, covering the cost of a daily lunch and a bottle of white milk during the milk break for grades Kindergarten through Six.

The bus routes and time schedule will be the same as last year. Pupils who ride on the buses are expected to return home on their regular bus unless they have a note from their parents for any change. All students are expected to remain on the school grounds during the school day unless they have a note to go downtown. If the permission to go downtown at noon is for all year, it should be stated in the note. When a student returns to school after an absence or tardiness, an excuse from a parent should be brought stating the reason for the absence. If a student is to be excused early, he should bring a note signed by a parent stating the reason.

The Vocational Classes at Lakewood and Sherman will commence on Thursday, September 5th, and all vocational students attended the session at Clymer the day before. Students who will be attending Special Education Classes in Panama and Ashville and those students scheduled for adjustment classes will be notified by mail of their starting date and time.

WELFARE AID RECEIVED.

Comptroller Arthur Levitt of the State of New York announced in Albany today the distribution of $32,969,900.00 for the month of September, 1968, to sixty-three Public Welfare Districts in the state. These monies represent the Federal and State shares of

THE CONSERVATIVE

LIST OF NOMINATIONS.

For The November Election.

— For Congressman —

LLOYD R. MURPHY

Of Allegany, Allegany Co.

The Proposed Chautauqua County Charter.

ARGUMENTS AGAINST.	ARGUMENTS FOR.
✝1. *The voters have only one vote on all issues, ie. reapportionment, new structure of government, appointed County Manager, and the other combined issues.*	✝1. *Voting on separate issues might not give a clear majority for one form of County government.*
✝2. *The Charter is not necessary to reapportion because reapportionment is mandated.*	✝2. *Present County government is illegal because it is not reapportioned.*
✝3. *The Charter opens the way for more expensive government. A number of new positions would be added to the payroll.*	✝3. *Any additional cost will provide effecient administration of the services the public demands.*
✝4. *Severs the tie between the Town and County government. Present Supervisors, outside the cities, serve on both Boards.*	✝4. *Town and County government have different problems.*
✝5. *An appointed Manager is remote from and not responsive to the public.*	✝5. *The County Manager should be appointed on the basis of experience and ability to carry out the policies of the County Legislature.*
✝6. *An elected Co. Manager would have to meet the people and learn their needs. His power would come from the voters.*	✝6. *Campaigning for election is a time-consuming expensive popularity contest.*
✝7. *A Board of non-professional Legislators might become a rubber stamp for the County Manager.*	✝7. *An elected Board would be a legislative, appropriating and policy making body.*

Fig. 1. Nineteenth-century style is cultivated by *Clymer* (N.Y.) *Independent* to reflect historic era and area.

got enough troubles of my own; why do you bother me with new ones in your paper?" Unfortunately, he must be bothered. "Man must choose between freedom and repose," said Jefferson. "He can't have both."

So it is the duty of a journalist to make sure that his readers do not sink into the repose of ignorance and thereby lose their freedoms. This may sound like flag-waving and starry-eyed idealism. Unfortunately, there are at this very moment brave newspapermen who are in dictators' jails—or even in the grave—because they faced the hard practicalities of their self-assumed responsibilities.

As soon as a piece of copy leaves the editorial desk, it goes to a factory, and so the editor is also a construction boss.

Despite the reluctance of most editors to acknowledge it, a newspaper plant is truly a factory. It manufactures a product at a cost and sells it at a price; the margin between is profit. Without some profit a newspaper cannot live; without a reasonable one, it cannot serve its community with adequacy or freedom.

Except on smaller weeklies where he can personally take part in each of the intricate steps of producing a newspaper, the editor doesn't operate a *Linotype* or press or make up his pages on the stone. Yet he must be as familiar with all the processes, their potentials and their problems, as an architect is with the construction business. Unless an architect knows how his blueprints are translated into steel and concrete, he cannot efficiently plan a building.

The blueprints the editor sends to the composing room directly affect the capabilities and efficiency of the mechanical departments. He cannot afford to waste their time on impractical tasks, nor can he demand less than professional standards from them.

The editor's third job is that of the merchant. He is constantly engaged in selling. He must sell the potential reader on picking up the newspaper in a cash transaction, off a newsstand or by subscription. He must sell the purchaser on the idea of reading all of the newspaper. He must sell advertising space. He must sell the reader on scrutinizing the ads. None of these things does he do personally. He does them—at a distance—by sales pitches that he builds into his newspaper.

To solve any of these problems is a man-sized job in itself. To solve all three sets of problems simultaneously is a staggering task. Yet the editor does them constantly, and with few exceptions he does them well.

A major tool for all three jobs is functional newspaper design. While this stone may not kill all three birds, it will whomp them quite satisfactorily.

Newspaper design is a combination of typography and layout; the arts and skills of photography, platemaking, and printing; and the effective use of machinery, equipment, and techniques in all of the mechanical departments of a newspaper. The newspaper designer must be intimately familiar with each department on the news and advertising sides of the paper as well as of the *back shop,* the mechanical department. He must combine a sense of esthetics with the hard practicality of the efficiency expert. He must be a working psychologist, melding many people with disparate skills and talents into a smoothly operating team. By its very catchall nature, newspaper design defies a neat academic definition.

Nor does functional newspaper design lend itself to epigrammatic definition. It is a philosophy that insists that every printing element and every arrangement of such elements perform a necessary job in the most efficient manner.

The yardsticks of *functionalism* are two questions which should be directed to every element, no matter how small or inconspicuous:

Does this element do a necessary job?

Can this job be done better, quicker, more efficiently, more profitably?

If the answer to the first is "No, the job is not necessary," that element should be thrown into the *hellbox* as quickly as possible.

Noncommunicative elements in a communications system are called *noise* by the theorists. One kind of noise, for example, is the static in a radio system. Static might be the eardrum-battering crash of an electric storm, or it may be a continuous, low, not unpleasant hum. But whatever its nature, static blurs the radio message.

So typographic static—noncommunicative elements—obscures the printed message, and a communicator simply can't afford to have the reader's attention distracted by nonfunctional noise.

Nor can the manufacturer afford to produce anything that cannot be converted into a profit, nor a merchandiser afford to disguise the sales appeal of a juicy lamb chop by too much parsley.

But if the first answer is "Yes, this is a necessary job," then we ask the second question, "How can we do this job better?"

Even casual inspection of newspaper files for the past three decades will show how dramatically the appearance of the typical American newspaper has been changed by application of the criteria of functionalism. Look at the typical *headline* complex of the 1930's. There was a *stepped head,* a *jim-dash,* an *inverted pyramid,* another jim-dash, a *crossline,* a dash again, perhaps a repetition of one or more of the *decks,* and, finally, the story.

To determine whether the theory of functionalism actually worked, early researchers directed their attention to the most inconsequential element in the complex, the jim-dash, a piece of *hairline* rule about 2 or 3 picas wide. When the first question, "Does this do a good job?" was asked, the answer was dull silence. Nobody knew what the dash was supposed to do, much less whether it actually did it. So the automatic reaction was, "Into the hellbox!" (Unlike the defendant in an American court of law, the typographic element must bear the burden of proof. It must do a demonstrably good job to survive the first question.)

With the elimination of these tiny jim-dashes, a plus was racked up in each of the three problem areas. The product was improved as a communication; the composing room was spared needless work (and thus expense); the sales appeal of the newspaper increased.

This sounds like the claim of a snake-oil peddler. But it is true. Let's examine these results and see whether the claims are valid.

The function of the headline, as of every display element and technique in a newspaper, is to direct the reader into body type. If our potential receiver reads only headlines and pictures, he is not well informed. Probably he is not buying our advertisers' merchandise in the ads and isn't a lively prospect for buying the next issue of our paper. Body type carries the overwhelming percentage of the information in a newspaper, and we must make sure that the reader consumes as much body type as he can with his quota of time, energy, and attention.

By eliminating jim-dashes within the headline, we speed the reading eye down to the body type. Granted, it doesn't take a lengthy period to "read" a jim-dash. But it does take some time, and even infinitesimal increments can add up to an appreciable total when they are used again and again.

But the real advantage in eliminating the dashes points up a fundamental truth of typography: Rarely do we find a nonfunctional element; almost invariably the nonfunctional is also the malfunctional.

If an element fails to do a good job, it usually does something that is bad. So with the jim-dash. Each of these tiny strokes is a barrier in the path of the reading eye, and any barrier, no matter how slight, slows the reading process.

When the eye is reading at a normal, efficient cruising speed, it sweeps back and forth almost like a pendulum. The smoother this motion, the more energy and attention the reader can devote to receiving the message. But when the eye hits a barrier, it is irritated, almost physically hurt. Worse, having passed the barrier, the eye only gradually smooths off a bumpy stride into an easy lope.

An appropriate analogy is the difference between driving a hundred miles on a freeway or on a local road. The time differential may be as much as an hour. Now the driver doesn't spend those 60 minutes waiting for red lights to turn green; the waste of time is in shifting gears and regaining cruising speed.

So elimination of the jim-dash has removed a barrier that, however slight, has lowered the reader's efficiency. We now do have better communication.

We also have a better manufacturing operation. The major wear on a Linotype is in the casting process, and it takes as much time and wears out as much machinery to cast a 3-em dash as it does to cast a 30-pica line of headletters. Eliminating dashes postpones the wearing out of machinery and thereby increases profit.

We have a more salable product when we use white space instead of nonfunctional ink. The reader describes a newspaper from which the nonfunctional has been stripped as "streamlined," or "clean," or "airy." Each of these is a compliment. The simplified style appeals to the reader's esthetic sense and persuades him to buy and read the paper.

By the same application of the criteria of functionalism, editors have eliminated most secondary decks in the headline. They have found that when the main head fails to lure the reader, rarely will decks attract him into the story. Indeed, decks may be malfunctional. If decks tell too much, the reader may feel that he already knows all about the story and may thus be encouraged not to read *body* type.

Here functionalism has resulted in reducing a job to its required minimum; all nonessential work and the elements that performed it have been eliminated. Product and production are improved.

In other applications of functionalism—converting four-sided boxes into sideless boxes, adopting flush-left headlines—the quality of the product remains constant but the production is markedly simplified. In another example, moving an *overline* from above to below a cut, where it becomes a *catchline,* the production steps remain the same but the quality of the product is improved. We shall look at these elements in detail in later chapters.

Functionalism, of course, extends far beyond the area of typography. It can be applied usefully to all editorial functions. Let's look at only one example, and this because it is involved in typography to some extent.

Periodic economy drives in any newspaper plant invariably focus attention on *overset,* unusable type so timely it cannot be saved for future editions. Obviously this is a waste of effort and material that erodes profits. Minimizing overset is an important responsibility of the copy desk. Yet this admirable objective can backfire. Too often something like this happens:

When the editor reaches his desk at the start of the day's cycle, he finds a long continuing story on his desk. He knows that there will be later developments that may require a new *leed*. So he holds the copy until the new leed comes through, edits it, and sends it to the composing room. He uses all the type and congratulates himself on avoiding overset. Yet this might not have been the most efficient way of handling the story.

In almost every composing room, we have "expensive time" and (relatively) "inexpensive time." Costly time is when the capacity of typesetting machines and men are strained to the utmost; cheaper time is during those periods of relative calm, when often a Linotype stands idle because of lack of copy.

Now if the desk had sent the complete, long story out for setting during cheap time, it need send out only the new leed during expensive time. The old typeset leed could be discarded and replaced by the new one. This would require more lines of type to be set, for the old leed would be overset. However, the total cost in time for the whole job would be less than when it is completely set on expensive time.

This accounting system may appear to have discrepancies. Unless the total work goes into overtime, how can simple distribution of work affect the total cost?

Composing rooms must be manned for peak demand. Every time a piece of copysetting is postponed from slack time to the maximum-demand period, it increases that demand and requires a larger work force to meet it. If typesetting could be distributed so no man ever sat idle, the total number of compositors could obviously be decreased.

Another important function of the copy desk is to maintain as consistent as possible a flow of copy to the linecasting machines. The nature of newspaper production inevitably creates peaks and valleys of demand on the composing room. But close copy control can bring this sharply fluctuating curve closer to a straight line even though the demand can never be kept exactly the same throughout the cycle.

A good *copy log* is an essential tool for the editor. This may be as elaborate or as casual as the desk desires. But it ought to be reevaluated from time to time to make sure that it is adequate for the needs of the moment. Minor changes may increase its usefulness to a major extent.

To maintain a log, the desk must have a simple way of converting reporters' copy into *column-inches*. This requires a couple of constants.

Fig. 1-B. Early American newspaper design. *Louisville* (Ga.) *Gazette,* founded in 1799, needed no headlines to build readership. Page size: 10 x 14½ inches. *Cherokee Phoenix* of New Echota, Ga., was bilingual, using Latin alphabet for English copy and, for Cherokee language, syllabary invented by great chief Sequoiah. Page size: approximately that of *Gazette.*

Typewritten copy will be double-spaced, of course, and that gives three lines per vertical inch of the sheet.

If the newspaper's body type is 8 on 9, there will be eight lines in a column-inch. Typically, there will be 31½ characters in an 11-pica line of body type, or 252 in a column-inch. The typewritten line should be established so it can convert easily. If it is set to 63 spaces, each vertical inch on the typewritten copy will make 2 column-inches in print. The copyreader need only measure the depth of a story and multiply by 2 to know the column-inches to note on the copy log. *Wire copy* can be converted just as readily.

All typewriters give three double-spaced lines per vertical inch. To find the number of type lines per column-inch, divide the depth of the slug—the type point size plus *ledding*—into 72 points. If type is set 8 on 8½, there will be 8.4 lines per column-inch (72 ÷ 8½). The number of characters per line of type can be determined by counting them on proofs or by using data from Mergenthaler Linotype Company's character-per-pica method of *copy fitting*. This is determined by the *lower-case-alphabet length* (*lca*) of the face.

A face with an lca of 111 points has an average of 3 characters per pica; that with an lca of 118 points has 2.85 characters per pica (*cpp*). Other data include:

$$116 \text{ lca} = 2.9 \text{ cpp}$$
$$120 \text{ lca} = 2.8 \text{ cpp}$$
$$122 \text{ lca} = 2.75 \text{ cpp}$$
$$127 \text{ lca} = 2.65 \text{ cpp.}$$

Now to determine the *copy factor,* the number which will convert the length of typewriter copy into the length of the equivalent body type.

Let's assume that the newspaper is setting editorial or feature pages in 14-pica lines, using a 9-point body type on a 10-point slug. The face has an lca of 127 points. One column-inch of type is 72 points deep. One line of this type is 10 points deep. So there are 7.2 lines of type per column-inch. A lowercase alphabet length of 127 points has 2.65 characters per pica, as indicated by the little chart two paragraphs ago. Our line (14 picas × 2.65) has 37.1 characters of type. (Be sure to hold the fraction; in a whole column of news matter, the fractions may accumulate to a substantial total.)

Now, by simple multiplication:

$$\begin{array}{ccccc} \text{Lines of type} & & \text{Type characters} & & \text{Type characters} \\ \text{per inch} & \times & \text{per line} & = & \text{per column-inch} \\ 7.2 & \times & 37.1 & = & 267.12 \end{array}$$

(Here we drop the fraction as insignificant in its final, nonrepetitive use.)

By the same method we find the number of characters in a column-inch of typewritten copy:

$$\begin{array}{ccccc} \text{Typewriter lines} & & \text{Characters per line} & & \text{Typewriter characters} \\ \text{per inch} & \times & \text{of typewriting} & = & \text{per vertical inch} \\ 3 & \times & 63 & = & 189 \end{array}$$

$$\begin{array}{ccccc} \text{Typewriter characters} & & \text{Type characters per} & & \\ \text{per vertical inch} & \div & \text{column inch} & = & \text{Copy factor} \\ 189 & \div & 267 & = & .7 \end{array}$$

A simple variation of this process puts the copy factor to use:

$$\text{Inches of typewritten copy} \times \text{Copy factor} = \text{Inches of type}$$

A typical story of 1½ pages would be 16 inches deep. To find out how much type this would make:

$$\begin{array}{c} \text{16 inches of type-} \\ \text{written copy} \end{array} \times \begin{array}{c} \text{Copy factor} \\ (.7) \end{array} = \begin{array}{c} \text{11.2 inches} \\ \text{of type} \end{array}$$

A new copy factor is required for each type-line length and/or each different lca, but this isn't nearly as complicated as it may appear. If decimals decimate you, have your bookkeeper work out the factor. Then use it. An accurate copy conversion will prove an invaluable tool to the desk and the composing room, too.

An efficient copy log is simply a list of consecutive numbers, in descending order, down a strip of paper with adjacent room for recording copy that has been sent to the composing room.

Let's assume that the numbers begin with 300, 299, 298, etc. Each number represents 1 column-inch of space. By inspecting page dummies from the advertising department or by communication from the person who decides the editorial hole for the issue, the editor knows how much space is available to him. He draws a line at that point on his log.

Let's assume that it is 287 inches.

The first story he handles makes 8 column-inches. He draws a line through 279 and, at the right, he writes the *slug line* of the copy. If there is anything unusual about the setting, he indicates that, too. Perhaps the copy is set 1½- or 2-column measure; maybe it has a 2-column leed; perhaps it is in *boldface*.

He writes a 3-line 24-point *head*. This will occupy 1 inch, so he draws a line through 278 and writes in the slug of the head and its specifications. A picture takes 16 inches and he crosses off 262, noting the slug and the dimensions of the engraving. Catchline and cutlines take 3 inches, and his running total comes down to 259.

The lowest marked number indicates the space still available. When that number becomes very low or when the deadline is near, the editor can begin making accommodations. If he knows a long story is still out and that it will use all, most of, or more than the remaining space, he can consult the copy log and decide which stories might be held for a later issue, which can be cut, or which discarded. On the rare occasions when he isn't using all his space, he can check to see what *evergreen* type (stories with no time factor) may be on the *bank* (stored in the composing room) or in his desk drawer.

He uses the log for dummying up and checking on the kinds of heads that have been written or that might be needed. If the log shows a great many 2-column heads, he may ask the *rim,* the subordinate editors, to write more 1- or 3-columners. If there aren't enough heads of a size sufficient to anchor inside pages, the fact is readily apparent and corrective steps can be taken before a minor emergency arises on the makeup *stone.*

Such a copy log is a flexible tool and imposes no burden on the desk. It can readily be modified to suit the needs or wants of a specific newspaper. For large papers, the beginning number may be higher, and instead of 1-inch increments, the gauge may show 2-inch, or even larger, steps. Each department can have its own log. The managing editor then can tell how much space is available on women's or sports pages, and if he needs to know how much is open in the whole paper, he can add up individual numbers easily.

Deskmen soon devise simple marks to note other details—for instance, whether a picture is self-contained or whether it accompanies a story. A scrawled V, lying on its side, can show the direction of *lines of force,* the way a picture is facing. *Sidebars* can easily be linked to their main stories. Body type set in measure other than 1-column should be tagged so it can be dummied into a wide enough area. The log might remind the editor that he's planning to handle a story in 1-up or a sideless box.

At 5- or 10-minute intervals, a red line is drawn across the log and the time noted. An unusually small amount of copy sent out during such an interval may indicate a bottleneck that must be broken promptly. The best way to avoid the intense demands of peak production is to avoid valleys in the production rate. If such periods of low copy-desk production occur daily and at about the same time in the cycle, the editor is warned against a chronically bad condition that demands immediate therapy.

A good copy log can also be a major factor in smooth news-mechanical teamwork.

The desk and the composing room are a closely linked team. This relationship cannot be overemphasized. The good newspaper manager will make it a continuing preoccupation to keep relations smooth. Unfortunately, in some newspaper plants, there is a serious lack of harmony between these two departments.

This is really not too surprising. Each department is made up of skilled craftsmen, creative people aware and proud of their talents. It should come as no shock that the prima donna attitude should rear its head on occasion. Both departments work under deadline pressures.

SUFFOLK SUN

Sunny, of Course

Sunny but cold. High about 46 today. Overnight low 25, Northeast winds, 10 mph. Milder Tuesday. Complete weather on 2-A.

VOL. 1, NUMBER — SERVING SUFFOLK COUNTY, LONG ISLAND, MONDAY, NOVEMBER 21, 1966 — 40 cents a week home delivered — TEN CENTS

Welfare Chiseling? Some Call It Survival

By JON MARGOLIS
Sun Staff Writer

When the Suffolk County Board of Supervisors last week adopted the highest budget in the county's history, the most expensive single item was $45 million for public welfare. The measure was accompanied by a chorus of political and citizen grumbling over "welfare chiselers."

A few hours after the adoption, a welfare chiseler, a 34-year old woman who here will be called Jane, began her nightly job as a waitress in a working man's bar in a poor area.

Jane is not typical of Suffolk County's welfare clients, but, perhaps more important, she is typical of what many people think is typical of welfare recipients. She is a Negro, and the mother of an illegitimate child. And although her job is both demanding and legitimate, she is cheating the taxpayers with every penny she earns.

Jane is a chiseler because she has not told the Welfare Department, which pays her $300 each month, that she earns $240 a month at her job. If she did, the department would cut her welfare payment to $60, because routine investigation has shown that this is all she needs.

Before Jane is judged, however, it should be noted that she did not apply for welfare to supplement her job earnings; she took the job because the welfare checks were insufficient to meet the needs of herself and her family.

"Mostly it's a matter of meat," she said. "If we just live off the welfare money, I can't afford no meat hardly. How can you raise up two boys on no meat?"

Welfare recipients, sometimes called the forgotten people of an affluent America, are never forgotten to the growing numbers of public assistance critics in Suffolk County and elsewhere. In this, the first of several articles by Sun staff writer Jon Margolis, the dilemma of welfare officials and the puzzlement of county budget architects are examined.

Jane's question represents the other side of the controversy over public welfare. While some complain of chiselers, of immorality by those on welfare, and on the injustice of asking hard-working middle class people to support those who seem to be lazy, others contend that it is the welfare client who is being denied justice.

Public welfare, subject to criticism from both sides, is becoming a major political issue in Suffolk this year. The basis of the issue is the county budget of $114 million, $45 million of which is for welfare.

The figures show that more than 30 per cent of county expenditures go to welfare. But like many statistics, they are misleading. Suffolk taxpayers do not spend 30 cents out of each tax dollar for welfare.

Much of the county's budget, for welfare and other items, is paid for by funds coming from the state, federal

Turn to Page 10A, Column 1

Jon Margolis

New Dawn: Sun Rises In Suffolk

The Suffolk Sun, the county's first daily newspaper, began publication this morning with a press run of 125,000.

The new paper's modern, six-unit Hoe press began to roll off the first copies of the 52-page paper shortly before 1 a.m.

Tension in the Sun newsroom began to mount about midnight as the deadline for the paper's first issue drew closer. Finally, at 12:15 a.m., news and sports pages held open for late-breaking stories and final scores were locked up, and the paper went to press.

After the presses rumbled to a halt about 4:30 a.m., a network of 809 carriers began delivering the paper before sunrise to the porches of 100,000 homes in western Suffolk and Riverhead.

The paper also went on sale at 648 newsstands at 10 cents a copy. The home-delivered price will be 40 cents a week.

The first issue climaxed more than 18 months of planning and preparation to fill what the Sun's publisher, Gardner Cowles III, called the "communications void" in Suffolk

"Suffolk County is faced with a variety of special problems generated by its rapid growth. So far there has been a communications void that has slowed the attack on these problems," Cowles said. "We hope to fill this vacuum by creating a forum for community leaders."

In its first editorial this morning, the Sun said it would have no political affiliation and that it would "serve no special interests, commercial or social, and will bow to no pressures except those of conscience."

The paper's editor, Cortland Anderson, said the Sun's 60 editorial staff members would serve the major new American preoccupation with community affairs.

"The challenge is to give local news the same quality of coverage, as deep and as thorough, as national and international news get," Anderson said.

The paper is being published by a staff of more than 225 full-time employes in a new, 32,000-square-foot plant at 303 Marcus Blvd., Deer Park. The one-story brick building was constructed for the Sun this summer at a cost of $675,000.

The Sun represents more than a $1 million pre-publication investment by its parent firm, Cowles Communications Inc., publishers of Look and Family Circle magazines and three other daily papers in Florida and Puerto Rico.

Cowles Communications, whose 1965 revenues total $137 million, also operates three television and two radio stations and an education division which publishes books and an encyclopedia. The Cowles family also owns the Minneapolis Star and Tribune and the Des Moines Register and Tribune

The paper's Deer Park plant has been picketed off and on this month by members of the Stereotypers' Union, challenging the right of the International

Turn to Page 2A, Column 3

—Associated Press Wirephoto

Inside Looking Out

Well, no one was really inside the mouth of this huge-molared hippopotamus. The picture was produced by Japanese photographer Atsuo Hirosawa, who placed a remote-controlled 35mm camera inside the hippo's mouth and waited outside while a Tokyo zoo keeper pried open its jaws. Hirosawa used a "fish-eye" lens to get this back of the throat view. The hippo cooperated throughout.

In Viet Nam

Bishops OK War If Aim Just Peace

WASHINGTON (AP) — U.S. Roman Catholic bishops said today that the presence of American forces in Viet Nam may reasonably be considered "justified." But they urged every effort to "create a climate of peace."

"While we cannot resolve all the issues involved in the Viet Nam conflict," they said, "it is clearly our duty to insist that they be kept under constant moral scrutiny."

This was the last of several major pronouncements flowing from the five-day session last week of the reorganized and renamed National Council of Catholic Bishops.

Entitled "On Peace," it said, in part: "Americans can have confidence in the sincerity of their leaders as long as they work for a just peace in Viet Nam. Their efforts to find a solution to the present impasse are well known.

"While we do not claim to be able to resolve these issues authoritatively, in the light of the facts as they are known to us it is reasonable to argue that our presence in Viet Nam is justified.

"While we can conscientiously support the position of our country in the present circumstances, it is the duty of everyone to search for other alternatives. And everyone—government leaders and citizens alike—must be prepared to change our course, whenever a change in circumstances warrants it.

"And we must clearly protest whenever there is a danger that the conflict will be escalated beyond morally acceptable limits."

The issue of Viet Nam has been a subject of hot debate among Catholics, as among other segments of the U.S. citizenry. At a news conference Friday night, it was announced that the statement was approved overwhelmingly—by a vote of 169 to 5 or 6.

...thers like it ...eated by the ... to attune the ... Among other ...s statement, ...e bars which ...ing in many ...d-up attacks ...ation. ...datory rule ...gical changes ...ding permis- ... of the Mass

Connor Denies Plan He'll Resign Post

WASHINGTON (UPI)—Commerce Secretary John T. Connor, President Johnson's first Cabinet appointee, denied Sunday a published report that he intends to resign in January.

"I have no present plans to return to private life," he said through a Commerce Department spokesman.

Balance or Else

Republicans Plot Budgetary Revolt

Reagan Urges Big War.....13A

WASHINGTON (AP)—Republican leaders are laying the groundwork for submission of an alternate budget if President Johnson fails to balance income and spending in his fiscal message to the new Congress.

Disclosing this Sunday, Senate Minority Leader Everett M. Dirksen of Illinois said this probably will be one of the steps taken by the election-revitalized GOP to offer the country "positive programs" rather than mere opposition to administration proposals in 1967.

"I think we will have support of the Republican members of the Appropriations, Finance and Ways and Means Committees in putting together a fiscal program," Dirksen said. "We hope to offer an alternative budget to cut government spending as a curb on inflation."

Dirksen noted that the 1946 Congressional Reorganization Act authorizes the preparation of a legislative—as well as a presidential—budget.

Although this provision remains in force—it has been ignored because of the difficulties encountered in early attempts to agree on expenditure figures.

"I remember that in trying to draft a legislative budget we had a meeting of 120 members of the House and Senate," Dirksen said. "Nothing could be accomplished with such a group, and a subcommittee of 20 was set up with Sen. Robert A. Taft as its head.

"That operation was unwieldy and nothing came of it. But I think we can get Republicans to agree on a budget."

The Illinois senator said the GOP position on a possible tax increase can't be determined until Johnson submits his budget in January. Although some individual Republicans have called for tax hikes, he said the party's position may not necessarily favor them.

Johnson has made no decision yet on on a possible tax increase. He hinted recently that mounting federal revenues may make such a boost unnecessary despite increased costs of the Viet Nam war.

Last January's estimate of a $1.8 billion deficit for the current fiscal year, ending next June 30, still stands. But it may have to be revised upward when Johnson asks supplemental funds in January for Viet Nam, civilian and military pay raises, the Cold War GI bill and other measures the 89th Congress passed.

Almost nobody believes the expenditures for the current year can be held within the $112.8 billion the President previously estimated. Almost everyone believes the new budget he will submit will be substantially higher, along with increased revenues.

Republicans will be watching closely what Johnson does about withholding expenditures from the $144 billion in appropriations Congress voted for the current and future years in its 1966 session.

—Associated Press Wirephoto

Ballot Day

Wilhelm and Amalie Houtzer, in native costumes, cast their ballots in Bavaria in the state parliamentary election. The eyes of West Germany and the world are on Bavaria, since the election result could influence formation of a new government at Bonn. (See story on Page 16A.)

G.I. Stricken

The 'Black Death' Haunting Asia

MANILA (UPI)—Plague, the "black death" that wiped out a quarter of the population of Europe during the Middle Ages, is again presenting the menace of "explosive outbreaks."

In Dallas last week, Army doctors announced that they had cured a 21-year-old soldier who contracted plague while in Viet Nam. It was, they said, the first case brought into the United States in 42 years.

But last month scientists from 16 nations held a five-day seminar at World Health Organization headquarters in Manila and faced some sobering statistics.

In one year 11 nations in the Southeast Asia-Pacific region reported that the number of plague cases had almost tripled. In 1965 there were 1,326 confirmed cases with 120 deaths. During the first 10 months of this year the figure had jumped to 3,293 cases and 211 deaths.

South Viet Nam, with 306 confirmed cases and 22 deaths, reported another 2,138 cases and 107 deaths in which plague was the "suspected cause."

In Viet Nam, with its rapidly shifting war-displaced population and critical lack of trained medical staff, there is little chance of keeping accurate count of the number of people who die of plague and are quietly buried.

Even trained doctors have a tough time recognizing the symptoms. The American soldier treated successfully in Texas after being shipped home from Viet Nam was at first thought to be suffering from hernia because of the swelling in his groin.

And plague is a permanent part of the scene in the United States in a belt running from California to Oklahoma. One or two cases a year are found, and prairie dogs, coyotes, rats and other wild animals provide a permanent home for plague-bearing fleas.

Inside the Sun

PEREIRA

FATHER Albert Pereira, who delivered sermons in a church attended by John F. Kennedy reminisces about him . . . 7B

SUFFOLK now has a s... for emotio... disturbed ... dren. But f... cial and ... problems s... persist . . .

THE Jets

It's Not Morning Without the Sun

Good morning.

This is the first issue of the Suffolk Sun.

The Sun will be delivered free to about 100,000 Suffolk homes for the next four weeks. In addition, it will be sold at more than 600 outlets throughout the county.

After the first four-week sample period, additional Suffolk homes will receive the Sun free. If your home is not in the first free distribution area, we invite you to buy it until it can be delivered to your home.

We hope you like the Sun. We're glad to be here.

Enjoy This Special Reading Bonus

The story of Lyndon B. Johnson for the past 35 years is a fascinating record of the acquisition and exercise of power. Today the Sun presents the first in a series of excerpts from the candid book, "Lyndon B. Johnson: The Exercise of Power," by Rowland Evans and Robert Novak, noted Washington observers. The story is on Page 8A.

THE EXERCISE OF POWER — LYNDON B. JOHNSON

Fig. 2. *Suffolk Sun,* Deer Park, Long Island, N.Y., is example of contemporary newspaper design. This is Vol. I, No. 1, appearing late in 1966. Circular tint block in nameplate is yellow, surprinted with stylized sun, shown same size, inset.

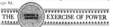

With time short, communication must be terse; there just isn't time for wordy amenities. Contact between departments is usually only at times of stress; when the pace is relatively slow and work proceeds normally, each department goes its own placid way. But when emergencies arise or the clock ticks close to press time, tensions and nerves tighten. And this is when editorial and composing must work face to face. Close and warm personal relationships can endure stress that between strangers raises temperaments to the flash point.

The relation of the mechanical departments to the news room must be clearly defined. The back shop is a service organization. It doesn't originate the material it works with, and only to a slight extent can it control its own operations. It is the copy desk that specifies what and how its copy is to be set and, very important, when. The composing room must perform its functions with engineering efficiency. It should call the attention of the news department to changes that can increase routine efficiency and to unusual circumstances that affect both departments. Often the press room must decide the pagination of an edition, how it is divided into physical sections, and where editorial can use advertising color for free. But the desk must retain—and fight for, if necessary—its directoral prerogatives. For the performance of the desk, far more than that of the mechanical departments, is judged by the typography and layout of each edition.

The editorial department, then, must also take responsibility for much of the composing-room costs. Unfortunately, and unrealistically, the composing room is often blamed for costs arising from specifications handed down to it. Overset; the slowing of Linotype production by odd measure; intricate setting or excessive swinging of magazines; overtime or extra manning to compensate for late copy or uneven copy flow—all add to comp-room expenses. But they are no more the fault of mechanical personnel than is the increased cost that results when an architect specifies a brick building instead of a wooden one.

The news room should not be interested in the creature comforts of the composing room. Printers are paid to work and, as good craftsmen, they enjoy doing their job. If that job is difficult and demanding . . . well, that's the job and that's what they are getting paid for. The desk should never lower the quality of the product to save the printer time or effort. Conversely, the desk should not complicate the work of the composing room if the result does not raise the quality of the product.

One of the ancient axioms is: "Anything that's hard to set or make up is hard to read."

If this axiom is true—as it is almost all of the time—then it isn't very smart to add to costs in order to make an inferior product.

The editorial department must be concerned with costs in all other departments, and vice versa, because all costs come from a common pocket.

But comp-room time has special interest for the news room. The longer it takes the mechanical department to produce the physical newspaper, the earlier the news deadline. The faster the mechanical departments can perform their part of manufacturing, the more time the desk has for late stories and buffing details to a fine luster.

Composing-room personnel applaud functional typography because it makes them more efficient. Editorial staffers sometimes are wary of functionalism because they believe it's just a blueprint for printers' comfort. Actually, functionalism is concerned with efficient production of a quality product. Any conveniences that may accrue thereby are pleasant, but only byproducts. Those conveniences, incidentally, usually benefit the desk as well as the composing room.

That is why it's a good idea to bring in key men from the composing room when new procedures or new typographic styling are contemplated. Printers are craftsmen, proud of a long heritage. Typesetters and makeup men must constantly make decisions affecting typography. They should be made aware of the basic principles that the newspaper will follow so they can make valid decisions on the spur of the moment. (Participation in planning also takes away the resentment that we all feel against having a flat dictum rammed down our gullets.)

Every aspect of a newspaper operation and product should be reassessed at frequent intervals. Interdepartmental sessions should be regular procedure at every newspaper. Needs that brought about certain practices may be outgrown. Changing conditions, equipment, or techniques may demand, or make desirable, new solutions.

Even if, after study, the decision is that the present way of doing things is the best, the editor at least has the satisfaction of knowing that his procedures are a result of a decision rather than of a legacy.

chapter 2

The Vocabulary of Newspaper Design

EVERY SPECIALTY has its own technical vocabulary. It may be a highly formalized lexicon like that of the physician, or it may be one as elastic as that of the printer, with meanings changing from region to region, even from print shop to print shop.

The printer, who contributes most of the newspaper designer's vocabulary, has an especially colorful jargon. In addition to the words and terms that had to be coined to describe his newly invented art of printing, the medieval printer used existing terms in ways deliberately fashioned to confuse the outside world. He told the world he was going to "chapel meeting," using that pious term to obfuscate that this was really a frowned-upon craftsmen's cell that would some day become a typographic union. He called his apprentice a *printer's devil* because he wanted the man on the street to regard printing with some degree of awe.

The jargon has expanded with new technology. The fifteenth-century printer would be baffled by the new language of computerized composing rooms and electronic typesetting. Yet he would be pleased at the great many words and terms that have endured since 1450.

Jargon is useful. It enables quick and accurate communication, and so the newspaper designer, who must work closely with the mechanical departments, will find their vocabularies useful tools.

In this book, as in any communication, a word means what the author wants it to mean. But he has the responsibility of making sure that it is translated properly by the reader. This is not to imply that the usage in this book is the only correct one; the reader may still use his own terms in his own communications.

This chapter will discuss the vocabularies of the typesetter, the makeup man, and the press room, because these are the ones the newspaper designer uses in his everyday work. Of these, the most colorful is that of type itself.

Since Gutenberg invented movable type around 1450, scores of thousands of modifications have been made on the forms of the Latin alphabet. This is the one that we use, along with all the nations of the Western world and with many of the East.

To be able to discuss any vast field, it is necessary to divide and classify its components. Many systems have been suggested, and some of them have been adopted for limited use. This book's aim is not to set up didactic pigeonholes but to facilitate study and discussion, so we shall employ the system that is most frequently used in the United States.

The first division of type is by *race;* in this system there are six races, five of which have major, or *ethnic,* subdivisions:

RACE	ETHNICS
Roman	Old Style Transitional Modern
Text, or *Black Letter*	
Monotone	Gothic Sans Serifs
Square Serifs	Egyptian American
Written	Script Cursive
Ornamented	Shaded Shadowed Novelty

The first race, *Roman,* with its corollary, *Italic,* heads our list because this is the style in which the Latin alphabet was first formalized in ancient Rome.

The various forms of the alphabet are excellent demonstrations that "form follows the tool." The characteristics of Roman are the swelling and thinning of curved strokes and the *serifs,* the tiny finishing strokes at the ends of main strokes. The swell-and-curve effect is produced by the first tool used in drawing the alphabet. This was either a flat, thin paintbrush—like the ones we use for painting a house—or a pair of pencils or charcoal sticks tied to the sides of a block of wood. With this tool the letterer drew his copy in erasable form across the masonry to see whether it would fit. When he drew the brush downward, it painted a strip as wide as the brush; when he moved it horizontally, the strip was only as wide as the thickness of the brush. A diagonal was somewhere between those widths and a curve varied from wide to thin. The markers fastened to a block drew a pair of lines far or close apart that duplicated the widths of the painted strokes.

As the stonecutter followed these patterns, he incised the main strokes as V-shaped grooves. But to finish the end of such a cutting, he used the narrow edge of his chisel in a stroke perpendicular to the groove. It was difficult to start and end the finishing stroke—the serif—exactly at the corner of the wider groove, so he began the finishing stroke outside the edge of the main one.

Then he found that there was danger of the stone crumbling at the T intersection between the main stroke and the serif. So he rounded off that corner; the serif was *bracketed* to the main stroke.

Although type designers no longer work with paintbrush and chisel, the characteristics of those tools are now an integral part of the design that we call Roman.

Italic is a Roman that slants to the right. It has the same varying width of curved strokes and serifs as does the Roman.

Most Italics are studiedly more graceful than Romans, reflecting the handwritten letterforms on which Aldus Manutius, an Italian printer and scholar, based his Italic designs around 1500. In some instances the serifs are replaced by *finials,* little curving strokes that clearly show the influence of the writing pen. Sometimes, especially on capital letters, a stroke is extended in a flourish to make a *swash;* this makes a *swashed* letter.

If the painter held his brush perfectly straight and made a circle, the widest parts of the stroke would be at 3 and 9 o'clock; only the narrowest dimension of the brush would deposit paint at 12 and 6. But this is an awkward way to hold the tool; the natural grasp will tilt the brush. So in the early forms of the alphabet, which we call *Old Style,* the brush was held so the heaviest strokes were at 2 and 8 o'clock and the narrow at 11 and 5. So all round letterforms, while actually standing straight, are on an axis that tilts slightly to the left. The difference between thick and thin strokes is readily apparent but not drastic. Both Romans and Italics may be in Old Style.

The major subdivisions of the Roman race are this Old Style and *Modern,* a style created by Giambatista Bodoni, another Italian type designer, around 1785. He designed his letters as *punches,* relief forms in

ROMAN	**The Times**
Oldstyle →	
Modern →	Post-Herald
TEXT	The Telegraph
MONOTONES	Independent
Sans Serifs →	
Gothic →	CHRONICLE
SQUARES	TIMES
Egyptians →	
Americans →	DAILY PRESS
WRITTEN	The World
Script →	
Cursive →	Mount HERALD
ORNAMENTED	STATENEWS
Shadowed	
Shaded →	The Advance

Example A. Races of type.

metal, that were driven into softer metal to make the *matrix,* the mold from which the actual type was cast. His tools influenced the letterform. He could cut far thinner strokes than the stonecutter could incise, and so the difference between thick and thin strokes was marked. The metal didn't crumble as stone might, and so serifs were thin, straight, and unbracketed. The axis of his round letter was perfectly perpendicular to the baseline.

The Italic letter is also designed in old and modern styles.

The most widely used newspaper head letter is Bodoni, a Modern Roman. The most popular body type, Corona, and all good newspaper body faces are Old Styles.

The fine-printing typographer needs further subdivisions such as *Venetian, Dutch,* etc., but for newspaper use we group all Romans and Italics that do not meet all specifications of Old Style or Modern into the *Transitional* category.

The second race of type is *Text,* or *Black Letter.* Interestingly, this was the first race committed to metal type. Here the original tool was an intractable quill pen that couldn't write a curve on rough parchment without getting caught and spattering ink. So the scribes converted round strokes into straight ones. To conserve the costly materials on which they wrote, they reduced the width of the letters. The identifying characteristics of Text are the straight lines which vary greatly between thick and thin and the condensed letterform that gives it its name of Black Letter. Over the centuries, curves have been added to the letterform, but it is still a basically angular design. Text has no ethnic subdivisions.

For newspaper use, Text is restricted to the nameplate and rare headings for obituaries and church or official announcements. Many newspapermen, and too many printers, call this race *Old English;* this is a misnomer. Old English is a Text, but to call the whole race Old English is like calling all automobiles Fords.

The third race is the *Monotones,* divided into *Gothics* and *Sans Serifs.*

In Europe, the Gothics are called *Grotesk,* an appropriate title. Original Gothics were *block letters.* All strokes are the same width throughout; there are no serifs; the letterform is rather constricted.

In original Grotesk, letterforms were made up of all straight strokes, just as those of Black Letter, except that there were no thin strokes. Eventually some strokes were curved, but they were tight, awkward arcs and the letterform was anything but handsome. It was this lack of beauty that gave the name Gothic. We should remember that their namesakes were the barbarians who terrorized Europe for centuries and that the term translates into "ugly." Many people think that Gothic refers to the angular but handsome architecture of ancient cathedrals and castles, so they incorrectly use "Gothic" to describe Text letters.

Sans Serifs are more rounded in form than Gothics and are beautiful in a sleek, mechanistic way. In the form we know best today, they were designed in Germany shortly after World War I.

There are some unobtrusive variations of the basically monotonal strokes of the Sans. Sometimes a curved stroke is *pinched,* thinned, as it meets a vertical one. If the curved strokes of a *B,* for instance, met the vertical stroke without pinching, the open area, the *void,* that is enclosed by the curves, would be so small that it might easily fill up with ink during printing. So the curves are squeezed thinner to provide an adequate void. This pinching is so slight that it is not apparent to the casual eye.

The distinction between Gothics and Sans Serifs is slight and often academic. Gothics are considered "less beautiful" than the Sans, but this is certainly a vague criterion. Gothics are usually more condensed than Sans and tend to be darker in tone. But these criteria, too, are a sometime thing. Contemporary Gothics are often nicely rounded and lighter in tone than their ancestors. The only infallible way to differentiate between the two divisions of the Monotone race is to learn to recognize specific letters and fonts. Even this is not always accurate because the terminology of type catalogs is so flexible that true Gothics are there sometimes called Sans Serifs and vice versa.

It doesn't matter too much in newspaper usage. The truly named Franklin Gothic is a favorite for banner heads; the Metros, contemporary Gothics, are excellent headletters. Spartan, Tempo, and Vogue are Sans that are widely used for heads and for such specialized use as stock markets, box scores, and classified ads, in body sizes.

Square Serifs are self-describing by name. The letterforms are monotonal, but they carry serifs. These are not the small, unobtrusive serifs of the Romans but are bold and brash, at least as heavy as the strokes of the letter itself. When the serif is the same weight as the body stroke, the letter is called an *Egyptian,* the name given to the whole race in Europe. When the serif is wider than the letter strokes, the form is called *American.*

For newspapers, Egyptian Square Serifs are a good headletter. Memphis and Karnak are popular in this group. American Squares are rarely used for news presentation. This is the letterform we associate with old circus posters, and the names are evocative: Playbill and Barnum, for P.T., the showman.

The Monotones and the Squares have letterforms that slant to the right, as the Italics do. Technically these are *Obliques,* and the normal letterforms are *Perpendiculars*. In popular usage, "Roman" is used to designate the perpendicular form of any race and "Italic" those which slant to the right. So we constantly hear reference to Spartan Italic or Memphis Roman. If everyone involved understands the meaning, this reference is acceptable. But the poor purists wince as much as they would at reference to an Oriental Caucasian or a Negro Indian.

The *Written* race is used rarely in news columns and then, usually, in headlettered headings. This race reproduces the flowing letterforms of handwriting. The two subdivisions have the same individual letterforms; in *Script* the letters are joined as they are in normal writing; in *Cursive* the letters are not joined, although the division between them may be so slight as to be almost invisible. Mandate, Mayfair, Coronet, and Hauser Script are *Ludlow* Written faces.

The final race is *Ornamented*. While the Ornamented are widely used for advertising, on the news side they are restricted to nameplates and occasional headings.

The subdivisions of Ornamented are *Shaded, Shadowed,* and *Novelty*. Shaded letters are those on which some modification has been made to the face of the letter. This may be as slight as a thin white line scribed within the letter. If this line runs down the center of the stroke, it creates an *Inline* letter; if it runs closer to one edge, it is a *shading line*. The whole face may be broken by parallel or crossed lines to give the effect of gray. This technique is often used with Text letters for nameplates; *Publishers' Auxiliary* used a Shaded Text for several decades.

Additions outside the letterform proper produce a shadowed letter. This may be a dark line as if the letter cast a shadow. (An interesting variation is that of *Umbra,* a 3-dimensional-appearing face in which the whole letter has been removed and only the shadow remains.) The addition may be more florid. During the Victorian era it was considered the ultimate in elegance to drape a letterform with leaves and vines and even to have sundry and assorted animals and people peering through and around the letter.

Shaded and shadowed letters are, of course, originally in other races. Usually the characteristics of the basic race are obvious, but if any additions have been made to the letterform, the mutant is ostracized from the original race and relegated to the Ornamented.

Novelty letterforms are those which are radically changed from those of other races. We are familiar with letters made of ribbons, flowers, logs, and planks. We occasionally see Latin letters made up of brush strokes to carry the flavor of Japanese, Chinese, Hebrew, or Arabic forms. Stenciled letters and those used for magnetic reading on checks and bank statements are classified as Novelties. This subdivision is used widely in advertising, but its editorial use is negligible.

From races and their subdivisions, classification carries down into *families*. Type families have their own names which, like peoples', come from several sources.

Many type designers give their names to their creations: Bodoni, Goudy, Cooper, Caslon. National backgrounds also give many names: Ionic, Caledonia, Old English, Eldorado. Or the name may be arbitrarily chosen: Corona, Tempo, Stymie, Century.

Type families are broken down into *series*. Each series bears the family name plus one or more adjectives that describe the variations that are possible to the letterform.

There are three things that a designer can do to a face without losing its family characteristics. He can change *weight, width,* and *angle*. The thickness of the strokes that make up a letter determines its typographic weight, or *color*. There is, unfortunately, little standardization in the terminology of weight. In the Spartan family, for instance, starting with the lightest, weights are called Light, Book, Medium, Bold, Heavy, Black, and Extra Black. In Futura, another Sans Serifs, the range is Light, Book, Medium, Demibold, and Bold. The heaviest form of Bodoni is variously called Bodoni Black, Poster Bodoni, or Ultra Bodoni.

When the thickness of strokes remains the same and the whole letter is squeezed together, the result is a *Condensed* face. When the form is stretched horizontally, an *Extended* face is the result. There are Extra Condensed and Extra Extended forms, too, but the normal and Condensed forms are, with very rare exception, the only ones used for news presentation.

The angle of letters is described as Roman and Italic and Perpendicular and Oblique. There is another, the *Backslant*, that tilts to the left. This is a very rare breed fortunately, because it is ugly and affected.

When a series carries only the family name, with no adjectives indicating variations, we assume that it is normal in weight and width and perpendicular in stance.

A series name may contain more than one adjective. We have, for instance, Cheltenham Bold Condensed Italic; what more could you do to a letterform? Or Spartan Extra Black Italic (which we know is truly Oblique!).

A *font* comprises all the letters, numbers, and characters necessary to set copy in one size of type. A font carries the series name plus a size, in points. A typical font would be "8-point Corona Bold" or "14-point Memphis Medium Condensed."

We must distinguish a font of type, consisting of one size of one series, and a font of linecaster *matrices*. In most cases those *mats* through 18-point carry two molds on each piece of brass, which is called a *matrix*. So a single font of matrices will produce two fonts of type.

A font is made up of *lowercase* letters—*minuscules;* the *uppercase*—capitals or *majuscules;* numbers; special signs, such as $, ¢, * etc.; and punctuation marks, called *points*. Some fonts also have *small caps*, letters in the form of capitals but about the size of lowercase.

The lowercase alphabet is made up of *primary letters, ascenders,* and *descenders*. Primary letters are those like *a, e, o, m,* and *s* whose height is defined by the *baseline* at the bottom and the *meanline* at the top. The distance between these lines is called the *x-height*, an important factor in body type, as we shall see later. Those letters which have "tails" projecting below the baseline—*g, j, p, q,* and *y*—are called descenders, and the tails themselves are also descenders. If the letter has an upward-projecting "neck" —*b, d, f, h, l, t*—both the projection and the letter to which it is attached are called ascenders.

The size of type and other printer's measurements are designated in *points* and *picas*. The American point system, in which a point is approximately $\frac{1}{72}$ of an inch (.01384 inch) and 12 points make a pica, was adopted in 1886, quite recently in comparison to the 500-year-plus history of printing.

Prior to the point system, the size of type was indicated by name. The tiniest were *excelsior,* 3-point, and *brilliant,* 3½. Maybe chauvinism was involved in giving the name *English* to 14-point and *Columbian* to 16. Few of the names remain in use. Older printers still refer to a 6-point slug as a *nonpareil*, and 5½-point, *agate,* is still referred to by name as well as number. But because agate is used mainly for classified advertising and tabular matter in news columns, the name is misused by giving it to any and all small type used for these purposes. Twelve-point type gave its name, pica, to the unit of measurement.

Often printers will use the word *em* as a synonym for pica, and this is an excruciating misnomer. An em is a measurement of area, the square of the point size of the type. Thus the em changes in dimension from font to font. In a font of 8-point, the em is 8 × 8, 64 square points; in 24-point, it is 24 × 24, 576 square points.

Only in the 12-point font is there a relation between the em and a pica; the 12-point em is a square of 1-pica dimensions. But equating the em of area with the pica of length is like using "acre" as a synonym for "mile."

A vertical half of an em is an *en*. This, too, will vary then according to the size of the font. For 18-point type, an en is 18 points tall and 9 points wide, for 24-point it is 24 high and 12 wide. Ems and ens are used for measuring spaces, especially between words, in the setting of type. In metal such spaces are *quadrats,* or quads.

Supposedly to avoid oral confusions, printers say mut and nut for em and en, but the difference between the sounds remains slight. It is an improvement when the printer says mutton quad to designate the em.

Other common spacing material is the *ledd,* a strip of metal 2 points thick. Ledd is here spelled phonetically; Mr. Webster prefers "lead." However, in newspaper usage "lead" may also be pronounced "leed," the beginning of a story. Often we must "lead a lead"—ledd a leed. That's perfectly clear when spoken across a composing stone. But to "lead a lead" is less than totally illuminating in print. Therefore, in this book, as increasingly in other technical writings, the phonetic form is used: ledd for a metal strip, leed for a story opening.

A *slug* is a 6-point-thick strip of spacing. *Reglets* are strips of wooden spacing material. Reglets come in various sizes, but most frequently the word, with no adjective, is applied to 1-pica widths, especially when used between columns of news matter. *Furniture* is larger rectangles of spacing material of hardwood or of honeycomb metal.

Another spacing unit is a *3-em space*. This is actually a one-third of an em of space. A 4-em space is a quarter of an em wide, a full em tall. Its actual size varies, of course, with that of the type being set. The 3-em space is the standard spacing between words for many styles of typesetting.

There is an extensive vocabulary of terms referring to the design of letterforms. We will take a fast look at them, although newspapermen will rarely have occasion to use them in workaday conversation.

The round part of a letter is the *bowl,* a term used primarily with letters such as *b* and *p;* the straight part of the letter is the *stem*. The entire *c* and the curved portion of *e* are also, but less frequently, referred to as bowls. The area within a bowl is the *counter,* or void. In many fonts there is a *ball* at the beginning of the arc of the *a* and *c*. (We might note here that there are two kinds of *a*'s. The one in the face you're reading now is a *Roman a;* when the letter looks like a *d* with the ascender sliced off, it is called a *Greek a,* as in the Italic form of this body type.)

In the early days of printing, typesetters sought to lighten their work by casting whole words or frequently used sets of letters on a single piece of metal. This was fine; to set "the," the printer had to handle only one piece of type instead of three. Unfortunately the temptation to make many words in one piece soon made the typecase so big that it was inefficient.

When two or more letters are thus cast on a single piece of metal, they are called *logotypes*—"a type of a whole word." Two or more letters that are connected, such as the *fi, ff, ffi* and *ffl,* are called *ligatures,* tied together. While ligatures are available in several newspaper body fonts, they are rarely used today in editorial composition but usually only for advertising copy. No regular logotypes are in common use today except those that identify news services by their initials—AP (Associated Press), UPI (United Press International), and CP (Canadian Press).

The *Linofilm,* a photographic typesetting machine, has revived the logotype in its original form. A single keystroke will set an entire word; these are all common ones, and they're usually short ones such as articles, conjunctions, and prepositions.

Because the nameplates of newspapers and the signature cuts of advertisers are often in the form of a *photoengraving*—all the letters or even more than one word on a single plate—these elements are commonly called *logos.*

Newspapers use either *hot metal* or *cold type.* Hot metal type is self-explanatory, although the metal has cooled before use. It is of two varieties. Most common is that produced by a *linecaster. Linotypes* and *Intertypes* are keyboarded linecasters. Using a keyboard vaguely similar to, though much larger than, that on a typewriter, the operator releases matrices (molds) of the required letters. These fall, solely by gravity, from a series of narrow *channels* in a metal receptacle called a *magazine.* When enough matrices to fill a given line length have been released and assembled in proper order, they are moved into position at the opening, the mouthpiece, of a *pot* containing molten *type metal.* This is an alloy of lead, tin, and antimony which has *eutectic* properties. This means that, unlike most substances except water, it expands as it cools. This assures that the metal will be forced into the tiniest recesses of the matrix and so cast a true letter. The hot metal is forced into the line of matrices and so is cast a line of type, from which the machine received its name, Linotype, with a capital to indicate its trademarked status.

The lines of type are called Linotype slugs, most frequently just *slugs*. This term should not be confused with the 6-point spacing material we've already noted.

Matrices are lifted to the top of the machine, slide across a triangular bar, and, using the principle of a lock and key, are released so they fall back into their proper channel, ready for reuse.

Spacing between words is done automatically to *justify* the line, aligning the left and right margins evenly.

Linotypes can cast line lengths up to 30 picas in type sizes from 5½- through 36-point in normal operation. Larger sizes can be cast in a few faces, but their use is uncommon.

For larger sizes, a Ludlow machine is used. This, too, is a linecaster, but it has no keyboard. The operator gathers matrices by hand, assembles them in a special receptacle, and casts a line of type up to 25 picas long. The matrices, or mats, are redistributed by hand.

Ludlow slugs are made so they can be linked into longer lines with no apparent break. They are T-shaped and require *underpinning*, supports of blank metal strips. This material, along with ledds, slugs, rules, and borders, is produced on a *stripcaster*, with the trademarked name of *Elrod*.

The second category of hot metal is *foundry type*. This consists of metal bars usually bearing a single letter. Foundry type is stored in a compartmented *California job case*, from which the typesetter picks the desired characters and assembles them with the necessary spacing in a *composing stick*. On dailies, this handset type is used only for large banner headlines; on smaller papers, all or most of the heads may be set by hand.

Cold type is type that is set photographically. The product of the phototypesetting machine is actually a picture of the desired characters assembled in lines and paragraphs, as *positive*, black-on-white images on photopaper or transparent film. Tonal values can be *reversed* chemically to produce a conventional film *negative* of clear images on a black background.

The most sophisticated of these machines are the *Linofilm, Photon, Linotron* and *Fototronic*. The *ATF Typesetter* is a less complex machine of slightly lower capabilities. These set both body and headline sizes.

The cold-type equivalent of the Ludlow are machines that, operating with manual levers and knobs, produce headlines in strip form. The best known are the *Typosetter, Hadego, Morisawa,* and *Headliner,* although there are many on the market. The *ProType* is the simplest, utilizing the operator's hands instead of mechanical devices to move and expose the film that creates the photo image.

Although, technically, cold type is only that produced photographically, there is a tendency to include in this category that composition which is correctly called *strikeon*. This is produced by some version of the typewriter. A raised character on the end of a metal arm strikes an inked-fabric or carbon-paper ribbon and thus prints the character onto a piece of paper resting on a rubber *platen*. Any typewriter produces strikeon composition. Refinements make it possible to produce justified lines, automatically or semiautomatically. The *Justowriter* is typical. From a conventional typewriter keyboard, the operator produces coded paper *tape*. This is fed back through the same or another machine which automatically types out the finished, justified copy. We shall discuss the capabilities of these methods in greater detail in Chapter 13.

Pasteon letters, black ones on white paper as well as black or white ones on clear plastic, are assembled and pasted together by hand in larger sizes. This is not very efficient, and so its use is limited in newspaper production to the biggest headlines or rarely used advertising fonts.

Hot-metal composition is assembled in long, shallow, 3-sided trays called *galleys*. A rather hurried impression of such type is printed on a small *proofpress,* and the result, a column of type on a long sheet of paper, is the *galley proof*. This is read by the *proofreader,* who is a printer and, in most daily and many weekly plants, is a member of the International Typographical Union, the ITU. Only special material— editorials, columns, or news stories with grave danger of libel—goes to the news room in galley-proof form.

When a complete newspaper page has been assembled, a *page proof* is made from it. This may be printed on a small press, or it may be a *beaten proof*. To beat a proof, the printer inks the page with a roller, a *brayer,* then lays a sheet of dampened paper over it. He places a small wooden block on the paper and beats it with a mallet. By moving the block over the entire printing area, he imprints a rough but adequate image of the paper. Page proofs are usually read by news-room personnel.

For book and much magazine work, proofreaders work in pairs. The proofreader reads the galley, the *copyholder* has the original copy. One of the team reads aloud and errors are corrected on the galley proof. Pressures of time make it impractical to use proofreading teams on newspapers so, typically, proofs are *horsed* by a single reader, who consults original copy only if there is a question about accuracy for which the answer is not obvious. If the paper has several editions, everyone in the news room usually reads the entire first edition, and corrections are made before the second one goes to press.

To correct an error in linecaster type, the entire line must be reset and the *error line* replaced. It is easy to place the *correction line* in the wrong place, or to remove a good line instead of the error line. Then we have a duplication of one line, with and without the error, and a gap where the erroneously removed line should be. So it is necessary to recheck, read a new proof, the *first revise,* to make sure that all errors were truly corrected.

There are two kinds of changes that can be made in type. Errors of the typesetter are called *typographic errors,* or typos. But when editorial changes are made in the type instead of on the original copy, such "corrections" are called *author's alterations,* AA's. There is no time in the newspaper production cycle for author's alterations. The only changes that should be made in type are those required for accuracy. If the type says that World War I started in 1913, a correction must obviously be made whether the error was a typo or whether the writer made the mistake. But literary changes, changing "holocaust" to "inferno," for instance, should not be tolerated in newspaper proofs.

The equivalent of galley proofs in cold type is a *photocopy* of the composition. The "page proof" is a blueprint made from the negative that will be used to produce an offset printing plate or a photoengraving. This will be discussed in more detail in Chapter 13.

Practically everyone involved in the newspaper between the copy desk and the mailing room is a "printer," but each has another name which more specifically describes his job. A *compositor* is a man who sets type, especially by hand. This name also applies to an *operator,* who runs a linecaster or the keyboard of a phototypesetting machine. He (or she; the female sex is well represented in the composing room these days) may also operate a keyboard that produces tape; then he is usually called a *tape puncher,* a term most often used when unjustified tape is produced. (This will be discussed in Chapter 3.)

The printer who makes up advertisements or newspaper pages by combining various printing elements is a *floor man* or *makeup man.* He may work in the *ad alley,* where advertisements are put together, or on the *news row,* which handles only editorial matter. Linecasting machines are also designated by these latter two terms. A *ring machine* is one that sets both kinds of copy and is used especially for setting corrections of typos.

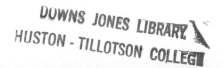

When copy comes from the desk or the advertising department, it is *on the hook*. In old days it was literally so, impaled on a large, curved hook. A *copy cutter,* or *copy marker,* is the first printer to handle copy. He actually cuts copy into component parts which must be handled by linecasters that carry the proper fonts. Or he may cut a long story into shorter portions—*takes*—which he will parcel out among various operators to speed the setting. Often he translates casual instructions, especially on advertisements, into precise fonts and measures.

The only editorial department members who work in the composing room are the makeup editors. They supervise the making up of pages, working opposite a printer, across the stone or *turtle*. The stone was once exactly that, a slab of polished marble. Today steel tables replace the stone but the ancient name remains. On this smooth surface, the many, various printing elements are assembled into an ad or a page. A turtle is a steel table on wheels just large enough to accommodate a single newspaper page.

The makeup editor may work with a *dummy*. The printer follows this guide until he reaches a stage where editorial judgment must be exercised—where to cut a story, how to trim an engraving, or how to avoid an unforeseen juxtaposition of headlines. Then the editor makes the decision. The editor may work without a dummy—especially on remake pages—instructing the printer where stories should be placed. In either case, the editor is strictly forbidden by union contract even to touch any typographic material.

Pages are made up in steel frames, *chases,* usually just big enough to hold one newspaper page. A *double truck* is a chase large enough for 2-page capacity; in it type can fill the *gutter,* the white space that normally separates facing pages. Double trucks are used mostly for advertising but are sometimes used for facing feature pages and, although quite rarely, for news pages. Double-truck pages are normally used only on the *inside spread,* the two pages at the very middle of a newspaper section, the only facing pages printed on the same sheet of paper.

When all elements have been placed in the chase, columns are justified, completely and exactly filled, by inserting or removing spacing material within the column. Then the page is held tightly in the chase by metal wedges called *quoins*. When two wedges are forced together, they form an expanded rectangle of metal which holds the page tightly in the chase. Quoins, today usually contained in metal boxes, are forced together by a T-shaped lever, a quoin key. Usually two or three sets of wedges are used on one side and two at the foot, of a page. When the page has been *locked up,* it is wheeled into the stereotyping room or to the press room.

Meanwhile another department has been preparing the pictures that will appear in the paper. For a letterpress newspaper, the *photoengraver* (naturally shortened to *engraver*) prepares relief plates, *photoengravings.* To print in simple blacks and whites, he makes a *line cut;* to reproduce the continuous tone of a *halftone,* he must *screen* the photo, breaking down its intermediate grays to a pattern of tiny dots of varying areas, for the printer has no gray ink with which to duplicate a photograph; he must create an illusion of gray by varying the ratio of black dots and white paper.

The fineness of such a halftone plate is determined by the number of lines of dots in a linear inch, the more dots the finer the detail. Newspapers that stereotype their plates use 55- or 65-line screen. Those which print directly from the original plates may use 85-line screens.

Newspaper engravings are most usually made of zinc. Those areas which must remain high, in relief, are protected by a coating of some acid-resistant material, then unwanted portions are eaten away with acid. A romantically named resin, *dragon's blood,* was once used as the acid-resistant material, but progress has eliminated the substance and its flavorsome name from the engraving department.

Both line and halftone photoengravings are often called *zincs,* even when magnesium alloy or copper is used for their making.

For offset newspapers, no relief elements are needed, of course. The platemaker does the equivalent of the photoengraver's work. He makes negatives of line and halftone work, then *strips in* these elements (fastens them in place) with negatives which carry the type material. Using the resultant combination negative, he *burns* a plate. By exposing a thin, sensitized zinc or aluminum plate to light projected through the negative, he makes those areas ink-attractive, while the rest of the plate repels ink.

The first American newspaper was the short-lived *Publick Occurrences Both Foreign and Domestick,* whose single issue was printed in Boston in September of 1690. This paper would be worth note, even if it were not a pioneer, for a charming phrase its editor used: The paper would appear monthly, he announced, unless "a glut of occurrences" demanded more frequent publication. Surely every hard-worked deskman would attest that occurrences come only in gluts these days.

For most of the 300 years since then—and even longer in Europe— *letterpress,* or relief printing, was the only method used. Type and printing blocks that are raised from the bearing surfaces capture ink and then deposit it on paper. Not till the 1930's was *offset lithography* used for newspaper printing. For two decades, until the 1950's, offset was such a rarity for newspaper production that it warranted no major discussion in textbooks or professional meetings. But the years after World War II saw so many newspapers turn to offset that for almost two decades this method of printing has rated ahead of politics and women as shop-talk topics.

We shall discuss offset in detail in Chapter 13; here we shall look at letterpress, still the major printing method for American newspapers, especially metropolitans.

Smaller newspapers, especially weeklies, may be printed directly from metal type on a *cylinder,* or *flatbed,* press. A sheet of paper is wrapped around a large cylinder and pressed onto the inked page-forms, which rest on the flat bed of the press.

But larger newspapers are printed on *rotary* presses. Here a strip of paper, the *web,* feeds off a roll and passes between two cylinders. One carries the page-form as a curved metal plate, the other is the *impression cylinder,* which presses the web against the inked type. Only after all the pages for one copy of the newspaper have been printed on the strip are they assembled in the proper order and cut into individual 2- or 4-page sheets.

To create this curved printing surface, the *stereotyping* process is necessary. The page is made up on a flat surface as for direct printing. A sheet of thin, flexible cardboardlike paper, the *flong,* is laid on the type form and pressed onto it under extreme mechanical or hydraulic pressure; this step is called *rolling a mat.* Now the paper is an accurate mold of the original page of type, the *stereotype matrix,* or stereo mat. This is bent into a semicylindrical form, and molten metal is poured onto it. The resulting cast, a *press plate, stereotype,* or *half-round,* is a replica of the original page except that its surface is curved. On the larger newspaper presses, the stereotype is a half-cylinder of about 14 inches in diameter. On smaller presses, it is almost a complete tube about 6 inches in diameter with a slot of about an inch that keeps it from being a true cylinder.

The printers who roll the mats and cast the plates have a union and a name of their own, *stereotypers.* The men who do the actual imprinting, who put images on paper, are called *pressmen.*

Normally the news room and press room have no need for direct contact, and so the pressman's jargon is rarely heard on the copy desk.

The only press function that has an appreciable effect on the desk is the method in which the paper is printed. In a *straight run,* two or more complete newspapers are printed at the same time from *duplicate plates* made by casting more than one stereotype plate from a single page matrix. For editions of many pages, the press room must make a *collect run.* Instead of several identical copies of the paper, only a single copy is printed at a time. The several sections that take the place of the duplicate copies are then gathered into one newspaper by the process that gives this method its name. Collect runs require longer time on the press, of course, to print a given number of copies, and so the news-room deadline may have to be moved up to allow the presses to meet truck, train, bus, and plane deadlines.

Printed papers are then handled by *mailers,* who, though they may be members of a printer's union, are really not printers. From the mail room, papers are hauled to various delivery points by truckers. On metropolitans, these men are usually members of the Teamsters Union. The editorial department has no working contact with these two groups, and so has borrowed none of their vocabulary.

An editorial department staffer can do an admirable job without mastering the language of the printer, but precise communication between news and mechanical departments is necessary to produce a quality product. All communication is more effective when a common well-defined vocabulary is utilized. Therefore it is well worth the little time required to master the picturesque terminology of the printing craft.

chapter **3**

Selection of Body Type

THE RECIPE for a tasty typographic dish is similar to that in any cookbook. First all the ingredients are listed, then instructions are given for mixing them into a gustatory masterpiece. So, in this book, we shall look at the typographic components of a newspaper and then discuss how to blend them into an appetizing whole.

The major ingredient of newspaper design is *body type*.

Body type is defined by only its use: in large masses, usually at constant line lengths, and justified. The composing room calls it *straight matter,* that set in conventional form with no variation. Contrasted to this is *display type,* that used for headlines of all varieties, editorial and advertising.

Size is not a factor. William Randolph Hearst used to have his editorials set in 14- and even 18-point type; in that instance those sizes were body type. In ordinary usage, 14's and 18's are used for headlines and are then display type. Twelve-point is frequently used for editorials as body type and, at the same time and often on the same page, is also used for small headlines.

Usually we consider body type as that in the 7- through 12-point range and display type as that in larger sizes. But this is a rough rule of thumb; use of type is the only precise indicator.

Body type is like the air we breathe. We can't live without oxygen, yet few people pay any attention to what they are drawing into their lungs. A newspaper can't exist without body type—97% of all the words in a paper are in this type—yet few editors give much heed to this essential part of their type library.

The editor faces two basic questions: "What type face shall I choose? How shall I use it most effectively?"

36

The first question must be answered infrequently; the second must be answered daily.

The choice of a news face is not one that is made often—or inexpensively. Linotype matrices are finely machined tools, and their cost is commensurate. With proper care, a font will last years, and replacement of worn ones is usually made by individual characters. It is rare when all the matrices in a newspaper composing room wear out at the same time and thus provide a logical opportunity to consider a new face. But matrices do wear out, and eventually it is more economical to replace a whole font than to continue to make piecemeal replenishment. This is certainly a time to consider the merits of all available news faces.

More rarely, such an occasion may arise when tape specifications are changed by the wire services, as happened in 1961 in Canada and 1963 in the United States.

The change of format is another time when a new choice of body type may be logical.

A publisher may also change his type to gain an edge on competition. A competitor's change of typeface—especially if properly promoted— may give an advantage that must be countered by the same tactics.

Finally, he may change type just for the sake of giving his readers something new and better. Fashion and automobile industries exploit new styling so expertly that the American public is intrigued by "the latest model" of anything from sneakers to limousines. Newspapers, too, can use a "new look" as the peg for successful promotion.

Whatever may prompt a publisher to choose a new body type, he should recognize this as a major decision and make it on the basis of sound thinking.

Body type is the newspaper's major tool of communication. The person who reads only headlines and pictures is poorly informed. Rigid restrictions on the length of a head often result in a statement that puzzles or misinforms the reader; the message of a photograph may easily be misinterpreted.

We must convert the "looker" at display elements into a "reader" of body type. We must lure him into body type and then keep him there until he is adequately informed. That means that he must "read" in the complete sense of the word.

We have all had the experience of reading only physically. In a dentist's office or in our own home while we wait for Junior to bring home the family car late of an evening, we may diligently process every word on a printed page—and not remember a syllable of what we "read." So the newspaper reader must actually receive and comprehend a message to complete communications.

To comprehend the message requires expenditure of attention and mental energy. The less the reader expends on the mechanical process of reading, the more he has to devote to receiving and comprehending the message.

When the reader's eyes become fatigued—even if the reader is not specifically aware of it—he lays aside his newspaper. The unread type is wasted. We seek to postpone the point of fatigue until at least the major portion of the information in an issue has been read and comprehended.

The choice of a new body type—if for no other reason than that it is a substantial investment—is usually that of top management. Usually committees—formal or informal—from the copy desk and possibly the composing room are involved in preliminaries. But the final choice is usually that of the publisher or editor. (Often one man holds both titles. In this book the terms will be used interchangeably in referring to the highest working executive at a newspaper.)

There are several basic requirements for body type. Each should be carefully evaluated. For although the factors are subtle—almost invisible—ones, they are of great, great importance.

This discussion is in the context of hot-metal type only because most newspaper body type today is in that form. Phototypesetter faces are, in most instances, made from drawings for metal type and, in print, are identical to the originals. So the following criteria apply to both kinds of type. They also apply to strikeon composition, that produced by machines like typewriters.

Readability

The primary requirement for body type is high *readability*. This is the quality that makes it pleasant and easy to consume large quantities of type. The word *legibility* is sometimes, and erroneously, used as a synonym for readability. In the precise usage of the typographer, legibility is that characteristic that makes a few words pop off the page, through the eye, and into the brain of the reader without his being aware that he is reading. Legibility is needed for headlines, tabular material, advertising copy blocks, and other brief quantities of type.

There are several factors which influence readability: the type design, its x-height, ledding, *measure,* and accent. We'll define each as we examine it more closely.

In type design, as in all art forms, the best criterion of quality is endurance. While the best news body types don't go back as far as Shakespeare or Rembrandt or Beethoven, they are old enough to merit the description of "classics."

Since the days of incunabula, type designers have played variations on the theme of the Latin alphabet, as we already noted in Chapter 2. Varieties available when newspapers began were already legion, but no type was designed specifically for newspaper use. Newspaper printers bought type where they could dicker for the best price, and they used whatever faces happened to be in their cases. Some faces were good, many were poor, most were indifferent. It really didn't matter much; in this country, at least, people were so hungry for newspapers and had so much time for reading them that any body type was more than acceptable. The printer used paper that was far better than today's newsprint, and he actually pressed the type into moistened paper so that each character was truly imprinted and clearly visible. Good thing, too, for paper was expensive and in order to make it go the farthest, type size was kept small.

The press used by colonial newspapermen and, for smaller papers, through the entire nineteenth century, was not appreciably different from that used by Gutenberg in ancient Mainz. It was made of iron instead of wood; that's all.

But the printing industry—and we must always remember that journalism is well described as "the press"—was the beneficiary of the industrial revolution. While we need not dwell on the colorful history of printing—several excellent books do that in fascinating detail—every newspaperman should be aware of those inventions which made his present career possible.

A major one was the invention of wood-pulp paper by a nameless Saxon weaver in 1840. Another, the American Richard Hoe's invention of the rotary press in 1846, took advantage of the stereotyping process invented by Lord Stanhope in England in 1805. By 1865 the principle of printing from a roll of paper instead of on individual sheets had speeded press productivity. Now newspapers could be printed swiftly on inexpensive paper; the way was opened to the rapid transmission of news to a mass market.

But two other inventions were still required to make modern journalism possible. One was Samuel Morse's telegraph in 1844, which enabled an editor to reach far out for fresh news; the other was Ottmar Mergenthaler's Linotype, which went into use in 1886. This overcame the final bottleneck.

Newspapermen had been chafing under the limitations of setting type by hand. What an irony it was to be able to print newspapers at more than 60,000 copies per hour but to have to wait while compositors picked individual pieces of type out of a case by hand!

Now type could be set mechanically at speeds four, five, or even more times greater than by hand. Actually, the Linotype doesn't set type; it manufactures set type, as was noted in the previous chapter.

This new machine offered—and still does, in fact—many advantages to newspapers. To the typographer, the major one is that each line of type is brand spanking new; handset type is reused and eventually shows wear. That sharp printing image pointed up typographic weakness, though.

Mergenthaler's first face—called, inevitably, Linotype No. 1—was 6-point, and that soon became "standard" for news body. But it wasn't until 1926 that type was specifically designed for newspaper use.

The first requisite of a good typeface is that it be "an honest design." That means that it must be unobtrusive, with no idiosyncrasies that call attention to individual letters. Each character must blend into words and sentences and even phrases so that the whole can easily be read without even noticing its parts. An honest design is also one that recognizes the special needs of specific printing jobs and meets them.

Newsprint, the relatively cheap, wood-pulp paper used for news-papers, is an obstreperous printing surface. It is hard, rough, and linty. The surface requires a letterform of sturdy lines that will be as visible "in the valleys" of the texture as "on the hills." The lint accumulates in sharp corners of the characters, soon becomes soaked with ink, then smudges the paper.

The ink is no pressman's delight, either; it is little better than colored kerosene. The ink dries by *absorption,* not by *oxidation,* as better inks do. It must soak into the fibers of the paper, and so it makes a fuzzy image.

In solid areas, news ink is only about 70% black. As newsprint is 10% gray—as opposed to 0% of white coated papers—the newspaper printer has only 60% of the gray scale to work with. To produce a clear image with these ingredients requires a well-conceived typeface.

"Form follows function" is an honored truism that good typefaces document. Look at the good newspaper body types, for example.

The first face specifically designed to conform to its function was Ionic

No. 5. Introduced in 1926, it was an instant success and became the first of the famous Legibility Group of body types which today still dress the majority of American newspapers.

Still another problem plagues those faces that must be stereotyped. We have noted in the previous chapter that stereotyping makes a mold of a flat printing form and from it casts a curved plate to fit on a rotary press.

The flong, of which the mold is made, is paper, made up of tiny cylinders of cellulose. Like logs floating down a stream, these cylinders tend to point in the same direction, up and down in relation to the regular newspaper page. When these little cylinders absorb moisture, as they must to make the flong pliable enough for molding, they expand in girth but not appreciably in length. The impression of the form is imbedded into the swollen fibers. As the flong is *scorched* (dried out) prior to the casting of the metal plate from it, the cellulose cylinders contract to their original size. Also contracted are the impressions of the type characters. This is the distortion the designer must guard against by the way he draws his letterforms.

Newspaper publishers have converted this liability into a dollars-and-cents asset. Because a flong shrinks sideways, it is possible to squeeze an advertisement and print it in an area considerably narrower than the plate supplied by the advertiser. But because ads are billed by vertical measurement, which is not changed appreciably by shrinkage, the narrowed ad will produce as much revenue as if it had not been shrunk.

Unless it is a deliberate attempt to shortchange the customer on the space he is buying, such planned and acute shrinkage is difficult to rationalize. It would seem much wiser to set columns narrow to start with and to keep stereo shrinkage to the minimum rather than making flongs that will shrink as much as 10% or occasionally even more.

The distortion of shrinkage is obviously a handicap to the readability of body type. It is all the more annoying because it is not uniform. The overall shrinkage of a whole-page flong can be controlled. But shrinkage is not always uniform; column 8 may shrink far more than column 3, for instance. This can easily be demonstrated. From any stereotype newspaper, cut out a single column, or portion thereof, from any page. Lay this clip on columns of other pages and see in how many instances the shrinkage has not been the same. So the column-widths vary; this means that body type—and halftone and *Ben Day* dots—are distorted in varying degrees. It takes real genius to design a body face that will be readable after it has gone through this torture.

The age of brilliance in newspaper body type design is past. The latest face is Aurora, cut in 1961. Several factors have contributed to the current eclipse of the news-type designer. One is the surge of phototype-setting that requires transformation of the great type libraries of Linotype and Intertype to photographic form. It takes an incredible amount of work to design a new font, work out proper spacing and placement on the matrix, draw enlarged letterforms, from them make brass templates from which punches are cut and matrices stamped. The highly skilled people who do this work are the same ones who are busy converting hot metal into cold type, and there have been just no men or machines left over to work with metal news types.

Equally pressing are financial aspects. There are 103 matrices in a regular newspaper body font. Fifteen of these are fractions and could possibly be eliminated. But the other 88 are essential; if only one of these is missing, the entire font is useless. There are at least a dozen significant news faces, and these are made in several combinations. Eight sizes are in common use. If you multiply all these numbers, you'll find that the inventory of matrix suppliers is truly astronomical. This ties up literally millions of dollars and requires highly sophisticated—and costly—inventory controls and whole regiments of stock clerks.

Because of this, plus a conversion of some of the market to cold type, the two major suppliers have classified fonts into two classes. Those with greatest volume carry a lower price; slow movers cost more, and eventually will price themselves out of the market.

But fortunately the designers of the past decades did their job so well that their faces are not in the least dated. (Excelsior, for instance, introduced in the late 1920's, was the second typeface in the Legibility Group; however, its design is so clean and sound that it was chosen by the *Christian Science Monitor* when it made its drastic restyling in 1963, and readers were enthusiastic about its highly contemporary feeling.) In Mergenthaler Linotype's latest Class I grouping, those faces that carry the lowest prices, there are 71 different fonts of news body type in 7- through 12-point. Intertype has almost that many. All are good ones.

The most widely used newspaper face, now and in the past, is Corona. Its popularity is well deserved; it meets all technical requirements with a comfortable margin of safety.

Corona, along with Ionic, Excelsior, Opticon, and Paragon, is part of the Linotype Legibility Group. Other faces in Linotype cuttings are News, Majestic, and Aurora. The most popular Intertype news faces are Ideal, Regal, Royal, and Imperial.

There are some faces which are not thought of as news type but which work well in that harness. Times Roman was designed for the *Times* of London, but some editors consider it rather bookish in flavor. Primer is used mostly for books and "fine printing" but works well for newspapers. Caledonia is so versatile that it can be used for practically any printing job. Fairfield Medium, used mostly for fine printing, makes a handsome body type for *Newsday*.

Individual characters among faces look so much alike that even an expert must make minute comparison to differentiate among them. But when they are compared in blocks, the differences become apparent. This is the only way that body type should be selected: after inspecting it in mass setting.

Each typeface has its own *typographic color*. Ionic and Corona are the darkest en masse; Paragon, the lightest.

It is interesting to note that darker faces rank high in the choice of contemporary readers. That may be why Ionic has been a favorite since its introduction in 1926 and has even shown a slight upturn in use during the past few years.

The use of tape-operated linecasters and strikeon composition adds new factors to decision making, which will be discussed a little later.

If one generalization can be made about the design of body type, it is the printer's observation that "You can see a pumpkin easier than a goose egg." This picturesque analogy means that a letterform that is well-rounded (based on a circular form) has higher readability than a more compressed, oval-shaped character.

When the difference between the typographical pumpkin and egg becomes pronounced, we call the oval form *Condensed*. Truly condensed letters are most commonly used in headletters. Differences in roundness in body type are more subtle but nonetheless important. The best way to determine even slight differences in the width of the letters is by the lca, lowercase alphabet length, discussed in Chapter 1. This is the length of the line formed by the 26 "little letters," the lowercase, or minuscules. These technical data are given in type catalogs.

One of the most widely used news faces is 8-point Corona with Bold Face No. 2; it has an lca of 118 points. Corona No. 2 with Erbar Bold has an lca of 126 points. Other Coronas, all 8-points, have lca's of 111, 121 and 128.

A face with a 126-point lca is 1.3% wider than one with a 111-point lca. This does not mean that each letter of the first font is that much wider than its counterpart in the second font. The *l* or *i* may be the same width in both faces. The difference will be most marked in the round letters like *a, e,* and *o.*

While the lowercase alphabet length is only an approximate measure for individual letters, it does show the roundness of the entire font; the longer the lca, the rounder the letters.

Type Sizes

The size of type is an obvious factor in readability. We need only to compare the 5½-point agate type of classified ad pages with the 120-point page-one banner head to demonstrate this vividly.

There is a definite long-range trend to larger type in papers. The first Ionic was a 6½-point. This caused a stir in the industry, for the most commonly used size up to then was 6-point. But when, a few years later, Excelsior, the second in the Legibility Group, was introduced, it was cut in 7-point; the trend to larger faces was begun.

The Newspaper Enterprise Association (N.E.A.) is a syndicated service with a clientele so widespread that it makes an excellent sampling of American dailies. Late in 1968, it conducted a survey of body types used by its clients. The results:

8 on 9	23.5%
9 on 9	20.6%
9 on 10	23.5%
Others	32.4%

The point size of a typeface is not a definitive measurement, alas, and this has created confusion for many newspapermen.

The point size really doesn't measure the type, it merely defines the size of the metal block on which the printing element is carried.

When a designer begins to draw an 8-point type, for instance, he knows that the distance from the top of the ascender to the bottom of the descender, plus a tiny shoulder of metal at the top and bottom, must measure exactly 8 points. He also knows that the baseline, the line that defines the bottom of such letters as *a, e, m,* and *w,* must be at a specified distance from the bottom of the metal block. This is called *standard lining,* and it assures that any and all 8-point type will align when mixed in the same line.

After that, the designer has practically unlimited freedom. If he

a

Selection of body type is the first, and most important, step in designing a readable newspaper. The newspaper reader expends most of his available time and energy on body copy. Good body type enables him to read more—and with greater pleasure—in any given period.

b

Selection of body type is the first, and most important, step in designing a readable newspaper. The newspaper reader expends most of his available time and energy on body copy. Good body type enables him to read more—and with greater pleasure—in any given period.

c

Selection of body type is the first, and most important, step in designing a readable newspaper. The newspaper reader expends most of his available time and energy on body copy. Good body type enables him to read more—and with greater pleasure—in any given period.

d

Selection of body type is the first, and most important, step in designing a readable newspaper. The newspaper reader expends most of his available time and energy on body copy. Good body type enables him to read more—and with greater pleasure—in any given period.

e

Selection of body type is the first, and most important, step in designing a readable newspaper. The newspaper reader expends most of his available time and energy on body copy. Good body type enables him to read more—and with greater pleasure—in any given period.

a. Corona No. 2
b. Ionic No. 5
c. Paragon
d. Opticon
e. Majestic

Fig. 3. Newspaper body types in Linotype Legibility Group. All are 8-point, set on 8½.

envisions a design with long necks and tails, he knows they can be only comparatively elongated; he must make the bowls of those letters small. The primary letters must then be small, too. With short ascenders and descenders, the bowls and the primaries are relatively large.

The reader considers the "size" of the letter that of the primaries. That's reasonable; ascenders and descenders are merely appendages. We don't consider a giraffe bigger than an elephant because his neck and legs are longer.

It is entirely possible to have a 9-point type that is actually smaller than an 8-point as far as the reader is concerned. Among various 8-points there are differences of actual size that are obvious even to an untrained eye.

So the editor must chose a body type with high primary letters, a tall x-height. This type is one where the x, along with the other primary letters, is as high as possible without converting circles into ovals. The x-height is the true measure of the size of type. Faces with tall primary letters are described as "big on the slug." This means that most of the bearing metal is devoted to the body of the letterform rather than to ascenders and descenders.

The Duplex

The *duplex* face on a Linotype matrix is a useful auxiliary to the regular typeface. On all body sizes and many display sizes through 24-point, a single brass matrix carries two molds. When the operator sets *on the rail,* he hangs the brass matrices on metal strips that lift the lower mold into contact with the casting mechanism. This is roughly the equivalent of using the shift key on a typewriter and bringing a second row of characters into position to strike the platen. However, the duplex molds on Linotype matrices do not carry the capitals; they are on separate, wider mats. The duplex usually carries the boldface or the Italic forms of the Roman face in the main position. But the duplex may be an entirely different face or even race. A popular duplex for Corona, an Old Style Roman, is *Erbar Bold,* a Gothic. In some fonts small caps are the duplex for punctuation marks.

Italic duplexes become fewer for newspaper use. Readers feel that Italics are hard to read. Actually, they aren't, but when we think a job is hard, we try to avoid it. Failing that, we do it with less than ecstatic joy. Neither alternative is conducive to high readership. Probably the adverse reaction to Italics on a newspaper page is due to their light typographic color. We have already noted that contemporary readers prefer Romans with darker color. To this taste the lighter Italics cannot be especially attractive. Thus boldface is the most widely used duplex.

The decision, then, is whether to use Roman boldface or the bold of another race. Linotype duplexes Corona with Erbar Bold and with Gothic; Excelsior and Opticon can carry Memphis, a Square Serif; News

Fig. 4. Big-on-slug characteristics shown in top line. All characters are 10-point, enlarged about 10 times. First *a* and *b* are Bodoni; center letters are Garamond; right, Times Roman. Note variations in apparent size.

is duplexed with Clarendon Bold, a useful and attractive accent. Inter-type duplexes Ideal with Gothic No. 3 and with Antique No. 1, a bold Italic, that is a little too bookish for best news use. Regal carries Cairo Bold, a Square, or Gothic No. 3. All newspaper faces are also duplexed with regular boldface, of course.

For the customary uses of boldface—conventional subheads, cutlines, boxes, etc.—there is no appreciable difference in functionalism between the regular bold, a bold Gothic, or bold Squares. The choice may well be made on the basis of personal preference for appearance.

Agate

The choice of an agate face is usually not that of the editorial depart-ment. The overwhelming proportion of 5½-point type is used for classified ads, and so the advertising department usually chooses that face, with editorial given little more than the opportunity to advise and consent.

Whoever gets to make the decision must first decide a basic choice: Shall we use Roman or Sans Serifs for our agate?

All the news faces, with a few insignificant exceptions, are cut in 5½-point. So there is a wide variety of Romans to choose from. In this size there are also enough Sans to offer adequate selection.

The trend today is toward the use of Sans Serifs for classified advertis-ing. On the face of it, that may seem an anomaly. We know that the Sans have low readability, yet newspapers set page after solid page in Sans. In many papers—notably the Sunday *Los Angeles Times*—the classified section will consistently run in the hundreds of pages. Almost every paper that runs such giant classified sections sets them in Sans Serifs.

The significant fact, though, is that no one reads page upon page or even column upon column of want ads. The person searching for a used bicycle couldn't care less about apartments for rent. Each reader reads only that small portion that interests him at the moment. He wants the information in each ad to come through quickly and accurately. He doesn't read in the graceful sweeps with which he consumes news matter; he reads a phrase at a time and evaluates it. So the normal stride in reading such matter is a choppy one that matches the literary style of such advertising.

On the news side, the same conditions prevail in the reading of matter set in agate—stock market reports, box scores, and similar tabular material. Here, too, although there is a large mass of such copy, the

AST BOOKKEEPER, experienced accounts receivable, state qualifications. Y 97 Times-Herald.

BOOKKEEPER, exp, complete chg, good salary, 9 to 5. W. M. Lederpush Loose Leaf Corp., 830 2d ave., City.

BOOKKEEPER ASSISTANT, payroll and accounts payable, 5 days, 35 hrs. State age, salary. Y 42 Times-Herald.

BKKPR and Asst., typing, 5 day, $60. NINTH AVENUE AGENCY, 2 9th av.

BOOKKPER, small facty payroll exp. size 13 pref., not essential. LA 3-2106.

BKKPR-STENO, exp; $58, 37 hrs; 2 wks vac. Associated Pencil, 39 Bway.

AST BOOKKEEPER, experienced accounts receivable, state qualifications. Y 97 Times-Herald.

BOOKKEEPER, exp, complete chg, good salary, 9 to 5. W. M. Lederpush Loose Leaf Corp., 830 2d ave., City.

BOOKKEEPER ASSISTANT, payroll and accounts payable, 5 days, 35 hrs. State age, salary. Y 42 Times-Herald.

BKKPR and Asst., typing, 5 day, $60. NINTH AVENUE AGENCY, 2 9th av.

BOOKKPER, small facty payroll exp. size 13 pref., not essential. LA 3-2106.

BKKPR-STENO, exp; $58, 37 hrs; 2 wks vac. Associated Pencil, 39 Bway.

AST BOOKKEEPER, experi counts receivable, state qua Y 97 Times-Herald.

BOOKKEEPER, exp, comp good salary, 9 to 5. W. M. Loose Leaf Corp., 830 2d a

BOOKKEEPER ASSISTAN1 and accounts payable, 5 da State age, salary. Y 42 Tim

BKKPR and Asst., typing, 5 NINTH AVENUE AGENCY,

BOOKKPER, small facty pa size 13 pref., not essential.

BKKPR-STENO, exp; $58, wks vac. Associated Pencil,

Fig. 5. Agate type for newspaper uses. Col. 1, Corona with Erbar Bold; 2, Ionic with Bold Face No. 2; 3, Spartan Book with Heavy. Each has lca of 88 points for wire-tape setting.

reader is interested in only a few stocks, the score of only one or a few ball games, his own name in a list of a hundred, etc.

Whenever the amount of reading at one time is small, the legibility of the Sans is an asset.

For advertising or news use, numbers are essential. Most of the information in a want ad is carried by numbers—the model year for used cars, capacity of the item, the price, and, absolutely essential, the phone number. Misreading any number in such data renders the ad useless. In editorial agate, the numbers are almost the entire message. The name of a stock is worthless without the closing price. We may want to know whether a player broke into the lineup, but we're far more interested in whether he is in the scoring column. Thus the design of the numbers in a font should be considered closely before a font is chosen.

Although we have been speaking about "agate," we should note that some newspapers use 6-point type for classifieds and news tabulations. The same factors for decision apply. Actually there is little practical difference between 5½- and 6-point type in horizontal measurement. Spartan Book, a widely used classified-advertising face, has an lca of 88 points in agate and of 89 points in 6-point. In the 9-pica column which most metropolitan papers use for their classifieds, the difference in lca's means only .18 character per line. That's in theory; in actuality, they set the same, line for line.

The important difference is in vertical measurement, of course. A newspaper column of typical 22-inch depth will carry 288 lines of agate but only 264 lines of 6-point. For smaller newspapers this difference, when multiplied by the line rate, is an attractive pile of cash. In editorial use, the difference becomes measurable in long stock tables, and while it doesn't convert as dramatically into money, the saving of space is definitely not inconsequential.

For even further savings of space, Spartan Book has been designed with ascenders that retain legibility even when partially chopped off. So agate Spartan can be cast on a 5-point slug. The abbreviated descenders are not as esthetically pleasing as they are in full form, but they do not affect legibility to any marked degree, and 316 of these lines can be stacked into a column, a gain of 243 lines per page!

Agate faces, like those in news sizes, are available for setting by wire-transmitted tape.

Spacebands

An important tool for readability is practically invisible—the space between words. It is produced automatically by *spacebands* that simply expand—like a wedge driven into a log—until all the available space in a line is evenly filled up.

The choice of spacebands can substantially affect the readability of all type, yet probably not one editor out of fifty even knows that there are five kinds of spacebands for linecaster use. It is rather difficult to make a rational choice when you don't know the alternatives.

Spacebands range from extra thin to extra thick, and obviously someone must specify on the order blank which style to buy. That ought to be the typographer's decision. But the mechanical department must be consulted, for the demands on this unobtrusive instrument run a comparatively wide range in the restrictive measure of newspaper composition.

Tight spacing is an important aid to easy reading. Good typographers specify *French spacing* in hand composition; this means that no gap between words can be greater than a 3-em space. (Remember that spaces are designated as fractions of an em; a 3-em space is actually a ⅓-em space.) Contemporary usage tends toward even tighter setting, 4-em spaces, but this controlled spacing is a luxury that can't be enjoyed under the pressure of newspaper deadlines.

The most useful spaceband style is the *special taper*, which can provide word space from .0369 to .1219 inches. This range is essential in tape operation and most efficient for manual operation, too. It provides the tight spacing conducive to good readability and yet can fill the line in those instances where there may be only two or three words—and spacebands—in a line.

The essential in good composition is, of course, the skill of the compositor. In punching tape or setting manually, he should be encouraged to *set tight*. This ungrammatical injunction means that he will get as many characters as possible in a line instead of taking the easy way out and avoiding more difficult hyphenation decisions.

Leaders

Leaders (pronounced *leeders*) are connective devices between two or more items on a line of tabulation. In newspaper usage a common example is the front-page index. We find leaders in some box scores and in budgets and similar tables.

Leaders are either dots or dashes, and there are from two to six of them in an em. This adds up to 20 different variations in style, and, again, someone must choose which one to use.

The use of leaders in various gaps between items cannot be determined by formula, but there is a rule of thumb that can be useful as a starting point: The maximum gap that can be spanned without the aid of leaders is one-third the point size of the body type, expressed in picas. So, using 8-point body type, we would use leaders to span any gap wider than 2⅔ picas or, for practical purposes, 3 picas.

If there is any doubt as to the need for leaders, use them, especially where there are many lines of tabular material and the eye might become confused as it matches up pairs or sets of data.

Faces for Tape Operation

Mechanization of typesetting by the use of tape is a major factor in the economic well-being of newspapers, and it is a factor in the selection and specification of news type.

Tape to operate linecaster keyboards is classified as *wire* and *local*. "Wire tape" is produced at a distant point, usually the offices of a news service. Holes in the tape are translated into electrical impulses which are transmitted by wire to the newspaper office. There the code is translated into two forms, a typewritten copy of the original message and a new perforated tape, an exact replica of that back at the sending point.

"Local tape," obviously, is that produced in the newspaper's own plant. At a keyboard, the operator produces perforated tape with or without *hard copy*, a typewritten translation of the coded tape which may be used for preliminary proofreading.

No matter what its origin, tape is fed into a unit on the linecaster. A *reader* deciphers the patterns of holes and actuates the keyboard according to instructions carried by the tape.

Advantages of tape operation are substantial and too well known to need elaboration here. There have been periods when tape operation was the difference between a sickly and a healthy newspaper as measured on the profit-and-loss statement. Sometimes tape has been the difference between a living and dead newspaper, too.

Local tape operation places no real restriction on the choice of news type. But there are real and sometimes uncomfortable restrictions which wire tape imposes on the designer and user of typefaces.

In designing a normal typeface, the designer may make any character as wide as necessary for harmony with the others in the font. But *unit matrices,* those for use with tape, must be designed to specifications that were set, alas!, not by typographers but by engineers. In any font of any face or size, the lowercase *e* must always be 10 units wide; the cap *M,* 18 units; the cap *A,* 14; and so on. For it is only by counting units that the operator who perforates the tape is able to tell when he has filled a line sufficiently. The Linotype operator need only look to see how three-dimensional matrices are filling a physically defined space. If he calls too many matrices out of the magazine, they will merely spill onto the floor, and the error is all too evident.

But the tape perforator has no such obvious gauge. He only punches holes in a strip of paper. A "line" in tape form is too long and the material too flimsy to measure mechanically. So the machine counts the number of units in a line by adding up the varying values for each character as they are keyboarded. Standardization is necessary so that an *h* in Spartan agate counts the same, in relation to its alphabet, as the *h* of 12-point Paragon.

These mechanical specifications are a handicap to designers, but those assigned to produce unit fonts have overcome this admirably.

There obviously must be a rigid relation of the tape to the matrices used on the tape-actuated Linotype. If the operator puts codes for 40 characters on a tape, this will make a neat 11-pica line of agate type. But if the same tape is used for setting 8-point Opticon, there will be about nine matrices that just won't fit into the 11 picas between the Linotype jaws. The tape puncher must know how many units of a specific face will fit into the desired line, set the counter on his perforator to that amount, then keep within that maximum. This is easy when tape is produced locally.

When wire is produced at a distance, however, the conditions reverse. Obviously Associated Press, punching tape in Radio City, Manhattan, can't transmit tape at different specifications to each of its members. One set of impulses may perforate tape in Poughkeepsie and Denver and all points hooked into the transmission. It becomes the need of the receiver to choose a face that will utilize this common tape. So a standardization was adopted: 8-set on 12 picas. This means that an 8-set face will just fill a 12-pica line when it has used up all the characters in a "line" of tape. "Set" is the width, in hundredths of an inch, of the brass matrix of the capital *M* of the given font. An 8-set font has a lowercase alphabet length of 118.1 points.

When that standard was adopted, the 12-pica column was standard for newspapers. Then came World War II. Among the many commodities to be rationed was newsprint, and it was allocated by weight. Immediately pressures built up to narrow the column. It was obviously advantageous to print as many columns as possible on each ton of newsprint. Columns were squeezed down, to get the maximum number of them—and of pages—from a newspaper's weighed ration.

Narrowing of columns was done independently, and the result soon neared chaos. The national advertiser never knew whether an ad would float in the ordered space or whether it would have to be trimmed down to fit. In 1951, agreement between the American Association of Advertising Agencies and the American Newspaper Publishers Association set 11½ picas as the standard on which national advertising would be prepared. An ad in this specification would fit in any newspaper that subscribed to the agreement.

Unfortunately, the narrowing of columns continued. Many astute observers believe this was a misjudgment. By now rationing had been removed; the economy had switched from military to consumer orientation. Now the publishers' aim was to save newsprint costs, for paper is sold just as it had been rationed, by weight. But a significant reality was overlooked.

Suppose a publisher changed his specifications from a 64-inch web, the roll from which pages are printed on a rotary press, to a 60-inch one. That's between 6% and 7% reduction in weight per roll. But the papermaker's cost didn't drop proportionately. In simplest terms, it meant that he only narrowed the width of the productive parts of his huge, blocklong machines. Depreciation, amortization, taxes, payroll, and utilities remained the same. For self-protection, he raised the price per ton so his revenue for a day's operations remained the same. There were other reasons for price increases, too. Inflation was setting in; the price of everything from milk to shoes to newsprint went up so inexorably that the consumer knew it was useless to protest. In the inflationary rise in paper costs, too few publishers noted that narrowing the web was only an apparent economy.

Finally 11 picas was established as a new advertising standard in

1953. But even this was not adhered to. Some newspapers engaged in sophistry. They cast their type on 11-pica slugs, all right, but they *jawed in* their linecasters 3 points at each end. So although the piece of metal that carried the type was the standard 11 picas long, the length of the line of type was only 10½.

Advertising columns and news columns must be the same width in a newspaper, of course. So when the ad column was established at 11 picas, news columns became, perforce, 11 picas too. But wire-tape specifications never quite caught up. Three years after the 11-pica standard had been adopted, the Associated Press established—and UPI concurred in—a new specification for their wire tape: 8-set on 11.9 picas! (Note that the period in the typographer's measurement is not a decimal point; the number after it is points. So 11.9 picas is 11 picas, 9 points.)

This standard was set as a concession to newspapers that were using 12-pica columns. They could accept the new tape and still maintain their old column width by expanding spacebands wider within a line of matrices. An expansion of 3 additional points is practical in newspaper lines of 11 to 12 picas. But lengthening the line beyond 3 points would demand more than maximum expansion from the spacebands and thus result in loose lines which could not be cast on the Linotype.

Obviously newspapers using 11-pica columns weren't about to widen them by 9 points and lose all the advantages—real and apparent—of a standardized column. They had to accommodate the different specifications by changing body type.

If a "line" of wire tape calls for enough 8-set characters to fill an 11.9-pica line of matrices, it will call out too many characters for a shorter line. The only way to use the tape for the narrower measure is to use a narrower typeface. For an 11.6-pica line, this requires a face with an lca of 113.2 points, a 7.66-set. For an 11-pica line, a 7.5-set face is needed; this has an lca of 111 points.

An 8-point face with a 118-point lca has the round design of the printer's ideal "pumpkin"; an 8-point with a 111-point lca is definitely a "goose egg."

But publishers accepted the wire-service standard and, in order to narrow their columns below 11.9 picas, adopted 7.5-set matrices. Almost all these were 8-point; a few 7- and 7½-points were still used.

Then new pressures began warping typographic standards.

In the very early 1950's, several major metropolitans adopted 9-point body type. The *Chicago Tribune* was a trailblazer, and dailies in the San Francisco Bay area were in the vanguard. It made sense to give the reader, who was being beguiled by larger television tubes and huge movie screens, a larger typeface to ease his overburdened eyes. Overburdened they certainly were. Statistics of the times showed that 75% of all American adults had some vision defects. Even youngsters of school age were far from eagle-eyed; one third of them—that was 3 million—had defective eyesight.

Bigger newspapers were not using tape at that time, a situation that has changed only slightly in the following decade, and so they could set in any size and lca and at any measure they darn well felt like. The results were good; readers were audible in their thanks, and excellent promotions extolled the virtues of the bigger face.

Soon papers that were committed to wire tape sought to join the parade. They demanded from type manufacturers 9-point faces that could be used with wire tape. That meant the designer had to retain the 7.5 set. The only room for enlargement was up-and-down.

The result was inevitable: a gangling, spidery face that pained typographers and gave no comfort or pleasure to the reader. At least one 9-point that gained considerable use was unmitigatedly ugly. But it became a status symbol to use 9-point, and type was chosen solely on the basis of that unrealistic measurement. Type manufacturers pointed out the anomaly. But in a free economy what the customer wants, the customer gets. He wanted—and he got—an inferior body type design.

There were sporadic suggestions that the wire specifications again be changed, but there is ingrained resistance to change. Fortunately in Canada, an influential committee of the Canadian Press, that country's wire news service, was directed by a man who knew type, William "Pete" Southam of Southam Newspapers. Under his leadership, CP adopted the logical standard: 8-set on 11 picas. The changeover was made without the utter collapse of typesetting that American skeptics had predicted. With that example as Exhibit A, publishers in the United States finally effected the same change.

While this was not a minor adjustment, it proceeded smoothly. Every American newspaper using wire tape had to adopt a face of 118.1 lca and have its machines ready when the tape changed at midnight of October 13, 1963. Success of that transition became ammunition for a new battle in the United States that is still only a skirmish at the time of this writing: to create a demand for two transmissions. One would be the current one for 11-pica columns, and a supplementary one would be at the length for optimum-format papers.

There are several excellent 8-set body faces, and so newspapers can again choose the fonts of higher readability rather than the uncomfortably squeezed-up forms of an 111-point lca, especially those in 9-point.

The typographer must choose a body type in unit matrices if, but only if, his newspaper uses wire tape. If it is using only locally perforated tape, any face at all may be chosen. For such fonts it is necessary to use a *multiface perforator*. The machine is given the information of the width of each character in a specific font so that it can properly count the building length of the line. The same information can readily be fed into the computer if it is used. With a computer, of course, the newspaper can take wire tape and convert it to the specifications necessary to set its own nonunit body type. These operations are so simple that they are negligible in consideration of a nonunit face.

Computerization for Typesetting

The 1960's may well go down in history as the age of computers. The ubiquitous electronic brains moved into newspaper plants, too. As in any large business organization, computers were valuable tools for accounting, advertising, and circulation departments. It was in the composing room, however, that computers became the glamour girls of the industry.

A truism that is often overlooked is that it takes human beings to set type. While there are mechanical devices that can scan typewritten copy and convert it into type without human intervention, they are still only laboratory devices. In this age of rapid technological advances, it is sheer foolishness to suggest that this lab tool will never become a working part of the composing room. But it is logical to assume that, unless the economics of the situation change drastically, the human typesetter will be around for a long, long time. The computer, as used now and as it probably will be for at least a generation or two, will merely take over the onerous, repetitious part of the job that slows down the human compositor.

A good Linotype operator can *hang the elevator* on his machine, call matrices out of the magazine, faster than the machine can cast a line and clear the way for the next group of mats. So he places no limitation on the productivity of the linecaster. But he cannot maintain this pace throughout a cycle. He must take breaks to decipher dirty copy, to confer with his foreman, to exchange amenities with co-workers, to take a walk to the water cooler or the rest room, to puff a cigarette, or just to stretch weary muscles. Each time he stops, the machine halts too, and a five-figure investment isn't paying for itself.

The operator of a tape perforator works in the same pattern, but his machine represents only a small portion of the cost of the linecaster, and so its momentary idleness does not affect the profit-and-loss statement nearly as much. It is obviously easier to move a strip of paper through a machine than to circulate matrices by means of heavy moving parts. So the mechanical limit on speed has been raised materially; the operator need not wait for his machine.

There are other advantages of tape. Tape is easily stored without the problem of weight and bulk that type imposes. So instead of actually setting type on Monday for a Sunday edition and having to store galleys of type, tape can be hung on a peg on the wall, and the actual typesetting postponed until late in the week. Or tape can be perforated during the day and be used during the night without the need for premium payments to the operator. The output of several keyboards can be fed into a single linecaster so that it can produce without interruption.

Tape perforating demands mainly typewriting skills. There are many people available who have such skills; to adapt them to tape punching requires minimal training. Linotype operators seem always to be in short supply, and for many newspapers the unavailability of operators is a constant problem. A familiar pattern is for printing skills to be learned on weekly newspapers, then for the craftsman to move on to larger papers. So smaller newspapers have a continuous problem of finding trainable people. Good typists are fairly easy to find, even in small communities.

Tape can, in effect, be transmitted by wire, or it can be moved physically. The latter is an advantage to smaller newspapers, especially weeklies. Women tied to their homes by small children can do full- or part-time typesetting right there. The tape perforator, a small and not ugly machine, is installed in the kitchen or a spare bedroom where the mother can work and still keep an eye on her children. At intervals a courier picks up the tape and transports it to the newspaper plant for casting. (Everywhere in this discussion where the operator has been referred to as "he," it might well be "she." Women do keyboard work well and are becoming useful as well as decorative additions to many composing rooms.)

Whether an operator actually works at the Linotype or on a perforator, a major function is decision-making. Is a line tight enough to cast? If matrices and spacebands do not make a solid side for the metal box in which the slug is cast, molten metal, pumped into that box under pressure, will be forced through the gaps as a *front squirt*. This is dangerous for the operator; a liquid at 535° is hardly a soothing shower.

The hardened metal must then be removed from the machinery in a tedious process that wastes much productive time.

As he approaches the end of the line, the operator must decide whether he has to hyphenate in order to create a properly filled line of matrices. This happens on an average of once in every five lines of 11-pica composition. Making a decision, even one of slight global import, takes time. Watching a Linotype operator in action, we are not aware of the time involved in reaching this decision. But although the process is hidden, decision-making takes a sizable accumulated slice of the operator's shift.

If hyphenation is necessary, the operator must be familiar enough with the language to break words at proper places. If he is unable to fill the line properly with whole words or syllables, he must resort to *letterspacing,* using up the necessary space with thin divisions within a word. The good compositor looks for a word of appropriate length for letterspacing so that only a single—and a complete—word is involved. He will also attempt to letterspace a word within the line; if the first or last word is so spaced out, it will have a worse effect on readability than when an interior word is so manipulated. All of this takes time.

This is the chore that a computer can do efficiently and swiftly because it is essentially a trial-and-error process. Is this line tight enough to cast? Answer yes or no. Can the next word be hyphenated? Yes or no. Will one or two syllables fill the line properly? Yes or no. A computer's function is merely to answer yes or no, and its advantage is its ability to decide between alternatives at extremely high speeds. Its function in the typesetting process is simply to free the human being from the need to choose alternatives.

Aided by the computer, the human being is merely the intelligent link between copy and type. He works at a highspeed keyboard which is like that of an electric typewriter with a few additions for the unique needs of the Linotype. He pays no attention to lines; in effect, he types one "line" for an entire paragraph, noting only the start of the graf, where an indent is required, and the end of graf, where space may be needed to fill out the line of type.

Working at a keyboard which requires minimum physical effort to actuate the keys and freed from the need to return the carriage at brief intervals, the human linotypist can handle a take of news copy in about 66% of the time required at the regular justifying perforator or 43% of that on the linecaster keyboard.

The product of such an operator is called *idiot tape.* This is not an accurate and certainly not a complimentary term. More descriptive, less derogatory—and not nearly as popular among printers, whose vocabulary is notably pungent—is the term *raw tape*.

Raw tape is fed through the computer, which breaks it into portions, each one of which will produce a justified line of type in the form of a linecaster slug.

There are several degrees of sophistication among computers used in this way.

The most advanced—and consequently the most expensive—has a huge electronic memory. Faced with the problem of hyphenation, the computer will first attempt to divide the word according to logical grammatical rules. The trouble is that English is not logical. By formal rules, the word "through" should be divisible as "thro/ugh" and "wolves" as "wol/ves." So the computer must check its memory to see whether the word under the dissecting knife is an exception to the rule. Because there are so many exceptions, the machine's memory must be huge.

The newspaper staff must check up on its electronic ally constantly and feed into its memory those exceptions which haven't previously been noted and which have resulted in gaffes in print. Proper names are particularly irksome.

Computers able to cope with all the ramifications of English aberrations are capable of handling all or most of the newspaper's accounting chores, and a large portion of its capabilities—and costs—can be allocated to other departments.

A simpler computer handles only tape and solves the hyphenation problem in the simplest possible way; it ignores it. The *Justape*—its trade name—places only complete words in a line, never hyphenating. It uses four kinds of spacing between words. In the first variation, it uses only spacebands between words. In the second style, it uses spacebands, then, if the line is still not tight, it will add a thin space to each spaceband or as many as are needed to fill. The third style adds an em space to each band until the line can cast. In the final variation, two spacebands with an em space between them may be used between words. (Spacebands cannot be side-by-side in a line.) In any style, if added word spacing doesn't fill the line to casting length, the computer will letterspace, seeking a single interior word of appropriate length.

With longer measures, hyphenation is needed less frequently, and so unhyphenated composition is not too deleterious to readability. In 11-pica lines, unhyphenated composition is far less desirable. Excessive spacing between words will fragment the line and break reading rhythm,

a

The Middies had heard of his ability to disappear on the slightest provocation. But the Army had another fleet-footed phantom for them to chase this afternoon, and on the second play he showed the Middies his heels.

On a short-side reverse, Whitey

b

The Middies had heard of his ability to disappear on the slightest provocation. But the Army had another fleet-footed phantom for them to chase this afternoon, and on the second play he showed the Middies his heels.

On a short-side reverse, Whitey

c

The Middies had heard of his ability to disappear on the slightest provocation. But the Army had another fleet-footed phantom for them to chase this afternoon, and on the second play he showed the Middies his heels.

On a short-side reverse, Whitey

d

The Middies had heard of his ability to disappear on the slightest provocation. But the Army had another fleet-footed phantom for them to chase this afternoon, and on the second play he showed the Middies his heels.

On a short-side reverse, Whitey

Fig. 6. Effects of stereotype shrinkage, left. a, no shrinkage; b, 3%, representing ½-inch shrink across whole page; c, 5%, total shrinkage of 13/16 inches; d, 7% shrink, 1⅓ inches.

Effects of ledding, below, a-1, 8-point solid; b-1, ledded ½ point; c-1, ledded 1 point.

All settings in 8-point Corona No. 2.

a-1

Probably at no other p newspaper history has th a need for printing news materially stepped-up sp were required during th hectic war years. It was midst of this strenuous pei the Linotype face knowi rona was developed . . . which answered the growi for a clean, easy-to-re: which would print clearl exceedingly high press sp this period, newsprint wa —and paper conservat quired the use of a comp for newspaper printing.

b-1

Probably at no other newspaper history has tl a need for printing new materially stepped-up s were required during tl hectic war years. It wa midst of this strenuous pe the Linotype face know rona was developed . . which answered the grow for a clean, easy-to-re which would print clear exceedingly high press s] this period, newsprint w —and paper conserva quired the use of a com] for newspaper printing.

c-1

Probably at no other newspaper history has tl a need for printing new materially stepped-up s were required during tl hectic war years. It wa midst of this strenuous pe the Linotype face know rona was developed . . which answered the grow for a clean, easy-to-re which would print clear exceedingly high press s] this period, newsprint w —and paper conserva quired the use of a com] for newspaper printing.

but economic pressures may decide that imperfect composition is better than no composition at all.

This discussion is no catalog of comp-room computers; it is merely a tiny sampling. As this was being written, a huge printing exposition was staged at Chicago. The whole giant amphitheater was jammed with equipment, and there were dozens of computers on display. Some were built right into the typesetting machines. Some were quite conventional by computer standards, but others were Buck Rogerish even to today's sophisticated graphic arts technicians. Some machines produce photographic type not by projecting its picture from a negative but by "drawing" the letterforms with cathode rays according to instructions given by computer memory.

No rational person would hazard a prediction as to when these science-fiction tools will become commonplace. But he wouldn't suggest, either, that this is far in the future. The speed at which new composing-room equipment is being developed is difficult to comprehend, and the only valid advice is, "Read the technical journals constantly. It doesn't take long for your knowledge to become outdated these days."

Computerization is a valuable tool in the composing room and, in the case of the *Linasec,* adds a lot of fun to the day's routine. But in the main, computers concern the mechanical staff. The typographer need not be involved in daily operations, but he should be closely involved in original planning and programming to insure that the best standards of composition are adopted. To lose readability for mechanical efficiency is a poor bargain.

The very length of this chapter reiterates its theme: The selection of body type, even though the typical editor will make it only once or twice in his career, is a major one that should be made only after painstaking evaluation of each available choice. To attempt to build a typographically sound newspaper with inferior body type is like trying to build a sturdy house with green, warped, or dry-rotted lumber.

chapter **4**

Use of Body Type

THE TYPOGRAPHER is like a bridegroom; much of his success depends on his first long-term decision, and he must live with his choice for a long time. But there are day-to-day amenities that also affect the situation. In the case of the typographer, he may make short-range decisions on ledding, measure, and the use of the duplex that can raise readability levels.

Ledding

Ascenders and descenders are a factor in a subtle influence on readability—*ledding,* interlineal spacing.

To the reader, the "space between lines" is that from the baseline of the first line to the meanline of the second. If descenders and ascenders are long, spacing between primary letters is esthetically pleasing. But newspaper faces are designed to be big on the slug, with blunted descenders, so the primaries are closer together.

Type set *solid,* without ledding, looks cramped and overpowering. The reader is discomforted, and most of the pleasure he ought to find in reading is dissipated. An unhappy reader, even if he doesn't know why he is, will not be a reader for very long. So some ledding is desirable for all news faces.

But excessive ledding is just as bad. A block of type with too much interlineal spacing looks as if it's falling apart; again a subconscious discomfort plagues the reader. It also affects the mechanics of his reading. The reader may actually lose his place as his eye moves back to the start of the next line.

Research and the perceptive evaluation of skilled typographers indicate that a half to a full point of ledding is suitable for type from 7- through 8½-point. From 9- through 12-point, 1 point of ledding seems the ideal.

A half-point of ledding improves the readability of agate to a marked degree, though most newspapers set this size solid. What's more, they often set the 5½-point on a 5-point slug, slicing off the bottom of the descenders to make it fit. This is because agate need not be especially readable; instead, it must be legible, as we noted in Chapter 3.

Adding a half-point of ledding to an agate line will require 9.9% more space. Think of this in terms of newsprint cost for metropolitans that daily run market reports and scores and hundreds of pages of classifieds; the difference between solid agate and that sliced down to 5 points can be measured in whole pages.

It's good to note that handset type is usually ledded 2 points; this is because the ledd is a strip of metal placed between lines. If thinner than 2 points, it is too fragile and hard to handle. In machine composition, however, the spacing is built right into the line of type; the block that supports the printing face is made taller in ½-point increments.

The size of the type block is determined by the dimensions of the *Linotype mold,* a little metal box in which the molten type metal is cast. This is a semipermanent fixture on the Linotype, and so ledding must be standardized. This is an important decision and should be an almost permanent one, although changes can certainly be made more easily than in that of the original body-type selection.

Measure

The *measure* is the length of the line in which type is set. It is the most important single variable in determining readability.

The *optimum line length* is the only typographic factor that can be determined by mathematics. It was first formulated by compositors whose instinct and experience led them to a conclusion. When scientific research was directed to the problem, it was found that the instinct of our grandfathers was sound. Science and art agreed exactly.

The formula: $O = lca \times 1\frac{1}{2}$.

O is the optimum line length. This is the measure which is read most easily, most quickly, with minimum fatigue and with maximum recovery from fatigue, and, most important, with maximum comprehension. This optimum is one-and-a-half times longer than the lowercase alphabet length.

Corollary formulas are: $Mn = O - 25\%$, and $Mx = O + 50\%$.

Mn is the *minimum line length* and *Mx* the maximum of what is called the *readability range*.

As we approach the limits of this span, reading becomes more difficult. Outside the range, difficulty is so great that the reader is consciously aware of it.

Translating these formulas into line lengths for newspaper usage brings important but often overlooked facts to attention. Newspapers that use wire-transmitted tape must use a face with a lowercase alphabet length of 118 points if they want a standard 11-pica column. For that lca the optimum line length is 118 points × 1½, or 14.9 picas. The minimum is 11.1 picas and the maximum 22.1 picas.

We see then that the standard column measure of 11 picas is already 1 point below the readability range, so any further narrowing by indenting is doubly foolish. It creates an inferior product, and it costs more to produce than a good one.

Type set at regular 2-column measure will be 2 to 4 points beyond the maximum of the range. This is not nearly as dangerous as violating the minimum, however, and we need feel no qualms at setting double-column measure. But we definitely should not set wider than 2 columns.

As a rule of thumb, the newspaper designer declares, "Never set type narrower than 1 column or wider than 2 columns."

Another valid observation is, "Anything that's hard to set on the Linotype is hard to read."

As we set narrow lines, *letterspacing*—spacing within a word—becomes necessary in inverse ratio to the line length; the shorter the measure, the greater the need for letterspacing. This is because there is often no opportunity to tuck in an extra syllable and there are fewer spacebands between words to expand the line so it can be cast. Letterspacing has to be done by hand, and the compositor may well spend more time dropping thin spaces between letters than in stroking the keys. Extra spacing between letters fragments words—and extra spacing between words fragments phrases—so they must be deciphered rather than read.

The temptation to drop under the minimum is greatest when half-column portraits, *porkchops,* are inset into single-column measure. The adjoining lines are often as narrow as 5 picas, and they are an absolute abomination to set and to read. An antidote to this typographic poison is suggested in Chapter 6.

Of course, indenting type—usually to create adequate *alleys,* white strips between columns—also brings the measure under the readability range. There are several ways to set indented type, with varying degrees of difficulty for the operator. The common specification is *nut-and-nut,* an en space at each end of the type. If this must be done manually, the operator's productivity is cut drastically. You can demonstrate this at your typewriter. Time yourself as you type 20 regular lines; now type the same 20 lines, but this time hit the space bar before you begin each line and again before you throw the carriage return at the end of the line. Your efficiency is obviously reduced. This is just about what we ask the compositor to do in setting nut-and-nut in manual operation. Nut-and-nutting can lose more than a half-column of type per operator in an ordinary day.

Another annoyance attends indented type. In galley proofs, slight indenting is not apparent, and thus frequently correction lines are set at full measure. In the page, this longer line sticks out not just like a sore thumb but like a whole arm.

On the other end of the range, mechanical difficulties also arise. The increment beyond 2-column setting is almost invariably 3-column, and this brings the need for *butted slugs.* Regular Linotypes cast slugs up to 30 picas long. Longer lines have to be set in two sections and butted together. This composition slows down the compositor because he must remember whether to place a space or an unhyphenated syllable at the end of a first section or a word or hyphen at the end of a second. This decision takes time and mental energy and breaks the mechanical rhythm of keyboarding. Butted slugs are not convenient to handle on the stone, and they have a tendency to pop apart in the form and create a disturbing gap on the page where none should be.

Settings beyond the maximum range most often occur in cutlines for 3-column or wider pictures.

Computerized typesetting removes all mechanical handicaps except that of butted slugs, but it does not put a poultice on the reader's pain.

The composing room is a factory, and the more the product line can be standardized, the more efficient the production line. For most newspapers, three settings are required: 1-, 1½- and 2-column. These do not place an undue load on the composing room, yet they take care of all needs. The 1½-column setting doubles over for 3- and 6-column pictures and, for papers in W-format, it may be the wide column, a need that is discussed in detail in Chapter 9. The double measure takes care of leeds on stories and even-column cutlines.

Because the regular 1-column setting is so restrictive to the reading eye, we should frequently use 1½-column—which is close to the optimum—and 2-column settings to give the eye a chance to stretch its cramped muscles. Newspapers that use wire tape, which produces only single-column setting, should use local copy to provide such optical rest breaks.

Two-column Leeds

Many editors like multicolumn leeds on important stories, often using larger type in the wider measure. Such leeds can give extra emphasis to a story, for the larger type may be more attractive and thus draw the

"MAC'S NIGHT" — Friends and associates of L. H. (Mac) McCullough paid tribute to his 37 years as general secretary of Beaver Valley YMCA during a testimonial dinner at the Brodhead Hotel last night. Pictured, from left are: seated, William Stein, president of the Beaver Valley YMCA, McCullough, and Mrs. McCullough; standing, A. Dean Heasley, master of ceremonies; Rev. O. K. Mellquist, pastor of the First Baptist Church, New Brighton, who gave the invocation and benediction; Robert G. Traugh, assistant state secretary of the YMCA; and Dr. Lawrence D. Smith, retired superintendent of Beaver Falls Area schools, keynote speaker.

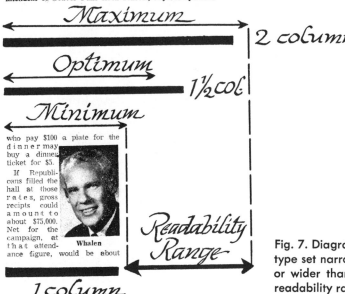

Fig. 7. Diagram shows how body type set narrower than 1 column or wider than 2 extends out of readability range.

reader from head to body more easily. It is a dangerous practice to set a narrow head immediately under a wider one; multicolumn leeds avoid such jamming. The eye gets a chance to stretch its muscles out of the confining 11-pica stride.

Multicolumn leeds are usually 2-column setting. Three-column leeds should be avoided. Even if the longer lca of larger type extends the maximum of the readability range, butted slugs should still be avoided. Leeds in 1½-column measure are pleasant, but the 1-column continuation must read out only on the right leg, and so flexibility in page layout is lost.

Multicolumn leeds should be at least six lines, and preferably eight, deep. A scanty depth is unpleasant by design criteria.

Ideally, changes in measure and body size should not occur between paragraphs nor happen at the same time. Assuming a 2-column leed in 10-point, the ideal transition would be 2-column 10-point, 1-column 10-point, 1-column 8-point, with the switch from 10 to 8 in the middle of a graf. Or settings may be 2-column 10-point, 2-column 8-point, 1-column 8, with the stepdown in width again within a paragraph.

The editor must usually eschew this typographic nicety for mechanical reasons. If both body types are on one Linotype, these progressions are not particularly difficult, but if the copy has to be divided between two machines, a break within a graf is impractical and collating the two takes of type is a nuisance.

Using any size type, the narrowing of measures should be within a graf. If the last line of a 2-column leed is a short widow, it is difficult to guide the eye to a 1-column setting reading out to the right. If the shift to 1-column occurs within a paragraph, the narrow measure can read out on either side.

If the change in measure is made within the same size type, we can make the shift in size at the end of a graf. It disturbs the purists, but the reader is not dangerously confused. But we should never change measure and size at once at the end of a graf. We would not, for instance, set one or two paragraphs in 2-column 10-point and begin the next graf in 1-column 8-point.

Flatout Technique

The major temptation for indenting type is that it permits the use of alleys instead of rules between columns. To do this, some papers adopt *open formats,* as discussed in detail in Chapter 9. But most papers are committed—usually by press capacity—to using column rules.

"Fresh air" in the typographer's language is white space. Injecting air into a printed page is as pleasant as opening a window in a stuffy room. Many editors seek to inject the fresh air of alleys into individual stories or sections, especially women's and feature pages. To effect this, they indent body type with the disadvantages already noted.

Nut-and-nut indenting, giving 4 points of space at each end of a line, plus that space normally occupied by the column rules, creates adequate alleys.

Indenting can also be done by *jawing-in* on the Linotype. A tiny cap is inserted at one side of the jaw, the area where matrices are assembled, and the other jaw, which is movable, is moved in. Thus the area into which matrices are gathered is decreased while the metal slug remains at 11 picas. This eliminates the need for the operator to drop in quads, but it still produces a line too short for easy reading. Jawing-in requires time to prepare the Linotype and is practical only when all type or all type produced on a specific machine is to be indented.

A much more practical method of achieving alleys is the *flatout,* or *1-up technique*. The latter term is more widely used and derives from the fact that the typographer *goes up one column,* uses one more column of space than of type. Typically, he would place only four 11-pica columns of type in a 5-column hole. This is called *4-across-5*. The 11 picas of the fifth column are distributed as white space to form wide alleys. Column rules are eliminated.

The advantages of this technique are solid. Primarily, it gives the fresh air of alleys without reducing the normal line length. It is extremely flexible. In most composing rooms, the fastest way to convert copy into type is to set it at 1-column measure; all wire tape is in single columns. If a major story breaks just before deadline, it can be rushed through into 1-column type, then used flatout to give it extra impact. If a later leed must be handled, the flatout material can be pushed together into normal form and the opened column used for bulletin material.

If the editor needs some device to brighten a dull page, he can use any standing type in 1-up form and so add air and interest.

While this technique is commonly labeled 1-up, flatout material may be half-up, 1½-, or 2-up as well. The number merely indicates the extra space that is used. Flatout matter may be regular 1-column matter or 1½- and 2-column type. If three legs of type set at 1½-column measure are used in a 5-column area, it is *half-up*. If used in a 6-column hole, it is *1½-up*.

The fewer the legs of type, the greater the width of the alleys. Two-across-3 will give 4-pica alleys, not only between the two columns of

Fig. 8. Flatout technique. *a*, *Pueblo* (Colo.) *Chieftain*, 1-column measure, 7-across-8; *b*, *Hamilton* (Ont.) *Spectator*, 1-column measure, 2-up, 4-across-6; *c*, *Elkhart* (Ind.) *Truth*, 1½-column measure, ½-up. *d*, *Ottawa* (Ont.) *Citizen*, 1-up in op format, 5-across-6.

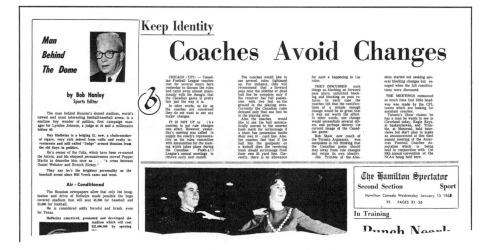

type but at the left and right margins of the unit. This may be too much for normal use. At the other extreme, 7-across-8 will give alleys of about 1.9 picas, a pleasing dimension. Six-across-8—in 2-up form—produces alleys of about 3½ picas, which are not too wide for the proportion of the type area. Three-across-4, then, is the narrowest flatout element for normal use.

A common and immediate criticism of this technique is that it takes

too much time on the stone. This is true only if the typographer hasn't done his homework. Widths of the alleys in flatout are not constant, as we have noted, and the extra space available doesn't always break down into neat and equal increments. Thus the typographer should give specifications for all the flatout elements to be used so the printer need not solve arithmetical problems on the stone.

Assuming 11-pica columns and 6-point column rules, these would be typical spacing instructions:

FOR 1-COLUMN SETTING, 1-UP

3-across-4	Type
3.6-pica space	3-pica space
Leg of type	Type
3-pica space	3-pica space

The 4-column area is 45.6 picas wide. Three legs of type occupy 33 picas. That leaves 12.6 picas of space to use as alleys. There are four alleys, at the left of each column of type and at the right of the last one. We want to work in ½- and 1-pica increments to avoid the need for using 2-point ledds for spacing, and so the extra 6 points is used in the first alley. If the shop should use 3-point spacing material, we could use 3-pica alleys at the left and right of the flatout element and 3.3 picas between type legs.

Another spacing instruction might be:

FOR 2-COLUMN SETTING, 2-UP

3-across-8	Type
6-pica #	6-pica #
Type	Type
6-pica #	6-pica #

The page width is 91.6 picas. Two-column measure is 22.6 picas and three legs (you'll note this element is called 3-across-8 instead of 6-across-8) will occupy 67.6 picas. That leaves 24 picas for use as alleys and four alleys into which to divide it.

Note that "space" has been abbreviated. We may even eliminate "pica" and abbreviate "type" to make this cryptic but adequate recipe:

6#, T, 6#, T, 6#, T, 6#

Data for each flatout element should be on a card above each page form on the stone. Following such instructions, the printer can make up an element like this in only moments more than, or even in the same time as, he would use for regular makeup.

These flatout instructions could be as many of the following as the newspaper's style requires:

1-column setting: 3-across-4, 4-across-5, 5-across-6, 6-across-7, 7-across-8, and 6-across-8.

1½-column setting: 2-across-4, 3-across-5, 3-across-6, 4-across-7, and 4-across-8.

2-column setting: 2-across-5, 2-across-6, 3-across-7, and 3-across-8.

When the editor indicates this technique on the dummy, he shows the area to be filled and in it writes *3-across-4* or the appropriate numbers. Only if type is in wider measure does he indicate that—*2-col., 2-across-5* or *1½-col., 4-across-8*. Telling the measure of the type merely makes it easier for the printer to find it on the galley.

To get the full benefit of flatout, the headline should be flush left in the area, not aligned with the first leg of type. It should extend across at least part of the last leg.

Some editors prefer not to use alleys at the left and right of the whole element. When flatout is used across the whole page, alleys at the outside are unnecessary; they simply dissolve into margins. Seven-column flatout —or across one column less than a full page in tab and other formats—is rare; we normally would prefer not to have a 1-column head next to such an element. Some editors do use it, though; then they provide only one alley at the side of a 7-column flatout. This space can easily be moved to the side at the inside of the page, leaving none at the margin.

But in elements of 4- through 6-column widths, alleys at the outside are pleasant, and I encourage their use. If the arithmetic of the situation requires, the alley at the right of the element may be eliminated but the one at the left is desirable; it is most conspicuous there.

There is a growing practice of using a decorative rule at the top and bottom of flatout elements to weave them together and also to emphasize the alleys. I prefer this addition, especially when the element is at the head or foot of the page. The rules are as wide as the open area; they are not cut off to align with the outside margins of the left and right legs.

One-up elements most frequently run at the page top or bottom, especially the wider ones. Four-column flatout is effective within the page, and 5-column elements are often useful in the page interior as under a floating flag. But 6- through 8-column flatout fragments the page horizontally, and it is rare when such use is effective anywhere except at top or bottom.

Pictures may, of course, be used instead of type in an area of flatout material. It is best to have some type—not just a picture—in each leg. But if a rule is used top and bottom, it will guide the reading eye enough so that it will be able to move across a full leg of art and read the type in the next column without any annoying interruption.

As with most new ideas, the biggest problem attendant on flatout is breaking inertia and adopting this useful technique. It soon becomes a facile tool, and editors who use it would not consider abandoning it.

Use of the Duplex

For this discussion we shall consider the duplex as a boldface, either Roman or Gothic. It is a valuable device for breaking up the deadly gray of large masses of body type.

The most common use of boldface is as a *subhead*. This is usually in the boldface capitals of the body type, centered, on a separate line between groups of paragraphs. Wire services now furnish subheads in this style on wire tape. Newspapers must then conform to this style, throw out all the subheads and reset them to local specifications, or lose harmony by mixing local and wire styles. This is another example of the encroachment of a distant technician upon the rights and responsibility of the local editor.

This conventional subhead is useful as a mild color device. This is its major and perhaps only function. I am convinced that few readers actually read subheads.

A 6-point slug should be dropped above each subhead so that the bold type will contrast against the white of the paper rather than the gray of the regular body type; a ledd below the subhead is pleasant but not necessary.

Flush-left subheads are used by a few papers. From a design point of view, it is a less than desirable practice. The subhead then aligns with the previous paragraph, but the next graf is indented in its first line. Thus the subhead is optically tied with the upper graf rather than the lower one.

A pleasant technique is to indent the subhead the same space as that of the paragraph start.

The *boldline* is a functional substitute for the subhead. The first line of a designated paragraph is set in bold with the first word or phrase in bold caps. A slug is dropped above it.

It jars the eye to mix bold and light in the same line. Don't do it. Some newspapers start a graf with a word or two in bold caps and then continue with light upper and lower case. This should be avoided. The whole line should be bold.

Care must be taken that the change from all caps to upper and lower case does not split a closely linked phrase. This is a bad break:

   a. | DR. CORNELIUS J. Brady testified at a |

The whole name should be capped, even though it does often create an awkward line like this:

   b. | DR. CORNELIUS J. BRADY testified at |

Avoid, if possible, setting the whole line in caps and, above all, do not let the caps run over into the second line. Each of the following is a misuse:

   c. | DR. CORNELIUS J. BRADY SAID |
         | that the new hospital would have |

d. | DR. CORNELIUS J. BRADY TESTI-
   | fied that use of hospital beds would

e. | THE CHIEF OF STAFF, DR. CORNE-
   | LIUS J. BRADY said hospital beds

Examples *c* and *d* are unpleasant, but if the usage is consistently to capitalize the entire boldline, the reader can forgive. Consistency helps atone for several typographic sins. (The axiom is "It is sometimes better to do something wrong consistently rather than do the right thing inconsistently.") But the style of *c* or *d* should not be mixed with the proper usage of Example *b*. The continuation of caps into the second line, as in Example *e,* should not be permitted. If such an awkward break occurs, the second line should be upper and lower case. Adoption of the proper style, *b,* will minimize the hyphenation of proper names in caps.

An extension of the boldline is the *bold graf,* a whole paragraph in boldface. The bold graf should have a slug at its top and bottom. The graf should not be indented; the horizontal strips of white are more effective than the thin vertical slivers of indenting, anyway.

Some editors dislike bold grafs because they feel that heavier type gives unwanted emphasis to the copy. If it does, we have a bad situation. If the story is written in the traditional inverted pyramid form, we need typographic color at places where the content just doesn't warrant emphasis. I feel, though, that the reader soon recognizes bold grafs as a typographical convention and not as a device to emphasize the content. Apparently a majority of editors agree. Among those in the 1968 N.E.A. survey, some 55% reported using bold grafs. Some 67% (this included some of the 55% mentioned) used conventional subheads and/or boldlines; 33% used no such color devices.

It is not necessary to remind professional newspapermen, but the student who may use this book is cautioned against using boldface or all caps to emphasize a word or phrase in newspaper copy. This is a common technique in books and magazines: " 'Yipe! *Yipe!* YIPE!' said Lincoln's doctor's dog." News copy must be written so the words, rather than the weight of type, give the needed emphasis.

Frequency of boldface color devices depends on editorial judgment. A story longer than 4 inches requires subheads or boldlines at about 3-inch intervals. A story 6 inches long requires one bold graf; after that such grafs should be about 4 inches apart.

Note that it is not necessary to have two or more subheads in a story; a single subhead can be entirely correct. The dictum that subheads cannot be used singly is a misapplication of the rules for breaking copy into literary subsections. The English teacher rightly explains that if you break a section, you must break it into at least two parts; if Topic *III* is subdivided, you must have at least sections *A* and *B*. If you have only *A*, it means that *III* has really not been subdivided or that the second part of the division has not been properly labeled.

But newspaper subheads have nothing to do with literary form or content. They are not labels of logical subdivision; they are merely visual devices that can be used exactly and only where the editor has decided optical relief is required.

Some editors feel that boldlines or bold grafs should not be used if the duplex is from a different race. They reason that the well-known phenomenon must occur: As the eye changes from one letterform to another in a block of copy, there is a break in reading rhythm. They think that a conventional subhead in a different race does not create this bad jarring because the subhead acts like a little headline that is read entirely separately from the body type.

I have no valid research data on the problem. I admit it is perfectly logical, but I find that it does not bother me, as a reader, to see a boldline or bold graf in a Gothic or Square duplex, though I think I would prefer these elements in regular boldface. But if I were an editor, I would not avoid these useful color devices only because my body type was duplexed with a bold of another race.

Some newspapers use a typographic *gimcrack* immediately above a boldline or bold graf. The most common gimcrack is a group of *asterisks* —*bugs* the printer calls them—usually three. Others—generically called *spots*—are stars, solid or outline; *bullets* (large periods); squares; or other shapes.

Both Linotype and Intertype offer a wide selection of gimcracks. The chosen one should have adequate typographic color. A bullet, for instance, should be about the size of the period of a font of 36-point Spartan Heavy; anything smaller is nonfunctional. An asterisk of a 24- or 30-point font of the same face is an attractive device and is more functional than the customary grouping of body-type "bugs."

Stars are attractive to most Americans because they connote the Glorious Fourth, Christmas, Hollywood, and other pleasant subjects. This gimcrack seems especially appropriate to newspapers named *The Star*.

Spots of even more specific connotation can be used pleasantly for specialized columns, departments, or pages. A tiny baseball would

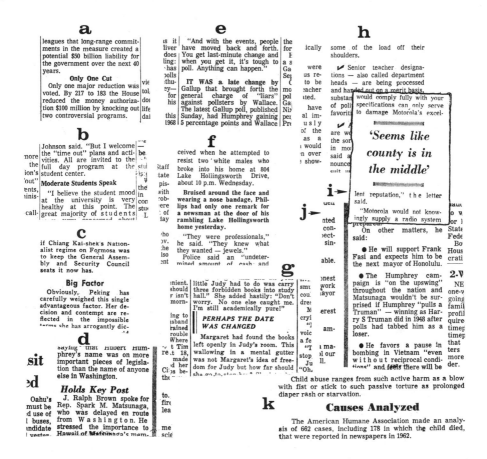

a

leagues that long-range commitments in the measure created a potential $50 billion liability for the government over the next 40 years.

Only One Cut

Only one major reduction was voted. By 217 to 183 the House reduced the money authorization $100 million by knocking out two controversial programs.

b

Johnson said. "But I welcome the "time out" plans and activities. All are invited to the full day program at the student center.

Moderate Students Speak

"I believe the student mood at the university is very healthy at this point. The great majority of students

c

if Chiang Kai-shek's Nationalist regime on Formosa was to keep the General Assembly and Security Council seats it now has.

Big Factor

Obviously, Peking has carefully weighed this single advantageous factor. Her decision and contempt are reflected in the impossible terms she has arrogantly dic-

saying that Hubert Humphrey's name was on more important pieces of legislation than the name of anyone else in Washington.

Holds Key Post

Oahu's J. Ralph Brown spoke for must be Rep. Spark M. Matsunaga, d use of who was delayed en route l buses, from Washington. He ndidate stressed the importance to vester. Hawaii of Matsunaga's mem-

e

"And with the events, people have moved back and forth. You get last-minute change and when you get it, it's tough to poll. Anything can happen."

IT WAS a late change by Gallup that brought forth the general charge of "liars" against pollsters by Wallace. The latest Gallup poll, published this Sunday, had Humphrey gaining 5 percentage points and Wallace

f

ceived when he attempted to resist two white males who broke into his home at 804 Lake Hollingsworth Drive, about 10 p.m. Wednesday.

Bruised around the face and wearing a nose bandage, Phillips had only one remark for a newsman at the door of his rambling Lake Hollingsworth home yesterday.

"They were professionals," he said. "They knew what they wanted — jewels."

Police said an "undetermined amount of cash" and

g

little Judy had to do was carry three forbidden books into study hall." She added hastily: "Don't worry. No one else caught me. I'm still academically pure!"

PERHAPS THE DATE WAS CHANGED

Margaret had found the books left openly in Judy's room. This wallowing in a mental gutter was not Margaret's idea of freedom for Judy but how far should she go to stop her? Sh

Child abuse ranges from such active harm as a blow with fist or stick to such passive torture as prolonged diaper rash or starvation.

k

Causes Analyzed

The American Humane Association made an analysis of 662 cases, including 178 in which the child died, that were reported in newspapers in 1962.

h

some of the load off their shoulders.

✔ Senior teacher designations — also called department heads — are being processed and handed out on a merit basis.

would comply fully with your specifications can only serve to damage Motorola's excel-

'Seems like county is in the middle'

lent reputation," the letter said.

"Motorola would not knowingly supply a radio system

On other matters, he said:

● He will support Frank Fasi and expects him to be the next mayor of Honolulu.

● The Humphrey campaign is "on the upswing" throughout the nation and Matsunaga wouldn't be surprised if Humphrey "pulls a Truman" — winning as Harry S Truman did in 1948 after polls had tabbed him as a loser.

● He favors a pause in bombing in Vietnam "even without reciprocal conditions" and feels there will be

i

j

Fig. 9. Techniques to relieve masses of body type: *a,* conventional subhead, centered, u&lc; *b,* flush-left subhead in bold u&lc; *c,* 12-point Spartan subhead, centered; *d,* 12-point Bodoni Bold Italic, flush-left; *e,* boldline; *f,* bold graf; *g,* 2-line subhead with decorative rule, used by *New York Daily News* in daily fiction feature; *h,* checkmarks for itemization; *i,* blurb set into body type; *j,* bullets for itemization; *k,* 12-point Poster Bodoni subhead in 2-column measure.

appropriately enliven a sports column; one of the many styles of crosses would be attractive on the church page.

Only one color device should be used. Gimcracks should not be used above regular subheads, nor should they be used to occasionally replace subheads.

The device, used alone, might change for a particular section or page, but there should be consistency within these areas.

By practical criteria, the boldline is the best color device. The bold graf runs a rather weak second. But if the newspaper uses wire tape with its built-in subheads, the editor must either reset more body type than the composing room prefers to or sacrifice consistency. In this case I would opt for conventional subheads throughout.

Sideless Boxes

Boxes are a classic and useful device for giving emphasis or interest to a block of copy whose size alone wouldn't do so. Functionally, the box is almost the equal of a small photograph and thus is valued as a component of a pleasing page pattern.

Making a *full box,* with four sides, requires 16 separate steps; to make a *sideless box* requires only three. The difference, when accumulated by the great number of boxes used annually, reaches substantial amounts.

We have already noted in the first chapter that replacing full boxes with sideless ones is an excellent example of functionalism: We maintain the quality of the product but lower the manufacturing cost.

Sideless boxes eliminate the need to measure and cut the side pieces, to *miter* the corners of all four sides, to fit those corners tightly, to set or cut the boxed material to the narrow measure. (We might note here that the injecting of vertical elements into a newspaper page is always a nuisance. Horizontal elements drop in easily in the normal makeup process; but vertical ones demand adjustment in the width of other elements to make necessary room at their sides.)

To make a sideless box, a decorative rule is used top and bottom only. The head is set short and flush left in a heavy type, the accent face if one is available. Body type is set boldface and indented 1 pica at the left only.

There are many styles of *decorative rule* to choose from. The most popular are Ben Day rules, in varying weight, that print lines in various tones of gray. Unfortunately, they often fill in during stereotyping and rarely print cleanly by that process. *Coin-edge*—technically, *broken*— rules give good color; so do the various *wave rules. Oxford rules,* a thick rule paired with a thinner one, are harmonious with a Bodoni head dress with its marked contrast between thick and thin strokes of the letter- forms. (A typographer's convention should be noted: Oxford should be placed so that the thinner rule is nearer the type with which the rule is associated. In a sideless box, for instance, the Oxford should be placed so that the thin rules face toward the boxed type; the heavy rule is then at

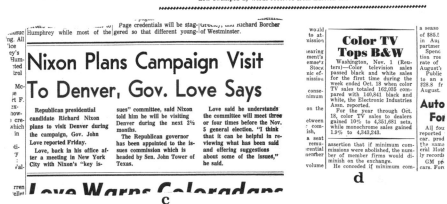

Fig. 10. Sideless boxes: *a*, boldface, indented left only, using head from regular schedule; *b*, 2-column in op measure, using accent face; both use wave rule. *c*, three legs of type, regular headletter, Oxford rule; *d*, regular body type, indented nut-and-nut, accent head, tapered dashes.

the "outside" of the box. The same placement applies when the Oxford is used with 1-up material. Often the typographer will observe, "This Oxford rule is upside down." Many people think he is joking, but he isn't. Any asymmetrical element, even a rule, has a top and a bottom.)

Body type within sideless boxes must be bold to be effective.

The full-pica indent does make the line too short, but in this case we believe that the benefit of the box outweighs the loss in readability. The shorter the block of copy, the less dangerous the drop in readability, of course. So boxes are kept short, preferably no deeper than 3 inches. Also, if they go much deeper, the box effect may be lost.

The full-pica indent is much more effective than 6 points at each side. And any indent less than 6 points is invisible.

Boxes may use 2-column settings; type is then indented 2 picas at the left only.

In open formats, those without column rules, the indent of a sideless box tends to dissolve into the alley and is not nearly as effective as when column rules are used. So in open format—but only in open format—matter in a sideless box may be set without indenting.

The box effect of unindented material is enhanced if the head is written very short—certainly no longer than half a column wide—and centered. Two-line heads may be used on such boxes far more effectively than on sideless boxes. Instead of a decorative rule, a *brace* may be used at the top and bottom of a full-measure box. The strong effect of apposition that braces create makes the box effect more apparent.

If body type of a different race is available, it should be used for setting the body of these non-indent boxes. Sans, Squares, and Gothics provide that contrast to regular body type that makes the box most effective as a color element.

Sandwiches

The duplex face is also used for *sandwiches,* a device for handling *reefers,* references to a related story on another page. A typical one might call attention to the full text, on an inside page, of an inaugural address or a court decision that is summarized in a page-one story. A sandwich is a tiny sideless box, without a head, which contains the reefer. To assure harmony, sandwiches should be made with the same decorative rule used for boxes. Reefer type should be boldface and brief, ideally no more than two lines; it is not indented.

The sandwich should be dropped into the story about 2½ inches from the top. The theory is that by this time the reader is interested enough in the story to make the accompanying inside matter of value to him. This interest should encourage him to interrupt his reading, take in the reefer, then continue reading below the sandwich.

The *preseed*—accent on the first syllable—is introductory matter before the story proper. It may be set in bold or in regular body type. Some papers use Italic for preseeds but the adverse effect of Italic on readability makes this a dangerous tactic.

Long Texts

Two techniques for breaking masses of body type have been perfected by Canadian newspapermen and have been adopted by some American papers. One is the use of large subheads, 14-point or even larger; the other is the *Canadian wrap.*

Large subheads, often called *divider,* or *breaker, heads,* are used with extremely large masses of body type, such as court orders, commission findings, formal addresses, etc. Fourteen-point seems to be the most popular size for breakers, but they may be in 12-point or, more frequently, 18- or even 24-point.

Setting these larger subheads is a nuisance; it requires another Linotype magazine. (It might be most effective to have the operator change magazines and set the subheads right into the text. To set all the dividers at once and let the stone-man collate them into the body type offers many chances for error.) However, a long official text without unusually strong relief elements will generally go unread, so it is worth the extra investment of this 2-magazine setting to assure readership. If we must shift magazines anyway, we might as well use large type; the difference between a 12-point subhead and that in body size is not great enough to warrant the cost of access to the second magazine.

The breaker must be written to size, as a headline is. If the unit count is such that only labels would fit into one column, the divider is often written in two lines.

Documents often have their own subheads, but these are not usually adequate as breakers. They are invariably labels, and most editors prefer more illuminating copy, with verbs. Document subheads do not occur as often as dividers are required. In most instances, the best results will come from breakers placed at intervals selected by the editor rather than by the author of the text.

These intervals are arbitrarily set by the desk. A common standard is that any story that runs deeper than one column should carry dividers. Other editors use them only on stories that run two or even three columns in length. These large subheads ought then to be used at about 10-inch intervals.

The content of dividers is far more important than that of conventional subheads, so the divider should be inserted at logical breaks in the text instead of at purely linear measurements. This may cause extreme variance in distance between breakers. If necessary, they may be as close together as 5 inches or as distant as 15.

The large subhead—in 2-column measure—is always used with a Canadian wrap. This is the disposition of 1-column body type in 2-leg units.

The head on a Canadian-wrapped story may be 2 columns or wider, but in an even number of columns. The story begins in column 1 and runs down, usually 4 to 6 inches, then wraps up to the head in column 2. At the squared-off bottom of these two columns is placed a 2-column breaker.

The second portion of the story starts right under this large subhead in column 1 and again wraps up to the breaker in column 2. A whole series of such wrapped units is piled up as a *chimney,* as in Example B-a.

If a headline wider than 2 columns is used, there may be two or more parallel chimneys (Example B-b).

If the group of Canadian wraps runs into the ad pyramid, the last portion of the story may run in a single column (Example B-c). It is not pleasing to the eye when this single column runs back up to a 3-column head though (Example B-d), nor should the story go from a set of Canadian wraps into a single-column leg and then begin again at the top of the page in 2-leg units (Example B-e).

If there are more than a single chimney of Canadian wraps, they should square off at the bottom. When the chimneys are squared off, four of them may be used clear across the page. A new 2-column unit must begin at the top of each set of columns, immediately under the main head.

Excellent examples of effective handling of large masses of text were given by a group of Florida newspapers, especially the *Tallahassee Democrat.* It used 2-column 2-line 36-point dividers over Canadian wraps to present the whole voluminous text of a proposed new state constitution. In a special 4-page pullout of a Sunday edition, body type was set at 13.9 picas. The labels within the document itself—article designations, for instance—were carried as reverses on Ben Day panels.

The *St. Petersburg Times* used conventional columns in a 4-page wrapper around a Sunday edition. It used eight large photos, and on each page was an 8-column banner in 96- and 72-point. The subheads were normal ones in bold body type; headings within the document made the copy. Two later revisions were presented in basically the same way.

New York State newspapers also had the problem of presenting a lengthy proposed constitution late in 1967, and many solved the problem by use of similar devices. Many editors will face the same problem of presenting a mammoth text in readable form, for political portents point to more constitutional conventions in several states in the near future.

The first Florida draft ran 59 solid typewritten pages. Not even the most conscientious voter can be expected to undertake the Herculean task of reading such miserable copy. It then becomes a clear obligation upon the newspaper to afford a physically readable version. It is doubtful whether the language of such documents will ever be gripping enough to fascinate the reader by content alone.

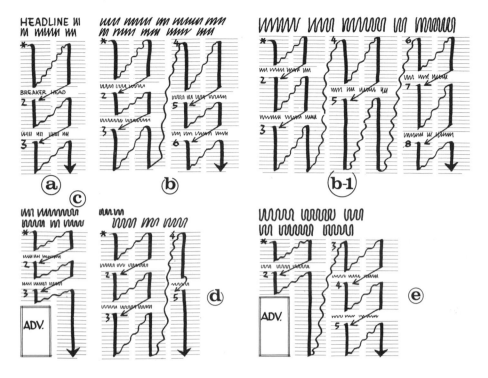

Example B. Canadian wraps.

Itemization and Tabulation

Itemization is a literary device that is being used more and more by newspapers. As news becomes more complex, often the only way that communication can be made clear is to break the story down into individual points, ticked off, as it were, on typographic fingers. The newspaper designer must cooperate with the copy desk to establish the style of this technique, for content will influence form of itemization.

Items should be short, a maximum of four lines. They are most effective when set off by a device that will signal the item without being too obtrusive. The simplest is a dash, but it is neither handsome nor visible enough. A bullet is effective; so is a star. A check mark seems appropriate, and it is distinctive enough to do its job.

Items may be effective in boldface. In that case there should be appropriate white space above and below. Items should not be indented except for the conventional paragraph start.

The bulkiest tabulations in most newspapers are the market reports. These are transmitted as tape by high-speed wire, and even metropolitans who don't use tape elsewhere use it here. Any size type may be used, but agate is most frequent.

Style of this copy is set by the press services. All the newspaper designer need concern himself with is the choice of leeders, as discussed earlier, and the *division labels*. In market reports, these labels are letters of the alphabet. They should be of strong color because, in addition to the obvious function of helping the reader find sections of the report, the labels must enliven the great gray masses.

Local markets—grain, livestock, produce, fish, minerals, etc.— usually are brief and really don't need to be set in agate to conserve space, but often the editor wants to maintain consistency of local with wire news.

Television program listings are usually tabulated for the convenience of the reader, but radio programs, because they change so little, are usually given as straight matter. Both regular and agate type are used for TV listings, and usually the choice depends on the tabulating style. If the grid pattern creates narrow areas, regular body type may not fit into the space. Once the pattern has been established, day-to-day changes are made mechanically, so it is wise to devote enough time in the first place to devise a system pleasant as well as functional.

Gimcracks—circles or tiny TV screens bearing numbers in positive or negative form—can dress up these listings. Usually these are used to designate local stations if the newspaper carries listings for those out of town, too. Whole-word logotypes are available for such common designations as color, special, and debut.

Athletic box scores are constantly used tabulations. These are usually set in agate, and wire tape is designed to set such copy in a typeface with a lowercase-alphabet length of 88 points.

Local tabulation is difficult to set; just as in typewriting, it is a nuisance. What this country needs (in addition to a good 5¢ cigar) is a new form for box scores that can be set as straight matter. A few sports editors have experimented with such style, but reaction has been less than enthusiastic—it's been totally invisible. Each sport has its own style for box scores, and woe to him who has the temerity to tamper with antiquity. So until someone has the genius and/or courage to create a good substitute, the editor is stuck with the imposed current and cumbersome style.

The practice of setting long lists of names in agate does not make a typographer starry-eyed, but editors who run such lists point out that few, if any readers, wade through scores or hundreds of names. They

Complete Text
Of First Draft
Of Constitution

Tallahassee Democrat

A Public Service
Presentation By
The Democrat

Here's First Draft Of Constitution

Preamble

We, the people of the State of Florida, being grateful to Almighty God for our constitutional liberty, in order to secure its benefits, perfect our government, insure domestic tranquility, maintain public order, and guarantee equal civil and political rights to all, do ordain and establish this constitution, first adopting and recognizing the supremacy of the principles stated in the following.

Rights Are Set Forth For People Of Florida

DECLARATION OF RIGHTS

Declaration Of Rights

SECTION 1. **Equality — inalienable rights — property rights of aliens.** — All persons are equal before the law and have inalienable rights, among which are the right to enjoy life and liberty, pursue happiness, to be rewarded for industry, and to acquire, possess, and protect property; but the ownership, inheritance, disposition, and possession of real property by aliens ineligible for citizenship may be regulated or prohibited by law.

SECTION 2. **Political power — government.** — All political power is inherent in the people. Government is instituted for their protection, security, and benefit. They have the right to regulate their government and to amend or repeal this constitution. The enunciation herein of certain rights shall not be construed to deny or impair others retained by the people.

SECTION 3. **Trial by jury inviolate.** — The right of trial by jury shall be secured to all. The number of jurors for the trial of causes shall be fixed by law.

SECTION 4. **Access to courts.** — The courts shall be open to every person for redress of any injury, and justice shall be administered without sale, denial or delay.

SECTION 5. **Religious freedom.**—The free exercise and enjoyment of religious belief and worship shall never be abridged, but this freedom shall not be construed to justify licentiousness or practices inconsistent with peace and safety. No person shall be incompetent as a witness or ineligible for jury duty or public office because of religious opinion. No preference shall be given by law to any religious denomination or mode of worship. No public funds shall be granted directly or indirectly in aid of any religious denomination or sectarian institution.

SECTION 6. **Habeas Corpus — suspension.** — The writ of habeas corpus shall be grantable of right, freely and without cost. It shall be returnable without delay, and it shall never be suspended unless, in case of rebellion or invasion, suspension is essential to the public safety.

SECTION 7. **Excessive fines — cruel punishment — detention of witnesses.** — Excessive fines, cruel or unusual punishment, corruption of blood, forfeiture of estate, indefinite imprisonment and unreasonable detention of witnesses are forbidden.

SECTION 8. **Bail.** — Until adjudged guilty, every person is entitled to release on reasonable bail with sufficient surety unless charged with a capital offense and the proof of guilt is evident or the presumption is great.

SECTION 9. **Prosecution for crime-indictments and informations - grand juries.**—No person shall be tried for capital crime without presentment or indictment returned by the affirmative vote of twelve members of a grand jury of not less than eighteen members, or for other felony without such presentment or indictment or an information under oath filed by the prosecuting officer of the court, except in cases in the militia.

SECTION 10. **Due process - double jeopardy - self-incrimination.** — No person shall be deprived of life, liberty or property without due process of law. No person shall be twice put in jeopardy for the same offense nor be compelled in any criminal case to be a witness against himself.

SECTION 11. **Rights of accused-speedy trial.**—In all criminal prosecutions the accused shall have the right to demand the nature and cause of the accusation, to be furnished with a copy of the charges, to have compulsory process for attendance of witnesses in his favor, to be confronted in any trial with the witnesses against him, to be heard in person or by counsel or both, and to have a speedy, public and impartial trial by jury in the county where the crime was committed, if such county is known. If such county is not known the indictment or information may charge venue in two or more counties conjunctively and proof that the crime was committed in such area shall be sufficient, but the accused may before pleading elect the county in which to be tried.

SECTION 12. **Right to work.** — The right of persons to work shall not be denied or abridged on account of membership or non-membership in any labor union, or labor organization; provided, that this clause shall not be construed to deny or abridge the right of employees by and through a labor union to bargain collectively with their employer.

SECTION 13. **Freedom of speech and press — truth as defense to defamation.** —Every person may fully speak, write and publish his sentiments on all subjects being responsible for the abuse of that right, and no laws shall be passed to restrain or abridge the liberty of speech, or of the press. In all criminal prosecutions and civil actions for defamation the truth may be given in evidence to the jury, and if it shall appear that the matter charged as defamatory is true, and was published with good motives, the party shall be acquitted or exonerated.

SECTION 14. **Costs, when payable.** —No person charged with crime shall be compelled to pay costs before a judgment of conviction has become final.

SECTION 15. **Right of assemblage—petition.** — The people shall have the right to assemble for lawful purposes, to instruct their representatives, and to petition for redress of grievances.

SECTION 16. **Imprisonment for debt.** — No person shall be imprisoned for debt, except in cases of fraud.

SECTION 17. **Bill of attainder — ex post facto laws — obligation of contract — limitations of actions.** — No bill of attainder, ex post facto law, or law impairing the obligation of contracts, shall be passed. No law shall be passed lessening the time within which civil action may be commenced on any cause of action existing at the time of its passage.

SECTION 18. **Public liability for torts.** — Sovereign immunity shall not bar recovery of compensatory damages from the state, its agencies or political subdivisions, for torts in proceedings brought after such notice and within such time as may be fixed by statute. Claims of less than one thousand dollars may be determined in administrative proceedings, and judicial proceedings may be tried without a jury, as may be provided by law.

SECTION 19. **Right to bear arms.** —The right of the people to bear arms in defense of themselves and of the lawful authority of the state shall not be infringed, but the legislature may prescribe the manner in which they may be borne.

SECTION 20. **Military subordinate to civil — quartering.** — The military power is in strict subordination to the civil. No member of the military shall be quartered on private property in time of peace without the consent of the owner, and in time of war all quartering shall be as prescribed by law.

SECTION 21. **Searches and seizures.** —The right of the people to be secure in their persons, houses, papers, and effects against unreasonable searches and seizures, and the unreasonable interception of private communication, shall not be violated. No warrant shall be issued but upon probable cause, supported by oath or affirmation particularly describing the place or places to be searched, the person or persons, thing or things to be seized, the communication to be intercepted, and the nature of evidence to be obtained.

SECTION 22. **Treason.** — Treason against the state shall consist only in levying war against it, adhering to its enemies, or giving them aid and comfort, and no person shall be convicted of treason except on the testimony of two witnesses to the same overt act or confession in open court.

How to Get Reprints

This is the complete text of the first draft of Florida's proposed new constitution.

It is being published by the Democrat as a public service so that the schools, civic clubs, study groups and others concerned about the future of their state will have available a convenient text to use in initiating discussion and debate on the proposals.

Reprints of this section can be had free at the public service counter of the Democrat. By mail, in order to help defray the costs of postage and handling, a charge of five cents a copy will be made. The charge will be two and a half cents per copy in quantities of 100 or more.

Please address your requests to:

CONSTITUTION
The Tallahassee Democrat
P. O. Box 990
Tallahassee, Fla. 32302

Symbol Of State Government Is Stately Capitol
. . . it is center of group of state buildings in Tallahassee

Tallahassee Designated As Seat Of Government

STATE BOUNDARIES — CAPITAL

Article I

SECTION 1. **Boundaries.**—The state boundaries are: Begin at the mouth of the Perdido River, which for the purposes of this description is defined as the point where latitude 30 degrees 16' 53'' north and longitude 87 degrees 31' 06'' west intersect; thence to the point where latitude 30 degrees 17' 02'' north and longitude 87 degrees 31' 06'' west intersect; thence to the point where latitude 30 degrees 18' 00'' north and longitude 87 degree 27' 08'' west intersect; thence to the point where the center line of the intracoastal canal (as the same existed on June 12, 1953) and longitude 87 degrees 27' 00'' west intersect; the same being in the middle of the Perdido River; thence up the middle of the Perdido River to the point where it intersects the south boundary of the state of Alabama, being also the point of intersection of the middle of the Perdido River with latitude 31 degree 00' 00'' north; thence east, along the south boundary line of the state of Alabama, the same being latitude 31 degrees 00' 00'' north, to the middle of the Chattahoochee River; thence down the middle of said river to its confluence with the Flint River; thence in a straight line to the head of the St. Mary's River; thence down the middle of said river to the Atlantic Ocean, and extending therein to a point three geographic miles from the Florida coast line, meaning the line of ordinary low water along that portion of the coast which is in direct contact with the open sea and the line marking the seaward limit of inland waters; thence southeastwardly following a line three geographic miles distant from the Atlantic coast line of the state and three leagues distant from the Gulf of Mexico coast line of the state to and around the Tortugas Islands; thence northeastwardly, three leagues distant from the coast line, to a point three leagues distant from the coast line of the mainland; thence north and northwestwardly, three leagues distant from the coast line to a point west of the mouth of the Perdido River, three leagues from the coast line, as measured on a line bearing 0 degree 01' 00'' west from the point of beginning; thence along said line to the point of beginning.

The legislature may extend the coastal boundaries to such limits as the laws of the United States or international law may permit.

SECTION 2. **Seat of government—location of offices.** — The seat of government shall be the City of Tallahassee, in Leon County, where the offices of the governor, cabinet members and the supreme court shall be maintained and the sessions of the legislature shall be held; provided, in time of invasion or grave emergency, the governor by proclamation may for the period necessary transfer the seat of government to another place. Other state offices and agencies shall maintain their offices at the places prescribed by law.

Government Branches Are Divided Three Ways

GENERAL PROVISIONS

Article II

SECTION 1. **Branches of government.** —The powers of the state government shall be divided into legislative, executive and judicial branches. No person properly belonging to one branch shall exercise any powers appertaining to either of the other branches unless expressly provided herein.

SECTION 2. **State seal and flag.**—The design of the great seal and flag of the state shall be prescribed by the legislature.

SECTION 3. **Public officers.**—No person holding any office of emolument under any foreign government, or civil office of emolument under the United States or any other state, shall hold any office of honor or of emolument under the government of this state. No person shall hold more than one office under the government of this state at the same time; provided, a notary public or military officer may hold another office.

Each state and county officer, before entering upon the duties of the office, shall give bond as required by law, and shall swear or affirm:

> **I do solemnly swear or affirm that I will support, protect, and defend the Constitution and Government of the United States and of the State of Florida; that I am duly qualified to hold office under the Constitution of the State; and that I will well and faithfully perform the duties of (title of office) on which I am now about to enter. So help me God."**

and thereafter shall devote personal attention to the duties of the office, and continue in office until his successor qualifies.

The powers, duties, compensation and method of payment of state and county officers shall be fixed by law.

Except as otherwise authorized or provided herein, no office shall be created the term of which shall exceed four years, and all offices shall be filled by election by the people or appointment by the governor.

Vacancy in office when not otherwise provided by law shall be filled by appointment by the governor for the remainder of the term if less than twenty-eight months, otherwise until the first Tuesday after the first Monday following the next general election. Vacancy in office occurs upon the creation of an office, upon the death of the incumbent, his removal from office, resignation, succession to another office, unexplained absence for six months, or failure to maintain the residence required when elected or appointed, and by failure of one elected or appointed to office to qualify within thirty days from the commencement of the term.

Each state or county officer shall, upon demand, furnish to the governor or either house of the legislature information regarding his executive or administrative duties.

SECTION 4. **Enemy attack — emergency powers of legislature.**—In periods of emergency resulting from enemy attack the legislature shall have power to provide for prompt and temporary succession to the powers and duties of all public offices the incumbents of which may become unavailable to execute the functions of their offices, and to adopt such other measures as may be necessary and appropriate to insure the continuity of governmental operations during the emergency. In exercising these powers the legislature may depart from other requirements of this Constitution, but only to the extent necessary to meet the emergency.

Legislative Sessions Scheduled Every Year; Reapportionment Set Up

THE LEGISLATIVE DEPARTMENT

Article III

SECTION 1. **Composition.** — The legislative power of the state shall be vested in a Legislature of the State of Florida, consisting of a senate composed of one senator elected from each senatorial district and a house of representatives composed of one member elected from each representative district.

SECTION 2. **Members-officers.**—Each house shall be the sole judge of the qualifications, elections, and returns of its members, and shall biennially choose its officers, including a permanent presiding officer selected from its membership, who shall be designated in the senate as President of the Senate, and in the house as Speaker of the House of Representatives. The senate shall designate a Secretary to serve at its pleasure, and the house of representatives shall designate a Chief Clerk to serve at its pleasure.

SECTION 3. **Sessions of legislature - adjournment.**—

(a) **Organization sessions.** — On the fourteenth day following each biennial general election the legislature shall convene for not more than three consecutive days for the exclusive purpose of organization and selection of officers.

(b) **Regular sessions.** — A regular session of the legislature shall convene on the fourth Tuesday in January of each year.

(c) **Special sessions.**—The governor, by proclamation stating the purpose, may convene the legislature in special session during which only such legislative business may be transacted as is within the purview of the proclamation or of a communication from the governor or is introduced by consent of two-thirds of the membership of the membership of each house.

Three-fifths of the membership of each house of the legislature, by demand made as provided by law, may convene the legislature in special session.

(d) **Length of sessions.** — A regular session of the legislature shall not exceed sixty consecutive days, and a special session shall not exceed twenty consecutive days, unless extended beyond such limit by a two-thirds vote of each house, during which extension no new business may be taken up in either house without the consent of two-thirds of its membership.

(e) **Adjournment.** — Neither house shall adjourn for more than three days except pursuant to concurrent resolution.

(f) **Adjournment by governor.** — If, during any regular or special session, the two houses cannot agree upon a time for adjournment, the governor may adjourn the session sine die or to any date within the period authorized for such session; provided at least two legislative days before adjourning the session, he shall, while neither house is in recess, give each house formal written notice of his intention to do so, and agreement reached within the period by both houses on a time for adjournment shall prevail.

SECTION 4. **Quorum - compelling attendance - procedure - open doors - journals - discipline.** — A majority of each house shall constitute a quorum, but a smaller number may adjourn from day to day and compel the presence of absent members in such manner and under such penalties as it may prescribe. Each house shall determine its rules of procedure.

The senate may close its doors to the public while sitting in executive session to consider appointments to or removal from public office. Other sessions of each house shall be public.

Each house shall keep and publish a journal of its proceedings, and the yeas and nays of the members on any question, shall, upon the request of five members present, be entered in the journal.

Each house may punish a member for contempt or disorderly conduct and may expel a member by two-thirds vote of its membership.

SECTION 5. **Attendance of witnesses - production of evidence - contempt and penalties.** — Each house when in session may compel attendance of witnesses and production of public and private documents and other evidence upon any matter under investigation before it or any of its committees, and may punish by fine not exceeding $1,000 or imprisonment not exceeding ninety days any person not a member who has been guilty of disorderly or contemptuous conduct in its presence or has refused to obey its lawful summons or to answer lawful questions. For making investigations between sessions the legislature may confer such powers upon any committee of legislators by a law limited to the committee designated, to a stated period of operation, and to the matters specifically assigned. The manner of exercising such powers, including the fixing of witness fees and expenses and appropriate right of appeal, shall be prescribed by law.

SECTION 6. **Form of bill-one subject - title amendment - enacting clause.** — Every law shall embrace but one subject and matter properly connected therewith, which subject shall be briefly expressed in the title. No law shall be revised or amended by reference to its title only. Laws to revise or amend shall set out in full the revised or amended act, section, subsection, or paragraph of a subsection. The enacting clause of every law shall read: "Be it enacted by the Legislature of the State of Florida."

SECTION 7. **Passage of bills.** — Any bill may originate in either house and after passage in one may be amended in the other. In each house it shall be read on three separate days unless this rule is waived by two-thirds vote. On each reading it shall be read by title only unless one-third of the members present desire it read in full. In each house passage of a bill shall require a majority vote. On final passage the vote in each house shall be taken by yeas and nays and entered on its journal. Each bill and joint resolution passed in both houses shall be signed by the presiding officers of the respective houses and by the secretary of the senate and the chief clerk of the house of representatives.

SECTION 8. **Executive approval-veto - item veto of appropriations - repassage.** — Every bill passed by the legislature shall be presented to the governor for his approval and shall become a law if he approves and signs it, or fails to veto it within seven days after presentation; provided, if during such period the legislature finally adjourns or takes a recess of more than thirty days, he shall have twenty days from the date of adjournment or recess to act on the bill. In all cases except general appropriation bills, the veto shall extend to the entire bill. The governor may veto specific items of a general appropriation bill except an expression of legislative intent as to expenditures.

When a bill or any item of a general appropriation bill has been vetoed by the governor, he shall transmit his signed objections thereto to the house in which the bill originated if in session. If that house is not in session, he shall file them with the secretary of state, who shall lay them before that house at its next regular or special session, and they shall be entered on its journal.

If each house shall reenact the bill or reinstate a vetoed item of an appropriation bill by two-thirds vote, the yeas and nays shall be entered on the respective journals, and the bill shall become law or the item reinstated, the veto notwithstanding.

SECTION 9. **Effective date of laws and censuses affecting laws.** — Each law shall take effect on the sixtieth day from the final adjournment of the session of the legislature in which enacted unless otherwise provided therein.

Each decennial census, for the purpose of classifications based upon population, shall become effective on the thirtieth day after the final adjournment of the regular session of the legislature convened next after certification of the census.

SECTION 10. **Special and local laws - requisites for enactment.** — No special law or local law shall be passed unless notice of intention to seek enactment thereof has been published in the manner provided by law in each county in the area to be affected thereby not less than thirty days or more than ninety days prior to introduction in the legislature. The fact that publication has been made shall be recited on the journal of each house and the evidence of publication shall be preserved with the bill in the office of the secretary of state. Such notice shall not be necessary when the law, except the provision for referendum, is conditioned to become effective only upon approval by vote of the electors of the area affected.

SECTION 11. **Types of special and local laws prohibited.** — The legislature shall not pass any special or local law pertaining to:

(1) Jurisdiction, duties, fees other than those for special county purposes, or election, including the opening and conducting thereof and the designation of places of voting, of any officers except municipal officers;

(2) Assessment or collection of taxes for state or county purposes, including extension of time therefor, relief of tax officers from due performance of their duties, and relief of their sureties from liability;

(3) Rules of evidence in any court;

(4) Punishment for crime;

(5) Grand or petit juries, including compensation of jurors, except establishment of jury commissions;

(6) Change of civil or criminal venue;

(7) Conditions precedent to bringing any civil or criminal proceedings, or limitations of time therefor;

(8) Refund of money legally paid or remission of fines, penalties, or forfeitures;

(9) Creation, enforcement, extension, or impairment of liens, on pri-

(Continued on next page)

Fig. 11. Voluminous text of proposed Florida constitution well displayed in *Tallahassee Democrat*. Cols. 3-4 are Canadian wraps.

look for only the one or few with which they have some connection. Pleasure in finding Junior listed with 187 other youngsters who made the honor roll is intense. The editor feels that such pleasure, even though it is given relatively few readers, is valuable as a public relations tool, if nothing else. On the other hand, he doesn't feel it's worth setting the list in regular body type. And after pointing out that masses of agate mar the appearance of a page, the typographer must accede to the editorial judgment of the desk.

Widows

A nicety that newspaper composition cannot afford is a preoccupation with *widows*. Even in a lexicon of unusual imprecision, the term "widow" stands out. Some typographers consider any line less than full as a widow; others contend that a widow is one less than a half, a third, or even a quarter of the full measure. Many newspaper typographers consider as a widow only a single syllable or a word of four or less characters.

Widows are anathema in fine typography. ("Fine" means that used for books and certain commercial printing and doesn't necessarily carry a meaning of higher quality.) There the author is called on to rewrite copy if the typesetter cannot eliminate the widow. Obviously this cannot be done with news copy.

In book work, the designer tries to avoid a widow at the top and bottom of a page. Sometimes he must change the depth of a pair of facing pages to eliminate this positioning, for two lines must be moved to take care of the widow. To move just the widow from the foot of one page puts it at the top of the next one. So the line above the widow must also be placed on the next page. This manipulation, too, is impractical in newspaper makeup.

As far as I'm concerned, I move a widow only if it is very short and at the bottom of an open column. I particularly avoid starting a second leg of type with a short widow if the first leg has been a long one. It is annoying for the reader to climb 8 or 10 inches to the start of the next column and find his arduous trip rewarded with only the hyphenated "ed" from the last word. In this case I would move the last full line to the top of the next leg. Fortunately, justifying the first leg is much easier in newspaper format than on the page of a book.

In magazines it is often style to fill out the last line of cutlines, and this usually requires painstaking writing. A few newspapers make the same effort. I'm agin' it!

A colleague of mine once deleted a word from the Gettysburg Address in order to make the type block a precise rectangle. This is heresy. The quality of typical newspaper cutlines rarely attains the heights of Abraham Lincoln's eloquence. But the principle remains the same. If the writer has done the best possible job, the typographer has no business changing the literary form to effect a pleasant geometric form. Even cursory reading of squared cutlines will often detect an unpleasant break in the flow of copy where a superfluous word or phrase has been added or a necessary one eliminated in order to avoid a widow.

Initials

The use of *initials,* another typographic nicety dearly beloved of book and magazine typographers, decreases steadily in newspapers. Where it is still retained, it is usually confined to editorial and feature pages. Initials have a fussy feeling that is not out of place in books and magazines, but to many contemporary eyes they seem inappropriate for a newspaper. More compelling reasons for their decline are the mechanical problems of setting initials and the danger of their breaking during the mat-rolling process.

There are two styles of initials. The *rising,* or *stickup, initial* aligns at the foot—at least in theory—with the first line of body type and projects above the type block. It is the easiest to set, and the white space built in at the right of the initial is advantageous. The *inset,* or *sunken, initial* occupies a rectangle cut out of the top left corner of the type block. By good standards, the initial should align at its top with the meanline of the first line of type and, at its baseline, with that of adjacent body type. This is practically impossible to achieve without manipulation on the galley. Even by disregarding this nicety, the fussing around to use a sunken initial doesn't bring any dividends.

I recommend vigorously against any use of initials. However, if an editor insists on using them, he ought to adopt the rising style.

Line Justification

The very first job printed with movable type had justified lines, lines aligning exactly at the right and left. There was good reason; the paper and vellum on which that printing was done was expensive, and setting type in this style minimized waste.

The practice has persisted even though it has meant countless extra hours of work for compositors since Gutenberg's day. Justification in hand composition is difficult and time-consuming; in linecaster composition, it is automatically performed by the spacebands.

Justified lines are a sign of typographic quality even to the layman, though he probably is not actually aware of it. School children producing play newspapers on a typewriter will work diligently to create justified lines, and this is far more difficult on a typewriter than in metal type. But they know that "this is the way a newspaper should look."

Some copy—notably poetry—is set unjustified, *ragged right*. This style emphasizes word groupings and focuses attention on a bard's well-turned phrases. For this reason, no doubt, this style is often used to enhance the deathless prose of advertising copywriters. But ragged-right setting is effective only for copy written for specific line-for-line duplication in type. Flowing copy, such as news stories, for instance, is best set justified.

Ragged-right setting is sometimes called *free line-fall,* when words are hyphenated but the line is not necessarily filled. Typewritten letters customarily are composed in this style. *English line-fall* never has hyphenation at the end of a line (hyphens must be used elsewhere, of course), and the type is not justified.

Recently, a few newspapers have been experimenting with the English line-fall. Their primary aim is to eliminate hyphenation and with it the time that is used in making hyphenation decisions. If a line of complete words will justify by the normal expansion of the spacebands, that's fine. If the leftover space is greater than the spacebands can use up, no syllable is put in nor is letterspacing used; enough spacing to fill is dropped in at the end of the line and the right margin is left ragged.

Cursory measurement indicates that on an average there will be one short line for every 4½ regular-length lines. As with all averages, though, the pattern of short lines is erratic. A dozen or even more lines may be full length, and then there may be three or four, or even more, consecutive lines of short and varying lengths. I haven't been able to determine which annoys my own reading eye most, an occasional short line or a ganging-up of them. Both are bad and have an inhibiting effect on my reading speed, comprehension, and—most certainly—pleasure.

The experimenters, though, are enthusiastic about the technique. They claim substantial savings in keyboarding time. Some of them concede that the esthetics do not meet their complete approval but insist that the economic savings are so great that the disadvantages pale in comparison.

While I applaud all typographic experimentation, I am pessimistic

ıngs Limit ın Sales

CAROL WILCOX
r Post Staff Writer

t Denver druggist
knuckled under to
and agreed not to sell
glue to minors—unless
with a model build-

east Denver residents
outside the Yale
, 3401 Downing St., on
ore's glue sales.
re's pharmacist, Ar-
ttini, and picketers'
l, reached a hasty
after protesters ap-

peared in front of the pharmacy
with cease-glue signs. The picketers were alarmed about neighborhood youth sniffing glue purchased at the drugstore.

One of the spokesmen, Mrs.
Faye Gomez, 1517 E. 36th Ave.,
said she and several other wom-
en presented Hayutini with anti-
glue petitions with 500 signatures about four months ago.

"We know it's the kids who
are doing wrong," Mrs. Gomez
said.

But, she said the best way to
curb glue sniffing is to persuade

"Geralyn doesn't sniff glue,
but some of the neighbor kids
have been trying to get her to.
I had some kids come to my
house and dare me to take pictures of them sniffing glue.
Now some of them are in Denver Juvenile Hall," Mrs. Gomez
said.

Protesters were objecting to
a rubber cement or airplane
glue Hayutin stocks which sells
for 15 cents for a tube containing ⅝th ounce. The tubes are
labeled, "Danger: flammable

Fig. 12. Unjustified body type from *Denver Post*. Of 45 lines shown here, same size,
11 are short; other six short lines are paragraph ends.

about the ragged-right technique. I have not seen substantive data to support the claims of economy. Nor can I rationalize them. The typesetter must still make a line-end decision. It is simpler than the previous one; he must merely decide whether the spacebands will be able to make a castable line or whether he has to drop in extra spacing at the end of the line. He doesn't have to decide whether or how to hyphenate. But I cannot, from my own experience, comprehend how the great claimed savings are effected by this slight difference in degree of decision.

If the linecaster has an *automatic quadder*—a device that automatically places spacing material so the line is flush left, flush right, or centered—this nonjustified technique is speeded up, of course.

We do not yet have any substantial research on the effect of the ragged-right margin on readership or readability. We have some studies that indicate that justified lines are read best, but these have not been in the exact context of newspaper pages. As an individual, I find the ragged style is annoying, but the typographer must always beware of leaping to the conclusion that his likes and dislikes are shared completely by the whole reading public.

Research often quoted in support of nonjustified composition has been done by Dr. John Scott Davenport and Stewart A. Smith for the Scripps-Howard Newspapers. Impetus for the study came from Ronald

White, the S-H engineering director, who, before a meeting of his group's editors, questioned the need for hyphenation. He suggested that hyphenation was not developed to aid readability but rather to set maximum words per line. But, he said, hyphenation saves only a negligible 2% of space. The advantages of simpler manual operation and—his concern at the moment—simpler computer operation and simpler, thus less costly, computers themselves could be substantial.

If words are never hyphenated but lines are justified, there will be great variation in word spacing, and this irregularity might adversely affect reading rhythm. If lines were not justified, word spacing could remain constant. What then, he speculated, would be the effect of the ragged-right margin?

The researchers added another variable, point size. They then could present eight different styles of composition; 7½- and 9-point type were each set (a) hyphenated and justified, (b) hyphenated but not justified, (c) justified but not hyphenated, and (d) neither hyphenated nor justified.

The findings indicated no appreciable differences in total words read, accuracy of reading, or comprehension. These data were eagerly accepted as proof that setting styles are a negligible factor in readability, but the researchers themselves flashed bright amber signals.

They pointed out, for instance, that the study was made after only a 20-minute exposure to the special newspaper that had been created for the test. Apparently none of the tested readers had reached the point of eye fatigue in any setting. To be more useful, the test would have had to cover longer periods of reading in a single edition as well as over weeks or months, long enough to determine the accumulated effect.

Respondents were exposed to the test matter under circumstances unlike that of the regular newspaper reader; there was no competitive material available, the reader was a truly captive audience; the sample population was not necessarily a good microcosm of the readership of a typical newspaper.

"Generalizations from these results to real-life newspaper reading behavior should be made with caution," the researchers warned. But—a danger with all statistics—the data were cited by others with greater partisanship than accuracy.

I certainly do not deprecate the Davenport-Smith study. It was honestly done and accurately reported. Inaccuracies resulted from the way the results were quoted and interpreted by others. We need much more research in this field, a point that this team also makes in its report.

Those who have adopted the new technique in their news columns report that they have received no adverse reaction from their subscribers. Yet other research, done on a scale yet too small to have statistical validity, indicates that more than half of the respondents thought that the new technique was the result of ineptness or carelessness.

It is this reaction that I fear. I think the newspaper can afford to do nothing that will harm its image of quality. Ever since the electronic media grabbed the market on immediacy of the news, a major strength of the newspaper has been its authority. People consistently said they would believe a story they saw in print although they might be skeptical about the same report that they had just heard on the air. This reliability is far too valuable to risk on any typographic innovation.

It is my fear—and I stress that it is only my opinion, not backed by sufficient research—that the reader may, if only subconsciously, get the reaction, "If the newspaper is this careless about the way it looks, it may be just as careless with its facts." I think that every reader has had similar experiences; surely we would not consider a poorly printed book as authoritative as one of sharp, clean impression. A hard-cover book carries more weight—literally and figuratively—than a paperback. An author who uses poor grammar and writes awkwardly does not have the authority of one who uses the language well. If we concede that poor use of the printing press or of the rules of English composition can have a deleterious effect on the reader, poor typography may have the same ill result.

If this premise has any validity, then we must wince when we see another abomination, *zombie composition.* Here all rules of hyphenation are ignored in order to eliminate absolutely all decision-making and thus speed composition. The typesetter puts as many characters as possible in a line. If the last word is not complete, he places the hyphen there with no regard to syllabification. These examples were taken from the first eleven lines of a random page in a booklet set in this style: su/mmer, John/'s, st/aff, wome/n's. The ratio—and horror—maintained throughout.

Without any claim to research, users of this technique blithely insist that "it has no effect on readership," that "hyphens are an artificial device," and that "the reader will quickly learn to carry over to the next line letters that do not make a syllable."

Many newspapers that use computers to justify tape are marred by improper syllabification, and reader complaints come quickly and loudly. To avoid these lapses, good newspapers feed corrections daily into the computer's memory. The computer's errors at least create "syllables." Each computerized "syllable" does have a vowel, even if it is silent in speech. If these relatively minor errors are disconcerting and annoying to the reader, it seems incontrovertible that random hyphenation will have worse effects.

In an era when craftsmanship and standards have been superseded by mass production and planned obsolescence, many printers have still maintained pride of craft. It seems a pity and a shame that the editorial department should encourage any abandonment of typographic standards. Of course, we should not maintain customs and amenities that have become nonfunctional. But neither should we let all our standards be set by the balance sheet and the computer. Most of the standards of the fine graphic arts craftsman evolved from the desire to create and maintain readability. That goal is just as valid—and more important—today as it was in the days of Aldus Manutius.

chapter **5**

Headlines

EVERY EDITOR has at least once experienced the anguish of a typographical error in a 96-point banner. He need not be reminded that headlines are conspicuous.

The very fact that heads are conspicuous makes them more interesting to the typical newspaperman. Changes in news coverage, reporting, writing, and editing are unobtrusive. Often a change in body type may pass unnoticed, or at least with silence from the reader. But a new headline schedule is obvious to the most untutored eye. And while most deskmen take their body type for granted and work with it without comment, it is a rare editor who doesn't vociferously express a constant need for more, better, or just plain different headline faces.

"Form follows function," so if we analyze the function of headlines, we can more effectively choose headletters and ways to use them.

A primary function of the headline is to evaluate the news. A major story will certainly not go with a 14-point head, nor will a brief about a fender-crumpler rate a 72-point banner.

The head summarizes the story. While we will never be content with having our reader get his information about the day's events only from heads, we do hope that he has at least a smattering of knowledge from such a cursory exposure to current events.

The head is one of the elements of typographic color that combine to make attractive page patterns. Headlines help define the personality of the newspaper. The difference between a paper dressed in a black Sans and one in an Old Style Roman is like that between a man habitually dressed in tweeds and one who wears only blue serge. Both content and headletter contribute to the image. The breezy flavor of the *New York*

Daily News heads contrast as much as their typography against the staid, in form and content, heads in the *New York Times*.

Most important, a headline is a salesman that says to the reader, "Here is a story of importance or interest. Read it right away!"

A good headletter enables the headline to perform each function well, but the content is of greater importance, and here the creativity of the headwriter is paramount.

Headline Content

There are two kinds of headlines, the definitive and the connotative.

The *definitive,* or *summary, head* boils the gist of the story into a terse sentence. The *connotative head* is a teaser, piquing the curiosity of the reader without telling him much, or anything, about the story. Teasers are most frequently used on features; straight news usually doesn't warrant the subtle levity usually found in the connotative head. Connotation need not be incompatible with somber subjects, though, as perusal of any magazine demonstrates.

The typographer's job is to transmit written information. Mostly he doesn't concern himself with the quality of content. Whether it's a sober presidential fiat or a lively World Series report, he puts it into typographic form that transmits the content in the most efficient way. Only with headlines is he involved with content as well as form.

A good headline must not require translation. It is a good technique to read a headline aloud to make sure that it says what the writer hoped it would. This may save embarrassment as well as miscommunication. Double entendres sneak into headlines with tantalizing frequency.

One of America's respected—and rather staid—newspapers informed its readers (in only one edition, it might be observed) that:

SOVIET VIRGIN
LANDS SHORT
OF GOAL AGAIN

There was undoubtedly mixed reaction on the part of the reader when he discovered that it was merely an agricultural fiasco: Virgin farmlands in Siberia had not met crop quotas. (We ought to note here that headline examples are given here in all-caps only to distinguish them from the rest of the text. This does not in the slightest way suggest that actual headlines be set all-cap.)

The VIRGIN head demonstrates the validity of the admonition that heads must be written as they are read, line for line. Closely linked phrases should not be split between lines. If the phrase "virgin lands" had been on a single line, the head would have been more accurate, if less piquant.

White House, Red China, and Sen. Kennedy are typical phrases that, in terms of communication, must be handled as a single word. Prepositional phrases obviously should not be split. But we must remember that what seems to be a preposition may well be an adverb:

SLAYER GIVES UP
AFTER WIFE'S PLEA

Headlines, typographically, should give the effect of a breathless courier blurting out sensational news. A recent research project showed that heads with three words per line were best recalled by readers. Presumably they had been drawn into the story too. Now this does not mean that the desk should always and only write three-word heads. The import of the finding is broader: that heads in a boom-boom-boom, boom-boom-boom pattern set up a staccato rhythm that creates the immediacy and excitement essential to the good headline.

Although "headlinese" is an artificial, created language, it has rules of grammar just as an organic language. Just as our living English is being adulterated by the lazy, careless, and ignorant, so is headlinese when it doesn't have the watchful protection of a discerning desk. Unfortunately, the newspaper that is lax and slovenly in its headline content is often just as inferior in standards for newswriting.

Headlinese eliminates articles. It says:

DELEGATION GOES
TO WHITE HOUSE

The slovenly headwriter will often add an article—or some form of the usually omitted "is"—to make the head fit better:

GOP DELEGATION GOES
TO THE WHITE HOUSE

This is not a hanging offense, but it jars the reader just as it would if you told him, not "I am going home," but "I am going to the home."

Headlines use commas instead of "and":

ALBANIANS, CZECHS
SIGN TRADE PACT

and the semicolon instead of a period:

WILDCATS WIN TROPHY;
JONES BREAKS RECORD

(An excellent rule of thumb: When a headline requires punctuation, it probably needs rewriting. A one-idea headline is the most effective; the reader can most easily decide whether or not he wants to read the story. Added phrases and thoughts, no matter how they are set off, blur the essence of the headline and make the reader's choice a little less clear-cut.)

Headlines use the historical present tense. BOMB EXPLODES means it went bang in the near past. BOMB EXPLODING is the simple present tense and BOMB TO EXPLODE is the future.

The past tense is used rarely in headlines. When it is, it generally refers to an event in the past that has just come to light:

VICTIM KNEW SLAYER,
DIARY FRAGMENT SHOWS

Other usage of headline tense is not a criminal offense, but it is a mark of the illiterate in this special language.

Admonitory heads are most annoying to the reader. These are heads where the subject is eliminated:

THROW MUGGER
IN CITY JAIL

We can only applaud the reader if he insists, "Throw your own mugger in jail."

But the primary topic of this chapter is the form of the headline, and so we must return from digression, no matter how interesting it may be.

Headline Form

Headlines should be simple in form and large in size.

Simplicity of headline form is endorsed by findings that 1-column heads are most effective when no deeper than three lines. The next-to-last line is often misread or unread in deeper heads.

Four- and even 5-line single-column heads are a Britishism that is beginning to creep into some American papers. They are not effective with readers used to U.S. newspaper style.

Multicolumn heads are most effective in 1- and 2-line forms. If the type is so large that only a word or two fills a line, a 3-line form is satisfactory.

Type should be as large as possible and appropriate. A line of 36-point is worth more than two lines of 18-point, for instance, and if we can reduce the number of lines without weakening the impact of the head, it will be more effective.

Type that is unusually large for the measure gains added impact from the unaccustomed usage. My newspaper once used a 1-column 72-point Spartan Bold head:

POOL

NOW

OPEN

The effect was striking, far more than if the type had been used more conventionally in a 3-column 1-liner.

Another aspect of simplicity is in the volume of a headline. We find that the most effective heads have a maximum of about 32 characters and spaces per line and 45 for the whole head, no matter how many extra lines. (Note that for this purpose, every character and space counts as 1. We do not weight the count according to the width of the character as we do when counting heads to see if they'll fit.)

Heads that exceed this rough and admittedly arbitrary limit become pedestrian and lose the terseness that attracts readers. Long words and unfamiliar words tend to weaken the impact and should be avoided. If there are too many characters in a proposed line or head, either a larger size type should be used or the head made a column narrower.

In 1-column heads there is little danger of using long words, for the inexorable limit of the column width restricts multisyllabophiles. The opposite may be a danger, though. The mechanical need for short words forces the headwriter into the Anglo-Saxon section of the dictionary. Here he finds words that fit. But short words usually are far stronger than longer ones. So the terse "hit" may be substituted for "point out," and the meaning is intensified beyond accuracy. This distortion by tersity is often cited by the reader to bolster a contention that newspapers sensationalize the news.

Simplification of the headline form has thrown out jim-dashes, as we noted in the first chapter. It has also eliminated most decks. The 1968 N.E.A. survey already alluded to showed that 65% of the responding newspapers had eliminated all decks. (Time out for definitions. A deck is that portion of a headline which is set in a single type style and size. It is made up of one or more *lines,* or *banks.* These synonyms are rarely used though, possibly because "line" more commonly refers to "cutline" and "bank" to the comp-room storage area. While the main portion of a headline is technically a "deck," that word is usually applied to second or third decks. "The deck" is invariably the second one.)

Rarely is a secondary deck functional, but exceptions should be noted. The *readout* from a banner may be functional by guiding the eye to the proper column. The *banner* is the main multicolumn head on the front page. Once it referred only to an 8-column, or full-page-width, head, but today it may be as narrow as 4 columns. It is also called a *streamer, screamer,* or "the line."

The need of a readout from a banner depends primarily on the point at which the story begins. If it is in the right third of the page, with no other heads right under the banner, the eye does not need a directional device to define its path. If there is body type of the story in each column under a banner, the readout head is not required. Rarely, though, can we dispose body type this way under banners wider than five columns.

Even when the readout head is not required to guide the eye, its "step-down" function may be desirable. The eye can adjust from a 48-point head to 8- or 10-point body type with no difficulty, and many editors are convinced that the drop from 60-point to body size is not too great. Most seem to believe that a banner in 72-point or larger definitely requires an intermediate size as a transition to body type. The readout then becomes a kind of decompression chamber.

If this funnel effect is functional, it may seem logical that we continue it down through a deck of 48-point, then 36 and perhaps 18, before the body type. But the law of diminishing returns sets in. So does another danger.

If a succession of decks summarizes the story in too much detail, the reader may decide that that's all he cares to know about the topic and omit reading any body type. Remember, the reader is conditioned to brief "news reports"; electronic media give only a sentence or two and inform us "and that's the story from Istanbul."

It is demonstrable that too much information in a headline does decrease readership. So we limit ourselves to a single deck as a readout.

When a 1-column head must hold the top of a column, we may want the extra ink of a deck just for the typographic weight it provides. A single added deck is the functional limit.

A 3-line deck seems to be the most pleasing from a design viewpoint, whether it's a readout or under a page-top head. If the weight of a readout is at least 36-point, this deck may be adequate in two lines. But a

1-column deck, whether it's under a banner or a smaller head, will usually require a 3-line form. A 2-line main head may look pleasant with a 2-line deck. But if the main head has three lines, the deck must, without exception, also have three.

If the deck is too flimsy, it will give the unpleasant effect of an after-thought, added only to fill in some unwanted blank area. The most unpleasant deck is a 1-liner in multicolumns. Whether this sliver runs under a 1- or 2-line main head, the deck itself looks distressingly out of proportion. Usually this style of head has a cluster of stars or asterisks or some other gimcrackery between the main head and the deck. This is nothing but parsley dressing a skinny lamb chop.

It is an easy-to-live-with rule of thumb that 1-line heads, other than the banner, never take a deck; that there shall be no multicolumn decks except as a readout; that there shall be no 1-line decks under any cir-cumstances.

A 1-column 36-point head could take a second deck in 14- or 18-point. A 24-point head could take a 12- or 14-point deck. A 30-pointer would take 14- or 18-point deck. A main head smaller than 24 can't hold a column-top on a full-format page. On a compact page, an 18-point main head might conceivably hold the top of a column with a deck of 12-point.

Flush-left Headlines

Simplicity of form suggests the use of *flush-left* headlines, and sound typographical principles second the motion.

To the best of the knowledge that we have at this time, flush-left setting is the most effective for heads, for it is based on the instinctive pattern in which the reading eye moves.

When the eye reaches the end of a line of type, it must, of course, sweep back to begin the next one. In this backsweep it returns to the benchmark, the *axis of orientation* (*A/O*) of that grouping of type. This is the start of the first line. If the second line is indented, the eye must then search for the beginning instead of finding it at the end of the backstroke. After it has read the second line, the eye returns left—not as far as the start of that second line—but to the start of the first line again; the axis of orientation remains constant. If the third line is indented beyond the second line, the eye must search a larger area before it can begin reading again.

This doesn't take a lot of time or energy. After all, the vacant area is usually less than an em; it's not a 5-acre field. But the major danger is the annoyance to the reader. When your telephone rings while you are busy, you reach without looking. If it's been moved, you must look and find before you can grasp. This, too, is a trifling expenditure of time and energy. But it is an annoyance that, repeated too often, will trigger an explosion of irritation. The reader doesn't explode when he is aggravated; he just quits reading, either right then or much sooner than we would prefer.

Any head with a ragged left margin is, therefore, nonfunctional at best. If it annoys the reader too much, it is malfunctional as well. Accordingly, flush-right heads are to be avoided. *Stepped heads*—the form in which the first line is flush left, the last flush right, the middle one centered—add another discrepancy. They have the undesirable ragged left margin, of course. But unless each line is written with far more care than is possible, the diagonal line created by the steps will vary in angle from head to head. This inconsistency is like a mosquito bite, not fatal in itself but unbearable in repetition.

Ragged right margins are not only permissible, they are desirable. An interesting questionnaire about headlines was directed to readers of the old *New York Herald-Tribune*. At that time its heads were written so each line was full. The headline, then, was justified composition, just like body type. Readers were asked to choose among adjectives that might describe the headline form as it affected them. "Formal," "stodgy," "hard to read," and "cold" were constantly chosen. When heads were written with studiedly ragged right margins, the reader changed his evaluation to "informal," "comfortable," "easy to read," and "friendly."

Capitalizing Style

Application of functionalism to headline forms will soon direct attention to capitalization style because this is a weighty factor in their effectiveness.

Standard headline style of capitalization is *upper-and-lowercase (u&lc, cap-and-lc, c&lc)*. Basically, each word is capitalized, but some newspapers amend the style to lowercase prepositions. This creates problems. In headlines, "to" is a verb in MAYOR TO SPEAK and so is "up" in BANKS UP MORTGAGE RATE. So do we cap them or not? This is a trifling problem but one that adds to the tension of making deadlines and destroys consistent style.

U&lc, *cap-and-down,* heads are a distinct improvement over the standard that preceded them, all-capital heads. All-cap setting is not efficient. We recognize words by their top silhouette. If you cover the lower half of a line of type set in u&lc or all lowercase, you find you can read it as readily as if you saw the whole line. But the top half of a line of caps is difficult, if not impossible, to read, because its top silhouette is basically a straight line.

Of course, the reader doesn't exert any great effort to decipher the all-cap line. If he can't make sense from the top half, he merely looks at the rest of the letterform. So he can read all-caps; he just can't read as quickly and easily as we want him to.

The fewer the words, the more easily the reader overcomes the handicap. So because there are only a few words in a head, the low legibility of all-cap is often overlooked. But we can test the effect in body type. Don't cheat now! Read every word of the following paragraph!

AS THIS PARAGRAPH DEMONSTRATES, ALL-CAPITAL SETTING IS NEITHER EFFICIENT FOR THE READER NOR PLEASING TO HIS EYE. WILLIAM RANDOLPH HEARST USED TO HAVE KEY GRAFS IN HIS EDITORIALS SET ALL-CAP. INSTEAD OF MAKING THE THE POINT EMPHATICALLY, AS HE INTENDED, SUCH SETTING ACTUALLY CUT DOWN THE READERSHIP AND ITS IMPACT.

Now that wasn't much fun to read, was it? And did you spot the typo in the last sentence? If you didn't, don't feel bad; it was a deliberate trap to demonstrate poor readability, and the most attentive and skilled reader will be blinded by the swarm of all those capitals.

The next experiment won't be as annoying because we're going to eliminate most of the capitals, retaining only the first in a word.

Upper-And-Lower Setting Is Admittedly Better Than All-Cap. But When The Style Was Introduced In The *Minneapolis Tribune* In 1908, It Brought Howls Of Indignation From The Traditionalists Of The Copydesk. We Now Have A Distinctive Upper Silhouette. But Each Capital Still Acts Like The Hook On A Barbed Wire Fence, Snagging The Reading Eye As It Moves Along And Diminishing Pleasure Even As It Reduces Reading Speed.

It's a real relief to get into the paragraph you're now reading, isn't it? This is because the style is one to which we have been accustomed since we first learned to read. This is *downstyle,* in which only the first word in a sentence and proper nouns are capped. In both instances the caps serve a functional purpose. They indicate the beginning of a sentence, and they make the fine but vital semantic distinction between a red man and a Red man or a democrat and a Democrat.

This ease and comfort of reading have been the main factors in the

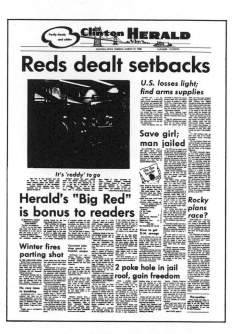

Fig. 13. Downstyle headlines can make heavy banners as in *Clinton* (Iowa) *Herald* and *Chicago's American,* opposite. Note unusual possessive case of nameplate.

adoption of downstyle for newspaper headlines. That downstyle heads can be written and set much more quickly and easily than other styles is a pleasant side benefit. Most editors who adopt downstyle heads are enthusiastic about them. I have known no instance where downstyle was given a fair trial and then abandoned. I do know some cases where the publisher abandoned downstyle after as little as one day or less than a week, far too short a period to test the value of the new style. We must wait until the novelty wears off before we can truly evaluate a new technique. Even a new automobile is awkward to drive for the first hundred miles or so. Downstyle heads, as any typographic innovation, should be used at least six weeks before a final evaluating. Even if a technique is abandoned, nothing horrendously bad can result in those six weeks. Irate readers are not going to storm the editorial office; downstyle can be used with impunity for the period necessary to give it a fair trial.

In fact, the reader is so quiet in his acceptance of new things that often the publisher is disappointed. But just as silence gives assent, so silence on the part of a newspaper reader is often an accolade. Many publishers have been complimented on a "new type" when downstyle heads were put into use; often the new style leads the reader to believe that pictures are larger or clearer. Unless the reader has not been prepared for the new style by advance promotion, it is rare for him to complain.

Windy, Warmer
Considerable cloudiness, windy and warmer today. High in the 60s. Tonight, windy, warmer, chance of showers. Precipitation probabilities, 20 per cent today, 50 per cent tonight. Tomorrow, showers and mild.
(Details on page 2)

Chicago's Sunday AMERICAN
Always On Top Of The News

5 STAR
★★★★★
COMPLETE

Vol. 87, No. 48   Nine Sections, Section 1   SUNDAY, APRIL 7, 1968   10   Phone: 222-4321   25 CENTS

GIs arrive here

LBJ federalizes national guard

Roosevelt road, 2800 block

WALLS of what once was a building stand starkly in smoking ruins left by one of numerous fires set by rioters on west side. This scene is in 2800 block of Roosevelt road.

Division and Larrabee streets

CROUCHED BEHIND vehicles and with rifles at ready, national guardsmen scan building at Division and Larrabee streets after snipers were reported in the area.

Madison street and Kedzie

LOOTERS walk freely with merchandise taken from stores along Madison street near Kedzie avenue.

[CHICAGO'S AMERICAN Photos]

Many Viet vets among army troops on patrol

By Robert Smith

A BATTALION of combat and riot trained regular veterans, between 800 and 1,000 men, is patroling Chicago streets today.

The soldiers are part of three brigades, made up of 5,000 soldiers from the 1st armored division flown in at the request of Mayor Daley and acting Gov. Samuel H. Shapiro to restore peace to the riot torn areas of the city.

At 12:01 a. m. today, President Johnson officially placed the elderal troops here, and federalized the national guard already on duty in the city.

"We are here to maintain law and order in this city," said Deputy United States Atty. Gen. Warren Christopher, who will direct the army and, with Mayor Daley, the regular army, and the national guard. "We are determined to do so."

Both the army troops and the national guardsmen will be under the command of Lt. Gen. George Mather, 3d army corps and commanding general of Fort Hood, Tex.

"A CONSIDERABLE number of the army men here are veterans of the Viet Nam war and all of them are riot trained," said Gen. Mather.

On the question of the use of guns or other weapons, he said:

"The orders that have been outstanding for some time will continue in existence. Only a minimum of force will be used as needed. No man will fire his weapon unles directed to do so by an officer."

Shortly after his arrival here, Gen. Mather and Christopher were taken on a helicopter tour of the burned out area. They met and conferred briefly with Mayor Daley and Police Supt. James B. Conlisk Jr.

Conlisk said the situation appears to be "reasonably under control," and added that the emergency is not over. Mather said the federal troops not patroling will be kept in reserve to be called out as needed.

IN HIS REQUEST for 5,000 federal troops along with 6,900 national guardsmen, Gov. Shapiro called the wave of rioting, looting, and burning in Chicago an "insurrection."

Shapiro sent a brief telegram to Pres-

The situation

• TWO POLICEMEN race into a building on N. Cleveland avenue and seize a sniper, to the relief of young guardsmen waiting in thick, black smoke for fire equipment to arrive at a burning grocery. A vivid insight into a city under siege. Page 2.

• ATTY. GEN. Ramsey Clark, in Memphis to spur the search for the assassin of Dr. Martin Luther King Jr., is optimistic the

killer will be found. An on-the-scene report by THE AMERICAN'S L. F. Palmer Jr. Page 5.

• A PLEA FOR shelter for Negro families left homeless by the rioting and fires met a gratifying response yesterday by suburban residents who are opening their homes to victims. Page 3.

• NEW RIOTS and looting plague other cities across the nation. A r undup with pictures on page 6.

ident Johnson at 5:30 p. m. requesting the soldiers after bearing reports from Mayor Daley and Brig. Gen. Richard Dunn that the situation here is worsening.

Johnson immediately approved Shapiro's request.

First federal troops arrived at O'Hare International airport at 9:40 p. m. They were from the 1st armored division. Fort Hood, Tex.

Headquarters for the regular army

[Continued on page 4, col. 2]

Quell D.C. violence

By Tom Leach
CHICAGO'S AMERICAN
Washington Correspondent

WASHINGTON—A tripling of federal troops and national guardsmen last night restored a measure of law and order to the nation's capital.

The massive display of force put a halt to burning and looting that had swept thru three Negro sections of the city for 3 days.

Mayor Walter Washington said late last night, "We're happy to say that the streets are calm." Officials pleaded for citizens to stay in their homes.

Most of the troops had their hands full protecting firemen, who have answered 540 alarms since violence began Thursday night.

The toll from the disorders stands at 5 dead, more than 750 injured [including

23 policemen and 16 firemen], and 3,263 arrested.

A curfew for all citizens was extended 2½ hours over the previous night's from 4 p. m. to 6:30 a. m.

The curfew will continue until complete order has been restored, officials said.

Sections of the city still smoking or burning resemble bombing scenes from World War II. Only gutted walls and empty shells still stand.

OFFICIALS DESCRIBED conditions in the capital as "serious," and thousands of troops are standing by to be called into the city if needed. Thru the day and last night, the troop force has increased f r o m 6,000 to more than 12,000.

In addition to the troops, more than 1,300 District of Columbia policemen are

[Continued on page 6, col. 6]

Negro plea: 'Save spirit'

ATLANTA ⟨P⟩—As the body of the Rev. Martin Luther King Jr. lay in public view last night, a group of students passed out handbills urging nonviolence.

"Even now the sirens are sounding. Why? Because black people are using the death of our great black leader for an excuse to rob and steal and destroy," the handbills said.

They were given to mourners going to view the body of King at Spelman college. They were signed by the Black Action committee, Morehouse college, a school in the same area which is King's alma mater.

Of King the statement said: "A white man killed his body, but black people are killing his spirit. A white man took his life, but black people are taking away his principles of nonviolence. . . .

"We are asking you in the King's name to respect his death. . . . Don't forget the King.

"Don't support or condone any violent action during this mourning period. Let us go this little way further with the King."

Chicago: A sad story

DEAD—10.

INJURED—Hundreds.

FIRES—Hundreds.

PROPERTY DAMAGE—Millions of dollars.

POLICE—10,500-man force on duty in 12-hour shifts.

MILITARY—6,900 Illinois national guard and 5,000 regular army.

ARRESTED—1,250.

LIQUOR—Sale suspended in these police districts: Wabash, Englewood, Fillmore, Wood street and parts of Kensington, Austin, Shakespeare, Deering, Marquette, and Chicago avenue. In other areas voluntary closings.

BUS SERVICE—Curtailed in 12-square mile area of west side from Chicago avenue to Cermak road, from Ashland avenue to Cicero avenue.

BOUNDARIES—Hardest hit was Madison street from Damen avenue to Cicero, Pulaski road from Madison to Roosevelt road and along sections of Roosevelt road. Also hit was the near north side from Chicago avenue to North avenue west of Wells street and the south side in an area around 63d street.

Postpone awarding of Oscars

The American Broadcasting company announced today that the Academy awards ceremony has been postponed from 9 p. m. tomorrow [Channel 7] until 9 p. m. Wednesday, out of respect to the Rev. Martin Luther King Jr.

An ABC special, starring Singer

Wayne Newton, also has been postponed from tomorrow until Wednesday.

The request for the postponement of the awards ceremony was made by Sammy Davis Jr. to Gregory Peck, president of the Academy of Motion Picture Arts and Sciences.

It is important to note that downstyle follows the capping style of ordinary body composition. Only the first word of a sentence is capped; we do not cap the first word of each line, a perversion occasionally seen.

Some editors, especially on women's, feature, and magazine pages, become so enamored of downstyle that they abuse by overuse; they don't use any capitals. The poet e. e. cummings used the no-cap style as an advertising gimmick. He had the right to spell—or misspell—his name any way he wanted to. And we have the right to perpetuate his whim, even if we are not required to. Many trademarks or registered trade names turn their backs on grammar. In the newspaper business, for instance, a phototypesetting machine is a ProType and an A/C/E Mixer is an Auto-Controlled Elektron. In technical writing we may cap the T in ProType or use slashes in the acronym of the Linotype. But for news matter it is just as correct to spell it Protype or ACE or auto-controlled.

It is not correct, however, to set proper nouns without caps merely to please our own whim or house style. *January* is *January,* never *january.* Capping proper nouns is a grammatical standard; the typographer can no more change the *F* in *February* to *f* than he can change the *a* to *e.* *Februery* is no more wrong than *february.*

We can sum up. All-cap setting should be avoided; upper-and-lower is acceptable; downstyle is the best that we know at the moment.

As in all typography, consistency is essential. We should not mix two or more capping styles. If we keep prepositions in lowercase in u&lc heads, standards should be well defined and policed.

Headline Spacing

A tiny indent at the left of a head does not affect the axis of orientation, but it does aid the legibility of headlines when column rules are used. If 1-column heads are indented 6 points and multicolumns a pica, this sliver of white aids the eye in lifting the type off the page and into comprehension. We assume that the head is written ragged at the right so there is room at that end, too, to grasp the headline.

Indenting at the left is useless with open-format alleys, though.

Headlines should not be ledded. The shoulder on the slug is adequate. Indeed, the type designer has spent much skill and time in determining that space to the thousandth of an inch. Extra spacing tends to fragment the head into lateral sections and thus to slow reading. Word spacing should be constant; an en or the regular narrow space is adequate. We don't want excessive word spacing, but we must also avoid too-tight spacing in order to squeeze in a poorly written head. With u&lc head styles, inadequate word spacing is unpleasant; with downstyle or all-cap, it destroys legibility.

Some newspapers insist that the banner be full. To achieve this, they will use wide spacing between words. Or, with a 2-line head, they'll set the top one flush left and the lower one flush right. This is awkward and inconsistent; the head should be written full or allowed to set short.

Specialized Decks

There are some useful headline forms which, although they may not seem so at first glance, are decked heads. These *specialized decks* are functional exceptions to our general no-deck style.

The *kicker* is a short head, usually *underscored,* above a larger main head. (This head has many synonyms, but these have regional usage, and "kicker" is accepted in most news rooms.)

Ideally the kicker should be no longer than one-third the width of the headline area. It should be one-half the point size of the main head. If the main head is 30 points, the kicker should be 18; the kicker on a 42-point should be 24; on a 60-pointer, a 36 kicker will do. The main head should have no more than two lines. No other regular deck should ever be used with a kickered head.

The kicker should be underscored unless it is in a heavy accent face. Ideally the underscore should be the weight of the stroke in the *l* or *i.* Obviously we can't have a different underscore for each size of a kicker; there must be a single rule that is adequate with all kickers. Too often the underscore is not heavy enough and is, therefore, nonfunctional. The rule should have a printing surface at least 3 points thick. A kicker that is not underscored may be so light that it just evaporates.

The underscore may be a simple straight rule. But Ben Day, coin-edge, and wave rules work well if they harmonize with the typeface and give adequate weight. The rule used for the sideless box can be used as the underscore, too. The only function of the underscore is to add typographic weight to the kicker; if it doesn't add enough weight, it should be eliminated as nonfunctional.

The main head under a kicker should be indented, generously and consistently. I prefer to indent 1 pica per column. If the back shop prefers, this could be 1 en per column. When the indent is based on the column width, it is easy for the typesetter to remember, and we have consistency with minimum fuss.

The short kicker creates an effective area of white at its right; the indent of the main head provides a balancing area of white at the left of the head. These two masses of white act as spotlights, focusing the reader's attention on the kicker.

The indenting of the main head is the major assurance that the kicker will be read. If the main head is set on the same vertical axis as the kicker, there is a danger that the reading eye will jump right over the kicker and into the main head.

The centered kicker is utterly malfunctional. It is inevitable that the eye, entering that area of the page at its top left, will be drawn to the nearer, heavier optical magnet, the main head, rather than the lighter and distant centered kicker. If the eye is led immediately to the main head and refuses to go into reverse gear to read the kicker, the smaller head is nonfunctional. The time and effort of writing and setting it are wasted. But the reading eye may be distracted enough to backtrack and read the misplaced kicker. Then what happens? It proceeds normally, downward, and finds itself right in the headline it has already read. In this case the eye often moves off to the right, seeking greener, still unexplored fields. Now the centered kicker is obviously malfunctional.

Dual kickers, one flush left and the other flush right, are nonfunctional. The left one will function as a single kicker; if the main head is indented, the kicker is functional. But the right-hand kicker can never be functional; it's too far off the normal reading path.

The *hammer head* is a new style that is also called the *reverse kicker.* It gets that name because the ratio of kicker to main-head size is reversed. It's also called a *barker,* after the carnival variety of salesman. The hammer packs the same wallop as does its namesake.

The hammer is twice the point size of the main head. It is flush left and underscored, not because the weight is required but to be consistent with the regular kicker. The hammer should be no wider than half the width of the headline area. This builds in a large, effective rectangle of white space at the right. To balance that, the main head is indented, not 1 pica, but 2 picas per column. If it is easier for the shop, this increment may be 1 em instead of 2 picas.

The narrowest hammer, or kicker, is a 2-columner; in one column the areas of white are far too small to do their job. The widest possible hammer is 6 columns, thus allowing a leg of type at each side. But a 4-column hammer is the widest effective one.

If the newspaper uses column rules and its style calls for the slight indenting of headlines at the left, the kicker and hammer may be indented that amount. As these heads are always multicolumners, the

Fig. 14. Hammer heads, above. SAVED, in caps, from *Charlestown* (W. Va.) *Gazette-Mail*; WAH!, in accent face, *Chicago Daily News*; ASSASSINATION and DEFICIT from *Ottawa* (Ont.) *Citizen*. In latter example, underscore broken to allow descender to protrude is nonfunctional.

Below, all from *Chicago Daily News*, a, wicket head, and b, tripod heads.

Literary Diary **Russia's rugged east**

(a)

Not in Plot *Actress Sharon Tate Nearly Drowns During Filming*

(b)

Guts -- Battered Johnson's courage typical

normal indent is 1 pica. The indent of main heads under the kicker, or hammer, is in addition to that pica. So, in three columns the kicker would be indented 1 pica and the main head 4 picas—that is, 1 pica per column plus the regular pica indent. A 3-column hammer would be indented 1 pica, its main head 7 picas.

The major advantage of the kicker and hammer is the white space that these heads build into a page. This fresh air is most effective when it is well defined by surrounding masses of body type. It is least effective when the space dissolves into that of the margins. Ideally, then, we should not use either of these heads at any margin. We heed this admonition literally in the case of the hammer. But, to be practical, we must make exceptions in the case of the kicker and permit its use at side margins. The kicker should not be used at the top of a page, though. Some editors modify even this specification and insist only that a kicker not touch more than one margin, head, or side.

Two other new headline forms, *side heads,* are seen on modern *hed skeds.* The *wicket,* named by the staff of the *Chicago Daily News,* where it is used well, is a short, 2-line head that runs at the left of a single line of larger headletters. In practice, the wicket is usually half the point size of the main head. Ideally, the wicket ought to be smaller, though, so the two wicket lines can fit between the meanline and baseline of the main head. This means a 14-point wicket would ride with a 36-point main head, 18 wickets with 48 mains, or 24 side heads with 60.

The *tripod head* has a single short line of larger type at the left of two lines of smaller type, a simple transposition of a wicket using the same type-size combination.

The left element of both the wicket and the tripod should be short; in the latter it is often a single word. There should be a minimum of space between the side head and the main one; 1 pica is enough separation, 2 picas should be the maximum.

It is essential that the space that separates the elements of side and heads does not align—or even come close to aligning—with a column rule or alley. If it does align—especially with an alley—the effect will be that of two heads, side by side. Especially with the wicket, the eye may be drawn to the main head, then attempt to start reading body type in the first leg under the main head instead of that under the wicket.

I confess personal coolness to the wicket and less than incendiary enthusiasm for the tripod. I would prefer to use either side head only on feature pages.

The side heads and the kickers, regular and reverse, are actually decks and do give the headwriter a chance to inject a second thought. But the main head should be self-contained. It is easy for the reader to overlook the kicker or wicket and even the tripod, and, should that happen, he should be able to get the accurate message from the main head alone. Too, if the kicker must be removed for reasons of space or position or if it is inadvertently omitted, the main head must stand alone. A Midwest editor recently used a qualifying kicker: MAYOR CHARGES. The main head was COUNCILMAN IS LYING. Yes, the kicker turned up missing in print, and the editor became the unwilling participant in a libel suit. Fortunately, the finding in the famous Sullivan case persuaded the plaintiff to drop the suit. But there is one editor who will never write any head that is dependent for sense on another deck.

Linked Headlines

Linked heads, also called *in-reading heads,* are an interesting tool that deserves more attention and experimentation. These are headlines that can be read separately but also make up a series of related reports.

A pioneer of the technique was the *Chronicle-Telegram* of Elyria, Ohio, and one of its earliest uses is still a textbook example. On the eve of the scheduled summit conference at Geneva in 1960, Soviet Premier Nikita Khrushchev refused to attend, ostensibly because an American U-2 spy plane had been shot down over the Soviet Union. World Communism mounted an attack of unusual virulence against the United States and against President Dwight D. Eisenhower personally, especially in Japan, which he was planning to visit a month later.

The *Chronicle-Telegram*'s 8-column banner was:

THOUSANDS RIOT IN JAPAN

Reading out in columns 6 to 8 was a 60-point Spartan Bold head:

IKE'S STAND . . .

Immediately under this story, which was squared off, was another head in the same 3-column, 60-point Spartan:

ENRAGES JAPAN . . .

Then, still in the same three columns and same face:

ANGERS REDS . . .

and, finally,

IMPERILS TRIP

The first head on Ike's stand might have been momentarily puzzling, but under the circumstances of saturation coverage by all media, the reader probably recognized the Washington datelined story quite easily.

The JAPAN head was on a Tokyo story about vicious protest riots, the REDS from United Nations, and the last one from Washington again.

The *ellipsis,* a trio of periods, is the typographic device for linking separate typographic elements. In body type, the second and succeeding elements also begin with the ellipsis; it might be useful to handle headlines the same way:

IKE'S STAND . . .

. . . ENRAGES JAPAN . . .

The linking technique effectively tied together various facets of essentially a single story even though they were filed at several distant points. Had they been carried with conventional heads, these stories might not have been as obviously related. Had the desk tried to tie together these several developments in a single wrap-up story, the reader might have been swamped with more details than he could comfortably handle.

Another set of in-reading heads were of varying widths and sizes:

BLIZZARD CRIPPLES MIDWEST

MIDLAND DIGS OUT . . .

BUT B'VILLE CUT OFF . . .

DEATH TOLL MOUNTS . . .

AS ALASKA BASKS AT 70

Linked heads may also be used to handle the smaller stories that result when a long and complicated report is broken down into self-contained components. A city council report, for instance, that would make such a mass of body type that a jump would be inevitable can be displayed in entirety on page one if it is divided into several smaller stories.

As the world becomes more and more interdependent, reports from widely separated sources become involved in common consequences, and what may seem at first to be very diverse events are included in a topic of single, major interest. Linked heads make it easier for the reader to recognize such intricate involvements while he can assimilate each story separately.

Nonfunctional Headlines

A major function of the headline is to lure the reader into the story. It is, in an inelegant but accurate analogy, the bait, while the body type is

Fig. 15. In-reading headlines in *Newsday*, left, and *Elyria* (Ohio) *Chronicle-Telegram.*

the trap. If we keep this comparison in mind, some common mistakes become apparent.

One is the use of a *skyline banner* alone. The skyline is a head at the very top of page one, above the flag. It is an effective makeup device if the story runs with it. But when the banner runs alone, it creates an illogical situation. After the reader has read the skyline and been persuaded that he should read the body type, what happens? He must search elsewhere to find the story! This is analogous to putting a piece of cheese in one corner of a room and hiding the mousetrap some distance away. We still need bait right in the trap, and so the first piece of cheese is just about as nonfunctional as it could possibly be.

Although skylines are dearly beloved by circulation departments, there is no convincing evidence that this device sells more papers at a newsstand or builds readership. These imagined assets are even more suspect when the skyline's story runs on an inside page or even in another section.

If a skyline must be used, the position of the story must be given clearly, in content and in form. In at least 14-point type, the page and column must be told for the story. Then the head on the story itself must be a paraphrase of the banner. The key word or phrase should be repeated.

Skylines are frequently used on sports pages that front a section. In a typical example the banner says: 'JACKS STAGGER TO 1-POINT WIN. Some 5 inches lower, in column 3, is the story with the head:

> COLSON DUMPS
> 34 COUNTERS
> IN DEFEAT

For either of these heads to serve a useful purpose, the reader would have to know that 'Jacks is short for Lumberjacks, which is the nickname for a local high school, and that they were opposing a team on which Colson plays. For sure, some ardent fans are so familiar with these facts that there is a logical connection between the skyline and head on the story. But to the typical casual reader, there is no clue in the story head that it is really a readout from the banner.

The story head should have been something like:

> LUMBERJACKS   LUMBERJACKS
> ALMOST NIPPED or GIVEN SCARE
> BY EASTERN   BY COLSON

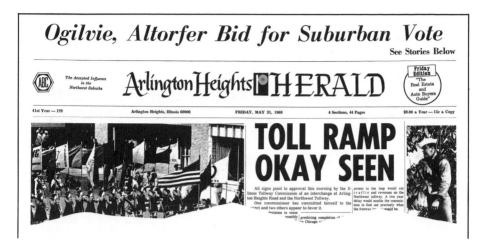

Fig. 16. Skyline banners. *Arlington Heights* (Ill.) *Herald*, story ran below fold of page one.

The keyword is "Lumberjacks," and it should be in the first line so that its connection with the skyline is at once obvious and immediate.

Notice that both suggested story heads are in the passive voice. This is contrary to the established dictum that only active verbs may be used in headlines. Granted, we want action in a head, but often a passive verb can be as colorful as an active one. The sense and flavor of a head should be the yardstick of whether it's a good one, not an arbitrary and artificial criterion of grammatical classification.

Misuse of typographic bait for the reader is also illustrated by the *layercake head.* This is a combination of two or more full-page banners, one on top of the other. The top head—or heads—on the cake are separated from their stories just as the skyline is. We must, again, attract the reader twice, for after he has read the layercake, he is still roaming around the page and must be lured again by the head right on the story.

Another malfunctional headline form is the *shotgun.* This gets its name from the fact that two stories read out of one head as two barrels project from the same gunstock. The shotgun is malfunctional because once the reader has been attracted by the head, he must decide which of the two stories to read first. The reader doesn't want to make even such a trifling choice. He wants to be told, clearly and unmistakably, where he is to go at any moment. He can't read two stories at once; the choice of which to read first has to be made by someone. That someone had better be the editor. If the editor is afraid to commit himself on the relative

The Miami Herald

Sunday

September 22, 1968

Sports

Sports on TV Today

PRO FOOTBALL

1:30 a.m. — Buffalo Bills at Cincinnati Bengals, Channels 5 & 7.
2:30 a.m. — Washington Redskins at New Orleans Saints, Channel 4.
4:00 a.m. — New York Jets vs. Boston Patriots at Birmingham, Channels 5 & 7.

Section

D

Florida Struggles Past AF, 23-20; Seminoles Hold Off Maryland, 24-14

Pajcic,
Sellers
Click

By FRED SEELY
Herald Sports Writer

COLLEGE PARK, Md. — Florida State gave Maryland a statistical beating here Saturday, but the Terrapins forced their visitors desperation tactics Seminoles esca 14 victory
It

Smith
Scores
Twice

By RAY CRAWFORD
Herald Sports Writer

TAMPA — Florida Gators, hoping to play under wraps, had to pull out all the stops Saturday to topple a spunky, under-rated Air Force team, 23-20.
Twice the Gators had to

Fig. 17. Layercake heads. In *Miami* (Fla.) *Herald,* top head's story reads in col. 8.

importance of associated stories, how can he expect the reader to assume the job?

Most frequently, stories under a shotgun have their own readout heads. This doesn't mitigate the ill effect of the head form.

The only time a shotgun should even be considered is when an editor makes a grandstand play of impartiality. During an election campaign, for instance, he may use a shotgun head and read out a story on each party, candidate, or point of view.

Other nonfunctional headline forms are used infrequently nowadays, although an occasional one still sneaks in to mar a page. In this category are:

1. The *stepped head,* a form in which the first line is flush left, the third is flush right, and the middle one centered.
2. The *inverted pyramid,* a head of centered lines, each shorter than the one above it.
3. *Hanging indent,* in which the first line is full and the second and succeeding lines are indented a specific and identical space at the left. The right margin may be flush or ragged.
4. The *chopped head,* a 2- or 3-line head in which the column widths vary from line to line. The top line might be five columns wide and the second line three. If a picture runs in the 2-column gap in the head, the effect is not quite as unpleasant as when body type runs up to the head in each column. But in neither instance is the chopped head attractive to American eyes. It is widely used in England, but we might speculate whether readers there really like it or accept it because they have been given no other choice.

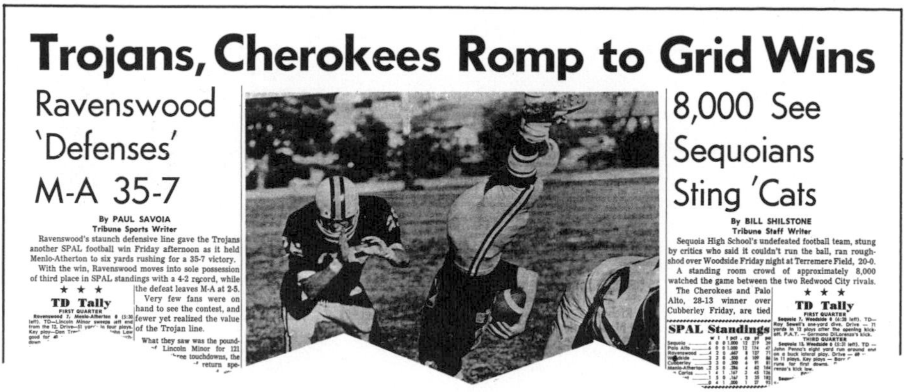

Trojans, Cherokees Romp to Grid Wins

Ravenswood 'Defenses' M-A 35-7

By PAUL SAVOIA
Tribune Sports Writer

Ravenswood's staunch defensive line gave the Trojans another SPAL football win Friday afternoon as it held Menlo-Atherton to six yards rushing for a 35-7 victory.

With the win, Ravenswood moves into sole possession of third place in SPAL standings with a 4-2 record, while the defeat leaves M-A at 2-5.

Very few fans were on hand to see the contest, and fewer yet realized the value of the Trojan line.

What they saw was the pound- ... Lincoln Minor for 121 ... touchdowns, the ... return spe-

★ ★ ★

TD Tally

FIRST QUARTER

Ravenswood 7, Menlo-Atherton 0 (5:30 left). TD—Lincoln Minor sweeps left end from the 12. Drive—51 yar... in four plays. Key play—Don Tre... good for ...

8,000 See Sequoians Sting 'Cats

By BILL SHILSTONE
Tribune Staff Writer

Sequoia High School's undefeated football team, stung by critics who said it couldn't run the ball, ran roughshod over Woodside Friday night at Terremere Field, 20-0.

A standing room crowd of approximately 8,000 watched the game between the two Redwood City rivals.

The Cherokees and Palo Alto, 28-13 winner over Cubberley Friday, are tied

SPAL Standings

★ ★ ★

TD Tally

FIRST QUARTER

Sequoia 7, Woodside 0 (6:28 left). TD—Roy Sewell's one-yard dive. Drive — 71 yards in 12 plays after the opening kickoff. P.A.T. — Germano DiLorenzo's kick.

THIRD QUARTER

Sequoia 13, Woodside 0 (5:31 left). TD — John Penna's eight yard run around end on a buck lateral play. Drive — ... in 11 plays. Key plays — ... runs for first downs. ...renzo's kick low.

Fig. 18. Shotgun heads. In *Redwood City* (Calif.) *Tribune,* TROJANS shotgun is used to give identical treatment to high school rivals.

5. *Hooded heads,* of which there are several variations.
   a. The *boxed head* is enclosed with a 4-sided box. This is philosophically unsound. It is not logical to place any barrier, no matter how slight, between the headline and the body type.
   b. The *hood* retains the top and sides of the box but removes the bottom rule, the barrier between bait and trap. This is an improvement over the full-box head, but the need for vertical rules has the same disadvantage as in making any 4-sided box.
   c. The *break-box head* is hooded with a 3- or 4-sided box, the top of the box broken so a smaller head may be set, centered, into the frame.
   d. A *breakline head* uses only the top line of the break-box.
6. *Flush-right heads.* With the ringing endorsement given to flush-left heads, it seems redundant to exhort against flush-rights. But editors—especially those of women's and feature pages—periodically succumb to the temptation to use them. It doesn't matter why a headline has a ragged left margin; that irregularity is irritating to the eye and should be eliminated.

British newspapers generally use these freak heads and this anarchic layout much more freely than their American counterparts. When British newsmen move to North America, as they have been doing rather frequently, they bring such mannerisms with them and inject them into the pages of their newspapers. The results are sometimes pleasant but usually dilute typographic harmony and consistency.

I don't want to suggest that the British are the only ones who endanger the purity of headline style. All deskmen are given to inspiration and like to invent new head forms. Sometimes results are happy, but usually not.

Unorthodox heads may be used on rare occasions when an unusual

Fig. 19. Malfunctional placement of headline elements. Eye reads from 1 to 2 and swings back to left. Attracted by second deck, it reads from 3 to 4. From 4 it is willing to return to 5 and begin reading toward 7. The farther it proceeds down this path, the more irritating it is to reverse up to 6.

story deserves unusual headline treatment. Effects, such as visual puns, can give pleasure to the reader and to the editor as well. When an oft-married actress finally became the legal spouse of an actor with whom she had cavorted on several continents, under a blaze of publicity pictures and minute-by-minute gossip-column coverage, a disenchanted editor expressed his surfeit by setting the story in agate and the headline in 8-point.

The prank of a journalism-fraternity initiation occasioned this head:

THXY STOLX ALL THX X'S
IN THX PRINTXR'S MACHINX

On another head the position of the bottom line pictured some Far Eastern advice to the White House:

YOGI ADVISES PRESIDENT:
‚STAND ON HEAD FOR PEACE'

We're all familiar with the phonetic heads used on spelling-bee stories or with the snow-capped type used on a blizzard or cold-wave story.

These typographic tricks are fun, but they should be used sparingly. The reader tires quickly of parlor tricks. Specific permission of a top editor should be required to break the integrity of headline style.

Jump Headlines

The practice of jumping stories from one page to another is declining —and for good reason, as we shall explore in Chapter 10. Possibly because of that decline, few editors pay much heed to *jump heads,* those on the type that has been continued to the later page. But there are still enough occasions when such continuation is absolutely necessary; when that does happen, there should be consistent and functional handling of the jump head.

Long before he actually reads the jump head, the reader should recognize it as such. When he has turned to the proper page, jump heads should be so distinctive that he can spot them instantly. Only then need he read headline copy to determine which is the particular story he is seeking. We need an obvious but appropriate visual signal to catch the searching eye.

The best device, in my opinion, is a star of the same point size as the head. The star starts the first line with a 6-point space between it and the words. Succeeding lines align under the first letter of the first line. The star may be solid or outline; in either form it serves its function as a signal the reader quickly spots.

A useful device is to run the star or a large bullet at the beginning of the *continuation line,* the line of body type that says "Continued from page one." This element runs between the headline and the story itself.

Another device is to use the key word of the page-one head as a small hammer or kicker on the jump head.

Some papers use a Ben Day panel with some kind of copy like CONTINUED FROM PAGE 1 above or below the jump head.

Whatever the device, it ought to be consistent with the typography of the newspaper. It should be easily spotted without being unpleasantly conspicuous. It should be easy to handle on the stone.

The jump head should be a news headline, not a label.

The headline on the jumped portion of a story should be the same size as it would be if it were a self-contained story. If a 10-inch story normally takes a 3-line 30-point, then 10 inches of jumped type requires the same headline weight. Some newspapers will run more than a galley of jumped copy under a single word in 24-point type. This may be adequate if that story is an absolute thriller, but if it's anything less than that, it needs a big head. When a properly heavy head is used, it permits a good page pattern. It may also draw readers who missed the start of the story on the front page. In many instances the reader will first enter a story on

THE TIMES-UNION

Greater
Rochester
Edition

56 Pages   Rochester, N.Y., Tuesday Evening, October 22, 1968   10 Cents

Spacemen Land Safe but ∩dsᴉpǝ ᑺoᙏu

Wally, Donn and Walt

Australian is a proud papa-papa-papa-papa-papa

BRISBANE, Australia (UPI)—Mr. and Mrs. Roger H. Braham, a country lawyer and his pretty 36-year-old wife uncorked a bottle of champagne last night and led the nation in ‑‑d New Year's Eve toast

weeks ago and plunged Australians into grief and mourning.

DOCTORS said one of the babies — three girls and two boys — was causing "a little ‑he others

Mrs. Braham — Mary Patricia—recovered so quickly from the 75-minute delivery period she was able to sit in a wheelchair and move to the nursery window to see the babies.

"Well, thank "

wife's when he was told his family had just doubled. He has a law practice in the small town of Tenterfield.

The Brahams have four other children ranging in age from 1-year-old twins to a 7-‑‑‑ ‑‑d daughter. A daugh-‑ The twins

examined Mrs. Braham in early October.

The odds for the birth of quints are about 42 million to one.

The oldest surviving set of two boys and three girls — now 24 years ‑‑ the Di-

---

⟵–·ⵀⵜⴰⵣ ∩ℓ˧6 oⱺⁱⱺ Laos Thailand

by
BRIAN COZIER
from the
Los Angeles Times

LONDON — From all over Southeast Asia, the past few weeks have brought news of intensified "revolutionary war" or even of entirely fresh outbreaks. Understandably, this news has gone largely unnoticed at a time when the eyes of the world are on Vietnam. Taken together, however, these events add up to a considerable potential threat, and force a reassessment of the famous "Domino Theory."

Very probably, ‑‑lutionary war" wasn't exactly wh ‑ Eisenhow ‑r had in mind w

Theory. It has always been temptingly easy to deride it.

The situation is dangerous and disquieting, though not uniformly gloomy: Some dominoes are more likely to topple than others.

Laos, Cambodia and Thailand can be considered together, for in all three the common factor is Vietnamese Communist irredentism.

HO CHI MINH'S ambition to reunite ‑what ‑‑‑‑‑ he ‑he "French Indochina em-

Domino Theory

OPINION

18th century, put a Khmer prince on the Cambodian throne and accepted tribute from Laos.

What is less well known is that Ho has consistently supported what used to be called the pan-Lao movement, to b ‑ the Lao-speaking inhabitants of ‑os and Northeast Thailand to-‑imately under North Vietnam-‑ ‑ ‑ur-

Hoa Binh, North Vietnam.

Of the three countries threatened by North Vietnam, by far the most vulnerable is Laos.

THE HISTORY of this buffer state is one of warring principalities ‑ ‑e Viet-namese Communist army ‑‑‑‑‑up-pet government in the n ‑

North Vietnamese troops were in his country. A more likely estimate today would be 40,000.

Attempts have been made to label the present fighting in Laos as a "war of the supply routes" since the main North Vietnamese military supplies to South Vietnam come through Laos along the "Ho Chi Minh Trail."

True enough, the capture of Nam Bac in northern Laos, by air-supported North-Vietnamese ‑‑‑‑‑ ‑‑‑ the current

SIMILARLY, the current fighting in Cambodia can be interpreted as an attempt to safeguard the sanctuary enjoyed on Cambodian soil by Viet Cong guerrillas from South Vietnam. But the long history of Vietnamese Communist subversion in Cambodia suggests there' more to it than that.

On Jan 27, Prince Sihanouk of Cardia blamed Vietnamese, Thai and ‑ nese Com ‑nists for a new revo‑ Battan ‑ ‑rovince, adjoining la ‑ ‑ ‑ he declared th ‑‑‑‑‑ th ‑

City's Fire Kills 5 Children
First In S. Suburban Home
Snow
May
Get
This
Deep

KENNEDY AND NIXON LOVE THOSE WISCONSIN BERRIES

Three Sox Place 1–2–3 For Most Valuable

Color Picture Of Nelson Fox On Back Page; Stories On Back Page And Page 62

Fig. 20. Trick heads. SPACEMEN in *Rochester* (N.Y.) *Times-Union* is literal presentation; stuttering head from *Elyria* (Ohio) *Chronicle-Telegram* announces birth of quadruplets; *St. Petersburg* (Fla.) *Times* creates visual pun on "domino theory." *Chicago* (Ill.) *Sun-Times* head shows actual depth of expected snow.

an inside page and then go back to page one to read the beginning.

It is essential that the jump head repeat the idea and the key words of the front-page head. A fairly common mistake is to use the jumped portion of the story as the basis for the jump head. This often is most confusing. Suppose the story is about tax legislation. The head on page one says:

SENATE OKs

SALES TAX

The portion of the story that starts the jumped portion tells about a futile delaying action by a senator. So the jump head says:

SMITH LOSES

BY 13 VOTES

The lack of obvious connection between the two heads and two portions of the story means that the reader has no easy clue to guide him to the jump he seeks. At least the key words of the main head should be repeated in the jump. Some newspapers duplicate the front-page head in copy, changing only the point size of the type.

Fig. 21. Jump heads: a, star and key words run under regular head; b, large star runs with regular head; c, key word and continuation line run under head; d, continuation line in large size; e, Ben Day panel; f, continuation line under head is flagged by large bullet.

Headline Schedule

Every newspaper should have a formal, codified *headline schedule*. This is a printed sample of every headline style used by the paper. Every head used should be on this hed sked; any head not on the schedule should be banned. There are two considerations for a schedule, the letters and the form in which they are used.

A good headletter must be legible; it should be attractive; it must have sufficient color to weave a good page pattern; it must express the personality of the newspaper; it must have an adequate unit count; it must be available in keyboarding. Physically, it must be sturdy enough to withstand wear and stereotyping pressure.

The Sans Serifs have the highest legibility of all type races, and so logically they are good choices. Some good Sans faces are the Spartans, available in seven weights; Tempo; Vogue; and Futura. In the Gothics, the Metros and Erbars are fine headletters.

While Romans have much greater readability than the Sans, they also

Fig. 22. Experimental pages give opportunity to compare proposed head schedules in Bodoni Bold and Memphis. Page pattern remains constant, only headletters are variables. Nameplate is simulated.

have legibility high enough so that the proper face makes an excellent headletter. The favorite Roman among American newspapers is Bodoni. Century Bold dresses a few papers, as does Cheltenham. Chelt, though, is a victim of its own popularity. It was the first face available both in Linotype and Ludlow matrices and in foundry type; no other face in history was as widely used. Thus Cheltenham is intimately identified with the early 1900's, and today it has a flavor so dated that it is difficult to use it for a contemporary effect.

Caledonia Bold is a fine headletter. But its handicap is a lack of sizes beyond 36-point. The *Toronto Star* is dressed in Caledonia, but for larger sizes it uses Ludlow matrices that were engraved individually rather than punched in mass production. Just as soon as larger sizes are commercially available, we can expect a boom in the use of Caledonia for heads.

Square Serifs have not been very popular as headletters for North American newspapers although they make good heads. Memphis, Stymie, Cairo, and Karnak are the best cuttings. Several excellent papers are dressed in Squares, and any editor who overlooks this race is missing a potentially good bet.

For practical purposes, though, there are only two headletters today, the Sans Serifs and Bodoni. These represent the great majority of all head dresses. The Squares don't excite many publishers; Century and Chelt are not as crisp as most editors would prefer; Caledonia is limited in range. What is needed is a face that gives the editor an altogether new choice. My nomination is Optima or a version thereof.

Optima is technically a Gothic. Actually, it is a Roman with the serifs removed. The swelling and thinning of curved strokes contribute pleasant color, and the sharp, unserifed main strokes give the crispness of the Sans. Optima is available only in body sizes and in European matrices. We might all hope that demand in this hemisphere will be great enough to warrant the substantial investment required to make a series in matrix form available domestically.

Lydian Bold is sometimes suggested as a headletter. It shares many characteristics with Optima. Lydian is a calligraphic Gothic; the effect of the chisel-shaped pen which drew the original letterform is very apparent. While this face is attractive for many uses, it has too strong a flavor for use as a headletter.

The most efficient head schedule is made up of one family of type. This assures fastest reading speed and taking the reader into body type as quickly as possible. Even the tiny changes between letterforms of differ-

The Press

Winner of the 1968 Pulitzer Prize for Meritorious Public Service

10 Cents Per Copy | Riverside, California, Tuesday Afternoon, October 29, 1968 | Five Sections—64 Pages

SUPPLY LINES BOMBED—Newsmap shows where U.S. B52s struck North Vietnam in heavy raids, smashing southern panhandle lines, military spokesmen said today. Smaller jets joined the attacks, flying 139 missions, the American sources said. (UPI Telephoto)

Sen. McCarthy gives vote to HHH, but little praise

Humphrey gratified by endorsement

By MERRIMAN SMITH

PITTSBURGH (UPI) — Vice President Hubert H. Humphrey today reacted with enthusiastic gratitude to the endorsement of his presidential candidacy by one of his former Democratic adversaries, Sen. Eugene McCarthy, and by Dr. Ralph D. Abernathy, who succeeded the late Dr. Martin Luther King Jr. as head of the Southern Christian Leadership Conference.

The Democratic presidential candidate heard of McCarthy's endorsement as he taped a television question and answer program here at the start of another intensive day of campaigning in an effort to win the heavily industrialized state of Pennsylvania.

HUMPHREY SAID it was "very gratifying" to hear McCarthy had announced his own support and had called upon his supporters to vote for Humphrey Nov. 5.

McCarthy, in his announcement made in Washington, said — so that party leaders understood he was not attempting to get back in their good graces — he would not run for re-election to the Senate in 1970 nor would he seek the Democratic presidential nomination in 1972.

"I am a very happy man," Humphrey said after learning of the McCarthy announcement.

At the same time Humphrey sent a telegram to Abernathy in Baltimore, Md., thanking him for his endorsement.

"I am deeply grateful to you for it," Humphrey said in his message to the Negro leader.

HE ALSO PRAISED the cross-country "get out the vote" campaign among Negro voters being led by Abernathy and his organization.

In the case of McCarthy, the vice president said he regretted the Minnesota senator's decision not to seek re-election but he felt there was a rewarding future ahead of McCarthy. Asked if he had any idea why McCarthy waited so long to state his position, Humphrey said, "Well, it takes time for wounds to heal."

He said he felt McCarthy came out for him as "the better alternative" in his current presidential race.

SILENCE BROKEN—Sen. Eugene J. McCarthy told newsmen today he will vote for Hubert Humphrey election day. He also announced he will not seek re-election as a Democrat in 1970. (UPI Telephoto)

Minnesotan will drop Demo races

WASHINGTON (UPI) — Eugene J. McCarthy today gave a lukewarm endorsement to Hubert H. Humphrey for president just one week before the election but said the Democratic nominee's position on Vietnam, military policy and draft reform "falls far short of what I think it should be."

To emhasize his stand, the Minnesota senator announced he would not stand for re-election to the Senate "from my party" in 1970 and would not seek the Democratic presidential nomination in 1972.

HOWEVER, McCARTHY refused to rule out the possibility of his creating a splinter party from the remnants of his unsuccessful campaign for the Democratic nomination as a "peace candidate this year.

In an exchange with newsmen after aides handed out his statement endorsing Humphrey, McCarthy was asked whether he was bowing out of all future Senate and presidential races. "It's still unclear," he replied.

Pressed further as to whether he was planning to form a new party, McCarthy only referred newsmen to his one-page statement and added: "It'll take a book to explain the situation."

The statement said he intended to vote for Humphrey, who defeated him for the Democratic presidential nomination, and recommended that his followers do the same.

McCarthy, in a brief interview with UPI, said he regarded his statement as a "positive" endorsement of the vice president. The statement, however, was less than enthusiastic.

"MANY, IF not most, of my supporters have, I believe, already made this decision," McCarthy said.

But lest anyone think he was giving Humphrey his endorsement as a means of getting back "in the good graces" of Democratic Party leaders, McCarthy delcared:

"I announce at this time that I will not be a candidate of my party for re-election to the Senate from the state of Minnesota in 1970.

"Nor will I seek the presidential nomination of the Democratic Party in 1972."

He issued the statement from his Capitol office, saying most Americans were "quite capable of making their own decision abcut the presidency."

After refusing, since he lost the Democratic nomination to Humphrey in Chicago in August, to endorse Humphrey or to tell his supporters what he would do on election day, McCarthy said in the statement just one week before the voting:

"TO THOSE . . .who may be waiting for my decision, I wish to announce that on Nov. 5 I intend to vote for Vice President Hubert Humphrey and recommend that those who have waited for this statement of my position do the same."

Planes and ships pound enemy areas

SAIGON (AP) — American warplanes and warships, including B52 bombers and the battleship New Jersey, attacked North Vietnam's southern panhandle yesterday with the heaviest blows in nearly a month, U.S. military spokesmen reported.

There were clearing skies across the panhandle, and Air Force, Navy and Marine jet fighter-bombers flew 139 missions, the largest number since 143 were logged on Oct. 3.

"THE ATTACKING crews continued to concentrate on road and river traffic, interdicting the southward flow of supplies and material," a U.S. communique said.

"Assessment of their bomb damage shows at least 25 trucks and 19 supply boats either destroyed or heavily damaged while numerous fires and secondary explosions were touched off. In addition, storage facilities and bunkers were struck repeatedly and two bridges were dropped."

Meanwhile 30 B52 bombers, carrying a bomb load roughly equivalent to that of 450 fighter-bombers, dropped 900 tons of bombs on enemy gun positions along the southern edge of North Vietnam.

Striking northwest of the allied combat bases at Con Thien and Gio Linh, the B52s touched off 27 second-

(See VIETNAM, Page A-2)

Waiting game played

Hanoi peace strategy depends on elections

By K. C. THALER

LONDON (UPI) — Hanoi's peace strategy is hardening amid indications the Communists want to await the outcome of the U.S. presidential elections before agreeing to negotiations, diplomatic sources said today.

The informants said that in the continuing debate within Hanoi's divided higher policy councils the hardliners have once more won the day, at least for the time being.

THEY REPRESENT the faction which thinks North Vietnam should await the outcome of the presidential election before committing itself to any firm course in negotiations for a Vietnam peace settlement.

The hardliners also want to have the problem of Viet Cong representation at the Paris talks settled in principle before concrete negotiations are set in motion, they said.

The diplomatic informants, whose government is in touch with Hanoi, conceded that they, too are left guessing about Hanoi's ultimate decision.

They feel Hanoi "means business" and wants a settlement, but is maneuvering for the best possible timing and the best possible terms.

In this tactical manipulating Hanoi is clearly anxious to avoid any impression that it is backing down or making concessions to the "imperialist Americans."

The recent publicity accorded to the soundings in Hanoi for an accord on negotiating terms may have played a part in the latest hardening of the regime of President Ho Chi Minh.

It is clear, they said, Hanoi will not make any "formal," let alone public concession in return for the cessation of all American bombing of North Vietnam.

Hanoi may do so quietly, but as soon as any public commitment is demanded or as soon any Communist "gesture" is publicly labelled as a concession, Hanoi is certain to pull back, they said.

This sensitivity is making, and will continue to make, contacts extremely difficult, they added.

The informants expressed the conviction, nevertheless that an American bombing halt would be followed by a go-ahead from Hanoi to negotiate.

BUT THERE was little doubt these negotiations will be "extremely tough" and that they will center largely on terms for American withdrawal.

On present indications Hanoi will delay a decision until after the presidential election for two specific reasons: Hanoi hopes the new administration may, after all, be more "co-operative" and that in any case it will provide continuity for the talks which they feel may not be secured if the talks were to be clinched now, with an outgoing administration.

Inflation jump slows

☆ ☆ ☆ ☆ ☆ ☆

But yearly total will set record

WASHINGTON (AP)—The government reported today the smallest monthly rise in living costs in a year, two-tenths of one per cent. Officials said, however, that 1968 is almost certain to wind up with the largest jump in prices in 17 years.

"It is safe to say the peak of the inflationary surge is past," said Arnold Chase, assistant commissioner of the Bureau of Labor Statistics, in reporting the comparatively small September rise.

The consumer price index for the month rose to 122.2, which means it cost $12.22 in September for typical family goods and services that cost $10 in the 1957-59 period on which the index is based.

The bureau also reported that the earnings of some 45 million workers climbed to an all-time high of $110.49 per week due to a four-cent jump in average hourly earnings. It was the largest gain in two years.

Wallace attacks news media, claims prejudice

BEAUMONT, Tex. (UPI) — George C. Wallace delivered one of his bitterest attacks on the news media last night, charging, "8hey're good at dishing it out but they can't take it."

Wallace, who has contended the news media are in a "conspiracy" to downgrade his candidacy, told a crowd at the South Texas Fairgrounds editors of big newspapers are guilty of "geographical bias" against Southerners.

"It takes 3,200 policemen to get me into the building at Madison Square Garden because of what they said about me, but when I say something about them they whine and say, 'you might get us hurt.'

"They're good at dishing it out but they can't take it. Well, I can take and dish it out."

Wallace planned to speak today at rallies in Enid, Okla., and Detroit.

The third party candidate, in talking at a $25-a-plate dinner attended by more than 700 in Beaumont, suggested that some of the newsmen "ought to take a balloon test before they report," a reference to the test given persons suspected of drunken driving.

He particularly scored the "platinum folks on television that look so suave. They're always talking about you and me."

Wallace predicted the news media would actually help him in the long run by solidifying his support in the southern and border states.

"I want to tell you folks that have written these things about us and said these things about us, you have made it possible for this movement to be solidified all the way from Wilmington, Del., and Baltimore, Md., to Miami, Fla., up to Oklahoma City and St. Louis, Mo.," he said.

Nixon says Democrats nominated wrong man

LAVONIA, Mich. (UPI)—Richard M. Nixon, in an obvious reference to Sen. Eugene McCarthy, said today the Democratic Party rejected a chance to nominate "a man of new leadership" and chose instead "a man of old politics."

Nixon commented on the nomination of Hubert H. Humphrey shortly after McCarthy announced his support of the party's presidential candidate. The two Minnesotans had battled for the Democratic nod.

Addressing a crowd in a banquet hall in this Detroit suburb, Nixon accused Democratic leaders of pulling "every trick you can imagine" in the last week of the campaign. He did not elaborate.

But Nixon said the Democrats were dealing in personalities instead of issues.

"One reason they are not talking about the real issues is that they could have nominated a man of new leadership but didn't," he said.

"They nominated a man of old politics."

The GOP nominee also repeated a charge he leveled for the first time yesterday, using the same language. He described the Democratic Party on the basis of its performance at its stormy Chicago convention as "that disorganized rabble," which he said could not be trusted to govern the nation.

The appraisal came as Nixon set forth another vote-seeking foray, one of several on which he is concentrating in the final weeks of the campaign. He planned a motorcade through Detroit suburbs and then was to fly to Syracuse, N.Y., in the evening.

To anyone who may have forgotten, Nixon yesterday recalled to mind the August scenes of disarray on the convention floor and violence on the streets of Chicago.

Speaking before 6,000 largely unmoved New Yorkers gathered at midday in front of the state Capitol at Albany, N.Y., the GOP presidential candidate pledged a leadership that could unite America.

"We cannot trust the next four years to that squabbling bunch at their convention in Chicago."

Directing a rally of about 15,000 last night in Pittsburgh's Civic Arena, Nixon referred to the Democrats this way:

"You saw it on television from Chicago. I say that disorganized rabble is not to be trusted—with the new leadership they presented to the people of the United States at their convention in Chicago."

'No demonstrations' noted

Czech leaders ignore chants

PRAGUE, Czechoslovakia (Reuters) — Czechoslovak authorities, with one eye on the Russian troops stationed in the country and the other eye half-closed, today continued to play down anti-Russian defiance yesterday by youths celebrating the 50th anniversary of the country.

"No demonstrations took place," police said last night. "Of course there were no arrests."

PRAGUE newspaper editors said their reporters covered the demonstrations but they did not think they would be able to write about them.

Thousands of youths marked the anniversary by booing Soviet troops, blocking traffic and noisily voicing demands for freedom.

(In East Berlin, an East German newspaper said today the demonstrations in Prague yesterday were staged by counter-revolutionary elements.

(The East German news agency ADN said the chanting of the youthful demonstrators in the Czechoslovak capital had found little sympathy among on-lookers).

Party and government leaders urged workers and youths not to demonstrate against the Soviet armies encamped on Czechoslovak soil. Soviet representatives warned that any disturbances would be put down by Soviet tanks.

Nevertheless thousands of youths burst through police cordons, chanting, "Russians go home," and booed Soviet troops armed with machine guns patroling the city center.

YOUNG WORKERS from Prague factories, and students jeered police tryin tgo disperse them and said, "out with the Russians. We want Dubcek (party leader Alexander Dubcek) and Svoboda" (both the name of the president and the Czech word for freedom.)

They sang national hymns, blocked road traffic and clambered up on the railings outside Hradcany, Prague's presidential castle.

As they chanted "give us liberty" outside, Dubcek, was inside giving a speech in which he defended the policies which in August precipitated the Warsaw Pact invasion.

Index to:

The Press

Ann Landers	A-12	Movies	A-18
Astro-Guide	C-14	Editorials	C-20
Business	C- 6	Sports	C- 9
Comics	C- 4	TV Log	A-19
Crossword	A-17	Vitals	C-14
Dear Abby	A- 8	Weather	C-14
Dr. Molner	C- 5	Women	A- 6

Weather: Cloudy, some drizzle. Yesterday's high, 85. Overnight low, 51. (Story on Page C-2.)

Fig. 23. Spartan, classic American Sans Serifs, makes effective headline schedule for *Riverside* (Calif.) *Press*. Key pages are in op format. Note unusual nameplate in large size of Modeled Gothic.

ing races are enough to make the reader hesitate as he shifts from one face to another. This breaks reading rhythm.

Having only one face in the hed sked assures that there will be typographic harmony under all conditions of page makeup. As many advertisements demonstrate, for instance, it is possible to combine type of different races into a single attractive layout. But the designer of such printing has more freedom and more time than is usually available to the newspaper layout man. A Century head might look well on a page of Spartan heads if it were isolated above the flag; in the center of the page, it might not harmonize at all with the Sans Serifs. The editor is too busy putting together a page to devote time to this unnecessary problem, so if he's smart, he'll just eliminate the problem along with the potentially incompatible faces.

An *accent face* is a handy addition to the schedule. It may be a highly weighted form of the headline family. For the Spartans—and any of the other Sans—it would be Spartan Extra Black or Tempo Black. For a Bodoni schedule it would be Poster Bodoni, Ultra Bodoni, Bodoni Black, or Bodoni Modern, all essentially the same face under different names.

If the accent face is from the same family as the regular headletter, the change in weight must be drastic. For a Square-Serifs sked, Memphis Extra Bold, Karnak Black, and Beton Extra Bold are heavy enough to accent the other three weights—Light, Medium, and Bold. But the other Roman headletters—especially Century, Caledonia, and Cheltenham—do not have a weight heavy enough to act as the accent. If these are used, the accent must come from out of the family.

A Square Serif can be used as the accent to a Sans Serifs or Roman schedule. The chosen accent must have adequate weight, and its design must be conspicuously different from that of the regular headletter. A Script or Cursive can be effective with both Sans and Roman schedules. Unfortunately, the good Scripts are all in foundry type. Ludlow's Coronet is pleasant on women's pages, but its Hauser Script and Mandate are too stylistic. Balloon, Cartoon, and Kauffmann Script—in foundry type—are good accents for almost any schedule.

The accent face is used for kickers, catchlines, and heads on boxed stories. If the accent is of exaggerated weight, as Poster Bodoni or Spartan Extra Black, it does not require an underscore when used as a kicker. This effects a substantial saving of time.

The accent may also be used as a 1-line head and is especially effective with 1-up material.

The Type Library

All the type—display and body—in a print shop constitutes its *type library*. The newspaper designer is constantly seeking to achieve the perfect library, either by one glorious purchase or by piecemeal addition to existing fonts on hand.

He is particularly interested in the head library, but it is difficult to reach consensus on the number of fonts necessary for a good headline schedule. Like Oliver Twist, the typographer and the desk will always respond, "More! More!"

The whole library, but especially the head library, should be lean. Only fonts that are definitely needed and widely used should be given house room. Functional duplicates should be weeded out, as should those faces that are incompatible without being genuine accents, those of poor design, and those which have become dated. Naturally, worn type or matrices should be scrapped.

Advertising type libraries are usually encumbered with a clutch of odd faces, accumulated over the years by the unsynchronized whims of many different people. These libraries, too, should be thinned out and organized. But the concern of this book is in the news row, not the ad alley.

If I were given a blank check for a headline schedule, I would choose the following faces:

        18-point, Roman and Italics
        24-point, Roman and Italics
        36-point, Roman and Italics
        48-point Roman
        60-point Italics
        72-point Roman
        18-point Roman and Italic of the accent face
        24-point of the accent face.

On most Linotype matrices 18- and 24-point faces are duplexed in Roman and Italics, so we get two faces from one font of matrices. It may be necessary, however, to use *single-character matrices* for the accent face. In that case we might choose Roman in both sizes or a Roman in the 18 and Italic in the 24, or vice versa.

We customarily use an Italic kicker or hammer above a Roman main head and vice versa. But this alternation of faces is not essential, and a Roman kicker is as effective as an Italic above a Roman main head. So if

THE REPORTER DISPATCH

82nd Year — No. 185 | WHITE PLAINS, N.Y., TUESDAY, OCTOBER 8, 1968 | PRICE TEN CENTS

Defiant M'Coy Bars Teachers

Scope

Westchester

Questions and answers on Medical Center planned in Valhalla.
Page 17

Westchester Board of Supervisors approves $2.4 million toward start of $54 million sewage plant upgrading program.
Page 25

Upcounty water district approved unanimously by supervisors.
Page 25

Supervisors agree to study a request to join forces with opponents of general aviation airport for Somers.
Page 25

Woodlands High School student has head — and feet in the clouds.
Page 25

Elmsford Mayor criticizes unsightly service station.
Page 25

Vietnam

American infantrymen kill 147 enemy soldiers in sweeps along the northwest approaches to the South Vietnamese capital.
Page 1.

Politics

Congressional candidates Reid, Davidoff, Burnet present views in Scarsdale.
Page 12

Nixon says, if elected, he would not step up the bombing of North Vietnam. He says he would seek broader negotiations.
Page 4.

Humphrey proposes that summit conferences be held annually between the United States and the Soviet Union.
Page 4.

A rally in a Baltimore sports arena is tailor-made for Wallace's style.
Page 40

National

Law enforcement officials express concern at the deterioration of police-community relations in the United States.
Page 13.

Gannett newspaper and media executives urged by Gannett Co. president Paul Miller to strive for "personal growth."
Page 17.

International

NATO foreign ministers meeting with Secretary of State Rusk agree that the strategic situation in Europe has changed as a result of the Soviet occupation of Czechoslovakia.
Page 13

Sports

Tigers stay alive in World Series as Mickey Lolich win second game over Cardinals.
Page 30

Herman Barron and Claude Harmon to renew long-standing links rivalry in Kent Classic Sunday at Fenway.
Page 31

Columnists Say:

BUCHWALD —Columnist finds way of curing a nuclear phobia.
Page 27

HARRIS —Nixon's leadership potential is capturing the eyes of voters.
Page 27

Special Pages, Features

Comics Page	33
Editorials, Comment	26, 27
Family Features	10, 11
Obituaries	2
Scarsdale Area News	14
Sports	30-32, 34
Stocks & Business	15, 19, 20
String Around Finger	28
Television	21
Theaters	28
Travel & Resorts	22, 23
Weather	2
Women's News	6, 8, 9

Second Class Postage Paid At White Plains, N.Y.

Today's Chuckle

Uncle Sam reports that there are 75 million people employed. He didn't say how many were working.

Won't Accept Orders

NEW YORK (AP) — A rebellious experimental school district in Brooklyn refused today to assign teaching duties to 80 unwanted teachers, a move that could trigger the third teachers strike in a month against the city's 1.1-million pupil school system.

The Board of Education said the 80 white teachers in the predominantly Negro and Puerto Rican district of Ocean Hill-Brownsville were assigned today to nonteaching duties, apparently carrying out the threat Rhody McCoy, Negro administrator of the community-controlled district, made Monday.

Meanwhile, the first sign of dissension within the leadership of the teachers union came with the disclosure that two union vice presidents who opposed going on strike again have been fired from their $13,500-a-year union jobs. The union gave other reasons for the action, however.

One of those fired, John J. O'Neil, said the union leadership was out to destroy the concept of community control of the school sistem. The union said the dismissals were part of a reorganization.

But as the school day opened, students and teachers at one of Ocean Hill's eight schools streamed into classes without incident. Some of the 80 unwanted teachers were among the 1,000 people who filed in.

Rows of police were stationed around the school and about 80 demonstrators sympathetic to the local board picketed at the nearest intersection.

Ignoring orders of the Board of Education, McCoy said Monday the teachers would be relieved of all classroom duties today and given nonteaching jobs.

Albert Shanker, president of the 55,000-member AFL-CIO United Federation of Teachers, said, "If horrible things happen tomorrow, then I will recommend a membership (strike) vote to be taken immediately."

The teachers have walked out twice since the schools opened for the fall term. The union says the issue is job security and contends the right of due process has been denied to the instructors by the Brooklyn district's local governing board.

PLANNING A TRIP — Apollo 7 Astronauts stand alongside the Apollo Mission Simulator and talk over plans for their 11-day orbital flight scheduled to start from Cape Kennedy, Fla. Friday. The three passed a rigorous four and one-half hour physical and then went into the simulator to practice critical portions of their flight. From left: Commander Walter M. Schirra Jr. Lunar Module Pilot R. Walter Cunningham and Command Module Pilot, Donn F. Eisele. — AP Wirephoto.

Astronauts Sharpen Skills

Apollo 7 All Ready For Orbit

By HOWARD BENEDICT
AP Aerospace Writer

CAPE KENNEDY, Fla. (AP) — The Apollo 7 astronauts sharpened their flying skills in a spacecraft simulator today as rocket, spaceship and all other elements of the mission were pronounced in excellent shape for Friday's launching of this nation's first three-man space crew.

Navy Capt. Walter M. Schirra Jr., the command pilot making his third trip into space, air Force Maj. Donn F. Eisele and civilian Walter Cunningham climbed into the simulator in midmorning and planned to spend several hours there. In the afternoon they were to attend a countdown review.

Meanwhile, the National Aeronautics and Space Administration announced that Wednesday it will roll to another launch pad the Saturn 5 rocket that is to boost the Apollo 8 three-man crew in December.

If Apollo 7 is successful, Apollo 8 may attempt to orbit the moon in a vital rehearsal for a manned lunar landing in 1969.

As preparations proceeded smoothly, Dr. George E. Mueller, the National Aeronautics and Space Administration associate administrator for manned space flight, said: "I feel Apollo 7 is as ready for flight as people can make it."

Schirra says the huge Saturn 1B rocket is almost as stable as the Brooklyn Bridge.

The vehicle "is almost overdesigned in the sense of safety and strength," Schirra said.

"It's very stable. This has eight engines on the bottom of it. One of those engines could fail and we would have no problems achieving orbit. In fact, two can fail as time goes on and we can still get into earth orbit," the 45-year-old astronaut said.

Blastoff of the Saturn 1B rocket is scheduled for 11 a.m. Friday. With its first stage generating 1.6-million pounds of thrust —more than the combined power of 100 jet fighter planes—the rocket will be the most powerful ever used for a U.S. man-in-space flight.

The 224-foot-tall booster is to hurl Apollo 7 into an initial orbit ranging from 142 to 176 miles high. By firing their spacecraft engine, the astronauts will shift this path several times, reaching a maximum altitude of 262 miles.

While circling the globe 164 times, the astronauts are to test all of the craft's complex systems to qualify the Apollo ship for man-to-the-moon missions.

Bulletin

By JESS PEARCE

ARDSLEY—

The Chase Manhattan Bank branch on Saw Mill River Road was held up at 11:25 a.m. today by a lone bandit.

The bandit, described as white, sandy hair and having a mustache, escaped with an undetermined amount of cash. He took the cash from one of the girl tellers on duty.

The robber drove north in a greenish gray Mustang, police said.

Twenty minutes later, Greenburgh police, on the basis of a bank employe's description, picked up a suspect at his home.

He was identified as Halsey Loder Beach, 22, of 43 Canterbury Road, in the Orchard Hill section of Greenburgh.

Police said the bank robber made off with $11,500.

Tax Revenues Show Increase In Westchester

WASHINGTON (GNS) — State and local property tax collections increased 12.4 per cent in the year ended last June to a total exceeding $29.1 billion, the Census Bureau reports.

The bureau provided collection figures for selected counties across the country, including Westchester, where property tax revenues totaled $230.8 million, about 10 per cent more than in 1967.

Rockland, where they totaled $49.5 million, 31.3 per cent more than in 1967.

NEW CUSTOMS JUDGE

NEW YORK (AP) — Samuel M. Rosenstein, a Louisville, Ky. attorney for 37 years, was sworn in Monday as a United States customs judge. He replaces senior Judge Webster Oliver, who resigned in June, 1966.

Cupid Bows To Inflation

(Council Stories On Page 13)

Dan Cupid is beginning to feel the pinch of the high cost of loving.

For those couples who are on their way to say "I do, I do," please be advised that the White Plains Common Council upped the price of marriage licenses last night from three to four dollars.

Mrs. Jessica Friese, city clerk, explains it this way: The price of a marriage license has always been $2 in the city.

In 1962 the State Domestic Relations Law ruled that a certificate of marriage had to be issued to the happy couple after the license was returned to city hall, and the payment for the certificate was fixed at $1, payable at the time the license was issued, for a total of $3.

Now the state has stated that the fee for the certificate can be raised to $2 with approval of the Common Council, or a total of $4 for the works.

And that's what the price is in White Plains for all altar-bound couples, as of Nov. 1.

147 Reds Killed

By GEORGE ESPER

SAIGON (AP) — American ground and air forces battled North Vietnamese troops along the northwesterly approaches to Saigon and killed 147 of them in a two-day fight that raged on and off until just after noon today, the U.S. Command announced.

U.S. casualties were 8 men killed and 13 wounded in the battle with troops from the 101st North Vietnamese Army Regiment, an old adversary that long has operated in the area 28 miles northwest of Saigon. This is about midway between the Cambodian border and Saigon along prime infiltration corridors leading into the capital.

While this was the heaviest fighting reported by both the U.S. and South Vietnamese commands, allied troops on massive ground sweeps up and down the country continued to uncover thousands of tons of enemy munitions, food and medical stockpiles apparently stashed away for future attacks.

The aim of the allied sweeps is to spoil enemy offensives across South Vietnam. U.S. officers claim that the seizure of more than 150 tons of war supplies in recent weeks has hurt the enemy and may delay, if not abort, some of his planned attacks.

A high-ranking U.S. officer, noting the huge finds of enemy booty, said, "One thing that has hurt them beyond physical punishment is the caches that have been discovered."

Blind Dater Ignores Envy

1,800 Girls: 1 Big Headache

By DEBBY RANKIN

CHICAGO (AP) — Many a man would envy James McDonough.

He has been assigned to recruit 1,800 girls, age 18 to 22, as blind dates for Air Force cadets and Naval Academy midshipment at a dance Saturday after the Navy-Air Force football game in Soldier Field.

But for McDonough, city commissioner of streets and sanitation, it's a big headache.

He was given less than two weeks to sign up the lasses.

The last time girls and academy men were matched after the game was in 1965, when 5,000 females applied to be dates for 2,000 males.

"But they had a couple of months to work on it," McDonough said Monday.

The lucky 1,800 girls—who must be high school graduates —will be allocated to the men according to lists provided by the academies.

And, true to military form, they'll be matched with the men by the number.

"They're given the name of their date—he's in Squadron 10, No. 7," said McDonough, who was appointed date-recruiter by Mayor Richard J. Daley.

"But they tell me that only lasts for a while," he added. "Then the guys start grabbing the best looking girl that comes along, and running."

Some 800 girls showed up Monday night for interviews with the screening committee in a normally masculine stronghold, the City Council chambers. Another session was scheduled for Tuesday.

The girls came in all shapes and sizes, said Mrs. Jane Byrne, a committee member well versed in such matters. She is commissioner of weights and measures.

The committee expects no trouble in easing the womanpower shortage and thinks it may have flooded the market with an SOS to 14 local colleges and universities.

About 500 coeds already have filled out the two-page application, which asks, among other things, for three references, "preferably your pastor, your school officials or employer."

Chicago, which will pay a $250,000 bill for transporting and entertaining the sailors and airmen has told the girls they'll have to provide their own rides home.

Institute's Discipline Strict

Self-Help Plan At Drug Center Separates Men From The Boys

(Editor's note: The following is the second article in a series of three on Renaissance, the self-help program in upstate Ellenville for 41 New York area and Westchester drug addicts.)

By SANDRA MILLER

To leave Renaissance Institute some day as successful "graduates"—addicts who are cured of the drugs and of the disease of despair—means many wonderful things to the residents there—things even as seemingly meaningless as, perhaps, a mustache.

That is because in their endless round of therapy sessions and duties at Ellenville the aims of their education are so thorough that not even a small mustache goes unnoticed as irrelevant.

The 25 male addicts now at Renaissance are not permitted to wear mustaches.

The symbols of manhood are denied them as luxuries for those who first prove, by their actions, that they are men and who don't sport a mustache as a crutch to cover inadequate feelings.

And acting like a man, even if they don't feel like one, is just what the addicts at Renaissance are forced to do.

Never Earned A Thing

"A drug addict never earned anything he wanted. He just always avoided it or took it," a Renaissance staff member, himself an ex-addict, told me. For tnis reason everything at Renaissance has to be earned. Each resident, the 25 men and 16 women, are given jobs to do every day such as dishwashing and cooking. And every person must work his way up the ladder to the "better" jobs.

Privileges also are earned by the fulfillment of duties.

Therapy includes "reality attack" sessions, which are held for about 8-10 people each, for two hours, three nights a week.

In them the addicts start talking about a topic, such as how it feels to be a man. The topic is probed and then the different

(Turn To Page 2., Please)

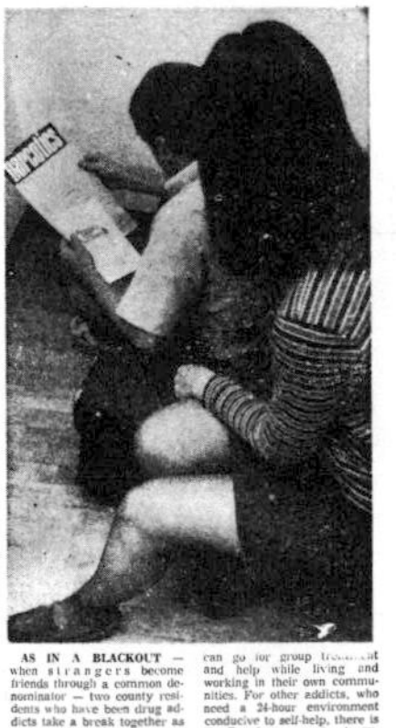

AS IN A BLACKOUT — when strangers become friends through a common denominator — two county residents who have been drug addicts take a break together as "brother" and "sister" during a weekend-long "marathon" therapy session with their Renaissance Institute "family" in Yonkers. They are looking over some literature on narcotics, at the Renaissance storefront center on Main Street, Yonkers, where addicts can go for group treatment and help while living and working in their own communities. For other addicts, who need a 24-hour environment conducive to self-help, there is the Renaissance center in upstate Ellenville. "Marathons" are held in both places: long discussions in a small group of addicts, who, after 24-36 hours together in one room, come to learn all about each other, and themselves. — Staff Photo by Art Sarno.

Fig. 24. Bodoni Bold, most popular of Modern Romans, makes head schedule for *White Plains* (N.Y.) *Reporter Dispatch*. Page in W-format.

we can have only one form of the accent face, it really isn't very important whether it is Roman or Italic. We'd probably choose one of each just for the sake of variety.

The proposed headline library would consist of six fonts of matrices for the keyboarded linecaster and three for the Ludlow. We might have to set the 36-point on the Ludlow, too, although we want to set as many heads as possible on the keyboard for maximum speed. We might set the 72-point in foundry type out of a California case, especially if we use no more than one line of that size per issue.

If this library had to be whittled down, I would give up the accent face. Under extreme pressure I would give up the 36 Italics and change the 48 to Italics.

On the other hand, if fortune were benign and we could expand our first selection, we would probably add the 14-point, duplexed in Roman and Italics. Then we'd add the 48 Italics. Depending on the normal tonal level of our pages, we might want a 96-pointer for banners, or we might find a 60 Roman more useful. We might add the 14 and/or 36 of the accent face. In the 14 we'd get the Roman-Italics duplex; the 36 would be a one-character matrix, and we'd probably choose the Roman form, although there is no compelling reason for the choice.

Don't choose a 30-point, no matter how generous your budget. There isn't enough difference between the 30 and the 24 or 36 to make this a functional face.

There are editors who insist on a Condensed 30 or 36 for their *A heads,* the biggest 1-columners on the schedule. They believe that this size is necessary to hold the top of a column; they also believe that the character count of the normal 30- or 36-point is too short to allow a good content in a headline.

I would never swap the low legibility of the Condensed for the added comfort of the headwriter. Writing headlines is an esoteric skill for which the headwriter is hired. Once he has mastered this art, it takes only a little more effort to write a head in normal letterform than in the Condensed, with its one or two extra unit-count.

In Bodoni, the only practical duplex is Roman and Italics. There are a few weird duplexes, such as Bodoni Bold Roman with Bodoni (Light) Italic or a 24 Condensed with an 18 Regular. But these are useful only in the ad alley, if there.

In Spartan, Metro, Memphis, Cairo, Futura, and Vogue, not only the Perpendicular-Oblique duplex but those giving two weights are avail-

Fig. 25. Century Bold, Transitional Roman face, makes headline schedule for *Champaign-Urbana* (Ill.) *Courier*. Note Condensed headletter in col. 1. Box at top of page in tan.

able. Metroblack is duplexed with Metrolite No. 2; Cairo Bold with Cairo (Regular); Memphis Medium with Memphis Bold; Spartan Book (the second lightest in a series of seven weights) with Spartan Heavy (the fifth heaviest).

Duplexed weights are useful for advertising but should be avoided for headline use. The difference between Roman and Italic lends pleasant but unobtrusive variety to a page; the difference in weight does not. In one way, the difference in weight is too slight to be effective; in another way, it is too great. If the lighter weight is used as the basic face, an occasional heavy head will look like measles. If the heavier face is the basic one, the light headline will almost disappear, and the page will look threadbare in that area.

In any headline schedule, one letterform should be the basic one. Usually this will be the Roman. Then there should be about four Roman heads for every Italic head. This ratio should be for the whole newspaper; it may change on any given page. In the women's or sports sections, Italics might be the basic head, and the ratio four Italics to each Roman.

Sheer chance may change the R-to-I ratio on a page during makeup. In this case the editor should make sure that there is not a 50–50 or even a 60–40 percentage. Either the Roman or the Italic must be conspicuously the dominant style, and the opposite letterform must obviously be an exception.

We must have a ratio of at least three basic heads to one alternate style; we can have as many as six to one. If we go beyond these limits, we're in typographic trouble. A ratio of three Romans to two Italics gives a pedestrian pattern, almost as bad as R–I, R–I, R–I. If there are more than six basic heads, the single alternate will be so outnumbered that it will be lost in the crowd. There ought to be one alternate head on every page, though, no matter how few basic heads there are.

Preparing a Head Schedule

When the typographer prepares a headline schedule, he must recognize the paradox that every newspaper already has one. Often this is a highly informal one, existing only in mental form between the deskman's ears or in disorganized form on tattered sheets of copy paper or dog-eared cardboards. But obviously there must be some established headline style even if it is not neatly committed to writing.

But when a new sked is drawn up—either because added headletters are available or a totally new head dress has been adopted—the typog-

Tampa Gets Post-Season Game

Tampa got into the football bowl business yesterday with the announcement that a post-season special will be held at the new Tampa Stadium Jan. 4.

The game will pit sectional all-star collegians of the 1968 season against each other on a generally North, East and Midwest vs. South and Southwest basis.

It will be an afternoon game and a color television contract has been signed with a private network which guarantees its sale.

Four of the coaches have been picked: Alabama's Paul Bryant and Florida's Ray Graves for the South, Purdue's Jack Mollenkopf and Army's Tom Cahill for the North. More will be named later.

Details are on Page 1-C.

The Weather SHOWERS Data on Page 2-A

THE TAMPA TRIBUNE

Final City Edition

Florida's Prestige Newspaper

74TH YEAR—No. 213 FOUR SECTIONS — 52 PAGES TAMPA, FLORIDA, WEDNESDAY, JULY 31, 1968

PRICE TEN CENTS
7 Days Home Delivery 60 Cents

Fulbright Leads In Arkansas

LITTLE ROCK, Ark. (AP) — Sen. J. W. Fulbright, D-Ark., whose outspoken opposition to the Vietnam war formed the major issue in the campaign, held a growing lead in his bid for renomination in Arkansas' primaries yesterday.

With 534 of 2,476 precincts reported, Fulbright had 24,659 votes, Jim Johnson of Conway 14,148, Bobby K. Hayes of Calico Rock 5,594 and Foster Johnson of Little Rock 1,276.

Fulbright, who came under sharp criticism from his foes for his war position, needed a majority of the vote to avoid a run-off set for Aug. 13, if needed.

Gov. Winthrop Rockefeller, the state's first GOP chief executive since Reconstruction, as expected, scored an easy primary victory over Sidney C. Roberts, an unemployed salesman from Little Rock.

With 224 of 280 precincts reported, Rockefeller had 15,676 votes and Roberts 565.

Rep. Marion Crank of Foreman, completing his 18th year in the Arkansas House, held the lead in the Democratic gubernatorial primary.

With 236 of 2,476 precincts reported, Crank had 5,213 votes, former Atty. Gen. Bruce Bennett 2,813, Mrs. Virginia Johnson 3,542, Frank Whitbeck 2,375, Ted Boswell 2,678 and former state Sen. Clyde Byrd 439.

Bill Alexander, an attorney from Osceola, led in the 1st District congressional race as Democrats nominated a successor to Rep. E. C. "Took" Gathings, who is retiring after 30 years in the U.S. House.

With 36 of 2,476 precincts reported, Alexander had 1,659 votes, Clyde Andrews 619, Henry D. Akins 329, Jack Files 379, Dr. Ralph R. Ratton 329, Lee Ward 341, Eugene T. Ridgeway 84 and Carroll (Bull) Durham 52.

Charles Bernard of Earle, a farmer, was unopposed for the GOP Senate nomination and Guy Newcomb of Osceola, a druggist, had no opposition for the GOP 1st District nomination.

Fulbright's war position became the major target of his three opponents as the senator waged his most extensive campaign since first being elected to the Senate in 1944.

In a statewide television appeal for votes Monday night, Fulbright said his opposition to the war was aimed at "stopping the killing of our men and to bring them home to their families where they belong." He said the war was costing billions of dollars that could be used to solve domestic problems.

Fiscal '68 Finished $25.4 Billion in Red

WASHINGTON (AP)—The nation's largest one-year deficit since the World War II period was reported yesterday by government officials closing the books on fiscal year 1968.

In the year that ended June 30, the deficit was $25.4 billion as expenditures outweighed receipts, $178.9 billion to $153.5 billion.

It was in line with unofficial guesses of $25-plus billion widely circulated in the closing weeks of the fiscal year, but it was a third above the $19.8 billion deficit forecast by the administration in January.

Although only half as large, the fiscal year 1968 deficit is the largest since the record highs of 1943 through 1945—$57.4 billion, $51.4 billion and $53.9 billion.

In a joint statement, Secretary of the Treasury Henry

(Continued on Page 11, Col. 2)

—Nation-Wide Strike Averted—

Steelworkers Given Record Pay Package

New Aircraft Carrier Kennedy Begins Trials

The attack aircraft carrier John F. Kennedy steams under her own power down James River at Newport News, Va., yesterday en route to her first builder's trials. The conventional-powered carrier will undergo 50 hours of trials some 150 miles off the coast. In background is the Newport News Shipbuilding and Dry Dock Co.

—AP

Totals 90 Cents An Hour

PITTSBURGH (UPI) — The United Steelworkers Union (USW) yesterday accepted a whopping $1.5 billion three-year wage package to end the threat of a strike against the basic steel industry.

The new contract for 400,000 union men employed in basic steel was estimated at 90 cents an hour—the largest package ever won by the union since its organization in 1937.

An industry source estimated the higher paychecks and fringe benefits would increase labor costs for the 11 basic steel producers by at least $1.5 billion over the life of the pact—or about a half billion dollars a year.

The added costs for 150,000 other workers in allied steel plants would cost an additional $561 million over the life of the contract, or an average $187.2 million a year. Wage contracts for these workers traditionally follow the pattern set by "big steel."

The top negotiators — USW president I. W. Abel and R. Conrad Cooper of U.S. Steel Corp. — appeared side by side at a news conference and both expressed satisfaction with the contract.

Cooper, however, conceded the pact was "substantially higher" than management had anticipated.

"It's a fine thing that a settlement has been reached in these negotiations without a strike at a critical time in our history," Cooper said. "Neither side took an inflexible position. The agreement was substantially higher than we had hoped for but it did not include all the things the union was seeking."

"I agree with Mr. Cooper that certainly neither of us are totally and completely happy with the result," Abel said.

But the union chief said he was "happy" with the pact.

Approval of the new contract by the union's top two policy-making bodies came only hours before the 11 major steel producers prepared to close their mills across the United States and Canada in preparation for a work stoppage at midnight Wednesday by 400,000 union members.

One producer, Jones & Laughlin Steel Corp., already had begun preliminary shut-

(Continued on Page 12, Col. 1)

USW's Abel (Left), Industry's Cooper

. . . announce agreement has been reached—(AP)

Russian-Czech Talks Extended

PRAGUE (AP) —Russia and its recalcitrant Czechoslovak ally extended their Cierna summit talks last night amid indications of tough bargaining. In the background, Soviet military and political maneuvers intensified pressure on the reformist Prague regime.

Highlighting the military phase was a report that Gen. Samuel Kodaj, a Czechoslovak army officer and member of Parliament who is opposed to liberalization, had a meeting Monday with "the Soviet army staff which is operating on our territory" since the end of Warsaw Pact maneuvers in June.

The trade union newspaper Prace said they discussed the situation at Strecno, a village in northern Slovakia. It is 150 miles northwest of Cierna and about 15 miles from the border of Poland, where informed sources have reported sighting substantial Soviet combat and supply equipment on the move since Sunday.

Tass said yesterday's session at Cierna, which is hard by the Russian frontier, "passed in an atmosphere of frankness and comradeship." The use by the Soviet news agency of the term "comradeship" seemed to indicate the leaders were holding their talks in a polite and businesslike way, without loss of tempers or harsh language.

"Frankness" is used in Communist terminology to mean differences of opinion. The combination of this with "comradeship" apparently meant that disagreements remained, but there was no im-

(Continued on Page 4, Col. 3)

Rusk Prods North Vietnam For 'Promise of Restraint'

EDITORIAL: "Dusting Off a Musty Question," Page 6-A.

WASHINGTON (AP) — Secretary of State Dean Rusk prodded North Vietnam's leaders yesterday to say — directly or indirectly — what steps Hanoi would take to reduce substantially the scale of fighting if there should be a total halt of U. S. bombing in the north.

Sharply discounting reports that Hanoi already is showing signs of military restraint, Rusk told a news conference that what is important in the situation is "not what happened yesterday but what will happen tomorrow, next week, next month. . ."

Rusk's statement appeared to go somewhat beyond the conditions for a bombing halt enunciated last February by Secretary of Defense Clark M. Clifford. There was no mention by Clifford of Hanoi's intentions for the future. Clifford held that "normal" resupply operations by Hanoi in moving men and supplies into the South would not violate the U. S. conditions for a show of military restraint.

Rusk contended that the United States had made a major move to de-escalate the war on March 31 when President Johnson ordered the bombing halted in almost 80 per cent of the territory of North Vietnam where 90 per cent of the population lives.

"We need to have something better than just a blank wall, something better than just committing ourselves to a course of action on our side, leaving the other side with complete freedom of action to move men and arms from North Vietnam into South Vietnam in whatever way they wish," Rusk said.

A newsman questioned Rusk about the lack of rocket attacks on Saigon in recent weeks. The secretary said that the presence of substantial enemy forces near major population centers and evidence from prisoners, defectors, captured documents and other intelligence "do not suggest there has been an effort to move toward peace by action on the ground."

He said regrouping and resupply may explain the lull in ground fighting. Allied

(Continued on Page 2, Col. 8)

Today's Chuckle

One nice thing about the old-fashioned blacksmith — when you brought your horse in to be shod, he didn't think of 40 other things that ought to be done.

INSIDE TODAY'S *Tribune*

CLEARED: Tampa doctor yesterday was freed of all charges in a police case controversy. 1-B

DOG DAYS: Tampans pant in 90-degree dog days. 2-B

PAY UP: Cabinet agrees Rep. Papy can pay up to $250,000 to settle fill claim. 7-A

Astrology	8-B
Business	5-C
Comics	6, 7-B
Crossword	8-B
Deaths	11-A
Editorials	6-A
Financial	6-8-C
Fishing	4-C
Goren	8-C
Graham	7-A
Landers	9-A
Morning After	1-C
Theaters	5-B
TV, Radio	4-B
Van Dellen	7-B
Wishing Well	6-B
Women	8-10-A

Sen. Fulbright and Wife Cast Their Ballots

. . . Arkansas foe of Viet war later was holding lead — (AP)

Coming August 5:

Faster Service for You

Starting Monday you will be able to direct dial the Tribune's Circulation Department.

For Customer Service, Dial 224-7881

For other Circulation business, Dial 224-7880

This direct dial circulation service is another step in the Tribune's continuing effort to better serve its readers and its community.

'No Retreat' Line—

GOP Said Listening To Ike on Vietnam

MIAMI BEACH (AP) — Republican platform writers are adopting the no-retreat-in-Vietnam line urged on them by former President Dwight D. Eisenhower, leaders hinted yesterday, despite cautious "de-escalation" proposals from the Rockefeller camp.

Eisenhower sent to the Republican platform committee hearings a special message urging that both parties reject any "camouflaged surrender." The United States should stress to Hanoi, he said, America's "patient determination to obtain security for the South Vietnamese."

Almost simultaneously, Gov. Raymond P. Shafer of Pennsylvania, political ally of Gov. Nelson A. Rockefeller, was urging upon the policy body a fresh assessment of the role of Americans as "policemen of the world."

There should be no jeopardizing of the Paris peace talks or damage to the morale of fighting men, Shafer said, but the new assessment "should lead us to de-escalation of the war and a de-Americanization of foreign involvement wher-

(Continued on Page 11, Col. 1)

Pa.'s Gov. Shafer

. . . urges fresh approach

Fig. 26. Most widely used face in American history, Cheltenham is used for headlines by *Tampa* (Fla.) *Tribune*.

Jet attacks feared, Canada halts Biafra airlift

Toronto Daily Star

four star ★★★★ edition

ESTABLISHED 1892   September paid circulation 372,565 copies per day   Thursday, November 7, 1968—76 pages   Monday to Friday 10c; Saturday 15c; Home delivery 65c

METRO WEATHER
Wet snow or snowflurries tonight and Friday. Colder. Low 25, high 40. Details page 2.

OTTAWA (CP-Special) — Canada's single Hercules transport plane, which has been flying food to the breakaway Nigerian province of Biafra, has been grounded indefinitely.

The decision to halt all Red Cross flights was made because the Nigerians won't guarantee the planes' safety on night flights into Biafra and the Biafrans won't approve day flights, Defence Minister Leo Cadieux said yesterday.

On Tuesday five persons were killed and 40 wounded when the Biafran airport where the Canadian flights had been landing was bombed and strafed by a federal Nigerian MiG fighter.

However, Cadieux told reporters the strafing "actually happened after we had grounded our plane because we didn't have authorization from Biafran authorities to fly by day."

A Nigerian government spokesman warned Tuesday in the federal capital of Lagos that Red Cross airlift planes—including Canada's Hercules—which are flying into rebel Biafra under cover of darkness, may be shot down. "This we will chiefly play," he added.

Prime Minister Pierre Elliott Trudeau told the Commons earlier this week that Professor Ivan Head, his personal emissary to Lagos, last week had been given assurances of the safety of daytime Red Cross flights. Nigeria's only condition at the time was that the flights not be used for arms shipments.

Word of the airlift suspension came as two more MiGs left for independent firsthand looks at the situation in war-torn Biafra and the Commons external affairs committee called for wider relief and observer operations.

The Commons committee report also urged Canadian readiness for peacekeeping duties after a ceasefire.

But the report failed to satisfy opposition party members of the committee who issued statements at their own—calling for Canadian efforts to halt arms shipments and seek a settlement of the civil war through the United Nations and the Commonwealth.

The Commons agreed to set aside a day later this month to debate the report. While the report was being presented, Ralph Stewart—

See JET, page 4

We're asked to help save 'thin red line'

LONDON (CP) — Margaret, Duchess of Argyll, today launched an appeal for Canadians to join in the final sport of a mannish petition being organized here to save the Argyll and Sutherland Highlanders because of its "outstanding record."

The famous Scottish regiment which held the "thin red line" at Balaclava is doomed to disbandment by 1971 under defence spending cuts announced by the Labor government.

The petition has already amassed 756,000 names from all over the world and the organizers are hoping for at least 1,000,000 names before it is presented to Parliament.

PLASTIC CORNEA IMPLANT, the first of its type in Canadian medical history, was performed at Scarborough General Hospital yesterday on a man who

—Star photo by Graham Bezant

was blinded by explosion 22 years ago. Part of old cornea was cut away and the clear plastic window was then implanted into tissues. More pictures on page 9.

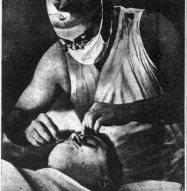

Nixon picks cabinet in Florida holiday spot

Special to The Star

KEY BISCAYNE, Fla. — President-elect Richard Nixon retreated to this island hideaway near Miami today and gathered a few of his closest advisers around him to decide on the administration that will take office on Jan. 20.

Nixon, his family, a few of his principal strategists and a press corps of 61 arrived here last night. Nixon planned to spend three days here, unwinding from the tension of the close election, and working on forming a cabinet.

Nixon's margin in the popular vote over Democratic presidential candidate Hubert Humphrey was still razor-thin as vote-counting continued today but he won or was ahead in states with 302 electoral votes—comfortably over the 270 he needed for election.

Humphrey rests up

With 94 per cent of all precincts reported, Nixon had 29,726,469 votes, Humphrey had 28,677,152 and third-party candidate George Wallace had 9,291,907.

Humphrey was also resting up from his tough, come-from-behind campaign that almost succeeded in catching the front-running Nixon. After conceding defeat and cheering up his downcast campaign workers yesterday, Humphrey said he was going to his lakeside retreat in Waverly, Minn., to stew the vote.

Nixon stopped off in Washington on his way here to visit former President Dwight Eisenhower, whom he served under as vice-president. Eisenhower is recovering from a heart attack at Walter Reed Hospital.

Delay expected

President Johnson returned to the capital from Texas for the 75-day home stretch of his presidency, pledging to Nixon "everything in my power to make your burdens lighter" during the transition period and seeking to make as much progress as possible toward Viet Nam peace.

However, the election of Nixon was expected to delay progress in the Paris peace talks for weeks and perhaps months.

Johnson offered Nixon government office space in Washington but the winner said he would continue to work out of his New York offices in the weeks ahead.

Selection of a cabinet. A White House staff and such other top aides as a budget director will be one of Nixon's first chores. He has maintained silence through the campaign about individuals who might serve but has said they will include Democrats as well as Republicans, businessmen, educationists and political leaders.

Among the prominent figures whom he reportedly is seriously considering for inclusion in his cabinet are the following:

• Governor John Volpe of Massachusetts. He is expected to be rewarded for his hard work during Nixon's campaign. He reportedly would like to be secretary of health, education and welfare but is more likely to be offered the transportation department.

• Governor George Romney of Michigan. He is another who is due a reward for campaign favors, even though Nixon lost Michigan. There is speculation that he might be named secretary of commerce. This would give him cabinet status in a post of minor importance where he could do little harm.

• For secretary of state, either C. Douglas Dillon, who has previously served as undersecretary of state and treasury secretary, or William Scranton, former governor of Pennsylvania.

• For treasury secretary, either Maurice Stans, who was director of the budget bureau under Eisenhower, or Arthur Burns, who was one of Eisenhower's principal economic advisers. Stans is regarded as a conservative economist. As investment banker now in New York, he was one of the inner circle of advisers who helped nominate and elect Nixon.

JUBILANT PRESIDENT - ELECT Richard Nixon retreated to an island hideaway in the Florida Keys with his family and advisers to select his new administration.

Robarts' man hedges over food tax

Ontario Revenue Minister John White has lost some of his enthusiasm for a provincial sales tax on food.

He said in an interview yesterday that the legislative committee on taxation, which he recommended it, may have been misled by faulty information.

While was chairman of the committee which brought down the report in September, shortly before he was appointed to the cabinet.

"I'm much more aware of difficulties in the proposal than I was previously," he said, although he added that he has reached no conclusions.

The committee had recommended that the sales tax be extended to food and children's clothing but he geared to a system of tax credits on the poor would not be hard hit.

Artificial cornea gives man his sight back in Canadian first

By LOTTA DEMPSEY
Star staff writer

A 49-year-old man, blind for 22 years, regained his sight yesterday when doctors gave him an artificial cornea made of plastic in the first operation of its kind in Canadian medical history.

"I can see, doctor. It's a little tender, but I can see," the patient exclaimed enthusiastically through the operation performed at Scarborough General Hospital.

The moment was a dramatic one for the Scarborough General corneal transplant team of ophthalmic surgeons, who wish to remain nameless.

More than 100 experiments were performed on rabbit corneas in Toronto before this first trial on a human was undertaken.

Those words, "I can see" shattered the quiet of the operating room as surgeons and nurses worked quickly and skilfully.

It took 32 minutes to perform the operation, in which the human cornea—the part of the eye that lets a person see—was removed and replaced by a clear plastic one.

The artificial cornea is about the size of a shirt button. It took a technician about an hour to shape it in preparation for the operation. He also had a spare one at hand.

Artificial implants are not to be confused with transplants of human corneas. The artificial cornea is designed for cases, like that of the Scarborough General patient,

See ARTIFICIAL, page 9

Appeal goes down to the wire

This year's United Appeal Campaign in Metro is as much of a cliffhanger as the U.S. presidential race.

That's the way campaign chairman, John P. G. Kemp put it today in the closing hours of a hard-fought drive to raise $11.3 million in six weeks.

Today he and 1,500 volunteer canvassers and workers, meeting for the final report luncheon at the Royal York Hotel, will watch anxiously right up to 12:30 p.m. deadline until the last donation is received.

When the campaign closes, computers will go to work and later today the 78 agencies will know whether there's enough money to operate full force in 1969 or if they've expect cut-backs in budgets.

Kemp said 96.9 per cent of the highest goal in history had been raised. But he also pointed out, even at this late date, there were still many areas in the campaign setup to report.

Kemp praised the 16,000 residential canvassers, most of them, women, who every year do "a hard job of footslogging and knocking on doors."

The residential division's goal is $875,000. Last year it reached $867,954 of the same goal.

Last-minute gifts or pledges may still be telephoned to 368-4241 or mailed to United Appeal Headquarters, 100 University Ave., Toronto 1.

LBJ's HEADING FOR HOME STILL A WHEELER-DEALER

By BILLY PORTERFIELD
Special to The Star

JOHNSON CITY, Tex. — Now that he's just about through on the Potomac, nobody who knows Lyndon Johnson expects him to doze away his remaining years on the Pedernales. The presidency wore him out for politics but it didn't nag his relish for life, Texas-style.

The man is only 60. He is big and tough and contrary, and if he didn't have his way with the country the way he thought he should have had, he'll have it down here in beer and barbecue country, for a long time to come.

It has nothing to do with politics, at least not politics per se. It has everything to do with the making of money and the use of it, which is power, which is influence, which is, well politics.

Off the pedestal

But it will be a different kind of politics than Lyndon Johnson knew as president. He has stepped off the pedestal and will be among the self-servers. The man from Johnson City has had a turn in the spotlight of history with the likes of Washington and Lincoln and FDR, and now heading home to wheel and deal with A. W. Moursund and all those country bankers.

But it won't all be boardroom intrigue and high finance. Between investments he'll come out in the open to lecture the young, this spring with a series of seminars at Rice University in Houston, and then next fall at the Lyndon Baines Johnson School of Public Affairs, now being built on the University of Texas campus, adjacent to the $12 million Lyndon B. Johnson Library, which, of course, will house the record of his administration.

Frustrated president

Although it has not been announced, the ex-president will probably find time to teach at his alma mater, Southwest Texas State College in San Marcos.

The prospect of LBJ holding forth in a classroom has history and government buffs all atwitter. The most consummate politician in the memory of the Senate and one of the most frustrated of presidents, embodied in one man, and there he stands before you, big and battle-scarred, made somehow magnificent by the storm of history through which he passed.

Cynics say he will use the classroom to expound upon the greatness of his many roles in Washington, and the intellectuals quip that he will give

See JOHNSON, page 4

Businessmen deplore 'defiance of the law'

The chairman of an Ontario Chamber of Commerce committee today expressed concern over a "deterioration of respect for law and order in society today."

R. T. Atherton, chairman of the chamber's administration of justice committee, told the Ontario cabinet he was worried about "open defiance of the law and humiliation of the courts and law officers by any person, group or body."

The chamber made more than 100 recommendations to the Ontario cabinet on topics ranging from national unity and academic parks to suggestions for how to make early control of pollution economic.

The chamber told the cabinet in a meeting at Queen's Park that a special committee has spent two years studying the "prime social problem" of law and order, and will soon come up with findings and recommendations.

The Ontario Chamber is a federation of over 220 boards of trade and chambers of commerce with a total membership of 50,000 businessmen.

President J. R. Meaken, publisher of the Sudbury Star, said "these people believe participating citizens at the total needs of their share a responsibility to look...

See BUSINESSMEN, page 4

Metro chairman defends airport

Get used to sonic booms: Allen

Get used to jet noise and sonic booms, Metro chairman William Allen told an audience yesterday—we can't afford to scrap Toronto International Airport.

Allen told the Electric Club that moving the airport elsewhere—as many port residents who helped nominate and elect Nixon.

would be a financial disaster to Metro.

Business and industry would follow the airport, he said.

"It is an absolute necessity that Metro Toronto have an overseas air terminal," he said.

The Department of Transport wants to expand the

airport and is running into opposition from Etobicoke officials and ratepayers' group.

Department of Transport statistics give the airport 6,400 employees who earn $50,999,000 a year. By 1985, the department estimates, the number will be 26,825 employees earning $236,-315,000.

Indirect employment will increase from 10,590 jobs today, with a payroll of $72,-116,000, to 22,530 jobs with a payroll of $158,605,000, the department says.

Allen said that big cities in the past had grown up along railway routes. In the future, he said, they will grow up on air routes and the cities without good airline services won't develop properly.

He said everyone living in big cities will probably have to get used to jet noise.

Listen to radicals, Pelletier tells college heads

By ANDREW SZENDE
Star staff writer

OTTAWA — Secretary of State Gerard Pelletier last night told Canada's universities and university administrators to start paying attention to student radicals and rebuild their universities from the bottom up.

Speaking at a banquet sponsored by the Association of Universities and Colleges of Canada, Pelletier said: "Surely your role must not be to maintain the status quo."

More than 800 university officials—many of them deans and administrators—sat largely unmoved as Pelletier, speaking in French, criticized them for being "a management institution," and urged them to "break down the barrier of the aristocratic university and rebuild it as a university of the people."

Although a simultaneous English translation of his speech was available, most in the audience did not use it and may not have understood...

"management institution," stood the full force of his remarks.

Pelletier, federal minister in charge of cultural and youth affairs, in effect said student radicals may not have gone far enough in their demands for university reform. Most administrators believe they have gone too far.

He said perhaps the only

thing students could be criticized for was for not suggesting "a completely different university than the one we know today."

Pelletier challenged administrators to decide whether they wanted to have a "university of reflection" producing the kind of

See PELLETIER, page 4

Toronto Daily Star

Pretty - - costly

Your child is unique, but trying to express her uniqueness by her fashion can cost dearly. The styles available are beguiling but expensive, and far beyond the reach of an ordinary working man with several children to clothe. Stasia Evasuk reports, page 62.

Section 1

Editorials 6
Can Mr. Nixon heal America's wounds?
Financial 17-19
Gary Lautens 5
Help Wanted 3
In the Courts 20
Milt Dunnell 10
Peter Newman 7
Races 16
Sports 14-16
Bridge 34

Section 2

Entertainment 28-25
Nathan Cohen 28
Patrick Scott 28
TV Listings 28
World News 32-38

Section 3

Ann Landers 71
Comics 60-61
Women's 62-70

Births and Deaths 42
Crossword 58
Metro News 28
Want Ads 42-58

Fig. 27. *Toronto* (Ont.) *Daily Star* is only metropolitan to use Caledonia Bold, Transitional Roman. Skyline banner, in Sans Serifs Oblique, in red.

DRIED UP SKIES

It should be dry and a little warmer on Thursday. High is expected to be in upper 80s. High Wednesday 84; low 59. Temp. at 1 a.m., 71.

FORT WORTH STAR-TELEGRAM

MORNING

32 Pages in 3 Sections

THURSDAY, JUNE 1, 1967 * * * * EIGHTY-SEVENTH YEAR, NO. 121

PRICE TEN CENTS

—Star-Telegram Photo

SMOOTH FLYING—Paul Rachal holds pictures of weather conditions existing when he made his May 23 New York-Paris flight.

Arabs Beef Ranks To Oppose Israelis

Jets Raid Complex By Port

Rails, Tanks Get First Bombing

SAIGON (AP) — U.S. Navy jets flew through heavy ground fire Wednesday to hammer targets near North Vietnam's port of Haiphong for the second straight day. American Air Cavalrymen and Marines fought North Vietnamese troops in two widely separated battles in the south.

The American Command said the Cong My complex of storage buildings, piers, railroad sidings and fuel tanks was hit for the first time in the war. The carrier-based pilots said their 1,000-pound bombs heavily damaged the site 3½ miles northwest of Haiphong.

The Loi Dong area four miles north of the city was bombed for the fourth time. Pilots reported leaving thick, black smoke over the area and said they also set off a large secondary explosion at a radar site three miles northwest of Haiphong.

One A4 Skyhawk from the 7th Fleet carrier Hancock was reported downed, the 565th U.S. plane announced lost over North Vietnam. The pilot was listed as missing.

A broadcast dispatch from Hanoi, the northern capital, said three U.S. planes were shot down. Pilots reported encountering antiaircraft fire and some missiles on the raids.

Tuesday's and Wednesday's strikes were the closest to either Hanoi or Haiphong in more than a week. There had been unconfirmed reports from Washington that American raids on the immediate Hanoi-Haiphong areas were being temporarily suspended.

—Star-Telegram Photo by Harry Cabluck

GIFT TO SCOUTS — O. P. Leonard, left, and Perry R. Bass exhibit statuette presented to Bass for the part he had in gift of land for scouts.

Britisher Delivers Warning

Restraint Plea Issued by U.S.

CAIRO (AP)—Arab nations took new military and diplomatic steps to buttress a united front against Israel Wednesday and Britain's Prime Minister Harold Wilson warned that a Mideast war could inflame the world.

The United States seized the initiative in debate at the United Nations. Ambassador Arthur J. Goldberg asked the Security Council to urge the Arabs and Israelis to cool off pending a diplomatic solution.

The council adjourned until Friday without acting on the U.S. resolution supporting Secretary-General U Thant's appeal for restraint.

Cairo radio reported Iraqi and Kuwaiti troops have begun arriving in Egypt to reinforce frontlines on the Israel border.

Egypt sent a high-level mission to Damascus apparently to enlist Syria's support for the new Egypt-Jordan mutual defense pact that brought Jordan into the anti-Israel front. Syria's Socialist regime continued its feud with Jordan with propaganda attacks on King Hussein.

There was no word on whether the Egyptian delegation was successful. It obtained the public support of President Abdel Rahman Aref on a similar mission to Iraq, which also has been on the outs with Jordan.

Prime Minister Wilson told the House of Commons the crisis has the earmarks of a holy war that could spread. Foreign Secretary George Brown warned that Britain would consider closing of the Gulf of Aqaba, Israel's trading lifeline to the East, an act of belligerence. He called on maritime powers to declare that the gulf is an international waterway open to vessels of all nations.

But Western diplomats in

Turn to Arab on Page 2

FLIGHT TO PARIS

Frog 'Airlift' Chilly Affair, But Ends Well

By JON McCONAL

When Paul Rachal retraced Charles Lindberg's historic Atlantic flight, he began with more fears for his cargo than his own welfare.

"The flight is a fairly simple process now," the 23-year-old Midland resident said of his 3,610-mile trip from New York to Paris. "It's down to a science."

Rachal had to come up with some science of his own to insure safety of the cargo — five horned frogs — which accompanied him on his May 23 flight in a single-engine Mooney Mustang.

The frogs, a gift from TCU's school spirit committee to a Paris zoo, almost didn't make the journey from Midland to New York.

"When I got there, they looked like chunks of ice," said Rachal, who was graduated from TCU Wednesday night.

The horned frogs had scooted to the back of the pressurized cabin where temperatures dropped to 10 below zero.

"I knew I'd be killed if I didn't deliver them," said Rachal. "They'd probably have held my diploma back."

While awaiting weather information, Rachal heated and massaged the frogs. They began to open their eyes. Shortly afterward, as Rachal nosed his airplane toward Europe, the horned frogs were blinking happily in their box beside the young pilot's feet.

"The wind and weather was perfect," said Rachal. "It just couldn't have been better."

Rachal said he didn't have Lindbergh's problem of 40 years earlier of fighting to stay awake.

"There was too much to do," he said. "I had to change the fuel from my cabin tanks to wing tanks and make position reports constantly."

During one of the position reports, the man at the other end of the radio asked:

"Jet?"

"No," replied Rachal.

"Twin engine?" asked the radio operator.

"Nope," answered Rachal.

"Single," stammered the radio operator.

"Yep," said Rachal.

When Rachal checked into the Paris airfield 13 hours and 59 minutes after starting, he had to circle the landing area 45 minutes before landing.

INSIDE INDEX

Houston's A. J. Foyt dodged a five-car pileup at the head of the mainstretch to win the Indianapolis 500 race Wednesday. Tuesday's leader, Parnelli Jones, was forced out of the race when his turbine car had gear trouble. Pace 1C.

George Dolan, who has been called (among other things) "The Hemingway of the Highways" and "The Falkner of the Farm Roads," has finally started to believe it. He's writing a book on his vacation. His Morning and Sunday offerings of trivia and treacle will be back in this space June 19.

2 Days Left To Ballot Absentee

Only two more days remain for Tarrant County citizens to vote absentee in the regional airport election.

So far, 340 persons have marked absentee ballots.

Absentee balloting, being conducted on the fourth floor of the courthouse, ends at 4:30 p.m. Friday. The regular election is Tuesday when polls will be open from 7 a.m. to 7 p.m.

If the elction passes, the North Texas Regional Airport Authority will be created. The authority, encompassing Tarrant and Dallas County, will administer affairs of a $250 million facility to be built near Grapevine.

JEST A MINUTE

Some people drive as if they were anxious to have their accident quickly and get it over with.

Airport Termed Key To Tax Load Balance

By MARTHA HAND
Star-Telegram Mid-Cities Bureau

EULESS — The surest road to a lighter tax burden for every homeowner in Dallas and Tarrant Counties is industrial development of this region, and is why the proposed regional airport is vital, Arlington Mayor Tom J. Vandergriff said here Wednesday.

"Everyone knows that the key to a good balanced tax role is industry," said Vandergriff.

"In order to retain lower tax rates for homeowners than are paid in other parts of the country, we have to continue to attract good industry to our area.

"But the first thing industry says to us today is, 'How close are you to Love Field or to the planned regional airport?' "

The nearness of air freight to any community will be the key to the economic vitality and health of that area, Vandergriff said.

"I am terribly concerned about this June 6 election," he said. "This just must not fail."

Vandergriff indicated that criticism of a suggested taxing method has confused voters.

He said, "No one can say that some kind of power has been set into motion to push this thing through. Some wrong things have been said."

"The average taxpayer over the next six or seven years will pay no more than $50 for this regional airport," he said.

Vandergriff told members and guests at a luncheon sponsored by the Hurst - Euless Chamber of Commerce at Western Hills that the airport will be self - sustaining as soon as the land is bought and it is in operation.

"There are many self - sustaining airports in the country," he said.

He said "having the world's best airport — a $250 million airport worth billions to the area — will be a good bargain for all area taxpayers."

Vandergriff said failure to build the big airport will turn Dallas, Fort Worth and the Mid - Cities into an economic minor league.

"I don't want Houston to get the ball — to have the airport for the jumbo planes and leave this area with a feeder airport — and in the minor leagues economically."

Dallas and Fort Worth residents interested in prosperity for the region should vote

Turn to Airport on Page 2

Boy Scouts Given 3,000-Acre Site

Related Map on Page 2A

Donation of a 3,000-acre camp site to the Longhorn Council of the Boy Scouts was revealed Wednesday night by Perry R. Bass, a director of the Sid W. Richardson Foundation.

Bass, himself a former Boy Scout, announced the gift at a dinner in the Crystal Ballroom of Hotel Texas.

The $500,000 piece of land was bought by the foundation. It is located at Lake Bridgeport in Wise County, about 40 miles northwest of Fort Worth.

It will be named the "Sid Richardson Scout Camp."

Stewart W. Devore, Longhorn Council president, said, "I think it will be one of the finest scout camps in America."

It is 10-times larger than any present Longhorn Council camp site and will be one of the largest in the state, he said.

Construction plans are still being made, Devore said.

But eventually, he said, the plot will contain 12 separate camp sites.

The site has 19 miles of shoreline. Scout executives described it as an ideal location.

Devore said the camp will fill council needs for more than 50 years.

O. P. Leonard, council vice president, presented Bass a bronze scout statuettee in recognition of the part he played in obtaining the land.

Mrs. Leonard presented Mrs. Bass a bouquet of red roses.

Bass said that about a year ago officials of the national scouting organization advised the Longhorn Council that while their present facilities were considerably more than adequate, suitable future camp areas were becoming rare.

He said they began then to search for a camp site "for the future." Their search, he explained, ended with the Bridgeport land purchase.

Devore remarked, "One can hardly imagine the great and lasting benefit to youth of this gift. Thousands of boys yet unborn will be the beneficiaries of this beautiful piece of property."

He noted that the council membership has grown 51 per cent in five years, and now has about 22,000 scouts.

Sunny Skies Follow Hail, Vicious Winds

May ended with a wet spurt Wednesday with cloudy skies dumping 1.48 inches of rain on the city in the 24-hour period ended at 6 p.m.

Most of the day, however, was fair and sunbaked.

The Weather Bureau predicted a warmer Thursday, with a high Thursday and Friday in the upper 80s and a low Thursday night around 70.

Forecasters say there's a 30 per cent chance of thunderstorms returning to the Fort Worth area Friday afternoon.

Late Tuesday and early Wednesday, spectacular electrical storms packing crop-pounding hail and elusive tornado funnels smashed across the state.

Wright Blames Thant's Pullout Of Troops for Crisis in Mideast

Star-Telegram Washington Bureau

WASHINGTON — Rep. Jim Wright of Fort Worth Wednesday condemned U.N. Secretary - General U Thant's action in withdrawing U.N. troops from the explosive Middle East.

Thant's decision, Wright said, is about as illogical as calling all the police out of neighborhood where a bank is about to be robbed.

"It permitted and abetted the development of the present crisis between Egypt and Israel, "the Fort Worth congressman said in a speech on the House floor.

Wright said he hopes a solution may be found short of armed conflict but that the United States and other responsible nations simply cannot stand idle and allow Egypt to close the Gulf of Aqaba as an international waterway.

To do so would be "a craven surrender of basic and fundamental principles to which this nation has been irrevocably committed for generations."

He called on the Security Council to assert the clear rights of peaceful commerce in the Gulf of Aqaba and to make clear that the United Nations will not tolerate violation of the territorial integrity of any nation in the area.

"In the tragic event that the United Nations should find itself incapable of acting, then the responsible nations of the world must form some concerted plan to assert and firmly establish the rights of all nations to the unrestricted use of the gulf," Wright said.

"It is important that this be done in concert rather than unilaterally," he added. "All nations have a stake in the preservation of the principles of free international shipping."

Conceding that Russia's intention is the greatest imponderable in the present crisis, Wright said the Soviet Union has an even greater stake than most nations in free and unfettered travel through the Bosporus and Skagerrak.

Wright, a U.S. delegate to the interparliamentary conference of 63 nations in Tehran last summer, said Israel must have faith that the United States and other peace-loving nations will act before it is too late.

If this action comes soon, and in concert with other countries, Wright said, there can be little question that President Gamal Nasser of the United Arab Republic will yield to it.

"Surely," he added, "he does not wish to provoke a bloody conflict from which he will again emerge defeated and discredited."

Fig. 28. Egyptian Sans Serifs dress *Fort Worth* (Texas) *Star-Telegram*.

rapher should start from scratch. The present schedule should be completely reconsidered and perhaps abandoned in entirety.

First the typographer should list all headlines possible with the head faces available. Let's assume this simple assortment:

18 Roman and Italic
24 Roman and Italic
36 Roman and Italic
48 Roman
60 Italic
72 Roman.

He'll start with all possible 1-column heads and describe them in the typographer's shorthand. (He uses *X* instead of *I* for Italics so he won't confuse *I* and *1*.)

1. *3 lines 36R, deck 3 lines 18X*
2. *3 lines 36X, deck 3 lines 18R*
3. *2 lines 36R, deck 2 lines 18X*
4. *2 lines 36X, deck 2 lines 18R*
5. *3 lines 36R*
6. *3 lines 36X*

Working from the heaviest to the lightest heads, he would finish with the notation: *1 line 18X*. This would be the lightest 1-column head on the schedule. A 1-line 18-point Roman would be the second-to-last head. (We assume that the Roman is a trifle heavier, optically, than the Italic of the same size.) There probably will be a couple of dozen or more 1-columners.

Then the typographer writes the specifications for all possible 2-column heads. The heaviest in this width would be a 3-liner, 36-point Roman. The 36 Italic 3-liner would be the next heaviest.

Two-column setting would give the first possible kickered head, and it would be the third heaviest: 2 lines 36R, kicker 18X.

Next would be a kickered 2-line 24-point head; then, 2 lines of 36; 2 lines 24; 1 line 36; 2 lines 18; 1 line 24, and finally the single line of 18. Always the Roman then the Italic. A single line of 36 could run with a kicker; that would come just ahead of the two lines of 24.

A single line of 24 with an 18-point kicker is not very pleasing because it doesn't have enough variation in size. By writing the 18-point kicker short and weighting it against two lines of 24, he can soften the handicap of inadequate variety in size.

Fig. 29. Carson City (Nev.) Nevada Appeal used American Square Serifs to convey flavor of Old West. Later schedule was changed to Sans Serifs.

SUPPLEMENT TO THE
Richmond
Times-Dispatch

The Southside Virginian

Wednesday, March 1, 1967

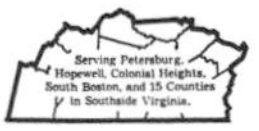

Serving Petersburg, Hopewell, Colonial Heights, South Boston, and 15 Counties in Southside Virginia.

Introducing The Southside Virginian

This is the first issue of something new in Virginia journalism, something unusual in American journalism: a publication for a sizable region with its own editorial voice and news coverage supplementing that of its metropolitan dailies.

Its foundation is a strong belief in the future of Southside Virginia. Signs of this future already abound and suggest the directions of development: the area's economy is growing stronger; resources for recreation are being developed, especially in the Buggs Island area; improved highways are swiftly shortening distances and giving the area's traditional unity an even more effective potential; educational possibilities are improving with better schools and colleges and with a share in the state's community college program; and industry is recognizing the area's possibilities, as in the planned establishment of the Brunswick Chair Corp., announced last week.

THE SOUTHSIDE VIRGINIAN'S HOPE is to help and share in the region's development. Already, announcements about this publication have put the spotlight on Southside Virginia in mailings to 3,500 leading national businessmen and in articles in a number of leading trade publications for newspapermen and national advertisers. The editorial goal will be to foster the growth of the region by encouraging and spotlighting the area, its interests, and its activities, and by constructively criticizing when that seems purposeful.

This publication's name was chosen because, of many suggestions, it most clearly and quickly emphasized that our aim will be to appeal to and to help represent the residents of Southside Virginia.

The name is not new, as Calvin Robinson pointed out in his "Father Darkleaf" column in the Appomattox Times-Virginian. "Appomattox County," he wrote, "once had a fine newspaper called The Southside Virginian. Away back in 1892, The Appomattox and Buckingham Times was established here and a few years later a rival paper, The Southside Virginian was established. Appomattox was hardly large enough to make two newspapers profitable, so the two were consolidated to form the present Times-Virginian."

We of the current Southside Virginian are confident our goals can be achieved partly because of the area's character and potential and partly because of the background of this publication. It is readily available to Southside Virginians at no extra charge as part of The Richmond Times-Dispatch and The News Leader going into the area Wednesdays. It is prepared in Petersburg by experienced newsmen and newswomen.

THIS NEW PUBLICATION gives the writers and editors an opportunity for intensive coverage of a most interesting area in a way that is not possible through the regular columns of the dailies. In this manner, The Southside Virginian seeks to fill a gap between the metropolitan dailies with their necessary emphasis on matters of world, national, and state importance and the weeklies with their necessary emphasis on matters of local importance.

In this spirit, The Southside Virginian seeks to do what the label on the map at the top right of Page 1 indicates: to serve the cities, towns, and 15 outlined counties of Southside Virginia.

In this spirit also, we welcome your reactions, comments, suggestions, and information about activities and developments that you think fellow Southsiders would want to read about, activities particularly that will help us realize the basic goal of working with Southsiders toward an attainable and bright regional future.

AGEE, OUTSTANDING FARMER, SAMPLES FINISHED PRODUCT

Year's Young Farmer

Cumberland Future Bright, Says Agee

By H. Hugh Moore

FARMVILLE — Robert L. Agee III sits in his big house in Cumberland County near Farmville, surveying his land holdings in a manner reminiscent of a pre-Civil War plantation owner.

There the similarity ends. For while the Civil War land baron sipped julips and chased the fox, Agee minds a herd of 120 Holstein cows and works a 16-hour day — every day.

AGEE IS one of Southside Virginia's many dairy farmers, a self-employed agriculturist who daily fights the battle of disease, drought and temperamental bovines. He is an average dairyman in those respects, but he's above average too. So much above that the Virginia Jaycees have named him the Outstanding Young Farmer of 1966.

Agee is proud of the award but it's hard to get him to talk about it. He'd rather talk about his native Cumberland County and adopted Town of Farmville just four miles away.

Born in the county, Agee is rapidly becoming a leader in the exclusively rural community. At 35, he is a member of the Cumberland Planning Commission and openly admits he is considering offering for election to the board of supervisors, "if not this year then in four years." If elected, he would hold a post his grandfather held for 40 years.

AGEE believes Cumberland's future is bright, despite a steady migration from rural to urban areas. He said he couldn't be specific but the planning commission and other agencies are working towards development in the county, particularly in the field of recreational facilities.

The outstanding farmer began dairying operations in 1949 with his father on 1,440 acres and a younger brother, Taylor, joined the partnership later. The Agees today, with help from two employes, boast a herd of 120 registered Holsteins, many of them prize winners. In recent years, the Agees have developed cattle breeding in addition to dairying. Five years ago the family sold a champion bull for $25,000 to the Curtis Breeding Service of Cary, Ill., a record sale for the southeastern states.

THE AGEE operation, named "Green Creek Farms," is a showplace for dairy operators and cattle breeders. At anytime, Agee said, the farm is host to other persons in the industry, and students from Virginia Polytecnic Institute sometimes tour the facility.

Agee's herd — he calls them his babies — have brought home numerous trophies and ribbons to "Green Creek Farms." The herd is rated 87 on a 100-scale, one of the highest in the state, Agee says, not without a trace of pride.

Married to the former Jane Fender of Buckingham County, Agee is the father of two sons, 6 and 9 years of age. He is a member of the neighboring Farmville Jaycee Chapter, president of his Sunday school class at Farmville Methodist Church and a member of the Holstein Fresian Association. He has frequently served as a judge for 4-H shows and is a leader in the Atlantic Holstein Club.

AGEE IS concerned that six of seven young men his age leave the Cumberland-Farmville area to seek employment elsewhere. "Most fellows leave right after school," he says. "I doubt if more than three or four members of my high school graduating class are still in the county." Agee completed high school in Cumberland and attended Hampden-Sydney College in 1948-49.

Blackstone Soldier Dies, Wins DSC

BLACKSTONE — A Blackstone man, described by his high school principal as "above average in every way," has been awarded the nation's second highest military honor posthumously.

Lloyd Fields Jr., 26, was killed in battle in Vietnam while serving as a lead scout for an American force attempting to clear a road held by Viet Cong forces.

The Distinguished Service Cross was presented to his parents, Mr. and Mrs. Lloyd Fields Sr. of Rt. 5, Blackstone recently.

SGT. FIELDS was an 'A' student in high school, Fitz Turner, principal of James Solomon Russell High School in Lawrenceville, said: "He (Fields) finished high school with but one idea in mind — to enter military service . . ."

The Blackstone soldier was credited with wiping out a Viet Cong machine gun nest and with saving the lives of many of his comrades. Maj. Gen. Victor J. MacLaughlin, commanding general of the U.S. Army Quartermaster Center and Ft. Lee, told Mr. and Mrs. Fields they can be proud of their son's action and his devotion to duty.

THE YOUNGER Fields was killed by a Viet Cong sniper April 13, 1966, while serving with Troope E, 17th Cavalry, 173rd Airborne Brigade. That unit was

See BLACKSTONE, Page 2

Integrate, HEW Tells Localities

By Allan Jones

Recent hearings in Washington demonstrate that Virginia school officials will be required to do more than they had anticipated under federal school desegregation guidelines.

Several local school officials who testified before a federal hearing examiner said they felt they were responsible only for dispensing information on how Negroes may transfer to white or predominantly white schools.

Most of them cited a provision of the guidelines declaring that "at no time may any official, teacher or employe of the school system, either directly or indirectly, seek to influence any parent, student, or any other person involved, in the exercise of a choice. . . ."

But representatives of the Department of Health, Education and Welfare countered by saying while local school officials cannot influence individual choices, they are required to seek community acceptance and support of school integration.

THE HEW spokesmen quoted from a different section declaring that "school officials must take steps to encourage community support and acceptance of their desegregation plan.

"They are responsible for preparing students, teachers and all other personnel, and the community in general, for the successful desegregation of the system."

The purpose of the hearings was to determine whether federal school funds should be withheld from the localities for failing to achieve a sufficient amount of student and faculty integration.

Testimony was taken concerning the Counties of Appomattox, Northumberland, Sussex, Southampton, Mecklenburg and Charlotte Counties. A seventh hearing will be held March 16 for Essex County.

An eighth school division, the city of Franklin, also has been cited for noncompliance with the guidelines, but no hearing has been set yet for that community.

IN GENERAL, the Virginia authorities who testified said they had confined their desegregation activities to explanations of how the guidelines work.

The testimony of A. B. Haga, superintendent of Mecklenburg County schools, was typical of that of most of the Virginia officials who appeared as witnesses at four days of hearings.

When asked what steps he had taken to gain community support of integration Haga said he met with principals and teachers and gave out information "as to what was expected of us." He then observed that he didn't know whether HEW would call that support.

Did Haga seek the assistance of any organizations in the community to make the county's free choice period more effective? "No, except to publicize it," Haga replied.

But under cross examination by Frederick T. Gray, counsel for the Mecklenburg School Board, Haga said he believed everyone in the county knew of the free choice period because all parents were required to fill out a choice form for their children.

Could Haga enlist organizations to assist him in the integration process? Haga said "I haven't felt so." When asked if he had tried to make the county's free choice plan work, Haga said "I think we have."

HEW SPOKESMEN also expressed concern over the amount of faculty integration in the six school divisions.

Federal civil rights advisory specialists testified they sought by means of

See INTEGRATE, Page 2

Local Conferences On Education Urged

FARMVILLE — A result of the third Governor's Regional Conference on Education held Monday at Longwood College in Farmville will be to hold further conferences on a local level.

A resolution offered by Delegate Dan Daniel of Danville and seconded by Garland Moss of Chase City, unanimously passed by some 900 Southside Virginians attending the conference, requested the regional conference chairman, Charles L. McCormick III of Halifax to appoint a citizen's committee on education for each county and city in attendance to promote local conferences similar to the regional conference "in order that all our citizens might be better informed of the necessity of Virginia's developing the potential inherent in our greatest resource, our young men and women."

THE RESOLUTION in part said, "The message heard at this governor's conference must be spread throughout Virginia if we are to meet our education obligation."

FORMER GOVERNOR HARRISON, a resident of Southside Virginia, presented the main address and set the theme of more local interest and increased county or local participation in the funding of education in the local area.

He said, "It would seem clear enough

See EDUCATION, Page 2

What's Inside

U. S. Army Photo

MRS. FIELDS ACCEPTS AWARD FROM GEN. MACLAUGHLIN; HUSBAND WATCHES

Untied Tobacco Issue Divides Growers, Buyers

By Spurgeon Compton

SOUTH BOSTON — Buyers and processors of flue-cured tobacco are opposed to any increase in the amount of tobacco sold in loose leaf form rather than the traditional method of tied bundles.

Tobacco growers on the other hand would like to sell all of their tobacco untied.

THESE TWO widely divergent views were made plain at a hearing called last Friday by the U. S. Department of Agriculture to seek some solution to the seeming impasse separating those who grow the tobacco and those who buy, process and manufacture it into cigaretts. Each group is motivated by economics.

The buyers claim that handling, transporting and processing loose leaf tobacco is slower and more costly than tied tobacco.

Farmers say that labor has become a critical factor on the farm, and with the rising cost of production, growers can no longer afford to tie the tobcaco before offering it for sale.

Historically, flue-cured tobacco has been sold in loose leaf form only on the markets of Georgia and Florida, while all leaf sold on markets in Virginia and the Carolinas has been tied into bundles before being placed in the auction warehouses.

IN 1962, the Department of Agriculture began experimenting with the sale of loose leaf on all markets, allowing growers in Virginia and the Carolinas to market untied tobacco for a certain number of sales days at the beginning of the auction season.

In 1962, only 48 million pounds of untied tobacco were sold on the traditionally "tied" markets. But by 1966, the amount of loose leaf offered for sale in Virginia and the Carolinas had jumped to 348 million pounds.

Complaints then began to be heard from the buyers and processors, who said they were not equipped to handle additional amounts of loose leaf. Furthermore, the buyers said handling and processing loose leaf consumed more time resulting in congestion at the redrying plants with a resultant slackening of demand on the auctions.

BUYERS FOR the foreign trade, especially, complained that manufacturers in their countries could not use additional untied tobacco and they would have to look elsewhere for their needs unless desirable grades of tied tobacco could be purchased in the U.S.

H. Itoh, a spokesman for the Japanese tobacco monopoly, made this plain at the hearing Friday. Itoh said in 1965, Japan, the third largest foreign customer for U.S. tobacco, purchased 55 million pounds of tobacco here. In 1966, Japanese purchases dropped to 45 million pounds because of the increase in loose leaf sales and the inability of Japanese buyers to secure the desired grades in tied form.

Spokesmen for five other buyers for the domestic and foreign trade voiced opposition to sales of additional loose leaf.

The solution offered by a majority of the spokesmen for the buyers would be to allow each farm in the Carolinas and Virginia to sell a certain percentage of its quota in loose leaf form during a specific number of consecutive sales days. The percentage of loose leaf sales to be alloted to each farm would be determined by the percentage of the overall crop which the buying companies felt they could handle.

The Virginia Farm Bureau Federation also advocated the percentage method of allocating loose leaf sales for 1967. But S. T. Moore, Jr. of South Hill, chairman of the farm bureau's flue-cured committee, said the tobacco industry should move as rapidly as possible toward selling 100 per cent of the crop untied.

On the other hand, Jack Hall, chairman of the Tobacco Advisory Committee of the National Farmers Union, called for extending the number of sales days for loose leaf tobacco from the 12 in 1966 to 20 in 1967.

INDIVIDUAL tobacco growers testifying at the hearing called for support prices on united tobacco "from the first day of the selling season to the last day." These included J. W. Kirk, who grows 10 acres of tobacco in Lunenburg County; Wilson Bagley, also of Lunenburg County and a number of growers from the North Carolina portion of the Old Belt.

Most of these growers said the solution to providing enough tied tobacco for the domestic and foreign trade would be a price differential which would make it profitable for farmers to take the added time and expense of tying the leaf.

A. R. Butler of Chase City said he would "tie every pound" of his tobacco if the companies would pay a higher price and made it worth his while. "All I'm after is the dollar, just like the buying companies," Butler declared.

THIS POSITION was supported, at least partially, by Maurice B. Rowe, Virginia's Commissioner of Agriculture.

He said a market price pattern which would reflect the added expense of tying tobacco would result in the tobacco being tied without complaint on the part of the grower.

Testimony taken here, as well as that heard at earlier hearings in Marion, S.C., and Wilson and Raleigh, N.C., will be considered by the Department of Agriculture in establishing regulations for the sale of the 1967 flue-cured crop.

Fig. 30. Contemporary Gothic heads are used in *Southside Virginian,* satellite publication of *Richmond* (Va.) *Times-Dispatch.* On this Vol. 1, No. 1, nameplate, box on col. 1 head and index head in col. 6 are in magenta.

Pope calls synod of bishops for '67; asks lay council

VATICAN CITY (NC)—In a news-packed speech to a group of cardinals meeting in Rome, Pope Paul VI announced that the synod of bishops which will help to govern the Church will be convened Sept. 29, 1967. He also announced the establishment of an international layman's council to assist with the lay apostolate movement and of a pontifical commission for justice and peace.

Other announcements during the speech, given Dec. 23, were:

- decrees dealing with the reformation of the curia have been drawn up and will soon be published.
- the pope will visit personally and by personal representation Rome parishes to promote contact between the people and their bishop.

THE SPEECH, WHICH was made at the annual Christmas audience granted to cardinals in Rome and members of the Roman Curia, was far different from past practices. Ordinarily popes in past years have delivered talks of a spiritual and meditative nature. This year's, however, was packed with facts and news.

One person present said that the assembled cardinals and prelates in the Hall of the Consistories sat almost motionless throughout the 3,000 word discourse. "You could hear a pin drop," he said, "especially when Pope Paul began discussing plans for the reform of the Roman Curia."

His desire to reform the curia has been known since almost the beginning of his reign three years ago, but so far only the Holy Office has been reformed. However, as if answering doubting Thomases, the Pope said: "Though this evolution of a traditional and fully active organization requires some time and a certain amount of gradual change

(Continued on Page 2)

Strolling up Hercules Hill

And once at the top, a delighted look around at the beautiful snow-bound countryside surrounding the Hercules Country Club off the Lancaster Pike—then a swift trip down via sled. Pam and Dave Moreland, Allen Segal and Tom Leedy make their slow way to the top, there to join the dozens of other youngsters who are finding that holidays from school and the big snow make a happy combination. See other snow photos by Lloyd Teitsworth on page 9.

DELMARVA
DIALOG
VOL. 2, NO. 18 | DECEMBER 30, 1966 | 10 CENTS

Secret ordinations cited in North Vietnam

MINEOLA, NY (NC)—A Vietnamese priest stationed here confirmed reports that men are being secretly ordained priests in North Vietnam in order to continue the Church's mission in the communist-ruled portion of that war-torn country.

Father Joseph Duc Minh, director of the Secretariat for Vietnam Missions and a native of North Vietnam, said he knew of several dioceses where seminarians—often Brothers and catechists—were living in pastors' homes and receiving basic education in Catholic theology. They are ordained when the pastors feel they are adequately prepared to carry on the duties of the priesthood, he said.

"I know of one diocese where 20 priests were ordained last year," Father Duc Minh said.

Methodists, Catholics come a little closer

By FATHER JAMES P. ROACHE

CHICAGO (NC)—Conversations between 24 representatives of the Catholic and Methodist Churches here "pointed up large areas of basic agreement and accented the truth that all Christians have much more in common than they sometimes realize."

The sessions (Dec. 18 to 20) "raised the hope of all its members that the way has been opened for further 'breakthrough' in discovery and mutual understanding," according to a "summary memorandum" presented to the participants at the closing session.

The conversations were part of a series involving the Catholic Church and various Protestant groups, growing out of statements on Christian unity of the Second Vatican Council. The sessions here were the second between representatives of the Catholic and the Methodist churches.

THE CATHOLIC participants were headed by Bishop Joseph B. Brunini, apostolic administrator of the Natchez-Jackson, Miss., diocese, and the Methodist group by Bishop F. Gerald Ensley, Columbus, Ohio, resident leader of the Methodist Ohio West Area.

FOCUS WAS ON THE nature of faith. Discussion papers were presented by Father Robert F. Quinn, CSP, Boston, director of the adult education and Christian Culture Lecture programs at the Catholic Information Center, and the Rev. John Deschner, Dallas, professor of theology at southern Methodist University's Perkins school of theology.

The faith that saves, in both Catholic and Methodist teaching, is the total commitment of the whole man who "gives himself entirely to God," the memorandum said. It was pointed out in the papers presented by Father Quinn and Dr. Deschner that saving faith is not merely an intellectual acceptance of the revelation of God.

Pointed up in the papers was the similarity of both Churches in adherence to traditional teachings and the summary memorandum stressed that both churches "have the right and duty to rethink and reformulate the store of traditional teaching in thought-forms and language which are valid and relevant to men in 'the modern world.'"

"THIS MEANS development—rooted in the Christian past, open to the present and future, under the perpetual guidance of the Holy Spirit," the memorandum said.

Bible study sessions during the conversations were led by Bishop James K. Mathews of Boston, resident leader of the Methodist Boston area, and Father Barnabar Ahern, CP, professor of Sacred Scriptures at St. Meinrad's, Ind., seminary.

Paul VI's plea fails; truce off

VATICAN CITY (NC)—The key to the ending of the Vietnam war is mutual good will exercized by both sides at the same time, Pope Paul VI declared in his 1966 Christmas message.

The end of the war depends on man's free will, he pointed out.

Referring to his proposal to extend the truce period from over the Christian holiday period to that of the Buddhist holidays in February, the Pope said: "One waits in hope that both sides may extend the truce and that from suspension of hostilities it may be possible to advance to negotiations in good faith, the only way of reaching peace in freedom and justice."

POPE PAUL'S comments on the Vietnam war came towards the end of the 2,000-word Christmas message broadcast to the world on the night of Dec. 22.

(So far both sides have failed to extend the truce as outlined by the pope. Vatican sources indicate that the pope is depressed over this failure.

(Earlier this week the United States

(Continued on Page 2)

Spellman visits Viet battlefront

SAIGON (NC) — Francis Cardinal Spellman of New York celebrated midnight Mass at Cam Ranh Bay within 400 yards of the South China Sea. An estimated congregation of 5,000 which began gathering at 7:30 p.m. included Army, Navy, Air Force, Vietnamese and Korean Catholics.

Wearing an Army fatigue jacket and a red pilot's cap, the cardinal arrived by plane from Saigon at 8:30 p.m. He was welcomed by Brig. Gen. M. E. Gates, commanding general of the Cam Ranh Bay Support Command. Father (Lt. Col.) Leonard Faznonsk of Scranton, Pa., headed the chaplains greeting the cardinal. A choir of 30 voices, directed by Sp. 4/c Alan Welinski of Santa Ana, Calif., sang Christmas carols before and during the Mass.

PREACHING after the Mass the cardinal said:

"I have no words to tell you how grateful to God I am for the privilege of being here in Vietnam for midnight Mass. I announce no news when I say that I am getting old and it is no wonder that for the past few

(Continued on Page 2)

Priests ask Bishop Hyle for pastoral reforms

A sharing of parish responsibility by the pastor with other priests and the laity and Religious of the parish has been recommended by the diocesan clergy committee on renewal.

The recommendation was contained in a press release issued earlier this week based on the Dec. 16 meeting. The next committee meeting is to be held today.

The 16 priest-members of the committee also suggested that the term "associate pastor" be used in referring to parish curates. This will "bring out more forcefully" the cooperation that should exist between the pastor and his priests, says the statement.

LENGTH OF SERVICE in each parish was also recommended by the priests. A pastor should serve a maximum of 10 years in each parish and an associate pastor, a maximum of five.

The term for the pastor "would afford a new challenge to the priest and give the parishes involved greater vitality as a result of new points of view and approaches to parish problems," reasons the statement.

The committee also recommended that seniority alone not be the criteria for selecting pastors. It recommended that ability and past performance also be weighed.

Regarding the associate pastors, the statement says a shift within every five year period would allow an associate "a wider field of experience in several parishes before he is assigned as a pastor."

The committee also recommended that a priest be permitted to retire at 65 from administrative responsibilities and required to submit his resignation to the bishop at 70. The statement added, however, that the bishop does not have to accept the resignation.

THE COMMITTEE also said that the diocese should provide suitable pensions for retired priests and asked that details of such a plan be taken up by the diocesan priests senate which will be organized once the present renewal committee finishes making its recommendations.

Regarding a sharing of responsibility with the parish laity, the committee recommended that the "main responsibility" for directing parish societies,

(Continued on Page 2)

Cardinal asks atheists for 'liberty' statement

RECKLINGHAUSEN, Germany (NC) — Vienna's Franziskus Cardinal Koenig, writing in the Catholic weekly, **Echo der Zeit**, here, challenged the atheist governments of the world to issue a document discussing universal religious freedom.

The Austrian prelate, president of the Vatican Secretariat for Non-Believers, invited atheists "to work out, according to the example of the Second Vatican Council, a document treating religious freedom based on the natural law."

POINTING out that Vatican II had not condemned atheism, Cardinal Koenig continued that the aim of the council was to offer the aid of the Church to those who needed it. The Catholic Church, looking after atheists as after all men, will not condemn. But the Church, the cardinal added, cannot accept a doctrinaire and unchanging atheism.

Because the Church is in some ways to blame for the growth of atheism, the cardinal explained, it will not shut its doors to nonbelievers, but rather holds its doors always open in the hope that there will be a reconciliation.

However, Cardinal Koenig emphasized, this reconciliation cannot come on religious or theological grounds but on the common desire of atheists and Christians for the full development of man. Therefore, he continued, dialog between atheists and the Church must be "a human dialogue of respect, love, peace and honesty."

ACCORDING to the Austrian cardinal, this includes a common effort to preserve world peace and a broadening of attitudes that will see both an atheist good will toward Christianity as well as Christianity's good will toward atheists in the hope of cooperation for the good of mankind.

The **Echo der Zeit** article ended: "The Church will condemn nobody; she is ready to cooperate with all men of good will. But she will stress that men may not be forced into atheism any more than they may be forced into belief in Christianity, since freedom of conscience, growing from the natural law, may not be abridged."

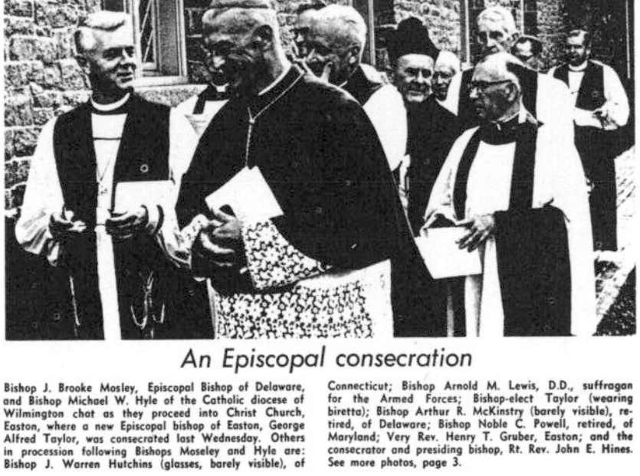

An Episcopal consecration

Bishop J. Brooke Mosley, Episcopal Bishop of Delaware, and Bishop Michael W. Hyle of the Catholic diocese of Wilmington chat as they proceed into Christ Church, Easton, where a new Episcopal bishop of Easton, George Alfred Taylor, was consecrated last Wednesday. Others in procession following Bishops Moseley and Hyle are: Bishop J. Warren Hutchins (glasses, barely visible), of Connecticut; Bishop Arnold M. Lewis, D.D., suffragan for the Armed Forces; Bishop-elect Taylor (wearing biretta); Bishop Arthur R. McKinstry (barely visible), retired, of Delaware; Bishop Noble C. Powell, retired, of Maryland; Very Rev. Henry T. Gruber, Easton; and the consecrator and presiding bishop, Rt. Rev. John E. Hines. See more photos, page 3.

Fig. 31. American favorite, Goudy Bold, Old Style Roman, is rarely used for headlines but is striking in *Dialog*, weekly of Wilmington, Del.

In 2-column measure he'll also have his first hammer. It would be written: *Hammer 36R, 2 lines 18X.*

As the measures get wider, the number of heads decreases. You can't use 18-point in any head wider than two columns, for instance. By the time the newspaper designer gets to eight columns, he may have only two heads, a 72-pointer with a 36 kicker and the plain 72. He might add two lines of 72 or a single line of 60, with or without a kicker.

Here, as elsewhere, the form of the letter will determine somewhat the headline form. If a single line of 60-point in 8 columns has many more than 32 characters, the typographer won't use an 8-column 60-pointer. If two lines of 72 have more than 45 characters, he won't use more than a 1-liner.

After all the possible head forms have been specified, the desk should evaluate them. It might decide not to use a deck on any head. That would eliminate the first four 1-column heads that were jotted down. The editor might decide that his narrowest hammer would be in 3 columns or that he would not use a kicker on an 8-column banner. The typographer wants to eliminate all heads that do not promise to give constant and good use. A good hed sked is all muscle; the typographer wants to get rid of the fat even this early.

Now the desk is given the job of writing heads to meet the specifications on the list. From a specimen book, from an old schedule, or by counting heads in another paper, the headwriter determines the character count for each head.

Each news room seems to have its own counting system. Any one that works is a good one. If there were one system considered "the standard," it would be the one that counts most lowercase letters as 1, the *m* and *w* as 1½, and the *i, l,* and punctuation as ½. Most capitals count 2; *W* and *M* count 3; *I* counts as 1. However, in some fonts the lowercase *f* and *j* are narrow enough to count only ½, and in other fonts the cap *I* may count only ½.

Some students, who like to shore up their memories with mnemonic devices, say, "Flitjays are skinny; whammies are fat." This incantation refers to a system in which the *f, l, i, t,* and *j* count ½ and the *w* and *m* are wide.

We may refine this counting system to increments of decimals. (The Linofilm, for instance, counts characters in 18ths of an em.) Or we may make it far more tentative, counting all lowercase as 1 and all caps as 2. I have seen deskmen write heads on the typewriter, counting all letters as 1. Then they check to see if there is an unusual number of capitals. If a

HEADLINE SCHEDULE

keyboarded from 4 fonts of Bodoni Bold

36 pt. Bodoni Bold

36 pt. Bold Italic

24 pt. Bodoni Bold Roman
24 pt. Bodoni Bold Italic

14 pt. Bodoni Bold Roman
14 pt. Bodoni Bold Italic

---

① **Anti-Rabies Serum Flown To Brookline**

Diseased Squirrels Roaming Streets, Attack Children

② **Quake Razes Chile Village**

Casualties Mounting As Fires Break Out

③ **Mayor Insists Police Chief 'Defied Me'**

Fig. 32. Headline schedule. This version, just before final revision, has several heads which would be eliminated. It does not show many possible heads which have already been deleted. Heads 1 through 42 are all set from four fonts of Linotype matrices. Courtesy Mergenthaler Linotype Company

(4) *Lonely Chimp Seeks Friends At Midnight*

(7) **Rain Forecast**

(12) **Dismiss Band**

(5) **Schools Open For Fall Term**

(8) County's Swim Pools Overload Waterworks

(9) *Church Council Elects Bennett as Moderator*

(6) *May Flowers Bloom Late*

(10) Fog Delays Wharf Job

(11) *Worm Turns; Car, Too*

(13) # Seven File in Race For New Judgeship

New State Law Calls For County Court To Open in June

No Panic

(14) # False Fire Report Evacuates Schools

Homer in 11th

(15) *Big Crowd Sees Tigers Win Game*

(16) Tax Increase Halts State Injunction

(17) *Clergymen Take Message to Rioters*

New Bridge Open

(18) Traffic Jam Over

Sheltered Lincoln

(19) *Storm Fells Elm*

(20) Snow Buries Valley

**Sneak Blizzard Takes
Heavy Damage Toll
On Budding Trees**

(21) Record Crops Seen

(22) *Storm Signals Up*

**(23) Congressional Delegation
Sets Up Shop in County**

**Seeking Voters Views
On Army Engineers
Flood-Dike Plan**

**(24) Hospital Maternity Ward
Rated Best in Midwest**

**Inspection Teams
Praise Records**

No Sissies

**(25) Boys Find Hair Dressing
Very Manly Occupation**

12 Minutes

(26) *Council Approves Budget In Shortest Session Ever*

(27) New Factory Starts Hiring For November Production

(28) *Massed Bands Beat Tempo For Giant Knights Parade*

Way for Road

(29) Radio Tower Topples

Daylight Time

(30) *Police on New Hours*

(31) Fire Sweeps Shoe Warehouse

(32) *Reservoirs All Overflow*

Final Testing Monday to Select

First American Man in Space

(33) Choice Down
To Only Four
Rocket Men

Secretary of State Accepts

Invitation to Speak Here

(34) Commencement Talk
Expected to Explain
Position on China

Fired!

(H)

Charter Commission Works So Speedily

Job Ends Months Before Appointments

Once in Swiss Tower

(35) **Ancient Church Carillon To Find Home in Museum**

South Seas Ahoy!

(36) *Family Starts New Cruise To Revisit Pacific Atolls*

(37) **City Sales Tax at Record High Barometer of Business Here**

38. New Strain of Broom Straw Rates High in Experiment

39. Onions on Menu
Now Strong Men Cry Too

40. Pheasants Plentiful
Game Bird Season Opens

41. Police Car Plunges over Cliff

42. Mayor Appoints City Clerk

Council Approves Projects on 10

* *Once in Swiss Tower*

Ancient Chu
To Find Hoi

Bodoni Bold 42 point (used on this banner) is the largest newspaper headletter available at the keyboard. It extends the Bodoni schedule so that on most pages no handset heads at all are required and, even on front and section pages, handsetting is reduced to the bare minimum. For larger sizes, Bodoni is available in several forms.

The addition of 18-point Bodoni Bold, duplexed with Italic, makes possible the heads marked * on this page plus many more. It can be used for the decks on heads 13, 20, 33 and 34, in three-line one-column heads and as kickers for head 14, 15, 18, 19, 35, 36 and 40.

* **Scouts Start on
Hike to Capital**

* **Templars to Elect**

* *Award Citation
To Women's Guild*

* *Report Burglary*

Spartans Take
League Lead
Over State

**Congress
Overrides
Tax Veto**

For metropolitan dailies that require stronger one-column heads, the 36-point (left) and 30-point (right) Bodoni Bold Condensed offers a practical unit count and strong impact. All are keyboarded

Britons man
Shastri reviews
Congo knot
British ato
Floods c
Floods

Fig. 33. Bodonis from 48- through 120-point sizes are set on Ludlow to complete head schedule. Courtesy Ludlow Typograph Company

line contains NAACP, for instance, they would have to recount by more precise measurement to make sure the line fits. If there are more *m*'s and *w*'s, caps or lowercase, than usual, they would recount the line.

Some counting systems give a value of ½ to spaces. It is better to count them as 1. In actual metal, the space should be a 3-em space. If we count *M* as 3 units, then word spacing, one-third of an em, will count as 1.

After the sample heads are all written, the composing room sets them. At this time the headwriter checks to see whether his counting was accurate. In actual production, a head written too long is immediately returned for rewriting. But in setting the tentative schedule, excess characters are merely left off. So the writer must look for those places where the system—or he—failed. For each particular head he notes the maximum, and in some cases perhaps the minimum, character count.

Now headlines are grouped according to optical weight, the heaviest one at the top, the lightest at the bottom. The designer tried to do this as he first wrote the specifications. But a head that seemed heavier than another as he visualized it may not weigh quite as much when he sees it as ink on paper.

The editor must decide on how heads should be ordered by the desk. The obvious way is to mark headline copy as we would that for an ad. The head is typed line for line as it's to appear in print. Then we'd write *36-pt. Bodoni Bold* and draw two parallel vertical lines at the left of the copy to designate flush-left setting. In case of a kickered head, we'd write the copy line for line. We'd designate the top line as *18-pt. Bodoni Ital,* and show that the underscore is *Rule #17* and the main head *36 Bodoni Bold*. At the left of the main head we'd draw a rectangle and within it a number to show how many ems the head should be indented.

These notations are used all the time in advertising work because each ad is a custom-built job and there is little repetition or opportunity for standardizing. But the copydesk is far too busy for all this writing; it wants to abbreviate. We can speed up writing directions by eliminating constant factors; if all heads are set flush left, we needn't specify that. We abbreviate "Bodoni" to "Bod" and "Century Bold" to "CB."

The simplest way, of course, is to use a code. So in most news rooms, heads are designated by a letter and/or number. The trouble is that the code generally has little if any logic, so it must be learned by sheer memorization. The code used by one paper I have worked on named as a "3 head" one with three lines of 24 with a deck of 12. Yet two lines of

24 with the same deck was a "G head"; without the deck it was a "17 head."

A good code must be logical; it must be simple; it must be accurate. To meet these qualifications, the *2-digit code* has been developed. It works well; I know of none that works better.

The first of the two digits designates the column width. Thus *1-1, 1-7, 1-18* all designate 1-column heads. All heads starting with *2* are 2-columners, etc. The second digit designates the comparative weight of heads within the given column-width. Thus, the heaviest 1-column head is coded as *1-1,* the heaviest 2-columner is *2-1.* The second-heaviest 1-columner is *1-2,* the fourth heaviest in 3 columns is coded *3-4.* Notice that weights are only relative. A *1-1* head, the heaviest 1-columner, may have three lines of 36-point while the *6-1* would be two lines of 72.

Advantages of this code are many. It is simple; two numbers—at the most, three—give all the necessary information to the back shop. The *3-7* head, for instance, might be kickered. When the compositor gets the copy, he looks on his headline schedule for *3-7.* There he is shown the face and size for both components of the head, the kind of rule to use for the underscore, and the amount of indent for the main head. There is little danger of misunderstanding.

When the head is indicated on the copy log, the simple code gives the editor all the necessary data he needs in the quickest manner. If he sees a great many *3-5* heads, he can specify a few *3-1* or *3-2* heads. If he notes that his biggest head is a *5-2,* he knows that his major story is a weak one or that it hasn't been given a head of enough weight. If the editor notices that there are no *4-1* heads, he really needn't stop to remember just what a *4-1* head is. All he needs to know is that the 4-column heads he does have out on the bank are comparatively weaker ones.

Some editors designate Italic heads with an X. Their top 1-column head, *1-1,* might have three lines of 36-point Roman. Three lines of 36 Italic would be coded as *1-1X.* Normally the Italic head is one number lower than the same one in Roman form, and in that case three lines of 36 Italic would be designated as *1-2.* Using the X instead of a number for Italics enables the editor to determine easily whether a proper ratio of Romans to Italic heads is being maintained.

For similar checking, some editors add *K* to kickered heads, as *2-7K.* Hammer heads are customarily noted simply as *2-H, 4-H,* etc.; there should be only one hammer in each column measure. But there will be several kickers in each measure, and so the editor must use the regular weight code as well as the K. The *3-4K* head is the fourth-heaviest 3-columner, as the numbers show; that it carries a kicker is important only to the editor in determining whether he has enough or too many kickered heads. Otherwise he would have to memorize the code numbers of kickered heads.

The 2-digit code makes it simple to count how many heads of a given width have been sent to composing. The editor simply notes the first digit in the code. If he notices that he is weak on 3-column heads, he may then determine the weights of the 3-columners already set and then designate the particular extra 3-column heads he needs.

Adoption of this code—or any other logically structured one—is usually met by resistance from the desk and/or the composing room. Rarely is any reason given other than the old and tired, "We've never done it that way before." No one can give a logical reason because there isn't any. One consolation for the person who pushes through the use of this code is that after six months everyone who is now anti will be just as vehemently pro. In every plant where the two-digit code has been introduced, any attempt to abandon it would be met after six months with stronger resistance than its adoption originally was.

A headline schedule should be used for approximately six months or a little longer, then be subjected to a final assay. At this time all those heads which have received only marginal use should be eliminated. If a real need has been shown for a head not on the schedule, that addition should be made. Only now should the head schedule be committed to final printed form. The sked should be an appendix to the typographic style manual and should also be printed on a single sheet of cardboard for use on the desk and in the comp room.

Form and content are equally important in the functionalism of headlines. The typographer must establish good headline forms, insist that the desk write only heads good in content, and then use them properly on the page.

chapter 6

Pictures

PHOTOJOURNALISM suffers from the too-many-cooks syndrome. Some newspapers do not even have a picture editor, and many of those that do fail to give him enough authority. As a result, too many unqualified and uninterested people are involved in the editorial handling of pictures, and standards are depressed because no one has the overall responsibility or power to maintain quality.

The picture editor must work in close cooperation with all editorial departments so that words and pictures can be combined in the most effective communications possible. But when a final decision is required, the picture editor should make it, subject only to appeal to the managing editor. All assignments for cameramen should funnel through the picture editor. The chief photographer should be responsible for equipment and housekeeping.

The typographer must be involved in establishing the basic newspaper philosophy on photography long before a shutter is clicked or a cameraman even leaves the office on assignment. His responsibility is nonverbal communication, and that's what pictures are supposed to be. In too many cases, though, the communicative function seems forgotten or deliberately ignored.

Good photojournalism actually begins with the editor, not the cameramen. Editors must know good pictures; they must use only good pictures and use them properly. They must reward good photography and penalize poor. They must establish sound ground rules under which the photo staff must operate.

The editor must recognize that clichés are as profuse and as deadly in nonverbal communication as in written copy. They may be edited out after verbal copy is written, but they must be eliminated before they are committed to film.

The list of photographic clichés seems endless: *The Handshaker, The Check-Passer, The Ribbon-Cutter, The Pointer, The Smiler-with-Approval* are all familiar, if not welcome, passers-by on the picture desk. Then there are the classical subjects, *Three Men and a Piece of Paper* and *Execution at Dawn,* where the subjects are lined up in petrified rigidity against a wall and snapped without mercy.

Every editor—and most readers—can expand this basic list with his own pet peeves. It is not the function of this book to tell how to avoid such clichés; there are many excellent volumes directed to this topic. But because the editor is responsible for the quality of photography, this book must exhort him to make a list of proscribed clichés and then to enforce it rigidly.

The editor must establish the rule that no more than five people may be in a picture. If this can be cut to four or even three, results will be still better. If there are more than five people, no one—including people in the picture—will take the trouble to read the picture and its cutlines. There will, of course, be rare instances when we want or need more people. A crowd shot of the audience at an athletic contest may have great appeal. An event of resounding importance might bring many of the famous onto one film; the inauguration of a president or governor comes to mind at once. But such events are infrequent.

The editor must enforce the ceiling of five in a picture. This is the cameraman's only hope for survival. When a dozen size-48 dowagers of the Daughters of the War of Jenkin's Ear insist on posing in their bosomy majesty, the cameraman must be able to blame a distant editor for depriving the public of this photographic gem.

The editor must also be specific about the time the cameraman waits for late arrivals for posed shots. The word quickly gets around a community that the *Daily News* cameraman won't wait more than ten minutes; this has a salutary effect on the chronically tardy. Without such a consistent policy, a photographer can waste hours every day.

The cameraman should be encouraged to break out of the common 3 x 5 proportion of news pictures. There is nothing wrong with the 3 x 5 ratio; in fact, it is based on the *golden rectangle* of the ancient Greeks, who delighted in reducing artistic ideals to mathematics. They determined that the ideal area was in the ratio of 1 to the square root of 2. For practical purposes, this is 3 x 5. Photo paper and film—indeed, all commonly used paper—is sized pretty close to this ideal.

Why take pictures like these?

Sports is where the <u>action</u> is. Yet we continue to shoot athletes in the most posed, artificial, hoked-up situations imaginable.

"Can't you hear my heart beat?"

Shortest player on the team gets a "lift" so he can read his big birthday card!

It's a bird. It's a plane . . . It's Picture Day!

Dick, Roy, and Rob play ball. See the ball?

See another kind of ball?

Draft choice "awaits" his fateful phone call!

<u>These</u> pictures tell a story:

A batter gets a ball on the inside.

Not what you'd call ideal football weather.

Fig. 34. *Photo-Letter,* published by Associated Press Managing Editors newsphoto committee, berates photographic clichés, especially in sports coverage.

A good cameraman likes to use up all his negative area; this makes sure that he has the maximum-sized image on his film. Thus it is not surprising that most pictures that hit the editor's desk are in the general shape of standard film and paper. Rewards—ranging from bylines to money—should be given to the photographer who breaks the golden rectangle. Any good picture that is 1-column × 6 inches, vertically or horizontally, ought to be rewarded. (Lew Alcindor and the Mackinac Bridge come to mind instantly.) The value of these tall and skinny or wide and shallow pictures to good page layout cannot be overemphasized.

The cameraman should be encouraged to provide adequate variety for the desk in color—tonal value, lines of force, point of view, length of range, and proportion or area.

A former student of mine, who has done memorable photographic coverage of the Vietnamese war, writes that even under the pressures of combat photography, he always tries to make sure that he has pictures with right and left movement, in vertical and horizontal composition, and in long, medium, and closeup range of every subject. Obviously this variety can't be achieved every time, but the cost of film is the smallest item on the photography budget and the insurance shots spare the editor the difficulty of having all pictures for a page or a layout facing in the same direction.

The photo staff ought to know the kind of print that the engraving— or platemaking—department prefers. There is little unanimity in these specifications. Some engravers abhor dull-finish prints; others are equally adamant against glossies. Some like to *shoot down* considerably, make the plate much smaller than the photo; others are happy with same-size copy. But whatever his standards, the platemaker is responsible for the quality of the printed image, and the staff should give him what he wants.

The editor should learn to read negatives, if only to make preliminary photo selections. If he can spare the darkroom the necessity of making contacts on everything in the shop, he may save crucial minutes before deadline or free photographers for more rewarding work.

When the chosen photo is on the editor's desk, he must take a series of crucial steps, each covered by an ancient axiom:

"Find the picture in the photograph."

"Harness the lines of force."

"Crop ruthlessly."

"Enlarge generously."

"Frame dramatically."

"Explain engagingly."

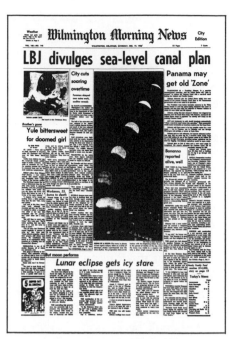

Fig. 35. Pictures far from customary 3—5 ratio add impact to page. *Wilmington* (Del.) *Morning News* has unusual multi-exposure of phases of moon's eclipse above city skyline. *Boston* (Mass.) *Globe* uses tall, narrow W-column cut on inside page. Shallow 8-column cut in *Binghamton* (N.Y.) *Press* adds interest inside.

Finding the Picture

Again we must define terms. A photograph is a chemical record of reflected light. Its quality depends on proper lighting, focus, and exposure. We can make a perfect "photograph" of a small area of a linen handkerchief, but it surely wouldn't add anything to a front page!

A *picture* is a communication. Its quality is determined by how well it communicates and how much emotional response it generates.

A good picture may be a poor photograph. At least one Pulitzer Prize was awarded to an atrocious "photograph" because the communication it conveyed as a "picture" was so powerful. It showed a woman jumping to her death from a burning Atlanta hotel where scores of other people died. Taken by a passing amateur with a box camera, the picture was blurred, grainy, and muddy, but it told a story and gripped the reader's viscera. But the Pulitzer has also gone to many superb pictures that were also excellent photographs. A good example is a picture of an East Berlin policeman jumping across a barbed wire barrier to the West and freedom. The drama was intense; the photographic quality impeccable.

We should always seek a combination of high pictorial and photographic quality, but the decisive factor in choice must always be communication.

Lines of Force

In selecting the pictures to be used in a newspaper, the editor must find the *lines of force* in a picture and harness them to build readership.

Display elements on a newspaper page may be likened to magnets that draw the reading eye. The eye is also influenced by what might be compared to wind streams, a more subtle—but also strong—influence. These are the lines of force in a picture. Lines of force are created by motion, real and implied, and by arrows that are formed, obviously or unobtrusively, by elements within a photograph.

The most obvious line of force is that created by a swiftly moving object. A thoroughbred racing to the Derby finish line carries along the reading eye as well as its jockey. The swifter the motion, the stronger the line of force. But even an object at rest creates force if it has an obvious front end. A locomotive standing at a station will sweep the eye toward the direction in which the cowcatcher is pointing. Even an automobile that has smacked against a telephone pole will force the eye in the direction of its former travel.

Strong lines of force are established by the direction in which the subject is looking in a photo. A profile of a person creates a maximum push. But even a head-on portrait can direct the reader sideways if the eyes are turned in that direction.

All arrow shapes in a picture strongly influence the reading eye. The most obvious is a pointing person. The reader's eye will follow the direction of that peremptory finger in a photo as readily as in the flesh. The parts of the human body constantly form arrows, less obvious but just as compelling. When hands are placed on hips, each elbow is an arrow. A shoulder or the head itself can be a pointer. Clothing or draping thereof makes strong arrows. The V of a man's jacket or the decolletage of a dress sweep the eye downward. Folds of clothing at the elbow, waist, or knee are effective arrowheads. Note how artists who do fashion advertising drawings emphasize the effect by stressing certain folds and eliminating others.

The eye is so susceptible to lines of force that it will create arrows where none actually appears in a picture. When two lines in a picture may meet somewhere outside the margin of the picture, the eye will extend those lines until they meet in a V and then obey the directions of that newly formed arrow.

Even a single strong line will carry the eye along to some extent. If there is anything vaguely resembling an arrowhead on it, that points the direction of the line of force. If the line has no head or foot, it will direct the eye to the right or downward. Actually such a line doesn't direct the eye; it merely adds momentum to the reading diagonal on which the eye is already moving.

Lines of force should always direct the reader into close and appropriate body type. But they can also lure the reading eye away from the area where we want it to stay. Usually the eye will return to its proper route, but the detour has been a waste of energy, time, and attention. If the picture faces into the page, the eye will more readily return on course, apparently by bouncing back off adjacent type. When a picture at the edge of a page faces off the page, the detour is longer and thus more debilitating to readers.

The ancient axiom "Pictures should face into the page" remains valid.

Cropping

We edit pictures, to a large degree, the way we edit written copy—by blue-penciling the extraneous.

When we have found the picture in the photograph, we crop out everything that isn't part of the picture, that doesn't communicate. Eliminating the nonessential assures us that the reader's time, attention, and energy won't be distracted by the useless or confusing.

The axiom "Crop ruthlessly" is explained by another: "Slash, don't slice!"

The mark of the professional—be he quarterback, Broadway actor, or picture editor—is that whatever he does, he does it so definitely that the audience knows he's doing it on purpose. It makes the spectator, listener, or reader uncomfortable if the performer is tentative. We expect the beginning duffer to baby up on a putt; we expect Jack Nicklaus to go boldly for the cup even though he is far away on a rolling green.

So if we have to cut into a photograph, we should avoid slicing a thin layer off the back of a head, the tip of an elbow, or an inch or two of the end of an auto. If we do that, the reader will get the uncomfortable impression that "somebody slipped up here."

In cropping a human subject, we must remember another axiom: "Don't amputate." If we crop at any joint of the body—finger, wrist, elbow, shoulder, or the equivalent of the leg—the reader is discomforted. If we want to show only a human head, we should never crop at the Adam's apple. We may cut immediately under the chin. But if we show any of the neck, we must show a small strip of shoulder as a base for the pedestal.

Although we should crop ruthlessly, we must remember that "negative"—blank—space is an essential for good pictures. If we have a picture of a sprinter, we must leave a little blank space for him to "run into." If we crop too close to the speeding figure, the reader will wince at the imminent collision between the runner and the edge of the picture. Large areas of gray sky are almost automatically eliminated by the cropper's blade. But these blank—void or negative—areas may contribute communication. Example C demonstrates how emotional flavor is controlled by cropping. Picture *a* is not particularly exciting or informative; the horizon bisects the photograph exactly, and the buildings are at the precise horizontal center. Breaking space into obvious divisions—halves, quarters, or thirds—creates a static composition with little appeal. In *b,* the vast sweep of the sky suggests isolation but with freedom. In *c,* the reader seems closer to the buildings, though they are the same size as in *b,* because he is "on the ground" already; isolation is decreased, but so is freedom. To crop picture *a* to the "essentials" of *d* would destroy pertinent communication.

Portraits should be cropped so that there is comfortable room at the top and sides. Usually the most pleasant effect is when the nostrils are at the center of the area or slightly above. The space at the sides of the head should be about twice as wide as that above the head. If there is an unusually large space in front of the subject, the psychological effect is one of hope and inspiration; if extra space is behind the figure, the mood is of ostracism, of hopelessness and despair. Such cropping, shown in Example C-d, is rare in news pictures. In feature shots, though, it can be a valuable tool to communication.

If the persons in a picture are adult and are shown full length, the editor should consider cropping at the bottom of the rib cage. With males, the portion that winds up in the wastebasket is that which most middle-aged subjects would prefer not to have called to public attention. If the subjects are women, we lose none of the interesting topography which we associate with that pleasant sex.

Of course, this line of demarcation does not carry the weight of legislation. I recall with profound admiration an editor in Illinois whose community had contributed Miss Something to one of the major beauty

a   b   c

contests. The staff photographer had made a beautiful picture of a beautiful girl wearing a minimal bikini, plus a bouquet of roses and a ribbon bearing her title.

"Fine," said Mr. Editor. "We'll crop it at the rib cage and run it on page one." That is exactly what he did, despite the pleading and argument of the staff, which was convinced that the boss had become *non compos mentis*. But he also added "Continued on page 7" and ran the rest of the picture there. This was one time when there was no loss in readership when a front-page item was continued inside.

The good cameraman does a lot—but not all—of the cropping with his camera. He excludes much extraneous material by moving close to his subject. This gives the largest possible image on the negative. He also crops on the enlarger, using only the pertinent portion of the film and again placing the largest possible image on the photo paper.

But the photographer should leave some room for the editor to crop.

d

e

f

Example C. Effect of cropping on mood of pictures: *a,* static; *b,* free, distant; *c,* earthbound, near.

Negative area around human face creates mood of: *d,* hope, freedom; *e,* depression, imprisonment; *f,* isolation. Photos by Jon Sagester, Ph1, U.S. Navy.

Fig. 36. Dramatic cropping in *Chicago* (Ill.) *Daily News* shows only half of model's face lifesize.

If the image is too tight in the glossy, the editor can't exercise his judgment.

If the newspaper uses a *mechanical engraver—Photo-Lathe, Elgramma,* and early models of the *Scan-A-Graver*—or is committed to same-size platemaker's copy, the photographer must, of course, do all the cropping on the enlarger. In that case the editor will indicate on the negative or contact prints where he wants the darkroom to crop the film.

When picture subjects are seated, it is almost automatic that they should be cropped somewhere around the waist. Nothing looks as ugly as

THE NATIONAL OBSERVER

Vol. 7, No. 46 © 1968 Dow Jones & Company, Inc. All Rights Reserved MONDAY, NOVEMBER 11, 1968 A National Weekly Newspaper Price 25 Cents

By Mark R. Arnold

'New York Is Fun, Exciting . . . and a Mess'

After Three Years of The Lindsay Style the City Is Closer to Chaos

A New Kind of Republican

Mr. Nixon Charts an 'Activist' Course

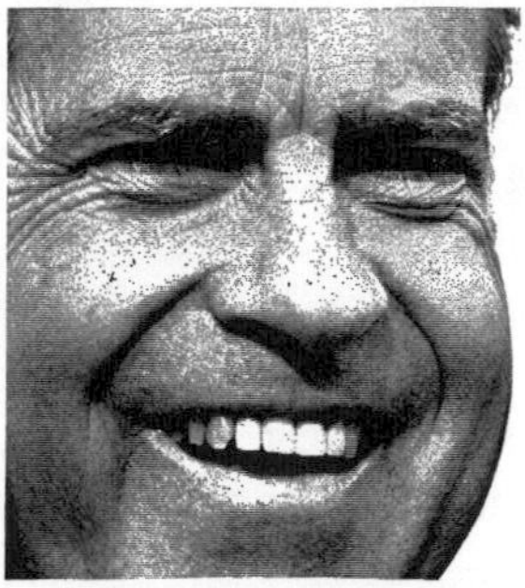

On The Inside

• Four Blocks of Frustration

• Election Box Score

• Distilling the News

After Patrolman's Death, His Record Becomes a Hit

Democrats Find Some Solace In Nearly Winning

Close Brush With Victory Reveals a Party Worth The Gathering Struggle

Fig. 37. Tight cropping enables *National Observer* to show President Richard M. Nixon's face lifesize. Engraving is in parallel-line screen.

a picture of a group seated at a table on a stage during a panel or public hearing. Awkward ankles and legs add nothing to the picture except confusion and ugliness.

The space between heads in a picture is almost always wasted. Unless the cameraman poses his subjects closely, a major portion of an engraving—and the paper on which it is printed—may be wasted. Subjects will not naturally stand close enough together to avoid such waste; the cameraman must overlap their shoulders.

Space between heads of seated and standing subjects is also wasted. By raising the seats or having the shorter people stand in back, the distance is minimized.

It is possible to tighten a photographic composition by actually cutting out figures in the photograph and pasting them together more closely. Cutting should be done along conspicuous lines in the picture, but it is not always necessary to cut along the outline of a figure. It and the whole background can be moved to a new position in many cases. After the picture has been cut, a soft lead or a grease pencil in black or red should be rubbed on the edge to prevent it from being glaringly conspicuous after the pasting-down. The engraving process softens detail, and such manipulation is rarely obvious to the reader.

As in all cropping and retouching, the editor must make sure that the essential honesty of the photo is not destroyed. In a routine picture, it doesn't alter the essence of fact if two people are moved closer in the photograph in order to achieve a tighter composition. But sometimes two bitter opponents are forced together by circumstances and go through the formality of shaking hands or posing. They may do so with icy politeness and at an exaggerated distance. To move them together by cutting and pasting is, of course, a falsehood as reprehensible as any other deliberate lie.

Another darkroom manipulation is *flopping the negative* on the enlarger or *not flopping* it in the platemaking process. This is erroneously called "reversing the print" because it reverses the direction of lines of force in a picture. Actually, in graphic arts terminology "reversing" applies only to the reversal of tonal values; a *reverse print* is one in which a white image appears on a black background instead of vice versa.

Flopping the negative should not be done except under the most pressing exigency. In most pictures there are signs of "right-handedness." If there is any lettering in the picture, it will appear in mirror form in a flopped print. Coats will button the wrong way; hair will be parted at an unaccustomed side of the head; pocket handkerchiefs or lapel pins will be switched. But even if there are no such obvious indicators, the marked difference between the right and left sides of the human face will create a feeling of incongruity that discomforts the reader. This will be greatest if the subject is familiar to the viewer, but it exists even if the subject is a total stranger.

Mortises

An interesting form of cropping is *mortising*—cutting out a portion of a halftone. The simplest mortise is the *notch,* where a corner of the rectangle of halftone is removed. Into the notch we may place type or head and/or body type. We may also place another halftone. If this inset cut is also notched, we have an *interlocking mortise.* This technique is too fussy for a newspaper. If the notch is a slight one, the effect is even more arts-and-craftsy and should be avoided.

An *internal mortise* is one cut into the middle of a halftone. A variation is the *bay mortise,* where the opening is surrounded on three sides by the halftone. These mortises may be so obtrusive that they're distracting and malfunctional. The bay mortise may distort or destroy the spatial relationship between elements at either side and thus fragment the picture into ineffective subdivisions.

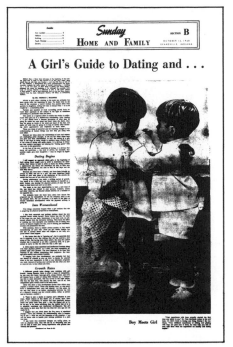

Fig. 38. Impact of large photos is demonstrated by two pages from *Evansville* (Ind.) *Sunday Courier and Press.*

A few editors insist that a mortise be tested by continuing the crop clear across the picture. If anything essential is eliminated by such cropping, they say, the mortise should not be used.

The truly valid criterion for a good mortise is our ubiquitous one of functionalism. A good mortise must give something to the picture that it would not have as a simple rectangle or delete something from the picture that would distract or confuse the reader.

A form of mortising which should be avoided with zeal is that which inserts a portrait into another halftone. This may be an actual mortise, where a separate cut is inserted into an opening of a larger one, or the inserted picture may be pasted onto the larger glossy and both made into a single engraving. In either case, the result is rarely happy. If the insert is in the same-size scale as the large picture, it will confuse the reader, for it will appear that the person was in the picture, but in some weird and unexplained position, when it was first shot. If the scale of the two pictures is drastically different, the reader will still be confused and annoyed. It is much better to use the portrait as a totally separate cut than to make an insert of it.

Perhaps the most drastic cropping is to eliminate the entire background around a figure, a *silhouette engraving*. In a *modified silhouette,* there are one or more straight sides, and the effect is that of the irregular figure emerging from a straight base or a rectangular background.

In the strictest sense of the word, it is cropping that produces engravings of any shapes other than rectangles: circles, ovals, rhomboids, etc. All these variations are commonly used only on feature or women's pages, and so their use is discussed in Chapter 12. The technique of subjecting a photo to several crops to make rectangles project in varying column widths is favored by sports editors, and use there is also covered in Chapter 12.

"Enlarge generously" is advice based on the fact that the impact of a picture increases with its size in geometric instead of arithmetic progression. A 2 x 10 picture is far more than twice as powerful as a 2 x 5. A provocative way of phrasing the axiom is: "A picture should be one column wider than you first think." This presupposes, of course, that the picture is a good one. If it isn't, it shouldn't be run at all. If a bad picture must be run for "political reasons," it should be as small as possible.

Another yardstick: "The size of a face in a picture should be that of a dime." Some editors think the dime size should be that of the human head, not just the face. Others think that a nickel should be used instead of a dime for measuring either the face or head size.

Canadian newspapers consistently use larger photos than those in the United States. Often portraits become almost life size, and they could actually be life size. If cropping is tight, a 3-column cut can show the actual size of a human face. A picture in that proportion allows the reader to feel he knows the subject almost intimately. We can see on the politician's chin the whiskers that he missed in a hasty campaign-trip shave that morning. We see how a matron's eyes crinkle in laughter. We can see the details of a doll clutched by the child hurt in a traffic accident. The larger the photo, the easier it is for the reader to put himself into the picture.

One of the memorable pictures taken during the days following the assassination of President John F. Kennedy was made from the top of the Capitol rotunda by Harry Leder, chief photographer for UPI Pictures. The old *New York Journal-American* blew it up to full-page size. In the 3-column size which many editors would have ordered, it would have been "just a picture." In its giant size, the impact was powerful.

If size is such an important factor in the usefulness of a picture, it is difficult to make a case for the half-column portrait, the porkchop. As an old picture editor, I insist that if a picture isn't worth one column, it isn't worth running at all, but many able editors disagree adamantly. They

Water-choked ravine claims Niles youth

A child's play in a flooded westside lawn ended in tragedy yesterday afternoon.

Randall S. Williams, 11, son of Mr. and Mrs. Ronald Williams, 1114 Weesaw Road, was drowned shortly after 5 p.m. when he was swept by flood-like waters into a drainage tile under Chicago Road near Sassafrass Lane.

His' body was recovered by police and firemen at 6:05 p.m. more than half-mile down the twisting, water-choked ravine, near Gettysburg Drive.

The youth was swept into the tile after the current broke the grip of a girl who was desperately holding onto him. Mary White, 14, 905 Topinabee Road, had grabbed the boy's hand when the boy began going under.

Two other companions tried to flag down passing motorists while Mary and Randy struggled in the water.

Two nearby residents, Paul Ritchie, 519 Meadow Drive and Ray McNeese, 523 Meadow Drive, formed a human chain to reach the two. But when they began to pull the force of the current tore the boy from the girl's grasp.

Firemen attempted to revive the boy when he was found and at Pawating Hospital additional efforts were made by Dr. John Strayer and Dr. John Doolittle.

Deputy Berrien County Medical Examiner Dr. John Bruni said death was caused by accidental drowning and placed time of death at 5:13 p.m.

The victim and other youngsters from the area had been wading in the water caused by the daylong rain. Normal drainage channels were overflowing throughout the city.

Sgt. Max Cole, first officer at the scene, said he believed if Ritchie and McNeese had not arrived when they did, both youngsters would have perished.

For nearly an hour police and firemen fought the current in the ditch searching for the boy's body. In places the water was over the heads of the men.

The men tied ropes around their waists and to each other in an effort to keep from being swept off their feet. At one point Sgt. Cole tripped on a submerged log and went under the water. As he struggled to regain his feet, he struck the back of his head on a second log.

In the water with Cole were Patrolmen William Mason, Gilbert Brazo, Fire Chief John Frucci and fireman Herman Exner.

Frucci was behind the three policemen holding a second line attached to them in an effort to help them brace against the current and Fireman Thomas Gunter and Fire Capt. Willard Harbaugh held a line on Exner.

City maps show the ditch or ravine starting southwest of Washington Street. It weaves between Meadow Drive and Hillcrest Road, then under M-60 Chicago Road, then southwest under Weesaw and Topinabee roads and then bends near Gettysburg Drive Next the ditch goes south where it is joined by another fork and both lead into the St. Joseph River between Laurel Drive and Topinabee Road.

The Chicago Road drain is about 50 feet long and measures 4 feet in diameter.

Run off water from the entire area feeds into the normally drv ditch.

Funeral services for Randall will be held at 10 a.m. Friday in the Pifer Funeral Home with the Rev. John Wyngarden, pastor of the First Presbyterian Church, officiating. Burial will be in Ottawa Hills Memorial Park, Toledo, Ohio.

Born in Toledo, Ohio on Sept. 3, 1956, Randall moved here with his parents from Menomnee Falls, Wis. in 1961.

Randall would have entered Ballard Junior High School this fall as a seventh grade student. He had attended the Westside elementary school.

In addition to his parents, he is survived by his grandparents, Mr. and Mrs. Frank P. Williams, of Charlotte, N.C.; two brothers, Ronald and Robert; and two sisters, Nancy Lee and Carol Lee, all at home.

A carrier for the Majerek News Agency, Randall was a member of the Boy Scout Troop, 71, of the First Presbyterian Church.

Upon family request, memorials may be made to the First Presbyertian Church Boy Scout Troop 71.

Friends may call at the funeral home after 2 p.m. Thursday.

Randall Williams

The Niles Daily Star

Vol. 83, No. 79 | 2 sections | Niles, Michigan, Wednesday, June 26, 1968 | 22 pages | 10 cents

Cloudy outlook

Heavy showers swamp area

Yesterday's downpour here and throughout Michigan and northern Indiana swamped the area with about four and a half inches of water, flooding drainge systems, streets and basements, and disrupting work and traffic.

Two deaths, one Niles youngster, were blamed on the deluge.

The weather outlook for today called for more rain. A 20 per cent chance for rain was predicted by the Weather Bureau for Thursday.

In Niles, the sewage treatment plant reported 4.49 inches of rain fell through 5 p.m. yesterday. More fell later. The downpour exceeded the 1966 June total of 3.75 inches, but was under the 4.84 record in June, 1967.

St. Joseph Airport in South Bend set an all time record rainfall for a 24-hour period with 4.70 inches during the downpour. The previous record was set August, 1966 with 3.70 inches.

The South Bend Weather Bureau said until yesterday precipitation this year was below normal but it now stands 2.90 inches above.

Because of the deluge, some roads in Niles were washed out and flooding was widespread. The waters rolled across roads, reached doorsteps and gushed into basements.

Arthur Reed, city engineer, said area creeks and ravines were full and overflowing.

S. A. "Tex" Brett, manager of the Board of Public Works, said the sewers were loaded down "pretty well" but everything went "real smooth" during the storm.

Mrs. Virginia Myers of Grathwohl Plumbing said "We had 17 calls in 13 minutes for jobs. People on Grant Street were above their knees in water," she added.

David Canavan of Tyler Refrigeration Division of Clark Equipment Co., said one shift was let off early because of an overflow of a roof drain. Canavan said the second shift did start on time, though.

Radio station WNIL reported employes needed a boat to get to their cars. Station manager James Mitchell said the water, however, drained off about 5 p.m.

Cass County roads were washed out in

Continued on Page 20.

Battle raging current

City firemen and police lash themselves together with a life line to fight the undertow during search for boy's body yesterday afternoon. At left in background is Fireman Herman Exner, in left foreground is Fire Chief John Frucci. Three policemen from left are Patrolmen Gilbert Brazo (white shirt), Bill Mason and Sgt. Max Cole. (Staff photo.)

Canadians give Trudeau clearcut mandate to rule for next 4 years

TORONTO (AP) – It was a Trudeau tidal wave, and it gave his party a clearcut mandate to rule Canada with a strength no party has enjoyed in six years.

In Tuesday's election Pierre Elliott Trudeau, who entered politics only three years ago, led his Liberals to the biggest victory any party has scored since John Diefenbaker's prime. Diefenbaker in 1958 spearheaded the Conservatives to a landslide triumph that was good for four years' control.

Trudeau became Liberal leader, and thus prime minister, by choice of a party convention two months ago when Lester B. Pearson retired. Tuesday Canadian voters had the chance to ratify or repudiate the choice. Their answer gave the Liberals the House of Commons majority they had never won under Pearson's leadership.

Trudeau on assuming the prime ministry vowed to improve his party's standing. As the leading party, even lacking a majority, the Liberals could call an election at a time they thought advantageous. Trudeau and his aides judged this a good time, and the bet paid off.

How did he do it? There is no question of Trudeau's personal appeal, evidenced in the reaction of happy throngs that greeted him on the campaign trail across the country. But as the campaign progressed he also showed himself a pragmatic and tough politician. He said the right things and made no big promises.

Though a native of Quebec, he didn't give an inch to those Quebeckers who want a special deal for that dominantly French-speaking province, or even to split off from Canada. There is one Canada, Trudeau said, and that's the way it's going to be. At the last minute, when Quebec separatists rioted in Montreal and hurled a bottle past the prime minister, he didn't flinch.

In contrast, the Conservatives, though also under new leadership, never caught popular fancy. Robert Stanfield, the Nova Scotian who replaced Diefenbaker last year, said as the returns rolled in that he had known 24 hours earlier that his party was beaten.

Stanfield is 54, only six years older than Trudeau, but to most Canadians, it appeared, his and the Tories' ideas were old-hat or at least not good enough.

The election was for 264 seats, with each citizen voting only for a legislator in his own district. Thus Trudeau's name was on the ballot only in a Montreal district, but voters nationwide knew whom they were supporting when they voted Liberal.

Tabulations today showed the Liberals were sure of 153 seats. The Conservatives had 70 and were leading in two contests. The New Democratic party took 23, the Creditistes of Quebec 15, and an independent 1.

The Social Credit party was eliminated from Parliament. It had four members after the 1965 election.

The Conservatives showed strength in the Atlantic provinces, winning 25 seats to the Liberals' 7. That trend was easily overcome in more populous provinces.

The Liberals led 55-4 in Quebec and 65-16 in Ontario. They picked up more than a dozen seats in the Prairie provinces and British Columbia.

Tragedy scene

Bystanders wait anxiously for word on the fate of 11-year-old Randall Williams who was carried through the Chicago Road storm drain tile to his death. Rescue workers searched almost an hour before recovering the body a half-mile down the flooded ravine. Mrs. John Frucci (in raincoat) watches while her husband, Fire Chief John Frucci directs rescue efforts downstream. (Staff photo.)

Saigon bound

Reds moving in fresh troops

SAIGON (AP) – U.S. sources said today two freshly equipped North Vietnamese regiments– possibly 5,800 men–are believed headed toward Saigon to join the enemy force threatening another attack on the South Vietnamese capital.

U.S. intelligence officers said the 32nd and 33rd North Vietnamese regiments were in Phuoc Long Province five days ago, 74 miles north of Saigon and 165 miles southwest of their previous headquarters.

The two regiments have been inactive for a year while refitting. They include veteran troops who fought in the 1965 Ia Drang Valley campaign, one of the bloodiest of the war.

The two regiments are normally headquartered along the Cambodian border just west of Pleiku in the central highlands. Apparently they moved down through Cambodia and crossed the border into Phuc Long. U.S. B52 bombers have been attacking their suspected positions in efforts to break up their troop concentrations and blunt their advance toward Saigon.

The eight-engine bombers flew eight missions Tuesday and Wednesday against enemy base camps and river loading points in Binh Long, Binh Duong and Tay Ninh provinces, west and south of Phuoc Long. These are considered the enemy's main infiltration corridors from Cambodia to Saigon.

The river points, 15 to 20 miles from the Cambodian border, are where rockets destined for use against Saigon are loaded on sampans after shipment down from North Vietnam through Laos and Cambodia.

Prisoner interrogations and captured documents have indicated the enemy plans for a third offensive on Saigon, expected to be as big as the second offensive May 5, when about 10,000 soldiers were sent against the city.

Allied troops have formed a ring of patrols around Saigon, but ground fighting has been in a lull for about two weeks.

Light rain

Cloudy and cooler today with light rain or drizzle at times. High in the mid 60s. Tonight will be mostly cloudy and cooler with a chance of showers. Low in the 50s. Thursday will be partly sunny and continued cool. High 65 to 70. Friday's outlook: Increasing cloudiness and warmer. (Complete forecast and temperatures on page 20.)

Fig. 39. Large photos add impact to top local story in *Niles* (Mich.) *Daily Star,* in op format.

insist that the porkchop is a useful device for breaking up masses of body type and that these small pictures can be used where the normal 1-column cut wouldn't work out.

Thus the porkchop is a typographic color element. When it is of the writer of a story or column, the picture also assures the reader that his newspaper is produced by human beings, not computers. Each of these is a legitimate function, and every editor must decide for himself whether this is the best way of performing that function.

A major liability in the use of the porkchop is the short lines of body type adjacent to the cut. Usually only 5½ or 6 picas long, they are dangerously under the minimum of the readability range and also are very difficult to set.

The solution is to leave blank the space alongside the little engraving. This gives several immediate benefits. The compositor is saved the trouble of a miserable typesetting job; the reader is spared an equally onerous chore. The white area focuses more attention onto the engraving, and thus its impact is increased. The "loss" of space is slight; usually there are no more than a couple of dozen words in the area alongside the porkchop.

The picture should be placed so it looks toward the inside of the column of type into which it is set. If the pose is head-on, the picture should go on the side of the column nearest the outside margin of the page. The porkchop should always be at the side of the column; to center it creates a tentative, rather unpleasant effect. In the blank area next to the picture, its identification may run, in one line or more. Most editors prefer to center the indent in the open area.

If the porkchop is that of the writer of a story or column, it is most effective in the headline area. If the author's name is used as a kicker, the porkchop may be placed under the kicker, at the left of the main head. The effect is pleasant.

The "regular" 1-column cut used to be 2 x 3 inches. Today there is a tendency to make the shape closer to a square. But the nearer a picture gets to a square, the more static and tepid it becomes. Cropping must be uncomfortably tight; the head looks like a shrunken one, gift-boxed by witch doctors. If a strip of shoulders is included and there is a little room at the sides and top, the face becomes too small to be truly effective.

A 1-column cut is a display element important in the creation of a pleasant page pattern. But it must also communicate.

What can a 1-column portrait communicate to the reader? That Joe Jones has the customary number and assortment of eyes, ears, lips, and

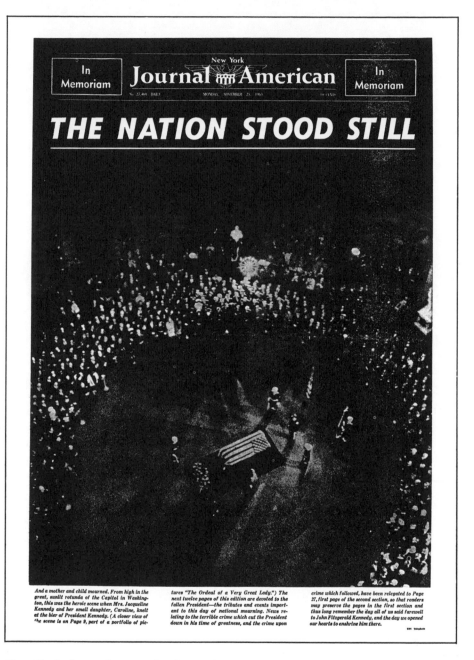

Fig. 40. Striking photograph of President John F. Kennedy's bier makes full-page cut in *New York Journal-American*.

THE DALLAS TIMES HERALD

CONTINUOUSLY PUBLISHED FOR 87 YEARS   THE TIMES 1876   THE HERALD 1886   CONSOLIDATED 1888

FINAL
EDITION

87th Year—No. 295 · · · ★   DALLAS, TEXAS, MONDAY EVENING, NOVEMBER 25, 1963   Telephones—   3 Parts Price Five Cents

Mourning Nation Bids Chief Farewell

Tip to FBI Warned of Oswald Death

Copyright, 1963, The Dallas Times Herald—Staff Photo by Bob Jackson

The President's accused killer as executioner's bullet pierces body.

Anonymous Call Forecast Slaying During Transfer

Nation Buries Its Chief

Fig. 41. One of most famous of American news pictures is displayed in half page of *Dallas* (Tex.) *Times Herald*.

Fig. 42. Treatment of half-column cuts: *a*, insetting requires adjacent lines of type at too-short measure; *b*, centered, and *c*, paired, avoid runaround setting; *d*, *e*, and *f* place cuts flush and use variety of identifications; *g*, name of column combines with cut and ident to create form of logo; *h*, fragment of 2-column heading.

noses is hardly edifying. We prefer to know what Mr. Jones *is* like rather than what he *looks* like. An interesting technique is that used by *Time* and *Newsweek*. On their cover portraits the background, by implication, tells much of the habitat, habits, and humanity of the cover subject. If we adopted the same style for 1-column newspaper cuts, we would certainly lose some detail of the subject's appearance. But we would, just as certainly, gain in learning what kind of man he is or at least what his line of work might be.

The sports departments of the *Detroit News* and the *Toronto Star* have a practice that any desk might well emulate. Whenever a sports action picture has a recognizable face—whether the photo is used in its original form or not—that face is cropped out and filed for future use in making a 1-column engraving. So the sports pages are spared the plague of wooden mug shots which drag the pace of these pages down to the pedestrian.

Often portraits isolated out of news action pictures may seem to leave much to be desired. Facial features may be obscured by the deep shadows cast by a baseball cap or by the mask of the football player. A driving shoulder or a swinging arm may hide part of the face. Yet the reader identifies people in the public eye—especially athletic idols—not by the sum of facial characteristics, but by the overall impression they

Valley Women Push for Culture on Home Front

Mrs. Edmund P. Goodwin has been the one woman who has contributed most to the Fine Arts Center. Although she did not hang the first exhibit in the library, she hung all the others for the next 12 years, in addition to all sorts of other chores. Retired now from routine hanging jobs, she has charge of the special exhibitions put on once or twice a year. This means she not only supervises the mounting of the exhibits, she also collects and researches the objects put on display.

Mrs. Goodwin's talents in other lines were used earlier in the Junior League of Roanoke, another feminine power in the area's cultural picture and joint purchaser of "Cherry Hill."

It was back in the early 1930s that the Junior League put on its first Children's Theater in the old Academy of Music. Mrs. Goodwin was to be found then nailing and painting scenery for the plays, a job she handled almost single-handedly for some years.

League members took the parts in the plays as well as staging and promoting them in the first years. Recently the entire enterprise has been taken over by a corporation which runs workshops in creative dramatics for children, stages a play with child actors and brings outside attractions spectacular for young audiences.

It was the Junior League which underwrote the Roanoke Youth Symphony until two years ago. And it was a woman who masterminded the venture.

Mrs. Whitwell W. Coxe, pianist and teacher, heard a young people's symphonic group elsewhere and could not rest until she had seen one established here. The 50-member orchestra is 10 years old and not only plays concerts for school children in Roanoke Valley, but also tours to small communities in Southwest Virginia.

Without the women of the Thursday Morning Music Club the city would have missed a great deal of the world's best in music.

Founded in 1908 by Mrs. George Gravatt, the club brought artists to Roanoke for a concert series early in its history. In 1947, after a lapse of 15 years, the group again started a series of musical importations which is still operating and is a vital part of the musical life of this part of Virginia.

Women play a supportive role in the affairs of the Mill Mountain Playhouse.

They sit on the board of directors, sell tickets and generally take care of the behind-the-scenes necessities.

It was a power-behind-the-throne part for women in the realization of the dream of a civic center for Roanoke. However, they will undoubtedly be heard from when the buildings are ready. Like the advertisement says, "Never underestimate the power of a woman."

When it's a cultural matter, the women are willing to flex their muscles.

Mrs. Harry Dixon Has a Maternal Stake in the Roanoke Symphony Orchestra

Fine Arts Center's 'Cherry Hill' Is Proper Setting for Mrs. E. P. Goodwin

Fig. 43. Connotative backgrounds add interest to portraits. When subject cannot be photographed in such setting, studio portrait may be cut out and pasted on appropriate background as here. From *Roanoke (Va.) Times.*

make while they are in action. An action shot, then, can identify a person better than a more explicit static pose.

Framing

Framing a picture in a newspaper page is as important as framing one in your living room. We have a wide variety of materials for frames on a wall; for frames in a newspaper page, the material is basically plain white space.

A few editors still enclose a halftone with a typographic box. This is not functional. If the box is thin, it blends into the photo and does no good. If the border is heavy, it fights the halftone.

The practice of putting a black *finishing line* around a picture as part of the engraving is almost obsolete. No matter what its other virtues or vices might be, the finishing line to the contemporary eye looks old-fashioned, even a little quaint.

Only white space can effectively frame a news picture. The effect is achieved by indenting the engravings. The increment of 1 pica per column is practical. But any generous increment may be used, for while the width of an engraving is designated in columns, the engraving department can be told to make, say, a 2-column cut at any size the editor has determined. We might prepare a chart for the engraving department like the following, based on 11-pica columns with 6-point column rules:

Chart A

ENGRAVING WIDTHS

1 column	...	10 picas
2 columns	...	20½
3 columns	...	31
4 columns	...	41½
5 columns	...	52
6 columns	...	62½
7 columns	...	74
8 columns	...	91½

(Although this discussion is in the terms of letterpress, it applies exactly to pages done by pasteup as well.)

This is based on a 1-pica-per-column frame. Notice that the 6-column engraving is indented 6 picas; so is the 7-column one. That is because the 7-column cut must run flush at one margin, which then becomes one side of the frame. We don't want to create a ragged page margin by indenting the cut there. If the page is in 9 columns, the 8-column cut would have the same indent as its 7-columner. For a tab, the 4- and 3-column cut would have the same indent.

When the engraving is run within the page, it is centered, and the indent is equal on each side. If the picture runs at the outside of a page, the engraving aligns with the outside edge of the type column. The more generous frame at the inside is balanced by the margin at the other side of the page.

The value of indenting cuts on a per-column basis is that as the picture widens, the frame widens proportionately.

Some editors prefer frames narrower than the ones produced by this method, so they establish arbitrary measures for engravings. A typical chart for an 8-column page (again using 11-pica columns and 6-point rules) would be something like this:

Chart B

ENGRAVING WIDTHS

1 column	...	10 picas
2 columns	...	20½
3 columns	...	32
4 columns	...	42½
5 columns	...	53
6 columns	...	63½
7 columns	...	76
8 columns	...	91½

Cutlines should align precisely with the sides of the engraving to tie the two elements closely together. If they don't, the lines may be indented conspicuously, at least 1 pica on each side for each column width of the engraving. Note that this indent is from the side of the engraving, not of the type column. For aligning cutlines, the following type measures could be used with various column widths of cuts:

CUTLINE MEASURES

	Chart A		Chart B	
COLUMNS	ENGRAVING WIDTH	TYPE MEASURE	ENGRAVING WIDTH	TYPE MEASURE
1	10 picas	10 picas	10 picas	10 picas
2	20½	20½	20½	20½
3	31	15 (2 legs)	32	15 (2 legs)
4	41½	20½ (2 legs)	42½	20½ (2 legs)
5	52	15 (3 legs)	53	15 (3 legs)
6	62½	15 (4 legs)	63½	20½ (3 legs)
7	74	20½ (3 legs)	76	15 (4 legs)
8	91½	20½ (4 legs)	91½	20½ (4 legs)

As these charts demonstrate, we can handle all cutlines with only three body-type settings. As with all arbitrary determinations, however, we face some situations that are not ideal. In Chart A, for instance, with a 4-column cut we will have only a 6-point alley between the legs of the cutlines. Again in Chart A, with a 6-column cut we would use only 6 points of space between legs 1 and 2 and between 3 and 4, and 1½ picas between legs 2 and 3. While this does not give us the most desirable alley width, we might make do in order to gain the advantage of standardization of cutline type widths. If this standardization does not seem very important to the editor or if he thinks that wider alleys are essential, lines for 4-column cuts could be set at 20 picas and those for 6-columners at 14.9 picas.

Alleys should be used in all cutline combinations even if alleys aren't used elsewhere in the paper. Cutlines should be short, and it's better not to have to cut tiny lengths of column rule to drop between ultrashort legs of type.

Some editors set cutlines for pictures of all widths in normal 1-column measure and use conventional column rules. This is standardization with a vengeance, for the effect is unpleasant. The eye bounces up and down on these short columns like a child on a pogo stick.

When alleys are used instead of column rules throughout the page or paper, they act as frames, too. Editors who have experimented with indenting pictures in the open format have almost unanimously decided that the effect is not pleasant or necessary.

Whether framing is created by alleys or by indenting cuts, the frame should continue all around the picture. There should be a minimum of a full pica of white above an indented cut. In an open format with 1-pica alleys, there should be 18 points of space above the picture.

When the catchline is used, it should be considered as the brass title plate affixed to the bottom of a wooden frame. The space occupied by the catchline slug is considered part of the bottom framing, and it is necessary to drop only 6 points of space between the engraving and the catchline.

The same amount of space, 6 points, is used when the cutline style doesn't use a catchline. This is not adequate to continue the framing effect, but if we use much more space there, there is a danger of splitting the cutlines away from their picture. So we choose the lesser of two evils, the lesser space.

A greatly exaggerated frame—the equivalent of the indent of a whole column or even more—will put unusual attention on a picture. A 1-column cut centered in a 2-column space, for instance, will have much, much more impact than a normal 2-columner does. This technique should not be used very often, but if you save it for a truly momentous situation, it is a formidable weapon to have in your arsenal.

Cutlines

Now that the picture is framed dramatically, we must explain it engagingly.

All pictures are more useful and more pleasant to the reader when they are accompanied by some verbal copy. In the simplest comparison, you might note your own reaction in a picture gallery. Those paintings that have a title—even though it makes no apparent sense—are more enjoyable than those without.

In newspaper use the type accompanying a picture is called the *cutlines,* or *lines,* always in the plural form. In magazines we usually refer to this copy as a *caption.*

There are four kinds of cutlines. The most common are just plain old "cutlines." When the text is unusually long, including material which would normally be carried in an accompanying story, it is referred to as the *comprehensives, comprees,* or *comps.* If just the name of a person runs with a cut, it is called, not surprisingly, the *identification,* or the *ident, line.* A second line that expands upon the ident is called the *expository,* or *expo, line.*

Just as the newspaper designer is concerned with the content of a

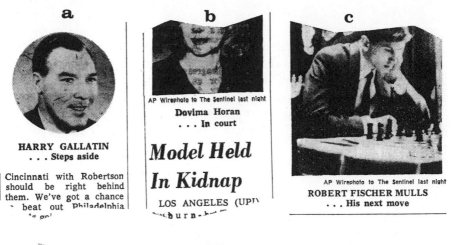

Fig. 44. Treatment of identification and ident-and-expo lines: *a*, conventional treatment with unconventional circular cut; *b*, ident in u&lc; *c*, in-reading from ident to expo; *d*, ident-and-expo in larger type for multicolumn cut.

picture as well as its form, so he should concern himself with the content and literary style of cutlines as well as their typographic form.

The writing of good cutlines is a fine art which is probably practiced at its peak on the picture desk of the *New York Daily News.* Any issue of that paper is a good textbook on line-writing.

Cutlines should say: (1) This is the reason why this picture was taken—and printed; (2) these are the people in the picture; and (3) here is something interesting which you might not notice or understand if we didn't call your attention to it. That's all!

If cutlines say any more than these two or three things, they may well be malfunctional. When the reader has consumed too-lengthy cutlines and goes to the accompanying story, he finds the leed is but a paraphrase of the lines. He may then decide there's not much point in rereading that information and may thus be turned away from the story.

Pictures are read as blocks of type are, from top to bottom. Experiments by *Look* magazine and others have shown us that the reader "looks" at a picture in a sweeping loop. The eye enters the picture just below the top left corner. In a counterclockwise motion it describes a circle, then continues in a spiral to exit the photo near the lower right corner. But when it "reads" the picture, instead of looking at it, especially when it must match faces and names, the reading eye follows its old top-to-bottom path. So the "first row" is the top row. Too many cutline writers confuse the reader by identifying faces in the bottom row first and working their way, in reverse gear, to what they call the "back row."

Functional cutlines start the identification process where the reader wants to, at the top left corner. Because of confusion which has been perpetrated, this row should be referred to as the "top row"; that can't be mistaken. The next row is the "second" or "middle," if that's the case. The last is the "bottom row." Within rows, identification is always left to right. This progression should be followed in all instances, even if the Grand Patron of the Loyal Order of Muskrats and his trusty lieutenants are comfortably ensconced in the center of the "bottom row."

If all persons in a picture need not be identified, we may use the same devices in cutlines as we would in describing the picture orally. We might identify a president as "waving hat" or a governor "at rostrum" or a halfback as "leaping for ball." We might use distinctive clothing to identify an ecclesiastical dignitary "in white robe" or a senator as "wearing fur cap." Other people in the picture may then be identified as left or right of the primary figure. It is best to designate a person as "left of the mayor" rather than "at mayor's left." In the latter case the reader must take the trouble to determine that the mayor's left is opposite the reader's left.

When several or many people must be identified but are not arranged in recognizable rows, two methods may be used. A number may be placed on each figure, and cutlines will identify persons by that number. We must strike a fine line here. If the number is not too obtrusive, it may be difficult to notice; if the number is large enough to be easily noticed, it may mar the photo.

A favorite method in book and magazine typography is the *keyline drawing*. The photo is run in its normal form. Near it is a simple line drawing of only the significant shapes; within these are numbers which the cutlines then identify. It is easy to do the keyline drawing by placing tracing paper over the photo. A red grease pencil or a Speedball pen, with a B (for "ball") point, is used for the tracing. Note that this is a drawing pen, not the conventional "ballpoint" that has replaced the pocket fountain pen.

Sometimes a figure in a photograph is pointed out by an arrow or a circle. This technique, which must be used with Spartan restraint, is *marker art,* discussed later in this chapter.

The style of cutlines—typographic and literary—must be consistent. Literary style will follow that of any news copy plus a few points unique to this particular form.

Cutlines should be paragraphed as all copy is, with eight lines the preferred maximum per graf. If identification is by row, each row should begin a new paragraph.

The editor must establish style for recurring phrases such as "left to right." Accepted forms are: *left to right, l to r, L to R, L–R, from left.* Personal preference determines which form to use.

My preference is the following:

> Mayor John H. Jones (in plaid jacket) accepts gift of an Andean wildcat from Justin De Morales, Peruvian consul.
>
> Present for the ceremonies in Council chambers this morning are: Top row (from left): John Doe, Richard Roe, Thomas Thumb, etc.;
>   Middle row: John Q. Publick, John Bull, Samuel Spade, Jackson V. Gleason, etc.;
>   Front row: Robert Roberts, Edmond Edmonds, etc.

Note that the identifications read out of a sentence with an action verb and that the verb is in the historical present tense. In a picture, the mayor is always "accepting"; it is a continuous, present action as long as the photograph exists. The action itself was in the past, and in the news story we say that the mayor "accepted." In cutlines, however, we do not use the past tense.

The transition between the action sentence and the identifications is marked by a colon. "Rows" are capped—*Top, Middle, Bottom.* The phrase "from left"—or its equivalent—is in parentheses, and another colon precedes the list of names. The last name in a row, and so in a paragraph, is followed by a semicolon, except for the final name, which is naturally followed by a period. Each row begins with a normal paragraph indent.

This style is suggested only as an example, perhaps as a point of departure for an editor to establish his own style. Any style that is grammatically correct and that makes it easy for readers to match faces in halftones and names in cutlines is equally valid. As with any style, consistency is a major virtue. All cutlines in a paper should follow the same style; there should not be separate styles for women's or sports pages, as is—alas!—often the case.

One phrase that should be totally tabooed is "pictured here." This insults the reader. He knows that this is a picture and that, obviously, something or someone is thereby pictured. It is more complimentary, as well as entirely accurate, to say, simply, "here is. . . ."

Credit lines or bylines are part of the cutlines, and a style must be established for them. Some editors prefer to set this matter in agate type which is usually run immediately under the lower right corner of the cut, in a few instances under the left corner of the cutlines. It is a nuisance to have to handle this extra typographic element; there is always the danger that the agate will become lost before it's collated with the cutlines; the imbalance of this extra line is unpleasant to some people.

I prefer to include the credit lines with the cutlines and run them, in parentheses, immediately after the explanatory copy:

> battled the blaze in subzero weather last night. (Gazette photo by John H. Gill)

Example D. Keyline drawing, right, used to identify subjects in photo above who are not in well-defined rows.

Associated Press, United Press International, or any other service might be identified the same way. The cameraman might be identified as "John H. Gill, Gazette staff cameraman," or in any other desired phrasing. With this style the credit line becomes an integral part of the cutlines. It won't get lost, and it won't be another element to add to a busy makeup.

The credit line might be set as the byline on a written story, usually centered bold caps of the body type. This can be run between the picture and the cutlines or immediately under the catchline, if that device is used. This style might be saved for a truly outstanding job of photo-journalism, keeping routine credits at the end of cutlines.

On very rare occasions, the cameraman might be credited in the cutlines proper:

> Moments after Gazette cameraman
> William J. Gleed took this picture,
> he was struck by a brick flung
> by someone in the building that

Photographers should be awarded bylines for the same reasons a writer is: to recognize good work; to build individual and collective morale; to acquaint the reader with a name, a person at the newspaper office. The reader is much more likely to call in story and picture tips to this person, even if they've never met, than to the impersonal, faceless newspaper.

Credit lines given to commercial studios are harder to justify. Some newspapers use this method of compensating the studio for making the glossy portrait for publication. But this is a cost that the subject ought to pay—and probably has paid for as a hidden item in the package. Some newspapers use such a credit line but also charge the studio an advertising fee. This strikes me as an unconscionable mixing of news and advertising or disguising of advertising as news. Court precedents seem to say that the subject owns reproduction rights of a portrait he has commissioned. So a bride-elect can give a glossy to a newspaper which can reproduce it without permission of the photographer or without a credit line for him—this despite the stern admonition often rubber-stamped on the back of the glossy that the studio retains all rights including mineral.

Typographic style for cutlines seeks three objectives: It should lead the reading eye directly and pleasantly from an easy-to-read halftone into the more difficult reading of type; it should help convey verbal information easily, quickly, and clearly; and it should tie picture and lines into a single integral visual unit.

Many editors choose boldface cutlines to meet these requirements. They believe that a block of boldface more closely approximates the tonal value of the engraving, and thus the two tend to look like a single element. The preference of readers for darker body type for stories would indicate that such type is more attractive to the eye which has just finished reading a halftone and that boldface will convey information speedily. We know that boldface is not pleasant in large masses of body type, though, so this is another reason for keeping cutlines terse.

Some editors set cutlines in a size larger than regular body type. If straight matter is set in 8-point, then either light or boldface 10-point is often used for cutlines.

Some editors prefer a Sans Serifs for cutlines. The color is usually attractive and compatible with that of the engraving. The high legibility of the Sans may be an incentive for the reader to jump right into type from the picture. The visual difference between cutlines and straight matter will be so marked that the reader automatically associates the lines with the cut.

Syndicated pictures delivered in the form of stereotype matrices include cutlines. These ought to be sawed off the cast and reset. Rarely will the typeface used for the matted lines be the same as that used by the newspaper for such setting. Nor, in most instances, will the measure coincide. The stereo flat casting process increases regular distortion. It all adds up to cutlines that are conspicuously disharmonious with those set by the paper's own comp room. On smaller papers, especially, there is a temptation to save time and money by using the matted lines, but the results are so poor that it becomes a false economy.

Display Lines

The transition from picture to words is so sharp that most editors apply a little typographic lubrication. The simplest is *read-through cutlines*. These begin—without a paragraph indent—with a word or phrase in caps. It may be a self-contained phrase:

> ROTARY PRESIDENT. John H. Stevens receives the gavel of the Midtown Rotary club as he assumed office today at a meeting

It may be the opening phrase of the cutlines:

> WINNING TOUCHDOWN is scored by Tommy Kranto as he hurdles from the 2-yard line in the Cougar-Viking game in Milwaukee

While the read-through is better than nothing, it's not much better. We need a more effective transition between picture and words and a more potent lure to draw the eye into the lines. The most effective is the *catchline*, a line of display type between the picture and the cutlines.

Catchlines, in content, follow their name; they're catchy. They should be connotative or provocative but never definitive; they should not be "little headlines." WILSON ELECTED BY KIWANIS is an adequate headline; as a catchline it's blah. On such a picture, in an Iowa newspaper, the catchline was CHAIR MAN BECOMES CHAIRMAN. Brother Wilson, in this case, was president of a chair-manufacturing company. (Let's note that catchline examples are given in all-caps merely to distinguish them in this text. In actual usage they follow the newspaper's capping style for headlines.)

Writers of good catchlines use alliteration. They perpetrate puns. They use familiar quotations or titles of books or plays or give them a twist to make them interestingly unfamiliar. Again, the *New York Daily News* is a daily textbook of superlative catchlines.

Catchlines may be centered or flush left. Flush left is pleasing to the eye when the credit line is a separate element riding at the right. I prefer centered catchlines whose symmetry, to my eyes, ties the picture and the lines most neatly into a single package.

A variation is the *sideline*. In content, the sideline is like the catchline, bright, breezy, and a bit irreverent. In form, it is set in one or more lines and runs under the picture at the left of the cutlines.

An obvious disadvantage of the sideline is that we may need several lines of display type instead of the single one of the catchline. We have to space around the sideline to make that area match the depth of the cutlines. An advantage of the sideline is that we can standardize on the width of cutlines. They can all be set the same measure, while the sideline becomes the variable to match different widths of pictures.

Both catchline and sideline are effective tools, and research has shown that their use can increase readership of cutlines and stories under the pictures as much as 25%. Every picture in the paper represents a considerable investment in photography and engraving, not to mention space. Any device that will produce up to 25% more dividends on an investment is worth considering.

The size of the display lines—catch or side—should vary with the width of the cut. A practical formula is: On 1-column cuts, use a 14-point catchline; on 2-columners, use an 18; on 3- and 4-columners, 24-point catchlines; on 5- and 6-columners, 36-point. On wider cuts, it

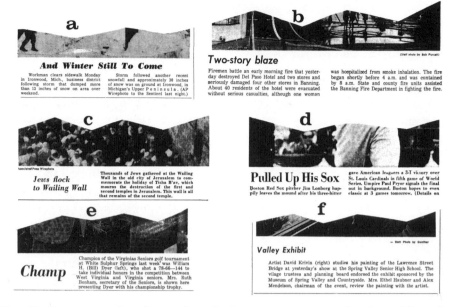

a

And Winter Still To Come

Workman clears sidewalk Monday in Ironwood, Mich., business district following storm that dumped more than 13 inches of snow on area over weekend.

Storm followed another recent snowfall and approximately 30 inches of snow was on ground at Ironwood, in Michigan's Upper Peninsula. (AP Wirephoto to the Sentinel last night.)

b

Two-story blaze

Firemen battle an early morning fire that yesterday destroyed Del Paso Hotel and two stores and seriously damaged four other stores in Banning. About 40 residents of the hotel were evacuated without serious casualties, although one woman

was hospitalized from smoke inhalation. The fire began shortly before 4 a.m. and was contained by 8 a.m. State and county fire units assisted the Banning Fire Department in fighting the fire.

(Staff photo by Bob Purcell)

c

Associated Press Wirephoto

Jews flock to Wailing Wall

Thousands of Jews gathered at the Wailing Wall in the old city of Jerusalem to commemorate the holiday of Tisha B'av, which mourns the destruction of the first and second temples in Jerusalem. This wall is all that remains of the second temple.

d

Pulled Up His Sox

Boston Red Sox pitcher Jim Lonborg happily leaves the mound after his three-hitter

gave American leaguers a 3-1 victory over St. Louis Cardinals in fifth game of World Series. Umpire Paul Pryor signals the final out in background. Boston hopes to even classic at 3 games tomorrow. (Details on

e

Champ

Champion of the Virginias Seniors golf tournament at White Sulphur Springs last week was William H. (Bill) Dyer (left), who shot a 78-66—144 to take individual honors in the competition between West Virginia and Virginia seniors. Mrs. Ruth Bonham, secretary of the Seniors, is shown here presenting Dyer with his championship trophy.

f

— Staff Photo by Gunther

Valley Exhibit

Artist David Krivin (right) studies his painting of the Lawrence Street Bridge at yesterday's show at the Spring Valley Senior High School. The village trustees and planning board endorsed the exhibit sponsored by the Museum of Spring Valley and Countryside. Mrs. Ethel Haubner and Alex Mendelson, chairman of the event, review the painting with the artist.

Fig. 45. Treatment of cutlines using display type: *a*, conventional catchline; *b*, flush-left catchline; *c*, double sideline; *d*, inset catchline; *e*, conventional sidelines; *f*, flush-left catchlines with cutlines indented at left for balance.

would depend on how the cutlines are handled whether they went clear across the picture or ran under only a portion of the cut. If a 2-, 3-, or 4-column cut were exceptionally tall, its large mass might call for a step larger display line.

Sidelines can be smaller than catchlines, for they can be written in two or more lines to gain sufficient mass to be harmonious with the engraving.

The general size of picture display lines will depend on the usual tone of voice of the newspaper. Editors who use large headlines will naturally use comparatively large catchlines.

Catchlines and sidelines may read into cutlines by the use of ellipses. These three little dots are handy devices to indicate continuity in copy even though there is a physical break in the type. A typical reading-in might be:

> ANOTHER OPENING, ANOTHER SHOW . . .
> . . . for Pit & Balcony will be at 8 tomorrow evening as the little-theater group presents "My Fair Lady" with a cast that includes two

Some editors use catchlines only with *self-contained pictures,* those with no accompanying story. When the cut does have a story, they use *read-throughs* or even no device at all. This logic is difficult to follow. If the catchline has any value, it ought to be used on all pictures. An accompanying picture should not be handicapped by depriving it of the pulling power of the catchline. If the catchline has no value, then it shouldn't be used on any picture, independent or dependent.

Well-written—that means terse—cutlines will produce only a small mass of type. This brevity may cause a problem. When cutlines are set in two or more legs, there should be at least four lines of type in each leg. Fewer lines give a skimpy effect and cause the reading eye to bounce up and down like a bicycle on a bumpy road. If there isn't enough pertinent information to provide adequate depth, we must reduce the number of legs or convert conventional cutlines into the *ident-and-expo* form, *i&e*.

Identification lines are usually set in bold caps, centered, in the normal cutline face. The expo line is set in lowercase, often beginning with an ellipsis. Thus:

JOHN H. HARRISON
. . . named superintendent of schools.

The advantage of this style is that the expo line may be removed on the stone if conditions demand; the ident will then stand independently.

Several leading women's sections are using expo lines on all portraits with engagement and wedding stories. With the former, the girl's name is the ident, that of her fiance the expo:

MISS JANET CARRUTHER
. . . engaged to Walter L. Borden III

With bridal pictures, her new, married name is the ident, her maiden name the expo:

MRS. ROBERT J. DUCLOS
. . . the former Miss Ellen Richards

Readers are enthusiastic about this technique, for it is easy to recognize a familiar name even though the picture might be of a stranger. After all, friends of a young man are greatly interested in whom he chooses as a bride, but without his name in the cutlines, they might well overlook the picture as having no personal interest.

The ident line need not be only the name of an individual, although that is its most frequent use. With a wide picture and little information to be carried, a single line of display type may be used. This, too, is an ident line:

Flames Spurt 200 Feet In The Air Above Broken Gas Main

This line was used, in 24-point, under a 7-column cut. The display-size ident line may be downstyle or, if necessary to match headline style, in u&lc.

Another useful technique is to use a catchline and a single line of a smaller display face as, in effect, the expo line. In content, this line might be the same as for a single ident line.

If the lines are comprehensives and there is much detail to present, we may wind up with too large a mass of boldface. There are two solutions. The first and most common is to restrict or abandon the use of comprees. This trend is strong. Editors recognize the pulling power of a headline. If they can justifiably handle copy as a story, with the magnet of its own head, instead of as comprehensives, readership may well increase.

Some editors set comprees as a regular news story and the catchline becomes the head. Others will set a specified number of compree lines in boldface and then continue right on in lightface to avoid the excess of bold.

Axioms: "Every picture must be identified" and "Every picture must have its own set of cutlines."

Often the person in a picture is so well known that it seems gratuitous to identify him. The news magazines often make oblique references to famous people. In the caption, *Sen. Balloo and friend,* the "friend" may be the president of the United States. But it is dangerous to assume that anyone is so well known that no readers will need to have him identified.

An interesting bit of research was done with a Midwestern paper. A 3-column head said: SAM JONES HONORED FOR 30 YEARS' SERVICE. The leed was almost identical: "Sam Jones, secretary of the Midlands town board for more than 29 years, was honored at a testimonial dinner Wednesday evening, etc." In the second column under the head ran Sam's picture, a typical 1-column cut, without any identification. In a survey, 94% of the people who remembered reading the story correctly identified the picture as that of ol' Sam. But the others identified it as that of the town chairman, whose name was in the third paragraph; as one of three town board members, who were mentioned in the second column, right under the cut; or as the minister who delivered the invocation and who was mentioned in the last graf.

With a tendency for odd camera angles and with the natural look-alikeness of people in the news, I have often found myself wondering just whose picture I was reading. No editor can take even a remote chance at misidentification; every picture must be properly identified.

Every picture should have its individual identification. Never should a single set of cutlines identify or attempt to identify two or more pictures.

Matching a photo or elements therein with words in cutlines is probably the most difficult job that we put to a reader. This job is complicated greatly when we force the reader to sort out one of a group of pictures, find that portion of the cutlines that applies to this picture, then begin matching faces and names.

A single catchline may be used for two or more pictures, but each picture should have its own cutlines, and they should run immediately under the picture. This is particularly essential for sequence pictures.

A single catchline may carry the whole sequence, or each picture may have its own display line. Each picture then should have its own cutlines. Ellipses are useful here to maintain continuity between segments of descriptive type.

A catchline might read: ONE LITTLE, TWO LITTLE, THREE LITTLE INDIANS. Cutlines might be:

> Linebacker Dave Grainger of the Michigan Indians seems to have brought Ohio's Steve Glazo to a grinding halt in this last-period play as . . .

Under the second picture, the cutlines continue:

> . . . Indian End Tony Macuzzo comes up to lend a hand. But Glazo shakes loose in a great second effort, staggers to the 40-yard line, where he . . .

And under the third sequence shot, the lines conclude:

> . . . sidesteps the Indian safety man and has nothing but open space between him and the goal line, which he soon crossed for his third TD of the day.

Sequence pictures may be the answer to the competition of television. Some fascinating research data indicate that we may remember visual experiences as a set of still photographs. It is interesting to search your own memory. Recall a particularly thrilling touchdown. Do you remember the whole run that preceded it? Or do you remember only split seconds thereof: a successful reversing of the field, the feint that suckered out the last defender, the happy leap as the runner crossed the goal line? If the theory is true, if we do remember in "still pictures," our sequence shots may be more meaningful than the continuous action that television can bring our reader.

If the action in a sequence is left-to-right, the pictures should run side by side. But if the action is right-to-left, then the sequence is most effective if the pictures run in a vertical column. In either case, pictures should all be of the same width, like frames of a movie. The reader is better able to orient the action in identical fields of view. (An interesting technique is to show a sequence of identically sized pictures and then to repeat one of them with all or part of the shot enlarged to show detail. But it is not good to change the size of pictures within the sequence because this confuses the reader.)

On occasion, the editor may be forced to run a right-to-left sequence horizontally. This means that the movement is opposite to that of the reading eye. In that case, cutlines must be written to read left-to-right. This may be awkward, but it's the only way we can hope to salvage any value from the sequence. Lines may be something like this:

> Steve Glazo, Ohio College halfback, sets a record with his third touchdown against Michigan Poly yesterday, after a 63-yard run during which . . .

Then:

> . . . he had feinted Indian Jappy Janaro into missing this tackle on the 40-yard line. Moments earlier he had shown great second effort . . .

And finally:

> . . . by breaking loose from two Indian defenders who apparently have him trapped here on the old Statue of Liberty play. (AP Wirephoto)

You may have noticed that nowhere have we mentioned the *overline* that used to be the traditional label on every news photo. The overline is, at best, nonfunctional; too often it is malfunctional.

A major function of a picture is to separate headlines on the same horizontal line and thus avoid tombstoning. When a picture carries an overline, that display type becomes part of the tombstone. But there is a graver non- or malfunction possible, as Example E indicates.

The eye enters this subdivision of the page at *A*. There it is drawn by two magnets, the small and distant overline and the large and near picture. There is little doubt; the eye will go directly to, and into, the picture at *B*. From there it proceeds in the sweeping loop that ends at *C*. The normal instinct of the eye is to move downward to *D*. Then the overline is left unread. It is wasted; it is nonfunctional.

But it is a truism of typography that rarely do we have a merely nonfunctional element. Almost invariably the nonfunctional becomes the malfunctional. This is well demonstrated with the overline.

Too often, as the eye proceeds from *C* to *D,* it is distracted by that overline. So, reluctantly, it goes up to *E* to see just what in the devil is there anyway. Now the overline is read; it isn't nonfunctional any more. But what happens then? From *F,* the eye must move onward—that is, downward. As his eye reenters the picture, the reader says, "What the heck! I've been here before!" and looks for somewhere new to go. That usually is somewhere off to the right, beyond *G.* Now the overline has become malfunctional, for it has led the eye on a wild-goose chase.

If the eye finds something engrossing in the area around *G,* it will probably never come back to the area below the picture. We have, then, placed a grave handicap on that part of the page. But even if the eye does return from *G* to *C* or *D,* that detour has been wasteful.

Research shows that the typical reader spends approximately the same amount of time with each issue of his newspaper, be it a fat Wednesday or Sunday edition or the comparatively slim Saturday or Monday. He has a fixed quota of time, energy, and attention to devote to his newspaper. It is the typographer's job to assure that he gets maximum information from the consumption of this quota.

We might use the analogy of an automobile with exactly five gallons of gasoline in its tank. We put a driver behind the wheel and tell him, "Drive to the state capital." If he drives carefully and skillfully, he will proceed some 75 to 100 miles up the road. But if he revs up his motor, then slams on the brakes; if he spins his wheels in a mudbank or snowdrift; if he misses a turn and travels four or five miles off course, he will ultimately travel only 60 to 80 miles toward his goal. The parallel is plain here, isn't it? If the eye—because of the malfunctioning of the overline—leaves the picture in Example E and detours to *G,* a certain percentage of the reader's mental "gasoline" is wasted in a detour, nonproductive mileage. This is energy he should have expended later on body type that may now remain unread and wasted.

Hand Art

All illustrative material that isn't photography is *hand art.* While newspapers haven't come full circle yet, they are using hand art enough today to remind us that all illustration used in newspapers until the invention of photoengraving in the late 1800's was pen-and-ink drawings. Hand art most often is line, but it may be halftone. Either variety provides interesting contrast to photography.

Some of that contrast comes from the personality of the artist, which

A B E Overline on Picture F

G

D C

Example E. Path of eye while reading photograph.

seems to come through stronger in hand art than in photography. That's why some editors refuse to use hand-drawn portraits with news stories; they insist that such art is an opinion, a subjective value judgment that should have no place in a factual report.

It is true that hand art seems most appropriate, and is used most frequently, on editorial, op-ed, and feature pages. Some hand art—the traditional editorial cartoon—is certainly most subjective. This is, of course, its special function, and we shall examine it more closely in Chapter 12.

In merely illustrative hand art, it is questionable whether any pictorial opinion expressed would be momentous enough to stir controversy or jeopardize objectivity. The *National Observer* and the *Christian Science Monitor* use serious hand art with great effectiveness in all kinds of stories and departments.

Much hand art is light in nature. Cartoons brighten up feature stories and little spot drawings (like those *The New Yorker* magazine uses so well) are effective on feature, fashion, food, and travel pages. Newspapers that don't have a staff artist can find useful hand art in advertising mat services. Growing popularity of light, cartoony illustrations for ads

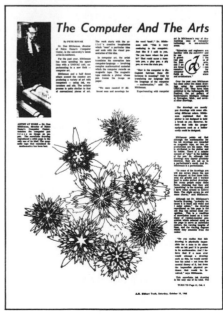

Fig. 46. Effective use of hand art: *a,* where photography is not feasible, used by *Milwaukee* (Wis.) *Journal; b,* where cameras are forbidden, as in courtroom, *Mattoon* (Ill.) *Journal Gazette; c,* when news source will not pose for cameraman, *Lighthouse,* feature section of *Virginian-Pilot Lighthouse* of Roanoke, Va.; *d,* in contrast to halftones, A.M., magazine section of *Elkhart* (Ind.) *Truth.*

The Virginian-Pilot

LIGHTHOUSE

Sunday, Oct. 13, 1968

Section
C

Editorials • Books
Analysis • Features

All You Need Is a Match, Man

A reporter talks to three admitted arsonists in the Washington riot last April after the assassination of Dr. Martin Luther King, but he gets the story of an unknown aspect of the riot—that a small group of black revolutionary activitists worked to keep it going.

A Chapter From "Ten Blocks From the White House"

Copyright 1968, The Washington Post

Picture by Frank Hoy, The Washington Post

A FEW DAYS AFTER the occupation of Washington ended, The Washington Post assigned a reporter to find and interview some arsonists to complete the picture of the April riot that was being assembled for this book. He began at once making contact with persons who might lead him to someone who would talk. At first, he was told that anyone who set fires would not agree to talk for publication. He persisted, suggesting that the interview be conducted with the arsonists wearing masks or hoods so that their identities would not be known. For nearly four months, there was no response.

Then, on August 8, around noon, the telephone rang.

"About the meeting. Do you still won't it?"

When the reporter said "Yes," he was told to expect another call around 10 p.m.

At 10:15 p.m., the same voice on the telephone told him to appear in front of a specified room in a shabby old hotel, in the heart of Washington's inner city. The reporter, who is black, said he would like to have another reporter accompany him.

"No, we don't w a n t anybody else. Just you."

Armed with a tape recorder, the reporter appeared alone at the hotel room and knocked on the door. After he identified himself, he was made to wait 10 minutes. Then the d o o r opened just a crack. A pair of eyes p e e r e d at him from two small h o l e s in a black hood and he was allowed to enter.

The only light came from a lamp on the floor of an open closet. It cast a dull, eerie glow on three hooded figures in the small room. One was the black-hooded man who had opened the door. The other two wore improvised hoods, made from white hotel linen, with jagged holes torn out for eyes and mouths. One had also covered himself with a bedsheet, f r o m his neck to his shoes.

Ground rules for the interview were quickly established. The reporter explained that the information was desired for use in this b o o k and that he might be required to tell the authorities what he k n e w about the meeting. The trio balked at the idea of using a tape recorder, but agreed w h e n the reporter promised to destroy the tape after the interview was transcribed. Presumably, they feared that their voices on the tape would provide clues to their identity. However, as the interview progressed, they began to warm up to the tape recorder and e v e n o rated into it. (The tape was destroyed as soon as the transcript was made.)

The interview proceeded for an hour and forty minutes. The room became stifling hot, and two of the men kept pulling their wet, sweaty hoods away from their faces. One man had a .45-cal. semiautomatic in his belt. Once,

hearing a noise in the hallway outside the room, he nervously drew it. The reporter did not, as far as he could tell, know any of the three hooded men.

The purpose of the interview was to learn about arson in the April riot, but, as the session went on, it became evident that the three men were purporting to describe an unknown aspect of the riot—the fact that a small group of revolutionary activists had worked to keep it going.

The three made no claim that they or their group were responsible for starting the disorder in Washington. To this extent, their story parallels the FBI's assessment that there was no plot or conspiracy to touch off a riot in Washington in April 1968.

They did claim, however, to have performed a catalytic role in the riot, by example and suggestion.

"A lot of areas we went into, man, there was nothing going on till we got there," one of them said.

The scope of their activity was limited, they said, by the relatively small size of their group and because Dr. King's assassination caught them by surprise. They took strong exception to the word "riot," preferring "rebellion" or "revolution" instead. They did not see what happened in Washington as a reaction to Dr. King's murder as much as an assault of a racist system, which, they believe, must be destroyed if black Americans are to survive.

The reporter felt that their basic story, told four months after the events of early April, was not inconsistent with what was known. This, too, was the judgment of senior reporters and editors who listened to the tape and examined the unedited transcript. It was decided that the interview should be published to help in understanding the reactions and attitudes held by some participants in the riot. The transcript was then edited for space and clarity, w i t h less relevant portions omitted.

'So I just stuck the cap on, lit it and threw it...'

Virginian-Pilot drawing by George Linyear

The room became stifling hot, and two of the men kept pulling their wet, sweaty hoods away from their faces.

THE REPORTER, Jesse W. Lewis Jr., assigned numbers to the three men who spoke to him as follows:

No. 1: I guess that what you want to hear about is what happened after Dr. King got killed. Right?

Reporter: Right. But specifically about burning.

No. 1: We've had ourselves somewhat organized in this city alone, I'd say, since about February. We felt for quite some time that it has been necessary to protect ourselves, to arm ourselves, in case The Beast does decide to come down on us. When Dr. King got killed, of course, it came as somewhat of a surprise to us—a hell of a surprise. It caught some of us off guard. But we still were able to do our thing. We had some of our equipment at close hand, where we could get to it easily, even with the curfew being in effect.

Reporter: When you say equipment, what do you mean?

No. 1: Cocktails, even dynamite. There were a couple of places in this town that were dynamited. A&P at Benning Road, Cavalier's on 7th Street, were dynamited, and a couple of other places. But to get to burnings and things. We were preparing to make our own move with the slightest motivation, with the slightest incident that we could use to move with. We had the reasons, but, in order to move, you must have the people behind you, also.

Reporter: You used Dr. King's murder as an excuse?

No. 1: No. That's not the wording I used, brother man. I said we needed an incident that would make it justifiable even in the eyesight of the mass of the people that do not agree with the term "black power." With the mass of people that do not agree with protecting oneself with a piece (gun) such as I have on my side, you see. We had some people who still think that the white man is a good man and he will set us free. Jesus with blue eyes and blond hair. I use the

white man as a beast, not only from anybody's terminology but from my own past experiences. I was raised in the south, man; I've dug on it there, you see.

Reporter: Thursday night, Dr. King was killed. What did you do?

No. 1: Thursday night. I was uptown when I heard the news. I was somewhere between U and Florida Avenue when we heard that Dr. King had been shot, and we were waiting news whether he would survive. Shortly afterwards, we heard that he had died from the gunshot. People were demonstrating, from the beginning of 14th and Florida, down 14th Street, to get the businessmen in that district to recognize Dr. King. This is to show our respect for the man, although our philosophies conflicted, you did it. But the mass of people fell in behind them. And from that, I think the first window that was broken was at one of the theaters on U Street. And, man, when that broke, that was, like —the shot that was heard around the world when the honkies were fighting against their own people.

Reporter: What was the first thing? What did you do? Do you you got to some equipment?

No. 1: I broke a window.

Reporter: You broke a window. With what?

No. 1: My foot, man. I put my foot through it. I wear combat boots most of the time.

Reporter: What was the first place you burned? Or threw a bomb?

No. 1: The first place that I personally b u r n e d? My first thing I did was not the part of burning, as much. I believe in a total type thing. So I just stuck the cap on, lit it, and threw it, you know.

Reporter: You put the cap on what?

No. 1: On a stick of 'mite.

Reporter: Where?

No. 1: A&P.

Reporter: What street?

No. 1: It's Benning Road, I forget the exact hundred block. These things don't register too well with me.

Reporter: How did you obtain the dynamite?

No. 2: Well, like in Maryland and Virginia, they have sites where they keep dynamite.

Reporter: Construction sites?

No. 3: Yeah. In the district, they raise the dynamite back to the place that's doing that job, you know. But like, out in Maryland and Virginia, they keep it in shacks on the site in many instances.

Reporter: It was stolen from there?

No. 3: It was liberated.

Reporter: Where did you learn to make Molotov cocktails?

No. 1: I learned in the service. Uncle Sam taught me in Army basic training.

Reporter: How do you make them?

No. 2: Simply by depositing gasoline into a glass container and p l a s t i c container and putting some type of combustible material at the top—and ignite it.

Reporter: Are you selective about what type of Molotov cocktails you use against a certain surface?

No. 3: When we had time. I know one group of brothers I was with—we didn't have time to do nothing but just pick up and go.

Reporter: Why didn't you have time? The policemen were nearby?

No. 3: Yeah. Well, the police were in the whole area; they were saturating the area. All we had time to do, like one instance, just drive up, hop out, hit it, and jump back in the car.

Reporter: Is there a place where Molotov c o c k t a i l s are made? And are stored?

No. 3: Now there isn't so much —there was a semiplace that was used before to store some gasoline, kerosene, and varsol, you know. We had a place—a couple of places—to store these things, and we would get it little by little. To build up. Because, like, the guns and everything—we didn't have the money we have now to buy guns off the

(See This is Really, Page C-2)

has enlarged the selection in all mat services, and the editorial department can often use these to good effect.

Simple line portraits are useful in column headings, and many syndicates furnish pictures of their writers in this form. Line portraits—either factual or in mild caricature—can be used for straight news stories or, especially, in background material. Some syndicates furnish, in periodical batches, such drawings of people who are in the news or can be expected to break into the spotlight.

Special Effects

Photography can, by special effects, be converted into the equivalent of hand art. The simplest technique is *linear definition,* which converts a continuous-tone photograph into a line cut. By using special photographic materials, film or paper, gray areas darker than 50% gray will reproduce as solid black and those less than 50% gray will become pure white. Middle gray tones are eliminated.

In such treatment it is necessary that shape of the subject be well defined by shadows and dark areas. If the original photoprint is made on highly contrasty paper, it is possible to tell whether the definition is adequate. If not, it is simple to reinforce or extend dark lines and areas with black India ink or the light ones with white poster paint. The platemaker, of course, shoots without a screen, so his camera will not record the minor tonal difference between the paint and the paper.

The engraver may replace his conventional square-gridded screen with *special screens.* With a *mezzotint* screen, the image is defined in patterns of larger irregular dots which give the effect of a crayon drawing. Or instead of dots, the image may be formed of *parallel lines* or *concentric circles* which vary in thickness to create the halftone effect. The axis of the circles, when on an important element in the picture, draws the eye to that point as inexorably as a whirlpool.

Halftone dots, which normally are no bigger than $\frac{1}{55}$ inch in diameter, can be blown up to many, many times that area. Most detail is lost in a plate made in the equivalent of a 12- or 18-line screen, but with a picture in which detail isn't essential, the highly visible dot pattern is striking.

With parallel-line screens, the lines are made heavy to intensify the unusual effect. But parallel-line halftones are made for everyday use, too, and here the halftone pattern is kept as inconspicuous as possible. Mechanical engraving machines, the Photo-Lathe and the Elgrama, use only parallel-line patterns to make their zinc or aluminum plates.

The Wichita Beacon

VOLUME 39   R   PRICE 10c   WICHITA, KANSAS, 67201, TUESDAY, JUNE, 21, 1966   AM 2-4211   28 PAGES   NUMBER 144

The Awesome Life Cycle of a Prairie Tornado

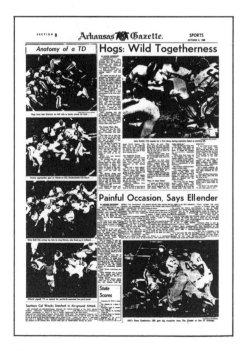

Ronnie Man, Waterville, Kan., caught this arresting photo sequence of a twister as it touched down June 5 near Enid, Okla.

Fig. 47. Sequence pictures. When action is left to right, sequence pictures are properly displayed in that order. From *Wichita* (Kans.) *Beacon.*

Fig. 48. Sequence pictures. When action is right-to-left, above left, or back to front, above right, sequence pictures are properly displayed vertically. Both from *Arkansas Gazette,* Little Rock.

STAR Report: Poverty in Minneapolis... *Like it is, Baby!*

By MAURICE HOBBS
Minneapolis Star Staff Writer

WHITE AND BLACK

I'm sitting at a new desk, smoking a good cigar and typing on a new typewriter, trying to tell another comfortable, well-fed man what it's like to be poor in this city.

Maybe the comfort is what makes it difficult.

FIRST in a series I should take an old typewriter and sit on the dirty, sagging porch of that graying duplex near Plymouth Av. There I could see the littered, hump-backed street and breathe the dust from the almost grassless front yard, and it would all get into my story.

When I first stepped onto that porch, some six weeks ago now, the house looked abandoned except for a couple of old bicycles lying on the floor. I pushed at the doorbell and—surprise—it rang.

"Who's there?" a woman's voice called. "Come in."

New linoleum had been laid over the small entryway floor, but in the living room, patches of decaying floor boards showed through holes worn in much older material. At the far end of the room, the linoleum trailed away into colorless tatters.

Woman With a Puzzle

The dining room didn't have even these shreds of linoleum to hide the floor. In that room sat the woman, 215 pounds, Negro, wearing a house dress, looking just-out-of-bed, resting in a red, plastic covered, wobbly, chrome-legged chair at a kitchen table.

She was working a TV Guide crossword puzzle, a pocket dictionary ready on the table next to the ash tray. Ground into the aluminum tray were the ashes from the long, filter-tipped mentholated cigarettes she smoked.

I sat down, and offered a suggestion for 17 Across in her puzzle: Ian, Fleming's first name.

She seemed open, friendly, likeable.

I wished we could just talk about anything—the weather or her children or whatever else offered itself—but not about this run-down house, or her stingy AFDC grant, or riots, or why some whites hate blacks and vice-versa.

But that was the job—to put together this report, a look at what it's like to be poor in Minneapolis. What it's like to live on welfare, in a shabby house, with never enough money. What it's like to walk on Plymouth Av. where plywood scar tissue still shows from last summer's wounds.

No Answer in Facts

We could put together all the facts, tell the reader that this percentage of people is unemployed, that children from homes in the poor neighborhoods don't get the same push into school or the jobs that keep the rest of us going.

But figures don't say why, and they don't take one real, living, breathing person and say: "This is where it's at. This is where poverty hurts."

This was the real person, and she knows where poverty hurts.

She answered my questions frankly, as freely

Minneapolis Star Photo by William Seaman
COLORLESS TATTERS OF LINOLEUM TRAILED AWAY TO A BARE FLOOR

as she could, and I told her we wouldn't use her name or those of her relatives and friends. She will simply be Mrs. Smith, mother of an 11-year-old daughter we'll call Marie and a baby boy we'll call Allen.

We tried some quick, easy facts first.

She had come up from Hooks, Tex., in 1956 when others in her family did. Fourteen years old, she was pregnant then with Marie.

She married a Minneapolis man soon after she arrived. Before she was 16 she was divorced, and before she was 20 she was on AFDC (Aid to Families With Dependent Children). Allen was born last July. Now 25, she is again pregnant and expects her third child in September.

We'd gotten that far when the front door opened and in walked a tall, heavy Negro woman, a man who looked small next to her, and two boys, one 4 years old, the other 5.

The woman sat down with us at that dining room table that belonged in the kitchen, the table that's the center of the house. (I was to visit

her more than a dozen times in the following days, and she was sitting there whenever I arrived, whether she was alone or with friends or sisters or aunts.)

The man who had just come in sat on a shabby, red-and-black couch that leaked stuffing at the seams. He took off his right shoe and stocking and began to dab at a bunion near his little toe with the glass rod from a mercurochrome bottle.

Who Were They?

The children pressed up against the table, staring at me, wondering, I suppose, who I was, as I wondered who all these people were.

Not until I asked did Mrs. Smith introduce us. They were her sister and brother-in-law, and their two children.

The interview started over and soon I was asking about the paper and paint peeling away from a pipe running from floor to ceiling in a

Turn to Next Page

Fig. 49. Photograph in *Minneapolis* (Minn.) *Star* gains strength from linear definition. This is page from tabloid section of reprints of outstanding report on POVERTY IN MINNEAPOLIS.

(The Scan-A-Graver, the most commonly used mechanical engraver, burns a dot pattern into a plastic; the *Klischograph* excavates a dot pattern into a type-metal plate.) There are usually 55 to 85 lines per inch on such plates, and the pattern is not noticed by most people. Still uncompleted research indicates that the pattern is most unobtrusive when the lines run horizontally. (This may be because the eye is accustomed to horizontal scanning on television screens.) The pattern becomes more apparent—and sometimes annoyingly so—when a horizontally lined engraving runs right next to one in vertical lines. The editor should, if he agrees with the basic premise, try to keep all his halftones in horizontal scan. Unfortunately, this may become difficult. Same-size photos are affixed to a scanning drum on the Lathe and Elgrama; after a simple setting by the operator, the cutting of the plate is automatic. Pictures must be placed sideways around the drum to effect horizontal lines in the plate, but to use all available space on the area and take full advantage of automatic operation, the operator often places one or more pictures so they are scanned in vertical lines.

If a narrow picture must be made singly, it can be done most quickly in vertical lines. Some editors prefer all halftones in the vertical pattern. Until research is further advanced, the editor must trust his own perception and taste. He should, however, establish one style and try for maximum conformity to it, for there is no question that inconsistency of scanning has adverse effect on the reader.

Special screens are most effective for feature and atmosphere pictures and for feature stories and pages or for magazine sections. They are not precise enough for news stories. Special screens are used far more often in the advertising than in the news columns in newspapers.

Expository Art

A form of hand art is *expository art,* whose growing use deserves cheers, trumpet fanfares, and perhaps even fireworks displays. *Expo art* consists of maps, charts, graphs, and diagrams. One of its specialized forms is *marker art.*

Expo art should be used when it can convey information more readily or understandably than photography or verbal copy or where it can augment other communication.

Maps become more useful by the day. New countries are being created at such a pace that only the professional geographer can be expected to know where they are located. If we are reporting on a political crisis in East Africa, a map may demonstrate how a country can be placed under intense economic, cultural, or military pressure from adjacent nations. Unless the geography is clear to the reader, he may not be able to comprehend the nuances of the story.

But even in more familiar locales, maps are useful. If you can, without hesitation, name the states that bound Iowa, you are probably a native Iowan or a student. Within a newspaper's own city, maps constantly become more necessary. In a typical American community some 25% of the people have moved within the past two years. Many of them—about half—come from out of town. Although the born-and-bred native may visualize perfectly the proposed route of a new throughway parallel to Oak, Summit, and Franklin, many readers won't have even a foggy idea where those streets are.

As cities grow and traffic patterns become more complex, even long-time residents tend to concentrate their activities into fewer areas and to use only a few routes to travel among them. So they, too, know less about local geography than their fathers did and will benefit from maps.

The value of a weather map in explaining meteorological forecasts is so obvious it can be the final exhibit for the plaintiff.

Graphs and charts have become as accepted a form of communication as the alphabet. It is somewhat surprising to recall that when I was in school—in comparatively recent times—it was necessary to run an explanation on how to read a graph with almost every such drawing that was used.

The person who communicates with expository art must be as scrupulous as the verbal communicator in conveying not only the truth but the whole truth. Misinformation can easily be conveyed by expo art. Although this is usually unintentional, the reader is as duped as if intentions were Machiavellian.

Distortion often comes from a natural need and desire to save space. Only a portion of a graph may be shown, for instance. Suppose that we are comparing a proposed town budget with that of last year. If the new budget is $42 million, a line graph showing it might extend the depth of the type page you're now reading. If last year's budget had been $38 million, the graph line would be four type lines shorter. Even if he didn't translate it into these exact terms, the reader would note that the proposed increase is some 10%.

But now suppose that the editor—or chart maker—wants to conserve space. He makes the graph show only indexes from $30 million to $50 million. The old budget would be shown by a bar eight type lines deep

Fig. 50. Expository art: *a*, maps expand verbal information in *Providence* (R.I.) *Bulletin*; *b*, data in Dow-Jones graph would literally require full column of verbal report in *Arkansas Gazette*, Little Rock; *c*, simple bar graph used by *Tucson* (Ariz.) *Daily Citizen* conveys comparisons clearly; *d*, line graph in *State Journal*, Lansing, Mich., is decorated with hand art.

and the proposed one would be 12 lines deep. It would appear, then, that the new budget is 50% greater than the current one.

This technique of showing only a portion of a chart is used frequently and, almost always, with no intent to deceive. But deception is inevitable.

Whatever expository art is used, the editor should be as wary of double entendre as he is in written copy. He must remember not only Murphy's Law but its first corollary. The law: "If anything can go wrong, it will." Corollary: "If anything can be misunderstood, it will be."

Maps

Maps are not difficult to prepare. Stock maps for many areas are sold at school-supply houses. State maps and those of their subdivisions can be obtained from governmental offices. Service-station road maps are generally inadequate; there is too much detail even for several colors to help sort it out. In black-and-white the confusion is insurmountable.

Copies of local maps should be Photostated in several sizes. When a story needs this expo art, the editor chooses the size that can best be cropped to show the area involved. Nonessential detail should be edited out. Arrows, X's, dotted lines, etc., can be drawn directly onto the map or on a transparent plastic *overlay* affixed over the map.

If whole areas have to be designated, an effective method is to use *Zip-A-Tone* or a similar *shading sheet,* which is sold at all art stores. These are sheets of transparent material on which are printed various patterns of dots or lines in black or white ink. A thin coating of wax on its reverse is all the adhesive needed. The shading sheet is laid over the map and rubbed at a couple of places with a knuckle to hold it temporarily in place. Then, with a *stylus,* a needle stuck into a pencil-like wooden cylinder, the area is cut out and the unwanted material removed. That left on the map is then smoothed down with the flattened opposite end of the stylus.

Designations of elements on maps may be lettered by hand, although this requires a skilled letterer to give the proper professional effect. It is better to typewrite names, either directly on the map or on strips of paper which are then pasted on. It is best to have the comp room set the necessary labels and furnish well-printed *reproduction*—repro—*proofs* to paste on.

Each time such type is set, several repros should be pulled. The names which are not used should be filed for the future. Eventually the file will be so complete that most maps can be prepared without requiring any immediate services from the composing room.

The *Washington Post* uses many maps and uses them exceptionally well. Some time ago I helped work on a style book just for its maps. While many—undoubtedly most—newspapers do not need or want all the refinements used by the *Post,* it is worth noting some excerpts from that guide.

Four typefaces are used. Geographic designations are in Bodoni Bold; political designations in Futura Bold and Medium. Man-made objects are identified in Futura Medium, and any other explanatory matter is in regular body type.

All names of water—oceans, seas, bays, rivers, lakes, etc.—are in Bodoni Bold Italics, u&lc. Surface features—mountains, deserts, forests, etc.—are in Bodoni Bold Roman, u&lc. Nonpolitical areas—the Piedmont, Lower Appalachia, timberline, etc.—are in Bodoni Bold Roman caps.

Names of countries are in Futura Bold, all-cap; states or provinces, Futura Medium all-cap; counties or similar subdivisions, Futura Medium, u&lc. Capital cities are in Futura Bold Condensed; key cities, the same face in all-cap. Metropolitan cities are in Futura Bold Oblique, all-cap, and minor cities in that face and upper-and-lower.

Streets are Futura Medium, caps and lowercase. All other man-made objects—buildings, monuments, dams, canals, parks, etc.—are in Futura Medium, all-cap.

When shading is required, land areas are shown by diagonal parallel lines and water areas by dot patterns.

The manual not only establishes the order of importance but tells what size type each will use. In a 1-column map, for instance, countries are shown in 24-point, states in 18 and so on down to roads in 10. In 2- or 3-column maps, countries are 36-point. If major area shown is, let's say, a county, it will take the 24-point in a 1-column map and lower elements have correspondingly larger type labels.

Other instructions show how painstaking attention is given to detail:

Condensed letters may be used or normal letterform characters letterspaced to fit available space.

The NORTH arrow should be unobtrusive. But when the map's north-south axis is not perpendicular, the arrow should be placed so it is not overlooked.

All maps of areas whose width is 500 miles or less, or those where distance is important in understanding the accompanying story, shall carry a distance scale. The desk that orders the map should designate when a scale is required.

Graphs

Simple bar graphs can be made directly from type rules. As these can be cut in 6-point increments, the desk can show quite precise variations. Different rules may be combined for clarity.

For the most precise measurement in bar graphs and for all others where circular, curved, or jagged lines are required, the graphs must be drawn by hand. This is usually not difficult and requires no special artistic skills or drafting. Labels can be handled as are those on local maps.

Graphs can be more meaningful or more interesting with the addition of decoration. This may be a simple sketch inserted in a blank area, or the graph may be overprinted in black or white on an appropriate photograph. It is best to draw the graph on a separate piece of paper and let the platemaker combine it with the photo.

Marker Art

A more frequent combination of photo and hand art is marker art. Also called *demo* (from *demonstration*) *art,* this technique might be the dotted path of a careening auto in a fatal crash. It might be the classical X that "marks the spot where." It might be an arrow pointing to a politician almost buried in a crowd of supporters. If such art truly adds to communication and if it does not detract from the photo itself, it can be a useful tool. But especially on sports pages, demo art is overdone to the point of insulting the intelligence of the reader.

On many sports pages, every football that appears in print is sur-rounded by a white circle as automatically as a halo appears around the head of a saint in an Italian primitive. When a cut shows three players leaping for a football hung starkly against the sky, we give the reader little credit for rudimentary comprehension if we insist on circling the ball. Stressing the obvious is pedantic, to say the least.

Tempera, poster paints, may be used for marker art, but it is far more convenient to use *draftsman's tape* and *stick-on* materials. Self-adhesive tape, in black, white, or a combination thereof is available in many patterns. It is dispensed from easily manipulated containers and can be used to make curves as well as straight lines. Stick-on material is printed—in black or white—on thin self-adhesive plastic sheets, like the shading sheets we've already noted. Many symbols—of which circles and arrows have many uses—are available. If the artist makes a mistake or changes his mind, this material—and the tape—can be easily peeled off without harming the glossy. Another benefit is that you can push around a roll of tape with impunity, but a jar of paint or bottle of ink is a constant hazard. It is one of the bitter laws of the contrariety of nature that ink will never spill on a duplicate picture but only on an irreplace-able one, and that paint will never splatter at the start of a job but only as the artist is affixing the final brush stroke.

Black or white letters, in a great many styles and sizes, are also available as stickons. This makes it easy to run headlines right onto halftones. This technique is pleasing to the typical reader, for it is an indication to him that someone took unusual pains in the preparation. Heads may be set as repro proofs and stripped onto photos by the

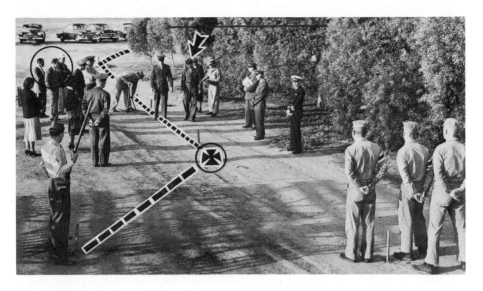

Fig. 51. Marker art in *San Diego* (Calif.) *Union* clarifies complicated situation. Dotted lines indicate paths of subjects; cross marks shooting where they met; arrow and circle identify principals at inquiry later.

engraver or platemaker, but there are advantages to having the head placed on the photoprint in stick-on letters by the editorial department. It keeps control of the process in hands of the person who creates the idea. It enables the editor to see what the effect will be before it is committed to metal. Often it saves critical time in the platemaking department.

But a disadvantage is that the letters will not appear as full black or white. In halftones there will always be shadow or highlight dots to convert the letters to shades of gray. Their outlines will not be as sharp as when the engraver makes a *combination cut,* in which the letters of a repro are captured on a line negative which is then combined with the halftone neg.

Instead of stick-on letters, the headline may be painted or drawn right onto the glossy. This is not very practical unless the lettering style is a very casual one. Attempting to duplicate the formal shapes of regular type takes far too much time, and the glossy surface of the photo is difficult to work on unless it is first sprayed with a clear plastic coating that creates a surface receptive to ink or paint.

Whether the stripped-in head is in black or white, it should be on a solid area of the opposite color. An irregular background disguises type like an autumn cornfield camouflages a pheasant. A proper area for the stripped-in head may be provided in the darkroom by *burning in* or *dodging.* Or it may be painted in with tempera.

A word should never run across two background tones. The entire word—and preferably a whole phrase—should always be on the same background. If the head must start on the picture and continue on plain paper, that break should come between phrases. If possible, that part which is stripped in should be a wicket or a tripod.

Of course, the headline can be inserted into an external or internal mortise in the photo, but the reader is not nearly as impressed by the effect.

Another combination of photo and hand art is sometimes used for features. A human head, in halftone, will have a little cartooned body in line. Or a cartooned background may be used for a photographed and silhouetted subject. The figure may be scissored out of a regular photo and pasted onto a sheet of drawing paper on which the background is later sketched. Or the subject may be photographed against a plain white background on which, in the photoprint, the background sketch is done.

If either technique is used, the person involved should be shown the combined art and be asked permission to run it. This is a simple courtesy, but it may also save legal complications.

Laws concerning the rights of people in photos are state legislation and thus may vary from one state to another, but the general attitude is that a newspaper can use a news picture without the permission of anyone in it. The reasoning is that by becoming involved in a news event—deliberately or by accident—the person has forfeited his right of privacy. It has also been held by several courts that when people knowingly pose for feature pictures, that cooperation gives tacit consent to the publishing of the picture.

But when manipulation by retouching, added drawing, or other techniques radically changes the content or mood of the picture, it has been held that the picture has been used without permission. A girl willingly modeled a fetching bathing suit and expressed pleasure that the picture was to appear in the newspaper. This implied permission. But a staff artist placed the halftone figure on the cartooned runway of a burlesque theater banked with leering males. The girl claimed, and the court agreed, that she had not given permission for such use of her picture. She logically emphasized that even the most intelligent person couldn't possibly have foreseen such usage and that her silence could not, then, give consent.

So it is wise as well as courteous to show drastically modified artwork to the people involved or, if there is not enough time, to explain in detail the proposed results.

It is not necessary to obtain signed *model's releases* from people in

Fig. 52. Stripped-in heads. Above, regular headline in *London* (Ont.) *Free Press;* below, Script in *Milwaukee* (Wis.) *Journal.*

any picture other than that to be used in advertising. To obtain such releases for news use even only occasionally might well open a Pandora's box, and editors generally warn their cameramen against starting any such precedent.

There have been no major court decisions that have penalized a newspaper for using a legitimate photograph that may make the subject look ridiculous. Harsh lighting from unusually high or low can make a person look like Frankenstein's monster. A normal blink of an eye or speaking lips frozen at the halfway point may make the subject look as vacuous as a mental retard. The camera may exaggerate a heavy stubble of beard or an unusually shaped nose. It may catch the person in an unguarded moment, making an inelegant or embarrassing gesture. Even though it may be entirely legal to publish such photos, common courtesy would consign them to the waste basket.

Good taste keeps most editors from using gory pictures of accident victims. Unfortunately, taste runs thin on occasion. The invasion of the privacy of Mrs. Ethel Kennedy at prayer at her husband's bier caused resentment among many newspaper readers.

Retouching

A great many of the typical pictures used by a newspaper would be improved by judicious *retouching*.

The finest retouching is done on the negative. The highly skilled and trained artists who do this delicate work require time and remuneration far too generous to be practical for newspapers. Airbrush artists work right on the glossy. They are used effectively by large newspapers though their work also takes time and money. But even small papers need the rudimentary retouching that can be learned by almost any staff member.

Such a retoucher should frankly admit his limitations and not try to exceed them. Generally speaking, he should not try to retouch the human figure but concentrate on the background. It takes very specialized skills to remove double chins, bags under eyes, and complexion blemishes. Unless the retoucher has this talent, he will probably emphasize physical imperfections rather than mitigate them.

But any craftsman can improve photo backgrounds.

In a typical newspaper, a surprisingly large number of posed pictures will have been taken in a single dining or meeting room. Especially if it is in a hotel or restaurant, this room will usually have vivid wallpaper. While this is pleasing to the diners' eyes, it creates nothing but problems for the photographer, for the geometric or floral patterns so warmly beloved by interior decorators emerge from heads of human subjects like elk horns or Medusa's hair. Ornate chandeliers or wall fixtures grow out of ears or necks.

Confusing backgrounds can be *ghosted out* by using *Bourges* (pronounced Burgess) *sheets* or their equivalent under several trade names. These are like shading sheets except that instead of regular patterns they carry layers of white of varying intensity. Placed over a picture's background, the white dims it as a snowstorm does a landscape. The subject, which is not covered by the sheet, is in full normal value, but it does not stand in artificial isolation as it would if silhouetted. It is still possible to discern the main elements in the background, but details are blurred and do not distract the eye. Ghosting in this way takes about three or four minutes for an 8 x 10 glossy.

The entire distracting background may be painted out, using gray poster paint. This paint is easy to apply; it dries quickly in a flat mass. There are no brush strokes or overlaps to disconcert the artist or viewer. Painting out the entire background gives an artificial, isolation-tank feeling to the picture, so it is best to paint a rectangle behind the figures or heads of the subjects. Often such rectangles are already defined in the picture by window frames, molding, draperies or similar linear elements. A gray rectangle behind a head will eliminate a lamp shade that looks like a hat or a reflection that elongates a nose to Durante dimensions. Yet the rest of the background remains to show the general setting of the picture.

The technique of gray rectangles is useful to define the shape of a head or body if dark hair or clothing blends into a black background or if blonde hair or light clothing dissolves into a bright background.

If changing the tonal value of the background destroys its validity, we may want to outline only a head or body. Assuming a dark head on a dark background: With gray tempera, draw a thin line around the top of the head from ear to ear. Immediately place your thumb on the wet paint and draw it down into the head. If you've done this skillfully or have been lucky, you'll find that the gray has blended softly into the dark of the hair and now gives the effect of a diffused highlight on the head. The same highlighting may be used on the shoulders of a dark jacket or dress. If the effect isn't what you want, don't give it another thought. Wet a piece of tissue with a touch of saliva and wash the paint off. It comes off easily and without residue. Then start the process over until you get an acceptable result. It takes far less time to do this than to explain it, and the little necessary skill is quickly acquired.

With blonde hair against a dark background, the head is again outlined in gray. But now the thumb smears the paint away from the head and onto the background. The effect is that of a soft shadow that defines the fair hair or light clothing.

Highlights on dark clothing or hair or shadows on light may be intensified by a layer of gray paint that is softened by pressing a thumb on it while it's wet.

Notice that we use gray instead of black or white paint. Full values of black or white are rare in photographs, and if we use these for retouching, the painted areas will be painfully conspicuous. The best retouching is the most unobtrusive. Gray will define either light or dark elements but will not be obtrusive itself. If the value of gray needs to be changed, it can be darkened by adding black India ink or lightened by mixing in white poster paint.

For retouching in paint, the staffer needs gray and white tempera, a bottle of ink, a small pointed No. 1 or 2 paintbrush—called a *bright*—and a flat brush about a half-inch wide—a *flat*. He should have a piece of glass or plastic—covers from food containers work well—on which to make sure the paint is of proper consistency and on which to mix in white or black.

Photo-supply shops have sets of paints in several values of gray, and with them it may be possible to match skin tones to paint out facial blemishes. It may be convenient to have several sizes of brushes. The best economy is to buy good brushes. A couple of dollars is not extravagant for a small brush. If washed and dried properly immediately after use, it should wear as long as some on my drawing board, which are over 30 years old and have been used steadily, almost constantly.

The retoucher should always pay attention to the way a man's jacket fits his neck; just a dab of paint can make a snug line from shoulder around neck. Any lingerie that shows on a female subject—a tiny shoulder strap or a strip of petticoat—should be touched out.

Picture Pages

Picture pages began as *tours de force*. They were a way for the newspaper to demonstrate its fantastic ability to take news pictures in quantity and to reproduce them within 24 hours. Readers were properly impressed, and such pages contributed markedly to increased circulation and higher readership. Good pictures still do that, but many editors believe that picture pages as such are becoming obsolete and that the same art can contribute more when scattered on several pages.

Part of the objection arises simply from the mechanics of producing a picture page, especially on a daily basis.

There is a tendency of the editor of the picture page to hoard good photography, leaving slim pickings for editors of other pages. And even in this heyday of pictorial journalism, there are still times when the photo budget is scrawny. Glossies which normally would be fired into the wastebasket are then used only because there is a given amount of space to be filled.

This is not to suggest that picture pages or *combinations—combos—* of pictures are without merit. On the contrary, grouping pictures on one subject will produce greater impact than the sum of the parts. Thus many editors are generous in providing space for a page or pages of pictures on a big news story even though they will not run a regular picture page.

No matter what the occasion on which pictures are comboed, the layout man should use the *hen-and-chicks principle*. This technique uses a dominant picture—the hen—as the nucleus round which smaller pictures—the chicks—are placed in a pleasing pattern.

The dominant picture should be at least 50% larger in area than the next largest one. If the "hen" is unusually light in tone, its area may have to be increased further to assure its dominance. Among the "chicks," pictures should not be of identical shape and size.

The editor should seek variety in picture pages. The most obvious is that of size and shape. But variety in tone, range, and angle is important. If possible, there should be variety in subject matter, too, although this may not be as obvious in the coverage of a single news event.

The editor should resist using all pictures with dark backgrounds or all in high key. He should vary the tone. Variety in range is achieved primarily by the cameraman. He will take long, intermediate, and closeup shots. The editor can control the range to some extent, however, by the way he crops and enlarges a picture. If he chooses to use only a small portion of a medium-range shot and then enlarges it dramatically, he has created a closeup. This presumes, of course, that the photographic quality of the original is so good that it can stand extreme enlargement.

Angle can be changed only by the cameraman; no manipulation on the desk can change a bird's-eye view into a low angle shot.

Each picture page or combo should have a block of body type of a minimum of about 1 column by 4 or 5 inches. This block of type is as effective an accent to a page of pictures as a halftone is to a page of type. Cutlines alone are not adequate for such an accent. If the page or combo is about a single subject, the type block ought to be on the same topic, but if the pictures are on various subjects, the type block need not be on the same subject as that of one of the pictures. Any good feature story will make an excellent foil to the photography.

The editor must remember another ancient axiom: "Don't use the same picture twice!"

This axiom shouldn't be given literal interpretation. It's a rare editor who would actually use the same glossy to make two engravings. But we frequently see two engravings which, although they seem to be totally different, are "the same picture"; they say the same thing. On a recent picture page on a new community hospital, there were three pictures which were identical as far as the message they conveyed. Each showed a medical technician looking through a microscope. The people vary; so do the jobs that they are performing. But to the reader there is only one "picture": somebody looking through a microscope.

There is one interesting exception to this "rule": A deliberate use

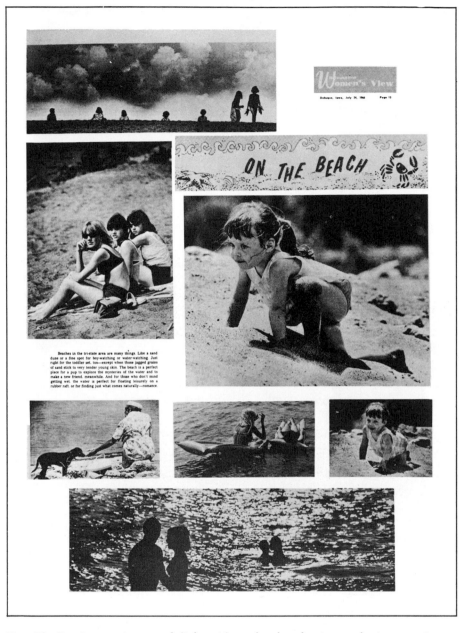

ON THE BEACH

Women's View

Dubuque, Iowa, July 24, 1966   Page 13

Beaches in the tri-state area are many things. Like a sand dune or a fine spot for boy-watching or water-watching. Just right for the toddler set, too—except when those jagged grains of sand stick to very tender young skin. The beach is a perfect place for a pup to explore the mysteries of the water and to make a new friend, meanwhile. And for those who don't mind getting wet, the water is perfect for floating leisurely on a rubber raft, or for finding just what comes naturally—romance.

Fig. 53. Dominant picture—of little girl, under head—gives cohesion to picture page from *Dubuque* (Iowa) *Telegraph-Herald*. Note use of Ben Day panel of section logo and of hand-lettered heading. Also note wide variety of size, shape, and tonal value.

The Washington Post
for and about WOMEN
SUNDAY, APRIL 23, 1964   H13

(Photo by Steve Szabo—The Washington Post)

Burr Gore Steers, 1½, with his mother. Other sons
are Newton Ivan, 8, and Hugh Auchincloss, 4.

Well Dressed–The Washington Way

By Dorothy LeSueur
Washington Post Staff Writer

AS SHE rounded the corner of the parking lot near the Elizabeth Arden Salon where once a week she undergoes the ritual of a sauna, massage, facial and pedicure, Nina Steers' figure was silhouetted by the mild April sun.

She wore a trench coat, the belt tugged tight around her narrow waist. Hers was a young, vibrant silhouette, casual, buoyant with the assurance of fashion knowhow.

The slender, tall, athletic young Washingtonian with trim legs and an almost sprinting gait was in a hurry as usual; clouds of still-damp dark hair fell in tendrils around her face (she had insisted that Salvadore comb her hair before it was dry).

IN AN ERA of tomboys with whacked-off hair shouting "down with elegance," Nina Steers remains confidently elegant and feminine. She is decidedly sensible about clothes and not influenced by the off beat.

"Miniskirts? They lack romance. Short, short skirts are revolting when legs aren't good. The length of my clothes usually depends on my mood."

If her moods change as rapidly as a magic lantern, her wardrobe does not. She has a collection of uncomplicated clothes that convey an atmosphere of permanence.

Hers is basically a city wardrobe—"I don't have a large group of country clothes. After all, we live in

the suburbs," she said, comfortably curled in a large chair, wearing Pucci's beige cotton pants and a bulky knit sweater.

THE Newton I. Steers live in Bethesda. He is an attorney and financial consultant and a former Republican State Chairman. He readily admits that his wife doesn't consult him about clothes.

"My only contribution is that I tutored her in college economics, and she almost failed the course." Nina Steers is, nevertheless, down to earth about the economics of fashion; she does not hesitate to discuss clothes in terms of money.

"I like American designers. Naturally, I love Norman Norell—his clothes are beautifully constructed—but who can afford him? The same is true of Galanos, who can be exotic . . . gruesome . . . or so romantic! For an expensive designer fashions, I often buy off-season."

She also appreciates such masters of design as Mainbocher, but doesn't feel a great need to wear such prestige fashions. "I have two Mainbocher suits, a gray flannel given to me as a Christmas present and a green check I bought on sale."

Donald Brooks and Rudi Gernreich have the simplicity and imagination that appeal to her.

WEEKDAYS, Mrs. Steers drives to Washington early, deposits two of her three children at school and gets to her office by 9 a.m. She is a reporter for the Chattanooga Times.

Although her days are lightly spaced with appointments and deadlines, she finds time for yet another project: writing a biography of her blind grandfather, the late Senator Thomas P. Gore of Oklahoma.

She is the daughter of Hugh D. Auchincloss and the former Nina Gore and stepsister of Jacqueline Kennedy.

SHE CONSIDERS knitted dresses particularly well suited to the life she lives. Like the Duchess of Windsor and others wise in the ways of fashion, she buys Kimberley's, which are well designed and well priced.

"A Washington dressmaker stitches up simple little dresses for me. They have six pleats, are made of Liberty cotton and are never in style," she added, characteristically.

IN A DECADE of hatlessness, Nina Steers wears hats. For rain, there's a sou'wester of red vinyl. A leghorn with a wide brim shields her from the sun. For windy weather, she wears a straw boater with a scarf that ties under the chin.

In cold weather, she keeps her ears warm with an Army-Navy design which she had copied in black seal and beaver by Gartenhaus.

"I have one hairpiece to wear in the evenings, and I want one of the new wiglets with bangs from Saks Fifth Avenue for the summer. Hair is so important.

"If you are good with your hair, it doesn't matter

See STEERS, H11, Col. 2

Nina Steers in Geoffrey Beene's dress (left) of paisley challis, which she ordered from a newspaper advertisement. To her surprise, it fit perfectly and became a favorite for informal evenings. Donald Brooks' sculpted one-shoulder dress has powerful black and white bias stripes twining the body. The dramatic jersey dress from the Park Avenue Room, Saks Fifth Avenue, falls in the new category of amusing fashions for evening.

Drawing by Sandra Leichman

See-through plastic raincoat with twinkling dewdrop rhinestones, from Dorcas Hardin, is summer-winter answer to the evening rainwear problem.

Fig. 54. Large and striking hand art combines with halftones for interesting women's page in *Washington* (D.C.) *Post*.

twice of the identical picture. A typical use might be of a current hero surrounded by a swarm of admirers. The first picture is a long shot, describing the event. Then, a small portion of the original shot is cropped out and blown up most generously. In this new size, details of the idol's face and form—and perhaps of a few nearby people—are presented in a size to be enjoyed by the reader. The effect of using two identical pictures in this technique is that of zooming in, as in motion pictures, from a long shot to a closeup. As with all striking techniques, this one should be used sparingly lest it lose its shock value.

Scaling

Newspaper pages are dummied up and often are made up in metal before the photoengravings are made. In pasteup, a window must be left for the picture, and this may have to be pasted in before the screened negative is available. Thus the desk must know exactly how large the finished picture is going to be after it has been reduced—the usual procedure—or enlarged from its original size. Determining the new dimensions is called *scaling*.

Slide rules—either conventional or circular—or quite elaborate pantagraphic devices are used in scaling photos. But I prefer a simpler method, that of the *common diagonal*. This is based on the geometric principle that the diagonals of rectangles of the same proportions create identical angles with the sides.

In this method, the editor draws the diagonal of the photo—or of that part of the photo that crop marks indicate should be used by the platemaker. (It doesn't matter in which direction the diagonal is drawn; I find lower left to top right is most convenient for me.) Now, along the bottom of the photo he measures off the width that the engraving is to be. At that point he raises a perpendicular until it meets the diagonal; that line indicates the height of the engraving. By drawing one more line, from that intersection to the left edge of the picture, the editor can see the actual area the engraving will occupy and will also be able to tell the approximate size of various objects in the photo as they will appear in reduction.

In newspaper usage, pictures are almost invariably reduced to a specific column width, and we must find the new height. On rare occasions, when the height of the engraving is known and we must determine its width, the common diagonal method works equally well. After drawing the diagonal, the editor marks off the desired height on the left margin of the glossy and draws the perpendicular to intersect the

'It Makes No Damn Sense'

By BILL LYON
Sunday Staff Writer

DETROIT — Hate is not a pretty thing to look at.

It showed in the snarling face of a curfew violator as he stood spraddle-legged, hands flat against the wall, submitting to a search by a sergeant from the 101st Airborne Division at Fort Campbell, Ky.

A neon sign blinked on and off, giving an eerie, unreal glow to the whole scene. The curfew violator did not conceal his hate.

"You the man, baby. You got the gun. What you gonna do with the gun, whitey?"

The hate also showed in the face of another sergeant from the 101st Airborne Division. This sergeant was a Negro.

He stood there in his flak jacket and helmet, tear gas grenades strapped to his chest, bayonet on his M-16, eyes scanning the rooftops for a sniper.

Less than a year ago those eyes were scanning the rice paddies of Vietnam.

"This isn't Detroit . . . this is Saigon," the sergeant said, softly . . . deliberately . . . and with hate.

"Just like Saigon. The guy who walks by you and smiles . . . he's the same guy who just might come up and stick a knife in you when you turn your back.

"I spent 13 months in Vietnam. I go back in September. I thought I knew what I was fighting for before. Now I'm not so sure.

"If this was what I was fighting for, it's not worth it,

"You get enough killing over there."

What about the civil rights cause?

"Civil rights?" the sergeant snorted.

"The idiots who started this used civil rights for an excuse . . . an excuse for crime.

"The idiots who did this . . . they're the guys who say they have nothing. So they don't want anybody else to have anything either. And if they keep this up, pretty soon nobody will have anything.

"It's all so senseless. This is the United States of America, man. But it's like another world."

Riot-ravaged Detroit, indeed, was like another world. Or, at least, like another city . . . in another time.

London must have looked like this during the blitz . . . whole blocks gutted out by bombs. But these bombs weren't dropped from any plane . . . they were bombs made out of lighted, gasoline-filled bottles hurled into shops and businesses by people gone mad . . . by people who live in houses on streets that turned into terror.

It was the costliest riot in history . . . in terms of money, in terms of lives . . . in terms of disgrace and shame and senselessness.

"It just makes no damn sense," the Negro sergeant kept saying, "no damn sense at all.

"We were killing each other a hundred years ago. Haven't we learned one damn thing yet?"

This sergeant, who had risked his life half a world away and was now risking it again in his own country, boiled inside . . . with hate and with questions.

"Your people, man," he pointed to a white reporter, "and my people . . . why can't we get together?"

It was a monumental question . . . perhaps the most important in the history of humanity.

What is the answer to that question?

"God, I wish I knew," the sergeant sighed.

"But," he said, waving his rifle at all the destruction, "this isn't it."

A CURFEW VIOLATOR is escorted by an Airborne trooper as another night of terror descends on Detroit.

GIS AND RESIDENTS of Detroit's west side stand in front of a store bearing the hastily painted "Soul Brother," which means the store is owned by a Negro.

HOLDING ONTO EACH other's clothing, Detroiters arrested for rioting and looting form a human chain as they are marched to jail.

Sunday
Staff
Photos
By
J. Bruce
Baumann

THE HANDS OF a suspected looter rise up, palms first, in Detroit's city jail, as he awaits legal action.

Fig. 55. One of facing full pages of *Sunday Courier and Press* of Evansville, Ind., that gave outstanding photo coverage of Detroit race riot although no actual picture of violence was used. Note unusual cropping of top picture.

diagonal. Scaling to predetermined height is used almost only in maga-
zine- or feature-page layouts.

On such pages there may be occasion when a photo must be reduced
to fit a specific area, with both height and width predetermined. In that
case the dimensions of the engraving are drawn on the photo as in
Example F. The diagonal of the engraving is extended to meet the edge
of the glossy. In Example F-a, the desired area of the engraving, 1-2-3-4,
is superimposed on the glossy. The diagonal 1-3 is drawn and extended
to 5. It is obvious that, by the distance of 5-6, the glossy is too wide to
reduce to the proportions of the desired cut. So the editor must narrow
the glossy by the amount of 5-6. This might be at the right of the glossy,
as indicated; at the left or partially at each side.

In F-b, the desired engraving is 7-8-9-10. As the diagonal 7-9 is
extended, it shows that the picture is too tall, by the space of 11-12, to
reduce to the desired area. So the editor must crop 11-12—or its equivalent elsewhere—from the glossy.

The drawing of these diagrams is not done directly on the glossy. It
may be done on an overlay of tracing paper or on a separate sheet of
paper on which the dimensions of the photo have been drawn. Even
easier is to use a plastic overlay which is gridded in 1-pica spaces. Any
straightedge can be the diagonal, and the editor can immediately determine the new dimension by the grid which marks the intersection.

Scaling may be done by simple algebra, too. The equation is

$$W:H = w:h$$

W is the width of the glossy and w that of the desired cut. (Always in
given dimensions of photographic elements, the width is first.) H is the
height of the glossy; h of the cut. In such an equation we must know
three factors to find the fourth. We know W and H, of course, and we
almost always know w. That leaves h as the unknown, x.

$$W:H = w:h$$
$$10:8 = 1\tfrac{3}{4} :x$$
$$10:8 = 1.75:x$$
$$10x = 14$$
$$x = 1.4$$

"The product of the means equals the product of the extremes." W times
h equals H times w. More simply, "The outsides equal the insides." W
and H, and w and h, must be in the same units of measurement.

The disadvantage of this algebraic method is that we often come up
with awkward fractions, some of which we can't even find on a ruler or a

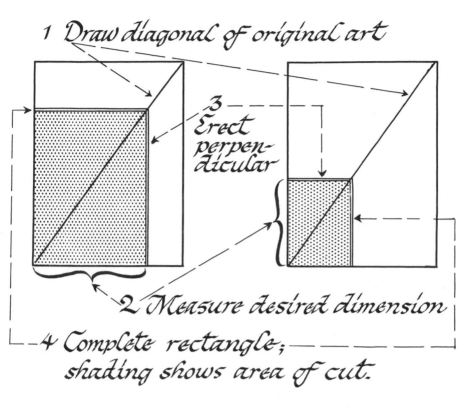

1 Draw diagonal of original art

3 Erect perpendicular

2 Measure desired dimension

4 Complete rectangle; shading shows area of cut.

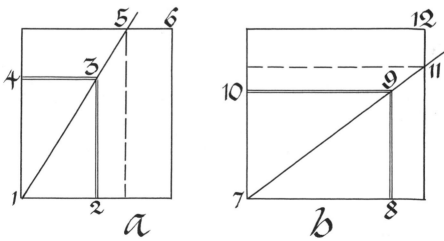

Example F. Common-diagonal method of photo scaling.

pica stick. And a pair of numbers isn't very useful in helping us visualize how the engraving and elements therein will look on our page.

Whatever the method used, all pictures should be scaled before leaving the news room, and the precise size of the engraving noted on the page dummy. It seems inconceivable that an editor could properly dummy a page without knowing exactly how large an engraving was going to be, yet I was in the composing room of a large and respected Manhattan newspaper when a picture page had to be made over twice because some deskman hadn't determined the correct size of an engraving.

Cropping Instructions

It is embarrassing, annoying, and sometimes costly when a picture fails to fit its allotted area. Customarily, a page is made up with only the base for the picture in the form. All other elements are already locked up, and the form is ready for stereotyping. As soon as the plate comes from the engraving department, it is placed on the base and the mat is rolled. This is usually right on the deadline; thus, if the plate doesn't fit, there isn't time to remake it. It has to be sawed down, perhaps losing important detail. If it's too small, it will float haphazardly in the open space, and its failure to align with the cutlines will show it was an accident.

Sometimes the dilemma is caused by faulty scaling. Sometimes it is due to instructions that were faulty in the giving or understanding or both.

Cropping should be indicated with grease pencil in the margins of the glossy; the photo should never be physically cut. No marking should be made on the face of the photo. If any writing is placed on the back of the photo, great care must be taken that it is written so lightly that it does not raise the surface of the emulsion. The bright lights of the platemaker will exaggerate this embossing, and the engraving might be rendered useless.

Two crop marks in one margin are adequate to show the horizontal part, and a pair in the top or bottom margin to show the vertical portion of a photo, that should be made into a plate. It is not necessary to indicate crops in both facing margins unless the cropped portion is on a new, tilted axis. If there is no crop mark, the platemaker will go to the margin of the photo.

To show the cropped area of the photo to be used for the engraving, the editor draws in the margin a pair of arrows, each pointing to one crop mark or margin. The tails of the arrow are within the extension of the used portion of the photo. Between the tails in the arrows in the bottom margin—those showing the vertical portion to be used—the editor writes in the dimensions of the engraving. Care must be taken that this is the dimension of the engraving, not the actual measurement on the photo, a common error. If the width of the photo is 5 inches and the number written on the photo is 5 inches, the engraving will be the same size as the photo. If this is actually what the editor wants, no reduction or enlargement, the correct instruction is S/S, same size.

The engraver needs to be told the screen to be used for making halftones. If the newspaper has its own engraving department, the screen is constant and known by the craftsmen, so no written instruction is necessary. But if, as is frequent, engraving is done in a commercial plant, the screen must be designated. This is usually written in the margin too. It is also wise to include the name of the newspaper.

A convenient device is to use a label affixed to the back of the glossy but projecting so it can be read from the front. Basic information is printed on this tab so the editor need only make a check mark or two to give necessary information to the engraver. The same technique can be used with a rubber stamp printed on the back of the photo. Some editors use gummed tabs in a brilliant color to indicate any copy—written or photographic—that requires unusual treatment.

The pyramiding growth of photojournalism in the past two decades is well indicated by the rising status of the picture editor. At the end of World War II, only metropolitan papers had such an executive. Today even small papers recognize the need for his specialized services.

Often the picture editor is also the typographer. In what are still a few instances—although the practice is growing—the combination of photo art and type usage is reflected by a new title, graphic arts editor. This is logical, for both type and art are tools for communication, and they must be used skillfully for that purpose.

chapter **7**

Constants

ALMOST ALL of the contents of a newspaper change drastically from one issue to another. Advertisements may on rare occasion be repeated, but the news is always fresh and different. Those few elements which do not change are the newspaper *constants*.

Like all familiar things, the constants are usually taken for granted. So much so, in fact, that they are often invisible to the editor and his staff. But the constants, too, should be subjected to the same continuing reassessment that the alert editor gives to other typographic elements.

No cow that wanders around India is more sacred than the newspaper's *flag,* or *nameplate*. This is the official version of the paper's title as it appears on the front page (and as it should appear whenever the name is displayed, as in house ads, on delivery trucks, and perhaps on the building façade). The term "masthead" is erroneous although frequently used.

The nameplate is a trademark, and it gains much of its value from continuity and repetition. The nameplate should not be changed on idle whim or as frequently as a shirt is. Neither should it be so sacrosanct that necessary changes are forever precluded.

A nameplate should be legible, distinctive, handsome, and appropriate. Not only should new flags be evaluated against these criteria; existing ones, too, should be reassessed.

Sometimes only a little polishing up is needed to bring the nameplate up to these standards. Letterforms may be sharpened, ornamentation simplified, idiosyncrasies of letter design removed, extraneous matter deleted from ears or folio lines. Such changes need not detract from the value of an accepted trademark.

If a completely new flag is being designed, the first decision is that of

212

the letterform. Any of the six type races may be used, and each is represented among American newspapers.

Text is the most widely used letter for nameplates. This is undoubtedly because of its connotations of well-established authority. (It is interesting, though, to note that the first two newspapers in Colonial America, *Publick Occurrences* of 1690 and *The Boston News-Letter* of 1704, had nameplates in Roman.) Text is adequate in legibility; it is handsome and distinctive. Whether it's appropriate depends on the nature of the newspaper. The personality of a newspaper is reflected by its flag just as the personality of a person is suggested by his clothing.

Both Old Style and Modern Romans, Sans Serifs, and Squares meet the first three requirements. So do many versions of the Written and Ornamented race. Whether they properly reflect the paper's personality must be decided by the editor.

Generally speaking, the nameplate ought not to be in the same letterform as the headline; there can be a danger of the flag getting lost on the page.

Choice of type will be influenced by the newspaper's name. The *Yuma Sun* in Arizona, with only seven characters in its name, or the *Bath Times* in Maine, with nine, can use a wider, bigger and more ornate letterform than can the *Hot Springs National Park Ouachita Observer* in Arkansas, with its 38, not to mention five spaces, or even the *Klamath Falls Herald and News* in Oregon, with its 25 and four.

The character of the community helps determine the style of the flag, too. A swinging town like Las Vegas would suggest a nameplate much different from that of restored Williamsburg.

Before even preliminary choice of letterface is made, the actual name should be set in any proposed type or traced from a type specimen book, for the combinations of letters within a name strongly affect its appearance. If the name starts with a capital *W, T,* or *V,* for instance, we would recognize that there will be a distressing gap between the initial and the next letter if Italics are used. This will require the correction of negative letterspacing. Some typefaces have unusual treatment of one or more of their characters. In Metro, for instance, the *f, i, j, l,* and *t* have distinctive finials. The cap *Q* and lowercase *w, x, y,* and *z* in many fonts have a pleasant flair. If such letters appear in the newspaper name, they may swing the choice of the face to their font.

The flag may be set in type, hot or cold; that gives wide selection. It may be hand-lettered; then there is truly no limit on the variety.

Most newspaper flags are in the formal letters that we associate with hot-metal type, though in many instances the letters are actually drawn by an artist. Lettering requires a highly specialized skill, and the publisher should be warned not to assign this job to anyone except a proven professional in this specialty. Even the best of artists usually encounters difficulty in designing a nameplate.

Obviously hand-lettered flags, especially those in *calligraphy*—"beautiful writing"—are comparatively rare. More's the pity. For there is a charm in this style that foundry type cannot duplicate, and the ability to tie together certain letters within the name makes a unique signature.

Only the characters required for the flag need be purchased as sorts of hot-metal type. Repros from metal type are inexpensive. Phototypesetting houses—many of which advertise in graphic arts magazines—will not only set a flag but even manipulate the words to fit certain areas for only a few dollars. The cost of hand-lettered flags will vary radically, from less than $20 to more than 10 times that amount. In this case, the rule of the marketplace usually prevails: You get only what you pay for.

The actual printing element of the flag that is locked into the page-form should be an engraving. Metropolitans use steel, bronze, or steel-faced engravings because they withstand wear so well and guarantee clean, sharp stereotype molds. Or a master plate is made of copper—which holds the finest detail in photoengraving but is relatively soft—from which are made *electrotypes*. These are exact replicas of the original plate made of copper or nickel by an electroplating process like that which puts the chromium on your automobile bumpers. The electros, which can be replaced rather inexpensively, are actually used in the forms. It is probably just as economical to make ordinary zinc line cuts and replace them frequently.

The original art, the platemaker's negative, or the master copper plate should be filed for making duplicates.

The largest type size available should be used for pulling repros of hot metal. Phototype or hand lettering should be at least 1½ times as tall as the engraved flag will be. This is to assure the sharp photoengraving that comes best from reducing original art. If the largest hot-metal type is only 42- or 36-point, it is sometimes useful to have the repro enlarged by Photostating. That enables the platemaker to shoot down and also permits easy retouching of ragged or spotted letters.

When the flag is engraved, it is easier to acquire the several sizes required for floating the flag. *Floating flags,* short ones that are moved around on the page, are very functional, and their use is warmly recommended. A full-page-width nameplate is like the lid on a kettle; the floating flag becomes an ingredient in a tasty typographic ragout.

Even when the front-page flag is the conventional 8-column one, a smaller nameplate is usually used on the section page.

The largest flag can be centered across the page-top or set into a 7- or 6-column space. The next smaller size can be used normally in a 5-column area, snugly in 4, and with lots of elbow room in a 6-column space. Two- and 3-column nameplates are also useful. In these two sizes it is usually necessary to break the name in two or more lines in order to retain enough size to make letters clearly legible. These narrowest flags can gain weight as reverses on gray or black backgrounds or when bordered with striking rules. Printing them in colored inks also increases their typographic weight.

Although floating flags are considered "contemporary," they go all the way back to colonial days. Nameplates on our earliest newspapers were relatively small, but as more publishers entered competition, the flags were enlarged to emphasize them. However, the Stamp Act of 1765, which hiked the cost of paper drastically, made it desirable to save space by reducing the nameplate not only in depth but also to widths less than full page.

During the colonial period the precedents were also set for the ornamented nameplates which today are constantly growing in popularity. To emphasize the speed by which news was brought to their readers—though it seems incredibly slow in this electronic age—those old newspapers ran pictures of galloping horsemen or swift ships with their nameplate. Later it became common to decorate the flag with the coat-of-arms or seal of state or city. This was reminiscent of the heraldry that identified officially printed proceedings of Parliament or the decrees of religious or secular rulers and gave an aura of authenticity and accuracy to the newspaper.

More frequently in the Wild West days, with home-town boosterism at its peak, the ornamentation of the nameplate enhanced civic pride, visualized hopes and ambitions, or exaggerated the size, beauty, riches, or importance of some tiny cattle town.

After more than a half century in which ornamented flags were out of style, the pleasant practice flourished again. The trend continues and is applauded for its contribution to good design, sales appeal, and preservation of history and romanticism.

The most discreet ornamentation comes from the letters in the name itself. The designer first looks for letters that he can swash by an

Fig. 56. Decorated nameplates. *Frankenmuth* (Mich.) *News* makes trophy case of nameplate. *Elko* (Nev.) *Daily Free Press* uses American Square Serifs and line drawing to evoke Wild-West background. *Ames* (Iowa) *Daily Tribune* adds device to mark its centennial and *Aalborg* (Norway) *Stiftsidende* has one, in red, for its 200th year.

Appropriate palmetto ornaments nameplate of *State* of Columbia, S.C., and Yankee Clipper that of *Day* at New London, Conn. Phoenix, symbol of Atlanta, Ga., identifies *Atlanta Times*. Favorite eagle-and-shield device decorates flag of *Mattoon* (Ill.) *Journal Gazette*.

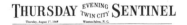

Times-Argus of Barre-Montpelier, Vt., *Daily Local News* of Chester, Pa., and *Arcola* (Ill.) *Record-Herald* use popular map motifs.

Daily Chronicle of Centralia-Chehalis, Wash., breaks folio rule to allow descender to project. Ribbon motif forms panel in flag of *Daily News*, published in Olathe, Kans.

Financieele Dagblad, Holland's national financial newspaper, has nameplate designed by American Arthur L. Koop, Jr.; it uses bold Italic *f* to decorate Squares.

Pocono Record of Stroudsburg, Pa., and *Emporia* (Kans.) *Gazette* use Shaded and Shadowed Ornamented letters. *Twin City Sentinel* of Winston-Salem, N.C., makes day of week integral part of nameplate.

Fig. 57. Three variations of flag for *Medicine Hat* (Alta.) *News* were tried before lower form was adopted.

Scotsman of Edinburgh, Scotland, modernized and simplified traditional nameplate through three steps, top to bottom.

ornamental elongation of one or more of its strokes. While swashed letters are usually the capital initial or the last letter of a word, interior letters, too, can be manipulated and made more decorative in this way. The cap *R* is always a good one to swash, as an initial or within or at the end of an all-cap word. The *Christian Science Monitor* extends the leg of the first *R* in its all-cap head but leaves the last one in normal form. Other capitals that lend themselves to such treatment are *A, F, G, H, K, L, M, N, P, Q, Y,* and *Z.* In lowercase, all descenders, plus *z,* can be effectively swashed.

A pleasant technique is to use a single fairly heavy rule under the nameplate and break it to allow the swash to extend. Swashes may be at the top as well as at the bottom of a letter, but usually the latter is most useful for design purposes.

Another design possibility is to join letters in a ligature or to overlap them. The specific letter combination of the newspaper name determines whether this is a feasible technique, of course. Overlapping is particularly useful with curved letters. Such forms seem farther apart than letters of straight strokes, and so they often demand that other letters in the word be optically letterspaced, their normal spacing extended to give uniformity with the excess space. Overlapping removes that need and adds charm to the word. The double-O combination is particularly suitable to this handling.

Combining Italic initials with Roman lowercase—and vice versa—can add interest to an all-type nameplate.

If a decorative element is to be added to the type of the nameplate, the choice is almost without limit. An obvious one is the visual reiteration of

Fig. 58. *Columbus* (Ind.) *Republic* uses nameplate in four widths. Even full-width nameplate is consistently floated into page pattern but always remains in top third of page.

the newspaper name—Sun, Star, Blade, Courier—which has Early American precedent. The seal of the city or state, the seal or trademark of the publishing firm, or a geographical point of interest is as good today as it was in Jackson's days. A little Chamber of Commerce-ism may creep in with the illustration of a geographical point of interest, historical memento or monument, or natural resource. The paper may brag a little by showing its own plant. Or the ornament may be an abstract one without symbolic significance designed just for this purpose.

The use of maps grows in popularity. These forms are attractive, especially when they have the distinctive silhouette of a Michigan or a Florida. They can also be informative if the geographical adjective is deleted from the newspaper name. When *The Hometown Star* becomes just *The Star,* the decorative map can also provide Hometown's orientation.

Usually, the ornament is most effective when it is placed within or between the words of the nameplate, perhaps even overlapping them a little. Decoration outside the area of the actual name may look extraneous.

Never should ornamentation be allowed to reduce legibility. If the decoration overlaps the letters of the flag, those letters should still be read easily. If there is important lettering in the ornament, as with a seal, it should be legible too. Fussy details should be simplified.

The many nameplates illustrated here show interesting use of several techniques. Your table of exchange newspapers, public libraries, and newsstands handling out-of-town papers will furnish many more idea starters.

That the nameplate is becoming less sacrosanct is demonstrated by the growing tendency to drape it with special decoration for special occasion. Growing in popularity is the practice of using a snowcapped flag on the days of unusual blizzards. So many American newspapers are in the tier of states where snow is commonplace that a large percentage can avail themselves of this device. I applaud it. It shows the reader that his newspaper is produced not by computers but by people who are as aware as he of the drifts that engulf their city. It rids the newspaper— even if only temporarily—of the stuffiness that usually pervades its columns. A storm worthy of such commemoration occurs so infrequently that the technique need not become boring.

A similar technique might be used for unusually hot or wet weather. Decking a nameplate with Christmas trimmings is not common, but neither is it a total rarity; however, I have never seen Easter or Thanksgiving hailed in this way.

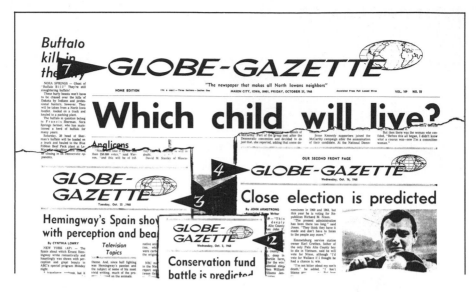

Fig. 59. Mason City (Iowa) *Globe-Gazette* uses flags of various sizes; narrower ones are designed in two lines.

Many newspapers are still hesitant about making even minor changes in their nameplate. The *New York Times* prepared its readers months in advance for the elimination of the period on its nameplate. I am certainly not one to defend a status quo that needs changing, but of all the changes that the *Times* might have made, this is the one that I was least happy about. The *Times,* the *Kansas City Star,* and the *Nashville Banner* were the only metropolitans I know that used periods on their flags. Yet it was a pleasant little touch that I hated to see removed, and I hope that papers which still carry the bullet will continue it.

There has been a tendency to remove the "the" from newspaper titles. No strong argument can be advanced pro or con.

As newspapers sought to broaden their circulation and advertising claims beyond a city or county, they often dropped place names from their titles. This has obvious disadvantages. A person living or visiting in Populated Area, Minn., and buying the *Evening News* on the street corner can reasonably assume that it is the local paper. But there are people who read newspapers at distant points, at newsstands or libraries, or who receive them through the mails. To them it is annoying to have to search for clues that might indicate the origin of the paper. I can testify to that, for I receive scores of strange papers every week; it is amazing how hard you have to hunt for pertinent place names. As a nonpaying reader, I may not be important to a publisher and he need pay no

Fig. 60. *Steamboat Springs* (Colo.) *Pilot* uses positive and reverse forms of new nameplate, in American Square Serifs, which was derived from one at top.

Worthington (Minn.) *Daily Globe* stylizes ornament and makes narrower version of new flag in two lines.

THE KNICKERBOCKER NEWS

Knickerbocker News of Albany, N.Y., decorates its nameplate seasonally.

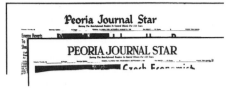

Fig. 61. Peoria (Ill.) *Journal Star* gives unusual treatment to nameplate, changing Cursive nameplate for evening edition to Transitional Roman for morning edition.

attention to my dislikes or annoyance. But my circumstances are shared by people who are important to the publisher, the buyers of national advertising space.

I have been told by space buyers that they would prefer to have newspapers identified by place names. If this is desirable for space buyers, it is essential for those who check tearsheets.

Apparently advertising agencies don't feel strongly enough about this to complain to ad representatives or space salesmen. But it seems to me that newspapers ought to check with major advertisers when they are tempted to delete geographical references in the nameplate.

A deletion from the nameplate that can easily be made is the designation of time or frequency of publication. The terms are removed from public usage long before they are taken out of the nameplate. At the turn of the century, when many weeklies became dailies, it was a mark of pride—and perhaps of necessity—to put *Daily* in the nameplate. When even small cities had two or more newspapers, it may have been functional to distinguish between the *Morning News* and the *Evening Gazette*. But today that need has apparently become obsolete. At least the reader doesn't think it important. It is as rare to hear a New Yorker ask for the *Daily News* as it is for one to ask for the *Evening Journal* in Scranton; it's just the *News* or *Journal*.

Minor changes in the name of a newspaper usually accompany a change in frequency, when a weekly or biweekly goes daily or a weekly becomes a biweekly. A merger may result in hyphenating the acquired name with the established one.

But rarely is a newspaper name changed entirely.

A notable exception recently took place in Columbus, Indiana, where an established newspaper changed its name without a merger or change in frequency. For some 87 years, with slight variations, it was called the *Columbus Evening Republican*. It was decided to simplify the name. "Columbus" was deleted because the paper was serving ever-widening suburban areas where many readers failed, or refused, to identify with the city. "Evening," it was decided, was superfluous. Identifying the newspaper with the title of a political party might make it difficult to maintain reader acceptance of its political neutrality. So the name was changed to the *Republic*.

The job of designing a new flag was given to an art studio that specializes in trademarks and corporate-identity devices. The result was striking. The name was set in letters that might be termed "Federalist" in their connotation. A federal eagle was added as ornament. Heavy Oxford rules framed the flag.

The design is used as any flag must be, in many different sizes, manners, and places. On the letterhead and business cards, the type is in a warm, tannish gray with the eagle in full black. On delivery tubes the entire design is white on black. On the building, trucks, and carrier bags, it is entirely black on white. It is a telling test of the quality of a design when it retains it characteristics in such a variety of uses. The *Republic's* trademark passes the test admirably.

Ears

Ears are the elements at the sides of the nameplate proper. Rarely are they functional; often they are malfunctional.

The only editorial matter in the ears that is consistently read is the weather report. But reader interest in this copy is so great that this position is not required to assure readership. The growing tendency to give greater emphasis to weather news and to run a more detailed report and forecast elsewhere on the front page makes the weather ear redundant even though it may be a convenience to the reader.

There is little evidence that other matter in the ears receives any reader attention. Inspirational quotations may bring a glow to the heart of the editor; his reader usually ignores them. If the habit has been built up over the years, a short editorial *bright* may have adequate readership in the ears. But available data fail to prove the efficacy of this treatment.

The right-hand ear usually carries the *edition logo*. For metropolitans, a few editions have unusual appeal to a certain clientele. Homebound businessmen may want to console—or torture—themselves with the closing market quotations. The Damon Runyon crowd wants the race results and nothing else. But it is doubtful that the average reader cares—or even knows—whether he has a 3-STAR FINAL or a RED-STREAK in his hands. It may be necessary to identify editions for office use by newspaper personnel. It may be desirable to do it for some street sales. But it is highly dubious whether the logos must be so conspicuous that they compete against the nameplate itself.

Sometimes the single-copy price is given in the right ear. This is most convenient for the transient buyer and this position might well be used especially for those editions with high street sales.

Folio Lines

Although few newspapermen give much thought to them, the *folio lines* are an integral part of the nameplate and should be tied snugly into its design. In strictest technicality, folios are page numbers alone. In newspaper usage, however, they include other data. On the front page, the day and date, the volume and number of the issue, and, especially if not part of the title, the name of the city of publication are considered part of the folios.

Although not strictly part of the front-page folios, the price of a single copy is always given in the folio area, and second-class-mail certification may be run there.

The price should be given in the simplest, most easy-to-read style, not "ten cents," but the simpler "10¢"; nor is it necessary to preface this information with the redundant "price." It is only the transient purchaser who needs to know the single-copy price; he wants to find it quickly and easily. The use of numbers and conspicuous position make this possible.

Often folio data are enclosed within two horizontal *folio rules*. The top one is nonfunctional, as there is no reason to separate the folio matter from the nameplate proper.

Inside-page Folios

Like many other newspapermen, I had long been under the impression that folio lines were required on all inside pages by Post Office regulations. This is an error that was reiterated by several local postmasters, who apparently were under the same misapprehension. But the fact is that postal regulations make no such demand. All that is legally required is a distinctive nameplate on page one and the second-class-mail indicia "on one of the first five pages, in a position where they may be easily located by postal employees and other interested persons." Although they are not required by law, folio lines ought to be included by voluntary action of the publisher.

Folios are not consistently needed, but whenever the need arises it is a strong one. The reader needs them when he follows a jumped story or seeks an indexed feature; checkers of advertising, especially national, can hardly work without folios.

The decrease in jumped stories may eventually obviate the need to identify pages for this purpose. But the growth of the number of pages in the typical newspaper makes the use of an index all the more important.

Inside-page folio lines should include the name of the newspaper, the place of publication, the day and date, and the page number. Only the latter is needed for the reader, but the ad checker needs all these data. It is annoying to him when a newspaper omits any. This, unfortunately, happens often.

The advertiser needs to know the date to determine whether the ad ran on schedule; the day is an added convenience but not vital information. The page number shows the position of the ad. The name of the city is most important. As a tearsheet reader for other purposes, I can testify that it is maddening to have a page identified only as coming from the *News*. There are probably dozens of *Newses* on the typical national advertising campaign. To determine which *News* supplied a particular tearsheet requires a process of elimination and deduction worthy of Sherlock Holmes. Often it is literally impossible to identify a tearsheet even after reading all the advertising and editorial matter on the page. The ad checker hasn't time to play such games, and the advertiser who refuses to pay for an ad in an unidentified page is certainly in the right.

Inside folio lines used to run clear across the top of every page in every newspaper. The practice today is to boil the folios down to one or two columns; only a comparatively few papers stretch the lines clear across the page. Eight-column folios waste space, almost one column-inch per page. That means a substantial linage for a typical newspaper in a single day, not to mention a month or year.

Folio lines should be set so they can be used in a single line in two columns or in two lines in one column. The page number is often set in a larger and/or bolder face. On even-numbered pages, the page number should be at the left, on odd pages at the right, of the other information.

Ideally the folios should run in the top outside corner. But this is not an absolute necessity. If the folios are at the top of the page, they will perform their functions adequately. If the editorial element in the top outside corner is wider than two columns, it looks awkward to have a 2-column folio line ride above it. So the folios should then be moved toward the middle of the page into the first 1- or 2-column space available.

The short folios, of course, run within the page; with editorial matter in the other columns, they align at the top of the chase. Occasionally a newspaper will run the folios in two columns but above the page proper.

There is no gain in space then, and a major reason for short folios is ignored.

A few newspapers run folio lines in the outside margin of the page proper. For letterpress papers, this can be done simply by mortising the page chase so the folio slug just fits. The folios themselves then run sideways to the page proper but the page number should be oriented in the same direction as the page itself. Usually there isn't enough space on offset plates to use this technique.

The Masthead

Masthead is the most misused word in the newspaperman's lexicon. Too many people use the word to refer to the nameplate, when it is actually a statement of ownership of a newspaper.

Traditionally the masthead has appeared on the editorial page.

The newspaper name is an essential element in the masthead. It should be in the very same form as in the nameplate. Day and date, volume and number, the name of the publisher—individual or corporate —and the place of publication are included. After that, variety sets in.

In the earliest days of American journalism, the editor, who was usually the publisher, too, displayed his name prominently. This was an act of courage and of courtesy. It took courage to identify the authorship of editorials that consistently raised the hackles of the authorities. But it was also a courtesy to the reader to identify the writer whose opinions were so prominently set forth.

The era of faceless journalism removed the editor's name from the masthead. But in recent years, there has been a renewal of the custom. Often names of executives other than the editor and publisher are included in the masthead. Indeed, the order in which the names are listed is an excellent indicator of the publisher's philosophy. If the business and advertising managers are listed before the editor, it is obvious that the newspaper is far more oriented toward making money than toward serving as a news medium.

Some weekly newspapers list most, or all, of their employees, including typesetters and bookkeepers. I'm in favor of including as many names as possible. I think that the more personal identification we can give to a newspaper, the more we lay to rest the evil of the anonymous machine which the typical reader often fears, especially in a one-newspaper or one-ownership city. I believe, too, that public identifica-

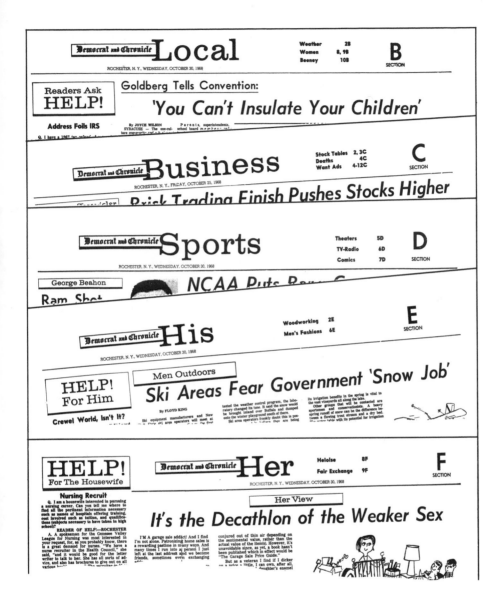

Fig. 62. Section-page logos of *Democrat and Chronicle* of Rochester, N.Y., display nameplate prominently despite small size. Note that HELP department offers specialized service to general readers in B Section and to men and women in E and F.

tion with a newspaper makes every person more careful and accurate in his work.

Customarily those indicia which the Post Office requires to identify publications entered as second-class mail have run in the masthead. But there is a tendency today to run this matter elsewhere. Sometimes, as we've already noted, this may be in the nameplate complex. Sometimes it appears on page 2 or 3. Then, usually, it is set in agate and treated as inconspicuously as possible.

The names of national advertising representatives are often listed in the masthead, as are those of organizations with which the paper is affiliated. The symbol of the Audit Bureau of Circulation is a familiar addition.

The masthead is an ideal trophy case for the newspaper to display the awards it has won. Many organizations that award prizes for journalistic excellence provide appropriate emblems to attest to that recognition. Some publishers affect false modesty and refuse to show their prizes. This isn't very smart. If the publisher expects some other medium to tell the world about the achievements of his newspaper, he should anticipate a long wait.

Usually the insignia of membership and awards are sufficient decoration for the masthead. If the nameplate is ornamented, no other decoration is required, but if the nameplate is plain and affiliations are merely listed in type, an added ornament may make the masthead more attractive.

Logos

Logotype, or logo, is a term of several meanings. In its purest sense, a logotype is a single piece of type, or a matrix, which bears two or more characters.

Because a signature cut is often made as a line engraving, a single typographic element, the word "logo" is used to refer to it whether that signature is used on an advertisement or as the nameplate of a newspaper. *Section* and *department logos* are display devices that identify subdivisions of a newspaper. The most common section logos are those for the women's and sports pages.

Section logos are rarely functional. If one is required to identify a section as the sports section, you really don't need a logo; you need a new sports editor.

The primary—perhaps sole—function of a section logo is not to

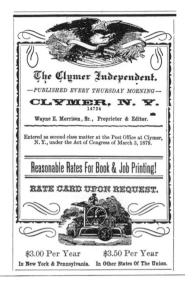
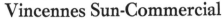

Fig. 63. Ornamented mastheads. *Clymer* (N.Y.) *Independent* uses period decorations. *Vincennes* (Ind.) *Sun-Commercial* has sketch of Abraham Lincoln visiting its office. *Philadelphia* (Pa.) *Evening Bulletin* and *Chicago* (Ill.) *Daily News* display their Pulitzers. *New York Times* uses handsome house emblem. *Sacramento* (Calif.) *Bee* runs legally required indicia unobtrusively on pages 2 or 3 so it need not take space in masthead. *Doings* of Hinsdale, Ill., shows major awards of year.

identify, let's say, the women's section but, rather, the women's section *of your newspaper.*

I was exposed to a pertinent experience some years ago while working with the *American Metal Market.* It is a daily in Manhattan that is the authoritative source of current prices for all metals from the common iron to the exotic berylium. Since 1882 it has been the bible of the industry, and every day millions of dollars of metals change hands at prices published in *AMM.* Some years ago the publisher was appalled at the results of a readership survey. Although many companies dated their subscriptions back to the 1880's and were apparently willing to pay the high rates of a specialized newspaper, nobody was reading it.

This seemed incredible; so further and deeper research was carried out. *AMM* is highly departmentalized; all data on a specific metal is in one page or section. When the paper arrived at the subscriber's office, each page or section was torn out and given to the specialist concerned. The steel or aluminum buyer would almost wear out his sheet as he referred to it constantly. But he never saw the whole paper and didn't identify his invaluable tool with *Metal Market.*

As a result, the *AMM* staff began running a miniature flag on every page. No matter whether a man used the tearsheet for uranium or scrap metal, he was aware of the paper from which it came. The next readership survey showed the accurate—and unusually high—readership.

The problem may not be as pressing for the general newspaper, but there may be a small segment of your readers who buy your paper just for the racing results or the late stock-market reports. If they read only one section of your paper, you want to make mighty sure they know they're reading the *Hometown News.* A section logo may be indicated, then. It is obvious that the main element of such a logo should be the newspaper name; as always when the newspaper name is displayed, it should be in the form of the page-one nameplate.

Department logos are artificial devices primarily used because advertising departments sometimes feel they will be persuasive to space buyers. But if book reviews get only a half-column of space once a week, it is doubtful whether the addition of a BOOKS logo will persuade publishers to buy the large space they take in the *New York Times* book magazine.

There may be some value in attracting the readers by the use of departmental logos. Common ones are ART, DRAMA, MUSIC, PETS, HOMES, etc. If headlines do their job properly, departmental logos are usually unnecessary.

Third Page

Beeline

Fastest line in town
Dial 321-1111

Cool

Tonight — Partly cloudy, low in upper 30s. Saturday—Mostly sunny, high in lower 50s. Sunday—Sunny, a little warmer.

Map and chart on Page 36.

Late Markets

Red Flash

Virginia Kay

I CONSIDER IT PART of my duties to keep you abreast of what the zanes are up to in New York NOW, and so I gladly pass on to you this info called by Daily News — Editor Milt Fre—'

CHICAGO DAILY NEWS
Sports

For the latest sports scores call 726-1242

Friday, October 20, 1967
Section Four ☆ Page 39

News lady

Person to Person

By Bonnie Larkin 321-2176

Dear Abby

She likes to bend the ears
of strangers with secrets

DEAR ABBY: Is there something wrong with me? Whenever I take a trip train. ! your real name and address at once, and I will send you the information you need im— asked to be an usher at his friend's wedding. He will h— — —'t a tuxedo for th—

Dr. John R. Richardson

Belief in the Lord
is indestructible

God is. This is the supreme affirmation of life. The Bible does not argue this fact. It assumes it as life's most obvious —xiom. "In the beginning God" is the majestic way the Bible — its —

Heloise

Russell Kirk

Fig. 64. Headings for regular features. *Chicago* (Ill.) *Daily News* uses lozenge-shaped panel for family resemblance but varies illustrations and tone. Note how panel on KAY heading is kept open.

Atlanta (Ga.) *Times* maintains consistent style of casual Script and line portraits.

Toronto (Ont.) *Daily Star* uses pennon notches on nameplate as well as heading panels, (next page).

If the decision is to use departmental logos, they should be harmonious with the nameplate and with section logos.

Standing Heads

Standing, or *label, heads* are unchanging ones, usually verbless and of a single word or phrase, used to identify regular, recurring features. When such heads are decorated, they are usually called *headings.*

Standing heads become fewer as editors seek to eliminate their static dullness. Often what used to be an independent standing head is now a kicker. The name of a column, department, writer, or locality, carried as a kicker, will attract the regular, rapid reader. The main head, summarizing the content of the specific column, may attract the transient reader who couldn't care less about YOUR HEALTH, DREW PEARSON, or WEST BOOTHILL but is interested in the topic of the day.

There are a few kinds of copy that require only a standing head, and any attempt to dress it up with a more elaborate display would be wasteful. Such copy might be local markets, comparatively insignificant or obscure commodities, tide schedules, traffic fines, divorces, etc. The accent face in the head schedule—if there is one—is effective for such heads. The label might be placed in a sideless box, and the rules used for that purpose will provide the desired family resemblance. Normally boxed heads are shunned as without philosophical justification for separating the bait from the trap. But in the case of standing heads, the color afforded by a boxed or sandwiched head often seems to outweigh the

Fig. 65. Headings. *St. Petersburg* (Fla.) *Independent* puts type in shield-shaped panels, often in color.

Sighting device identifies all standing heads in *Christian Science Monitor.*

Courier-Times, New Castle, Ind., uses simple but effective style with parallel rules and accent face.

liabilities of such a head. If the body type is brief enough, the whole story may run in a sideless box.

Headings are always ornamented and often hand-lettered. Thus they are an almost irresistible temptation to the artist. The result is a hodge-podge of styles, typefaces, pictorial treatment, and typographic color.

Consistency is essential for good headings. There must be a strong resemblance among all headings in a paper. If there is variety, it should be slight and within the framework of such resemblance. Often there is no discernible difference between a heading and a department logo.

Headings can be effective when they are designed into a headline complex. Often they are inset into body type; this is less than desirable, for even if the adjacent lines are within the readability range, the change of measure in body type—a *runaround*—in order to provide space for the inset, reduces efficiency in typesetting and reading.

All newspaper constants share one disconcerting characteristic: They wear out.

The familiarity of the constants often makes them invisible to the staff. We rarely look—really look—at the very commonplace. Therefore badly worn constants may mar otherwise immaculate pages. The only practical solution is to assign to one staff member the responsibility of examining every standing element in the paper immediately after each press run. He ought to have a check list to assure that he has really looked at all standing matter, from the nameplate to the classified-ad rate card. Any element that is worn should be replaced immediately.

Even offset newspapers may have "worn" elements, not from physical deterioration but from reshooting reproduced instead of original art. This problem is explored further in Chapter 13.

Care devoted to keeping the constants constantly clean is often called "polishing the brasswork." This activity has no more practical value for a newspaper than it does for a soldier or a bank. Shiny brass buttons don't increase the firepower of a regiment by a single round; shiny brass door handles don't increase the assets of a bank by one penny; shiny, clean newspaper constants don't add one reader or one line of advertising. But shining the brass gives real psychological advantages. An organization that takes pride in its own appearance can expect greater respect from outsiders. An immaculately polished bank or newspaper carries that aura of authority and reliability which is essential to both institutions. A staff that can be proud of the appearance of its newspaper always does a better job.

chapter **8**

Editorial Color

Editorial color (printing with colored inks) might, by applying a little poetic license, be considered a component of newspaper typography. Two factors have markedly increased its use in the past two decades: advertising and offset.

Advertisers have found that the addition of color gives them extra selling power much greater than the extra cost of such ads. The addition of one color, for instance, will increase the pulling power of an ad by some 65%, while its cost has increased only 35%. The spread between these two figures is "free advertising." When color is made available for advertisers, the editorial department can share the extra cylinders required on the press by assuming only the slight cost of an extra printing plate.

Not only has offset made color economically feasible for even smaller newspapers, but its rapid growth, example, and competition have also spurred letterpress users into advertising color and, of course, the attendant inexpensive use of editorial color.

After generations of black-and-white printing, the newspaperman has found new tools for communication in the rainbow. And new terms have been added to his lexicon. The dictionary of color is a thick and varied one, but the newspaperman need learn only a few of the most rudimentary terms.

Hue is that characteristic that identifies color for the human eye. Hue is, for instance, that quality which makes red "red" or blue "blue." Hue is also the product resulting from mixing any two colors—orange from red and yellow, for instance. *Chroma* is the quality of brightness in a color. A peacock blue has a higher chroma than navy blue, for instance.

Value, or *tone,* refers to the darkness of a color. By adding a little black paint to a can of any color, we create a *shade;* adding white paint to a color produces a *tint.* Brown is a shade of orange; pink is a tint of red. In newspaper printing we make shades by surprinting a pattern of black dots on a color area; we make a tint by screening a printing plate, putting a pattern of white dots on its surface. Value is measured on a *gray scale.* If we make a black-and-white picture, all colors are reduced to various kinds of gray. A red sweater will appear as very dark gray; the blue of a summer sky will be a pale gray. The red has high value; the blue has low.

*ROP—run of paper—*is a familiar phrase in newspaper plants. It means color printed without the use of special presses. It also means ads—b&w or color—that run anywhere in the paper, not only in specific positions.

Opposed to ROP color are the *preprinted advertisements,* of which there are two basic kinds: *Hi-Fi* and *Spectacolor* ads. Hi-Fi's are printed in a continuous "wallpaper design." The ad is designed so that the cutoff may vary, yet the complete ad will appear on each page. In this style, there are no top or bottom margins; the ad bleeds off the paper. Specta-color ads are placed precisely on the page, their imposition being con-trolled by electric scanners that operate at the high speeds of regular newspaper presses.

These preprinted ads are produced on rotogravure presses. Instead of being cut into pages, the paper is rewound. The printed roll is shipped to the newspaper, which threads it into its regular webbing and prints on it in black as it would on blank paper.

When Spectacolor is used for advertising, it is usually available for editorial use, too. The advantages are obvious. No printing method can reproduce full color on newsprint with the brilliance and fidelity of rotogravure. The disadvantage of this method is the long lead time that is required. It has been customary to have a gap of six weeks between the time copy went to the platemaker until the preprint appeared in the newspaper. That meant, of course, that only feature material could be used for editorial color art. Cutlines can be printed by the newspaper's own letterpress, of course, so it is possible to get a fairly timely angle on the feature. Suppose that a Spectacolor ad is to run on March 30. Copy has to be on hand in mid-February. The editor decides to use a spring-time feature; it isn't difficult to get a pretty girl surrounded by flowers in a nearby greenhouse. This full-color picture is printed on page one. On the day of publication, cutlines are written to match the situation. If spring is on schedule, the lines refer to the latest additions to the landscape. If the weather is behind the calendar, the lines refer to the pictured flowers as mere visions of a winter-weary public. Planning feature pictures for use a month and a half later is no great tax on editorial ingenuity.

There is a remotely possible complication in the use of a picture like this springtime shot. A big story may break on the scheduled day that demands the whole front page or at least the elimination of the competition of the color picture. If such a story is a sad one, of a death or assassination of a great man or of a cataclysmic disaster, the color subject may be entirely inappropriate. But alternatives are practical. Usually preprints do not have to run on a specific day; the ad and its accompanying editorial color can be postponed a day or two. Or the editorial color may run on a section page instead of page one; the shift in position will have no effect on the ad, and as long as he's on the last page of a section, the advertiser will not object. If the preprint must remain on page one, the headline of the big story can be beefed up and its accompanying pictures made larger to outweigh the color. The possible dangers are so slight that no editor would hesitate to risk them for the very real advantages of preprints.

The *Detroit Free Press* has been highly successful in using offset instead of gravure for preprinting. The conversion has led to a substantial saving in required lead time, a portion of which is directly attributable to the fact that *FP* is now able to use a local offset printer instead of having to transport printed rolls from a distant gravure plant. When gravure and offset color reproductions are seen side by side, the gravure is obviously more brilliant. But when preprint offset is compared only to the black-and-white letterpress on the same page, its quality impresses staff, reader, and advertiser. The *Free Press* anticipated that the lead time would be cut down to one working week, and its goal may well be reached by the time this book is published.

Newspaper color is classified as *process* and *spot,* or *flat.* Process color is the reproduction of the full spectrum of nature. Original art for process work is usually a color photo, although any continuous-tone artwork, such as paintings, may be used. Process color utilizes an optical sleight-of-hand. Tiny halftone dots of the three primary colors are printed side by side in varying ratios of size and number. The eye does not register these as individual colors but mixes them optically; instead of seeing scores of yellow dots nestling close to blue ones, the eye sees the whole area as green.

Original continuous-tone color work is broken down into its primary components by optical filtering, *color separation.* By placing a green transparent substance before the lens of the platemaker's camera, the blue and yellow rays that make green are blocked from the film, and only the red rays can pass through to create a negative. The result is "a picture of the red portion of the original." This color separation is subtle; the camera detects hues in nature that the eye never sees. Each of the three color separations—red, blue, and yellow—is used to make a halftone plate, which prints the appropriate color of ink.

Mechanical scanning devices are slowly taking the place of filter separation for making process-color plates. Simply, the machines scan the original and take out each of the three primary colors. Often there is no intermediate step of separation negatives; the machine makes the printing plate simultaneously with the separating process. These machines have successfully passed their initiation under field conditions and produce excellent work. The saving in time and effort is substantial, and their end products are often better than those involving human intervention.

European innovations use colors other than the combination used in the United States. This is not sensational; we have already modified the original concept of using primary colors. We use cyan instead of the truer blue, which we commonly think of as the primary color, and the printer's magenta is several steps removed from the primary red. It doesn't matter how we divide the spectrum as long as its subdivisions, made by color separation, are reproduced precisely by appropriate ink. The Germans, especially, have met with success in using different arcs of the spectrum, with their "blue" plate using an ink that the layman would describe as "almost green."

In this country, the Bureau of Advertising has perfected newspaper inks called *AdPro,* which, while they stay within the conventional ranges of primary colors, result in truer reproduction and brighter hues.

Black is not truly a color; it is *achromatic.* Thus it does not combine with the primaries to create new hues. But black plays an important role in good color printing. It gives greater depth to the various shades of the true colors, and it adds detail that sharpens the picture.

Letterpress newspapers customarily eliminate the black plate and stick to three-color process instead of the four-color process used by magazines. The rationale is that the same plate that carries the black portion of a four-color picture must also carry the type and black-and-white halftones that make up the rest of the page. This plate is not available to

The Skokie Life

A Lerner Newspaper covering the village of Skokie

Vol. 21—No. 48   Four Sections, 68 Pages   THURSDAY, MAY 23, 1963   10 Cents Per Copy   Want Ads: Section Three, Pages 10-19

The paper
with the
want ads

Nilehi 'wins' by 3-2 margin

By FREDA ARON
LIFE Correspondent

THE PEOPLE of Niles Township approved the rate referendum raising the ceiling of the educational fund of High School district 219 by 21 cents.

This makes the present ceiling $1.3901 per $100 assessed valuation. That is the amount the Board of Education of the Niles Township High Schools may spend on the instructional program in its schools.

The educational fund, known as the housekeeping fund of the schools, covers teachers salaries, supplies, materials and expenses under the heading of "instructional program."

RAISING educational fund ceiling does not mean the board will spend at full amount immediately, or all at once, but that the amount of expenditure.

Supt. Clyde Umbrella said the board are committed to making that the last seen at least 2 years, but how far money will go in the West increasing expenses is the unknown factor.

While it can be said that the vote was a landslide, it most certainly was more convincing than the one in Palatine only last month when the school district referendum won by

11 votes. Niles Township brought in almost a 3 to 2 vote, or a majority of 842 votes of approval.

A BREAKDOWN of LIFE-land villages reveals some surprising facts. Skokie, where the rumbles were loudest (and some areas showed severe symptoms of rejection), came through with a 401 majority for the referendum. Only 3 of the polling districts in Skokie, out of 13, brought in a majority of negative votes; Menoon (197 no's to 186 yes's), Edison (257 no's to 152 yes's) and Fairview North (122 no's and 112 yes's).

Niles barely skirted through with an approval majority of 47 votes. In the school district (71) where taxes are the lowest of all LIFE-land communities, there were 142 against and 105 for the referendum.

Morton Grove, which was rather non-committal throughout the referendum campaign, rejected the referendum by 42 votes —505 to 547 against.

LINCOLNWOOD made the best showing with almost a 5 to 1 majority of yes votes.

The turnout, while not spectacular, was not considered bad for a referendum. There were 6,704 voters of which 3,781 voted yes and 2,938 voted no.

Dr. Tom Koerner, coordinator of the referendum campaign, said the victory belonged to the advance work of the Citizens Advisory Committee, who took on as their first assignment a concentrated program of disseminating information about the rate referendum to the entire community of Niles Township.

An additional factor in the victorious vote was the combined efforts of the PTA groups in Niles Township schools.

THE MAN responsible for the rate referendum preparation and follow-through, retiring Supt. Clyde Parker, stated he was leaving with a feeling of wrapping it all up and leaving the new man (Supt. Charles Einberla) free of financial worries for the new year.

"This an dthe long-range plan are my last two big projects here and though no one is really satisfied with a small margin, this has been a satisfactory vote, about a 800 majority out of nearly 7,000. Just 1 above 50 per cent pleases me. We are saved."

The icing on the cake is spread even more thickly when Dr. Parker retires with the knowledge that he has never lost an educational rate referendum in the decade he has been in Niles Township. In the whole of 30 years spent at the superintendent's helm, Dr. Parker has lost only one referendum.

Has Jaffe fired first in bid for mayoralty?

By CHARLENE LOUIS
LIFE Correspondent

SKOKIE — Niles Township Democratic Committeeman Raymond V. Krier's naming of Aaron Jaffe as deputy committeeman last week has turned thoughts in Skokie beyond November's national election and focused them on Skokie's own next April.

To many, the appointment affirms their conviction that Krier is grooming Jaffe to confront Mayor Albert J. Smith for the top job in Skokie. It seems almost certain that Smith would like to retain the mayoralty, if he can.

Jaffe is noncommittal about it now. He told The LIFE, "We have to concentrate on the June 11 primary and the general election first."

WITHOUT A DOUBT, he sounded like a candidate last week as he chided Mayor Smith before the party membership. Jaffe referred to the mayor as "Mr. Magoo," that little man well known for his nearsightedness.

He did so, Jaffe said, because once again Smith was telling the press that all is right in Skokie when it is not. Just as he did over the radio the day after the super storm, the deputy continued.

All is not right in Skokie financially, Jaffe told the Tribune two weeks ago, Jaffe declared.

NOT WHEN the village manager has presented the board with a budget that requires a utility tax and the sale of public land to balance it to cover a $1.7 million deficit, he added.

This may appear to be candidate's talk.

Jaffe does appear to have the support of the precinct captains. They gave him a standing ovation as he stepped forward to speak.

While everyone appears certain that Jaffe is the frontrunner today, there are some in Krier's own party who question the wisdom of the committeeman's naming Jaffe as his deputy.

TO THESE MEN, close identification with a national party is the "kiss of death" in Skokie.

Traditionally, Skokie likes its mayors to be a little on the independent side. Deputy committeeman, they say, is about as close as you can get partywise.

Perhaps the influence of some of Krier's "Young Turks," has prevailed. They have told this reporter personally, "If we go down this time, it's going to be with our own people."

They also want the party running locally under its own banner, rather

than as the Civic Achievement party or some other meaningless label.

FOR A LONG TIME, those in the know in Skokie have been predicting an election that will face-off Democrats against Republicans, without an independent party, like the Skokie Caucus party, needed to form a coalition.

One by one the leadership of the Caucus party have been drifting under the Republican wing, including such notables as Jean Doney and Shirley Neuman. There no longer is the charge against the Caucus party, as there was at one time, that it is Democratic dominated; it is now the reverse.

Currently even Harvey Schwartz, Caucus kingmaker and Skokie corporation counsel, has said that he is serving on a committee working for the election of Rumsfeld and Ogilvie. Although he has not joined the Republican party, he says, that could be in the cards.

Mayor Smith breaks tie

Skokie votes to amend liquor code

SKOKIE — In a 4-3 vote, broken by Skokie Mayor Albert J. Smith, the Village Board voted Monday to amend the liquor code so that no liquor establishment may be closer than 200 feet to another.

The amendment, affirmed by Trustees Calvin Butker, John Banghart, and Walter Flintrup, removes the original concept of the law limiting one liquor license to a block.

The reason for the change in the code was the recent realization by the village that Skokie has varying block sizes, ranging from 150 to 1,200 feet. It seemed very possible to many that this could indeed provide a loophole in the law, which was written to prevent clustering of liquor businesses.

TRUSTEE BERNARD Kaplan again led the fight to prevent a change in the law, which he considers to be one of the most constructive pieces of legislation this board has designed. Prior to the vote, he charged, "We've not plugging the loophole; we're opening the dikes.

Voting with him against the change were Trustees Robert Morris, and Herman Schmidt. But neither supported Kaplan in his try to remove the loophole between liquor business to 600 feet.

Trustee Calvin Butker could not agree with his fellow attorney Kaplan that the board is opening a Pandora's

Box. He wanted the legal loophole plugged and argued that what this amendment does is prevent the clustering of liquor business on corners, which is the real problem.

CORPORATION COUNCIL Harvey Schwartz stated that the change does not weaken the ordinance, but strengthens it.

Mayor Smith, who is also liquor commissioner here, added: "I can see to it that licenses will not be clustered in one block.

"With the limitation on the number of liquor licenses here, there is little to worry about."

The board also listened to another problem during the Monday night hearing, but of a different nature.

COMPLAINTS were heard by the village fathers against the Royal "Q" billiard parlor at 8806 Bronx.

It is, at least on the outside, a hangout for the motorcycle gangs, juvenile delinquents, and drag racers in this area, it was charged.

Several instances of women being insulted, and men accosted by these hoodlums were related. It was also mentioned that people are afraid to shop in the area.

The village has the police power to close the establishment at any time Village Manager Gordon Thorn seemed to be seeking that authority.

However, the board expressed concern that closing up the parlor would only be sending the problem elsewhere.

THE OWNER appears to be able to police his establishment but not what goes on outside.

The board will receive a report on the matter next week.

In other business, the board:

● Confirmed the appointments of Glenn Hartmanr, 4811 Davis, to the Skokie Fine Arts commission; and David Stone, 4449 Davis, to the Skokie Beautification commission.

● Affirmed the request for a special use permit to install additional drive-in windows and office space for the Skokie Trust and Savings bank.

● Delayed indefinitely the request to vacate the east-west alley south of Golf and east of Laverne.

About that weather...

WGN-TV WEATHERMAN Harry Volkman talks to a group of students at Orchard school for Special Education, 8600 Gross Point, Skokie, about his specialty. Also pictured are Mrs. Julia Molloy, principal-director of Orchard school, and pupils Julie and Dennis, who are pinning a red apple insignia boutenier on Volkman's lapel.

Today's Focus

Section two

Today's graduate: how he's changed

★

Roosevelt controversy bugs a reader

★

Hunger: as American as apple pie?

★

J. Edgar Hoover resignation hinted

★

How maverick Yorty views the world

★

Nigeria: bloody African battleground

Baseball off limits in street?

SKOKIE—Did you know that Skokie does not have an ordinance prohibiting baseball playing in the streets? You may not, but it seems that some of the teenagers do.

This is what the Skokie Board of Trustees learned recently when they were presented with an ordinance drafted to regulate street baseball playing.

The idea brought protest from those seated in Village Hall.

Skokie Corp. Counsel Harvey Schwartz did not appear enthusiastic over the proposal. He practically proclaimed that it would not be strictly enforced.

THE NEED for some kind of law, however, finally came out when it was learned that Skokie's police officers are being told, "Get out of here, copper, there's no law against it," when they try to break up rowdy ballplayers, the kind of players who think nothing of breaking young trees and other things while playing ball.

Trustee Walter Flintrup declared that he does not equate ball playing with breaking trees. "You're branching out from kids to young hooligans," he said.

"It's no joke," Thorn assured Flintrup. "Our biggest problem is our juveniles, who are knowledgeable of our law."

Another man said, "When someone cries 'copper,' these kids do not run." No one appeared ready to question if the village was better when they did run.

Fig. 66. Spot color in constrained use by *Skokie* (Ill.) *Life*. Arrows indicate elements in VanDyke brown.

register until the last news is in, while the primary plates can be registered on the press just as soon as the last previous run has been completed. Also, the black form must be remade to handle edition changes and replates for any reason. The brief periods available for such remaking do not allow sufficient time for registering in the black of the process picture. If the black is eliminated from the process art, the three primaries always remain in register, while any changes can be made on the rest of the newspaper page without affecting the color reproduction. Unfortunately, elimination of the black results all too often in a reproduction that is washed out and lacking those details which add life and crispness.

Offset newspapers usually do not remake for editions. Even if they did, the problem of register is far simpler on offset plates than in letterpress. So the black plate ought to be—and customarily is—retained for all process color.

Spot color is anything that isn't process color. Spot or flat color uses inks of the desired hue rather than creating the illusion of that hue by the optical mixing of primary colors.

On the advertising side, inkmakers work closely with the fashion industry. If a retailer wants to use the popular color of the high-style season in his advertisement, the newspaper orders ink of that hue. Pictures printed in "alfalfa green" will match exactly the color of the original dress, shoes, or hat.

Spot color may be used to print line or halftone. It can be used to create new hues, usually by printing screen patterns of two or more colors on the same area. Sunday comic strips are excellent examples of the versatility of spot color. *Beetle Bailey* uses color most simply, in large areas of primary color and only a little blending to create the army khaki which clothes most of its characters; large areas are left white. *Peanuts,* too, uses color in simple hues and masses. In *Terry and The Pirates,* George Wunder uses color in subtle hues and values. The most sophisticated user of spot color is Harold Foster, whose *Prince Valiant* absolutely refuses to recognize any limitation of color imposed by flat hues.

Sunday comics are either preprinted outside the newspaper plant or are supplied in stereotype matrices for each color. But daily comics are supplied only in black-and-white. At least three newspapers, the *St. Louis Post-Dispatch,* the *Daily Oklahoman* in Oklahoma City, and *Today* in Cocoa, Florida, make a highly promoted asset of daily comics in color.

Their methods are the same—and ingenious. The black plate is cast and printed in a blue that is light enough to be invisible to the plate-maker's camera. This is the *key plate* for the artist. Over it he places three pieces of transparent plastic as overlays. On these the artist paints the primary colors, one on each overlay. A special paint is used. This shows the artist how the individual colors and the new hues they create will appear in print. At the same time, the paints produce the proper values so that the colorblind engraver's lens can reproduce them in Ben Day patterns of the necessary tone.

The technique is admirably adopted to all spot-color artwork and can expand the possibilities for the staff artist even as it saves him substantial amounts of time.

Editorial color is usually predicated on advertising color. When the advertiser has bought the capacity of one or more color cylinders on the printing press, the editorial department can use that added color at the low cost of an additional printing plate. So on most papers, editorial color is used only as an exploitation of ad color. If the advertiser uses process color, the editorial department may also use process, or it may use any or all of the standard process colors as spot color.

But if the advertiser is using spot color, editorial use will depend greatly on the exact hue. At least it should so depend; when the news desk doesn't pay attention to the color available, the result may be less than happy. If the advertiser is using a primary or secondary color, almost any hue will work well for editorial spot color. But if the ad uses a fashion-world hue, the color may not be versatile enough for editorial purposes. In an ad, "boudoir pink" can show the precise hue of a selection of lingerie. But a front-page tint block or border in this color may be ridiculously inappropriate. Therefore the desk should always find out exactly what hue it is when spot color is offered for editorial use.

A single color should not be used for printing editorial halftones. Few colors have enough body to handle halftone detail adequately; some colors are unusually inappropriate for the subject of the picture. Warm colors do not fit cool scenes; cool colors are usually unpleasant for the printing of skin tones. A "little green man" may be a friendly fellow in science fiction, but in newspaper reproduction he is less than pleasant.

Color may enhance a halftone as a *tint block* over which the halftone is printed in black. Or the color may be used for a *duotone*. Duotone is used here in its strict sense; often the word is misused to describe two-color process work. A genuine duotone is a reproduction printed by two halftone plates made from the same black-and-white original. One plate prints a light ink, the other dark ink. In newspaper usage the dark ink is black and the light one is that used for advertising spot color. The result is a new third hue; the original two cannot be discerned.

Color should not be used for printing body type and rarely for headlines. The ink that has enough strength to make type readable usually irritates the eye. Color may be used as a tint block, a background for the surprinting of black type. In this case color must be screened down to a very low value. The full value of the color and the hue itself will determine what percentage of gray the tint block should carry. It must be light enough that the surprinted type is easily read. That may mean screens as low as 15% or 20% for such full-bodied colors as red, brown, orange, blue, and green. Only yellow can be used as a background in its full value. In fact, black printed on yellow has a legibility even greater than black on white.

If spot color is used with line art, the technique should be bold and free, and register should be loose. With *loose register,* plates may be out of alignment by as much as a full pica without destroying the effect of the picture. Detail should all be carried in the black plate, and the color should be broad and bold, laid down in large areas and in free brush strokes.

Color can make a good newspaper page more attractive, but it can't do much for a poor page. As a matter of fact, the addition of color to a poor page may make it worse.

Editorial color must be used functionally. Process color should not be used just because press facilities are available. Many news pictures actually have more impact in black-and-white than in full color.

The platemaker, in relief or offset, can't produce a plate better than the original art, so, whether using b&w or color, the editor should insist on top photographic quality. Only when the content of a photo is so strong that it cannot be left out of the paper can the editor afford to overlook technical deficiencies.

A page must be good in black-and-white or it can't be good in color. So all principles of good layout apply whether a page is chromatic or achromatic.

Color should be used in no more than three places on a page. These color areas may be large or small. But they should be kept simple in silhouette to be most effective. Color areas should be kept widely dispersed.

Circulation managers dearly love front-page banners in color, especially for street sales. It's interesting to note that under normal reading

Fig. 67. Hi-Fi ad pattern. Arrows on page from *Elko* (Nev.) *Daily Free Press* show how display element repeats in wallpaper pattern. Elements at right are of same depth but at different interval. Center panel is in yellow with black surprinting done locally. Note bleeds at all four sides.

conditions, changing a black headline to color has no measurable effect on readership of specific stories. Of course, a color banner may raise street sales without increasing the readership of their stories. But it makes no difference whatsoever to the job of the layout editor whether a head is printed in black or color.

When full-color photos are run in a combination, it usually adds to the impact if some b&w pictures are used in the layout. This should encourage the picture editor to replace inferior color shots with good black-and-whites.

Color, spot or process, is relatively inexpensive in time, materials, and labor for offset newspapers. There is then a temptation to overuse it or to use it nonfunctionally, a temptation that is minimal for letterpress operations. In either case, color should be used not because it is cheap or convenient, but only because it serves to enhance communication.

chapter 9

Format of the Newspaper

HAVING BROUGHT LUMBER, brick, and nails to a site, we are ready to build. Having determined the best forms for typographical components, we can start putting them together to make a newspaper. We must establish a principle of typography for the construction of a newspaper, then particularize it for the layout of each page.

The first decision a publisher must make on typography is that of the newspaper's format. Webster defines format as "the general physical appearance" of a publication. In newspaper usage, this is usually particularized to the size of the page, the number of columns, and the method of separating columns.

Newspaper format is either full or tabloid.

Full format uses a page of approximately 15 × 22 inches. Variations may add or subtract as much as 2 inches.

Full format may have six through nine columns.

Tabloid, or *compact, format* is usually in five 11-pica columns on a page approximately a horizontal half of the full format. Four- or 6-column tabloids are not rare. The difference between tabloid and compact format comes from typographic and layout techniques rather than page size. Differences in editorial content are just as important as the visual one.

The first tabloid, and still the classic example, is the *Daily News* in New York City, the paper with the largest circulation in the country. The dimensions of the *News* were determined on two bases: (1) the page was half of a full-format page so two tab pages could be printed in the same area of paper and of press cylinder as a full page, (2) the resultant page was a convenient size for reading on subways and other public transportation.

The Weather
Tonight
Snow
TEMPERATURE TODAY
Maximum 38; Minimum 29

The Kingston Daily Freeman

Get All the News
In The Freeman,
Leading Ad Media

VOL. XCVIII—No. 22 CITY OF KINGSTON, N. Y., TUESDAY EVENING, NOVEMBER 12, 1968 PRICE TEN CENTS

Dick Hints Peace Progress

By MERRIMAN SMITH

NEW YORK (UPI)—President-elect Richard M. Nixon, endorsing the lame duck Johnson administration and saying its members speak for him, hinted that "some very significant action and progress toward peace" may come before he takes office in 69 days.

Nixon, standing beside the man he will succeed Jan. 20, warned the "parties on the other side" Monday that the two administrations stand united on Vietnam, the Middle East and relations with the Soviet Union.

The president-elect said Johnson and Secretary of State Dean Rusk could conduct negotiations knowing "they could speak not just for this administration but for the nation and that meant the next administration as well."

Nixon's endorsement of Johnson's Vietnam policy moves over the next two months will put added pressures on the Saigon government of President Nguyen Van Thieu to reverse its stand and send a delegation to the expanded Paris talks, diplomatic sources said.

The president-elect conferred with Johnson Monday and was briefed by his top aides on foreign and domestic policy.

Nixon said the White House talks were helpful in "seeing to it that in the next 60 days—this very critical period—rather than havng the lapse of a lame duck presidency, in effect we might have some very significant action and progress toward peace."

Neither Nixon nor his aides would elaborate on the reference to the possibility of progress in the Vietnam negotiations.

Nixon, said there are too many critical international problems facing decision in Washington and the country could not afford a gap of two months in which no action or no negotiations could occur.

"If progress is to be made in any of these fields, it can be made only if the parties on the other side realize the current administration is setting forth policies that will be carried forward by the next administration," Nixon said.

After his afternoon meeting at the White House, Nixon flew to his headquarters in New York to continue putting together a new administration and preparing a budget for submission to Congress shortly after inauguration day.

Flying north from Florida Monday, Nixon and his wife went to the White House for lunch with the President and Mrs. Johnson. Then after a brief two-man meeting in the President's office, Nixon received nearly an hour and a half of briefing in the Cabinet room from ranking administration experts on foreign relations. Johnson arranged for Nixon to hear from Rusk, Secretary of Defense Clark M. Clifford, Gen. Earle G. Wheeler, chairman of the Joint Chiefs of Staff Central Intelligence Director Richard Helms and Walter W. Rostow, a foreign affairs specialist on the Johnson staff.

Johnson said he and Nixon realize the American people had a right to expect their government "to function efficiently at all times and he and I are going to do everything we possibly can to see that the wheels of government operate with maximum efficiency not only from now until Jan 20 but for all time to come."

Johnson indicated he anticipated further consultation with the president-elect before inauguration.

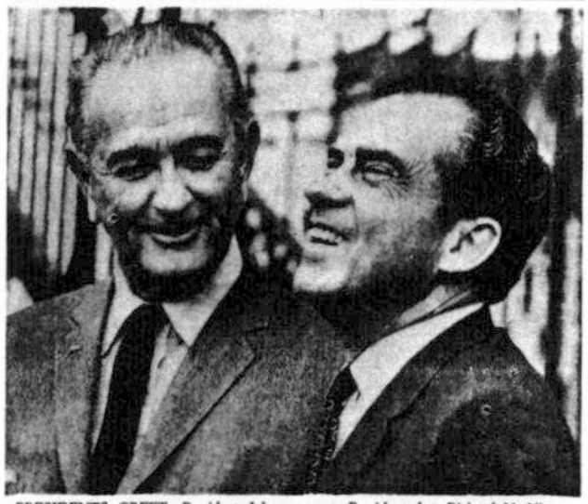

PRESIDENTS GREET—President Johnson greets President-elect Richard M. Nixon as the latter arrived at the White House for lunch and a meeting with the Chief Executive. (UPI TELEPHOTO)

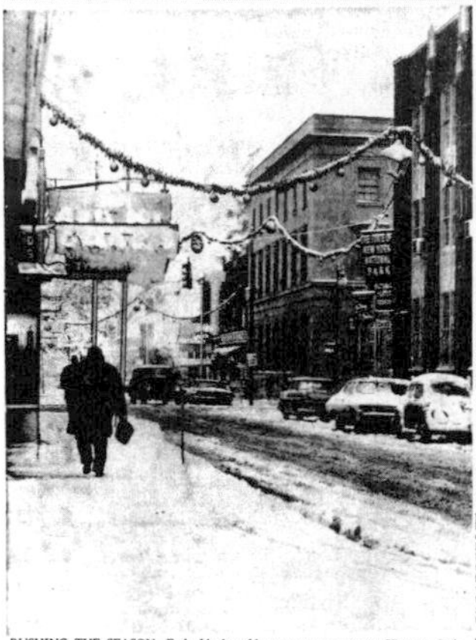

RUSHING THE SEASON—Early blanket of heavy snow coats uptown Kingston. Buffled walkers lend a mid-winter look as they hurry down John Street. (Freeman photo by Kruh)

The Dreary Forecast: Snow and More Snow

By JEAN F. DOLAN

The first major snowstorm of the not yet winter season hit Ulster County early this morning, snarling traffic, downing tree limbs and closing schools.

With official winter more than a month away according to the calendar, many motorists were caught without the protection of snow tires and chains.

The forecasters peered into their snow covered crystal ball and came up with predictions which varied from three to five and eight to 12 inches during the six to 12 hour storm. Anyway you look at it that's a lot of snow for early November.

City Department of Public Works crews were out early this morning salting hills, bus routes and hospital accesses. The plows are on ready in case the accumulated white stuff reaches pushing depth.

Another factor which hampered travel and caused headaches for Central Hudson crews were falling trees and limbs. The heavy snow driven by northeast winds overloaded trees still wearing their fall foliage. Much of the trouble which accompanied Sunday's two to six inch snow fall was repeated over a wider area today.

The state highway department was harrassed by equipment breakdowns and downed limbs all over the county. County highway department reported sanding crews and scrapers on the job early this morning trying to untangle the creeping cars.

State Police reported that Route 209 near Kerhonkson was completely blocked at approximately 9:30 as skidding vehicles clogged the road.

The reports of power interruptions throughout the area swamped the switchboard at Central Hudson. As heavy snows snapped tree limbs and power lines over a wide section of the Mid-Hudson valley, repair crews rushed to the scenes of trouble.

The N.Y. Telephone company faced a similar situation plus the overload of calls from stranded travelers trying to reach help and inform waiting employers.

Social and civic events were canceled left and right througout the county.

The heavy snow which spread north and west across the state throughout the day came in from the south. Heavy snow warnings for Southeastern New York including Ulster County were out through tonight. By tomorrow the entire state will be under the cloud of rain and snow with heavy squalls predicted for the shores of Lake Erie and Ontario.

New York City had rain, sleet and winds gusting to 63 miles an hour just before dawn today. Snow was falling in the Southern Tier but the Mid-Hudson Valley was bearing the early brunt of the southern-born storm.

Last year's first major snowstorm of the season was a more timely Christmas season dumping of up to 10 inches in Kingston Dec. 28 and 29. Although the snows came Nov. 9 in 1967 it was a respectible half inch dusting which quickly melted.

This year's first was up to four inches on Nov. 10 followed by this unseasonable mess. And there is little consolation in knowing the area is not alone in the wide-spread wet blanket.

Family of 7 Perishes In Sullivan Holocaust

By WALTER S. CLARK

A family of seven perished early today when fire of undetermined origin erupted in their bungalow home at Camp Hemlock on Burlingham Road in the Sullivan County community of Bloomingburg about three miles north of Middletown.

The victims of the tragic blaze, which was discovered by a neighbor at about 4:30 a.m., apparently were suffocated before their bodies were burned, authorities said.

State Police identified the dead as:

Donald Terwillier and his wife, Margaret (ages not available) and their five children, Peter, 8 ,Catherine, 7, Donald Jr., 6, Angel, 5, and Otis 4.

According to investigators the fire was discovered by Jesse Hinkley, who resides next door. He was awakened by crackling of flames and smoke. Hinkley hurriedly donned his clothes and drove a quarter of a mile through blinding snow and over slippery roads to the home of Bartley Smith, where he used the telephone to notify fire officials.

Firefighters from Bloomingburg in command of Chief Harry Kramer made the run to the scene of the blaze within 15 minutes. On arrival they found the frame bungalow completely engulfed in flames.

Within minutes firemen were directing hoseline streams of water into the roaring flames that were fanned by a strong wind.

About 20 minutes later firemen discovered one body in the burning building. Fire officials immediately summoned state troopers from the Ferndale Station and notified Sullivan County Coroner Dr. Sidney P. Schiff, who went to the fire scene to take part in the investigation.

Troopers and firemen with Coroner Schiff searched through the burning embers of the house, handling piece by piece as they sought the bodies of the other victims.

All of the seven bodies were found burned almost beyond recognition on the beds in the two bedrooms of the small residence.

Preliminary examination by the coroner and physicians indicated that Terwilliger, his wife and five small children died of suffocation before the flames reached them.

Volunteer firemen experienced considerable trouble as they drove their cars over snow-packed roads to get to the fire scene.

The Terwilliger family lived at the bungalow the year round, state police were told, although most of the dwellings in Camp Hemlock are used only as summer camps.

It was not known whether a heating unit of whether defective wiring started the blaze which completely destroyed the dwelling.

Camp Hemlock, a popular summer resort in the Bloomingburg area, is operated by Charles Tarrow. No estimate of the loss was reported.

The bodies of the victims were removed to a morgue. State police sought relatives to notify them of the tragedy.

Terwilliger had been employed at a box factory in Middletown.

Harry Schirick, 78, Dies; On Court Bench 26 Years

Retired Supreme Court Justice Harry E. Schirick, 78, of 1 Albany Avenue, Kingston, died this morning.

From warming a bench as a rookie big league ballplayer with the St. Louis Browns in 1914 to serving 26 years on the Supreme Court Bench, Justice Schirick's colorful career continued until his retirement in 1960.

Born in Ruby, Ulster County on June 15, 1890, he was one of a family of ten children—seven boys and three girls. All of the justices' brothers and sisters are deceased. One brother was killed in World War I.

Justice Schirick moved to Kingston with his family at the age of four and one-half years, graduated from elementary school and the old Kingston Academy and later received his law degree from Cornell University.

It was during the summer of 1914 that the justice was signed by the St. Louis Browns, then managed by Branch Rickey.

Later Justice Schirick, in pursuit of a law career, became associated with the late Judge Frederick Stephan of Kingston. A Democrat, he was elected City Judge in 1916 and was reelected in 1920.

From 1920 to 1934,. Judge Schirick was a law associate of Frank Brooks at 44 Main Street, Kingston until he was appointed by Gov. Herbert Lehman to fill a Supreme Court vacancy. The appointment went into effect Jan. 1, 1935 and the following year Justice Schirick ran for election to a 14-year term. His running mate was Justice Francis Bergan of Albany. At the expiration of the 14-year term, Justcie Schirick was endorsed for a new term by both Republicans and Democrats in the Third Judicial District.

Guest of honor at a round of testimonials given by a number of bar associations and judiciary groups at the time of his retirement, Justice Schirick was also cited for his role as a dynamic political figure.

As Democratic county leader, he won a majority on the Board of Supervisors, a feat that Democrats have not repeated since (40 years).

In 1958 he was feted by the Old Timers Baseball Association and was given the associations' annual award for being "the

Continued on Page 8, Col. 5)

Hercules Explosion Injures 2 Workmen

PORT EWEN—An explosion at the Hercules Powder Company plant that rocked the Port Ewen area this morning, severely injured two workmen and damaged the fuse press house where the blast occurred.

Admitted at Benedictine Hospital where they were rushed following the blast were John Emmick, 51, of 66 Harding Avenue and James Williams, 28, of 13 Russell Street. Their conditions were described as fair.

A company official said Emmick and Williams were the only two workmen in a concrete bay in the 20 x 60 foot building when the explosion occurred at 4:20 a.m. They were reportedly pressing fuse powder, it was said.

The cause of the explosion was not immediately determined, but officials of the company were investigating.

The Hercules official said it didn't appear that damage to the structure, which was divided into concrete bays, was extensive although inspectors were examining the structure.

The official also noted that he was awaiting word from the company physician about the extent of injuries suffered by the two men.

Early reports showed Emmick sustained multiple puncture wounds. Williams received blast injuries and possible punctures of the eardrums from the noise of the explosion.

Both Williams and Emmick have been employed by the Port Ewen firm several years. It was reported that other workmen attracted to the fuse press house rushed to the aid of the two injured men.

Paging the Inside News

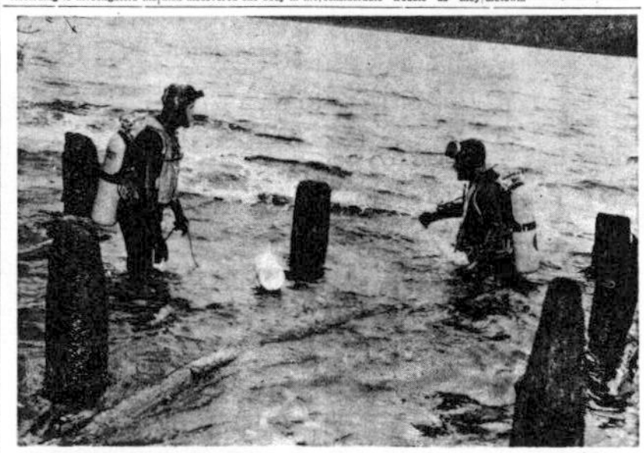

SEARCH CONTINUES—State Police Scuba divers have been combing the bottom of the Hudson River for five days in search of evidence that might aid in the solution of the unsolved murder of 23-year-old Robert D. Gallo of East Kingston. The victim was shot while hunting near his home on Oct. 20. Participating in the search which was halted temporarily on Monday were (l-r) Trooper B. S. O'Connor and Robert M. Malloy. They are working with Troopers J. E. Storch and R. W. Thorpe under command of Senior Trooper R. S. McDowell. (Freeman photo by Kruh.)

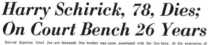

Fig. 68. Full format is that of *Daily Freeman* of Kingston, N.Y., in eight columns. Note effective use of horizontal layout.

Fig. 69. Poster format of typical tabloid newspaper was created and is still used by New York Daily News. Note treatment of back page.

Aiming his publication at the subway set, Captain Joseph Patterson added to the appeal of a convenient size by editorial treatment that delighted the same group of readers. Love nests, murders, assorted scandal, and human interest were displayed by headlines brash in form and content. Photographs, still scarce and small in the conventional newspaper of 1919, became profuse and large in the *News*. Cameramen were as irreverent as reporters, and "candid photos" were a major stock in trade. Cutlines were artfully written to enhance the lure of the picture, and the *News* is still a textbook for this demanding and specialized form of writing.

Circulation of the *News,* ever since its birth, is the best indicator of the popularity not only of this newspaper but of the techniques it introduced. But a large percentage of Americans, many of whom were *News* readers despite their protestations, clucked their tongues at this tabloid and the imitators which inevitably sprang up. "Tabloid" became a term of less than profuse compliment; it was a synonym for the "yellow journalism" of the preceding generation.

The typical front page of a tabloid is in *poster makeup*. There will be a large picture, one or two headlines, and no body type. The lead story will be on page 3. There, too, will usually be the stories for other front-page heads. The back page of the tab is usually the sports page and carries its own nameplate. Often it, too, will be made up in poster style, and then there is the unusual situation of the reader going backward into the paper to read the stories. More often than on page one, there may be body type on the back page—say, a complete short story or a bulletin.

In the 1930's a new breed of tabloid was born. It used the smaller page size but never poster layout. Its appearance was that of a small full-format newspaper; its content was as sober as that of full-format papers. After World War II, many such smaller papers were begun because the size can be produced on presses that were more readily available in that era of intense shortages of peacetime equipment.

Publishers of such newspapers chafed under the undeserved opprobrium that "tabloid" meant to many people. So when the automobile industry made "compact" a respectable term, publishers borrowed the word to describe their product. The new label caught on only slowly, and even today "tab format" is generally used unless the need for fine distinction requires "compact."

The decision between full and tab format is usually based on available press capacity. This is most frequently the case when printing is directly from type or by offset. Most presses using stereo plates can handle either format equally well.

There are other considerations, of course. (The advantages of tab format apply to compacts, too, so although "tab" is used here, "compact" may be substituted at any time.)

1. Reader convenience is a definite asset. While subway, bus, and train readers are generally found only in metropolitan areas and their number shrinks constantly, the convenience of the smaller page is pleasant to the at-home reader, too.
2. A tabloid is a bulkier newspaper. The reader feels he is getting more for his money. An 8-page full-format paper feels skimpy and flimsy in his hands; the same amount of paper in 16 tab pages is a thicker and more pleasant package.
3. The small page affords greater flexibility in adding pages. When two full-format pages are added to accommodate extra advertising, the ad-news ratio may go out of balance. Only half as much area need be added with a tab page. (Two points must be remembered: Two pages are the smallest increment for enlarging or decreasing the size of the paper; full pages must be added even though the advertising itself fills far less than that area.)
4. Departmentalization is easier because a whole small page can be devoted to one department. On larger pages, more than one department may have to run on the same page.
5. It is easier to keep an entire tab page free of ads, for better editorial display, than an entire full-format page. This may be especially useful in making possible an ad-free editorial page for a small newspaper. Weeklies often have a severe problem in obtaining an open editorial page.
6. Advertisers are benefited by the smaller pages.
   a. Because fewer stories can be displayed on the front page, the editor must run good ones on inside pages. The reader is accustomed to this, and may give more attention to tab inside pages. This increases reader traffic and ad exposure.
   b. Smaller ads gain prominence on smaller pages. (Often this permits higher rates in tabs. This can be advantageous to the publisher. The cost of setting and composing local advertising is affected to a large degree by its area; if a smaller space in a tab can produce as much revenue as a larger area in a full format, the net profit is greater.)
   c. It is easier to sell an advertiser a full tabloid page than a large page. There is an advantage in a full-page ad, no matter what format. If the tabloid advertiser can achieve this advantage with only a 10% or even a 20% increase over the space originally planned, he may be more easily motivated to do so; a far greater percentage of increase is required to fill a whole full-format page. (Tabloids can accommodate full-format complete-page ads by running them sideways on two tab pages.)
   d. The tighter departmentalization that a tab affords makes it possible for

advertising to be placed more appropriately adjacent to an editorial department.

Each coin has "tails" as well as "heads." The tab's disadvantages are:

1. The term "the little paper" is still used deprecatingly against the tab format in some areas. This depends, of course, to a large extent upon competition. If the competitor has a full format, he may encourage such comment, or it may spring up spontaneously among readers. In the past there was widespread prejudice against tabloid format, either because of its unfamiliarity or because of its association with sin-sex-and-sadism journalism. This antipathy has almost disappeared, though.
2. Tabloid format requires a higher percentage of the paper area for margins. If a sheet of paper that accommodates a full-format page is used for two tab pages, the division between the two tab pages uses approximately 10 column inches, some 6% of the total area. The annual accumulation of this loss is substantial.
3. Page justification and lockup is increased by the extra number of pages. While it takes a little longer to place the material needed to fill a full-page chase than to place that for a tabloid form, the final lockup process takes about the same time for any page.
4. It may be necessary to add pages to obtain workable areas for placing advertising. A tabloid section may have room for five more full columns of advertising, but it is divided into 1-column strips; thus to place a 4- or 5-column ad, it may be necessary to add another page. That means adding the reverse side of the page also, of course, and thus the ad-news ratio may go awry. (The same problem plagues full-format pages, of course, but the larger the page, the less the danger of having unusable areas of open space.)
5. The smaller page size may encourage smaller advertisements when the advertiser realizes that he can dominate a page with less space than is required on a full-format page. (The antidote of higher rates is not always possible, especially in a competitive situation.)
6. Matted ads larger than a tab page may create problems. The center spread can accommodate a full-format page advertisement, as we have already noted, but there is only one center spread available. Ads deeper than 15 inches may run sideways across the spread or even on facing pages. Although this is less than desirable, many tabloid papers use this method, even for a full 8-column advertisement. But, unless the ad has a strip of white where it can be divided into two sections, this requires rearranging of the stereotype material. Often it requires special permission of the advertiser that may be difficult to obtain from national ad agencies.
7. The bulk of a large daily in tabloid form may negate the advantage of the more convenient page size. The full-format newspaper is quickly and easily

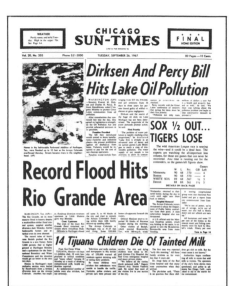

Fig. 70. Compact formats. *Alhambra* (Calif.) *Free Press* and *Chicago* (Ill.) *Sun-Times* use 6-column format. *Crown Zellerbach Times* of San Francisco, Calif., is in more typical five columns. MOONLIGHTERS head and parallel rules in nameplate of *Free Press* are in cyan; boxes in *Sun-Times* ears are red.

divided into sections. A tabloid is a single section; any division is usually an artificial one that the reader doesn't make instinctively. When a tab runs greater than about 36 pages, it becomes a heavy and awkward bundle to handle while reading.

There is, though, a solution to this problem. The single section of a tabloid may be divided into subdivisions by using one or more _pull-outs._ This is a group of pages that the reader is asked to remove from the original package to make a second, separate section. The pull-out may be identified by turning it upside down. As the reader moves normally through the paper, he comes to the pull-out. He sees its last page, reversed in position in relation to previous pages. The hope—and it's usually realized—is that the reader will lift out this portion. It's easy for him, of course. He need not look for the other end of the pull-out; he just wraps his finger around the gutter margin of the first page and has the removable portion in his hand.

Newsday, a Long Island, New York, tabloid, identifies its pull-out sections by using a semicircle cut out of the margin. This acts like the _thumb index_ of a dictionary. To produce such a cutout index requires an attachment to the press, of course. The research-minded mechanical crew at _Newsday,_ which developed the technique and machinery, says it's no problem at all. There is a question, of course, as to whether this capital investment would be profitable to a paper with a circulation smaller than _Newsday_'s 427, 393 (Audit Bureau of Circulation, October, 1968).

In theory, at least, a tabloid can be divided into several pull-outs. Let's assume an issue of 24 pages—just for the sake of illustration, not because a small paper like that needs subdividing. In the simplest scheme, pages 9 to 16 would be the pull-out. This 8-page section would be turned so that page 16, upside down, would follow page 8. After the section had been removed, page 17 would follow directly after 8. The page numbering we use here need not be used in the actual paper, of course. Our 17th page could be numbered as 9 and the pull-out's pages be numbered independently.

If we want to break down the 24 pages into three sections, the first section could contain pages originally numbered 1 to 4 and 21 to 24. The second section could be pages 5 to 8 and 17 to 20; these would be upside down in relation to the first section.

The third section would be pages 9 to 16. These would be upside down in relation to the second section in which they appear, but they would be right-side-up in relation to the first section.

8. Tabloid format usually requires more "excelsior" than full format. This is editorial content whose main purpose is to fill in space around advertising. Ideally, this matter should have the same news value as that on an open page. Good inside-page content can teach and encourage the reader to

Fig. 71. Diagram for sectioning of tabloid or compact newspaper.

recognize that even this copy is well worth reading. But it requires extra work on the desk to keep this copy from becoming merely padding to keep ads from rattling around on a page.

When a publisher adds up pros and cons, he usually faces the same disquieting data which attend so many editorial decisions. The choice is almost never between something that's 100% good and zero percent bad. Usually the choice is somewhere between 45% and 55% or even 49% and 51%.

Then purely mechanical factors become more decisive. Press capacity is a major factor; we want to use the maximum cylinder area of the press. There is no point in amortizing or moving masses of machinery that don't produce a printed image.

Tabloid pages can efficiently be made up in full-page chases, so rarely is the composing room equipment a decisive factor.

If the paper is produced or printed in a central plant that is used by more than one newspaper, it may be advantageous to choose a tabloid format merely because all other publications produced by the plant are in the same format. The efficiency of standardization is great.

The competitive situation may swing the decision. The publisher may want to challenge the competitor in identical terms; if the competitor is in full format, the challenger may choose the same page size to make his superiority more obvious. He may just as logically decide that his newspaper may achieve its own identity more readily with a radically different appearance.

Tabloid advantages may be greater in special circumstances, and so it has become commonplace to run special sections in tab format and insert them into the regular full-format newspaper. Many merchandising events lend themselves to this technique. It is easy to fill an entire section with the appropriate editorial support which is valuable not only in selling space but making it produce sales. Radio-TV sections and Sunday magazines are customarily in this format.

In full format, the decision as to number of columns is predicated on press capacity. In conventional full format, the 11-pica column is standard. Advertising—national and in stereo matrices supplied for local use—is prepared in this increment. While a very few newspapers still use a measure up to 12 picas, this is wasteful in the context of salable space.

Seven-column format is not rare, but eight-column is customary in full format. Six-columns may be used in both tab and full format. The only difference is that the six-column full page is about 33% longer than the tab page.

Nine-column pages are more common among weeklies than in dailies in the United States, but in Canada the nines are common among dailies. Most weeklies in this format adopted it after a narrower column was adopted as standard for national advertising in 1953. Papers then using 12-pica measures—and, in a few instances, even wider lines—found that they could get the ninth column in their chases and on their presses with relative ease after they changed to 11 picas.

The esthetics of the 9-column page leave much to be desired; the economics are most attractive, however. With little extra cost, the newspaper's space is increased 12.5%. Typesetting costs advance proportionally, of course, but lockup time is increased only very slightly over that for eight columns. Press time remains constant, as do attendant expenses. The big advantage, however, is in reducing the need for going to extra pages to accommodate advertising. Especially on smaller papers it is a distinct asset to be able to place a 5-column and a 4-column ad on the same page. In an 8-column format, the 5-column ad would force the 4-columner to another page, and often that has to be an added page.

Because newspaper readers are human and therefore creatures of habit, the full format has the advantage of "looking like a newspaper." This is nothing to dismiss lightly. People associate format with content, and are often uncomfortable when a familiar association is changed. A magazine in *Look*'s format had better have plenty of pictures, and one in the size of *Reader's Digest* is expected to carry brief articles. Newspapers, too, must conform to preconceptions of appearance and contents.

Habits change, though, and it is primarily mechanical factors that keep most American newspapers in full format and will continue to do so until present presses are worn out.

WEATHER
Cloudy, clearing tonight. Cloudy periods, milder Friday. Low tonight 30. High tomorrow 50.

THE TELEGRAM

82 PAGES
91ST YEAR

TORONTO, THURSDAY, MARCH 23, 1967

10 CENTS
367-4500

NIGHT EDITION

1867 | 1967

A CHILD . . . a prayer book . . . and, in stained glass, the figure of Christ crucified. The spirit of Easter is everywhere in this study of a five-year-old Maureen O'Neill, of Ravencliff cres., Agincourt, inside Regis College chapel on Bayview ave. The window is one of the Stations of the Cross created for the Jesuit community by artist James Patrick Morrish. This is a time to pause and meditate, as thousands of Torontonians in city and suburb flock to church. (See times of Church services on Page 31.)

Richard Cole, Telegram

WARRENDALE:

Auditors' report causes a storm

John L. Brown, fired last year as executive director of Warrendale, authorized funds that went to his wife, a brother and himself — without telling his board of directors.

This is revealed in a special auditors' report by a Toronto firm of accountants tabled in the Legislature yesterday.

The investigation into expenditures at the former private treatment centre for emotionally-disturbed children ended when the Province took over the centre last Sept. 7.

Mr. Brown is a New Democratic Party candidate for the next Provincial election in the Toronto riding of Beaches-Woodbine.

The report says it appears Mr. Brown was paid for holidays twice the same year; raised his own salary; paid his wife for 18 days after she quit working at Warrendale and employed his brother at excessive rates.

Deputy NDP Leader Ken Bryden said it wasn't an auditors' report at all but a "desperate attempt at a political hatchet job" and the "dirty work of the Government."

Mr. Brown, former Warrendale director, told a Queen's Park press conference today that the entire auditors' report was "a pack of lies" put together by a Tory firm."

He said that the attack was politically inspired because the Government had wanted to defeat him at the polls.

Liberal Leader Robert Nixon said the auditors had shown "serious inconsistencies." He demanded the Government "tell the whole

See BROWN Page 13

The high cost of Government

$255,200 hike for Senate

By ROBERT MacDONALD
Telegram Staff Reporter

OTTAWA — The Senate — the Valhalla of the politically faithful — will cost Canadians more than $3,000,000 this year.

That's a hike of $255,200 over 1966.

The senators will pick up $1,300,000 in salaries; $60,000 for travelling plus $300,000 in expense allowances.

The 1967-68 budget for the Senate also contains an increase in supporting staff. There will be 227 in the administration staff compared to 200 last year.

Salaries alone for the staff will jump to $979,300 compared to $898,000 last year.

Although many people have called for abolition of the Senate over the years, its cost keeps mounting for day-to-day business.

Publishing Senate debates — debates where as few as 10 or 12 senators attended — will cost $90,000 compared to $80,000 in 1966.

Printing of other publications — reports and similar material — will jump to $140,000 from $120,000.

And there is a $60,000 item in the budget estimates for new furniture.

Cost of telephone calls and telegrams for the senate

See SENATE Page 13
See also Page 4

BUTTER UP 2c

A Federal Government decision will boost the price of butter two cents a pound. Report on page 12.

KATHLEEN QUINNEY

Mother, 20, turned to burglary to feed family

Garnishees against her husband's wages forced a 20-year-old pregnant housewife into a burglary spree, Magistrate P. J. Bolsby was told yesterday.

Kathleen Quinney, mother of a nine-month-old baby, said she was unable to feed her family on the $27 a week that remained from her truckdriver husband's salary.

Salvation Army Major Thelma Worthylake said the pregnant woman was refused welfare because her husband was employed.

Mrs. Quinney, a slightly-built girl appearing much younger than her 20 years, said she had to choose between hunger or crime.

She chose crime and is now in prison awaiting sentence on March 29.

She entered a home on Codsall ave. by forcing a door, smashing windows and causing $70 worth of damage to the house. But she left empty-handed.

Magistrate Bolsby remarked that she showed great determination in becoming a burglar.

She smashed windows of a second house and stole a dress worth about $25. Returning to the same house two days later, Mrs. Quinney jimmied the rear door, but left without taking anything.

Then she returned to the first house and stole a purse with $16.

Mrs. Quinney then changed her methods. She began talking her way into houses.

She asked the owner of a house on Clinton st. if she could use the phone, and

See MOTHER, Page 2

Finance firms strangle town say workers

ANSONVILLE, Ont. — (Special) — This remote Northern Ontario paper mill town of 3,500, with about its entire working force in debt, wants to run its two finance companies out of town.

Some 1,200 paper mill workers, who with their families make up about 3,000 of the town residents, claim the firms are financially "strangling" them with multiple wage assignments that sometimes exceed their wages.

Last week, a delegation of mill workers led by Doug Thompson, president of the Pulp and Sulphite Workers' Union local 90, told the town council that unless the firms are forced to leave they will be run out of the town, 50 miles northwest of Timmins.

Mr. Thompson estimates that the mill workers between them owe some $6,000,000 aside from mortgages on their homes.

While some of these loans,

See FINANCE Page 9

There will be no editions of The Telegram next Friday. Publication will resume on Saturday. Friday's comics are in today's issues.

NOW
tv weekly
(Complete program listing)
Free with today's Telegram
In The Southern Ontario Television Viewing Area

Bulletin

Canada was knocked out of the Scotch Cup today — for the first time in nine years — losing to Scotland, 6-5. Sweden beat the U.S., 7-6.

Yorkville 'festering'

Liberal MPP George Ben said yesterday Yorkville is festering with drug addicts, venereal disease carriers and corrupted youth. He called for a breaking-up of the area.

See FATHER Page 9

PRUDENTIAL
FINANCE

Behind-the-scenes story

To the public, all was well with Prudential Finance Corp. until Nov. 1, 1966, when the company missed an interest payment, but what went on behind the scenes was revealed yesterday.

Actually Prudential was in bad financial shape for six years before its collapse. And the situation had been steadily worsening.

Two reports tabled in the Legislature told how assets of the company, that went bankrupt with a deficit of $17,000,000, had been inflated over the last few years to make it look as though there

was more than enough money to pay off debts.

Take for example the Muir Park Hotel in Toronto. Clarkson, Gordon & Co., chartered accountants, told how its value was written up more than 400 per cent. in one year.

It was bought by Ontario Metal Specialties, a Prudential subsidiary, for $870,000 on Jan. 9, 1965.

Ontario Metal Specialties paid $170,000 cash and assumed a $700,000 mortgage. Improvements of $463,447 raised the value to $1,333,447.

A further $450,000 was added by Prudential Fi-

nance as a finder's fee and on Dec. 31, 1965, the property was sold to another Prudential subsidiary, Filton Realty Co. Ltd. for $3,586,634.

Mercantile switch angers U.S. bank

By RON COLLISTER
Telegram Ottawa Bureau

OTTAWA — Canada today stands accused of "nationalizing" the Mercantile Bank as the battle over the fate of the U.S.-owned bank erupts again.

And there were rumors here today the U.S. State Department may make another attempt to have the Prudential subsidiary changed. The department stepped in without success earlier in the controversy.

Before First National City Bank of New York, owner of Mercantile, find its broadside of criticism, Finance Minister Mitchell Sharp was peacemaking in Ottawa.

He offered Citibank an annual exemption from the law so long as it moved "in good faith" to sell Mercantile shares to Canadians.

On Tuesday the Commons had dropped a bombshell in voting to give the Government power to choose the day when Citibank must un-

Ontario Metal got 10 per cent. of the mark-up and Triangle Equipment Ltd., another company controlled by Prudential president J.

B. Brien, got 90 per cent. — or $1,620,000.

In talking the reports by Clarkson and the Ontario Securities Commission, Financial and Commercial Affairs Minister Rowntree said it was impossible for the Government to legislate morality, but promised to "bring to justice every person responsible for these reprehensible acts."

And he told a press conference that despite new securities legislation that had been passed, there was no guarantee a Prudential

See PRUDENTIAL Page 15

load 75 per cent. of Mercantile shares.

An hour after Mr. Sharp appeared before the Senate banking committee and

See MERCANTILE Page 8

$Full page report — 27

Inside

A SUPPLEMENT FOR YOUNG CANADA IN TODAY'S PAPER

Fig. 72. Nine-column format. Large picture in *Toronto (Ont.) Telegram* is brilliant rotogravure Spectacolor.

The earliest American newspapers were small; *Publick Occurrences* was only 7¼ x 11⅜ inches. When invention of the Linotype alleviated the horrendous problem of setting sufficient type, newspapers grew larger in format and number of pages. The all-time record—with no challenger in sight—is held by the single issue of the *Illuminated Quadruple Constellation,* also published in Boston, on July 4, 1859. With a name like that, it needed a generous page just to contain the flag. It had eight 35 x 50-inch pages, each with 13 columns of 13½-pica measure. In case the delightful statistics don't mean anything to you, note that these pages were more than four times as big as today's "large-size" newspapers.

Current contender for the largest American newspaper page is the *Inquirer and Mirror* of Nantucket, the picturesque island off the Massachusetts coast. *The Inky M,* as its readers affectionately refer to it, was founded in 1821. Its page is 22 x 30 inches and has nine 12-pica columns.

Open Format

There are several subdivisions of full and tab format, and to avoid complete confusion, we must stop to sort out and define a few more terms.

Closed format is the conventional one that separates type with column rules. *Open format* replaces column rules with alleys, which ought to be at least 1 pica wide but frequently are narrower.

Maximum—max—format is one that places the maximum number of standard columns on the sheet of paper. For the discussion here the "standard" is assumed as 11 picas.

Conventional format is *maximum closed format.* When alleys replace column rules but the number of legs of type remains the same, the result is *maximum open format.* But neither adjective—max or closed—is ever used except in technical discussions like this when precise meanings must be expressed.

There are three variations of open format which are not maximum format and so carry their own labels. These occur when the space used for alleys is so great that it would be possible to put another standard column on the page simply by replacing alleys with column rules. These four formats—all comparatively recent—are optimum format; W-format; Chicago, or Detroit, format; and 7-format.

Optimum Format

Optimum—op—format spreads five or six wider columns across the normal 8-column page and allows alleys in place of column rules. It gets its name from its column width, which is at or near the *optimum line length* for the body type used.

The distinction must be made between the 6-column page in 11-pica columns, a max format, and the 6-column op page of approximately 15-pica columns. Because the op format is so new, it is often a matter of pride to claim to have the first in a state. When that claim is made for "a 6-column format"—in 15 picas—it is often challenged by a newspaper which has used six 11-pica columns for a long time. So "op format" should never be described as "6-column format."

The first notable use of the 6-column op format was by the *Wall Street Journal*. At that time, it is supposed, the choice was made to give the *WSJ* an unusual appearance that pointed up the distinctive area of news that it covered. Because it was such a specialized publication, its format had no apparent influence on general circulation newspapers.

It was a younger sibling that caused real ripples of interest in the newspaper world. The *National Observer* was begun by the Dow-Jones Company, publishers of the *WSJ,* to utilize printing facilities that were standing idle over the weekend, when the business paper didn't publish. But it is just coincidence that the baby adopted the 6-column format of its big brother.

When the *Observer* was in planning, its planners deliberately ignored all existing specifications. The decision for six columns was based on accommodating the optimum line length. The decision on the format came only after the body type had been selected. It was 8½-point Ionic, a longtime favorite news face that had just been cut in 8½. Its 131-point lowercase-alphabet length produces an optimum line length of 16.4 picas.

In order to provide a full pica of white space as an alley between columns, the measure was set at 15½ picas (15.6 in print-shop usage). Six such columns fit perfectly onto the page width which was, of course, the same as that of the *Wall Street Journal*.

The unique nature of the new newspaper and the high reputations of the men behind it focused attention on the *Observer*. Its format was hailed by professional newsmen and readers alike. But because it was a weekly and because it was, at least to some degree, more specialized than

Fig. 73. Optimum format as introduced by *National Observer*. Note customary use of large halftone and large art. Headline schedule in Caledonia Bold.

the typical paper, the *Observer* did not become the real bellwether for op format.

That significant role was played by the *Christian Science Monitor* in 1965.

The *Monitor,* since its inception in 1908, has almost without exception been on every list of "the 10 best newspapers." The depth and accuracy of its reporting and the authority and impartiality of its editorial content, not to mention its wholesome ethical stance, gave the *Monitor* a readership among professional journalists that few other newspapers have attained. Any example it sets gets wide and intense scrutiny. It is important, too, that the *Monitor* is a daily newspaper and that it remakes extensively for five editions.

The *Monitor* had reached a stage in its history when reevaluation of its function and performance was logical. At that time it was decided to shift the emphasis of its coverage. Rising sophistication and deeper involvement of its readers demanded greater depth reporting. Inability of print media to match electronic communications in immediacy of news coverage was aggravated by problems of the *Monitor*'s global circulation. Even the fastest of jet planes which carry printed paper or page mats to distant points are lumberingly slow in comparison to radio waves or television images bounced off satellites.

So decision was made to anticipate news breaks as much as possible, to give background stories before the event. What was in effect almost a new product deserved new packaging, the *Monitor* editors decided. The result of almost a year of planning was the op format. But this time "optimum" translated into a 5-column page.

An unusual factor was injected into the *Monitor*'s problem. It carries a great number of small advertisements sold by local representatives in communities throughout the country. Many of these are one column wide—and that column is 11 picas. Indeed, many of these ads have run in local newspapers and come to the *Monitor*'s Boston plant as stereo mats. It was beyond possibility to convert these ads to a wider measure with correspondingly higher rates per column-inch.

These small ads usually run in only one edition. So pages have to be made over much more extensively than in a typical daily. These ads are grouped by locality or subject matter and so the task of *laying the ads* is complicated. These factors added up to the inevitable: Advertising must stay on 11-pica columns, and editorial measure must accommodate itself to the ad pyramid.

A tentative decision was to go to a 5-column format. The measure was

THE CHRISTIAN SCIENCE MONITOR

BOSTON, MONDAY, MARCH 1, 1965 — *An International Daily Newspaper* — VOL. 57, NO. 78 TWO SECTIONS — EASTERN EDITION ★ 10c

FOCUS on science-technology

What's ahead...

Gemini, the American two-man spacecraft, storms into space with its first astronauts late this month or early next.

But this and other early Gemini flights won't answer the central question in manned space travel.

Can man be weightless for a week, two weeks, or more, and function normally?

Soviet space physicians, whose cosmonauts have flown longer than any other—five days—are still uncertain.

Later Geminis will help answer the question. If the answer is no, then manned exploration may be set back years—until engineers find a practical way to create artificial gravity in spaceships.

⊕

Early Bird, another space forerunner, will fly in late March.

It will be the first of the commercial communications satellites. Eventually a full-fledged network of lofty satellites will be launched by the Communications Satellite Corporation.

Early Bird will perform like a humming bird. It will hover in a "stationary" orbit 22,300 miles above the Atlantic. If all goes well, it will be used commercially for the first time in May.

Satellite networks to come will add vast new channels to world communications. There will be no wait then for a call to London or Beirut. It may even cost less.

⊕

High-flying balloons will soar this month over India.

The balloon-borne instruments will study the precise composition and energy of cosmic rays. Thus, hopefully, will be found a clue to the enormous forces that created them.

Trends...

Nuclear-weapons know-how continues to spread. Four countries have the bomb—Britain, France, the United States, and the Soviet Union. Communist China has exploded a test device, but, it is believed, does not yet have a bomb.

A dozen others have bombmaking potential: Canada, Italy, India, Indonesia, West Germany, Japan, Sweden, the United Arab Republic, and probably Australia, South Africa, and Switzerland.

Are any of them actually making one? West Germany and Japan are legally forbidden to. Otherwise, the answer is hard to pin down. Some nations receiving atoms-for-peace aid are diverting some facilities for the development of weaponry.

Plutonium is a by-product of all reactors. Out of it, bombs can be made. All United States-aided peaceful reactor projects have procedures to prevent plutonium from being diverted to bombs. Some other international projects are likewise safeguarded.

But many are not. The International Atomic Energy Agency administers a safeguard system only if a nation allows it. The United States has gone along reluctantly with this lack of safeguards.

Many United States officials urgently ask how long this can continue? It is a diplomatic volcano that may erupt at any time.

How and why...

The United States is taking the first steps to tap the riches of its continental shelf.

Alaska's Democratic Senator, E. L. Bartlett, has introduced a bill for a five-member marine exploration and development commission. It would spend $50,000,000 a year and manage a $100,000,000 trust fund—all aimed at developing the resources of the nation's undersea shelves.

Continental shelves rarely run deeper than 600 feet below the water. They stretch as far as 300 miles to sea before dropping off into the oceanic abyss. The United Nations last summer recognized exclusive American rights to this vast offshore real estate.

Men are learning to live on it. This summer the United States Navy will put 10 men in a chamber 250 feet under the water off southern California to live for extended periods.

⊕

Those 12,000 pictures from Rangers 7 and 8 already are helping scientists make maps of the moon.

Using light and dark splotches from Ranger 7's lunar close-ups, geographers have made out heights of features, surface textures, and directions of slopes. A map based on the closest Ranger 7 photograph shows height contours at four-inch intervals.

But no maps yet show what the lunar surface is made of. Will men landing there sink out of sight in a sea of dust? Or will they walk around on foamy crust? We may not know for sure until the first astronaut sticks his foot in it.

Where to look

Arts-Entertainment	8	Home Forum	12
Women Today	10	Sports	14
Business	15	Family Features	19

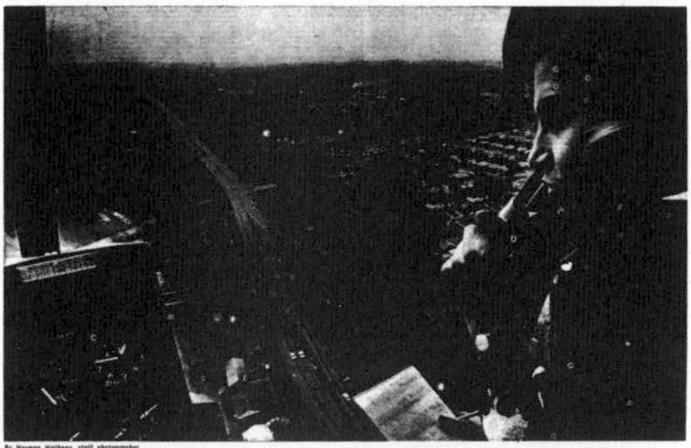

By Norman Matheny, staff photographer

Traffic watch

Washington women 'traffic reporters' are up in the air. They're supposed to be. One of the two, Miss Marie McDonald, broadcasts information and warnings on traffic conditions from her bird's-eye view overhead. Washingtonians listen in on Station WWDC's copter traffic service during morning and afternoon rush hours.

Monitor's new look

The Christian Science Monitor today introduces major typographical changes designed to make the Monitor easier to read:

- **The traditional eight-column newspaper layout is replaced with a five-column width for news and feature matter, a very desirable length of line for readability.**
- **The size of the body type has been enlarged from 7½ point to 9 point, a 20 percent increase, to improve its legibility.**
- **Headline style has been streamlined. Capital letters have been eliminated except on the initial word and on proper names.**
- **Column rules have been removed. White space is used more generously.**

Accompanying these changes are editorial improvements:

Special columns of opinion on national and world news have been moved from the news pages to the editorial page, sharpening the distinction between news reports and news commentary.

The daily "Focus" feature, starting today on Page 1, will note trends, focus on what's ahead, and pinpoint highlights in major news areas.

A new feature entitled "The news — briefly" will appear on Page 2 to summarize important spot news breaks.

These and other changes are part of a long-range program to provide even greater service to Monitor readers and advertisers. The Monitor's exclusive, in-depth coverage of national and world news topics will be expanded. Other changes will be introduced in coming months.

Further details: Page 2

U.S. signals loud and clear on Vietnam

By Joseph C. Harsch
Special Correspondent of The Christian Science Monitor

London

For another week the soldiers have been largely marking time in Vietnam while the diplomats continued to grope toward some possible resolution of the contest there.

The groping has not produced results yet visible to the general gaze, but there could be some progress behind the scenes. This is the type of negotiation which is conducted more by Indian smoke signals than by written communications or direct conversation.

Washington was making two kinds of signals during the past week. One was more direct American use of armed force. The other was restraint which tacitly but clearly told of readiness to settle on fair terms.

There is and need be no mystery about the Washington position. It was being read accurately in Communist capitals. But the reading was interrupted during the week by the march of Gen. Charles de Gaulle of France into the middle of a rather delicate situation.

London's loyal rôle

The joint French-Soviet proposal for a Vietnam conference was more accurate as a measure of the middle position France has taken up between Washington and the Communist world than helpful toward a settlement in Vietnam itself. London, as from the start of the Vietnam crisis was playing the role of loyal ally.

The French intrusion is unhelpful in that it could encourage the North Vietnamese to stiffen their terms. The Communist demand is for American military withdrawal first and political neutralization afterward. The American position is for an end to Communist aggression and subversion first and neutralization afterward.

Probably nothing important will come of the long-range signaling unless or until North Vietnam is convinced that the United States intends not only to stand firm on its position but will also back it up with increasing use of direct force.

Stability vital

Another needed foundation for a settlement is political stability in South Vietnam.

Optimists among the diplomats working in the operation think that some real progress toward a settlement might become visible by midsummer. Pessimists say Washington might be able to hold its position in South Vietnam for another year.

Meanwhile, the West Germans provided an interesting example of how rusty a great power can be when it begins to play power politics again after years of passive diplomacy.

This past week the West Germans tried to cope with the arrival of East Germany's Walter Ulbricht in Egypt. They seemed to make every mistake conceivable — and a few more never dreamed of. At the end, the world watched the extraordinary spectacle of the leader of a Communist satellite government being treated to a royal welcome in Cairo.

The West Germans are left in the embarrassing position of having let Cairo appear to dictate German foreign policy. At least Bonn has suspended arms aid to Israel.

Justice poses U.S. paradox

Several important decisions of the Supreme Court of the United States in recent years have compelled profound changes in American criminal justice. In this and a series of following articles, The Christian Science Monitor explores these changes and how they affect the police, the courts, and the public.

By Nobuo Abiko
Staff Correspondent of The Christian Science Monitor

Chicago

"Our country is overwhelmed by crime," cries a big-city police superintendent.

Newspaper headlines echo him daily. Police ledgers bulge with bookings. Courts strain with criminal cases.

Federal Bureau of Investigation reports show that crime is increasing everywhere—not only in the teeming cities but in the suburbs and countryside. They show that it is growing five times faster than population. This, says the president of the American Bar Association (ABA), is "the single most shocking statistic."

Crime, without doubt, is one of the severest problems taxing American society today.

Landmark decisions

Like the police superintendent, many Americans feel "overwhelmed." When the sun goes down, they do not walk the streets of cities. They do not stroll in New York's Central Park, or Philadelphia's Fairmount Park, or Washington's Rock Creek Park.

But Americans today feel baffled, too. And some, infuriated.

For they often read of criminals "going free" on legal "technicalities." They read of courts reversing convictions. They hear of judges dismissing cases for lack of evidence.

Perhaps the police seized evidence unlawfully. Perhaps they held a suspect too long for questioning. Perhaps the man confessed but had no lawyer with him. And so he is freed.

These and many more. All stem from landmark decisions of the Supreme Court of the United States in recent years. And

★ Please turn to Page 6

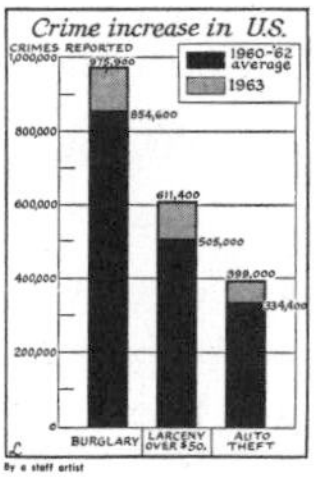

Crime increase in U.S.
CRIMES REPORTED
1,000,000
800,000
600,000
400,000
200,000
0
1960-'62 average
1963
975,960
854,600
611,400
505,000
399,000
334,400
BURGLARY
LARCENY OVER $50.
AUTO THEFT

By a staff artist

Inside East Germany:

How a police state 'prospers' . . .

By Harry B. Ellis
Staff Correspondent of The Christian Science Monitor

Leipzig, Germany

Around the table in the dark little room sat five schoolboys, eating an afternoon sausage.

They were of prep-school age, attending a state-run school of the Communist (East) German Democratic Republic.

Their school was in the countryside, many miles from Leipzig, the nearest big city. At the end of our talk I asked these boys a question.

They looked at each other, smiled, and nodded. Yes, I was the first American they had ever seen.

Soviet soldiers

I had tried this question elsewhere in my journey throughout East Germany (the DDR). Outside Berlin, I had found few East Germans under 25 years of age who had talked with an American.

This was startling. Americans, in and out of uniform, are an everyday sight in the (West) German Federal Republic. Many streets and apartment houses are a salt-and-pepper mixture of American and West German tenants.

Their children go to school and play together. Once I had asked a West German girl in her early 20's what the war had meant to her.

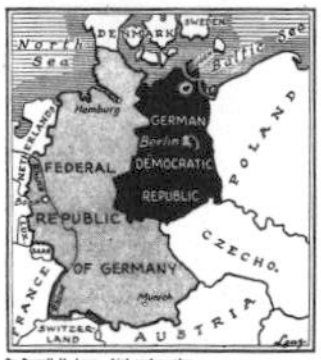

North Sea
DENMARK
SWEDEN
Baltic Sea
Hamburg
GERMAN
Berlin
DEMOCRATIC
REPUBLIC
FEDERAL
REPUBLIC
OF GERMANY
POLAND
CZECHO.
NETHERLANDS
LUX.
SAAR
FRANCE
SWITZERLAND
AUSTRIA
Munich

By Russell H. Lenz, chief cartographer

"Growing up with Americans," she had replied. Now she worked for an American company in West Germany, as did thousands of her compatriots.

East of the Iron Curtain, in the Soviet Zone of Germany, Americans are invisible. East Germans, of course, have their counterpart.

An estimated 350,000 Soviet soldiers, organized in 20 divisions, are stationed in East Germany. Many East Germans see Soviet soldiers every day, particularly in and around garrison towns.

But they seldom speak to them. They could do so, for the study of Russian has been compulsory in the DDR since its founding.

"I would not want to be a Soviet soldier here," an East German Communist told me. "They are forbidden to mix at all with our people. If they do, they are punished."

This annoys many East Germans, who would like a chance to practice their Russian, which often rusts into disuse after school.

There are German-Soviet friendship societies throughout the DDR. But East German Communists assured me their meetings were stiff, formal, and uneasy—particularly for the Soviets.

The Soviet Army is not in East Germany to fraternize. Those 20 divisions have a different function — to shield the Communist regime of Walter Ulbricht against internal or external attack.

Reds bolster army

Not for the sake of Mr. Ulbricht. But to buttress the western flank of the Soviet system in Europe.

These Soviet forces bolster an East German Army of about 80,000 men, plus another 70,000 special border and security troops.

The East German Navy of four destroyers and 150 smaller vessels is manned by 15,000 sailors. Fifteen thousand DDR airmen make up an Air Force of 400 Soviet-built planes—MIG-19 and MIG-21 fighters, and MIG-15 and MIG-17 fighter-bombers.

The intelligence and security apparatus of the DDR is thought to employ visibly 16,000 persons, with secret agents and informants running into the hundreds of thousands.

Police state symbolized

Experts of the West German Social Democratic Party estimate that 12,000 persons are political prisoners in the DDR.

The German Democratic Republic is a police state, symbolized to the West by the Berlin wall, which seals off escape for East Germans.

But to say that the DDR is a police state and to stop there would not be enough. Conditions are changing inside East Germany, and they point to a strengthening of the Communist regime.

Not to a liking of it, necessarily. Communist rulers of the DDR are not naive enough to expect that. But they are working subtly to convince 17,000,000 East Germans that the system under which they live is there to stay.

With Soviet power at their backs, with the Berlin escape hatch closed, DDR leaders have gained time and room for maneuver.

2nd Cl Post Pd at Boston, Mass., and add'l offices

March 1, 1965

Fig. 74. First issue of *Christian Science Monitor* in 5-column optimum format. Note promotional story in col. 2.

16.9 picas with alleys at 18 points. When later a 9-point Excelsior was chosen as body type, the column width was only 3 points from the exact optimum line length.

Three of the 11-pica columns would fit into a 2-column area in the new measure; six "old" columns would fit on three of the "new" ones; eight narrow columns would equal the five wider ones. If ads could be *squared off—blocked*—at any of those three widths, news and advertising matter would mesh smoothly. Such squaring-off is contrary to a long-cherished belief that advertising must be *next to reading matter* (*NRM*, as ad-insertion orders insist) to assure them the readership they need. Actually, this is a myth; *buried ads*—those which do not touch news matter—lose no measurable readership because of their position.

The *Monitor* had buried some ads in the past. The mass of small ones it had to lay made it virtually impossible for each to be NRM. But ads were grouped under geographical labels, and advertisers had long known that people in Cincinnati, for instance, would look for the name of their city and then read the ads below.

Despite misgivings the advertising department began a 2-month experiment. Still within the 8-column format, they began blocking ads, arranging them in 3-, 6-, and 8-column rectangles instead of the conventionally stepped pyramid. There were occasions when the rectangle could not be filled; a corner was, in effect, notched similar to a mortised engraving. But on a surprisingly huge percentage of pages, blocked ads were not only possible but practical. With this assurance, the editorial department could then proceed with its plans for a 5-column format. When the ad-layer couldn't square off the block, he noted that fact for the copy desk. The news department then prepared *N-matter,* (for "narrow"), copy in 11- or 22.3-pica measure, copyfit to plug the hole exactly. This proved no problem at all. Most N-matter is especially tailored for a specific spot in an ad block. Some *time* (or evergreen) material in N-measure is kept on the bank for unforeseen or overlooked chinking that may be required.

The "new" *Monitor* was announced to readers and advertisers before the changeover, and when it appeared it was greeted enthusiastically. Circulation and advertising revenue immediately moved in the proper direction on the charts—upward.

It remained for another honored newspaper enterprise—the *Courier-Journal* and the *Times* of Louisville, Kentucky—to finish the major trail-blazing. These papers, too, are consistently listed as among the great newspapers of America. Great editors on both the sister publications had made their places in history, not only of the Fourth Estate but of the

Fig. 75. Accommodation of 11-pica advertising to op-format news matter: *a*, 1-column N-matter squares off pyramid; *b*, 2-column N-matter; *c*, unobtrusive hole is left blank rather than attempt to fill area above ad with shallow (9-line) N-matter.

country. The *Courier-Journal* had supported Ottmar Mergenthaler in the research that begat the Linotype; the *Times* had sponsored and was the first to use Spartan Bold, still today the newest headletter and the first designed specifically for headline use.

After an overwhelmingly favorable experiment with a single issue in six columns, the format was made permanent in 1965.

First the Louisville papers had to grapple with a problem the *Monitor* had been able to avoid: advertising rates. Selling advertising space by a line or an inch is obviously an anomaly. Both the *agate line* and the inch are measurements of distance, but the newspaper was selling area. The effect was that of selling acres and billing in yards. A Louisville column-inch in the new format was 1½ times larger in area than the former; rates had to reflect the increase. For local transactions it was simply a matter of educating the advertiser; it was obvious to him then that the new rates were not an increase in cost.

For the national advertiser a new problem was present. Local ads

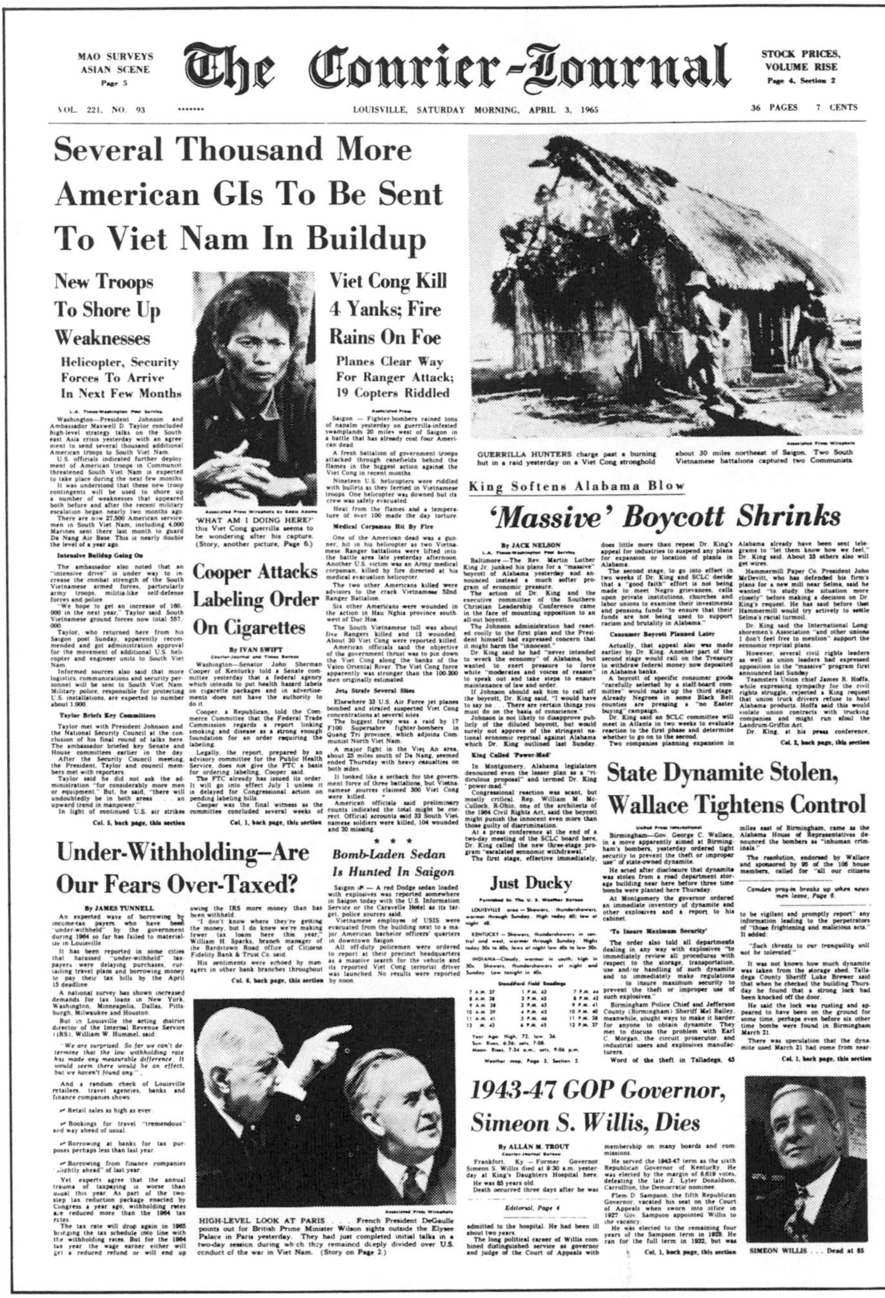

MAO SURVEYS ASIAN SCENE Page 5

The Courier-Journal

STOCK PRICES, VOLUME RISE Page 4, Section 2

VOL. 221. NO. 93 ••••••• LOUISVILLE, SATURDAY MORNING, APRIL 3, 1965 36 PAGES 7 CENTS

Several Thousand More American GIs To Be Sent To Viet Nam In Buildup

New Troops To Shore Up Weaknesses

Helicopter, Security Forces To Arrive In Next Few Months

L.A. Times-Washington Post Service

Washington—President Johnson and Ambassador Maxwell D. Taylor concluded high-level strategy talks on the Southeast Asia crisis yesterday with an agreement to send several thousand additional American troops to South Viet Nam.

U.S. officials indicated further deployment of American troops in Communist-threatened South Viet Nam is expected to take place during the next few months.

It was understood that these new troop contingents will be used to shore up a number of weaknesses that appeared both before and after the recent military escalation began nearly two months ago.

There are now 27,500 American servicemen in South Viet Nam, including 4,000 Marines sent there last month to guard Da Nang Air Base. This is nearly double the level of a year ago.

Intensive Buildup Going On

The ambassador also noted that an "intensive drive" is under way to increase the combat strength of the South Vietnamese armed forces, particularly army troops, militia-like self-defense forces and police.

"We hope to get an increase of 160,000 in the next year," Taylor said. South Vietnamese ground forces now total 557,000.

Taylor, who returned here from his Saigon post Sunday, apparently recommended and got administration approval for the movement of additional U.S. helicopter and engineer units to South Viet Nam.

Informed sources also said that more logistics, communications and security personnel will be sent to South Viet Nam. Military police, responsible for protecting U.S. installations, are expected to number about 1,000.

Taylor Briefs Key Committees

Taylor met with President Johnson and the National Security Council at the conclusion of his final round of talks here. The ambassador briefed key Senate and House committees earlier in the day.

After the Security Council meeting, the President, Taylor and council members met with reporters.

Taylor said he did not ask the administration "for considerably more men or equipment." But, he said, "there will undoubtedly be in both areas . . . an upward trend in manpower."

In light of continued U.S. air strikes

Col. 5, back page, this section

Associated Press Wirephoto by Eddie Adams

'WHAT AM I DOING HERE?' this Viet Cong guerrilla seems to be wondering after his capture. (Story, another picture, Page 6.)

Cooper Attacks Labeling Order On Cigarettes

By IVAN SWIFT
Courier-Journal and Times Bureau

Washington—Senator John Sherman Cooper of Kentucky told a Senate committee yesterday that a federal agency which inteads to put health hazard labels on cigarette packages and in advertisements does not have the authority to do it.

Cooper, a Republican, told the Commerce Committee that the Federal Trade Commission regards a report linking smoking and disease as a strong enough foundation for an order requiring the labeling.

Legally, the report, prepared by an advisory committee for the Public Health Service, does not give the FTC a basis for ordering labeling, Cooper said.

The FTC already has issued its order. It will go into effect July 1 unless it is delayed for Congressional action on pending labeling bills.

Cooper was the final witness as the committee concluded several weeks of

Col. 1, back page, this section

Viet Cong Kill 4 Yanks; Fire Rains On Foe

Planes Clear Way For Ranger Attack; 19 Copters Riddled

Associated Press

Saigon — Fighter-bombers rained tons of napalm yesterday on guerrilla-infested swamplands 20 miles west of Saigon in a battle that has already cost four American dead.

A fresh battalion of government troops attacked through canefields behind the flames in the biggest action against the Viet Cong in recent months.

Nineteen U.S. helicopters were riddled with bullets as they ferried in Vietnamese troops. One helicopter was downed but its crew was safely evacuated.

Heat from the flames and a temperature of over 100 made the day torture.

Medical Corpsman Hit By Fire

One of the American dead was a gunner, hit in his helicopter as two Vietnamese Ranger battalions were lifted into the battle area late yesterday afternoon. Another U.S. victim was an Army medical corpsman, killed by fire directed at his medical evacuation helicopter.

The two other Americans killed were advisors to the crack Vietnamese 52nd Ranger Battalion.

Six other Americans were wounded in the action in Hau Nghia province southwest of Duc Hoa.

The South Vietnamese toll was about five Rangers killed and 12 wounded. About 30 Viet Cong were reported killed.

American officials said the objective of the government thrust was to pin down the Viet Cong along the banks of the Vaico Oriental River. The Viet Cong force apparently was stronger than the 100-200 men originally estimated.

Jets Strafe Several Sites

Elsewhere 33 U.S. Air Force jet planes bombed and strafed suspected Viet Cong concentrations at several sites.

The biggest foray was a raid by 17 F100 Supersabre fighter-bombers in Quang Tri province, which adjoins Communist North Viet Nam.

A major fight in the Viet An area, about 25 miles south of Da Nang, seemed ended Thursday with heavy casualties on both sides.

It looked like a setback for the government force of three battalions, but Vietnamese sources claimed 300 Viet Cong were killed.

American officials said preliminary counts indicated the total might be correct. Official accounts said 32 South Vietnamese soldiers were killed, 104 wounded and 20 missing.

★ ★ ★

Bomb-Laden Sedan Is Hunted In Saigon

Saigon (AP) — A red Dodge sedan loaded with explosives was reported somewhere in Saigon today with the U.S. Information Service or the Caravelle Hotel as its target, police sources said.

Vietnamese employes of USIS were evacuated from the building next to a major American bachelor officers' quarters in downtown Saigon.

All off-duty policemen were ordered to report at their precinct headquarters as a massive search for the vehicle and its reported Viet Cong terrorist driver was launched. No results were reported by noon.

Associated Press Wirephoto

GUERRILLA HUNTERS charge past a burning hut in a raid yesterday on a Viet Cong stronghold about 30 miles northeast of Saigon. Two South Vietnamese battalions captured two Communists.

King Softens Alabama Blow

'Massive' Boycott Shrinks

By JACK NELSON
L.A. Times-Washington Post Service

Baltimore—The Rev. Martin Luther King Jr. junked his plans for a "massive" boycott of Alabama yesterday and announced instead a much softer program of economic pressure.

The action of Dr. King and the executive committee of the Southern Christian Leadership Conference came in the face of mounting opposition to an all-out boycott.

The Johnson administration had reacted coolly to the first plan and the President himself had expressed concern that it might harm the "innocent."

Dr. King said he had "never intended to wreck the economy" of Alabama, but wanted to exert pressure to force white "moderates and voices of reason" to speak out and take steps to ensure maintenance of law and order.

If Johnson should ask him to call off the boycott, Dr. King said, "I would have to say no . . . There are certain things you must do on the basis of conscience."

Johnson is not likely to disapprove publicly of the diluted boycott, but would surely not approve of the stringent national economic reprisal against Alabama which Dr. King outlined last Sunday.

King Called 'Power-Mad'

In Montgomery, Alabama legislators denounced even the lesser plan as a "ridiculous proposal" and termed Dr. King "power-mad."

Congressional reaction was scant, but mostly critical. Rep. William M. McCulloch, R-Ohio, one of the architects of the 1964 Civil Rights Act, said the boycott might punish the innocent even more than those guilty of discrimination.

At a press conference at the end of a two-day meeting of the SCLC board here, Dr. King called the new three-stage program "escalated economic withdrawal."

The first stage, effective immediately, does little more than repeat Dr. King's appeal for industries to suspend any plans for expansion or location of plants in Alabama.

The second stage, to go into effect in two weeks if Dr. King and SCLC decide that a "good faith" effort is not being made to meet Negro grievances, calls upon private institutions, churches and labor unions to examine their investments and pensions funds "to ensure that their funds are not being used to support racism and brutality in Alabama."

Consumer Boycott Planned Later

Actually, that appeal also was made earlier by Dr. King. Another part of the second stage would call on the Treasury to withdraw federal money now deposited in Alabama banks.

A boycott of specific consumer goods "carefully selected by a staff-board committee" would make up the third stage. Already Negroes in some Black Belt counties are pressing a "no Easter buying" campaign.

Dr. King said an SCLC committee will meet in Atlanta in two weeks to evaluate reaction to the first phase and determine whether to go on to the second.

Two companies planning expansion in Alabama already have been sent telegrams to "let them know how we feel," Dr. King said. About 25 others also will get wires.

Hammermill Paper Co. President John McDevitt, who has defended his firm's plans for a new mill near Selma, said he wanted "to study the situation more closely" before making a decision on Dr. King's request. He has said before that Hammermill would try actively to settle Selma's racial turmoil.

Dr. King said the International Longshoremen's Association "and other unions I don't feel free to mention" support the economic reprisal plans.

However, several civil rights leaders as well as union leaders had expressed opposition to the "massive" program first announced last Sunday.

Teamsters Union chief James R. Hoffa, while expressing sympathy for the civil rights struggle, rejected a King request that union truck drivers refuse to haul Alabama products. Hoffa said this would violate union contracts with trucking companies and might run afoul the Landrum-Griffin Act.

Dr. King, at his press conference,

Col. 2, back page, this section

Just Ducky

Furnished by The U. S. Weather Bureau

LOUISVILLE area — Showers, thundershowers, warmer through Sunday. High today 60; low at night 48.

KENTUCKY — Showers, thundershowers in central and west, warmer through Sunday. Highs today 50s to 60s; lows at night low 40s to low 50s.

INDIANA—Cloudy, warmer in south; high in 50s. Showers, thundershowers at night and Sunday. Low tonight in 40s.

Standiford Field Readings

7 A.M. 37	1 P.M. 43	7 P.M. 44
8 A.M. 38	2 P.M. 45	8 P.M. 42
9 A.M. 38	3 P.M. 45	9 P.M. 41
10 A.M. 39	4 P.M. 45	10 P.M. 40
11 A.M. 41	5 P.M. 46	11 P.M. 38
12 M. 43	6 P.M. 45	12 P.M. 37

Year Ago: High, 72; low, 36.
Sun: Rises, 6:26; sets, 7:08.
Moon: Rises, 7:34 a.m.; sets, 9:06 p.m.

Weather map, Page 3, Section 2.

State Dynamite Stolen, Wallace Tightens Control

United Press International

Birmingham—Gov. George C. Wallace, in a move apparently aimed at Birmingham's bombers, yesterday ordered tight security to prevent the theft or improper use" of state-owned dynamite.

He acted after disclosure that dynamite was stolen from a road department storage building near here before three time bombs were planted here Thursday.

At Montgomery the governor ordered an immediate inventory of dynamite and other explosives and a report to his cabinet.

'To Insure Maximum Security'

The order also told all departments dealing in any way with explosives "to immediately review all procedures with respect to the storage, transportation, use and/or handling of such dynamite and to immediately make regulations . . . to insure maximum security to prevent the theft or improper use of such explosives."

Birmingham Police Chief and Jefferson County (Birmingham) Sheriff Mel Bailey, meanwhile, sought ways to make it harder for anyone to obtain dynamite. They met to discuss the problem with Earl C. Morgan, the circuit prosecutor, and industrial users and explosives manufacturers.

Word of the theft in Talladega, 45 miles east of Birmingham, came as the Alabama House of Representatives denounced the bombers as "inhuman criminals."

The resolution, endorsed by Wallace and sponsored by 95 of the 106 house members, called for "all our citizens

Camden pray-in breaks up when newsmen leave, Page 6.

to be vigilant and promptly report" any information leading to the perpetrators of "those frightening and malicious acts." It added:

"Such threats to our tranquility will not be tolerated."

It was not known how much dynamite was taken from the storage shed. Talladega County Sheriff Luke Brewer said that when he checked the building Thursday he found that a strong lock had been knocked off the door.

He said the lock was rusting and appeared to have been on the ground for some time, perhaps even before six other time bombs were found in Birmingham March 21.

There was speculation that the dynamite used March 21 had come from near-

Col. 1, back page, this section

Under-Withholding—Are Our Fears Over-Taxed?

By JAMES TUNNELL

An expected wave of borrowing by income-tax payers who have been "under-withheld" by the government during 1964 so far has failed to materialize in Louisville.

It has been reported in some cities that harassed "under-withheld" taxpayers were delaying purchases, curtailing travel plans and borrowing money to pay their tax bills by the April 15 deadline.

A national survey has shown increased demands for tax loans in New York, Washington, Minneapolis, Dallas, Pittsburgh, Milwaukee and Houston.

But in Louisville the acting district director of the Internal Revenue Service (IRS), William W. Hummel, said:

"We are surprised. So far we can't determine that the low withholding rate has made any measurable difference. It would seem there would be an effect, but we haven't found any."

And a random check of Louisville retailers, travel agencies, banks and finance companies shows:

- Retail sales as high as ever.
- Bookings for travel "tremendous" and way ahead of usual.
- Borrowing at banks for tax purposes perhaps less than last year.
- Borrowing from finance companies "slightly ahead" of last year.

Yet experts agree that the annual trauma of taxpaying is worse than usual this year. As part of the two-step tax reduction package enacted by Congress a year ago, withholding rates are reduced more than the 1964 tax rates.

The tax rate will drop again in 1965 bringing the tax schedule into line with the withholding rates. But for the 1964 tax year the wage earner either will get a reduced refund or will end up owing the IRS more money than has been withheld.

"I don't know where they're getting the money, but I do knew we're making fewer tax loans here this year," William H. Sparks, branch manager of the Bardstown Road office of Citizens Fidelity Bank & Trust Co. said.

His sentiments were echoed by managers in other bank branches throughout

Col. 6, back page, this section

Associated Press Wirephoto

HIGH-LEVEL LOOK AT PARIS . . . French President DeGaulle points out for British Prime Minister Wilson sights outside the Elysee Palace in Paris yesterday. They had just completed initial talks in a two-day session during which they remained deeply divided over U.S. conduct of the war in Viet Nam. (Story on Page 2.)

1943-47 GOP Governor, Simeon S. Willis, Dies

By ALLAN M. TROUT
Courier-Journal Bureau

Frankfort, Ky.—Former Governor Simeon S. Willis died at 9:30 a.m. yesterday at King's Daughters Hospital here.

He was 85 years old.

Death occurred three days after he was admitted to the hospital. He had been ill about two years.

Editorial, Page 4

The long political career of Willis combined distinguished service as governor and judge of the Court of Appeals with membership on many boards and commissions.

He served the 1943-47 term as the sixth Republican Governor of Kentucky. He was elected by the margin of 8,619 votes, defeating the late J. Lyter Donaldson, Carrollton, the Democratic nominee.

Flem D. Sampson, the fifth Republican Governor, vacated his seat on the Court of Appeals when sworn into office in 1927. Gov. Sampson appointed Willis to the vacancy.

He was elected to the remaining four years of the Sampson term in 1928. He ran for the full term in 1932, but was

Col. 1, back page, this section

SIMEON WILLIS . . . Dead at 85

Fig. 76. Optimum format. First metropolitan dailies to adopt 6-column op format were *Louisville* (Ky.) *Courier-Journal*, morning and Sunday, in Bodoni, and . . .

MILD
and partly cloudy tomor-
row, high in the mid-60s.

THE LOUISVILLE TIMES

FINAL
HOME

VOL. CLXII—No. 131 ★★★★ LOUISVILLE, TUESDAY EVENING, APRIL 6, 1965 40 PAGES SEVEN CENTS

Reds Close Road To Berlin For 2nd Day, Buzz Airport

City Forester William Heffernan examines an oak sapling in city's nursery at Shawnee Park, near Shawnee Golf Course clubhouse.

Neglect Threatens 70-Year-Old Trees On City Parkways

By WILLIAM GREIDER

Tommy Horton directs a power sprayer's blast of chemicals up into Shawnee Park trees.

State School Fund In Red; Help Sought

6 Americans, 120 Reds Die In Viet Battle

Quake Took Mother And Home

Catholic Marriage Law Faces Major Revision

Guiana Ex-Premier Is Visiting In Cuba

Friend Weatherman Rates A Nice Bow For Tomorrow

IS ORDINATION ACCORD POSSIBLE?
Test Confronts Church-Merger Talks

On The Inside Of Today's Times

Fig. 77. . . . evening *Louisville Times,* in Spartan Bold head schedule. Note how each maintains individuality despite common format.

could simply be reset to the new measure, but national ads are made up to 11-pica column widths. It would be uneconomical for an advertiser to prepare advertising only for the Louisville papers, no matter how important the market they covered. In fact, in order to eliminate the need for different ad widths, the "standard" column had been defined. But Barry Bingham, the publisher, and his associates had long been considering a single-rate plan for their newspapers. This would eliminate the differential between local and national rates which favored the national advertiser.

We ought to digress for a closer look at such rates. There are two reasons customarily cited to justify higher national rates. It is conceded that for the typical local advertiser some circulation of any newspaper is nonproductive. The larger the city, the more it is obvious that even the best advertisement will not draw a customer clear crosstown, and almost every newspaper has some circulation far out of its trading area. But the national advertiser presumably reaches a prospective customer wherever he may live. The Ford Motor Company, for instance, doesn't care whether one of its cars is bought in the north or south section of Chicago or whether a copy of the *Milwaukee Journal* is read in that city or in California; the total circulation is usable on a national basis. Rather than a "higher national rate," say proponents, a "lower local rate" prevails to compensate for "waste circulation."

The other reason concedes that the national rate is higher and then justifies it by citing agency commissions. In theory at least, advertising agencies are compensated for their efforts not by the client whose advertising they prepare but by the publications in which the ads are placed. The mechanics of payment is a 15% commission which the agency charges the publication; this is analogous to the commission paid a travel agent by transportation companies or to the commission paid newspaper space salesmen. The agency also claims a 2% discount for payment made within 30 days. Additional commissions may be taken by other service agencies involved in an ad campaign. One of these is American Newspaper Representatives (ANR), an organization that sells and services national advertising for small dailies and weeklies. Its commission is 13%, over and above normal agency commission.

Many publishers chafe at paying these commissions, and frankly raise their "regular" or local rates to cover this "extra cost." The flaw in this reasoning is a failure to recognize that these commissions pay for necessary services that must be rendered even though the cost is often disguised on the local level. It costs money to hire a salesman, whether he's an individual calling on Main Street merchants or an organization selling to national organizations. It costs money to check ad runs, pull tearsheets, mail such proof of publication, and bill the client. All these services are rendered by ANR and similar service groups that usually operate as adjuncts of state press associations.

An even greater cost is that of preparing local advertising in the newspaper's composing room. National advertising is usually in mat form, and local efforts are merely those of making a flat cast and, perhaps, setting a line or two of type for the signature of the local outlet. Even this minimal effort is reduced if the ad comes in the form of an electrotype or plastic plate.

So the economic justification for two rates becomes quite tenuous.

In Louisville, as in a few other cities, the conclusion had been reached that a single rate would be attractive to national advertisers and thus make newspapers more competitive to the electronic media, especially television, that had cut alarmingly into national ad budgets. It was decided that the new rate would go into effect when the new format was adopted. It meant that the national advertiser would pay no more for any ad than the then-current costs. If the ad floated in a wider area, he was not charged extra for that white space. The width of that framing would depend on the width of the ad. A full-page ad has no extra margin, whether it is measured as eight columns or as six. While the full-page ad didn't get a free frame of white, there was a cost saving. For newspaper space, unlike that in magazines, is not sold by the page but by the column-wide agate line. The full-page buyer at Louisville now bought only six columns, not eight.

The papers made the changeover painless for the advertiser who didn't want to float ads. For the first year of the new format, they offered to resize advertising by making line engravings from slick proofs. This did not require as much photoengraving as might be expected, however, for advertisers found that "standard" ad sizes for magazines would fit neatly into the new newspaper format. In many instances the same plate could be used for both. Even when halftones in an ad had to be reshot in a coarser screen, there was the advantage of using the same *mechanical* for both platemakes.

The effect on advertising linage was electric. In the first six months of 1966, general linage plus automotive rose 7.9% in 52 cities documented by *Media Records*. In that period, the same advertising categories rose 22.57% in Louisville.

All advertising linage at Louisville rose 30.35% during the first year of the new format, and though the one-rate plan lowered national rates by margins of 25% to 41%, advertising dollar volume increased.

There are many advantages to the op format. From an editorial point of view, a line length at optimum is an asset because it enhances communication. The reader likes the longer measure, too, even if he doesn't understand the technicalities involved.

Seven hundred readers were surveyed in Louisville. Among men, 72% called the new line length "easier to read"; 26% could detect no difference, and 2% thought it more difficult. Among women, 64% found the new measure easier to read, 35% found no difference, and a solitary 1% considered it more difficult to read.

The papers, setting 8-point Corona on 8½, use a 14.3 line with 9-point alleys. Only one setting is used for all news. The editorial page is in five columns and the classified in nine.

The wider columns allow more effective display of photographs. There is no pressure to use small cuts that fail to communicate. Now a 1-column cut in op measure has almost as much impact as the old 2-columner, and the fewer columns seem to give extra prominence to pictures.

There are some editorial disadvantages, as George Gill, managing editor of the *Courier-Journal,* has enumerated. There are usually fewer stories on page one, six to eight major heads as compared to the 10 to 12 that were par for the 8-column course. There is a tendency for stories to run longer, and more policing is required to keep them taut. For this purpose, all local stories are kept to a maximum of 20 column-inches; copy that would extend a story is handled as a sidebar. Wire pictures often have to be blown up to fit wider columns, and this creates problems for the platemaker if the quality of the original is not high.

But the new format has had no apparent inhibition on the layout man. Both papers remain newsy and interesting, and each maintains its own personality. Just as they were in 8-column format, the *C-J* is conservative in its Bodoni headletter and the *Times* remains in a higher key with its Spartan Bold head schedule.

The mechanical advantages of op format are so great that they would make the changeover worthwhile even if the quality of the product were not raised.

A major saving of time and money results from a reduction in the number of casting operations necessary to fill a page with body type. The major wear on a linecaster occurs to the casting mechanism; the other parts of the machine do relatively light duty. If each time the linecaster goes into the casting cycle, it uses up 45 characters in the copy rather than 30, the casting operations are reduced by a third. This saving is anything but inconsequential. Another way of phrasing this is 25 casting operations in 14-pica measure produce as much type as 32 casts of 11-pica lines.

The longer the line, the less the percentage of it is spacing between words; longer lines then give proportionately more characters per line. Mr. Gill reported that at Louisville they get 3% more copy in an area when setting is in op lines.

Another costly process is hyphenation, another end-of-line operation. The more characters in the copy that an operator can use up before he has to end a line, the faster he can set any given story.

Longer lines have more spacebands, and thus there is greater tolerance in the length of a line long enough to cast. The operator can assemble a justifiable line without the need for an unsightly 2- or 3-letter syllable which is so often required in an 11-pica line. Letterspacing within a word, which usually has to be done by hand, is required in approximately one line out of 22 in 11-pica measure. (In 6-pica measure, it occurs about once in every six lines.) In a 15-pica line, letterspacing is virtually eliminated.

Six-column pages can be made up more quickly on the stone. After all, the compositor lifts approximately a third to a half more type with each *take* that he handles. And he has to justify the length of one-third fewer columns.

There is another mechanical advantage that is rarely considered. In Louisville, all body type is set in one size and at one measure. That means that any straight-matter machine can set any copy that the desk sends out. This relieves some of the jams that occur even in the best copy flow on an average paper; often a multicolumn leed or an odd-measure cutline has to be held until the machine equipped for such setting becomes available. Meanwhile other machines may be momentarily idle because they cannot handle that special copy. Standardizing at one setting not only saves money, it also moves the editorial deadline back a few minutes and gives some extra time for late stories or for more painstaking handling on the desk.

That standardization not only makes all Linotypes instantly interchangeable in function but reduces the inventory of molds and liners required for different settings.

Computerization of typesetting reduces a few of these mechanical advantages, but the major ones still pertain.

These mechanical advantages are not merely theoretical. Albert Leicht of West Virginia Institute of Technology found that 30 linecaster operators whose performance he analyzed could set about 35% more copy at 15 picas than in 11-pica measure. Adjustments must be made for corrections, though, for a correction line requires more typesetting in the wider measure. But after such adjustment, it was found that total production was 17% higher.

In one actual newspaper operation, it was found that efficiency in making and locking up pages rose 18%. Increase in the amount of required Ludlow composition was 17% because the new format lends itself to larger headlines. However, the overall efficiency of the combined processes was 13%. The newspaper where these statistics were compiled prefers to remain anonymous, but I can attest to their validity.

Many newspapers—their number increases constantly—use the op format only on *key pages,* those that carry no advertising. Thus they maintain old standards and old rates for advertising while they enjoy the benefits of op on sufficient pages to establish a new standard there. Some papers sell, sometimes as premium space at premium rates, a single large ad on a key page. If this is the conventional 4- or 8-column ad, there is no problem of adjusting to the new column. If it is in any other number of columns, the ad is made up to the new specifications.

Op format can be adapted to the tabloid, or compact, page, too; four columns of type run on the page that would otherwise accommodate five. Five standard columns plus four 6-point column rules give a type page 57 picas wide. For a 4-column page, we need three alleys, so we have 54 picas for type. Dividing that width by four, we come up with $13\frac{1}{2}$ picas as the measure for the type column.

The reduction of the number of columns per page doesn't seem to be a very heavy handicap to editors who use this format. They consistently lay out interesting and newsy pages.

An interesting format that defies neat academic classification is that of *Newsday.* Its basic format calls for five 12-pica columns with 6-point column rules. But Floyd H. Main, the production manager, points out that "actual pages rarely are made up to this specification. Editorial matter is set in 14.6, 18, 20, and 24.6 picas. About the only time a 12-pica column is used for news is when a 4-column-full ad is dummied on a page.

"The $14\frac{1}{2}$ measure converts the page into one of four columns (op format for this page size) and the 20-pica measure makes a 3-column page. The 18-pica matter is column-and-a-half to the 12-pica setting and is doubled over into a 3-column hole. With all these settings we can use alleys of at least a full pica."

An interesting practice at *Newsday* is to keep all editorial areas in full-page depth for ease in makeup and to assure adequate areas of news

Fig. 78. Optimum format in compact pages. *Trib,* satellite of *Chicago* (Ill.) *Tribune,* uses four columns. *Towne Courier* of East Lansing, Mich., is in three columns. Each page is 11½ inches wide. *Trib* is 15 inches deep; *Courier,* 16½ inches.

matter on all pages. On full-format pages, such deep "wells" of editorial matter are undesirable; on tab pages this liability does not exist. To achieve such areas, *Newsday* consistently buries small ads. Its experience reinforces data that show that such ad placement is no handicap to the pulling power of advertising.

W-Format

No one knows where the 7½-column, *W-format,* began. Many newspapers experimented with this form in the early 1960's, but none has irrefutably established its claim as the originator. *Today* in Cocoa, Florida, was the most publicized of the early users.

The objective of the W-format is to replace column rules by alleys. The typical column rule used to be hairline on 6-point; this has been gradually reduced so that a 3-point body is common. But the minimum width for an alley is a full pica. If type is set perfectly, 9 points may be sufficient to separate columns. However, in typical newspaper composition, plagued by the too-narrow measure and pressures of deadlines,

Coshocton's weekly

The Commentator

"Nothing worthwhile is achieved without enthusiasm"

ONE COPY PER FAMILY

POSTAL PATRON LOCAL

BULK RATE U.S. POSTAGE **P A I D** Permit No. 3 Coshocton, O.

Coshocton, Ohio. July 5, 1967. P.O. Box 224   Call 622-0912   Vol. 1, No. 11   10c

The editor's corner
By Don E. Beattie

People often inquire where one gets the ideas for stories that appear in a newspaper — any newspaper.

The answer is relatively simple: From people themselves.

No newspaper worth reading is actually the product of the creativeness or imagination of its staff. It's the reader who makes a newspaper good or bad.

This may sound contradictory, but it isn't.

Almost all of the good stories that appear in a newspaper are the direct result of a suggestion, a tip or a letter to that newspaper from a reader.

That is why we in the business are always ready to listen and examine any suggestion a caller or letter-writer has to make.

Some don't jell

To be sure a lot of the ideas suggested don't jell. And they don't always make good yarns.

But it is certainly true that there are a flock of good stories about people everywhere, every day. You just have to have a lead, a tip or stumble on them yourself.

That is what makes the business so fascinating.

To give you an idea of what I mean, take last week for an example.

I set out for West Lafayette to gather some information on the plans and programs for the Homecoming celebration there, slated Aug. 3, 4th and 5th.

That was my objective.

I wasn't quite certain who was in charge and who should be seen. So I stopped to chat with Rev. C.F. Roberts at his drug store on Main St.

Ideas just emerge

He gave me some names and some ideas on the topic I had in mind. Seems he was among the first leaders in the West Lafayette Chamber of Commerce and was one of the Chamber's first officers.

From his place of business I went up the street to Rev. Charles Ireland's home. There I inquired more about Homecoming.

Rev. Ireland gave me the names and places to find the people to charge this year. And as we talked he told me about his trip to England and his exchange pastorship with Rev. T. Lesley Thexton, who will be in West Lafayette for five weeks starting next Sunday.

As we talked an interesting story emerged. The Ireland family obviously is thrilled and excited about the coming experience and the results of our chat are found today on Page 2.

Quite a stunt

I didn't go out seeking that one, it just of fell into my lap.

Later the same day I talked with Don Jackson, Chamber president, and got a rundown on his organization for the Homecoming.

So I stopped at the West Lafayette General Store to snap a picture of Clarence Gress and Art Emler, two of the committee chairmen for Homecoming.

They obliged for the picture and as we chatted, they told me of their humorous and useful experience at playing "Lum and Abner" in their store one day back in the early 1950s.

They hauled out pictures and newspaper accounts of the event and related it with obvious enjoyment.

It seems that one evening as they closed up, Art said to Clarence, "Why don't we come to work tomorrow dressed as Lum and Abner"?

Those folks are nuts

They did. And both looked the parts, as pictures prove.

The day went on in hilarious style. People dropped in and some failed to recognize the operators and their wives, who were also dressed up specially.

Art recalls that one new delivery man came in from his truck, took a look at them and went back to tell the regular driver and said, "Sam, those people in that store are nuts."

Sam had been visiting the store for years and he said, "Why, you must be mistaken, I know those folks and they're fine people."

"Well," the first man said, "if you think so, go in there and take a look at them. They're nuts."

Visitors came to the store from miles and miles around. A ledger shows 282 people stalked in to see Lum and Abner.

Quite a tale and quite a stunt.

People are interesting

Which gets again to the point: Here is a fine feature yarn I plan to do soon. A general store that is really a general store, just as they were years and years ago.

West Lafayette has one and there's another down by Wills Creek. There aren't many around any longer.

There's gonna be a fire

There's gonna be a fire in our town tomorrow.

Yes sir, a planned one.

And it will accomplish a couple of good things.

First, it will save the taxpayers about $325 in wrecking charges.

Second, it will give the Coshocton city fire department a realistic rehearsal.

You might add, too, that it probably will entertain a flock of Coshocton people who enjoy watching fires.

The house to be burned at 6 p.m., Thursday is pictured above. It is located on Cambridge Road, at the entrance of the location of Coshocton's new senior high school building.

The Board of Education has arranged the blaze with city officials, thus saving an estimated cost of $325 to tear down the old structure and clear the grounds.

Firemen will utilize the burning as a practice session and all precautions will be observed to be certain the practice is just practice.

Meanwhile the Board of Education is moving forward with its plans and designs on the new high school structure.

Last week the Board completed the sale of the bonds, at an interest rate of approximately 4 1/4%, a rate considered extremely beneficial at current interest charges.

Supt. Roy McKinley says the interest rates will figure at that amount after allowances are made for the premiums paid.

The Board also has moved forward on securing additional bond in the site area. Purchase of the property adjacent to the old house for $50,000 was approved last week and negotiations on the sale are in final stages.

This addition will allow the Board more flexibility in its initial layout and planning stage and will also afford added buildings for possible use as administrative headquarters.

Architect Jack Tribble is proceeding with the completion of plans following approval from state educational officials and the Board plans to have the specifications and plans ready for bidding this fall.

Construction will start early next spring with completion set for the opening of school in 1969.

Homecoming near, West Lafayette is getting ready

Homecoming is a traditionally big time in West Lafayette.

It's nearing that time again.

On Thursday, Friday and Saturday, Aug. 3, 4 and 5th, West Lafayette turns into "another world".

It will again this year, too.

Don Jackson, president of the West Lafayette Chamber of Commerce, is head man of the organizational structure for Homecoming and he has the community leaders at work in preparation.

The group of committee people meet at 7 tonight at the Rate Stand for a report session and to move things along.

Jackson has lined up another impressive crew of people to put the show on the road this year.

Dr. Robert Arnold, West Lafayette dentist, is chairman of the parade committee. His is the big chore and all details to be completed are his responsibility.

Such as the entering floats and parade units for the Thursday evening extravaganza, this year with "Song Titles" as its theme.

Mrs. Floyd (Nancy) Gress is chairman of the Rate Stand committee, a huge undertaking that will feed thousands.

She is assisted by Mr. and Mrs. Glenn Hill, Mr. and Mrs. Dale Gress and Mr. and Mrs. Robert Cox.

Tom Berry heads the program committee, which arranges all the events in the three-day festival. He is aided by Henry Young and Jim Ronahauen, Arthur Emler is in charge of merchandise certificates to be given as prizes.

The Horse Show committee is headed by Gene Durben and Mrs. Pearl Beall is chairman of the Homecoming Queen committee.

Mrs. Beall is taking entries for the Queen contest. A young lady must be between 16 and 21 and a resident of the Ridgewood School District. Anyone interested should get in touch with Mrs. Beall — and soon!

Ernest Holmes is ground committee chairman and Gen O'Neill heads the rides committee. Cashiers are headed by Harold Ott and include Duke St. John and Taylor Lymesmmayer.

Clarence Gress is lone man on the eats procurement committee, a chore he has handled for many, many years.

Chairman

Don Jackson is president of the West Lafayette Chamber of Commerce. This job has its regular duties, but among the most pressing is to organize and guide the structure that creates Homecoming each year. Jackson has the job well in hand and reports progress on all fronts for The Aug. 3, 4 and 5th event.

Working pair

Two fellows who each year are busy men over Homecoming are Arthur Emler, left, and Clarence Gress, right. The working pair operate the West Lafayette General store, but for Homecoming they are chairmen of the merchandise certificate committee and the food procurement committee, respectively.

He is a charter member of the Chamber, founded about 1942.

The program this year will include the parade at 7 p.m. Thursday, the crowning of the Queen following the parade and a dance featuring Johnnie Andrews Friday night, the Horse Show on Saturday and square dancing Saturday evening.

The usual rides and games will be featured, coupled with drawings for merchandise prizes each evening. Drawings are at 10:30 Thursday and Friday and at 11 p.m. Saturday.

"We're expecting this to be another great event," Jackson says, "and we are looking forward to the thousands of visitors it brings to our community."

Each year, officials say, people who have lived in West Lafayette over the years return, visit relatives and friends and "just have fun" at the Homecoming events.

It won't change this year. Except that probably it will be "bigger and better".

"That's our goal," Jackson says confidently.

Fig. 79. Optimum format is effective for weeklies. *Coshocton* (Ohio) *Commentator* uses five columns at 15½ picas with 3-pica alleys. Picture top right is green-black duotone.

spacing between words is often 9 points or even wider. If the eye has been skipping across this much space between words, it will hurdle that space between columns just as easily. The result is confusion.

It is not possible, then, merely to remove the column rules; extra space must be added to the alleys. For many papers, this extra space is impossible to obtain without widening the paper, too costly an investment in the opinion of many publishers. Nor can type columns be narrowed further without serious complications.

The answer was found in the W-format. In 8-column format such a page has six columns of 11-pica type and a seventh column which is approximately 1½ columns wide. The leftover half-column is used to expand the alleys.

The wide column is called the *W-column* and gives its name to the format. Width of the W-column is determined by plain arithmetic. Start with the width of the type page. From it subtract 66 picas (the six normal columns), then 6 picas for the alleys. What's left is the width of the W-column.

There may have to be some adjustment to the measure of W-matter. Ideally, that column should be no wider than 1½-column setting. At that measure, W-matter can be doubled over and used in a 3-column hole on a nonkey page. This flexibility is advantageous. If replating forces W-matter off the key page, it need not be reset to use it elsewhere.

Sometimes this readjustment of the W-measure requires widening the alleys. If every alley must be widened, it is wise to increase them to 18 points. There is nothing magic about this number, but it does simplify the arithmetic of spacing materials on the key page. Sometimes it is necessary merely to broaden one alley; that is usually the one that separates the W-column from the regular ones.

Using a unique measure for W-matter is not a high-yield editorial complication. It merely means that the desk has to keep a fairly accurate copy control and set only enough W-matter to fill the column; this is too simple to fret about. Copy for the W-column must be selected so there will rarely be need to pull it out of that position.

Many papers run a news summary, index, weather report, and/or similar copy in the W-column and thus eliminate the need for remaking that area.

Most newspapers that adopt the W-format start by using the wider column at the left of the page. Then they experiment with running it at the right. The next step is placing it near the center of the page. After that, if the editor is inventive and the W-column is not devoted to a

Surveyor Sending Back Photos

A 'Soft' Landing on Moon

★ ★ Late News Edition

THE KNICKERBOCKER NEWS

No. 29–Vol. 283 Second Class Postage Paid at Albany, N. Y. Albany, N. Y., Thursd: March 18, 1966 Published Daily Except Sunday Price Ten Cents

Two Ministers Quit Schenectady Posts Over Church Role

By MARY ANNE WEBER

Two Schenectady ministers have revealed plans to leave the active ministry because of serious questions they have about the present role of religion and the church.

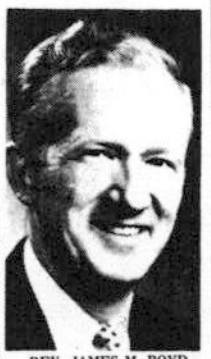

REV. JAMES M. BOYD

The Rev. James M. Boyd, pastor of the First Methodist Church in Schenectady and the Rev. John Waggy, his assistant, have received their bishop's permission to be relieved of duties at the First Methodist Church in July. Mr. Boyd has been reassigned to teach philosophy at Drew University in New Jersey and Mr. Waggy has status, which means he may work outside the ministry, probably in government or the Peace Corps. These are the two alternatives usually offered to Methodist ministers, since there is no such thing as actual resignation from the ministry.

Church Lags Behind

What do the two men question?

"I question why the church constantly lags behind in answering real social questions," says Mr. Boyd. "I question the unwillingness of people to let go of old images . . . their unwillingness to allow something new—new forms of worship, dance, film, contemporary music. The institution has tried to make sacred what is temporary and historical."

Mr. Boyd explained he felt that customs and traditions, which were merely a matter of history were considered sacred.

Said Mr. Waggy, "As far as I am concerned, the church is not a good secular institution, the professional leadership is not professional. They take something secular and make it into something sacred.

As an example he said he felt that "manipulation in the church becomes the movement of God's spirit or God's will instead of being frankly called manipulation.

"The Institution really can't deal with issues of contemporary society in any adequate way. It is always being dragged along." So the Church finally lets the Negro in the front door. So what! What's been won?", he asked.

Rigidity of Church

Mr. Waggy, who was more caustic in his comments than the pastor and more pessimistic, often referred to the rigidity of the church and the fact that it was constantly being "dragged along" by change rather than initiating it.

Regarding a solution, the two men differ.

Mr. Boyd would work for a renewal of the church, although it is a renewal that would shock and disturb most ortho-

Continued on Page 2-A

Ky Forces Take Over In Hue

SAIGON, South Viet Nam (AP) — Premier Nguyen Cao Ky's troops took over the Buddhist stronghold of Hue today without any resistance from the Buddhist-led mobs and antigovernment troops that have held the northern city in open rebellion since mid-March.

The junta's forces seized Hue's radio station and other strongpoints in the city 400 miles northeast of Saigon a day after the ruling generals came to a political agreement with their Buddhist opponents in Saigon.

Hue was the last territorial strongpoint of the antigovernment forces. Its recapture was a major victory for Ky, who has managed to stay in power with the support of his fellow generals and the Unitde States despite the massive campaign mounted against him by the Buddhists.

Armed Groups

Armed Buddhist groups were seen in the old part of Hue, across the Perfume River, government sources said, but they offered no resistance hours after the seizure as dusk settled over the city. A dozen government tanks and several armored personnel carriers watched over the radio station, the U.S. military compound and the bridge linking both banks of the city.

After weeks of street disturbances by Buddhist youths, Saigon took an unnaturally calm look. However, some radical Buddhist elements pretested the Buddhist - government compromise agreement to add 10 civilians to the ruling directorate of 10 generals.

American planes staged massive raids on North Viet Nam for the third consecutive day, concentrating again on antiaircraft and missile sites in 68 missions. Pilots also reported destroying a 20-truck convoy. Three more planes were shot down, raising the number lost over the Communist north to 254. One pilot was rescued.

Ground Action

Only sporadic contact with the Communists was reported by American ground forces in South Viet Nam, continuing a week-long pattern.

U.S. casualties declined last week from the record level of the week before, while government and enemy losses were about the same. The U.S. command reported 87 Americans killed, 605 wounded and two missing. A government spokesman said 240 South Vietnamese were killed and 55 missing, while the enemy toll was put at 1,173 killed and 197 captured.

Following up its seizure on May 23 of Da Nang, the other Buddhist stronghold, the junta's troops swept into Hue without a shot after the departure of units of the dissident-riddled 1st Vietnamese division.

No opposition was reported from members of the Buddhist struggle movement there led by the monk Thich — Venerable — Tri Quang, leader of the Buddhist rebellion in the north. More than 1,000 students sacked and

Continued on Page 2-A

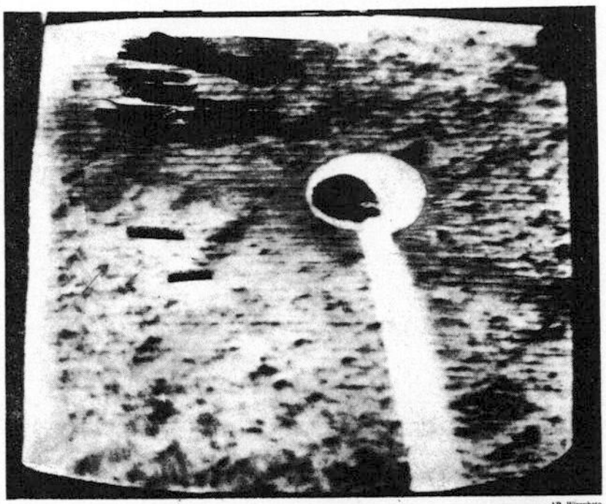

AP Wirephoto

SURVEYOR ANTENNA IN THE PICTURE—One of the Surveyor's antenna is shown in this picture transmitted to earth by the spacecraft after it had landed on the moon early today. It was transmitted in the form of 600 separate lines and copied from a monitor screen at Pasadena's Jet Propulsion Laboratory. The moon's surface is in the background . (Another Surveyor picture from the moon on Page 19-A)

Gemini 'Bug' Caught; All 'Go' Friday

CAPE KENNEDY (UPI) — With their latest obstacle locked, luckless astronauts Thomas Stafford and Eugene Cernan went back to the old waiting game today while technicians readied the Gemini 9 spaceship for a new orbital flight attempt.

Everything appeared "go" for the new 9:39 a.m., EDT Friday attempt to send the frustrated astronauts on a

PICTURE ON PAGE 2-A

chase in space after a target satellite that whirled overhead in a near perfect orbit. It was launched on schedule Wednesday.

Engineers were confident they have eliminated the computer guidance system "bug" that cropped up at the last moment Wednesday and set the ambitious rendezvous and spacewalk flight back two days.

The failure was traced to two of about 3,000 similar electronic

Continued on Page 2-A

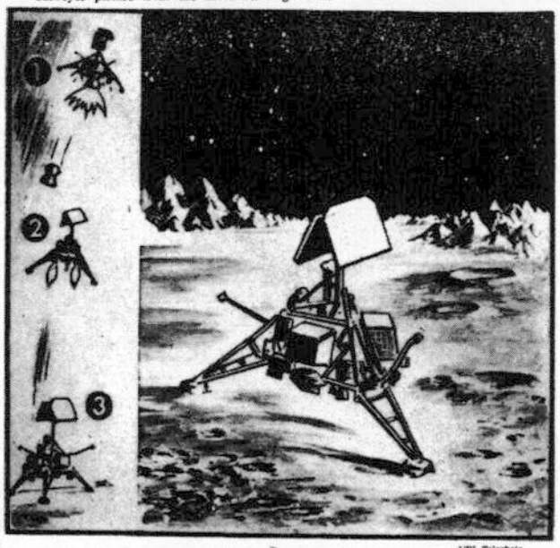

UPI Telephoto

HOW SURVEYOR LANDED — Artist's drawing shows how the Surveyor spacecraft made a soft landing on the moon early today. The descent to the lunar surface was made when the main retrorocket on the underside of the spacecraft was fired (1), slowing the craft from 5,900 mph to 400 mph. Vernier rockets slowed the craft (2) when it was at an altitude of 14 feet to 3½ mph. The touchdown (3) was at 8 mph.

Cameras To Function For 12 Days

PASADENA, Calif. (AP) — Surveyor 1, in an amazing first-try success, televised excellent closeupsfrom the moon today after an apparently perfect gentle landing in the Sea of Storms.

Scientists, after viewing the first 144 pictures showing hte 620-pound craft in good condition on a broad and featureless plain seemingly hard enough to support a manned landing craft, hailed it as a technical and informational triumph.

The spidery vehicle, laden with complex and sophisticated instrumentation, climaxed a 63-hour, quarter-million-mile flight from earth by braking to a soft landing at 2:17:37 a.m. — precisely on schedule and within feet of its target. It came to rest nearly vertical and so far as is known, undamaged.

At a morning news conference at the Jet Propulsion Laboratory, which guided Surveyor's flight, project officials made no attempt to hide their joy. "Extremely excellent" and I don't expect to see anything like this again in my lifetime" were two of the comments.

Level Surface

Dr. Leonard Jaffe, project scientist, said of the pictures: "They show a surface generally level, as expected, with objects that appear to be rocks and boulders, or fragments, from close to the spacecraft for as far as the eye can see, apparently to the horizon.

"Some appear to be a foot across. Some are much less than an inch. There are craters, one 10 feet across about 25 or 30 feet from the spacecraft."

R. F. Garbarini, of the National Aeronautics and Space Administration said "This in my opinion puts the Surveyor program ahead a year. We thought it would take three or four flights to get the craft operational. This means future Surveyors should provide more information about more sites than originally planned. It also means the Apollo manned spacecraft landing system, similar to Surveyor's, has been proved out."

3 Years Late

Surveyor 1, three years late due to a multitude of problems, was given small chance of success on the first launch due to its complexities.

Rep. Joseph E. Karth, D.-Minn., head of a committee which once criticized the program as poorly managed, offered "the congratulations of all American people" to the officials.

Jaffe, commenting on a photo that showed a shadow around one of Surveyor's three padded feet, said this indicates that impact was hard enough to cause a slight depression — a few inches deep — in the lunar crust. He said it appears about the same as that which would have made in sandy soil on earth.

The photos were first televised on a screen at the laboratory. Most were fuzzy and hard to distinguish, showing legs and other parts of the spacecraft and murky views of the plain.

Later, photographic prints obtained by electrical impulses on film, were distributed. They were strikingly clearer and showed much more detail. Ultimately, color shots will be obtained from among the hundreds of shots expected to be made over 12 days.

Jaffe said some of the initial

Continued on Page 2-A

Travia Lines Up Votes

Wage Bill Approval Expected in Assembly

By GERRY MCLAUGHLIN
Associated Press Writer

Assembly Speaker Anthony J. Travia arrayed his Democratic majority today for swift passage of a minimum-wage bill that would increase the pay of between 600,000 and 800,000 workers in New York State now earning less than $1.50 an hour.

The Democratic speaker moved for Assembly concurrence to a measure approved by the Republican - controlled Senate Wednesday. It would raise the state's hourly wage minimum from $1.25 to $1.50.

Senate approval of the wage proposal accompanied major developments on these other subjects Wednesday:

NEW YORK CITY — Over angry protests from Democrats, the Senate sought to force a 10-cent increase in New York City's 15-cent transit fare. Republicans did so by killing a bill that would give the Transit Authority $69 million to help relieve the transit system's financial deficit and maintain the 15-cent fare.

MEDICAL AID — Democrats rejected all but one of four proposals offered by Republicans in a move to revise the controversial state law providing medical care for the needy. The one provision on which there appeared to be agreement would provide $2 million to reimburse localities for any in-

Continued on Page 2-A

★ ★ ★

Fare Hike Battle Rages

By EMMET N. O'BRIEN
Gannett News Service

State Senate Majority Leader Earl W. Brydges made the big gamble—he stood firm on a fare increase to make the New York City subways self-sustaining.

Democrats shouted at him that he was hurting the subway commuters, but the Niagara Falls Republican led the fight against a bill permitting New York to give money to the Transit Authority that operates the subway-bus system.

"My purpose," said Mr. Brydges to a Senate that had just finished a hot debate over minimum wages yesterday, "is to defeat this bill. The end result will be an increase in fares for New York City to a realistic 25-cent level."

The posture he struck reflected the upstate Republican position on the complicated New York City fiscal issues. With a 25-cent fare—to be imposed, if ever it is, by the Transit Authority—the city would save $88 million it plans to turn over

Continued on Page 2-A

Warming Up

FAIR, COOL TONIGHT, WARMER TOMORROW

TODAY'S TEMPERATURES
(To 1 p.m.)
High 63 Low 40
(Weather Map on 3-C)

Rusk Arrives At NATO Base

BODOE, Norway (AP) — Secretary of State Dean Rusk arrived in Norway today for a two-day visit.

He flew from Helsinki to the NATO base outside this arctic port.

In Helsinki, Rusk spent a brisk sunny day in consultations with President Urho Kekkonen and leaders of Finland's new government which includes Communists for the first time since 1948.

INSIDE HIGHLIGHTS

52 Pages
Three Sections

Classified Ads	10, 11, 12, 13, 14, 15-C
Comics	13, 14-C
Earl Wilson	16-A
Editorial Page	18-A
Feature Page	16-A
Local News	14, 15-B; 1, 2, 3, 6, 16-C
Obituaries	5-C
Society, Women	B Section
Sports	7, 8, 9, 10, 11-C
Theaters	10, 11-A
TV-Radio	17-A

TODAY'S CHUCKLE—New Yorker: "What a day; I lost my job. Lost my wallet. My wife ran away with a salesman. The Yanks lost to the Senators. Imagine that! Leading by three in the eighth and they blow it to the Senators."

Flying Trip

Rocky in Washington For Medicaid Parley

Governor Rockefeller planned a flying trip to Washington today to discuss with federal officials a controversial state program that has been described as the most liberal in the nation for medical aid to the needy.

The late afternoon conference was scheduled in the midst of heated debate over proposed modification of the measure the Republican governor signed a month ago and since has defended.

The advocates of modification are Republicans, most of whom voted in favor of the measure and then ran into a barrage of criticism from constituents, including physicians, who consider the law too lenient.

The law is one open to all states as an arm of the federal medicare plan for persons 65 or older. The state laws, however, provide for medical assistance to all "needy," regardless of age. The states must establish the definition of needy.

Basically, the New York law would permit payment of medical bills for any family of four with a net annual income of $6,000. Net annual income is computed by deduction of income taxes and health insurance premiums from the gross earnings.

An estimated seven to eight million persons would be eligible, although state officials expect only two million applicants in the first year, including present relief recipients.

Judge Names Colleague's Son to Case

NEW YORK (AP) — Manhattan surrogate Joseph A. Cox says he has named the son of surrogate S. Samuel DiFalco as special guardian of 35 minors involved in an estate estimated to be worth $5 million.

Judge Cox, who said he had appointed Anthony DiFalco as a guardian "three or four times" previously, estimated the fee for the younger DiFalco at "maybe $500, but certainly not more than $1,000."

He and Judge DiFalco, the only two surrogates in Manhattan, are handling separate aspects of the case, which involves the estate of Orme Wilson. Judge DiFalco said Tuesday that his son "has never been professionally engaged in any proceeding before me at any time. . ."

Son Assigned To Dad's Ship

PEARL HARBOR (AP) — Chief Boatswain's Mate Ben Blakeman, 52, El Monte, Calif., got a letter from his seaman apprentice son Wednesday about his first Navy assignment. He thinks the boy is in for a surprise.

Bruce Blakeman, 20, will serve aboard the Polaris submarine Tender Proteus, but he doesn't know his father got orders this week transferring him to the same vessel.

Another son, Dave, 21, is a seaman stationed aboard the destroyer Hopewell in the South China Sea.

Fig. 80. *Knickerbocker News* of Albany, N.Y., was in 8-column full format before converting . . .

Nov. 22, 1963

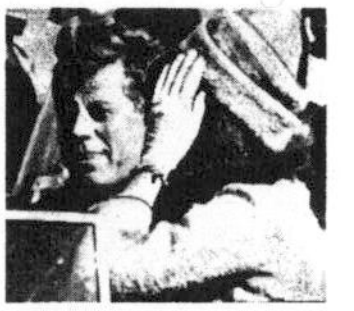

"Arnold Rowland and his wife stood close together on the grass, with the young husband busy glancing elsewhere. He saw a man in the Texas School Depository window with a gun. "Want to see a Secret Service agent?" he said. Mrs. Rowland turned and he pointed. Arnold knew of protection all over the city for the President. It didn't surprise him that there was a man in a window, with a rifle sloping across the front of his body, pointing downward."

"In the jump seat of the President's car, Gov. John Connally, a hunter, knew the sound. The expression under the pale cowboy hat changed to open-mouthed disbelief. His mouth formed the words not yet on his tongue: "Oh, no, no, no," as his head swung to the left to see the President."

"The great head that was sinking to the left came up in the rifle sights, again and the trigger was squeezed. As before, the explosive sound swelled through the plaza. This bullet entered the right rear of the skull."

"At the hospital entrance, Emory Roberts, agent in charge of this shift of Secret Service, opened the limousine door on Mrs. Kennedy's side, saw the President face down on Mrs. Kennedy's lap and said "Let us get the President." Mrs. Kennedy said "No." The last sentences she said in the car were to agent Clint Hill: "You know he's dead. Let me alone."

Press aide Malcolm Kilduff swallowed hard and said: 'Mr. President . . .' The tall Texan brought his head up sharply; Mrs. Johnson turned as she was about to sit, and held a hand against her mouth. This was the first time that Lyndon Baines Johnson had been so addressed. This was the first time he KNEW he was the 36th President of the United States."

"The Gaelic antidote to grief is whiskey: (Kenny) O'Donnell, turning to Mrs. Kennedy, said: 'I'm going to have a hell of a stiff drink. I think you should too."

"Supervisors of Arlington National Cemetery were summoned. Though darkness enveloped it now, they could show plots of the cemetery. For the usual burial, a 4-foot-by-8-foot section is allocated. A 3-acre area, including the plot where the President nad stood (several weeks earlier when he had said 'I could stay here forever') was taken for him."

"On shortwave, the word went to the White House. The 35th President of the United States was on his way 'home." Hurriedly, a triangular piece of crepe was hung on the front door of the main entrance. Sleepy guards were whipped by words to attention. Officers strode up and down in the darkness, sabers against shoulders. A big black catalfalque in the East Room waited for him as it had waited for others . . . the hearse entered the driveway . . ."

From:

'The Day JFK Was Shot'

Starting Monday in

THE KNICKERBOCKER NEWS

THE KNICKERBOCKER NEWS

★ Late News Edition

No. 32—Vol. 121 Published Daily Except Sunday Albany, N. Y., Friday, Nov. 22, 1968 Second Class Postage Paid at Albany, N.Y. Zip 12201 Price Ten Cents

10 to 15 Pct. Reduction Expected

Franc Will Be Devalued As Check on Money Crisis

By GEORGE THOMSON

BONN, Germany (AP) — The French franc will be devalued, West German Finance Minister Fraz Josef Strauss said today.

He told reporters the French Cabinet will have to decide the extent of the devaluation.

He spoke as the three-day emergency conference on the international monetary crisis was ending.

Informants said after Thursday's 17-hour session it appeared the franc would be reduced either by 10 per cent, from 20 cents to 18 cents, or by 15 per cent to 17 cents.

A spokesman for the office of French Premier Maurice Couve de Murville said in Paris there would be no announcement until after the French Cabinet meets on Saturday.

The conference appeared to be nearing an end. Britain's chancellor of the exchequer,

Washington's View of Monetary Crisis: Dollar Will Come Through Unscathed.

ON PAGE 5-A

Roy Jenkins, left the meeting shortly after noon and the Swedish delegation was reported on its way home.

Only the amount of the devaluation was unsettled, sources said after Thursday's 17-hour session. It appeared the franc would be reduced either by 10 per cent, from 20 U.S. cents to 18 cents, or by 15 per cent to 17 U.S. cents. A value in between also could be chosen.

To bolster the new value of the franc, the 10 nations at the conference were getting together a line of credit in other currencies which France could use to halt the flight of capital from French banks.

Admitted Certainty

A West German source said $2 billion would be subscribed by members of the "Group of 10" at the Bonn meeting, the Western world's leading financial powers. The Bank of International Settlements in Switzerland reportedly offered an additional $950 million.

Members of the French delegation admitted privately that devaluation of the franc was certain. But it was a severe blow to President Charles de Gaulle, celebrating his 78th birthday today. A week ago he

Continued on Page 2-A

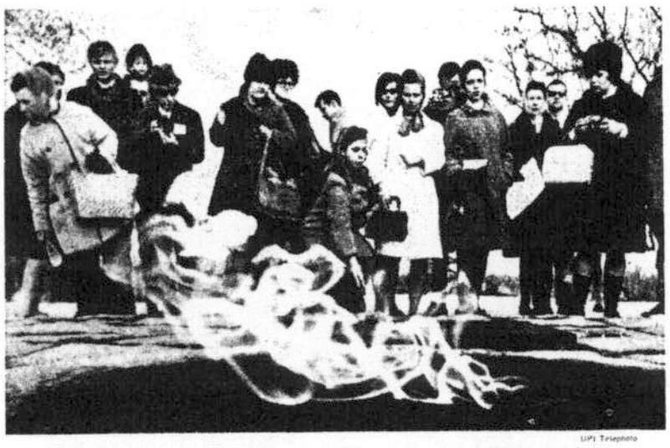

UPI Telephoto

5 Years Ago Today . . . The Nation Remembers

The Eternal Flame in Arlington National Cemetery continues to burn at the grave of John F. Kennedy today—the fifth anniversary of his assassination—and crowds like this one continue to file past it to pay their respects to the late President.

Jerusalem Car Blast Kills 10

JERUSALEM (AP) — More than 400 pounds of explosives in a parked automobile blew up in a crowded marketplace in the Jewish sector of Jerusalem today. Hospital officials said 10 persons were killed and 70 wounded.

It was the worst carnage to result from sabotage in the 20 years of the Jewish state's existence.

At least two Arabs were among the wounded.

Police picked up more than 10 Arabs for questioning or to protect them from possible mob violence.

Premier Levi Eshkol interrupted a vacation, hurried to Jerusalem and called a special Cabinet session.

The death car was parked on Agrippas Street, in the Mahaneh Yehuda market area. It blew up at 9:30 a.m. as some 3,000 persons were doing their Sabbath shopping.

A policeman said about 20 kilos—440 pounds—of explosives were packed into the death car.

"I ran outside and saw half a dozen fires in the shops," said one resident of the area, Rahamin Elmalak. "I ran to a barber shop to try and help. I saw people dead and burned. The seats were splashed with blood.

"It was the most terrible thing I ever saw."

Acting Mayor Mordechai Ish-Shalom and top police and army commanders inspected the area.

Police crawled on their hands and knees, picking up every bit of blackened metal.

About 20 autos were destroyed or damaged.

Police and troops sealed off the area, fearing more bombs might have been planted there.

Arab East Jerusalem also was closed to traffic from the Jewish sector to head off anti-Arab rioting.

The blast left a five-foot-wide crater in the street outside a hairdresser's shop.

A dozen ambulances converged on the market, using their sirens to get through the crowds running from the scene.

It was the third bomb attack inside the Holy City in recent months. At least a dozen Israelis were injured in the earlier incidents.

A Flame, A Cross, A Family

By HARRY F. ROSENTHAL

WASHINGTON (AP) — At night you can look westward across the Potomac from Washington and see, high on a hillside, the restless flame that marks the grave of John F. Kennedy. And you think of five years ago today.

By day you stand at that serene place and let your eyes sweep the grandeur of Washing-

Five Years Ago Today; The Scene at The K-N.

ON PAGE 12-A

ton, taking note of the plain little white cross a few steps to your right. And you think of all that has happened in that five years to one proud family, the Kennedys.

John's assasination . . . the plane crash that nearly killed Edward . . . Robert's election to the Senate . . . his campaign for

Continued on Page 11-A

Action Line

Action Line solves problems, cuts red tape, stands up for your rights. Write Action Line, The Knickerbocker News, 24 Sheridan Avenue, Albany, N. Y. 12201.

Q—If the president-elect dies between the time he is elected and Inauguration Day, does his vice president become our president? If so, does the nation then survive without a vice president for the next four years?—Mrs. W.F. Donovan, Mechanicville.

A—Technically there is no president-elect until after the electors of the 50 states cast their ballots which they do this year on Dec. 16. Should the president die after this, the vice president would become president. The Constitution says nothing about what would happen if the winner of a presidential election should die before the Electoral College votes in December. As to the vice presidency, a 1967 amendment to the Constitution provides that if the office of the vice president is vacant, the president shall nominate a vice president who shall take office upon confirmation by a majority vote of both houses of Congress.

Action Line

Q—In a recent discussion, a friend of mine told me that too much sleep causes cancer. Is this so?—D.M.U., Loudonville.

A—Your friend probably was thinking somewhat vaguely, of the recent release of statistical data compiled by the American Cancer Society to the effect that heart failure and stroke were prevalent to some extent, among people who slept 10 hours or more a night. No specific conclusions were drawn and it had nothing to do with cancer.

Action Line

Q — I am trying to find a movie poster of "The Endless Summer." — Debbi Joyce, West Coxsackie.

A — Marboro, 56 West Eighth Street, New York City, has a large stock of posters, including this one.

Action Line Gets Action

Our coat of arms from the Sanson Institute of Heraldry has come, and we are so grateful to Action Line. — Mrs. T.W.S., Nassau.

I have received my refund check from World Field Researdh. Thank you for your assistance. — Mrs. R.T., Guilderland.

Sound Off

I'm sounding off for the little birds, which can't sound off for themselves. With the coming of winter it would be nice if people would dispose of their unused bread, cake and the like by feeding it to the birds. An empty tummy isn't nice to sleep on, even in the bird world.—R.N., Albany.

U.S. Returns Red Fire From DMZ

SAIGON (UPI)—U.S. artillery shelled North Vietnam for the first time since President Johnson called off all bombardment of the Communist nation, American headquarters said today.

Two salvos from U.S. guns Thursday silenced two antiaircraft machineguns that opened

War Developments Sour Peace Talks.

ON PAGE 5-A

fire first on U.S. spotter planes from the northern half of Vietnam's border Demilitarized Zone (DMZ).

Hanoi Radio disputed the report. Its broadcast heard in Tokyo today said allied artillery and naval guns had hit three villages in the northern DMZ four times previously—on Nov. 16, 17, 20 and 21.

The United States, the radio said, "must bear full responsibility for all the consequences" of the "extremely brazen provocative acts."

Gen. Creighton W. Abrams'

Continued on Page 2-A

Flames Light Up Sky

New Explosion Dims Hopes for 78 Miners

MANNINGTON, W. Va. (AP) — A new explosion, sending flames shooting upward like a flash of lightning, hit the coal mine today where 78 men have been trapped in burning passageways for two days.

The blast at 2:50 a.m. shook the company store more than four miles away.

It was the latest in a chain of explosions that started Wednesday morning and trapped 78 of the 99 men working the early shift in the Mountaineer Coal Co. No. 9 mine. The other 21 either escaped or were pulled from the mine.

"I felt the impact on my face," said 19-year-old Rich Opyoke who was standing on a bridge near the store.

Leonard Gross, publications director for Consolidation Coal Co., Mountaineer's parent firm, pinpointed the explosion at the intake shaft on Mod's Run, one of the many passageways of the sprawling mine complex spread over a seven-mile area.

"There has been no assessment of the intensity of the explosion," Gross said immediately after the blast. "However, it was reported that flames erupted from the portal."

He said this was the spot

Continued on Page 2-A

Nice and Fair

FAIR TONIGHT, INCREASING CLOUDINESS TOMORROW.

TODAY'S TEMPERATURES

High 43 Low 31

(Weather Map, Details on Page 3-A)

This Boy Had A 'Fine' Meal

MISSOULA, Mont. (AP) — Police Court Judge Wallace N. Clark received a check and a note from an out-of-county parking meter offender which read:

"This check covers the payment of two tickets, one for Nov. 10 and one for Nov. 12 which my son ate. Thank you."

INSIDE HIGHLIGHTS

38 Pages

Three Sections

Comics	13, 14-C
Classified	9, 10, 11, 12, 13, 14, 15-C
Editorial	12-A
Financial	4, 5-C
Health Column	7-A
Jeane Dixon	14-C
Local News	1, 2, 3, 16-C
Charley Mooney	1-C
Obituaries	10-C
Society, Women	B Section
Sports	6, 7, 8-C
Suburban	3-C
Theater	6-A
TV-Radio	10-A

TODAY'S CHUCKLE — It **used to take two bales of cotton to make a woman's dress. Now a silk worm can do it on his day off.**

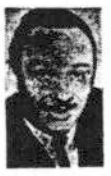

Off the State Cuff

Burns May Be Named As National Chairman

By ARVIS CHALMERS
The Knickerbocker News Capitol Reporter

John J. Burns, New York State Democratic chairman, is being considered for appointment as national Democratic chairman.

The inside party talk is that Mr. Burns is one of several national figures in the running for the job. Lawrence O'Brien said he would give up once the election campaign was over.

Mr. O'Brien ran the Humphrey campaign, but insisted that he was temporary even before Mr. Humphrey lost.

New Yorker Burns is in the picture for these reasons:

He represents a big state that gave Mr. Humphrey a big plurality. He is close to the Kennedy political family, yet he isn't so closely identified with partisan politics within the Democratic Party.

As state chairman, he managed in personal appearances around the state to help solidify his party in the November election.

And, he's had a faculty of being able to make friends quietly without bombardment or pressure.

In a call inquiring about the Washington report, Mr. Burns said his personal choice would be for Larry O'Brien to continue as national chairman.

Other names being mentioned for national chairman are Senator Fred Harris of Oklahoma and Terry Sanford, former governor of North Carolina.

For the political sophisticates in New York, it makes sense that John Burns might be chosen, depending, of course, on the national party thinking on how best to recoup during the four year Nixon administration.

AIRLINE SPECIAL: Th. flight schedules out of Albany

Continued on Page 2-A

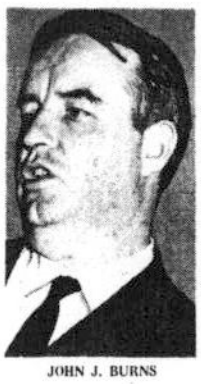

JOHN J. BURNS

Fig. 81. . . . into W-format. Wider W-column is apparent only in ACTION LINE setting. Remainder of depth is taken up in picture and banner.

regular department, he finds that there are countless patterns into which the wide measure may be woven.

It is necessary to have a complete column of W-matter, of course, but it does not have to run in one continuous vertical element; it can be broken into segments. The top of the second segment must align immediately under the bottom of the first one and so on, but it can be in any of the seven columns.

When the W-column is moved into the page, the alley at its right or left will not align with that adjoining the regular columns above or below it. This disturbs some editors but it need not. In fact, it is desirable to avoid an alley that runs without interruption for the full length of a page.

Pictures may run in the W-column, either as a 1½-cut or extending out into one or more of the regular columns. One-up elements may run in part of the W-column.

Most newspapers came to the W-format from the conventional full format. But *Today,* the Florida daily that was begun to serve the Cape Kennedy area, chose this format in its initial planning. The birth of a daily newspaper—especially one that begins as an entity rather than being an expansion of a nondaily—is always an exciting event and attracts intense interest from all newspapermen. So, although many papers were already using the W-format, *Today*'s selection of that format focused great interest on the technique and speeded its adoption by other papers.

Today uses the W-format only on key pages, but judicious planning was able to provide a relatively large number of key pages free of advertising. Other pages are in 8-column format, but the staff keeps a resemblance among all pages, key and inside. The W-column is almost without exception kept at the left of the page. On non-key pages, whenever possible, 2-column matter runs all or most of the way down the left of the page. So the pattern of a wider element at the left and regular ones on the rest of the page is maintained throughout the paper.

The only newspapers that use the W-format throughout—at least as this is written—are the Free Press publications in Fairfax County, Virginia. In 1966, these papers were bought jointly (and later sold) by the Gannett Newspapers and the Byrd interests of Virginia. Therefore it was natural that they should look at *Today,* also a Gannett property, as a model for the drastic restyling that was undertaken after the purchase. As a logical extension, it was decided to use the W-format on every page, even those with advertising. The result was happy and practical.

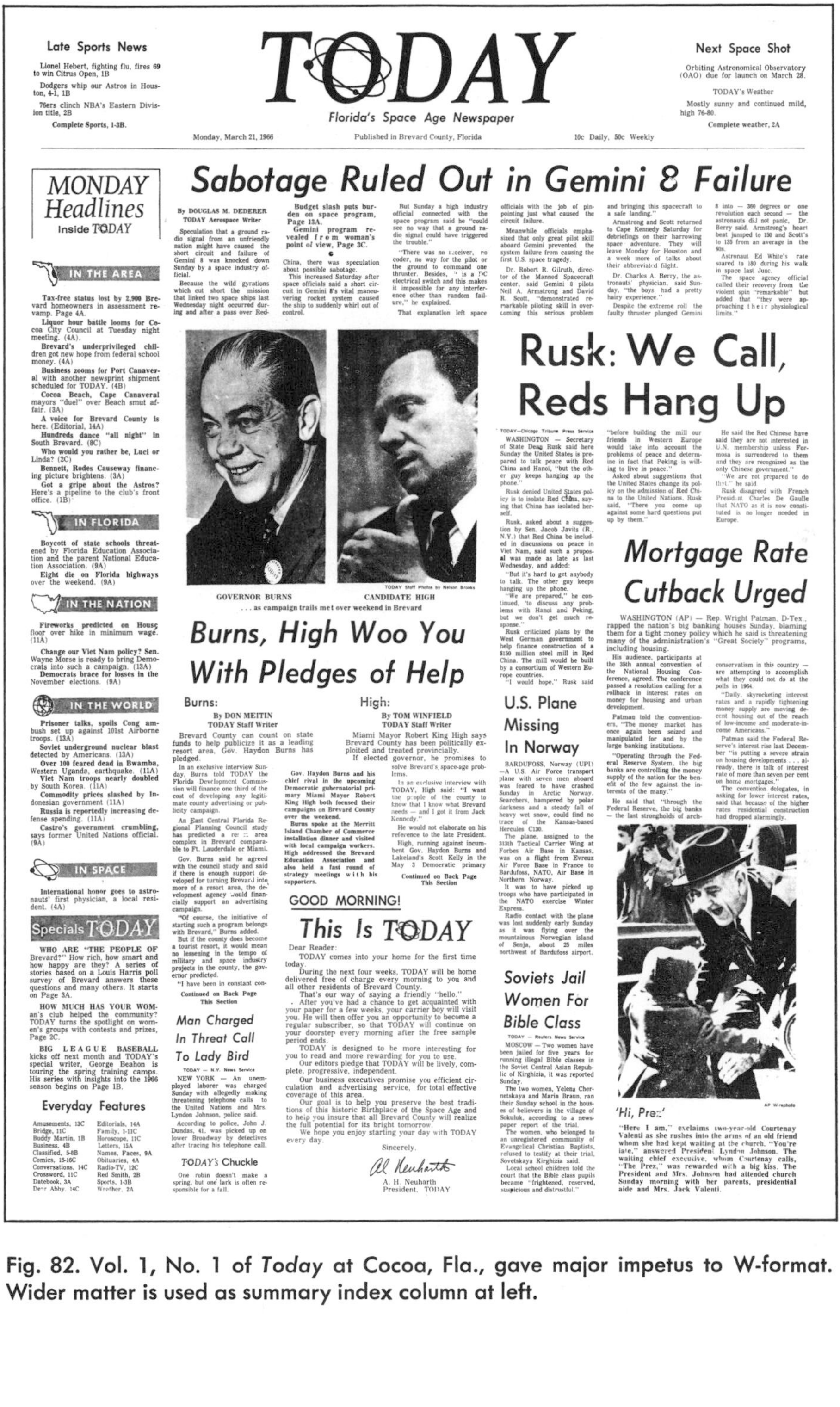

Late Sports News

Lionel Hebert, fighting flu, fires 69 to win Citrus Open, 1B

Dodgers whip our Astros in Houston, 4-1, 1B

76ers clinch NBA's Eastern Division title, 2B

Complete Sports, 1-3B.

TODAY

Florida's Space Age Newspaper

Next Space Shot

Orbiting Astronomical Observatory (OAO) due for launch on March 28.

TODAY's Weather

Mostly sunny and continued mild, high 76-80.

Complete weather, 2A

Monday, March 21, 1966 — Published in Brevard County, Florida — 10c Daily, 50c Weekly

MONDAY Headlines Inside TODAY

IN THE AREA

Tax-free status lost by 2,900 Brevard homeowners in assessment revamp. Page 4A.

Liquor hour battle looms for Cocoa City Council at Tuesday night meeting. (4A).

Brevard's underprivileged children got new hope from federal school money. (4A)

Business zooms for Port Canaveral with another newsprint shipment scheduled for TODAY. (4B)

Cocoa Beach, Cape Canaveral mayors "duel" over Beach smut affair. (3A)

A voice for Brevard County is here. (Editorial, 14A)

Hundreds dance "all night" in South Brevard. (8C)

Who would you rather be, Luci or Linda? (2C)

Bennett, Rodes Causeway financing picture brightens. (3A)

Got a gripe about the Astros? Here's a pipeline to the club's front office. (1B)

IN FLORIDA

Boycott of state schools threatened by Florida Education Association and the parent National Education Association. (9A)

Eight die on Florida highways over the weekend. (9A)

IN THE NATION

Fireworks predicted on House floor over hike in minimum wage. (11A)

Change our Viet Nam policy? Sen. Wayne Morse is ready to bring Democrats into such a campaign. (13A)

Democrats brace for losses in the November elections. (9A)

IN THE WORLD

Prisoner talks, spoils Cong ambush set up against 101st Airborne troops. (13A)

Soviet underground nuclear blast detected by Americans. (13A)

Over 100 feared dead in Bwamba, Western Uganda, earthquake. (11A)

Viet Nam troops nearly doubled by South Korea. (11A)

Commodity prices slashed by Indonesian government (11A)

Russia is reportedly increasing defense spending. (11A)

Castro's government crumbling, says former United Nations official. (9A)

IN SPACE

International honor goes to astronauts' first physician, a local resident. (4A)

Specials TODAY

WHO ARE "THE PEOPLE OF Brevard?" How rich, how smart and how happy are they? A series of stories based on a Louis Harris poll survey of Brevard answers these questions and many others. It starts on Page 3A.

HOW MUCH HAS YOUR WOMan's club helped the community? TODAY turns the spotlight on women's groups with contests and prizes, Page 2C.

BIG LEAGUE BASEBALL kicks off next month and TODAY's special writer, George Beahon is touring the spring training camps. His series with insights into the 1966 season begins on Page 1B.

Everyday Features

Amusements, 13C	Editorials, 14A
Bridge, 11C	Family, 1-11C
Buddy Martin, 1B	Horoscope, 11C
Business, 4B	Letters, 15A
Classified, 5-8B	Names, Faces, 9A
Comics, 15-16C	Obituaries, 4A
Conversations, 14C	Radio-TV, 12C
Crossword, 11C	Red Smith, 2B
Datebook, 3A	Sports, 1-3B
Dear Abby, 14C	Weather, 2A

Sabotage Ruled Out in Gemini 8 Failure

By DOUGLAS M. DEDERER
TODAY Aerospace Writer

Speculation that a ground radio signal from an unfriendly nation might have caused the short circuit and failure of Gemini 8 was knocked down Sunday by a space industry official.

Because the wild gyrations which cut short the mission that linked two space ships last Wednesday night occurred during and after a pass over Red China, there was speculation about possible sabotage.

Budget slash puts burden on space program, Page 13A.

Gemini program revealed from woman's point of view, Page 3C.

This increased Saturday after space officials said a short circuit in Gemini 8's vital maneuvering rocket system caused the ship to suddenly whirl out of control.

But Sunday a high industry official connected with the space program said he "could see no way that a ground radio signal could have triggered the trouble."

"There was no receiver, no coder, no way for the pilot or the ground to command one thruster. Besides, it is a DC electrical switch and this makes it impossible for any interference other than random failure," he explained.

That explanation left space officials with the job of pinpointing just what caused the circuit failure.

Meanwhile officials emphasized that only great pilot skill aboard Gemini prevented the system failure from causing the first U.S. space tragedy.

Dr. Robert R. Gilruth, director of the Manned Spacecraft center, said Gemini 8 pilots Neil A. Armstrong and David R. Scott, "demonstrated remarkable piloting skill in overcoming this serious problem and bringing this spacecraft to a safe landing."

Armstrong and Scott returned to Cape Kennedy Saturday for debriefings on their harrowing space adventure. They will leave Monday for Houston and a week more of talks about their abbreviated flight.

Dr. Charles A. Berry, the astronauts' physician, said Sunday, "the boys had a pretty hairy experience."

Despite the extreme roll the faulty thruster plunged Gemini 8 into — 360 degrees or one revolution each second — the astronauts did not panic, Dr. Berry said. Armstrong's heart beat jumped to 150 and Scott's to 135 from an average in the 60s.

Astronaut Ed White's rate soared to 180 during his walk in space last June.

The space agency official called their recovery from the violent spin "remarkable" but added that "they were approaching their physiological limits."

TODAY Staff Photos by Nelson Brooks

GOVERNOR BURNS — CANDIDATE HIGH

... as campaign trails met over weekend in Brevard

Burns, High Woo You With Pledges of Help

Gov. Haydon Burns and his chief rival in the upcoming Democratic gubernatorial primary Miami Mayor Robert King High both focused their campaigns on Brevard County over the weekend.

Burns spoke at the Merritt Island Chamber of Commerce installation dinner and visited with local campaign workers. High addressed the Brevard Education Association and also held a fast round of strategy meetings with his supporters.

Burns:

By DON MEITIN
TODAY Staff Writer

Brevard County can count on state funds to help publicize it as a leading resort area, Gov. Haydon Burns has pledged.

In an exclusive interview Sunday, Burns told TODAY the Florida Development Commission will finance one third of the cost of developing any legitimate county advertising or publicity campaign.

An East Central Florida Regional Planning Council study has predicted a re[illegible] area complex in Brevard comparable to Ft. Lauderdale or Miami.

Gov. Burns said he agreed with the council study and said if there is enough support developed for turning Brevard into more of a resort area, the development agency would financially support an advertising campaign.

"Of course, the initiative of starting such a program belongs with Brevard," Burns added.

But if the county does become a tourist resort, it would mean no lessening in the tempo of military and space industry projects in the county, the governor predicted.

"I have been in constant con-

Continued on Back Page This Section

High:

By TOM WINFIELD
TODAY Staff Writer

Miami Mayor Robert King High says Brevard County has been politically exploited and treated provincially.

If elected governor, he promises to solve Brevard's space-age problems.

In an exclusive interview with TODAY, High said: "I want the people of the county to know that I know what Brevard needs — and I got it from Jack Kennedy."

He would not elaborate on his reference to the late President.

High, running against incumbent Gov. Haydon Burns and Lakeland's Scott Kelly in the May 3 Democratic primary

Continued on Back Page This Section

GOOD MORNING!

This Is TODAY

Dear Reader:

TODAY comes into your home for the first time today.

During the next four weeks, TODAY will be home delivered free of charge every morning to you and all other residents of Brevard County.

That's our way of saying a friendly "hello."

After you've had a chance to get acquainted with your paper for a few weeks, your carrier boy will visit you. He will then offer you an opportunity to become a regular subscriber, so that TODAY will continue on your doorstep every morning after the free sample period ends.

TODAY is designed to be more interesting for you to read and more rewarding for you to use.

Our editors pledge that TODAY will be lively, complete, progressive, independent.

Our business executives promise you efficient circulation and advertising service, for total effective coverage of this area.

Our goal is to help you preserve the best traditions of this historic Birthplace of the Space Age and to help you insure that all Brevard County will realize the full potential for its bright tomorrow.

We hope you enjoy starting your day with TODAY every day.

Sincerely,

Al Neuharth

A. H. Neuharth
President, TODAY

Man Charged In Threat Call To Lady Bird

TODAY — N.Y. News Service

NEW YORK — An unemployed laborer was charged Sunday with allegedly making threatening telephone calls to the United Nations and Mrs. Lyndon Johnson, police said.

According to police, John J. Dundas, 41, was picked up on lower Broadway by detectives after tracing his telephone call.

TODAY's Chuckle

One robin doesn't make a spring, but one lark is often responsible for a fall.

Rusk: We Call, Reds Hang Up

TODAY—Chicago Tribune Press Service

WASHINGTON — Secretary of State Dean Rusk said here Sunday the United States is prepared to talk peace with Red China and Hanoi, "but the other guy keeps hanging up the phone."

Rusk denied United States policy is to isolate Red China, saying that China has isolated herself.

Rusk, asked about a suggestion by Sen. Jacob Javits (R., N.Y.) that Red China be included in discussions on peace in Viet Nam, said such a proposal was made as late as last Wednesday, and added:

"But it's hard to get anybody to talk. The other guy keeps hanging up the phone.

"We are prepared," he continued, "to discuss any problems with Hanoi and Peking, but we don't get much response."

Rusk criticized plans by the West German government to help finance construction of a $150 million steel mill in Red China. The mill would be built by a consortium of Western Europe countries.

"I would hope," Rusk said "before building the mill our friends in Western Europe would take into account the problems of peace and determine in fact that Peking is willing to live in peace."

Asked about suggestions that the United States change its policy on the admission of Red China to the United Nations, Rusk said, "There you come up against some hard questions put up by them."

He said the Red Chinese have said they are not interested in U.N. membership unless Formosa is surrendered to them and they are recognized as the only Chinese government."

"We are not prepared to do that," he said.

Rusk disagreed with French President Charles De Gaulle that NATO as it is now constituted is no longer needed in Europe.

U.S. Plane Missing In Norway

BARDUFOSS, Norway (UPI) —A U.S. Air Force transport plane with seven men aboard was feared to have crashed Sunday in Arctic Norway. Searchers, hampered by polar darkness and a steady fall of heavy wet snow, could find no trace of the Kansas-based Hercules C130.

The plane, assigned to the 313th Tactical Carrier Wing at Forbes Air Base in Kansas, was on a flight from Evreuz Air Force Base in France to Bardufoss, NATO, Air Base in Northern Norway.

It was to have picked up troops who have participated in the NATO exercise Winter Express.

Radio contact with the plane was lost suddenly early Sunday as it was flying over the mountainous Norwegian island of Senja, about 25 miles northwest of Bardufoss airport.

Soviets Jail Women For Bible Class

TODAY — Reuters News Service

MOSCOW — Two women have been jailed for five years for running illegal Bible classes in the Soviet Central Asian Republic of Kirghizia, it was reported Sunday.

The two women, Yelena Chernetskaya and Maria Braun, ran their Sunday school in the houses of believers in the village of Sokuluk, according to a newspaper report of the trial.

The women, who belonged to an unregistered community of Evangelical Christian Baptists, refused to testify at their trial, Sovetskaya Kirghizia said.

Local school children told the court that the Bible class pupils became "frightened, reserved, suspicious and distrustful."

Mortgage Rate Cutback Urged

WASHINGTON (AP) — Rep. Wright Patman, D-Tex., rapped the nation's big banking houses Sunday, blaming them for a tight money policy which he said is threatening many of the administration's "Great Society" programs, including housing.

His audience, participants at the 35th annual convention of the National Housing Conference, agreed. The conference passed a resolution calling for a rollback in interest rates on money for housing and urban development.

Patman told the conventioners, "The money market has once again been seized and manipulated for and by the large banking institutions.

"Operating through the Federal Reserve System, the big banks are controlling the money supply of the nation for the benefit of the few against the interests of the many."

He said that "through the Federal Reserve, the big banks — the last strongholds of arch-conservatism in this country — are attempting to accomplish what they could not do at the polls in 1964.

"Daily, skyrocketing interest rates and a rapidly tightening money supply are moving decent housing out of the reach of low-income and moderate-income Americans."

Patman said the Federal Reserve's interest rise last December "is putting a severe strain on housing developments . . . already, there is talk of interest rate of more than seven per cent on home mortgages."

The convention delegates, in asking for lower interest rates, said that because of the higher rates residential construction had dropped alarmingly.

AP Wirephoto

'Hi, Prez'

"Here I am," exclaims two-year-old Courtenay Valenti as she rushes into the arms of an old friend whom she had kept waiting at the church. "You're late," answered President Lyndon Johnson. The waiting chief executive, whom Courtenay calls, "The Prez," was rewarded with a big kiss. The President and Mrs. Johnson had attended church Sunday morning with her parents, presidential aide and Mrs. Jack Valenti.

Fig. 82. Vol. 1, No. 1 of *Today* at Cocoa, Fla., gave major impetus to W-format. Wider matter is used as summary index column at left.

20c
112 Pages

SUNDAY TELEGRAM

Forecast
TODAY: Variable cloudiness; high near 70; low tonight 50-55. Monday: Continued mild; chance of showers.

VOLUME 93, NO. 23 — ELMIRA, N. Y. SUNDAY, OCT. 13, 1968 — TWENTY CENTS

School, College Grid Scores

HIGH SCHOOL			
Edison	19	Trumansburg	30
Wellsville	12	Athens	29
Watkins Glen	7	Odessa - Montour	28
Romulus	6	Lakemont	0
Spencer - Van Etten	13	Towanda	46
Groton	6	North Penn	14
Penn Yan	53	Corning West	41
Geneva DeSales	0	Notre Dame	6
Dundee	33	Wyalusing	41
South Seneca	0	Sayre	7

COLLEGE	
Penn	10
Cornell	8
Syracuse	50
Pittsburgh	17
Ohio State	13
Purdue	0
Penn State	21
UCLA	6
Notre Dame	27
Northwestern	7

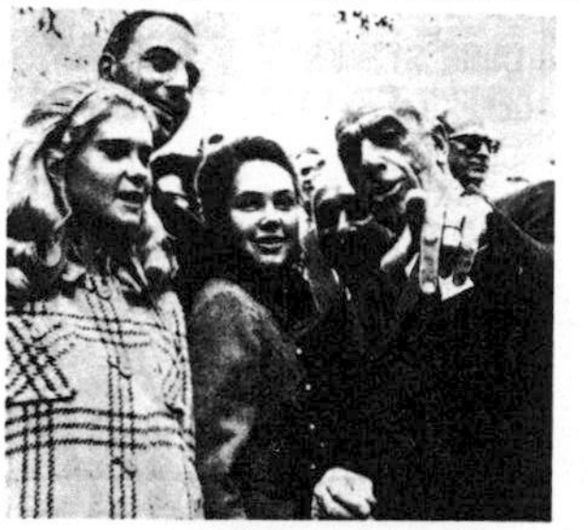

Parade Guests Patricia (left) and Julie Nixon, daughters of GOP presidential candidate Richard M. Nixon, follow the point of Italian Ambassador Egidio Ortona during the Columbus Day parade in New York City. Fortune Pope, the parade's grand marshal, is behind Julie. Flu prevented Vice President Hubert H. Humphrey from reviewing the parade. Nixon was resting in Florida. (AP Wirephoto)

Apollo Plays Space Tag With Tumbling Rocket

SPACE CENTER, Houston (AP) — Plagued by a cold, command pilot Walter M. Schirra Jr. gunned his Apollo 7 spaceship in pursuit of a wildly tumbling target in space Saturday, then played tag with it in a make-believe rescue of two astronauts lost in moon orbit.

"It's tumbling rather wildly so we want to stay away from it," the astronauts reported about the spent second stage of the Saturn rocket they had chased across the skies high over the Pacific.

Fighting a tight time schedule, Schirra, who had imposed a television blackout on the ship, concentrated on firing the spacecraft's big rocket engine packing more power than a jet fighter.

"Yaba daba doo!" Schirra exclaimed when he first fired the rocket. "That was a ride and a half."

• • •

After the maneuver was completed, Schirra broke away from the rocket for the last time. He also told the ground controllers that he would use the ship's portable television camera to give America a look at the astronauts in space sometime Monday morning.

The Apollo 7 inched as close as 70 feet of the tumbling rocket and jammed on the rocket brakes to avoid getting too close. Then it hovered there for nearly half an hour.

With astronauts Donn F. Eisele and Walter Cunningham at his side Schirra took more than three hours to close the 80 mile gap between Apollo 7 and the rocket, working out his own flight path by computer, sextant and telescope.

• • •

The astronauts reported a progressive dirty window problem. "The center hatch window now is pretty badly blurred just barely usable for detecting the horizon . . . very fuzzy through it," Schirra said. There is also a film on another window making it unusable for picture taking, and "interestingly enough small hairs like fuzz" are forming on all five spacecraft windows.

Schirra reported to doctors late in the day that his temperature is normal, "I haven't been coughing and there's nothing in the lungs." Still he said, his nose was full and he wanted to clear it up.

Doctors told him to take two aspirin every four hours and a decongestant every eight hours. Schirra replied, "Roger, I'll follow that schedule until I land, run out or feel better."

Apollo's medicine chest carries 24 decongestant pills, 72 aspirin.

The rendezvous, first for Apollo, came just a little short of three years after Schirra, piloting Gemini 6, performed the first rendezvous in space, dancing his spaceship around orbiting Gemini 7.

The Apollo 7 trio had kicked away from the Saturn 4B second stage Friday night, gradually losing it in space. Then, at 12:28 p.m. CDT Saturday, early in the second day in space, Schirra fired his hefty 20,000-pound thrust spacecraft engine.

It shot Apollo 7 into a higher orbit, some eight miles above the Saturn and more than 80 miles ahead of it.

Then at 2:04 p.m. Schirra hit the mighty rocket again and brought the Apollo 7 arcing down. Using his small attitude control rockets on the side of the spaceship, Schirra jammed on the brakes and tweaked his 15-ton ship as near as he dared to the cartwheeling SvB.

"They're braking like hell," a ground controller reported, picking up the action on his control console. Although they were in radio silence during much of the maneuver, the astronauts said they came in "right up the pike."

It is the basic maneuver a moon pilot would have to use if the space cab taking two astronauts to the moon's surface were disabled and stranded in lunar orbit. Should that happen, the lone pilot in the mothership would have to swoop down on the space cab to rescue his fellow fliers.

The rendezvous maneuver was a crucial test for the spaceship's prime engine. It is the one system aboard the spacecraft which has no backup. For the moon flight it must be tested to perfection.

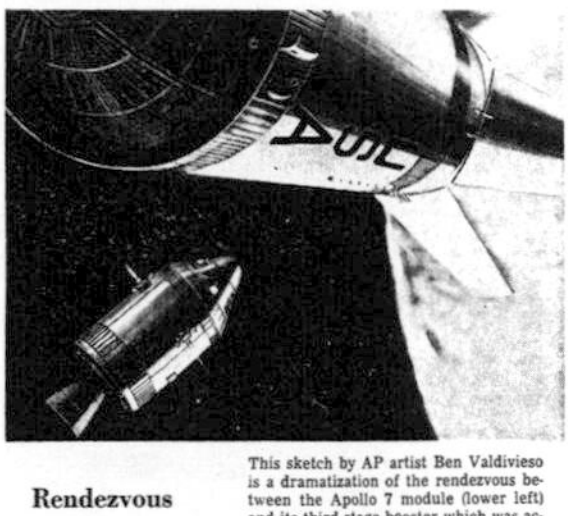

Rendezvous This sketch by AP artist Ben Valdivieso is a dramatization of the rendezvous between the Apollo 7 module (lower left) and its third stage booster which was accomplished Saturday.

Marines Repel Attack

SAIGON (AP) — U.S. Marines repelled a strong enemy attack near the Thuong Duc Green Beret camp Saturday despite virtually no air support because of bad weather.

A few fighter-bombers and C47 gunships equipped with rapid-firing machine guns managed to find holes in the cloud cover to strafe the North Vietnamese, but the heavy overcast prevented saturation strikes of enemy positions.

After a 3½-hour battle with small arms, machine guns and artillery, the enemy pulled back. The Marines counted 31 North Vietnamese dead and reported eight leathernecks killed and 20 wounded.

• • •

The firefight raged in jungled foothills 27 miles southwest of Da Nang, an area where there are believed to be between 5,000 and 7,500 North Vietnamese troops. The Marines, from the 5th Regiment, 1st Division, were part of a large allied force that was sent into the area a week ago to relieve pressure on the Thuong Duc camp.

Far to the south, enemy mortarmen pumped 24 rounds before dawn today into My Tho, a province capital 35 miles southwest of Saigon in the Mekong Delta. It was the second time in three days the city had been shelled. Ten persons were reported wounded.

• • •

A few minutes earlier, mortars fell into a Vietnamese army position about one mile northeast of My Tho, killing one soldier.

Deeper in the delta, a pacification team lost one man killed and four wounded in turning back a predawn attack. Two civilians were reported killed. There was no word on enemy casualities.

Another seizure of enemy war materials in the Saigon area was reported today by the U.S. Command. It said U.S. 25th Division infantrymen, acting on a defector's information, turned up a cache of 50 mortar rounds, 10,000 rounds of rifle ammunition and 100 grenades about 25 miles northwest of Saigon.

Television from Space Canceled by Schirra

SPACE CENTER, Houston (AP) — Due to circumstances within their control, Navy Capt. Walter M. Schirra and his two fellow Apollo 7 astronauts were not seen on live television from space Saturday.

Schirra had opposed carrying a television camera on the 11-day Apollo mission, but he lost that fight. The first telecast was scheduled for Saturday morning at the end of the 16th orbit.

About an hour before the scheduled telecast, as the commercial television networks were readying their equipment to relay it, Schirra told ground controllers in a no-nonsense voice: "At this point, TV will be delayed, without any further discussion until after the rendezvous."

• • •

It wasn't long before astronaut boss Donald Slayton got on the air.

"Apollo 7," he began. "All we've agreed to do on this particular pass is to flip the (on-off) switch on. No other activity is associated with TV. I think we're still obligated to do that."

Schirra, with irritation in his voice, said: "We have not eaten at this point. I have a cold. I refuse to foul up our timelines at this point."

There was nothing but silence from the ground.

A few minutes later, Paul Haney—the public's link with the spacecraft and Apollo control— announced: "This is a matter in which the control center decided they should accept the crew commander's judgment and that it would overload them to attempt this before the rendezvous (with the spent second stage of the launch vehicle).

As captain of the ship, Schirra can overrule his boss—as he did in this case.

Schirra was unhappy with the quality of the television picture in an earlier test from an airplane. "The world is not going to see much," he commented.

Late in the afternoon Slayton pressed Schirra for a commitment on the television project. Schirra agreed to do it after the 45th revolution. That revolution comes sometime on Monday morning.

U.S. Distress Voiced Over Coup in Panama

WASHINGTON (AP) — Secretary of State Dean Rusk voiced the "profound concern to the United States" Saturday over the military takeover in Panama. But Washington showed little optimism over prospects for undoing the coup.

—The United States has a special interest in political stability in Panama, the site of the vital U.S.-run canal connecting the Atlantic and Pacific.

—Coming so soon after the Oct. 3 ouster of Peru's constitutional government, the Panamanian coup raised apprehension that other overthrow-minded groups in Latin America might be tempted to follow suit. The United States is pledged to democratic constitutional processes in the hemisphere.

As Rusk put it in a special statement issued while high officials huddled over the Panamanian crisis:

"We are deeply distressed to learn that the Panamanian national guard has overthrown the recently inaugurated president . . .

"We have a close relationship with Panama and a stake in the stability of the isthmus in view of our presence there as stewards of the vital Panama Canal.

"This coup d'etat must be equally disturbing to our sister republics in the hemisphere"

• • •

Covey T. Oliver, assistant secretary of state for inter-American affairs, and some other high-ranking authorities were reported at their desks all night following reports of the overthrow late Friday evening—but what practical action the United States might be able to take remained, in their opinion, in some doubt.

The State Department announced U.S. diplomatic relations with Panama and economic aid were "in a state of suspension"—a definition which falls short of a formal break between two governments. As applied to Peru, it meant a period of no official contacts pending a study of the situation to see who should in fact be dealt with as the new government.

Washington sources acknowledge that the United States could swing a lot of leverage in Panama, where the expenditures related to the Canal Zone have a large impact on the small country's economy. But they are wary of any move that might be interpreted as interfering in that nation's internal affairs and thus could backfire.

• • •

Developments in Panama Saturday included these actions:

A two-man military junta was installed by the National Guard to rule the country.

The ruling junta imposed a 9 p.m. to 5:30 a.m. curfew on the capital.

Ousted President Arnulfo Arias at a meeting with reporters in the Canal Zone said, "I'll return at the first opportunity, when conditions of security are re-established."

Arias himself, along with cabinet colleagues, was given safe haven in the U.S.-controlled Canal zone.

Good Reading Inside

Sitting High

Tree - top sitting competition at Cohocton includes 84-year-old woman. Page 3B.

Dramatic Recovery

General Eisenhower will be 78 Monday. A victim of repeated heart attacks he has made a dramatic recovery. Page 9A.

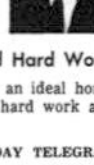

A Barn, Stones and Hard Work

A Valley couple have made an ideal home with the remains of a barn, field stone, hard work and imagination. Page 1C.

Five Centuries of Delay

Hometown Fetes Columbus

FUNCHAL, Madeira (AP) — Christopher Columbus was finally accorded full honors Saturday on this Portuguese east Atlantic island he once called home. After more than 25 years in a storehouse, a bronze statue of the Genovese discoverer was unveiled in a park near the sea.

The second-highest official in the Portuguese government, Minister of State, Alfredo Vaz Pinto, and the U.S. ambassador to Portugal, W. Tapey Bennett, were on hand for the solemn ceremony.

For centuries, Columbus had been considered something of a mountebank in Portugal

The Portuguese claim he used their seafaring knowhow for his famous voyage to America without acknowledging the help. He is said to have learned invaluable navigation secrets from his father-in-law, the governor of an island in the Madeira archipelago off the coast of northwest Africa.

• • •

Columbus lived on Madeira from 1478 until he left for Spain in 1485 to get backing for his voyage. He had two children by the governor's daughter, Filipa Moniz Perestrello.

His proposal to find a new route to India was rejected by the Portuguese Maritime Council in 1482 as "vain and fantastic."

Before the turn of the century, Madeira officals razed the house where Columbus was supposed to have lived. In 1941 the island ordered a statue of Columbus, but after it was delivered by Lisbon sculptor Antonio Maria Ribeiro, it was stowed away in a warehouse.

In 1953, local protests prevented the Funchal town council from erecting a new square to be graced by the stern-looking statue.

But time turned the balance in the explorer's favor. Last year, for the first time, official ceremonies were held in Madeira to mark Columbus Day.

Lack of Quorum Balks Congress

WASHINGTON (AP) — The House, stymied for lack of a quorum, met for an hour Saturday without even taking up the one remaining task facing Congress—final adjournment.

Both the House and Senate will meet again Monday but there is little likelihood they will be able to bring the 90th Congress to its official close at that time, either.

Rep. James G. O'Hara, D-Mich., is blocking House approval of an adjournment resolution by insisting that a quorum be present to act on it. That is 217 members, but with election day nearing, members have been departing in droves and only about 35 attended Saturday's session.

• • •

O'Hara is holding up adjournment in retaliation against the Senate Republicans' action in killing a bill that would permit free broadcast debates between presidential candidates. The Senate Republicans boycotted a session at which it was to be considered, preventing the Senate from getting a quorum.

O'Hara says he won't relent and permit final adjournment until the Senate revives the debate bill. There is nothing to indicate any such change in the Senate position.

McCarthy Endorses Muskie, Not HHH

LOS ANGELES (AP) — Sen. Eugene J. McCarthy endorsed Sen. Edmund S. Muskie for vice president Saturday, but said endorsement of Hubert H. Humphrey for president is "still an open question."

"I'm for Muskie for vice president," the Minnesota senator told newsmen. "That shows you what this campaign is coming to."

• • •

McCarthy, who lost the Democratic presidential nomination to Vice President Humphrey, was here to lend his support to several California Democratic candidates whose positions he agrees with.

In reply to questions, he denied withholding support from Humphrey to gain concessions on the Vietnam war, which he opposes.

"I've not raised the ante," he said. "We're still playing the same game."

Nixon Raps U.S. Policy On Cuba

Associated Press

Richard M. Nixon said Saturday that the Democratic administration has "talked tough and walked on eggshells" in dealing with Communist Cuba.

In a statement issued in Key Biscayne, Fla., where he is resting and conferring with aides, the Republican presidential nominee said Cuba "cannot remain forever a sanctuary for aggressions and a base for the export of terror to other lands."

Nixon did not spell out just what he would do differently in Cuba.

A mild, intestinal flu caused Hubert H. Humphrey to cancel a planned appearance in New Yor City's Columbus Day parade and a tour through Harlem.

• • •

But the vice president taped a speech, broadcast on nationwide television Saturday night, proposing a 10-fold increase in federal funds to fight crime. He said that he, like most Americans, was distressed and outraged at crime and violence, but added, "Americans don't want a national police force" which, he said, could lead to a police state.

Third-party presidential candidate George C. Wallace spoke to a crowd of more than 10,000 at the Mormon Tabernacle in Sale Lake City. He drew applause when he said people should work for what they get and pledged to return domestic institutions to local control.

TRAWLERS DETAINED

ACCRA, Ghana (AP) — The government announced Saturday it was detaining two Soviet trawlers for violating Ghana's territorial waters Thursday.

Fig. 83. W-column is unobstrusive in *Elmira* (N.Y.) *Sunday Telegram*. Less than column of W-matter is used in col. 6; balance of space is filled by banner, pic and doubled-over 1½-column setting. Note unusual handling of price in left ear instead of customary right one.

Fig. 84. Page 3 of *Rockford* (Ill.) *Morning Star* uses W-format in 9-column page with advertising. W-matter runs in well under NAME QUEEN head. Ads are in regular 11-pica increments.

Ads are layed only in the 6-column area, and the W-column runs the full depth of each page. Eight-column ads pose no problem, of course; the W-column ends at the top of the ad. When a 7-column ad must be layed, the space adjacent to it is filled with regular 11-pica type. If desired or necessary, local advertising can be made up to occupy the W-matter or extend from it. Such an ad would then be 1½-, 2½-, 3½-, or so on columns wide.

The fact that the W-format can be used on conventional ad pages intrigued many editors who have been indenting body type below 11 picas to achieve an open format with alleys. Usually this technique was used on women's and feature pages, sometimes in sports pages. At this writing, several papers are experimenting with the W-format on women's pages carrying advertising.

The W-format is especially attractive to editors of editorial pages. Editorials are usually written to fill a specified area, and they can be used for the W-column. Or the top part of the space occupied by a W-column and two N-columns can be divided into two legs for the setting of editorials. It is advantageous to have some regular-width columns on the editorial page. It simplifies typesetting, for one thing. Another advantage is the flexibility of use of editorial-page matter on regular pages. Often background material, originally planned for this page, is perfectly compatible on news pages and can be easily shifted if plans change. For papers that have an *op-ed* (opposite editorial) *page* that carries advertising, it is advantageous to be able to move type from this page to the editorial page and vice versa.

We should note that the W-format may be used on any full-format page. A newspaper in a 7-column max format could adopt W-format by using five N-columns and a W-column. A 6-column full format would require a 5½-column pattern to become W-format. Tab pages rarely lend themselves to the W modification.

Chicago or Detroit Format

An interesting modification of the W-format is the *Chicago,* or *Detroit, format.* This is the result of experimenting by Roy Fisher and Creed Black at the *Chicago Daily News* and, at the same time but independently, by Martin Hayden and Paul Poorman at the *Detroit News.* This format uses four legs of 1½-column type and one of 2-column length. This in itself uses eight full columns for type. To create an open format requires that the settings be narrower than actual 1½- and 2-column measure.

WEATHER
Clearing and cool
(Details on Page 6A)

The Detroit News

THE HOME NEWSPAPER

Markets
Pages 9 to 11D
Races
Page 6D

FRIDAY, SEPTEMBER 27, 1968 — 96th YEAR No. 36 10 CENTS

Shorter auto warranties stirring new U.S. wrath

By BOB IRVIN
Detroit News Automotive Writer

Government economists believe the auto companies will save more than $300 million by restricting new car warranties.

And this means the dispute between the government and the industry over new car prices didn't end with Chrysler's $34 price rollback yesterday.

Criticism is now focused on the cutback in new car warranties which accompanied the price increases announced by Chrysler, Ford and General Motors.

Some sources in Washington say the warranty changes represent a sizeable hidden price increase for consumers and a huge savings for the companies.

They estimate that by cutting the basic new car guarantee from two years to one year the companies will save $40 a car—or more than $300 million a year. And they believe the eventual cost to the customer will be at least $78.

AUTO CRITIC RALPH NADER says he believes the $78 estimate is conservative and the cost to the consumer may run as high as $125 because the car owner will have to pay the retail rate for repairs formerly performed free under the warranty program.

The automakers began to lengthen warranties in 1961, extending them gradually over several model years. They were credited with these added costs by the Bureau of Labor Statistics as it computed real value of the cars for its consumer price index.

Some of the governemnt's figures were expected to be released today by the office of Senator Warren G. Magnuson, Washington Democrat and chairman of the Senate Commerce Comittee. The report was prepared by the Federal Trade Commission.

In addition, Senator Philip A. Hart, Michigan Democrat, is starting a full-scale investigation of automobile servicing which will touch on warranty work done at dealerships. The probe will be conducted by the Senate antitrust and monopoly subcommittee, of which Hart is chairman.

The auto makers won't estimate their savings on the warranty cutback, but General Motors Chairman James M. Roche said it was taken into account in setting new car prices.

However, if the Washington reports about how much money is being saved are correct this would explain why the companies announced $50 to $55 increases instead of a $100 hike at a time when labor and material costs are up sharply.

THE BIG THREE FIRMS all claimed the increases were not enough to offset rising costs. Chrysler reemphasized this yesterday when it bowed to pressures of the market place and the government and scaled down some of its prices.

Under the new price schedule, Chrysler said its 1969 model cars now show an average sticker price increase of $55 or 1.8 percent. This was well below the average increase of $89 or 2.9 percent first announced by Chrysler last week.

The rollback had been expected since GM and Ford undercut Chrysler in pricing new model cars. Ford announced a $50 increase Wednesday while GM posted a $52 hike Monday. Both firms said their increases averaged 1.6 percent.

American Motors Corp. is expected to announce its 1969 prices when the models go on sale Monday. After Chrysler's rollback, a spokesman for AMC admitted his company "can do little else" but follow the pattern set by the Big Three.

A more detailed look at Chrysler's prices, including comparisons with the other manufacturers, is on Page 7B.

Contact 10

CONTACT 10 is Detroit's newest and largest information breakthrough, a 10-man Detroit News task force assigned to solve your problems, answer your questions, look out for your interests. It's backed by Michigan's largest news gathering force—and it's free. Write Contact 10, Box 2458, Detroit, Mich. 48231. Or call anytime at 222-8800.

Tomorrow night the Red Wings and the Montreal Canadiens will play a benefit hockey game to raise funds for the Old Newsboys' Goodfellow Fund. But pennant fever has slowed ticket sales. Can Contact 10 put a bug in someone's ear and tell people tickets are on sale at Olympia, Grinnell's and Hudson's? —L.M., Detroit

We'll do that—and more. As fast as we called them, the Greater Detroit Board of Commerce, Marathon Oil Co., Chrysler Corp., Max Fisher, Douglas and Lomason Co., Look Magazine, Simon-Michelson and the National Bank of Detroit whipped out pens and wrote checks for hundreds of tickets—thus striking another blow for the slogan: "No Kiddie Without a Christmas."

Contact 10 »

My son, Capt. Richard A. Sperling, served a year in Vietnam and was recommended for the Distinguished Service Cross. The award hasn't come through yet and he'll be separated from the service at the end of the month. Can you speed things up? —R.F.S., Beverly Hills

You have a date at 10 a.m. next Tuesday in Cleveland, Dick's present duty post, when he'll be decorated for "extraordinary heroism . . . in conflict with armed, hostile forces."

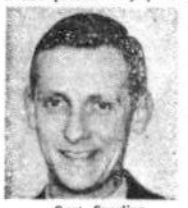

Capt. Sperling

Dick, a 1960 graduate of Birmingham's Seaholm High, won the D.S.C., second only to the Medal of Honor, for action March 16, 1967, when a heliborne assault force ran into an ambush and a helicopter was shot down in flames. Dick, piloting another copter, immediately landed in a clearing about 500 feet away, ran through the jungle "repeatedly subjected to sniper and mortar fire" to reach the crew of the burning craft, led them through a "hail of bullets and shrapnel" to his ship, helped them aboard and took off just as the enemy penetrated the tree line.

Contact 10 »

Last week I watched the premiere of "Mod Squad," a TV show about a trio of young officers on the Los Angeles Police Department who infiltrate teen-age groups suspected of illegal doings. Does the Detroit Police Department have a "mod squad?" —J.M.L., Lincoln Park

No organized squad, though police certainly do use the tactic of infiltration, says Inspector Charles Mayrand of the Intelligence Bureau. One such instance, says Mayrand, occurred two years ago when a police team—man and woman — infiltrated a group of students and dropouts suspected of trafficking in narcotics near Wayne State University. The policeman, known to the group as Louie, grew a beard, spent four months with the group and arrested all 25 of them. His work led to the convictions of all but one.

Contact 10 »

My son filled out a contest blank at Frank's Nursery in Lincoln Park. A few days later a man from Encyclopaedia Britannica called and said Henry won a free trip to Las Vegas or Miami Beach for three nights and four days. Then the man came to our house, told us we had to pay for the trip. I think they are making us pay extra because we are Negroes. —Mrs. E.R., Detroit

The Encyclopaedia Britannica people were misleading, not prejudiced. The blank your 11-year-old filled out was part of a sales device Britannica uses to get a man to your home to sell encyclopedias.

The salesman you spoke to on the phone was supposed to say your son had won a free "hotel accommodation in Las Vegas or Miami Beach," not a "free trip." But as Britannica's Chicago-based public relations director, William Healy, told Contact 10, "We're not responsible for what individual salesmen say on the phone."

After the call from Contact 10 Britannica rushed Program Manager Earl Cutler to your home, who apologized for his salesman's exuberance, promised to reward your Henry with a new set of the Junior Britannica.

Contact 10 »

I'm den mother of a Cub Scout pack that needs beer bottles for their Christmas project. They plan to make candle holders for their parents out of Michelob bottles, which have an unusual and graceful shape. My husband and I don't happen to be beer drinkers and have no way to accumulate enough bottles for the project. There are 10 boys in my pack, and we need two bottles for each boy. I may take to drink if I can't find them! —Mrs. S.Z., Dearborn Hts.

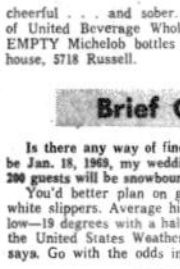

A Scout is brave, thrifty, cheerful . . . and sober. Robert F. Byrne, president of United Beverage Wholesalers, Inc., has a case of EMPTY Michelob bottles for you at the United warehouse, 5718 Russell.

Brief Contact

Is there any way of finding out what the weather will be Jan. 18, 1969, my wedding day? I'm wondering if my 200 guests will be snowbound. —J.K., Detroit

You'd better plan on galoshes to cover those dainty white slippers. Average high for that day is 33 degrees, low—19 degrees with a half-inch of snowfall. That's what the United States Weather Bureau Climatological office says. Go with the odds in your favor.

Contact 10 »

I would be grateful to you if you could contact a symphony orchestra for me and ask what they call their flute players. I'm sure they are called flutists, but Mom insists they are called flautists by anyone who knows anything about music. We keep having heated arguments. —B.B., Royal Oak

Cool down, Barb. Flautists are flutists and flutists are flautists. Same difference.

To Our Readers: While it isn't possible to answer, or even acknowledge, all your calls and letters, we will consider each and print those of most general interest.

Ball to guide HHH on foreign policy

By J. F. TER HORST
Chief of Our Washington Bureau

SAN FRANCISCO—Hubert Humphrey says that George W. Ball, resigning his Johnson administration post as ambassador to the United Nations, "will be my chief foreign policy adviser."

Former UN Ambassador Arthur J. Goldberg also will play a prominent role in Humphrey's underdog drive for the White House, the Humphrey camp announced late yesterday.

Both Goldberg and Ball have criticized administration policy in Vietnam. Goldberg recently came out for an immediate halt in the bombing of North Vietnam. Ball had been recognized as the "devil's advocate" in Johnson policy consultations, arguing against escalation of the war in Asia.

President Johnson late yesterday named J. R. Wiggins, published of the Washington Post, to fill in as the UN envoy for the remainder of the President's term. Wiggins, 64, is a strong supporter of the administration's war position.

Although critics of Mr. Johnson's Vietnam policy seem to be swinging to Humphrey's side, Humphrey insists that it is not a "quiet signal" to war doves.

THE VICE-PRESIDENT, buoyed by brighter signs on his campaign horizon after three days in California, made this statement as he followed up the announcements that Ball and Goldberg will play prominent roles in his race for the White House.

"Absolutely not," Humphrey said when asked if the news about Ball and Goldberg constituted a hint to backers of Senators Eugene McCarthy and the late Robert F. Kennedy that he is shifting away from LBJ policy on Vietnam.

"If I find that the situation in Vietnam or in Paris requires a statement from me, I'll not signal it quietly," the Vice-President said in a TV interview here.

But he added that before many more days he also expects McCarthy—"my friend of 20 years"—to come to his banner, rather than face the prospect of Richard M. Nixon in the White House.

Humphrey said Ball, former undersecretary of state for Presidents Kennedy and Johnson, quit his UN post for the sole purpose of helping the Humphrey campaign as chief foreign policy adviser.

GOLDBERG, Ball's predecessor at the UN, former Supreme Court justice and labor secretary under Mr. Kennedy and Mr. Johnson, will be cochairman of United Citizens for Humphrey-Muskie. His prime assignment will be to swing New York's fractious Democrats and Liberals to Humphrey's cause.

Humphrey carefully refrained from saying that the new additions to his staff mean something more than meets the eye.

But he did say that as his chief foreign adviser, Ball would be able to tell him "if there are any mistakes in our Vietnam policy." Humphrey added that he was sure there have been "some" mistakes.

Humphrey's optimism was such late yesterday that he even fired off a telegram to

(Concluded on Page 16A)

Kiefer staff calls attack vindictive

By BERL FALBAUM
Chief of Our City-County Bureau

Administrators of the Herman Kiefer branch of Detroit General Hospital today vehemently denied that the conditions at the hospital are "shocking."

The charges, which were made by the Detroit-Wayne County Health Department before the City Council two weeks ago, were branded as "purely personal and vindictive" by the administrators today.

The answer came in a long report mailed to the Council, more than 100 members of the county Board of Supervisors, and other key city and county officials.

THE REPORT CAME along with a covering letter written by John F. Dodge Jr., attorney for the Kiefer medical staff. It included an answer to all the charges and was signed by 28 medical directors of the hospital.

Dr. George Pickett, the new acting city-county health commissioner, told the Council two weeks ago that because of inadequate medical procedures at the hospital "unnecessary deaths" were occurring. Other health officials charged that maggots were found in the food at the hospital.

"The purpose of this well planned and coordinated attack was quite obviously to discredit the administrative and medical personnel of the hospital," said Dodge in his letter.

"It is even more important that you also understand that this attack was a smoke screen covering the real issues involved," he said.

DODGE SAID the real issue was the demand by former Health Commissioner John J. Hanlon to adopt a new treatment of tuberculosis instituted in Denver, Colo.

(Pickett replaced Hanlon Monday when the former commissioner resigned to join the U.S. Surgeon General's office).

"Dr. Hanlon knew, as his cohorts now know,

(Concluded on Page 16A)

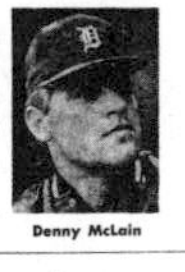

Denny McLain

Today's Tiger poster

Page 12D

With Series tickets or not, you'll want big News Guide

So who is Gagliano?

The Detroit News' special World Series Guide, part of Monday's editions, will be complete to the most minute details. It will be a 76-page tabloid section with facts, figures and pictures, handy for ready reference as you watch Detroit's first World Series in 23 years on television. Or if you're one of the lucky ones the News' World Series Guide can easily be taken to the ballpark with you.

There will be sketches on all the Tigers and all the Cardinals, including Phil Gagliano, a prize utilityman. For nostalgia, there will be histories of all past Tiger World Series back to Ty Cobb.

The News' World Series Guide will be freshly up to date. The baseball season ends Sunday—and on Monday you will have final statistics in the Guide on the World Series participants.

The job of assembling all the data for your World Series information is being handled by a task force headed by News Sports Editor Bob Sieger. Doing the writing and compiling are News baseball writer Watson Spoelstra, sports columnist Pete Waldmeir and sports writers Larry Middlemas, Jerry Green and Bill Halls.

Look for your special World Series Guide in Monday's News. It will make an excellent souvenir of Detroit's most thrilling baseball year.

For special home delivery of Monday's News, including the 76-page World Series Guide, telephone The News' subscription department at 222-2600.

Or, for postage-paid delivery to relatives and friends of the World Series Guide and 10 World Series issues of The News (Oct. 2-11) for $1, see Page 8D of today's News.

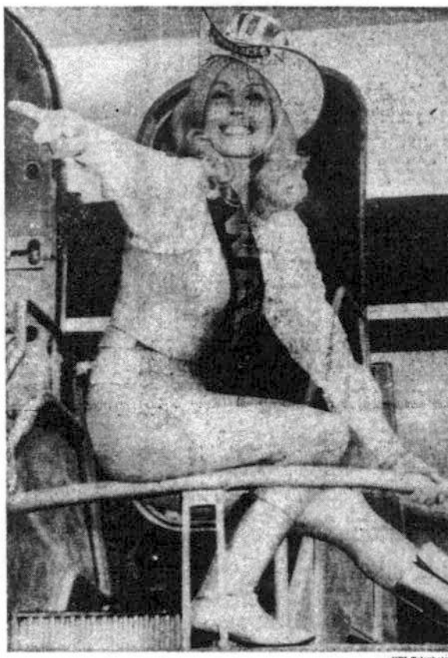

—UPI Telephoto

Ja-Neen Welch decked out in her Wallace campaign outfit

Aides fire blond

Indian love song played for Wallace

From UPI and AP Dispatches

MONTGOMERY, Ala.—Ja-Neen Welch is a striking, shapely, coal-eyed blond who has hinted she wants to marry George C. Wallace. She is part French, part Cherokee.

Wallace spokesmen say she wanted to put the Indian sign on the former governor's presidential campaign.

Dick Smith, a Wallace campaign aide, pooh-poohed talk of a romance between the Indianapolis advertising woman and the third-party presidential candidate.

Miss Welch "popped up two or three times on the campaign trail and now she's saying all these things," Smith said yesterday. "The governor knows nothing about her." She has been fired, he added.

WALLACE HEADQUARTERS here issued a statement saying Miss Welch's remarks were "false, untrue and calculated to damage the candidacy of George C. Wallace." Wallace himself had no comment.

Reports linking Miss Welch and Wallace, whose wife Lureen, the governor of Alabama, died of cancer May 7, appeared Thursday in several newspapers.

Contacted in Indianapolis, where she runs an antique shop and an advertising agency, Miss Welch said she "wouldn't mind being" the next Mrs. Wallace, but was not at liberty to say whether they would be married.

Miss Welch, once married and the mother of a son, said she was born in Columbus, Ohio, is "part French and Cherokee Indian" and that "people usually use 26 as my age."

She said she met Wallace in Chicago three months ago.

"I have extrasensory perception," she said, "and I predicted that he would be elected president and that I would be there when he took the oath of office.

"I wouldn't mind being Mrs. George C. Wallace. We are both single and he's a wonderful person."

SHE ADDED that she planned to see him again next week, either in Indianapolis or Montgomery.

Ja-Neen, wearing a spectacular white mini-dress, cowboy hat and calf-length boots, alighted from the Wallace airplane when the campaign party arrived at Daytona Beach, Fla., last Friday and rode in the official motorcade to a political rally in Orlando.

Ja-Neen said she didn't wish to discuss rumors of a romance further "until I find out about this business with Dick Smith."

"The trouble with the Wallace staff," she said, "is that they have too many chiefs and not enough Indians."

ON ONE CAMPAIGN swing, Miss Welch kissed and hugged Wallace for photographers at an airport news conference, but Smith said "she will no longer have anything to do with the campaign, you can get on that."

Wallace headquarters said another picture

(Concluded on Page 16A)

Today's index

SEPTEMBER
22 23 24 25 26 27 28
29 30
OCTOBER
1 2 3 4 5
6 7 8 9 10 11 12
13 14 15 16 17 18 19

Fig. 85. Detroit format as used by *Detroit* (Mich.) *News*. This pattern, using four 1½-column legs and one double-column setting, is also known as Chicago format.

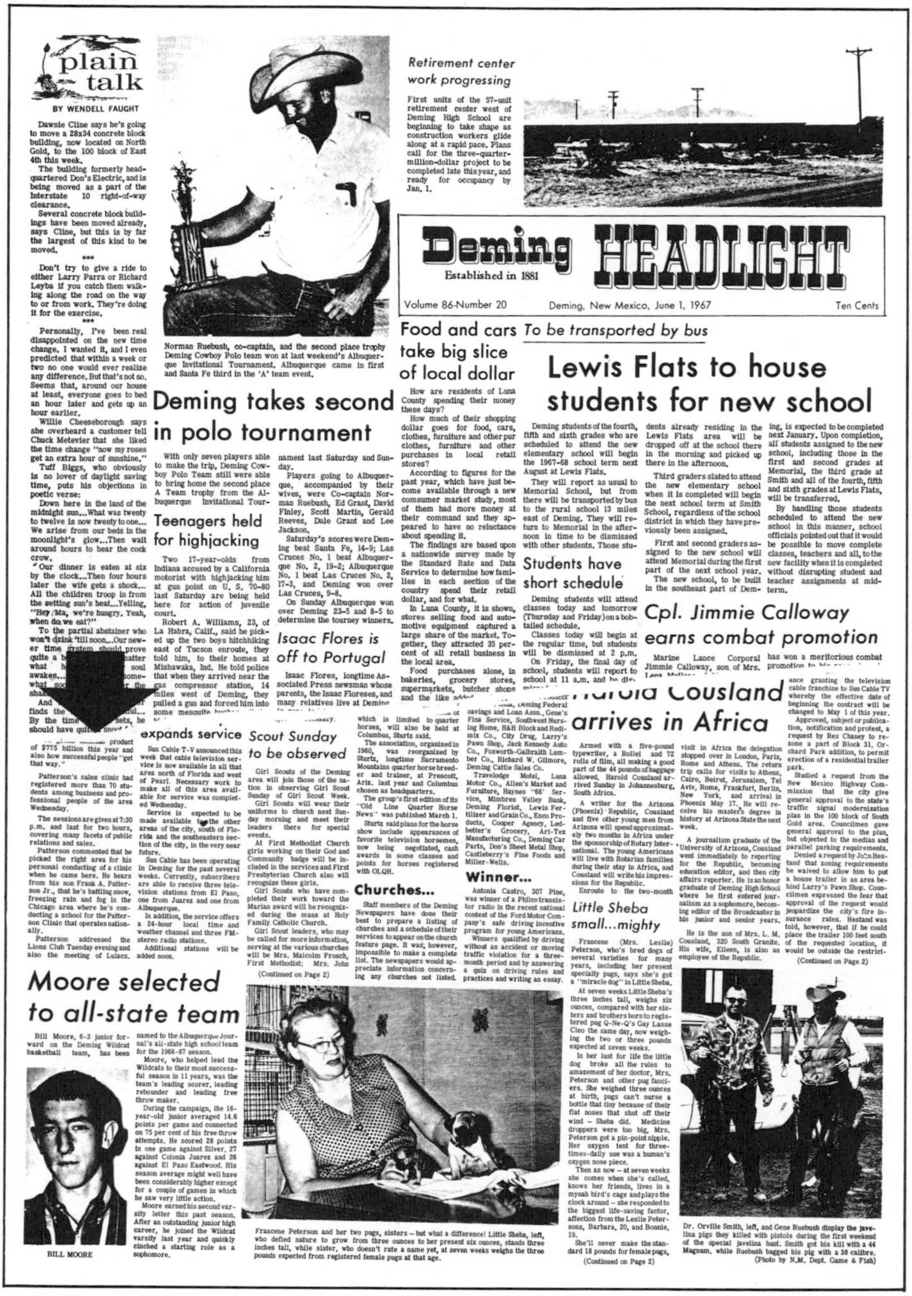

plain talk

BY WENDELL FAUGHT

Dawsie Cline says he's going to move a 28x34 concrete block building, now located on North Gold, to the 100 block of East 4th this week.

The building formerly headquartered Don's Electric, and is being moved as a part of the Interstate 10 right-of-way clearance.

Several concrete block buildings have been moved already, says Cline, but this is by far the largest of this kind to be moved.

***

Don't try to give a ride to either Larry Parra or Richard Leyba if you catch them walking along the road on the way to or from work. They're doing it for the exercise.

***

Personally, I've been real disappointed on the new time change. I wanted it, and I even predicted that within a week or two no one would ever realize any difference. But that's not so. Seems that, around our house at least, everyone goes to bed an hour later and gets up an hour earlier.

Willie Cheeseborough says she overheard a customer tell Chuck Metevier that she liked the time change "now my roses get an extra hour of sunshine."

Tuff Biggs, who obviously is no lover of daylight saving time, puts his objections in poetic verse:

Down here in the land of the midnight sun...What was twenty to twelve is now twenty to one... We arise from our beds in the moonlight's glow...Then wait around hours to hear the cock crow.

Our dinner is eaten at six by the clock...Then four hours later the wife gets a shock... All the children troop in from the setting sun's heat...Yelling, "Hey Ma, we're hungry. Yeah, when do we eat?"

To the partial abstainer who won't drink 'till noon...Our newer time system should prove quite a b[illegible] matter what h[illegible] soul awakes... [illegible] somewhat so[illegible] the shak[illegible]

And [illegible] finds the [illegible] ul... By the time [illegible] sets, he should have quit[illegible]

[illegible] product of $775 billion this year and also how successful people "get that way."

Patterson's sales clinic had registered more than 70 students among business and professional people of the area Wednesday.

The sessions are given at 7:30 p.m. and last for two hours, covering many facets of public relations and sales.

Patterson commented that he picked the right area for his personal conducting of a clinic when he came here. He hears from his son Frank A. Patterson Jr., that he's battling snow, freezing rain and fog in the Chicago area where he's conducting a school for the Patterson Clinic that operates nationally.

Patterson addressed the Lions Club Tuesday evening and also the meeting of Lulacs.

Norman Ruebush, co-captain, and the second place trophy Deming Cowboy Polo team won at last weekend's Albuquerque Invitational Tournament. Albuquerque came in first and Santa Fe third in the 'A' team event.

Deming takes second in polo tournament

With only seven players able to make the trip, Deming Cowboy Polo Team still were able to bring home the second place A Team trophy from the Albuquerque Invitational Tournament last Saturday and Sunday.

Players going to Albuquerque, accompanied by their wives, were Co-captain Norman Ruebush, Ed Grant, David Finley, Scott Martin, Gerald Reeves, Dale Grant and Lee Jackson.

Saturday's scores were Deming beat Santa Fe, 14-9; Las Cruces No. 1 beat Albuquerque No. 2, 19-2; Albuquerque No. 1 beat Las Cruces No. 2, 17-3, and Deming won over Las Cruces, 9-8.

On Sunday Albuquerque won over Deming 23-5 and 8-5 to determine the tourney winners.

Teenagers held for highjacking

Two 17-year-olds from Indiana accused by a California motorist with highjacking him at gun point on U. S. 70-80 last Saturday are being held here for action of juvenile court.

Robert A. Williams, 23, of La Habra, Calif., said he picked up the two boys hitchhiking east of Tucson enroute, they told him, to their homes at Mishawaka, Ind. He told police that when they arrived near the gas compressor station, 14 miles west of Deming, they pulled a gun and forced him into some mesquite [illegible]

Isaac Flores is off to Portugal

Isaac Flores, longtime Associated Press newsman whose parents, the Isaac Floreses, and many relatives live at Deming [illegible]

Retirement center work progressing

First units of the 57-unit retirement center west of Deming High School are beginning to take shape as construction workers glide along at a rapid pace. Plans call for the three-quarter-million-dollar project to be completed late this year, and ready for occupancy by Jan. 1.

Deming HEADLIGHT

Established in 1881

Volume 86-Number 20 — Deming, New Mexico, June 1, 1967 — Ten Cents

Food and cars take big slice of local dollar

How are residents of Luna County spending their money these days?

How much of their shopping dollar goes for food, cars, clothes, furniture and other pur clothes, furniture and other purchases in local retail stores?

According to figures for the past year, which have just become available through a new comsumer market study, most of them had more money at their command and they appeared to have no reluctance about spending it.

The findings are based upon a nationwide survey made by the Standard Rate and Data Service to determine how families in each section of the country spend their retail dollar, and for what.

In Luna County, it is shown, stores selling food and automotive equipment captured a large share of the market. Together, they attracted 35 percent of all retail business in the local area.

Food purchases alone, in bakeries, grocery stores, supermarkets, butcher shops and the like [illegible]

To be transported by bus

Lewis Flats to house students for new school

Deming students of the fourth, fifth and sixth grades who are scheduled to attend the new elementary school will begin the 1967-68 school term next August at Lewis Flats.

They will report as usual to Memorial School, but from there will be transported by bus to the rural school 13 miles east of Deming. They will return to Memorial in the afternoon in time to be dismissed with other students. Those students already residing in the Lewis Flats area will be dropped off at the school there in the morning and picked up there in the afternoon.

Third graders slated to attend the new elementary school when it is completed will begin the next school term at Smith School, regardless of the school district in which they have previously been assigned.

First and second graders assigned to the new school will attend Memorial during the first part of the next school year.

The new school, to be built in the southeast part of Deming, is expected to be completed next January. Upon completion, all students assigned to the new school, including those in the first and second grades at Memorial, the third grade at Smith and all of the fourth, fifth and sixth grades at Lewis Flats, will be transferred.

By handling those students scheduled to attend the new school in this manner, school officials pointed out that it would be possible to move complete classes, teachers and all, to the new facility when it is completed without disrupting student and teacher assignments at mid-term.

Students have short schedule

Deming students will attend classes today and tomorrow (Thursday and Friday) on a bob-tailed schedule.

Classes today will begin at the regular time, but students will be dismissed at 2 p.m.

On Friday, the final day of school, students will report to school at 11 a.m. and be dis[illegible]

Cpl. Jimmie Calloway earns combat promotion

Marine Lance Corporal Jimmie Calloway, son of Mrs. Lena [illegible] has won a meritorious combat promotion [illegible]

expands service

Sun Cable T-V announced this week that cable television service is now available in all that area north of Florida and west of Pearl. Necessary work to make all of this area available for service was completed Wednesday.

Service is expected to be made available to the other areas of the city, south of Florida and the southeastern section of the city, in the very near future.

Sun Cable has been operating in Deming for the past several weeks. Currently, subscribers are able to receive three television stations from El Paso, one from Juarez and one from Albuquerque.

In addition, the service offers a 24-hour local time and weather channel and three FM-stereo radio stations.

Additional stations will be added soon.

Scout Sunday to be observed

Girl Scouts of the Deming area will join those of the nation in observing Girl Scout Sunday of Girl Scout Week.

Girl Scouts will wear their uniforms to church next Sunday morning and meet their leaders there for special events.

At First Methodist Church girls working on their God and Community badge will be included in the services and First Presbyterian Church also will recognize these girls.

Girl Scouts who have completed their work toward the Marian award will be recognized during the mass at Holy Family Catholic Church.

Girl Scout leaders, who may be called for more information, serving at the various churches will be Mrs. Malcolm Frosch, First Methodist; Mrs. John

(Continued on Page 2)

[illegible] which is limited to quarter horses, will also be held at Columbus, Sturtz said.

The association, organized in 1960, was reorganized by Sturtz, longtime Sacramento Mountains quarter horse breeder and trainer, at Prescott, Ariz. last year and Columbus chosen as headquarters.

The group's first edition of its "Old Line Quarter Horse News" was published March 1.

Sturtz said plans for the horse show include appearances of favorite television horsemen, now being negotiated, cash awards in some classes and points for horses registered with OLQH.

Churches...

Staff members of the Deming Newspapers have done their best to prepare a listing of churches and a schedule of their services to appear on the church feature page. It was, however, impossible to make a complete list. The newspapers would appreciate information concerning any churches not listed.

[illegible] Deming Federal Savings and Loan Assn., Gene's Fina Service, Southwest Nursing Home, H&H Block and Redi-mix Co., City Drug, Larry's Pawn Shop, Jack Kennedy Auto Co., Foxworth-Galbraith Lumber Co., Richard W. Gilmore, Deming Cattle Sales Co.

Travelodge Motel, Luna Motor Co., Allen's Market and Furniture, Haynes "66" Service, Mimbres Valley Bank, Deming Florist, Lewis Fertilizer and Grain Co., Enco Products, Cooper Agency, Ledbetter's Grocery, Ari-Tex Manufacturing Co., Deming Car Parts, Don's Sheet Metal Shop, Castleberry's Fine Foods and Miller-Wells.

Winner...

Antonia Castro, 307 Pine, was winner of a Philco transistor radio in the recent national contest of the Ford Motor Company's safe driving incentive program for young Americans.

Winners qualified by driving without an accident or moving traffic violation for a three-month period and by answering a quiz on driving rules and practices and writing an essay.

[illegible] Cousland arrives in Africa

Armed with a five-pound typewriter, a Rollei and 72 rolls of film, all making a good part of the 44 pounds of baggage allowed, Harold Cousland arrived Sunday in Johannesburg, South Africa.

A writer for the Arizona (Phoenix) Republic, Cousland and five other young men from Arizona will spend approximately two months in Africa under the sponsorship of Rotary International. The young Americans will live with Rotarian families during their stay in Africa, and Cousland will write his impressions for the Republic.

Enroute to the two-month visit in Africa the delegation stopped over in London, Paris, Rome and Athens. The return trip calls for visits to Athens, Cairo, Beirut, Jerusalem, Tel Aviv, Rome, Frankfurt, Berlin, New York, and arrival in Phoenix May 17. He will receive his master's degree in history at Arizona State the next week.

A journalism graduate of the University of Arizona, Cousland went immediately to reporting for the Republic, becoming education editor, and then city affairs reporter. He is an honor graduate of Deming High School where he first entered journalism as a sophomore, becoming editor of the Broadcaster in his junior and senior years.

He is the son of Mrs. L. M. Cousland, 320 South Granite. His wife, Eileen, is also an employee of the Republic.

[illegible] ance granting the television cable franchise to Sun Cable TV whereby the effective date of beginning the contract will be changed to May 1 of this year.

Approved, subject or publication, notification and protest, a request by Rex Chaney to rezone a part of Block 31, Orchard Park addition, to permit erection of a residential trailer park.

Studied a request from the New Mexico Highway Commission that the city give general approval to the state's traffic signal modernization plan in the 100 block of South Gold area. Councilmen gave general approval to the plan, but objected to the median and parallel parking requirements.

Denied a request by John Hestand that zoning requirements be waived to allow him to put a house trailer in an area behind Larry's Pawn Shop. Councilmen expressed the fear that approval of the request would jeopardize the city's fire insurance rates. Hestand was told, however, that if he could place the trailer 100 feet south of the requested location, it would be outside the restrict-

(Continued on Page 2)

Little Sheba small...mighty

Francene (Mrs. Leslie) Peterson, who's bred dogs of several varieties for many years, including her present specialty pugs, says she's got a "miracle dog" in Little Sheba.

At seven weeks Little Sheba's three inches tall, weighs six ounces, compared with her sisters and brothers born to registered pug Q-Ne-Q's Gay Lasse Cleo the same day, now weighing the two or three pounds expected at seven weeks.

In her lust for life the little dog broke all the rules to amazement of her doctor, Mrs. Peterson and other pug fanciers. She weighed three ounces at birth, pugs can't nurse a bottle that tiny because of their flat noses that shut off their wind – Sheba did. Medicine droppers were too big, Mrs. Peterson got a pin-point nipple. Her oxygen tent for three-times-daily use was a human's oxygen nose piece.

Then as now – at seven weeks she comes when she's called, knows her friends, lives in a mynah bird's cage and plays the clock around – she responded to the biggest life-saving factor, affection from the Leslie Petersons, Barbara, 20, and Bonnie, 19.

She'll never make the standard 18 pounds for female pugs,

(Continued on Page 2)

Moore selected to all-state team

Bill Moore, 6-3 junior forward on the Deming Wildcat basketball team, has been named to the Albuquerque Journal's all-state high school team for the 1966-67 season.

Moore, who helped lead the Wildcats to their most successful season in 11 years, was the team's leading scorer, leading rebounder and leading free throw maker.

During the campaign, the 16-year-old junior averaged 14.6 points per game and connected on 75 per cent of his free throw attempts. He scored 28 points in one game against Silver, 27 against Colonia Juarez and 26 against El Paso Eastwood. His season average might well have been considerably higher except for a couple of games in which he saw very little action.

Moore earned his second varsity letter this past season. After an outstanding junior high career, he joined the Wildcat varsity last year and quickly cinched a starting role as a sophomore.

BILL MOORE

Francene Peterson and her two pugs, sisters – but what a difference! Little Sheba, left, who defied nature to grow from three ounces to her present six ounces, stands three inches tall, while sister, who doesn't rate a name yet, at seven weeks weighs the three pounds expected from registered female pugs at that age.

Dr. Orville Smith, left, and Gene Ruebush display the javelina pigs they killed with pistols during the first weekend of the special javelina hunt. Smith got his kill with a 44 Magnum, while Ruebush bagged his pig with a 38 calibre. (Photo by N.M. Dept. Game & Fish)

Fig. 86. One-up page pattern. *Deming* (N.M.) *Headlight* was in conventional 8-column format with 10½-pica columns and 9-point alleys, lower fragment. Converting to seven 11½-pica columns enabled use of larger, 9-point body type and full pica alleys. Inside pages remain in nine columns.

The major advantage of the Chicago format is that it eliminates the cramped 11-pica column; most of a page is set at a measure very close to optimum. It is easy to accommodate these measures to a pyramid of 11-pica advertising. An obvious disadvantage is that it doesn't utilize the 1-column setting provided by wire tape and so can be used only by those newspapers that set their own type.

This is a handsome format that is worth examining and that might well be adapted to key pages—the only way it is used at this writing—or throughout the paper. It can be modified to 7- and 9-column max pages; it won't work on compact pages.

7-Format

A less desirable variation of open format is the *7-format*. This is an entire 8-column page in 1-up, seven columns of 11-pica type. Seven-format must be distinguished from a normal 7-column page in maximum format, on narrower paper.

A major advantage of the 7-format is that it provides an open page without any special setting. Only 11-pica setting—manual or from wire tape—or conventional 1½- and 2-column variations are used; the desk does not have to worry about exactly filling a W-column. A disadvantage is that the alleys seem a little too wide for many editors. Seven-across-8 for a single story is fine as 1-up in a regular closed format, but as 7-format it tends to create an esthetic effect of a fabric woven too loosely.

Supposing an 8-column format using 6-point column rules, the type-page width is 91½ picas. If we use seven 11-pica columns of type, that leaves 14½ picas of space. Divided into six strips, that makes alleys of 29 points, 2.5 picas. These are so wide they tend to fragment the page.

Another disadvantage is that ads will not fit neatly unless they are set at odd measures. In full format, a 2-column ad would be 22.6 picas; a 3-columner, 34 picas; etc. In 7-format, a 2-column ad would be 24.5 picas; the 3-columner would be 37.10; and so on. If nothing else, the arithmetic gets complicated. Of course, ads can retain the old measurements and not suffer if there is extra space at their sides, especially if the ads are unbordered.

Turning the Rules

Most of this chapter has been devoted to the elimination of column rules, replacing their ink with white space. But there is occasion when it

Fig. 87. Turning the rules. Monroe (Mich.) *Evening News* turned rules on outside pages to mourn President John F. Kennedy's death. *Sandusky* (Ohio) *Register* obtained like effect by replacing column rules with heavier ad border; *Waterbury* (Conn.) *Republican* used same technique on editorial page.

seems appropriate not only to retain the rules but also to emphasize their blackness. It took a national tragedy to recall this old custom that deserves preservation: *turning the rules*.

This is an expression of mourning produced by turning column rules upside down in the chase and printing with their broad, irregular foot instead of the thin face. The black mourning bands so printed were first used by a Colonial newspaper in Philadelphia in 1765 the day before the detested Stamp Act went into effect. They marked the death of a freedom. Decades later the same typographic crape was hung on newspaper pages that reported the death of George Washington. Throughout the years rules were occasionally turned on the death of other prominent leaders or of the editor of a newspaper.

The custom had almost died out, however, until the assassination of John F. Kennedy prompted some editors to revive the custom. In many composing rooms, this caused consternation among younger printers who had never heard of the practice, much less seen it. For me it brought poignant memories. I had been with *Stars & Stripes* in France when Franklin D. Roosevelt died, and the French printers who made up the paper were completely baffled by this unprecedented procedure.

A few papers marked President Kennedy's death by using regular wide rules that printed sharp, clean strips of black. It may be a cavil, but I prefer the actual turning of the rules. A value of tradition is that we repeat ritual without demanding logical explanation. And, to me at least, the irregular bands printed by the bottom of the rule express a spontaneous and unstudied grief that is appropriate to deep emotion.

I hope that the custom continues. We know that the death of some men will bring unusual grief to a community or a nation. It may be the stature of the man or the unusually tragic circumstances surrounding his death. The newspaper that shares this mourning visibly with its readers humanizes its institutional presence.

Many tightly knit groups have special symbols to denote their sorrow at the passing of a close comrade: the riderless horse of the Army, the purple-swathed cathedral of the church hierarchy, the tolling of alarm bells for firemen. The death of a publisher or editor might just as well occasion the turning of the rules of his newspaper by his journalistic companions.

The publisher, then, has more options on format than his predecessors had. He should base his decisions on these factors:

Fig. 88. Conventional 8-column format is opened by elimination of column rules in *Mason City* (Iowa) *Globe-Gazette*. This is typical contemporary format.

1. The format must be attractive, to maintain and increase circulation in the face of increased competition.
2. The format must permit setting as close to optimum measure as possible, making reading easy, convenient, pleasurable, and rewarding.
3. The format must permit maximum efficiency on the desk, at the Linotype, and on the stone.
4. Finally, the format must reflect the personality of the newspaper.

These are all sound technical criteria for a good format. One more—less precise but valid—is the personal taste of the publisher or editor.

Typography, whether it involves the Bible or a newspaper page, is an artistic creation. A newspaper page is like an oil painting. After all the technical yardsticks have been used to measure its quality, the ultimate decision is the viewer's "I like it." If the publisher chooses a format because "I like it," it is certainly his prerogative. He should not choose a technically unsound format, but within the principles of sound typography there is still room for personal evaluation and choice.

chapter 10

The Front Page

LAYING OUT THE FRONT PAGE is probably the most exciting and pleasurable task of the editor. It comes at that point of the production cycle when adrenalin is high in the blood. Exhilarated and challenged by the deadline, the editor is eager for a chance at creativity that was not present during the often routine chores of copy editing.

All creative people need an audience; and the editor knows his front page will be seen—perhaps even admired—by even the most casual of readers.

Even a superlative job of reporting and editing is subtle. It can't be recognized unless it is read, and maybe not even then. But the layout of the front page is obvious long before the page is read. No one can ignore it.

For more than a century, the editor made up his front page by instinct. And he usually did a pretty good job of it. Today we still can't design a good page entirely by instrument, but we needn't fly entirely by the seat of our pants.

There are a few axioms that apply to page layout.

Turn for a moment to the next page of this book. What is the first word that you read on it? Yes, the word in the top left corner of the page.

The same answer would apply to any page, be it printed or written (except for one like this with a distinguishing pattern to indicate the start of a chapter). For from the first moment a parent takes a baby on his lap and shows him a picture book, the child is oriented to the top left corner as the "beginning" of a page. Whenever we're involved with written communication—and printed pages are just that—we instinctively begin to write or to read at that point.

The top left corner is called the *primary optical area,* the *POA*. Here we begin reading as unconsciously as we run to first base after we've hit a baseball or stay on the right side of the street while driving.

By that same training, we know that when we reach the lower right corner we have finished the page; we turn it or proceed to the adjacent one. So the lower right corner is our goal, conscious or subconscious. It's the *terminal area.*

In simplest diagram, then, the path of the reading eye is from top left to lower right, the *reading diagonal.*

The eye, of course, doesn't streak down this diagonal like a sprinter down his lane. It courses back and forth like a little boy in a park. He can be lured by ponds, hotdog stands, and strange animals; the eye is attracted by *optical magnets.*

We can dramatize this fact by thinking of a newspaper page as a sheet of plywood and the reading eye as a steel ball bearing. The wood is tilted gently so that when the ball is placed on the northwest corner, it will roll down to the southeast one. We can draw the ball off this path—the reading diagonal, of course—by placing magnets near its path.

Two things affect the pulling power of a magnet—its size and its proximity to the object. The larger one will draw the ball unless the smaller one is much closer.

We are particularly concerned with the *fallow corners,* top right and lower left. Strong magnets are needed to draw the eye into those areas.

We must always remember that wherever the eye finds itself on a page, it will resist having to move in "reverse gear," either upward or to the left. It is willing to return to the axis of orientation to read successive lines of a block of type, but it surely doesn't want to move any farther beyond this line to the left and never higher than the current position on the page.

This doesn't mean that the eye absolutely refuses to back up. But it refuses to do so happily. When it is distracted to a point where it does go in reverse, it does so reluctantly and with irritation. We don't know exactly how often the eye will accept being irritated by such tactics. But we do know that it will ultimately reach that point where not only will it refuse to back up, it will refuse to read anything further.

The comparison of layout to other visual arts is emphasized by the classical reverse-S pattern for paintings. This sweep, called "the most beautiful curve that man can draw," captures the eye at the POA, leads

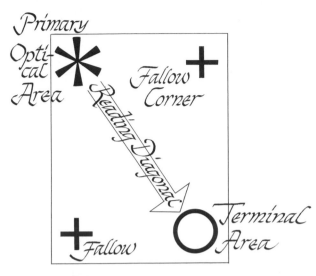

Fig. 89. Diagram of eye movement in normal reading path.

it through both fallow corners and finally to the terminal area. When this curve is simplified into a straight line, it is our familiar old reading diagonal.

Laying Out the Front Page

The first step in designing the front page is to place a strong *attention compeller* in the primary optical area. As the eye enters the page, it must be grabbed immediately by some element that is so interesting that the reader will want to enter the page and remain there to read. We must remind ourselves that the function of page makeup is to lure the reader into body type, to make sure the reader reads the first three paragraphs of each news story.

The attention compeller may be a picture, a strong or unusually interesting headline, or a box.

A picture is the strongest attention compeller. Unfortunately, we can't use a picture in the POA of each front page. For among other considerations, we want to make each front page as different as possible from all its predecessors. The most damaging thing a potential reader can say about a newspaper is to look at it and inquire: "Is this today's paper?"

The layout of page one must be so fresh that there is no doubt whatsoever that this paper is hot off the press. That precludes using a picture in the POA each time. Even drastic changes in the shape and size of a picture in that position will not be enough to break the stereotype.

Rarely will a 1-column headline be adequate in the POA. This is especially true if a picture runs in column 2. The almost inevitable progression in this case is for the eye to jump right across the 1-column head and into the pictorial magnet to its right. The wider the picture, the stronger its pulling power and the surer the eye is to leap across the first column. Should that happen, it is doubtful that the eye will backtrack to read the story in column 1.

The second layout step is placing the flag. If it goes clear across the page, its position is automatic. But if it's a floating flag, it must be treated as a display element and made part of the page pattern.

It doesn't matter on which side of the page a short flag is run. If it is anywhere in the upper third of the page, it will adequately identify the newspaper. Those editions sold mainly off newsstands may have to have the flag closer to the top. But the editor should know by his own observation how his paper is sold. In most instances the papers are piled on a horizontal counter or shelf and the whole top half of the front page is visible. Wire racks that display only the top strip of a page are usually reserved for out-of-town papers. The number of such sales is so minute that there seems to be little need to let it affect page makeup, certainly not of all editions.

Now the editor works in the top right fallow corner.

Traditionally, the leed story is placed in the top right corner. This is based on instinctive common sense. For a couple of generations, each daily newspaper and many weeklies had a full-page banner head on every issue. In those days the column width was 12 or even 13 picas. So by the time the eye had been carried as much as 18 inches across the page, it made sense to pull it down into body type without further delay. To make the eye back up to any column other than the eighth brought danger of losing it to fatigue. Today, even though the full-page banner becomes rarer, convention still puts the leed story in the top-right area most of the time on most papers.

This is all right; at least we know we have something potent to attract the eye into this fallow corner. Some editors are experimenting with using the leed story in other positions, notably in the POA. This can be effective, but then the editor must find some other magnet adequate to pull the eye into the fallow corner.

Abandoning the full-page banner has not lost any pulling power for the editor. Although circulation managers insist on such a banner, especially for street sales, there are no conclusive data that attest to its pulling power. On the contrary, we find that the reader is attracted more by a banner of less than full-page width than by the one that extends clear across the page. Indeed, the story under an 8-column banner is often one of the least-read on the page. The rationalization is that a full banner may optically become part of the nameplate and thus be almost overlooked, an effect even stronger when the full-page banner runs every day.

Another factor is that the leed story often has little drama. A cursory inspection of your files will show that often the No. 1 story comes from Washington or the state capital; it is important because of its effect on the lives and pocketbooks of the citizenry, and the editor properly plays it as the leed. But it doesn't have personal impact on the reader that a story of lesser importance may have. When the leed story is about murder, calamity, or personality, it gets high readership. But it would get that reader interest no matter where it runs on the page. It seems that it is the topic, rather than page position, that gives a story readership. Of course, the prominent position and large headline on the leed story are factors in building readership. But it takes more than typographic devices to lure a reader into a complex budget story or into one on the intricacies of technical legislation.

Whether the banner requires a readout head will depend on two factors, the size of the banner headletter as discussed in Chapter 5, and the point at which the story reads out. If there is any danger that the reader will be confused as to where the story begins, the readout should be used to take him by the hand and lead him into body type.

The editor has now placed three elements, the flag and those in the top corners. He then leaves the top of the page and goes down into the *basement,* the lower half.

Despite the huge street sales of metropolitan newspapers, more than 90% of all the newspaper circulation in the United States is home delivered. In Canada the percentage is even higher. This means that the major job of "selling" the paper is not off a newsstand but off a table in the reader's home.

If we flip a coin, it will come up heads 50 times, tails 50 times; if we place a newspaper casually on a table, it will come up "tails" almost as often as "heads." The top half will be showing about 55% of the time; apparently there is a slight inclination toward placing the paper face up, so that the purely random 50–50 ratio doesn't obtain.

But even if the paper lies tails-up only 45% of the time, that is often enough to indicate that we must also place strong sales appeal in the lower half. The editor who fails to dress the basement of his front page is like the baseball player who fails to take along a bat to the plate four out of ten times. It is true that with a bat, he can't be sure he'll get a hit, but without a bat he can be absolutely sure that he won't. A weak lower half

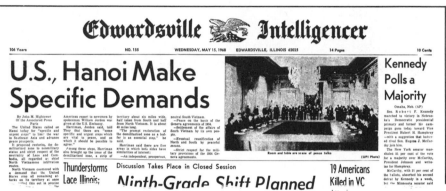

Fig. 90. Left-hand leads are effective in *Oshkosh* (Wis.) *Daily Northwestern* and *Edwardsville* (Ill.) *Intelligencer.*

of a front page may not lose all potential readership. Habit may prompt the regular reader to pick up even a completely uninteresting newspaper. But as more readers become transient and as competition for their time and attention grows more intense, no editor can rely solely on reader habit to sell his paper.

Another axiom: "There should be at least one strong picture and two multicolumn heads below the fold on page one."

One of such heads may well be the *basement banner.* While the definition for such a head is vague, it is generally accepted that it will be at least 48-point in size and four columns wide. Some editors think that a 5-columner is the narrowest to qualify as a basement banner.

The editor seeks to *anchor the corners,* placing strong display elements in them. Research shows that pages with well-anchored corners have higher readership than those whose corners just evaporate into the atmosphere.

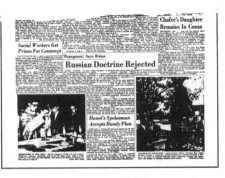

Fig. 91. Basement treatment. Lower half of page (top left) is devoid of all display elements. Upper right, *Mason City* (Iowa) *Globe-Gazette* uses multicolumn heads and horizontal makeup to add sales appeal to basement. Lower left, *Garland* (Texas) *Daily News* and (lower right) *Newport* (R.I.) *Daily News* use pictures to anchor lower corners and add appeal to basement.

Pictures and boxes are excellent anchors. Flatout matter can be effective as an anchor, if a rule is used to make, in effect, a sideless box.

The terminal area especially needs an anchor, although we cannot minimize the need for such element in the lower fallow corner as well.

A multicolumn head will anchor a corner if it's no more than 3 inches from the bottom of the page; a 1-column head must be even closer to the bottom, but the weight of a head which would normally run on a 2-inch story is not strong enough to anchor the corner. So a 1-columner is no practical tool.

With the lower corners adequately anchored, the editor leaves *downstairs* and goes to the top of the page again.

Across the top of the page there is always danger of *tombstoning*, heads running side by side. Editors have always recognized the hazards of this form of jammed heads but never quite analyzed the danger. They believed that the eye would read from one head into the next and that they could remedy this by using adjacent heads in markedly different size and form.

While there could possibly be confusion from reading together a pair of headlines, the real handicap imposed by tombstones is that the reader is exposed to conflicting persuasions at the same time. Each headline seeks to draw him into its story. But instead of making the choice of which story to read, he is apt to decline both stories and go elsewhere on the page where the decision has already been made for him by the editor. So, axiom: "Headlines should be as widely separated as possible."

Pictures are the ideal element to break tombstones. Note, however, that if the picture carries an overline, this type becomes part of the tombstoning.

Boxes are fairly good devices for breaking the stones. On the face of it, this seems an anomaly. For the box carries a headline and, one might assume, a box between two headed stories merely adds another choice as to what should be read first. But pragmatic observation leads to the firm conclusion that boxes do break tombstones. They are not as effective as pictures, but they are adequate when art is not available.

Armpitting is another incipient danger at the top of the page. This is the practice of placing a narrow head immediately under a wider one. This inelegantly named practice is easy to avoid by simple obedience to an ancient axiom: "There must be at least eight lines of body type between heads in the same column."

As stories are placed across the top of the page, they should normally break to the outside of the page. This is to leave room at the center of the page for later placement of display elements to break up unattractive concentration of body type.

A dollar bill is an excellent gauge for determining permissible density of text type. When the bill is held horizontally anywhere on a newspaper page, it should touch at least two display elements. Some editors insist that the bill touch two optical magnets whether it is held vertically or horizontally. (The latter method means that a 2-column story could be no deeper than 6 inches, the length of a bill.)

The dollar gauge is, as are most of our criteria, an approximate measurement, and any editor can make constant or occasional amendments to the method to suit his own tastes or needs. Some editors cut a rectangle of cardboard to the proper proportions so they can place it on the page dummy as a check. Some makeup men use the currency on the stone during the makeup process.

As placement of stories works down to the center of the page, the editor enters another danger area. The hand, with fingers loosely open but not widely spread, is placed on the mathematical center of the page. From wrist to finger tip it should touch at least three major display elements.

Fig. 92. Anchored corners. *Waterloo* (Iowa) *Daily Courier* anchors lower left with strong head. This is 8-format page; inside pages are in nine columns.

Bremerton (Wash.) *Sun*, next page, anchors three corners with editorial elements, uses display ad for lower left. Note impact of large picture. This is W-format on 9-column page.

Now we see why it is better to break page-top stories to the outside. These stories, because of the importance that gives them top position, are usually long ones. If they are read out into the center of the page, there soon is a morass of body type into which no display elements can be injected.

The reading diagonal should be sketchily defined by heads. We don't know why, but pages where the diagonal is at least suggested by display matter are pleasing to readers.

As the makeup proceeds down the page, the editor should get all the necessary strong display elements below the fold.

Finally, small stories are placed to fill holes in the form. The page is complete, and it's sound.

A casualty of contemporary makeup is the 2- or 3-line filler that used to delight editors and readers of another generation. These conveyed such breathless intelligence as: "The average depth of the Gollyhoolee River is 11½ inches." To a river lover this information can bring a warm glow; to the typical reader it is something he can quite definitely live without. Functional newspaper design insists that the space occupied by these fillers can more easily and attractively be used for white space.

Another casualty of this page pattern is an old office law that head-lines had to become progressively smaller down the page. No head could be larger than the one just above it in the same column. Some news-papers were even more adamant: Each head in a column had to be

THE BREMERTON SUN

Volume 69, Number 41.   BREMERTON, WASHINGTON Thursday, May 23, 1968.   10 CENTS PER COPY

Harriman Says Peace Negotiations May Fail

PARIS (AP) — Ambassador W. Averell Harriman, conceding that the U.S.-Vietnam peace negotiations could fail, said today: "You can't keep talks going just as a propaganda medium."

North Vietnam's envoy to the discussions, Xuan Thuy, had raised Wednesday the possibility of failure. In the same speech he appealed to U.S. and world opinion to put pressure on Washington to end promptly and unconditionally all bombing and other acts of war against North Vietnam.

Harriman was asked today when he left his office in the U.S. Embassy whether he considered Thuy's statement a threat.

He replied that he didn't take it as "much of a threat," that it seemed to him to arise naturally from other subjects Thuy had been discussing. Then Harriman added: "It's always a possibility, you know, that these talks would break down. The talks can just as well break down on the United States side if they (the Americans) think they (the North Vietnamese) are taking advantage of the restraint in the bombing."

Harriman cautioned against taking his discussion of the problem as any prediction of collapse.

"My own judgment," he said, "is that we're here for a long time, that the other side feels they want to have talks, and certainly President Johnson has shown every indication of wanting to come to agreement.

"But both sides have got to show some willingness to talk substance, willingness to move ahead.

"You can't keep talks going just as a propaganda medium. We have to move into a period of more productive results."

Four times American and North Vietnamese negotiators have met in the past 16 days, and four times they have either away slightly beaten in their original positions.

U.S. spokesmen have called the North Vietnamese "stubborn." The Vietnamese called the Americans "obstinate."

The stumbling block is always the same—North Vietnamese insistence on an unconditional end to U.S. bombing of their country and U.S. insistence that "reciprocal restraint" on Hanoi's part must accompany a halt in the bombing.

"The talks are frozen," said one neutral diplomat after Wednesday's three-hour meeting. The talks are in recess until next Monday.

To the meeting Wednesday, Thuy renewed an appeal from Harriman that both delegations stop making their conference statements public.

Harriman said this would "make possible a more useful and meaningful exchange of views."

America Warned On Talks

WASHINGTON (AP) — A blue-ribbon citizens group including former President Dwight D. Eisenhower voiced fear today that many Americans have been misled into expecting "too much, too soon" from U.S.-North Vietnamese talks in Paris.

Americans think of negotiations as a road to peace but there is unmistakable evidence Hanoi's leaders consider negotiations as another way to fight a war, said a special panel of the Citizens Committee for Peace with Freedom in Vietnam.

It warned against neglecting to "win at the conference table what we have not won on the battlefield" and against "letting the conference table what we have fought so hard for in our so much to protect."

Without the formal complaining for "a reasonable time" prospects for a peaceful settlement, it rated poor the chances for productive negotiations now.

The 1,700-word statement on "Negotiations: Hopes versus Realities" was issued by a 14-man special panel on negotiations.

The citizens committee was organized last fall by former Sen. Paul H. Douglas, D-Ill., and includes both living ex-presidents—Eisenhower and Harry S Truman — in its nationally known membership of about 100.

Police Warn De Gaulle They'll Support Strikers

PARIS (UPI)—French police threatened today to strike in support of the millions of workers who have paralyzed France with nationwide strikes. A police strike could bring anarchy to a nation already in chaos.

Police unions met today and declared they may refuse to follow orders that would conflict with the interest of the other workers. They promised government failure to negotiate an end to student unrest which led to student-police battles today, and against charges of "police brutality."

Observers recalled that a strike by Paris policemen and their march on the National Assembly 18 years ago signalled the start of the fall of the Fourth Republic and the rise of President Charles de Gaulle to leadership. Then, too, they protested government failure to protect them against accusations of brutality.

The threat to refuse to obey orders was as close as they could come legally to declaring themselves on strike. It came as the nation faced the threat of new student uprising in Paris and trouble Friday when sympathetic West German students said they would try

to enter France in support of French students.

A national religious holiday, Ascension Day, paralyzed even further a nation where 9 million workers were on strike—some estimates ran as high as 10 million—and other millions were locked out or unable to get to work. Almost the entire 13 million-man work force was affected.

President Charles de Gaulle met for nearly four hours today with his cabinet but there appeared no immediate way out of France's agony.

The National Union of Police Officials met this afternoon and said it "hopes the public power will not systematically oppose the police and the workers." The union warned that this might pose "serious questions of conscience."

A communique said police "would in no case serve a regime that did not respect them" and that they "understand perfectly what motivates the workers on strike." And in a warning of new tribulations for the 16-year-old Gaullist regime the police "deplored" a 1948 law forbidding them to strike.

North Vietnam Troops Reoccupy Shau Valley, Resume Hue Threat

SAIGON (UPI) — North Vietnamese troops have reoccupied the A Shau valley just one week after allied troops ended a costly sweep through the Communist stronghold, U.S. military sources said today. The Communist move meant a renewed threat to the city of Hue.

The A Shau valley is a 25-mile-long gateway to Hue and the coastal areas from the Ho Chi Minh trail a short distance west through Laos. It was occupied by American and South Vietnamese at a cost of 142 U.S. dead and 548 wounded. Vietnamese losses were not announced.

During the 28-day-old allied occupation of the valley, 738 Communists were killed and six prisoners taken with vast supplies of weapons. But the Americans also lost 128 belongings shot down.

When the operation was completed, Lt. Gen. William B.

Rosson said newsmen it had ended the immediate threat to Hue, the ancient imperial capital. He said U.S. planes would keep the entire area under "interdiction" by bombing attacks but that the monsoon rains made occupation too difficult.

Communist occupation was disclosed as Hanoi Radio broadcast an editorial in the official Communist daily Nhan Dan calling allied Operation Delaware which cleared out the valley a major American defeat.

It said more than an entire U.S. division was involved but that the Viet Cong and North Vietnamese "meted out severe punishment."

Hanoi claimed more than 2,200 U. S. and South Vietnamese troops were "wiped out," nearly 200 aircraft shot down or destroyed on the ground and more than 100 vehicles wrecked in a "heavy defeat" for the United States. It said the allied

operation failed to lessen the predicament of the Americans in the northern provinces.

American bombers kept the pressure on supply lines in the southern panhandle of North Vietnam today, dodging what pilots described as increasingly heavy antiaircraft fire since the Hanoi - Haiphong area was put off limits April 1.

U. S. headquarters reported two American planes lost in 135 missions Wednesday. Radio Hanoi said four American planes were shot down.

The two planes were matched by an increase in the number of missions flown. During March, while the northeast monsoons were still producing heavy cloud cover, the air war more than three years ago. One of the planes lost Wednesday was a Navy photo-reconnaissance RF9 Crusader, the other an Air Force F4 Phantom.

In February nine American warplanes were announced lost over the North. In March the number went to 11. During April, the first month Johnson's curtailment order was in effect, 16 U.S. planes were reported shot down.

The increase in losses was matched by an increase in the number of missions flown. During March, while the northeast monsoons were still producing heavy cloud cover, the air war more than three years ago. One of the planes lost Wednesday was a Navy photo-reconnaissance RF9 Crusader, the other an Air Force F4 Phantom.

In February nine American warplanes were announced lost over the North. In March the number went to 11. During April, the first month Johnson's curtailment order was in effect, 16 U.S. planes were reported shot down. The loss of the two planes raised the total reported lost in combat in the North to 18 in May and 841 since the start of

City Plans To Be Discussed

The first public report on Bremerton's civic auditorium study and an outline of city development plans will be given Monday evening at a special forum dinner meeting sponsored by Bremerton Chamber of Commerce.

Richard McEyina of Development Research Associates, the Los Angeles firm engaged by the city for the auditorium study, will give an illustrated report on what facilities and features could be included in a civic auditorium.

Bremerton Mayor Glenn K. Jarstad and other city commission members will outline plans for the city's new street system, parks, utilities, expansion, housing, beautification, a new zoning ordinance, new building code, annexations, a golf course, off-street parking and other items.

The meeting, which will be open to the public, will be held at Elks Temple, Fifth Street and Pacific Avenue, beginning at 6:30 p.m. Reservations may be made by contacting the Bremerton Chamber of Commerce office, Elson 5-8080, by 5 o'clock tomorrow afternoon.

Navy Dilemma

Home Hunt Lags

With the supercarrier USS Ranger's arrival only 18 days away, housing has been found for less than 25 per cent of the families who will be coming here aboard her.

Despite an areawide plea for housing, only 13 rooms, five apartments and two trailers have been located to take care of Ranger families, a Puget Sound Naval Shipyard spokesman said today.

"And these all are for couples only. We still haven't anything to take care of families with children," he added.

According to a survey taken aboard the ship last week, Ranger families need 58 one-bedroom units, 38 with two bedrooms, 16 with three bedrooms, and a few four-bedroom places.

"There has been talk of housing the people on the other side of the Sound if room can't be found here but so far we've only been able to find 16 places scattered between Burton and Tacoma ... and they start renting at $165 a month," the shipyard spokesman said.

"These people would be wiped out by that kind of rent. Also, there's the

transportation problem," he added.

The Ranger, just back from a deployment to the Vietnam war zone, is due to arrive at the shipyard the morning of June 3.

Current scheduling calls for the ship to be here for two months of repair work.

At latest count, about 128 families will be aboard the ship for the trip from Alameda, Calif. It is anticipated that some will drive here from California, he added.

Persons with housing space which could be made available for Ranger families in June and July are urged to contact the PSNS Housing Office by telephone at 478-2710 or 478-2583, or mail a description of the units to: Ranger Housing, Puget Sound Naval Shipyard, Bremerton.

"The Navy community and the men of the Ranger appreciate the offered help being made to find housing for these people and hope that enough space will be found to take care of them by the time the ship arrives," the shipyard spokesman added.

Marchers Arrested In D.C.

See Early Story Page 1
WASHINGTON (AP) — Police began a mass arrest of demonstrators in the Poor People's Campaign today but called it off after filling two paddy wagons when the group agreed to leave Capitol Hill.

The process of making the first arrests in the campaign was well under way when it was interrupted, apparently by the intervention of a Justice Department official and Rep. William F. Ryan, D-N.Y.

After a hurried consultation between the police officials and Ryan, the loading of the demonstrators stopped.

Their leader from Resurrection City, U.S.A., the Rev. Jesse Jackson, summoned to the scene, led them quietly from their position outside a House office building.

Police said an estimated 20 demonstrators arrested before the action was halted will be booked on charges of unlawful assembly. About 75 persons had been involved in the demonstrations.

The group had given repeated warnings that the group singing and clapping hands on the sidewalk outside the office building was violating the law and subject to arrest.

The group arrested was the overflow of a crowd of about 300 that had gone to Capitol Hill to protest a new welfare law.

Picketing on the Capitol grounds is against the law.

Haiti Halts Travel To Site of 'Invasion'

PORT AU PRINCE (UPI) — The Haitian government today maintained a ban on travel to the city of Cap Haitien, reported site of an invasion aimed at the overthrow of President Francois Papa Doc Duvalier.

The government said it had defeated an invasion force of about 50 Haitian exiles and mercenaries who landed both Cap Haitien and the capital with a B25 bomber.

Nevertheless highways to Cap Haitien were closed. All flights to this northern coastal city, Haiti's second largest with 36,-000 residents, were canceled.

All cable communications leaving the country had to be taken to the presidential palace —Duvalier's residence — before they could be sent.

Duvalier declared a state of emergency and received "extra-

ordinary powers" from the National Assembly Wednesday. But they brought no apparent changes to the daily routine of Port Au Prince.

Duvalier has ruled the small French-speaking country with no effective opposition since 1957.

Witnesses to the Monday attack of the B25 said three or four small bombs fell near Duvalier's residence but they and the explosions were so small they first were thought to be fireworks. They caused no apparent damage.

The Weather

Cloudy, a few sunny periods, showers, today and Friday. Highs 65-65, Low 45-50. Winds southerly, 10-15 mph.

Rap Brown Gets 5 Years On Violation of Gun Laws

NEW ORLEANS (AP)—H. Rap Brown was convicted Wednesday night of violating the National Firearms Act and was given the maximum sentence of five years in prison and a $2,000 fine.

Brown, 24, chairman of the Student Nonviolent Coordinating Committee, was freed on bond pending appeal after the bi-racial jury returned the verdict in federal court.

Under terms of the $15,000 bond, Brown's travel was restricted to the Southern District of New York State.

The immediate sentencing by U. S. District Judge Lansing L. Mitchell was at the request of William M. Kunstler, of New York, chief defense attorney for the Black Power advocate.

Kunstler included a plea for leniency, describing the government case as an effort to "silence" Brown, a frequent and fiery speaker at civil rights rallies.

"It is time this persecution must stop and this is persecution of the most blatant sort" cried Kunstler. "We recall that everything Adolf Hitler did was legal."

"The issue of black or white was only brought into this case by the defen-

ant," shouted U. S. Atty. Louis LaCour. "We deeply resent statements making such a comparison to Hitler."

Brown was convicted under a section of the act forbidding anyone under indictment on a felony charge to transport a gun across state lines.

Photo caption: H. RAP BROWN

---

smaller than any above it. Unless stories ran fairly long or the column were headed by the largest possible head, it was possible that an editor would run out of sizes before the column was filled.

Whatever justification this policy had—if it ever did—certainly no longer applies. The result of this step-down in size means that the bottom of the page gets grayer and grayer. We know today that we need larger

Fig. 93. Jammed head. Top fragment shows tombstoning across page-top; arrows, a, indicate armpits. In lower fragments, arrow b shows how overline becomes part of tombstone and prevents picture from breaking such a jam.

heads down in the page. If failure to anchor a corner loses readership, allowing the whole page to gray out must have even worse effects. It is impossible to create a pleasant page pattern if, by fiat, the page must be top-heavy. We have already discussed the need for strong display down in the basement; this is impossible to achieve if heads get progressively smaller. And as the reading eye becomes fatigued, it is revived by strong display elements.

We used the analogy of a newspaper page as a sheet of plywood to demonstrate the effect of optical magnets upon the reading eye. We might continue the illustration to point out another layout requirement.

We should picture the page as a sheet of wood hanging on a pivot at the *optical center,* 2 inches above the mathematical center. Each display element should be thought of as a piece of wood. Its area will correspond to that of the typographic unit; its thickness will be relative to its typographic weight. As the element is dummied in, we should visualize it as nailed to the plywood page. The page will swing on its pivot.

To keep the page in balance, we may place another element of the same weight at the same distance from the pivot. Or, as we'd balance youngsters on a teeter-totter, we can place a heavier element closer to the pivot or a lighter one farther away. The optical weight of elements cannot be determined as precisely as that of our analogous piece of wood. The editor must determine his own set of weights and measures. There are some generalities which may be helpful to him:

1. Display elements on the right side of the page weigh a little more than those on the left.
2. Elements in the top half of the page will be a little heavier than identical ones in the basement.
3. Pictures in dark tones are heavier than those in higher key.
4. A horizontal picture outweighs a vertical one of the same area.
5. An exaggeratedly horizontal or vertical picture will weigh more than one of the same area closer to a 3 x 5 ratio.
6. A 1-column sideless box will balance a conventional 1-column portrait.
7. Lines of force in a picture will make the page tilt in their direction and thus increase the balancing effect of the cut.
8. Colored ink will add about 25% to the weight of a black-and-white element.

Some editors try to get a strong element right on the optical center, actually defining the pivot on which the page hangs. This does give a pleasant effect, but it will too often create problems that seem unworthy of the benefits that might accrue. To define the small area of the pivot, the element must be small, too. Generally we place large elements where we need them and fill in the blanks with smaller ones that are easier to maneuver. If we must place the smaller one first, it may become difficult to accommodate longer stories to the pattern.

As we nail more typographic elements to the plywood, it becomes almost impossible to balance it exactly. But this is no disaster; we really don't want perfect balance. Slight imbalance adds a dynamic thrust that brings life and interest to a layout. Perfect balance is static, not very interesting to the reader. He prefers a page that is neither precariously unbalanced nor rigidly upright.

Symmetrical layout—a perfectly balanced page—should be avoided as a matter of principle. To create such a pattern means that everything on our news budget—type or art—comes, in fact, in equal pairs. This is obviously fallacious. To reduce the situation to the classical *absurdum:* On the day a man first sets foot on Mars, what is the story that will exactly balance this report to make a symmetrical page?

The balanced page should be used only on those occasions when an editor wants to point up parallels, even if they aren't totally accurate. During an election campaign he might give equal space to both parties, candidates, or sides of an issue just to demonstrate the long-range neutrality of the newspaper. On any given day he might overplay one side or downplay the other just to maintain the fiction that each candidate has produced exactly the same news in quality and quantity as the other.

This technique would not usually create a whole page in symmetry; two or three stories, often running out of a shotgun head, would be all the copy involved.

Editors disagree vehemently over artificial handling of the news. Some point out an obvious advantage: When partisans complain about election-campaign coverage, the editor need only whip out his trusty pica rule and demonstrate that each side got exactly the same linage as the other. Another editor would play a story for what it is worth by his professional criteria, and stand on his judgment against the inevitable screams of the disgruntled. To resort to artificial equality of coverage, he insists, is to penalize the good campaigner and newsmaker and to shelter the inept—or even the dishonest—against his inability or fear to meet issues.

Even on those rare occasions when there are two stories of approximately equal value, they won't automatically be of the same length. So the editor must cut arbitrarily or jump one or both of the stories to present them on a page in perfect symmetry.

Picture Placement

"Pictures above type" is an axiom useful in all layout, editorial or advertising. For it places elements in the order in which the eye prefers to read them.

The normal progression is picture, cutlines, headline, story.

If the headline is above the picture, there is a danger that the eye will go into the photo first, never reading the head, or having to back up, with reluctance and annoyance, to read it. Even if the headline is heavy enough that it will catch the reading eye before the halftone does, it is a poor technique to place type above the picture.

For there should be no barrier between headline and body type. A 3-column picture under a 3-column head is a barrier clear across the path of the eye. Even if only a 1-column cut is used with a 3-column head, it should not be placed in the first column with body type under it. There it would be an interruption to the eye moving from head to body.

If a head *canopies*—runs across—a story and a picture of any width, the story must read right out of the head. Normally the pictures would be at the left; under a 4-column canopy, for instance, the halftone would be in columns 1–2 or 1–3, the story reading out in column 3 or 4. If other factors demand, the picture may be in the right-hand columns under the head. The important thing is that the story read directly out of the head.

The power of a picture to pull readers into accompanying stories is

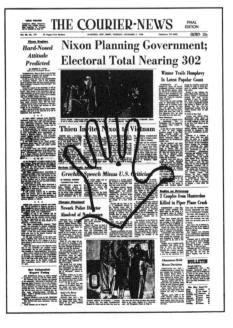

Fig. 94. Mid-page danger area. Space covered by partially opened hand should have at least three display elements. Meeting requirements are pages from *Biloxi* (Miss.) *Daily Herald, Plainfield* (N.J.) *Courier-News* and *Abilene* (Texas) *Reporter-News*. On latter, strip of stars and right ear are in red. Dots indicate mathematical center of page.

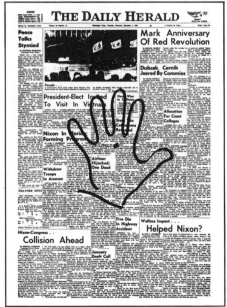

most effectively used when the picture runs with a headline of exactly the same width and exactly under the cut. A 4-column picture should not have a 3-column accompanying head under it; then a tombstone will be inevitable, or just as bad, body type will have to run right under the picture. Nor should the 4-column art ride above a 5-column or wider head; this effect is not esthetically pleasing. If a 4-column head accompanies a 4-column cut, it should not extend to the left or right of the picture; this occasions a tombstone and is esthetically unpleasant.

Even if there is no accompanying story, the head under an independent picture is best at the same width and immediately under the art. The two elements are separated by a cutoff, of course.

It is not very effective to run a picture alongside its accompanying head. If such placement is the only possible one, the picture should be at the left so the eye reads from the stronger to the weaker element. It is of little use to run a picture at the end of a story; this is giving the quarry the bait after it is already in the trap.

If the picture must, by force of circumstances, run in these positions, an arrow within one element should point to its companion piece.

Cutlines should be under the picture. Sometimes this is not possible, and the lines must run above or to one side of the cut. In this case, too, arrows are effective, and there should be an exaggerated amount of white space—at least 2 picas—above the cutlines.

A total waste of pictorial magnetism is separating picture and story on different pages. To run a picture on page one and the story elsewhere is like putting a chunk of cheese in the kitchen with a little sign: "The trap is in the basement; go look for it." To run the story on the front page and the picture inside is like putting the trap in the kitchen with a sign that says: "The cheese is in the basement."

When there is great volume of picture coverage of a story, it is functional to run a combo on an inside page or pages. But even then at least one strong picture should accompany the story on page one. Pix may run in a strip across the top of the head. This requires pictures of the same depth. When this is not possible, the pictures may be placed as an upside down L or U, and the head and story tucked into the mortise, as it were.

An antiquated rule says that no halftone may be placed on the fold. There is no real justification for this. Most editors will avoid placing a 1-column picture, especially a portrait, on the fold. They reason that relatively fine details are important in a small photo and that these details may be abraded during the delivery process if they are placed at the point of greatest wear on the paper. But large pictures can be very

Hempfield Dumps Vikings, 25-12

By PHIL MUSICK
Tribune-Review Sports Editor

Battlin' Bobby Gorinski did everything but swallow the football at halftime, but even his line-battering slashes were not enough to dent a tenacious Hempfield defense and Mt. Pleasant will have to wait at least one more season for its first victory over the Spartans.

A slim, but vocal crowd of 5,000 chilled fans waited and waited for Gorinski's powerful bursts to finally take their toll on Hempfield's defensive line, but the young Spartans, led by

Hempfield's Leo Henry (33) bursts through a huge hole on a 42-yard TD run behind block thrown by Spartans' Rick Druschel (76).

"old" senior linebacker Mike Stefanik, never ran out of gas and Hempfield registered a 25-12 victory.

The Spartan triumph, which closed out Hempfield's 1968 season at 6-3-1, sounded a death knell for Mt. Pleasant hop-

Fig. 95. Canopy. Proper method of linking picture and story is by canopy, arrow within body type is not needed. Below story and picture are not properly linked. Strong line of force in picture points away from story and further divides elements.

Humphrey Thinks Peace Talk Path Will Be Smoothed

Considers Thieu's Objections 'Political Problems At Home'

YOUNGSTOWN, Ohio (AP) — Vice President Hubert H. Humphrey predicted today "good sense will overcome any immediate emotional reaction" by South Vietnam in its refusal to join the Paris peace talks.

Humphrey refused to discuss the negotiations in detail, but noted that South Vietnamese President Thieu "fully approved the bombing cessati-

and "may be having some political problems at home—I am in politics and I can understand some of that."

Humphrey, campaigning in this industrial northeastern Ohio area before a heavy day of campaigning around New York City, also reacted strongly to news that Richard M. Nixon had been critical of the U. S. space pro-

CAMPAIGN HAZARD   Vice   paign handshaking while —

effective when wrapped around the fold. If nothing else, they give reader appeal to both halves of the page.

Unrelated pictures should be kept isolated from each other lest they compete too vigorously and immediately for reader attention.

Horizontal Makeup

In functional newspaper design the editor will use *horizontal makeup* as much as possible. Disposing body type in horizontal areas makes the mass appear smaller.

In a test of makeup, ten-year-olds were shown a quantity of 1-column body type and asked: "How long do you think it will take you to read this?" When type was in a single column, the estimate was, "Ten units of time." When type was doubled over in two columns, the answer was, "eight." When arranged in three columns, the estimate was that the type could be read in five units. Note that the experiment was concerned only with the estimate, not the actual reading time. Neither in this research nor in any other has it been shown that the shape of a mass of body type has any effect on the actual reading speed. But the estimate the reader makes of reading time is significant to the editor.

In an important way, a newspaper page is comparable to a highway billboard. The poster must be read the first time the passerby sees it; no one in history has been known to back up his car to reread a billboard.

Unlike the driver who passes the billboard, the potential reader will come back to his newspaper pages or some of their individual elements. But the best time to catch a reader is the first time he sees the newspaper, the page, or the story. Each time the reader postpones the actual plunge into body type, the slimmer are chances of his coming back.

If the reader sees a story that he estimates will take 2 minutes to read, he will be much more likely to begin the job than if he thinks it will take 4 minutes. As horizontal placement reduces the time estimate, it draws more readers the first time.

When type is arranged in a horizontal mass, the bottom edge should be fairly straight. But it need not be squared off entirely. Squaring off will result in a tombstone or require a head of at least the same width. Neither of these alternatives is desirable at all times. It will not destroy the efficacy of horizontal makeup to leave the bottom ragged enough to avoid a tombstone.

One-up is, of course, an adaptation of horizontal makeup.

Horizontal makeup must be used, as are all typographic techniques, with discretion. Sometimes a deskman is carried away and tries to use only multicolumn heads. This may distort the value of a news story; some are worth only a 1-column head. It creates an annoying problem on the stone when no 1-columners are available to fill up the little chinks that are usually left in and around horizontally displayed elements. An occasional single-column head also is a pleasant accent to the wider heads of horizontal makeup.

The Chimney Technique

Paradoxically, the opposite of horizontal makeup, the *chimney* technique, is also effective on occasion.

Piling up a series of heads or pictures of the same width creates the

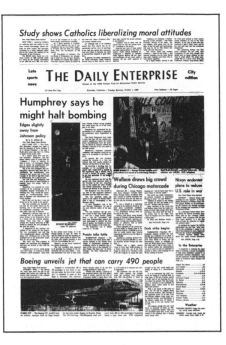

Fig. 96. Horizontal layout. *Cleveland* (Ohio) *Plain Dealer* has no single-column head on front page. *Belvidere* (Ill.) *Daily Republican* has only one; note reverse-plate flag. *Riverside* (Calif.) *Daily Enterprise* emphasizes horizontal strips at top and bottom of page. *Times Herald-Record* of Middletown, N.Y., divides page into four horizontal modules.

chimney, or *tower*. This gives a strong vertical thrust to the page and can be used to counteract excessively heavy horizontal weights. Two- and 3-column chimneys have the greatest vertical force, but 4-columners are effective, too.

Chimneys are strongest when used in the high columns with a floating flag.

The chimney must have sharp sides. If we start a chimney of 3-column heads, for instance, we shouldn't sandwich a 2-column or 4-column element into the stack. A narrower picture can be used in the tower when it is canopied under a head of the proper width.

A chimney can be made of pictures, too, and this device is very effective. The pictures may be on one subject (sequences are well handled this way) or may be unrelated to each other.

Pictures and stories may be combined in a chimney, but such a tower is usually not as effective as that made of only verbal or only pictorial elements.

The chimney technique is always good on compact or full pages, but it is particularly useful with 9-column pages.

The 9-column page, in open or closed format, poses vexatious problems. Physically, the page is just too wide to hold and handle comfortably in reading. Esthetically, it's squat and awkward. But economic pressures that we have already noted are great, and the editor who has a 9-column page must live with it.

He is in a quandary, though. He wants to use horizontal makeup to increase readership, but each such element he puts in emphasizes the width of the page. The chimney technique enables him to use these horizontal bricks yet build a towering complex to slim the page like vertical stripes in a dress trim down a female figure.

Tall, thin pictures, used outside the chimney, also help counteract the too-wide appearance of the 9-column page.

Sidebars

The sidebar is a story closely related to a main story and in close physical proximity to it. The common device to indicate a sidebar is a star or a group of them above its head. This is inadequate.

The deskman and his colleagues know that a star means a sidebar. The reader doesn't. And it is certainly of no value as a directional device; which way does a star point?

Another ineffective device is to remove a cutoff rule above the sidebar head if it runs under the main story or to delete the column rule between the two stories if they run side by side. To the desk, this removal isn't casual. The dummy must indicate it, and the stone must be checked to see that the removal has been made. So the editor is well aware of an unusual situation. But this is too subtle, in printed form, to help the reader. If cutoffs have already been eliminated as part of functional newspaper design, this technique obviously can't be used.

The arrow is an excellent device for tying related elements together. It is the most functional of directional devices. Used on all kinds of signs and in advertisements, the arrow's effect on the reader is immediate and unmistakable.

The arrow should be broad and short. It is available in solid and the more desirable outline form in 8-, 10-, 12-, and up through 24-point sizes.

If its height is that of the width of the alley or column rule, the arrow can run sideways in that area and tie together side-by-side stories. If the arrow points only downward or runs within the column, any size can be used, of course. The *Hartford* (Conn.) *Times* was among the first American papers to use this device to tie the sidebar to the main story. The desk finds it a useful tool. It can tie a story to a picture if the elements cannot be run pic-above-type. And if cutlines must run at the side of the picture, the arrow ties them neatly to the art.

Positioning of the sidebar and content of its headline should be used to indicate association with the main story. The sidebar should not arm-pit the main head; the minimum separation of eight lines of body type applies in this case, too. It doesn't matter whether the sidebar is placed to the left or right of the main story.

If related stories run on inside pages, they are referred to by sandwiches, as we've already noted.

The Fixed Column

Many newspapers run the editor's personal column or one of light miscellany on page one, column 1, in every issue. This is most common on weeklies, but many metropolitans use the same technique. It is there that Arthur Brisbane's unique writings always appeared in Hearst papers; that's where Atlantans read Ralph McGill's trenchant observations, and Dallas readers enjoy the froth of the popular "Big D" column.

On oldtime weeklies, the editor had a sound reason for running his column in a fixed position. He was assured that there would always be room for his own copy, no matter when he got around to writing it. If it were a column of short, random items, it was often written in bits and dribbles. Often it was the last thing to be locked into the last form, and so it contained the freshest news.

These columns, no matter what the size of the paper, consistently have the highest readership of any editorial matter. To capitalize on this popularity, dailies also run them on the front page even though there are no longer pressures of time. But that very popularity is a reason why the column needn't run in this position. It would probably have just as high readership on any other page. This drawing power might be used to attract readers to the editorial page or the local news section or any other that the editor wanted to encourage.

Spiking down a whole column of space for a continuing feature places a handicap on the makeup man; on an 8-column page it cuts down his area for maneuvering by 12½%. This makes it more difficult, of course, to achieve the markedly different front page the editor seeks for every issue.

The makeup man should have the privilege at least of lowering the column heading to anywhere in the top of the page. If the column must run on the front page, ideally its placement should be allowed anywhere on the left half of the page, even well below the fold.

The Index

Sometimes the fixed column is the *summary index*. The simple *list index* often runs in column 1, but it is so short that it can anchor the lower left corner and yet leave most of the first column for regular news display.

Metropolitan newspapers, with their scores or even hundreds of pages, certainly need an *index*. It is expecting too much of the reader to flip through all those pages to find the sports section or the editorial page. For smaller papers, however, the value of an index is debatable.

If the paper has no more than four sections, if pagination is consistent, and if the total pages are no more than 48, it is my feeling that an index is not required. If the reader can be assured that sports news is always in the third section, it is not asking too much to have him riffle through 12 or 16 pages to find what he seeks.

The simplest index would probably list: amusements, business, classified advertising, comics, crossword, editorials, family or women, obituaries, radio-TV, sports, state—and perhaps local—news, and weather, plus the most favorite columnists. Those departments which always get a

Fig. 97. Chimney technique. *Hornell* (N.Y.) *Tribune* builds two chimneys, one of photos in W-column, another of heads in cols. 6-7.

Sunday Pantagraph of Bloomington, Ill., opposite, builds 3-column chimney at left of page. Note use of art with heads. Note, too, unusual accent face in hammer in cols. 6-7.

section page need not be listed nor need those with an easy-to-find and regular position—comics on the second-last page, for instance.

The simple index lists mainly departments; the summary index lists individual stories with a sentence or two in recap. These must then be classified. *Today* does this fairly typically. It devotes its entire W-column to the summary and breaks it down into SPACE, of great interest to its Cape Kennedy readers; WORLD; NATION; FLORIDA and AREA. It also lists three or four SPECIALS, usually features that are not important enough to be included in the summaries. EVERYDAY FEATURES lists, without any explanatory matter, such items as bridge, comics, editorials, letters, weather, etc.

A few newspapers run such a summary inside, usually page 2. Its primary function is to enable the hurried reader to get a capsule report of the news in a few minutes. Whether this is good or bad is debatable—and unknown. It may build circulation among those who enjoy the convenience; but it may also cut down readership because the reader may not feel impelled to travel through the entire paper or even to go to another page.

Whatever the form of the index, its own position should be constant. The size of a summary will preclude its being moved around casually. The simple index ought not to be moved more than one column horizontally or 3 inches vertically from its customary position. The index is usually in a full or sideless box and, in this form, is effective as a corner anchor.

Illinois Shows Signs of Humor

There are signs that this isn't a dog-eat-dog world after all. At least there are signs of good humor in Illinois.

Take the sign in a Chicago Chinese restaurant: "We chop our own suey."

Or the note on a windshield on Ash Street, in Springfield: "I have just run into your car. People have seen me and are watching me write this. They think I am giving you my name and address. They are wrong."

In Peoria maternity shop: "We Provide the Accessories After the Fact."

In window of Urbana loan company: "We serve the man who has everything . . . but hasn't paid for it."

In pet shop in East St. Louis: "For Sale—Saint Bernard puppies. Guaranteed double your dog in a month, or your money back."

On the back of a large truck motoring through Marion: "Avoid Probate: "Don't Pass on My Right Side!"

On meat market in Danville: "Your friendly used-cow dealer."

Posted on lawn in Joliet: "Sick lawn: Absolutely No Visitors."

Over the bar in Rockford tavern: "We have a pay-as-you-glow plan."

A gas station near a ramp entrance to Northwest Tollway advises: "Buy here—no price war on I-90!"

In Oak Park bake shop: "Apple Turnovers!"

Near fire hydrant at the entrance to Centennial Building, in Springfield: "Park now, pay later."

In window of Decatur reducing salon: "Come in and Shoo and Fat."

In Elgin Italian restaurant: "Have you tangled with our spaghetti?"

Near boatyard outside Niota, on the Mississippi: "Trespassers will be drowned."

In Mattoon garage: "We stand in Front of our brake jobs."

Posted in a cemetery in suburban Chicago: "Persons are prohibited from picking flowers from any but their own graves."

Over a display of pamphlets on diets, exercise, and figure control in Galesburg dime store: "Please pay at the candy counter."

Over the box office of a small movie theater in Freeport: "First run, if you haven't seen it."

Over the bar in downtown Chicago hotel: "Scotch and Soda $1. With consultation $2."

On the outskirts of a small town in Hardin County: "Slow. No hospital."

Highway sign on Route 101, near Brooklyn: "Crossroad ahead, better humor it."

The Sunday Pantagraph

Bloomington-Normal, Ill.
Sunday, Nov. 17, 1968

Section D — Features

Faculty Member's Play To Be Premiered at ISU

Jail Visitor

Town preacher, played by Allan Sincox (lower left), is welcomed to jail by sheriff (Harry Hughes). Minister is visiting two hitchhikers held in jail, portrayed by Michael Dice, left rear, and Robert Mays.

The premier performance of "In Emerald," original play by Lonn Pressnall of the Illinois State University theater staff, is slated for presentation by University Theater players through Saturday.

All productions will be in Mable Clare Allen Theater in the Centennial building starting at 8 p.m.

Tickets are on sale in the theater box office Monday through Friday from noon to 1:30 p.m. and 4 to 6 p.m The number to call for telephone reservations is 438-2375.

Dr. Ruby A. Hauseman, assistant professor of theater, is directing the production. She describes the action of the play which takes place in Emerald, USA, a small provincial town.

"Two hitch-hikers, one from Minnesota and the other from Ontario, Canada, are apprehended in Emerald by law officers. They are charged for hitch-hiking, sassing an officer, driving with a "funny" license plate and possession of alcoholic beverages. The play develops the conflict between the hitch-hikers and the townspeople."

Members of the cast are Harry Hughes, ISU sophomore from Pekin as Sheriff Eugene Lark; Anne Crawford, graduate student from Johnson City, Tenn., Mrs. Mardi Lark, and Phil Gibboney, junior from Lewistown, as Deputy Fred Dass. Michael Dice, Country Club Hills senior as Ray Hickman, and Robert Mays, freshman of 1017 W. Wood, as Kelly Michael Harlan, play the hitch-hikers.

Others in the cast are Linda Zoucha, junior from Arnold, Neb., as Ginny Tilton; Allan R. Sincox, sophomore from Dixon as the Rev. E. Clifford Waters, and Robert Griffin, graduate student of Mineola, N.Y., in the role of Judge Tilton.

Ruth A. Wenk, freshman speech major from Woodstock, is the assistant director.

Set designer is Charles E. Howard, associate professor of theater, while Jerry L. Davis, assistant professor, is in charge of lighting. Graduate assistant Patricia Campbell of Toledo, Ohio, is the costumer.

Pressnall, the playwright, joined the ISU faculty in September, 1967. A native of Nebraska, he completed his undergraduate work at Peru State College, Peru, Neb., and received a master's degree in speech at the University of Illinois. He is an instructor in theater at ISU.

Education Never Finished Today

By David Nydick
UPI Education Specialist

Education is rapidly becoming a lifetime activity. Many adults participate in continuing education programs. The purposes are many and include improvement of ones vocational ability, recreation, and personal interest.

As a result, a high percentage of college students attend on a part time basis. In addition many adults are completing high school or going to trade and other specialty schools while holding full time positions.

Colleges usually estimate that a student should spend two hours of study time for each hour of class time. Depending upon the nature of the course, trade and technical programs will also require study time.

Before becoming a part time student, it should be remembered that the courses and study will probably take place after a full day of work. Sufficient time should be planned for meals and rest. It is most difficult to concentrate on learning when one is hungry or tired.

A student in a part time program will only get out of a course what he puts into it. In order to benefit the most from a course, careful planning will be necessary. The following should be considered.

The choice and number of courses are important factors if a student is going to be successful. These two factors should be considered together. Some courses involve only class time with additional laboratory work while others involve extensive outside study time. The number of courses taken should be based upon these considerations in relation to the individual's available time.

Study periods should be scheduled for times when the student is well rested. Morning hours are ideal. Fatigue naturally occurs after a day of full time work followed by classwork.

Vim

Ives Views Pop Music With Twinkling Eyes

HOLLYWOOD (AP) — Burl Ives, 59, maintains a youthful view of the pop-music scene.

Burl Ives

To the big daddy of folk singers the Beatles are "marvelous." Bob Dylan is "terribly gifted," Donovan is "wonderful," Peter, Paul and Mary are "great, and so is Lou Rawls."

Said the man-mountain of a minstrel: "There's nobody that really annoys me. Tiny Tim—I think he's great fun."

Ives spoke during a midday break in his career as dramatic actor—one of several lives the onetime Illinois farm boy juggles.

Sometimes he writes books—"seven or eight so far, including one of short stories, an autobiography and a mulligan stew, a little bit of everything."

Sometimes he's a camper-truck vagabond visiting, as he did this summer, scenic spots of Canada, California, Arizona and New Mexico. "I like to bat around," he says.

Basically—although he won an Oscar as a supporting actor in "The Big Country" in 1959—he is what Carl Sandberg called "the mightiest ballad singer of any century."

His Falstaffian bulk clad in buckskins for a guest role in Fess Parker's "Daniel Boone" television series, the bearded balladeer was now also a philosopher.

"Everything is in a state of change. Change is the only thing that's changeless. When you realize that, you do not get attached to the present."

In his own music, Ives said, "I change my style from flowing phrase to the more dramatic, to the style of the day. I don't know that I keep up, but I'm not tied to 'Jimmy cracked corn'."

2nd Term

Grant Renewed

The Negro Ensemble Company, which made a firm impression in its first season with four productions, will begin its second terms Dec. 17 under a new Ford Foundation grant of $750,000 covering two years.

The schedule of four productions at the St. Marks Playhouse will begin with "God Is A Guess What?" (sic) by Ray McIver which will run through Jan. 12.

Lonne Elder's "Ceremonies in Dark Old Men" is slated for Feb. 4-March 2. Three one-act plays, not yet chosen, will make up the third production, March 25-April 20. A musical, "Man Better Man" by Erroll Hill, will be presented June 24-July 20.

The company will appear for two weeks, May 5-17, at the Aldwych Theater in London as a participant in the Royal Shakespeare Company's annual World Theater Season. It will present Peter Weiss' "The Song of the Lusitanian Bogey," which was part of last season's program. And one of this season's plays. **(UPI)**

Music Teachers Clinic Planned

Music teachers from throughout Illinois are expected to participate in a "new music" clinic at Illinois State University on Saturday, Nov. 23.

New materials for band, orchestra and choral groups will be performed by six ISU vocal and instrumental organizations and the University High School choir.

Co-sponsored by the ISU music department and Educational Music Bureau, Inc., Chicago, the clinic will focus on selection techniques for music educators.

Dr. Joseph E. Wilson, head of the department, conceived the affair as an annual presentation at ISU.

There will be no fee for attendance.

Registration will be at 8:30 a.m. in the Centennial Building. Sessions will be held in the lecture hall and elsewhere in the building through 4:45 p.m.

Music materials will be displayed in the lobby. Complimentary scores will be available for clinic participants.

Paul E. Rosene of the music department is handling information on the clinic at ISU.

Best Sellers

Fiction

"The Salzburg Connection," MacInnes.
"Airport," Hailey.
"Preserve and Protect," Drury.
"The Senator," Pearson.
"Couples," Updike.

Nonfiction

"The Money Game," Smith.
"Memoirs," Krock.
"The Rich and the Super-Rich," Lundberg.
"Between Parent and Child," Ginott.
"The American Challenge," Servan-Schreiber.

Mason in 'Consent'

HOLLYWOOD (UPI)—James Mason returned from film making in Australia to report to New York and location shooting on Columbia's "Age of Consent."

New York Company To Revive 'Carnival'

The annual Christmas holiday musical revival at the New York City Center will be "Carnival," a great hit of the 1960-61 season.

It will be played by the City Center Light Opera Company Dec. 12-Jan. 5. This is its first revival in New York.

Sexy Subject

By JACQUELINE KORONA

EAST LANSING, Mich. (AP) — Michigan State University has announced plans to bring the topic of sex—long relegated to gab sessions in dorms—into the classroom this winter.

The university will conduct a seven-week colloquy on "Sexuality: A Search for Perspective," aimed at informing both students and faculty "not in terms of sex acts or sex behavior but in human relationships."

Orchestra Night Set In Peoria

The Peoria Symphony Orchestra will present its second concert of the season Tuesday at the Shrine Mosque in Peoria. The performance will begin at 8:15 p.m.

The concert has been designated "orchestra night." Members of the orchestra will be the soloists.

Season tickets are being handled by Mrs. David Rittmiller, 4129 Devon Lane, Peoria.

Orders Stopped on 1969 Coin Sets

The United States Mint surprised the nation's coin collectors with the announcement that the mint stopped taking orders for the 1969 proof coin sets on Nov. 6 of this year.

The mint's maximum production of more than three million sets has been reached and all orders received after Nov. 6 are to be returned to the senders.

Proof coin sets consist of one each of the five denominations of circulated coins from the cent through the half dollar.

Production of the 1969 sets will not begin until 1969 and will continue throughout the year.

One of the oddities of the coin world is the clogged letters on coins. A clogged letter happens when a chip breaks off of the die along the edge, sometimes inside the loop of the letter. The characters most often clogged are the numbers "6" and "9" and the letter R in the word Liberty. This is an oddity and not a major "find."

Quite often beginning collectors often mistake minor details or oddities for a major "find" only to be disappointed when they are told that what they have is fairly common or of no value.

The Joint Commission on Coinage will meet again in Washington in December and this time its major consideration will be the question of what to do with the government's hoard of three million silver dollars. Although the overwhelming majority of collectors prefer distribution to the hobby, it is possible the Commission may decide to have the government melt the coins down. The melting down should end the sticky problem of distribution though several ideas have been advanced to the commission.

Children's Theater Starts Future Stars on Their Way

Now in its 21st year at the fabled Atlantic City Steel Pier, the Tony Grant Children's Theater is the only complete theater in the country that devotes itself entirely to the discovery, development and display of the budding talent in young teen-agers and children.

Singer-actor Frankie Avalon, who now is one of the country's top stars earning about $18,000 a week, chuckled as he recalled when he got his start in Grant's productions for several summers.

"It's amazing the experience it gives you," he said. "He taught me how to bow, how to get on stage and how to wait for the applause."

Connie Francis, Peggy March and Ronnie Fields, who won an award last year for doing the choreography for "Cabaret" also got their starts in the Steel Pier Children's Theater.

Grant travels all over the country auditioning acts to appear on the Pier. Last winter, from November to May, Grant reviewed nearly 5,000 acts throughout the country.

He selected 240 acts for the 10-week season—24 acts are used every week. The show is entirely new each week. There are four shows a day comprised of 12 acts. And every act has a backup act.

Grant says that the total number of performers in his acts adds up to about 150 youngsters weekly. **(AP)**

Stamp Nook

New Luxembourg Stamps Aid Handicapped Children

By Ron Andre

Luxembourg has announced its annual Caritas set of stamps for issuance on Dec. 5. There are six stamps of this new semi-postal series in values of 50c plus 10c, 1.50F plus 25c, 2F plus 25c, 3F plus 50c, 6F plus 1F and 13F plus 6.90F. This totals 35 francs which would be 70 cents in United States money. The surcharge value on the set goes to help handicapped children.

All the stamps bear likenesses of children with the exception of the lowest value which shows the Medico - Professional Institure created on the initiative of the Luxembourg League for Mentally and Cerebrally Disabled Children. The home houses children of from 15 to 20 years of age.

The Caritas set is an annual event for Luxembourg.

Oct. 24 was the first day of issue by the Republic of Rwandaise of its new set of six stamps honoring the Mexican Olympics. The usual Olympic insignia of rings is included in the design with each stamp showing a different sport. The layout of each stamp is well executed to make it a nice-looking set. Values were 20, 40, 60, and 80 centimes and 38 and 60 francs.

The Republic of Rwandaise has also issued a set of 10 attractive flower stamps showing a variety of flower on each stamp. The top value of this second set is a 100-franc stamp. The official rate of exchange shows the Rwandaise franc to be worth 2 cents in United States money with the unofficial rate at a little over one-half cent per franc.

Three of New Luxembourg Stamps

Ed Ames--His Wife Owns Him

By Joan Crosby
NEA Entertainment Editor

Ed Ames had just completed a successful engagement at the Empire Room of the Waldorf-Astoria Hotel, and he was heading back to his California home to rest for a month.

But don't bet on it.

Big Ed, whose RAC Victor albums have been consistent best sellers, is one of the world's most energetic men. "I don't know where he gets all the energy," his petite wife, Sarita, said.

At the moment, Ed is busy launching his own production company which is seeking scripts for Broadway productions, with or without him in them, and signing artists for the company's record label.

An opponent of hard rock, and outspoken about it, Ed nevertheless has signed a rock group to record. "Tentatively we will call them The Human Touch, but that may be changed," he said. "But they will sing clean, happy songs, not acid, sex-laden, hate-filled songs."

Ed also is very close to signing for another TV series. But unlike Daniel Boone, which he left this year after four seasons as the Oxford-educated Indian, Mingo, this would be a musical variety series.

"It's a different kind of approach to a variety series," he added, "and getting the format set takes a lot of work. All three networks are interested in it, and there is a film company involved in the production."

Ed's company is called Sarita Productions, and his wife is actively involved in the administration. "Actually," Ed smiles, "I'm under contract to her. She owns me."

Ed Ames

Uganda Visit
His Concepts

Africa the Moon," on the Congo bor-
spent a der, and game preserves in Ken-
ud huts ya and Uganda; interesting an-
ty, and ecdotes, and the firm opinion
Trinity that "Africa isn't as primitive
yd, Pa., as we think."
in Kay- "Operation Crossroads: Af-
"Opera- rica," founded six years ago by
i" pro- Dr. James E. Robinson, former
a few Harlem clergyman, has sent
d hut over 1,000 Americans on assist-
t that." ance projects to Africa.
Ameri- Robert, like many other stu-
n who dents, raised about $1,000 of the

cil Eyes School Boar

LIUS   funds," the Mayor said.   The board annually consumes
apparently   STATE LAW strips the Coun-   about one third of the city's rev-
nnual inde- cil of any control over how the enues. This fiscal year the Coun-
of the way   board spends its money. But cil has allocated it about $13.6
tion spends "we have to appropriate the   million.
today that, money," the Mayor said, "and Board President Keith B. Hook
al Council   at least we should know how it said today he had assumed that
night, the   is spent." independent audits of the
sent agreed Other councilmen who were at board's finances were being
h an audit   the meeting said one question made already. He agreed that
he balance   the Council hopes an audit would "if they aren't they should be."
s are au-   answer is whether the board de-
e of great   liberately consumes surpluses at THE MAYOR said the coun-
evaluating   the end of each fiscal year to cilmen at the meeting Wednes-
equests for make its budgets seem tight and day night did not decide whether
             buttress its requests for larger to order an audit of the board's
             ones. last fiscal year, which could be
                  used in deliberations this Winter

The Hartford Times

Thursday, Octob

d Report Due
School Need

l is the survey will follow at 9:30 present teacher salary sched-
a p.m. ule without the raises proposed
Jni- City share of the Harvard for instructional employes.
uct study costs would be $2 r. Meinke has recommend-
s. and board members v employe salary sched-
aily ready asked th me effective for what-
tion appropriat the present budg-
an fi

Appea

Fig. 98. Sidebar treatment. Outline arrows, above, used by *Hartford* (Conn.) *Times* to indicate sidebar and to tie together picture and story. Flat black triangle is used by *Detroit* (Mich.) *Free Press*, below left, and black arrow, below right, in experimental page by *Detroit News.*

BOB HOPE accepts a gift from Gen. William Westmoreland when he puts on his first show in South Vietnam at Saigon's Tan Son Nhut Airport. That's actress Carol Baker applauding. — AP Photo

Bob Hope in Vietnam

Reds Don't Have a Blast
At This Christmas Party

BY BOB HOPE

SAIGON — Well, here we are in South Vietnam, this time without a welcome from the Viet Cong.

Last Christmas the Reds blew up a U.S. officers' billet 10 minutes before we arrived.

I'm not a bit nervous. I may even sleep on top of the bed this time. Carol Baker told me she's never been in a combat zone before, and when I said I heard differently, she explained, "Well, not this kind of combat."

MY FIRST audience here was a group of 10,000 soldiers in an open. Martha Raye met us at the airport and Cardinal Spellman got here Thursday. It must be a lonesome Christmas back in the states.

WE WOUND UP our tour of Thailand Thursday with two more shows.

The first was near the Laotian border, for about 1,500 U.S. airmen and the 79th Australian Air Squadron, which is part of SEATO.

We worked on a stage set up on a section of runway and it was an interesting experience. I've been heckled during a performance, but this is the first time I've had my hair parted in mid-joke by a blast from a jet.

Before taking off for our second stop, we did a radio show for the 40 guys who man "Green Mountain," a rebel and beautiful Queen Sirikit. It was a memorable evening and the food was great. But I wish Les Brown hadn't asked for a doggy bag.

And Love It
GIs Play Santa
To Viet Orphans

VUNG TAU, South Vietnam — UPI — American soldiers poorly provided Christmas to 61 chi in an

Hope Jeers
War Foes;
GIs Cheer

From UPI and AP
SAIGON — U.S. demonstra tors against the U.S. re Vietnam were targets Hope

offa Goes to Prison
upreme Court Rule

ott
ster
ls

ay
Protest
ng' Plan

8-Year
Sentence
Affirme

BY TOM JOYCE
WASHI GTON, De
a on an 4-3 de-
the U.S. Supreme Co
day upheld the jur
ering convictions of
ster President Ja
Hoffa and three co
ants.

TEAMSTERS' TOP TWO PARTED BY HIGH COURT RULING
Hoffa (Left) Now Will Hand Reins to V-P Fitzsimmons — UPI Telephoto

Fitzsimmons Is Hoffa's Sub

By JIM CRELLIN

One of Teamster President James R. Hoffa's closest and most trusted friends, Frank E. Fitzsimmons of Detroit, will run the 1.7 million-member Teamsters Union when Hoffa goes to prison.

Hoffa today ordered Fitzsimmons to the Teamsters headquarters in Washington immediately upon hearing that the U.S. Supreme Court

▼

Detroit Teamsters
Shocked, Furious

By JIM CRELLIN

"I think it is a shame that the highest court in our country has upheld his conviction which was reached through perjured testimony and lies from the government's star witness," Riddle said.

"They took a man right out of jail to testify against Jimmy," he said.

Riddle said he talked to his sister, Viola, who is Hoffa's daughter, shortly after learning of the decision. He said he did

Legislatur
May End
Georgi T

WASHINGTON, Dec. 12 The Supreme Court ruled tod that the Georgia legislature decide the deadlocked governo ship race between Dem and former Rep. Howard M. Calloway Gov. Carter C. Maddox and Re can Howard M. Calloway

See HOFFA—Page 11A

Jumping Stories

Editors used to pride themselves on the number of jumps they could make off page one. They were convinced that readers wouldn't turn to inside pages unless forced to by a jump. But this technique that they prized so much was at best nonfunctional and frequently malfunctional.

We find that when the typical story jumps off the front page, 70% of the readers who are still with the story will refuse to jump. It is a rare, rare, rare story that will have 100% readership of even the leed; most stories lose readers en route. So by the time a story gets to the jumping point, the 30% of the readers that it may hope to carry to an inside page is going to be a small percentage of the whole potential readership. There will be mighty slim dividends for the investment of setting the jumped type. In this case, jumping is certainly nonfunctional.

But suppose the reader does jump; there is always the chance that he will not return to the front page but continue reading on from the jump page. This means that other copy on page one, as well as all that on intervening pages, will be unread. It is clear that jumping can be highly malfunctional.

Even if the reader jumps off and returns to the front page once or twice, he will not do so indefinitely. More and more editors are limiting the number of stories that may be jumped off page one; many ban jumps entirely. Some stories, of course, have so much inherent interest to the reader that he will follow a jump with eagerness.

But what does the desk do with stories that are too long to run in their entirety on the front page? The stories that typically run long are almost always concerned with governmental units, meetings of township, county, village, or city boards, or school boards. These can easily be broken in logical and self-contained shorter stories. A school-board meeting might consider teacher appointments, plans for a new school, preliminary budget figures, and effects of new state legislation. Putting all these into one story will result in several galleys of type—and an inevitable jump. It also means that the typical reader will become tired or bored long before he has finished this reading marathon. If each of the major topics on the agenda were handled as a separate story, jumps could be eliminated. And important news would be hailed by its own headline instead of being buried in the customary tabulation of "The school board also. . . ."

When stories are thus broken into smaller units, several of them might run on page one. A reefer should call the reader's attention to related

Fig. 99. Index treatment. *Elkhart* (Ind.) *Truth* has unusual index at top right of page; art border is linked to that of flag. *Elmira* (N.Y.) *Star-Gazette* combines simple listing with four summaries in terminal-area box. *Pueblo* (Colo.) *Star-Journal and Sunday Chieftain* has two indexes, simple list at foot of col. 1, listing in display type at TA.

THE RHODESIAN summit talks collapsed and Premier Ian Smith prepared to fly home, declaring that Prime Minister Wilson's concessions were insignificant. Page A.

VIOLENCE IN the Irish civil rights controversy spread to Dublin and six plicemen were injured in a battle with 400 demonstrators outside the British Embassy. Page A.

ONE OF THE five surviving sextuplets in Birmingham, England, died after surgery for an intestinal ailment. Page A.

SLOGANS TO be used in the Soviet Union's observance of the 51st anniversary of the Bolshevik revolution made no mention of Czechoslovakia and had no fraternal greeting from Albania or Yugoslavia. Page A.

NIGERIA will attempt to negotiate a settlement of the civil war with the rebel Biafrans. Page A.

GEN. CURTIS LeMay, Wallace's vice presidential running mate, said the U.S. should resume full-scale bombing of North Vietnam and close the port of Haiphong. Page 2.

Top of the Morning

STUDENTS for a Democratic Society have called for a nationwide student strike and big-city demonstrations on Nov. 5 to express disdain for the presidential campaign and the election process. Page 7.

THE SOVIET newspaper Pravda said extremist Israeli leaders are pushing the Mideast situation into another military confrontation with the Arab nations. Page A.

THE NEWEST Seattle SuperSonic was on the NBA club's bench last night. Guard Lenny Wilkens, obtained from Atlanta for Walt Hazzard, predicted playoffs for Seattle. Page 36

MARTIN Johanson, founder of the Millionair Club Charity, celebrated his 81st birthday at a party attended by 300. Page 21.

PRESIDENT JOHNSON signed a bill extending subsidies on U.S. merchant ships. Page 6.

THREE NEW Congressional Medal of Honor winners were honored with a plaque at Washelli during a dedication ceremony. Page 21.

THE UNBEATEN Los Angeles Rams got a late-game field goal to edge the defending National Football League champion Green Bay Packers, 16-14. It was the Pack's third loss in five games. Page 36.

EMMETT WATSON, P-I columnist, went to the Washington-Oregon football game and performed a good deed for an urchin at the stadium. The good deed backfired, though, and to top off the day's miseries he saw a coworker beat the Huskies with a field goal. Page 13.

Seattle's Greene Equals Record

CHARLES GREENE of Seattle raced to a record-tying 10 flat time in his heat race of the 100 meters as the Olympic Games competition opened yesterday in Mexico City. For P-I Sports Editor John Owens' on-the-scene report turn to Page 35.

LOOKING MORE like an English lord than a former longshoreman, Eric Hoffer, P-I columnist, came to Seattle yesterday. He took in the scenery, took a deep breath and said, "Just like home!" He's from San Francisco. Page 12.

THE NEW GRIFFIN HOME for boys was dedicated yesterday, and Friends of Youth, Inc., announced at the same time that construction will start soon on a second such residence. Page 13.

IN TODAY'S P-I

Four Sections

SEATTLE

Post-Intelligencer

THE VOICE OF THE NORTHWEST

Monday, October 14, 1968

SUNRISE

S★★ MA 2-2000 10¢

THE WEATHER — Periods of rain today and tonight, showers and partial clearing tomorrow. High near 53; low tonight about 45. YESTERDAY'S WEATHER: High 56; low 49. Record low: 36, Oct. 13, 1890. Table, Page 34.

Full Text, Page B

O'Connell Makes Savage Defense

BY SHELBY SCATES
P-I Political Writer

Atty. Gen. John O'Connell combined a televised defense of his Nevada card-playing yesterday with a savage attack on Dan Evans, "a governor who lies."

The Democratic candidate for governor was fighting for his political life in response to a Seattle Times article which said he wrote a "$10,000 check" payable to a Las Vegas hotel in December, 1965.

In the roughest outburst of the campaign thus far, O'Connell charged that Evans, the Republican incumbent seeking re-election, did not tell the truth when he stated that he had no knowledge of the document prior to publication of the news article.

EVANS REACTS

Gov. Evans last night said he was away from his Olympia executive mansion with his family all yesterday afternoon and did not watch television.

Later, where he was attending a four-hour session with advertising and public relations people in the board room of the Cole and Webber Advertising Agency, the governor said he was aware that O'Connell had said that Washington has a "governor who lies."

Vigorously, Evans added:

"Don't worry! I'll have plenty to say about that!"

He declined to make any further comment until a transcript of the taped recording of the program is completed for his personal reading.

Neal McReynolds, the governor's press secretary, said "we" taped the O'Connell telecast while it was in progress.

ANOTHER DEBATE

The two candidates meet face to face Wednesday night in a televised debate certain to be heated by their recent exchanges over the $10,000 document.

The document described by the Times as a "check" was actually a "line of credit," said O'Connell in his telecast, and it was never cashed.

O'Connell admitted a penchant for card-playing and said he was in Las Vegas in Dec. 1965 for a bout with the blackjack dealers.

"All this (the article) discloses is that I have played cards for money under legal circumstances," he concluded.

Displaying newspaper photos of the $10,000 document, O'Connell said it was not precisely as he recalled it.

"This is not a check," he said. "And they referred to it as a check . . . nor was this cashed."

He noted that a corner had been torn from the document and said "up here should be maybe the words 'line of credit' maybe 'non-negotiable' maybe 'please hold' or words to that effect."

A campaign aide said such lines of credit are established with a gaming house for their protection. They may or may not be negotiated, depending on the player's losses.

Regardless, O'Connell said he did not lose $10,000. O'Connell did not explain why the line of credit was as high as $10,000.

"I lost $900 and I recall it specifically because I wasn't very happy about it," he said. "When I returned I sent the hotel

JOHN O'CONNELL
Attacks Governor

the money that I owed them and about the same time I received a call from the hotel saying their accounting office had

Please turn to Page B, Column 1

Apollo Whirls On; Crew Sets TV Stage

SPACE CENTER, Houston — (UPI) — Apollo 7 and its jaunty crew soared smoothly around earth yesterday on their 11-day trial for a flight to the moon, fighting off colds and bracing themselves for televised "show business."

"We're just pumping along," reported Walt Cunningham in the third day of the textbook flight, much of it spent in minor equipment repairs.

He said spaceship commander Walt Schirra appeared to be defeating his cold. Cunningham took a pill himself to ward off developing symptoms of the same virus.

CHEERED

Schirra's improved health and the completion of about half of the important tests of the entire flight seemed to bring good cheer to Schirra, Cunningham and Eisele. They joked with ground controllers occasionally throughout the day.

Early today, however, the astronauts launched a "witch hunt" for an unexplained problem that knocked out all the alternating current electricity on their spacecraft for five minutes.

Flight director Eugene Kranz said at the space center if the condition had continued it would have meant the end of the 11-day mission.

But Cunningham, systems engineer in the spacecraft was able to reset the electrical supply and Kranz said he did not consider the mission to be in danger at the present.

Today the astronauts plan to appear on live television right after they wake up.

During the afternoon, Eisele used his spacecraft scanning telescope to spot Orion and about 10 other stars in broad daylight, practicing navigational procedures for moon trips.

Flight director Glynn Lunney estimated in a briefing that the mission of Apollo 7 has already completed about half of its objectives.

The crew spent some time working on a troublesome cooling unit, although it was not critical to the flight's success.

However, the crew complained that two bags of chocolate pudding had burst their seams, rendering them impossible to eat although the chocolate did not escape into the cabin. The astronauts, having problems with a hand camera, took it apart and later reported it was "working fine with a combination of oil and grease removal and nose cream."

Optics problems hampered their efforts, but the astronauts proved they were able to spot the burned-out top stage of their Saturn 1 launcher orbiting more than 300 miles away from them.

The long-range sighting was one of their few assignments during a quiet afternoon in space. Their cone-shaped spaceship was flying 185.5 to 140 miles above the earth, while the launcher spun around the earth

Please turn to Page 7, Column 3

4 Found Dead In North End

Four members of one family were found dead yesterday in a North End home at 134 NE 61st St.

They were Jack C. Johanson, 35; his wife, Katherine, 33; their daughter, Tina Marie, 2; and a family guest, Mrs. Johanson's half-brother, Pfc. Edwin Mathews, 19, stationed at Ft. Benning, Ga.

Coroner Leo M. Sowers said the four were last seen Tuesday and had been dead since about then. Autopsies to determine the cause of the deaths were set for today.

Sowers said there was no evidence of violence or foul play.

FURNACE

Relatives told police the Johansons had their old furnace converted to gas last Tuesday. It was reported that a crack was found on the inside of the furnace and that

Please Turn to Page 6, Column 1

Snipers Fire On Panama Guard As Arias Vows War

Junta Installs New Cabinet

PANAMA — (AP) — Snipers opened fire last night on National Guard soldiers after the junta that overthrew President Arnulfo Arias installed a provisional civilian-military government, naming a guard leader as president. Arias pledged a "total war" against the new regime.

(Two National Guard soldiers were killed and at least two civilians wounded in the Caledonia and Maranon areas of Panama City, it was reported by United Press International.)

From his refuge in the U.S.-administered Canal Zone, Arias, ousted after 11 days in office, predicted his followers would soon start a general strike backed by urban guerrillas searching out guard leaders.

'DEATH'

Unless the military chiefs "leave the places they control," Arias said, "there's going to be death and desolation."

The shooting was about a mile from the presidential palace where Col. Jose M. Pinilla was sworn in as provisional president. Pinilla, who helped lead the bloodless coup that deposed Arias Friday night, said the new government would stay in power only until conditions permit the restoration of "civilian authority."

The new government includes eight civilians picked to serve as cabinet ministers.

MANIFESTO

In a statement to the Panamanian people that bore his signature, Arias declared: "The time for action has come. To the streets men and women of my country, this is the moment for going out on the streets to fight. The order of the day is to take up arms against the little group of military traitors of the fatherland."

The manifesto was taped for broadcast over a pro-Arias clandestine radio station.

The fighting subsided after approximately one hour. Crowds drifted from the streets without prodding from the Guard.

In his oath-taking statement, Pinilla stressed the provisional character of his government. He said: "We do not believe in staying in power indefinitely. This is but an historical parenthesis which would end as soon as the conditions of law and order are restored."

CHARGES

The message, read by the minister of the presidency, says attempts by Arias to "destroy representative democracy" led to the action against him. Arias, the message claimed, violated the constitution by removing a supreme court justice. The statement also said Arias sought to alter the National Guard's chain of command.

At Pinilla's side during the ceremonies was Col. Bolivar Urrutia, described as a member of the government although his precise position was not made clear. When a first post-Arias government was announced Saturday, Urrutia and Pinilla were identified as its co-leaders.

Today's Chuckle

After you lose your membership in it, the younger generation seems pretty bad.

Reds Mauled; Green Beret Camp Safe

SAIGON — (UPI) — South Vietnamese troops mauled North Vietnamese regulars around the Thuong Duc Green Beret camp in a 12-hour battle that ended yesterday, and a large communist force was reported retreating from the An Hoa Valley outpost near Da Nang.

"I believe there is no longer any danger to the Thuong Duc camp," a U.S. official said of the strategic fortress which blocks a major communist infiltration route to Da Nang. The victory eased the general threat to Da Nang itself.

U.S. spokesmen estimated that 400 communists had been killed in the battle of Thuong Duc since Sept. 28, including 40 in fierce fighting Saturday night that raged hand-to-hand at times.

CASUALTIES

Overall allied losses in the two weeks of sharp combat included 22 U.S. Marines killed and 27 South Vietnamese killed. More than 80 U.S. Marines and more than 100 South Vietnamese were wounded. There were other undisclosed U.S. losses aboard several helicopters shot down.

Allied forces pursuing as many as 2,000 North Vietnamese infantrymen pushed unmolested yesterday through the rain-soaked jungles near Thuong Duc, 25 miles southwest of Da Nang, as U.S. B52s blasted the surrounding plains to block escape routes.

Below Saigon, U.S. land, sea and air forces yesterday battled a Viet Cong unit caught on a river bank, American spokesmen said.

They said at least 24 communists — and no Americans — had been killed in the fighting 30 miles below the capital.

The fighting has raged since a 9th Infantry Division patrol spotted the guerillas and drove them across rice paddies.

SWEEP

The South Vietnamese infantrymen sweeping the battlefield reported only light contact, indicating the communists may have withdrawn or have been battered by B52 pilots who dropped more than 300 tons of bombs on the valley only three miles from Thuong Duc.

To the south of Thuong Duc, 70 miles below Da Nang, American soldiers patrolling the coastal plains traded fire with a communist unit using Russian-made rifles and automatic weapons.

The Reds wilted in the face of heavy fire from U.S. helicopter gun ships, and withdrew late Saturday night leaving 18 comrades and eight weapons on the battlefield. There were no U.S. losses, spokesmen said.

To the north and south of Saigon, communist gunners fired a heavy barrage of 171 mortar rounds into South Vietnamese installations and cities in a series of attacks late Saturday and yesterday.

Fig. 100. *Seattle* (Wash.) *Post-Intelligencer* runs summary index above flag. Reverse head of index and SUNRISE ear are in cyan.

stories on inside pages. Readership of such inside stories will be markedly higher than that of jumped stories. If stories are locally written, it is easier for the reporter to write several short stories than one of *Gone With the Wind* length. If the long story is on the wire, it will require a new lead for each subdivision, but this is a simple task.

Following a jump story is annoying to the reader. If stories must jump, the desk should make the reader's job as simple as possible. The ideal jump is to the last page of the first section. The reader need not look for folio lines, he need not fold and unfold his paper; he merely flips from one outside page to the other.

An interesting technique has been used for many years by Scandinavian newspapers. When the reader comes to the jump, he merely turns his paper end-over-end. On the back page, the continuation of the jumped story is in the same column as it was on the front page. These jumped stories are, of course, upside down to the regular orientation.

Some papers run half the back page upside down, using self-contained stories as well as jumps to fill the area. The other half may run sideways as a tab page or it may be a half-page ad, either oriented to the editorial copy or made up as a full tab page and running sideways.

The advantage of this technique is that the reader always knows where to follow a jumped story; it is convenient to turn to the jump page. By using only half the jump page for editorial copy, it cuts down the area the eye must search to find the continuation.

A few American newspapers have adopted this practice, and each reports that reader reaction—after a moment of eyebrow raising—has been enthusiastically favorable.

Unfortunately the back page of section one, though it really is not a particularly desirable position, is so much coveted by the advertiser that he is willing to pay a premium for it. So in many cases, the editor must find a different jump page. His second choice should be page 2. Again the reader need not look for page numbers. He is instructed to "Turn to next page" and all he need do is flip a single leaf.

Page 3 is the next most desirable page for jumps.

(An interesting aside. The *National Observer* treats its readers politely. There is no peremptory "Turn to page 2." Instead the pleasant advice is "Turn to page 5, please." This unexpected courtesy has not gone unnoticed by the reader. Many a letter to the editor has expressed appreciation for this common civility.)

Under no circumstances should a story jump out of one section and into another. As any reader knows, the neat package that is the news-

U.S. Hopeful Despite Paris Peace Talks Snag

Weather Forecast

Portland - Vancouver — Fair Thursday after morning fog. High, 70; low Thursday night, near 45.
Portland Temperatures — High, 69; low, 46.

The Oregonian

VOL. CVIII—33,767   ★ ★ ★ ★ ★   THURSDAY, OCTOBER 24, 1968   92 PAGES   PRICE TEN CENTS

Door Open To Action By Hanoi

Harriman Hints Secret Sessions Now Under Way

By HEDRICK SMITH

PARIS — The United States apparently did not receive a satisfactory answer from North Vietnamese negotiators Wednesday to the latest American proposal for an end to bombing of the North and broadening the Vietnam talks to include South Vietnamese representatives.

But after the negotiating session, an American spokesman said the U.S. remains hopeful, suggesting that delicate negotiations are still under way. Later, allied diplomats said the "door is still open."

William J. Jorden, the American spokesman, put a generally pessimistic interpretation on W—

The Oregon Poll

Senate Race Trend Hints Photo Finish

Teachers Turn Down NYC Offer

Board Proposed Reinstatement For Ousted 79

NEW YORK (AP) — An embattled Brooklyn local school district offered a new peace proposal Wednesday, aimed at ending tie-up of the 1.1 million pupil public school system, but it was rejected by striking teachers.

Elsewhere on New York City's chaotic labor front, firemen joined policemen in a work slowdown for more pay.

The patrolmen were continuing to fight crime here—

Students Begin Trek Back to Classrooms on Tuesday

Prairie State's North Campus To Open Sept. 23

Parents: If your children are always out of the house, coming home late and continuously on the move, there is a reason for it.

What these youngsters, ranging in age from four to 24 or maybe higher, are doing is re-enacting the life of Paul Bryan and trying to crowd 30 days of living into one, or two.

Yes, the nemesis of the young — school — is back once again to take those kids off your hands, and what's more give the— of America a much-needed education.

CHICAGO HEIGHTS STAR

SKyline 5-6161

68th Year   40 Pages — 4 Sections   SUNDAY, SEPTEMBER 1, 1968   Ten Cents Per Single Copy   ★   No. 44

SKyline 5-6161

MACH Pleads Case

REJECT TAX CUT APPEAL

Mothers Want School Lunch Policy Revoked

More than 500 mothers of school children in Lynn have petitioned the School Committee to alter a long-standing schedule and allow youngsters to remain at the schools through the lunch period.

A delegation of about 30 of these mothers attended last night's meeting of the School Committee and when they left they received a promise that a study of their proposal would be undertaken by Supt. of Schools Lawrence G. McGinn.

The present schedule in Lynn elementary schools calls for a 9 a.m. start in classes, dismissal of pupils for a lunch period from 11:45 a.m. to 1 p.m. and resumption of classes from 1 to 3 p.m.

The mothers' group asks that the pupils be allowed to remain at their desks through

the lunch period and eat their lunches in the school.

Mrs. Carol Meechin, 17 Hilda Road, served as spokesman for the group.

She said that the group would like to see full sessions at the elementary schools especially during the winter months. Mrs. Meechin pointed out that all neighboring communities of Lynn allow elementary school youngsters to eat their lunches in schools and called on the committee to abandon a policy that "made no sense."

Committeeman Robert E. Webber then suggested that the matter be studied by Supt. McGinn and that a full report be made to the committee.

Committeeman David L. Warden said he sided with the mothers adding the committee had been delinquent in the past by not revoking this policy.

Warden said that he did not think Supt. McGinn, was "for this new idea philosophically," and also expressed doubt as to the wisdom of any study noting that in the past other petitions by residents to the committee "had been studied to death."

Warden's statements were greeted by a loud round of applause from the mothers.

Jeers and other sounds of disapproval erupted from the mothers' side when Committeeman William R. Fallon criticized Warden for his statements and proceeded to defend the school administrators as "men who never ducked any issues." Fallon called on Warden to apologize to Supt. McGinn for the comments he had made concerning the superintendent.

See SCHOOLS On Page 2

Daily Evening Item

VOL. 173 — NO. 81   22 PAGES   LYNN, MASS., FRIDAY, SEPTEMBER 13, 1968   593-7700   TEN CENTS

Fortas Refuses Committee Bid To Testify

Stay Alert — It's Friday The 13th

It's Friday the 13th, for the first time this year. The only other one comes in December. To most everyone it's just another day, and possibly — To some of the

Senate Group Re-Opens Hearing On Nomination

WASHINGTON — (AP) — Justice Abe Fortas of the Supreme Court refused today to appear before the Senate Judiciary Committee for further testimony on his nomination to be chief justice of the United States.

Fortas declined invitation to

Saugus Vows To

Fig. 101. Skyline treatment. Functional readout directly from top-of-page banner makes useful technique. *Portland* (Ore.) *Oregonian* reads out in col. 8; note Square Serifs head schedule. *Chicago Heights* (Ill.) *Star* reads out at left. Unusual headline treatment features above-flag story in *Lynn* (Mass.) *Evening Item*.

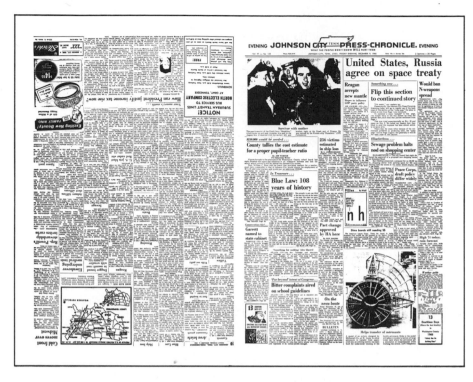

Fig. 102. Handling of jumps. *Johnson City* (Tenn.) *Press-Chronicle* runs back page of first section upside down to handle jumps. Page opposite shows how reader follows jump. At point of jump off page one, reader turns over paper lengthwise, continues reading in same column as indicated by arrows. Page-one story in cols. 6-7 first day gave instructions.

paper when it comes into a home is soon fragmented into individual sections. It is maddening to become so involved in a story that you are willing to follow it to page 28, and then to find that page 28 is in the second section, and then, finally, that you have no idea where that section has gotten to! This practice is almost infallible assurance that no one will follow the jump.

Stories should not be jumped off inside pages; the reader finds this an unpleasant practice. But if the editor just has no choice, inside jumps should always be from even pages to the next page. That keeps the jump on the same 2-page spread and all the reader has to do is turn over his paper to follow; he doesn't have to peel off, and flip over, a single page. A story should never jump more than once. If it is that long and that important, it is worth moving ads to open an adequate editorial hole on a single page.

A story in anything but a tab format should never be jumped back-

STATE

JOHNSON CITY TENN. PRESS-CHRONICLE.

STATE

WHAT THE PEOPLE DON'T KNOW *WILL* HURT THEM

Vol. 47 — No. 125   Phone 928-2141   JOHNSON CITY, TENN., 37601, FRIDAY MORNING, DECEMBER 9, 1966   Daily 10c — Sunday 30c   2 Sections — 28 Pages

Johnson announces space treaty with Russia

Adult education program OK'd ...
Cost of education aired by county school board

By JIM TURNER
P-C Education Writer

Figures brought to the attention of the Washington County school board last night revealed once again that education is an expensive business and that the county school system is still far behind the Johnson City system.

Supt. William C. Hunt told the board that providing teachers for a teacher-pupil ratio comparable to that of Johnson City would require the employment of 46 to 48 additional teachers and would cost an additional $250,000.

236 missing ...
Survivors of sunken ship sought in Aegean

ATHENS (UPI) — A vessel of the ferry in heavy seas between intense force, including plane and warships, searched the stormy Aegean Sea Thursday for survivors of the ferry liner Heraklion that broke apart and tore before dawn. The Greek Ministry of Merchant Marine said 236 persons were missing and feared drowned.

Survivors said a huge truck aboard the vessel broke loose and battered a hole in the side of the ferry in heavy seas before dawn Thursday, sending it to the bottom in a matter of minutes. Many passengers were asleep.

A statement issued by the Ministry early Friday said there were 46 survivors, but in Venice, Italy, the Tripolos Line, which owns the Heraklion, reported that a sister ship, the Minos, had picked up 62 survivors.

The 8,900-ton ferry was hit by mountain waves early Thursday and went down like a stone, apparently before many passengers had a chance to escape from below decks.

It was not immediately clear how many persons the ship was carrying. The passenger list showed 281, but crew members said the naval general staff said 46 members of the Greek Navy also were on board, and it was possible that more or all of them may not have been included on the passenger list.

City tobacco mart average at $69.78

Wet tobacco caused a slight drop in average per hundred weight on the Johnson City tobacco market yesterday.

Burley averaged $69.78 per hundred pounds and brought $207,394.40 on 296,975 pounds, average at $69.78. Sales were held at Carty's and Growers Co-op No. 1.

Sales today will be at Mason's No. 1 and Big Burley No. 1 warehouses.

Mountain City sales saw 127,866 pounds sold for $94,130.04, an average of $69.84 per hundredweight.

Other area markets:
Greeneville — 788,444 lbs. for $553,982.90, avg. $70.24.
Newport — 329,039 lbs. for $228,853.88, avg. $71.16.
Rogersville — 264,968 lbs. for $185,838.76, avg. $70.02.
Morristown — 525,710 lbs. for $368,050.39, avg. $69.45.
Kingsport — 264,914 lbs. for $184,706.34, avg. $66.38.

'Country Girl' presentation enjoyable

By CHARLES ARMSTRONG

Frank was hardly a Ulysses, whose wily was faithful to his strong and invincible train, but his Country Girl showed a nobility comparable to the honored Penelope.

Frank, the slashing theatrical great played by Barney Barbera, appeared on the stage last night at the Little Theatre production a man through with all of life except what he could drain from a bottle.

But he had a last chance from a tough-skinned director named Bernie, played by Bill McKinNon, who had worked as a hat check in theatre which owe Barney Frank's name.

A script handed Frank to read by Bernie seemed cold and stale until the exuberant director reminded the fading actor's own drinking binge and he did not know the part possessed.

(See PLAY, Page 16)

United Fund membership meeting set

The annual membership meeting of the Johnson City United Fund will be held at the City Chamber of Commerce.

Every member and everyone urged to attend.

The United Fund and reservations may be made by calling 928-3331.

New board members and officers for the coming year will be elected and routine business considered.

(See BOARD, Page 14)

Temperatures to begin falling

Thunderstorms, the crest of a warm spell and a gentle combe following of Blair's unusual warm temperatures.

The breath-taking of yesterday, and today's high of 76, may all be working or breaking the unseasonably nice, fine, and general mists, more warm, warm, warm.

At 9 p.m. the temperature was 68, and temperatures.

Weather Table

14 SHOPPING DAYS LEFT

CHRISTMAS SEALS fight TB and other RESPIRATORY DISEASES

'Elastic' water

Discoverer David James demonstrates the unusual properties of 'elastic' water which keeps flowing out of a beaker even after the beaker has been tipped upright after it is once started. The Cal Tech graduate projects some 90 per cent pure water but the other one-half per cent is a chemical polymer, polyethylene oxide. The long molecules of the chemical give the water a molasses-like quality and the weight of the liquid pulls itself out of the beaker. James said one way to stop the process is to cut the "water" with a pair of scissors. (UPI Telephoto)

Just like in May

Yesterday's May-like weather that sent temperatures soaring into the 70s in the area brought out the youngsters at East Tennessee State University for a leisurely stroll around the campus. This may well be the scene again today, as unseasonably warm weather will continue until tonight when temperatures will begin to drop.

Longer holiday truce possible

AUSTIN, Tex. (UPI) — President Johnson moved on two fronts Thursday in his quest for peace—announcing a U.S. space treaty with Russia in "sympathetic consideration" to an extended Christmas truce in Viet Nam.

Johnson made it clear to newsmen about the space bomb agreement, which bans bombs from outer space and guarantees free access to the moon.

Waiting on letters of intent ...
Council fails to approve Carter shopping center

ELIZABETHTON — The city council last night delayed the approval of a proposed new shopping center on Stateline Road.

City housing group OK's pact change

By OLIN ROGERS

The Johnson City Housing Authority approved an amendment to the contract with the local building firm.

13 Deathless Days
(Since the last fatality) In Washington County
1966
"Safety Has No Quitting Time"

Based on observance of Sabbath ...
Over a century ago legislature passed first version of controversial Blue Law

By JOHNNY JONES

'Jump page' goes to last page today

"It's easier," our readers say.

Consequently, the Johnson City Press-Chronicle will today go to regular use of the back page of this section as the "jump page," the place to which stories from Page 1 are continued.

13
Deathless Days

Commission to discuss issue today ...
Public sentiment is aroused by Blue Law

By BILL JENNINGS

Unquestionably, enforcement of Johnson City's "Blue Law" Sunday ran afoul of public sentiment.

It has proven to be a hot item for City Commission — in fact, that a meeting has been called for today to discuss this controversial issue.

On the news beats

American Legion collects $74.10 at Salvation Army's dime board

The American Legion Kings Mountain Post worked the Salvation Army dime board during yesterday's splendid weather and collected $74.10.

Other units collected $64.24 including the American Legion, according to Maj. H. R. Lawson.

Board
(Continued From Page 1, Col. 1)

Elizabethton
(Continued From Page 1, Col. 7)

Blue Law
(Continued From Page 1, Col. 4)

WRECK INJURES THREE — Three persons were injured last night in front of Boones Creek High School when these two cars collided. A 1960 coupe, driven by Mrs. Glenna Richardson, 3221 Antwood Ave., Kingsport, struck a slowly moving auto driven by ... — tia engine dr-

ward. Tabs customarily use the back page as the display for sports. From there reefers or jumped stories customarily take the reader backward into the paper. The tabloid reader has grown accustomed to this practice; he is also used to stories that jump off page 3, the main news page in this format. But the reader of full-format papers finds it most annoying to follow a jump backward or from inside pages. In these instances the loss of readership is even higher than on a jump off page one.

Spacing and Justifying

In the past, white space in a newspaper just happened. Every possible square pica was filled with type and only when there was just no way to obliterate white space was it allowed to remain. Today space is a tool of the makeup man; he does not leave it to chance but specifies where it is to be built into the page.

The desired open look of the contemporary newspaper depends on fresh air, and the designer must police the space on his pages. It is always a temptation to the printer to steal a little space in order to squeeze that last leftover Linotype slug into the form.

Management must lay down strict laws that the minimum space is inviolate. There must be no encroaching upon this space without specific permission of a top editorial executive. Any exception is like a small hole in the dike that swiftly becomes unmanageable disaster.

Here is a suggested spacing formula:

A. Use 1 pica of space:
    1. under flag
    2. above any picture within the page
    3. between catchline and cutlines
    4. between cutlines and related head
    5. between cutlines and cutoff rule
    6. above and/or below sideless box
    7. above and/or below 1-up material enclosed in decorative rule
    8. at end of a story, replacing 30-dash
       note: When story jumps, there is no space between last line of story and continuation line
    9. between 2-column leed and second leg of 1-column type

B. Use 6 points of space:
    1. between picture and catchline
    2. between headline and story
       note: No interlineal spacing within head

3. Between headline and byline
4. between byline and story
    note: No space between byline and identification line (Staff writer, *Journal* correspondent, etc.)
5. immediately inside decorative rule in boxes and sandwiches and that used to enclose 1-up material
6. above and below sandwich
7. under inside folio lines
8. above regular subheads
9. above 14-point subheads
10. under cutoff rule below pictures and banners
11. under portraits using ident lines
12. under identification lines
    note: No space between ident and expo lines

Fig. 103. Spacing chart. Note that to make diagram clearer, actual spacing of examples has been exaggerated on occasion.

    13. above the ad pyramid
    14. at the end of first leg and start of second in a Dutch wrap

C. Use 4 points of space:
    1. under 14-point subhead

The best way to convey this information is to paste up all examples of all occasions for such spacing and indicate the proper amount as in the accompanying illustration.

This suggested spacing can be changed to meet local needs and preferences, of course, but it is close to the minimum. Spacing for hot metal should be in 6-point and 1-pica increments as much as possible just for convenience. In pasteup, any increment can be used, but it is best to settle on a couple of basic units so metal gauges can be prepared for them, as we shall discuss in Chapter 13.

Filling out columns of type in a page so they are all the same depth is called *justifying,* the same term used for adjusting type lines to the same width. This adjustment of column depth can be done by adding or subtracting space when type lines alone do not fill the space precisely. But because the spacing between typographic units is designated as minimums, in practice justification is done by adding space, ledding.

Axiom: "Ledding is always done from the top." Ledding from the bottom, or in random paragraphs within a story, is slovenly craftsmanship that annoys and sometimes confuses the reader. It should never be tolerated.

The following procedures should always be followed in justifying columns:

1. First add 2-point ledds to the space at the end of each story. Begin with the top story and work downward as far as necessary.
2. Add 2 points space under each headline, beginning with the top one and working downward.
3. Drop 2-point ledds at the end of each paragraph. Begin in the top story and work down as far as necessary.
4. Add 4 points space above each picture beginning with the top one in the column. If the cut is multicolumn and there is not room for extra space in adjacent columns, do not add any in the column being justified.
5. Finally, add 2 more points space at the end of each story.

If these steps do not fill a column, it is probable that the dummy has been improperly prepared, and the desk should change placement of stories. In extreme situations, the five steps above may be extended by dropping 2-point ledds between lines of the top story beginning in the first graf and continuing as far as necessary.

By this suggested system justification is easy and quick, an important factor under the guns of deadlines. But some newspapers prefer to justify columns solely by ledding out body type. In this case, ledding should first be done in the first graf of each story in the column; a ledd should be dropped below the last line of the paragraph too.

If more spacing is required, second paragraphs should be ledded, again starting with the top story and working downward as far as is necessary.

It may be a little easier and quicker to do all ledding within one story, but the effect is not as pleasant as with the technique suggested here. If all ledding is within one story, it must be the top story in a column. Never, never should ledding begin from the bottom of a story. Worse yet is ledding at the bottom of a column which is at the center of a story that continues in the next column.

Good ledding techniques are the hallmark of quality craftsmanship. It is one of those unobtrusive details that contribute to superlative typography.

Two- to 4-line editorial fillers are no longer used for justification. Short stories that may be used for filling should always carry a real headline, in size larger than body type.

On inside pages, all typographic elements, including folio lines, should be placed directly against the top of the chase so that they will align at the top of the printed page.

Thirty-dashes are no longer used to designate the end of a story; they are nonfunctional. When the reader gets to the end of a story, he has little choice; he stops reading—not because he gets an end-mark signal, but because he has run out of type. If he is so naive that the lack of a 30-dash encourages him to read everything on the page, that's all the better.

Cutoff rules—horizontal division lines printed by the same material used for column rules—are used only rarely in functional newspaper design. Cutoffs are required only:

1. under a picture when the head below it is unrelated to the art
2. under a banner when an unrelated head or picture must be armpitted
3. in a Dutch wrap (This is discussed in the next chapter.)

While cutoffs are usually plain hairline rules, in a few newspapers a decorative rule is used. The object is to add a little typographic color and to reiterate that color which is used to establish a distinctive identity for the newspaper. This is a pleasant technique if the decorative rule is not too dark and if it is used very sparingly. The *National Observer,* for example, uses this technique well.

Cutoff rules are not required above ads in the pyramid. Many newspapers use a cutoff above an unbordered ad to make it more convenient for the advertising biller, but the cutoff is not required for separating news from ad material.

Page Patterns

You may have noted that nowhere in this chapter have page patterns been classified and labeled, as used to be the practice in books of this kind. I confess that I did this, too. But the fallacy was exposed as I scanned thousands of newspaper pages to find the illustrations for this book.

It is almost impossible to find a pure sample of a formal page layout. This is because the editor is not concerned with producing textbook examples. He doesn't even think in those terms. He never says: "Now I shall lay out a brace-makeup page"; his interest is presenting in the best possible way his news budget. Usually this is done by combining features of several formal page patterns.

Discussion may be facilitated, though, by laboratory examples, even if they rarely—or never—occur in real life. To establish the lexicon, here are listed those which are considered basic page patterns.

Symmetrical pages are balanced as closely as possible. An element in column 1 is counterpoised by the very same kind of head or size of picture in column 8, and so on. But even the most conservative of the editors who favor this style rarely creates a completely symmetrical page. If he uses a single 1-column cut, for instance, he can't get perfect balance even if he tries.

A variation of this pattern is the *frame* makeup. Single stories run the full length of columns 1 and 8. If the story in the last column jumps off the front page, there is no jump line. The reader is expected to flip the page and continue reading in column 1 or page 2 just as if this were a book instead of a newspaper.

Quadrant makeup divides the page into quarters, with each segment made up as an independent unit with a strong attention compellor. The four quarters are approximately balanced on each other so that no one significantly dominates the others.

In *brace makeup,* a picture runs in a top corner and one or more heads run into the engraving from the side, bracing it like a board might wedge a beam into the corner of a ceiling.

Some books list *dynamic balance, horizontal,* and, sometimes, *func-*

tional, as page patterns. Actually, any page that isn't symmetrical is in dynamic, informal balance. Horizontal makeup may be used in any page pattern. And any page pattern may be functional under the proper circumstances.

Vertical makeup is somewhat like the antimatter of the physicist; makes interesting conversation but who has ever seen it? The vertical page pattern is supposed to be made up in two segments with no element crossing the column rule or alley between columns 4 and 5. In theory, then, the reader can fold the page vertically for easy reading on a bus or subway. New Yorkers do fold their newspapers this way; they have to in crowded subways and buses. But I have never seen readers in other cities—including those with subways—fold their papers this way. Nor have I seen a newspaper—in Manhattan or elsewhere—made up in this style.

In *circus,* or *razzle-dazzle, makeup,* no holds are barred. Heads are big and usually complicated. Pictures are often handled with intricate mortising or silhouetting. If color is available it is laid on with a heavy hand. Everything is emphasized. The poor reader is a spectator at a three-ring circus, not quite knowing where to look at any given moment. I would nominate Portuguese newspapers as the heavyweight champions in this division. Customarily they will use literally dozens of different typefaces on a page—often each line of a head will be in a different font—and a wide variety of highly decorative borders and rules.

Dummies

All this discussion is predicated on the basic assumption that the news desk dummies up page 1. (It should dummy all pages, of course.) The dummy should be prepared on the desk even if, as on large metropolitans, a makeup editor is assigned to work on the stone, or, on weekly papers, the editor has the pleasure of actually putting together his front page in metal.

It is a saddening surprise to find that many editors have abdicated their right and responsibility to design their pages. No matter how skilled the printing craftsmen are, they have enough mechanical problems to solve in locking up a form. They don't have the time, the training, or the information to create a good front page—or any other page.

Dummying of a front page has been described as "solving a jigsaw puzzle on the turntable of a record player." For every time a story is placed, even tentatively, in a page, it affects the placement of all other

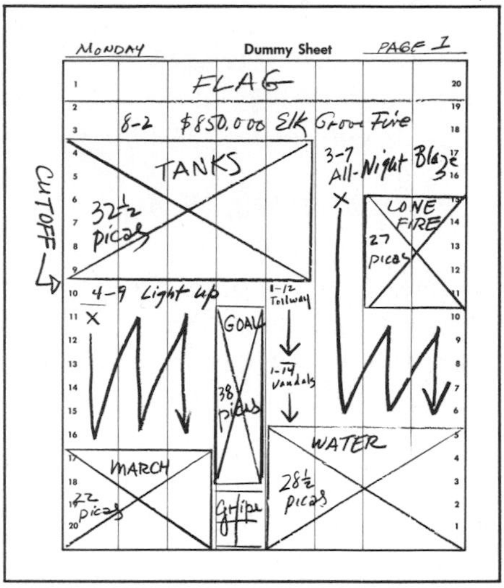

Fig. 104. Page dummy. Sketch dummy on 8½ x 11-inch sheet gives instructions for making up page of *Arlington Day,* Arlington Heights, Ill., opposite. Note how X marks start of story and arrow-lines show how type runs. Note cutoff-rule instruction in cols. 1-5 under TANKS picture.

elements. And as the news budget changes from minute to minute, the situation that determines good makeup changes also. Thus the desk must be making constant revisions on its dummy, whether on a daily or a weekly paper. Many editors prefer to do their first dummies mentally, committing them to paper only at the last minute.

Dummies are most conveniently drawn on preprinted blanks. Most common are 8½ x 11-inch sheets, but smaller ones are used by some papers. Specifications are given in a pictorial shorthand. Heads are designated by their code numbers and the first word or two of copy; their exact depths must be indicated on the dummy. Body type is shown by a straight line down the column it occupies. In multicolumn disposition, these lines are connected, thus showing the path of the eye as it moves from column to column. Some editors indicate the start of the story by a large asterisk; an arrowhead points to the line showing the exact point of the ending.

Pictures are shown by a rectangle with intersecting diagonals, boxes by a rectangle enclosing a cross. If style is to minimize cutoffs, a heavy horizontal line indicates where one is to be placed. If cutoffs and column rules are normally used, their deletion is shown by a wavy line that marks out the printed rule and the drawn cutoff on the dummy.

Special handling, such as 1-up, is shown by writing the information—3-across-4, etc.—on the dummy.

This shorthand has been developed for the convenience of the deskman; it conveys maximum information with minimum writing. But it is a means, not the end. The desk should modify or amplify this system as

WEATHER
Tonight: Partly cloudy and mild; Low in the 50s. Tuesday: Partly cloudy; Chance of showers; High around 70.

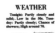

40 Per Cent Chance of Rain

The Arlington Day

Your Home Newspaper

Telephone
255-7200

Volume 2, Number 183 | Monday, October 23, 1967 | 217 S. Arlington Heights Rd. Arlington Heights, Ill. 60005 | 12 PAGES | Newsstand Price 10 Cents

$850,000 Elk Grove Fire

Tanks containing volatile chemicals at the Penray Co. in Elk Grove Village's Centex Industrial Park burst into flame as firemen from seven communities begin arriving on the scene. (Maxine Tyma photo)

All - Night Blaze
Battled by Firemen
From 7 Communities

Firemen from seven northwest suburban communities spent Sunday night battling a blaze that destroyed the Penray Chemical Co., 1801 Estes, in Elk Grove Village's Centex Industrial Park.

Elk Grove Village Fire Chief Virgil Bottler estimated the loss at $850,000.

The fire, fed on ether and alcohol used to make an automotive additive, threatened a large area of the vast industrial park, forcing firemen to deploy additional equipment to water down roofs of many nearby buildings.

THE BLAZE was discovered at approximately 10:20 p.m. and the first fire unit from the Elk Grove fire department immediately issued a call for all available help.

The first call for assistance was received by the Mount Prospect fire department at 10:22 p.m. The department dispatched its snorkel truck an engine company, and six men to the scene.

Less than an hour later, the village's Salvation Army Canteen truck was sent to the scene as firemen realized that they would spend the night battling the raging fire.

Arlington Heights received a call for manpower and equipment and sent an aerial ladder, an engine, and a squad of firemen. Rolling Meadows' fire department was also asked to send aid and the department sent one truck and three men.

A TENSE moment occured shortly after units began arriving on the scene. Mount Prospect's snorkel truck had just taken up position on one side of the blazing structure when Elk Grove firemen realized that an underground propane tank was located directly under the snorkel truck.

Firemen hurried to disconnect the truck from a pumper truck and moved to another location. A short time later the tank ruptured and exploded, sending a ball of fire several hundred feet into the

Water from a leaking hose floods the area, reflecting the silhouettes of firemen pouring water into the burning Penray Co. building Sunday night. (Joe Edwards photo)

A lone fireman backs away as an explosion rips open tank of chemicals (Bob Richardson photo)

sky. The explosion was heard as far away as Mount Prospect and the entire sky was momentarily lit by orange flames.

As firemen were forced to pull back due to intense heat, another call for help was issued. Palatine's fire department responded, sending one truck and several firemen. A civil defense light truck from the Skokie fire department was sent to the scene and an engine company from Des Plaines was sent to standby in the Elk Grove fire station in case other fire calls were received.

FIREMEN were prevented from entering the burning building by intense heat and smoke. The plant contained two other underground propane storage tanks and at least one of them was believed to have exploded.

After one explosion, aerosol cans containing the product manufactured at Penray skyrocketed high in the sky and rained down on firemen and spectators.

Police from Elk Grove patrolled the entire industrial complex, watching for other fires that could start from burning embers carried by the wind.

Elk Grove's snorkel truck, purchased earlier this year, was used almost continually in its first major blaze.

EARLY Monday morning, fire officials at the scene issued an appeal for gasoline. Trucks at the scene, with gas tanks holding between 40 and 50 gallons each, were dangerously low on fuel. A fireman estimated that the trucks were using up gasoline at the rate of 10 gallons each hour. Gasoline tanker trucks were rushed to the scene, however, and none of the equipment had to be taken out of operation.

Cause of the fire, the worst in the village's history, was undetermined pending investigation by village, state and insurance company officials.

'Light Up and Give' Tonight

"Light Up and Give," is this evening's motto in the Arlington Heights United Fund drive which seeks to raise $32,000 from the residential areas of the village.

About 1,400 solicitors wearing the AHUF badge will storm the village's more than 13,000 homes with the United Fund Appeal. They are expected to begin the drive at 6 p.m. and the AHUF has asked all residents to turn on the porch lights of their homes as a reminder of the drive.

Arlington Heights tonight will join 81 suburban communities which are participating in the Metropolitan Crusade of Mercy this year.

THE GOAL for all divisions has been set at $50,000 which will be spent locally. The crusade may give AHUF another $17,000.

The crusade's total goal has been set at more than $24 million in the 1967 campaign.

AHUF has six other divisions besides the residential and James E. Mason, general chairman of the drive said that the whole system is ready to "go"

IN ADDITION to the seven divisions, the Northwest Community Hospital and the Northwest Mutual Insurance Co. are staging their own drive.

"May people have been helpful this year," said Mason.

"The Illinois Bell Telephone Co.'s data processing division stuffed, printed and sealed the residential mailings, a total of 11,391 pieces of mail," he said.

AN ELECTRONIC data processing system operated under the guidance of several Arthur Andersen Co. employes has made it possible for the drive to list and identify each residence in the village.

Gordon Glorch is the chairman of the residential division. He has reported that this year the availbility of more workers than in the past should result in a substantial increase of contributions.

Last year residential contributions reached $28,000. The total local campaign collected $45,000 and the crusade gave AHUF $12,000 more.

HERE ARE the health agencies to be supported by the Metropolitan Crusade of Mercy.

Clearbrook Center for the Retarded, Arthritis Foundation, Mental Health Association of Greater Chicago, Kidney Disease Foundation, Heart Research, Cancer Research, Cystic Fibrosis, Cerebral Palsy Research, Multiple Sclerosis, Leukemia Research, Muscular Dystrophy Research, Hospital Free Bed Fund and Northwest Cooperative Community Mental Health Clinic.

The service agencies are: Salvation Army; United Service Organizations; Boy Scouts; Girl Scouts; Goodwill Industries; Young Men's Christian Association and Camp Fire Girls.

THE OFFICERS, directors administrators and solicitors give their services voluntarily.

The following are the other divisions of AHUF and their chairman:

Rod McLennan, in charge of School Districts 214 and 25; Irv Robbin and William Griffith, Commerce and Industry division; Richard Impey, professional division; Don Morton, special gifts; Stewart Grant, government division; Irv Crystal, clubs and organizations.

The special gifts division was organized this year and has started a "Century" group. A donation of $100 or more entitles membership to this group.

Two teenagers who volunteered to march for the Arlington Heights United Fund campaign tonight are Linda, 16, (left) and Cindy, 14, Schmidt, daughters of Mr. and Mrs. Harry Schmidt of 686 E. Ivy Ln. The girls are students at Wheeling High School and volunteered to canvass the Ivy Lane area. Wearing their identification badges, they do some necessary paper work before ringing doorbells.

Tollway Access Ramp Decision Expected Nov. 8

A decision is expected Nov. 8 on whether access ramps will be constructed at Arlington Heights Rd. and the Northwest Tollway.

A meeting is scheduled on that date between the Illinois Tollway Commission and members of the Tollway Access Committee, which represents the villages of Arlington Heights, Elk Grove and Mount Prospect. The committee is headed by Carl F. Mees of Arlington Heights.

Vandals Hit Library

Vandals entered the Arlington Heights Memorial Library and caused interior damage to the site at 500 N. Dunton

Robert Kim, an electrical contractor, told Arlington Heights Police Friday oil was splattered on cement walls and floor of the building and two locks were damaged on 'toors.

ROLLING MEADOWS COMMUNITY CHEST, INC.

Only 36 per cent of Rolling Meadows' goal has been collected in the drive for the Metropolitan Crusade of Mercy. This 'thermometer' stands in a corner of the Meadows Shopping Center.

Gripe Of The Day

To spend all summer taking care of your lawn and then get all the weeds from the lawn next door. S.V.D.

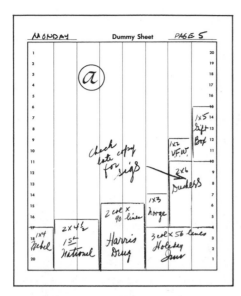
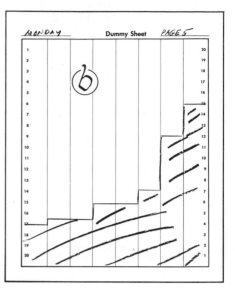
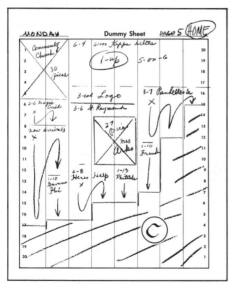

Fig. 105. Inside-page dummies. Advertising department dummy, *a*, shows individual ads. Editorial page receives dummy, *b*, showing only total ad pyramid and around it builds page dummy, *c*, from which page of *Arlington Day*, Arlington, Ill., was made up.

required to be sure that the stone has all needed information in unmistakable form.

On multi-edition papers it is convenient to use dummy sheets of different colors, corresponding to the edition for which they are drawn.

The width of elements is easily and sketchily shown; their depth must be indicated as accurately as possible, for it is this dimension that is the important variable. Usually 1-inch increments are printed on the dummy sheet, but the desk ought to work as closely as a half- or even a quarter-inch. For pasteup, more precise measurement is required; this is discussed in Chapter 13.

Student journalists can develop the mechanical skills of drawing dummies by working backward. They can take printed newspaper pages and convert them into dummies. This is a useful way to sharpen the ability to visualize a printed page from the hieroglyphs of the dummy.

I find it useful to maintain a rough *running dummy* as copy is read. As soon as a story, with its head, art, and any other accompanying material, has been sent to the comp room, it can be positioned on the dummy. If it is bounced out of this placement, it is easy to erase and revise the dummy. This isn't neat but it doesn't have to be. For, just before closing time, a final dummy can be redrawn. This may sound like a lot of work but it truly isn't. Redrawing even an intricate page dummy will take no more than 120 seconds. And it has been demonstrated over and over again that every minute the desk spends on the dummy will save several minutes on the stone.

Use of the copy log is important to record the exact dimensions and specifications of all material handled by the desk. If no running dummy is maintained, information on the log is essential to making out the final dummy.

Usually the same deadline is set for several pages, but the desk must try to keep an even flow of page dummies. If the sports editor sends out all page dummies for his section at one time, he will swamp not only the composing room but the mat rollers and stereo casters as well. Flattening off the hills and valleys of page makeup is as important as leveling the flow of copy to the Linotypes.

For inside pages, of course, the advertising department must prepare the ad dummies first. The ad layer sends the original dummy to the composing room and a carbon, or simplified copy, to editorial. There are advantages in the desk's using a carbon; this can help prevent awkward association of news and ads, for advertisers are identified on such dummies but not on simplified ones.

Dummies may also show *second-impression pages*. Whether a paper is printed on sheets or on a roll of paper, one side must be printed before the other one. The page which is printed last will usually have better detail in halftones; the page printed first may be smeared or offset as the second imprinting is done. On new or well-maintained presses, the difference between first- and *second-strike* pages is so slight it is invisible. On worn presses it may be intense. On flatbed presses pages 2, 3, 6, and 7 are first-strike; 1, 5, 6, and 8 are second-impression. On web-fed presses, page one is always second-strike, as is the last page of the first section. But other second-impression pages will vary depending on the size of the edition and the webbing pattern required.

Many editors make a fetish of holding good art for second-impression pages, often when there isn't even need to do so.

Dummies are the vital communication between the architect and the actual builder of newspaper pages. They are as important as the blueprints in manufacturing processes. It seems odd that any competent editor would neglect or minimize the use of this tool. Among the ancient axioms this is one of the most important: "All pages should be dummied as completely as possible."

chapter **11**

Inside Pages

WHILE FRONT PAGES are conspicuous, most of a newspaper consists of inside pages. Many of these carry advertising as well as editorial matter, so new factors enter the problems of layout.

Unlike front pages and the comparatively few key pages, the typical inside page is a joint effort of the editorial and advertising departments. The editor must make his layout conform to a heterogeneous area of advertising over which he has no control; at the same time he must create pages that will attract, hold, and serve the reader.

The primary function of any newspaper page is to transmit information. Advertising does this; in many cases there is as much news in advertising as there is in the next column of editorial matter. But it is the editorial content which is the most important; advertising revenue is only a side product of good news transmission.

This chapter will look at the advertising portion of inside pages first, not to slight the news content but only because the ad pyramid is, chronologically, built into a page before the editorial matter is displayed.

Display Advertising

In some newspapers there is so much rivalry between news and ad departments that they seem to forget they occupy the same boat on a stormy sea. Each must become aware of the aims and problems of the other, recognize that not only the end but also the means are identical for each, and perfect the close cooperation that is necessary to produce good inside pages.

The publisher is the one man directly charged with the responsibility of the whole newspaper enterprise rather than of one of its subdivisions.

Therefore he has the primary job of making decisions when departmental responsibilities and problems overlap. This happens in the placement and typography of advertising, and establishing policy about this requires top-management decisions.

The importance of advertising revenue is so great that it is easy to confuse priorities. Everyone concerned with a newspaper must remind himself that the reader, not the advertiser, is the major consumer. This is not to suggest that we must scorn advertising and the advertiser; it is a rare newspaper that could exist without ad revenues, and there is surely nothing demeaning to a newspaper or to any of its personnel to compete for advertising dollars.

The best way to compete for ad revenue is to produce a good newspaper. Newspaper advertising has a long history of success primarily because it is welcomed into the typical American home. That welcome depends largely on the news that is conveyed. Without that news, the paper becomes a circular, and the waste factor in this form of advertising is scandalous.

Good editorial content creates *reader traffic* throughout the paper. Reader traffic creates *reader exposure* to individual pages and advertisements. Without this exposure, ads can't do their jobs.

We have always felt that circulation figures were an excellent indicator of the readership of a newspaper. They are, but they are a delayed measurement. Circulation may continue for a period, because of habit, after readership has already dropped.

The best indicator of readership is the local advertiser. If ads in a newspaper are not doing their proper job, the merchant will increase his sales resistance to that newspaper's advertising salesmen. The retailer probably will neither know nor care just why his advertising isn't pulling its weight any more. But the alert publisher will know that a major factor undoubtedly is due to lower reader traffic, a sure sign of dropping reader interest.

So for economic reasons, the publisher must maintain editorial quality throughout the newspaper. There is an ethical factor, too. If the reader sees an attractive, newsy front page, he is entitled to believe that the rest of the package is of the same high quality. To allow a sharp drop in quality between page one and inside pages is comparable to a farmer putting a layer of big shiny apples on the top and filling the rest of the basket with culls. He is not likely to get the customer back again.

Except for the few key pages that run without advertising, the layout of inside pages depends greatly upon the number of ads and their placement on each of these pages.

The publisher spends much time determining the news-advertising ratio; he ought to spend more time pondering the placement of advertising. His isn't the task of placing individual ads; the publisher should concern himself with the general *progression* of the paper's contents. How much advertising, for instance, should be on a section page? If the overall content of advertising in an issue is 60%, should each inside page come as close as possible to a 60–40 ratio, or should some pages be loaded heavily with advertising to open up others? How many key pages should be kept ad-free? How much can he allow the display of news to be affected by selling or permitting preferred position for ads?

The newspaper industry must dispel insidious myths, some that it created itself. It's going to take more time and effort to do this than it did to create the fallacies in the first place. But the destruction of the myths is imperative.

All of these center on the so-called "preferred position."

There is, for instance, a belief that right-hand pages are more effective for the advertiser than the opposite ones. Carried to its logical extreme, this would fill all odd-numbered pages with advertising and all even-numbered ones with editorial content.

There is a belief that ads will draw best if they run in the low-numbered pages of a newspaper. Many publishers cater to the demand by numbering each section independently. Instead of going from pages one through 48, let's say, they will number the first section A-1 through A-16, the second, B-1 through B-8; the next starting with C-1, etc. This yields several low-number pages and, apparently, several pages desirable enough so that the advertiser feels favored of friendly fate when his ads wind up there.

As with most myths, some of these began as truth, but misunderstanding or misinterpretation has robbed them of validity.

Advertisers cite statistics that indicate that ads in the front of the paper have higher readership than others. But closer study proves that instead of being a good ad because of its up-front position, it gets that position because it is a good ad. The "good ad"—one that meets well-defined criteria of merchandise, copy, art, typography, and layout—gets high readership just because it is good. No research has ever demonstrated that readership comes from position.

Typically, an advertiser gets up-front position by seniority and volume. That means that, in most cities, the largest department store has worked its way up to pages 2 and 3. The same longevity and volume that earn this position are often associated with the use of a good advertising department or agency that makes this advertising the best in the newspaper. It's no wonder, then, that such advertising would have high readership. It would have the same readership if it consistently appeared on page 22 instead of 2.

A few publishers have whispered about changing a historical attitude. They believe that newspapers might compete better against television by adopting the opponent's tactics and giving "prime time" to the national advertiser. It has been in national advertising that the electronic media have made major inroads on newspaper ad revenue. One school of thought believes that wooing back the departed national advertiser is essential. They contend that local advertisers are pretty well compelled by circumstances to advertise in the local newspaper. So, they reason, if they offer the "prime time" of up-front position to the nationals, they may be able to regain at least part of those departed dollars. Local merchants would have to be content with higher-numbered pages.

The danger of this reasoning is apparent. Maybe the local advertiser has to use newspaper columns—today. But if he is a captive—and exploited—customer now, you can wager blue chips that he will leap to any feasible alternative as soon as one appears. Besides, this practice will reinforce the myth of premium position. We must recognize that, while this position is actually not better than any other, the merchant thinks it is and this makes up-front more desirable to him.

The solution is to make other sections of the paper attractive to the local retailer and make him want to move his advertising there. Food stores, for instance, insist that their ads run on inside pages. Their successful ads there demonstrate that up-front position is not required for high readership. Good editorial content and presentation are obviously the key to attention for inside pages.

Some observers, friendly as well as hostile, believe that sheer volume of advertising may be causing diminishing returns. They contend that on certain days the newspaper is so bulky that no reader has—or chooses to devote—the time to read all of it.

As far as the advertiser is concerned, however, it isn't necessary that every reader read every page. He wants readership of those who are in the market for his products or services. It doesn't harm anyone when I fail to read an ad for baby food; my offspring are long past the stage when I'm a customer for such food. But the advertiser wants to make sure that I'm exposed to ads for men's wear, tires, and golf clubs.

It seems that publishers will have to departmentalize their newspapers more. Then the reader can choose those portions of the paper in which he's interested or for which he has time. This is going to mean grouping

Fig. 106. Advertising pyramid. Improperly building ads up to left, *a*, gives primary optical area to advertisement. Proper pyramid to right—*b*, from *Pontiac* (Mich.) *Press*—opens POA for editorial art. Page, *c*, from *Kokomo* (Ind.) *Tribune*, shows proper pyramid in op format. Note that all ads are in op width. Arrows indicate 1-column ads; that in col. 2 is smallest sold, 1 x 1.

of advertising more than of editorial content, however. And in order to do this, newspapers will have to dispel another myth: that an ad must be isolated from all competitive advertising to do a good job.

Apparently the only skeptics are grocers; they insist that their ads run in the food section, surrounded by competitors. More typical of the believers of the myth of isolation are automobile advertisers. Insertion orders for national auto linage bear the stern admonition, sometimes even in red ink, that not only may no other auto ads appear on the same page, they shouldn't even be on the facing page. It is ironic that so many automobile dealers don't find such isolation desirable for their sales-rooms. They locate on the city's Auto Avenue, obviously seeking out their competitors as neighbors.

Departmentalizing advertising as tightly as editorial matter might help the reader cope with mammoth newspapers, but publishers may have to set a limit on the number of pages in an issue. This might be an advantage to the advertiser that could be translated into higher rates, so that dollar volume could be maintained without increasing or even maintaining the number of pages printed. If a half-page ad in the future produces as much profit as a full-page does now, the advantage is obvious.

While such a decision is being pondered, the reader's interests must constantly be remembered. No matter how many pages—or how few—an edition contains, there must be enough editorial content to keep the reader informed and to give him his subscription money's worth. The wise publisher, formally or by custom, sets a minimum number of columns of news matter for each issue, even those which do not carry enough advertising to support that much space.

A pressing question concerns pages 2 and 3. How much advertising should run there?

When the reader has enjoyed a good front page and turns to the next one, he must be instantly assured that his pleasure is going to continue. If he sees nothing but advertising in his first glimpse of the inside of the package, he may get the impression that there's not enough news inside to make it worth his while to continue flipping pages.

Yet if pages 2 and 3 are too wide open, it may take so much time to read their contents that the reader is throughly fatigued and satisfied—and again discouraged from continuing on inside pages. A couple of the nation's finest newspapers are actively wrestling with this question. It appears that a 50% advertising content on these two pages may prove just about ideal. If the ad space is a horizontal half-page, it offers the advertiser opportunities for pleasant and unusual designs. The rectangular space at the top of the page would be the most efficient for news display.

Some excellent newspapers use page 3 as a second front page, often labeling it as such. This technique is a good one. It gives more opportunity for the lively display of news; it is especially effective for local or area news for larger dailies.

Each such ad-free key page contributes to the continuing problem of ad placement. If the overall ratio calls for 35% news content, the 65% of advertising that doesn't run on a key page obviously has to be distributed on other pages.

The percentage of full-page, double-spread, or double-truck ads is a major factor in ad placement. The more of these a newspaper has, the easier it is to create key pages. But not all newspapers are blessed with an abundance of these ads. Smaller papers have fewer full-pagers as a percentage as well as on a numerical basis. In smaller communities, the typical ad is rather small, and placing many small ads takes more time, worry, and pages than the same area in fewer, bigger ads.

The combined pressures of the advertiser seeking preferred position and of maintaining the ad-news ratio create a misuse of what ought to be a key page or one with very little advertising. This is the *section page,* the first page of each section beyond the first. This is known by a variety of names, among them *break, split, Z, title,* and *wrapper pages.* Another term is a *front;* this is a noun, never an adjective for "page."

Someone has persuaded the advertiser—maybe he did it to himself—that a section page is a highly preferred position. On some papers this space carries a handsome premium rate; on many, it is a reward granted to a valued space buyer. The gilt of the section page may tarnish under logical evaluation, though.

We know that it doesn't take long for the neat package that is delivered to our reader to be broken down into separate sections. Each section becomes a separate newspaper. Each section page is truly a front page that must attract the reader and persuade him to pick up, then read, this newspaper.

If a full-page ad covers the section page, what does this smaller package look like? A handbill or circular! There is little incentive to the reader to pick up this batch of newsprint. Indeed, as we know well, the mortality rate of such advertising is high. If a section of a newspaper looks like a circular, it may meet the circular's common fate, immediate relegation, unread, to the wastebasket.

Advertising on the section page should be kept to no more than a quarter page. There must be a nameplate on this page. There must be the same exciting headlines, attractive pictures, and functional display on the split page as on page one.

If a section page doesn't have this treatment, especially if it carries a full-page ad, everyone involved is short-changed. The lack of section identification may make it inconvenient for the reader to find some page or feature for which he is looking or to which he has been directed by the index. Moreover, if the reader doesn't know that this is a news section, he may discard it without reading it at all and thus lose some of his purchase price. All advertisers in such a section, on the front as well as on inside pages, probably will lose traffic and exposure.

The back page of the whole newspaper or its sections is also erroneously considered desirable position. This is the unthinking carry-over of a characteristic of the back page of a magazine.

The back cover of a magazine is preferred position. By the law of averages, the back cover will be lying exposed on a table in the reader's home almost as often as the front cover will. But the back page of a newspaper is rarely exposed as it rests in the home. Almost always the newspaper lies folded, with the back page effectively hidden.

A few publishers use the whole back page for editorial purposes. Several excellent papers (the *Elyria Chronicle-Telegram* in Ohio, for example) devote that page to editorials. A few, such as the *Lowell* (Mass.) *Sun,* make the back page the second front page.

The rationale is interesting. These publishers believe that it's valuable to leave a pleasant taste in the reader's mouth as he finishes his newspaper. They point out that the typical paper gets progressively duller as the reader moves through it. Usually it winds up with a classified section—admittedly not attractive to the browsing reader—perhaps the comics, finally the back page completely filled with an ad or with a tiny editorial area that precludes attractive display. Instead of concluding, like a good musical composition, with a well-defined chord, such a newspaper just peters out with the squawks and wheezes of an expiring bagpipe.

Another long tradition ought to be reexamined: the placing of classified ads at the back of the paper. There probably is—or at least was—a reason for that once upon a time, but it seems lost in antiquity. Just why must these ads bring up the end of the parade? They could just as well occupy any other area. They aren't attractive enough to begin at page 2, of course, but they can be sandwiched in almost any other place.

The customary procedure is to *back the section down,* determine the last page and then count backward enough pages to accommodate the varying volume of classified. The first page of the want-ad section is not necessarily filled with ads; editorial filler material occupies the rest of the columns. This procedure is necessary when the last classified page is the second- or third-last page of the paper. But the count-back can begin at page 35 or 36 as well as at 95.

If this advertising is anywhere other than at the end of the paper, it is just as logical to begin it with a full page and count forward until all the ads have been placed.

Weekly newspapers, especially those which have to print in two or more press runs, traditionally keep classifieds on the last run to accommodate late ads. But some papers run classifieds successfully in the first run and run the few late ones unclassified, tucked into any appropriate space in the last run. These papers find that the late ads are consistently few and pose no great problem. Yet the transposing of the classified section pays a handsome dividend. Too often the first run has to be filled up with second-grade copy just because it's available early. Then, when the last forms are being made up, much better but later material has to be condensed severely or even left out just because there is no room. By using early space for bulky classified, most of which are early-set material, last-run space is made available to fresher news.

The most pesky myth to rear its ugly head is that advertising must be next to reading matter, NRM. This is most insidious with national advertisers, for every insertion order has "NRM" preprinted as a standing instruction.

It is true that reading matter brings attention to ads. But this results only from a long and consistent pattern of placing editorial matter of high quality throughout the paper. The reader must know that it will be constantly worth his while to read through the whole paper. But reading matter does not have to lead every reading eye to a specific ad. There is absolutely no data to suggest that a buried ad, one that is not touched by straight matter, loses even a small percentage of its potential effectiveness. A few newspapers have experimented with the filling of entire pages with small ads and there is no appreciable handicap to any buried advertisement. The Sunday *New York Times,* for example, uses this procedure.

Two things affect the pulling power of an ad: the quality of the ad itself and the quality of the newspaper in which it is delivered.

If the overall quality of the paper is to be maintained, it is essential that the desk not be boxed in by mandatory position for ads. When preferred space is sold or permitted, it means that the advertiser is influencing the arrangement of the newspaper. He isn't qualified; he doesn't have the skill and training, and he certainly doesn't have the knowledge of the contents of a specific issue that is required to package those contents properly.

The ideal inside page would have a rectangular portion of the page in advertising and another rectangle open for editorial display. For the news department needs not only space but space in usable shapes. Such squaring-off of advertising is practical; the *Christian Science Monitor* proves that every day.

But "political" considerations may make the *pyramid* the most practical for ad placement. Actually this pattern is only the lower portion of one side of a pyramid.

The pyramid should build up to the right on all pages. A carry-over from the 1920's is the practice of building ads to the outside corners, to the left on even-numbered pages, to the right on odd ones. The theory is that a pleasant double-page symmetry is thus effected. That may well be, but no one sees it! A double spread is just too large to be seen at the distance at which the reader holds a newspaper, about 14 inches. He doesn't read it with both pages spread wide. He can see only one page at a time; its symmetrical balance with an invisible page has absolutely no bearing on the reader's comfort, convenience, or pleasure.

When ads are pyramided to the right, it opens the primary optical area for editorial display. The *POA* is the top left corner of every page, odd or even. If ads are pyramided to the outside corner, it means that on even-numbered pages the POA will be devoted to advertising, and the editorial content is thereby slighted.

A pyramid to the right creates a subtle but potent psychological effect. As the eye moves across the page from left to right in reading, columns get progressively shorter. So as the reader becomes fatigued, he is faced with smaller tasks. He is encouraged to continue across the page.

The pyramid should be flattened as much as possible. This will help leave a usable depth of space clear across the top of the page. Some newspapers have attempted to keep page-top space open by fiat. They establish rules that a 2-column editorial hole must be at least 4 inches deep, a 3-column area at least 6 inches deep, and so on. They also insist that any editorial space be as close as possible to square. By this rule, the desk cannot be given 8 inches in one column and only 2 in another; there would have to be a 2 column x 5 inch block or a 2 x 4 with a little 1-column 2-inch projection. Usable formulas are difficult to establish and difficult to achieve.

But it is possible and it is wise to establish policy that will forbid *ribbons*. These are flat, wide strips of editorial space across the top of the ad pyramid. Some newspapers allow a ribbon as shallow as four lines of body type. Space like that just cannot be used effectively. But because it is charged as "news hole" in accounting, the editorial department is being short-changed on its budgeted space.

Some newspapers decree that a strip at least 4 inches deep be kept open at the page top. An advertiser whose ad projects into this strip must pay for a full column; no editorial matter is run above such an ad, the space is left blank. This is not only practical; it is also reasonable. On a page 21 inches deep, an ad 18 inches deep has the same impact as one that fills the column; space should be priced on that basis.

Columns should not be completely filled by piling up smaller ads. That usable 4-inch strip for editorial matter should be left across the top of every page except, of course, when a single ad fills a whole column or columns.

An abundance of smaller ads may have to be arranged in a *double pyramid* to render at least lip service to NRM instructions. In this case the left pyramid should be kept lower than the right one, primarily to assure adequate area in the POA.

When the double pyramid is used, it should not be allowed to create a *well,* a sharp V-shaped editorial hole between ads, especially one that goes clear to the bottom of the page.

There ought to be advertising at the foot of every column. Below the fold, on inside pages, editorial matter loses much effectiveness. Some authorities believe the loss is as much as 50%. No matter what the percentage, it is certain that there is serious loss, so we want to keep as much advertising as possible in the basement. By placing the stones of advertising in the bottom of a jug, we can force the water of news matter to the top of the container where the reader can easily drink it.

A variation of the well pattern is called *magazine placement.* This builds up pillars of ads on both sides of a page with a few columns in the center of the page entirely open for news matter. This is obviously poor placement. It gives the POA to advertising and puts almost half of the editorial content below the fold.

The worst placement of advertising is as *islands.* In this pattern, ads are floated at random on a page. Many of them, then, are above news. By American custom, this says to the reader that certain ads are more important than certain news matter, for the reader has been taught that the higher an element is on the page, the more important it is. This depreciation of news is certainly repugnant to all editorial staffers. It

Fig. 107. Ribbon treatment: a, *Arkansas Gazette* of Little Rock, Ark., uses 8-column banner; b, Oklahoma City (Okla.) *Times* uses only 7-column banner to reduce number of characters in head; c, Syracuse (N.Y.) *Herald-Journal* uses porkchop cut to shorten headline; d, Philadelphia (Pa.) *Evening Bulletin* fills ribbon with several stories and allows cols. 5-6 to run naked; e, Boston (Mass.) *Globe* uses 3-sided box around side-headed story.

ought to be as disturbing to the ad staff, too, because, by implication, it makes the newspaper an advertising circular and erodes that salable advantage of newspaper advertising which we have already examined.

A very recent device, *Flex-Form* ads, flies in the face of all these negatives to inject an exciting new factor in the creation of inside pages. The idea was born at the *Journal* and *Star* at Peoria, Illinois. The *Buffalo* (New York) *Courier-Express* was an early user, and in Canada the Southam Newspapers pioneered the technique.

Flex-Form (or FlexForm, without the hyphen) allows the advertiser to use any shape he desires for his ad. It floats, with no other advertising on the page, completely surrounded by editorial matter. Usually the shape is that of letters or numbers or a product, although the artist is allowed absolute freedom. It may be b&w or with color. Color is most effective as a tint block.

The newspaper designer looks upon Flex-Form with violently mixed emotions. The technique violates all present principles of ad placement. It dominates the page, not only by its unusual silhouette and color, if any, but also because it rides above some editorial matter and because there is no editorial art. All this is on the debit side of the editor's ledger.

But there is a major item on the credit side; this is the first opportunity that newspapers have provided for the advertiser to use creativity since run of press (ROP) color was offered in 1937. Today color is primarily an advertising tool rarely used all alone for editorial purposes. So it is interesting to note that the *Milwaukee Journal,* which has been an exemplary pioneer ever since, had used color for editorial purposes as early as 1891.

A grudging concession on the part of a few newspapers allowed the use of L-shaped ads. But even these were often only two adjacent rectangular ads because the artist was not permitted to treat the L as a single area. Most newspapers today still require that ads be vertical rectangles, and thus the advertiser and the desk are both denied the advantages of a horizontal ad.

Innovation was stifled, and there has been little attempt to use newspaper space in a creative way. But there are many opportunities for the ad designer to create exciting newspaper advertisements, if only the publisher will let him!

A few years ago the *Buffalo* (New York) *Evening News* began a contest for creative use of newspaper space. One prizewinner advertised fast developing service for movie film. On a right-hand page was the ad,

Fig. 108. Well placement. Deep chasm between ads wastes editorial space because news matter below fold loses effectiveness. Also note POA given to ad.

showing a series of blank movie frames, all in black-and-white. The reader was invited to hold the page to the light. When he did, the frames were filled with color pictures—showing through from the next page!

Some other notably successful ads actually used in newspapers utilized a narrow paper roll that created a half-page flap that combined with a regular full-page ad that it overlaid.

Another imaginative ad consisted of three lines of huge type, printed in a pale, pale blue—under a regular classified ad page!

But most newspaper ads are woefully restricted in physical appearance. And now comes Flex-Form!

The newspaper designer must applaud the imagination and daring that gave birth to the new concept. If it becomes as commonplace as ROP color, Flex-Form will present the editorial desk with some problems it might as well learn to live with.

The striking ad must take the place of editorial art; any news photos would lessen the value of the free silhouette of the ad. A major problem will be to handle the top of the page without art. It will usually require an 8-column banner to avoid tombstones. One-up—6- or 7-across-8— will be effective.

Example G is a promotional piece from the *Courier-Express*. (The concentric arcs were in color.) It was the first time the desk had worked with the technique, and the errors that it discovered then have since been well corrected. No longer are tombstones permitted at the page top. Kickered heads are distracting on a page like this.

The tombstone—MERCY GUN and R.F.K.'s—should be avoided in columns 1 to 4. The POZNAN head in column 8 should not align with the edge of the ad but be dropped down some 3 inches, to about the middle of the short arm of the *E*. The small head at that position in column 7 should be eliminated by lengthening the FEET story. Another small head in column 3, in the bowl of the *C*, should also be eliminated. The ORDER head in columns 2 to 4, mostly hidden by the arrow, should be moved away from the *E* into columns 1 to 3. The HOFFER story in column 1 carries a head light enough to avoid fighting the ad.

To make the ad most effective, the editorial portion of the page must be quite light. There must be headlines, of course, but they should be smaller than normal except when immediately under a portion of the ad. There must be a head under each horizontal edge of the ad; it should be just as wide as that element.

The editorial desk must estimate type accurately and tailor stories to fit specific areas. The advertising department should urge advertisers to avoid using b&w ad shapes that will completely surround editorial matter, as in the bowl of a *B* or *R* or of a number like *4, 8,* or *9*. News copy so surrounded loses all editorial value, and it also blurs the distinctive outline of the ad; it is best to leave such enclosed areas blank. If color delineates the shape of the ad, news may run completely enclosed, but the headline should be light. If color is not used, the ad will require a fairly heavy border to define the unusual shape.

All this makes the news markedly subservient to advertising, and this must be acknowledged as a grave deficit. But we might all hope that this innovative thinking will open new avenues for the creativity that will not encroach so harshly on the news content of the page.

It is necessary to have a well-defined policy on ad placement that both ad and news departments value and agree on, for it is always easier to lay out a paper properly the first time than to revise individual pages. The desk should have the right to ask that ads be moved in order to accommodate important news. But this authority should be used rarely. Even while pages are still in the dummy stage, it may create an expanding ripple of problems to move an ad. Once the ad has been placed in a chase, moving it means diverting time and effort that are necessary to meet deadlines.

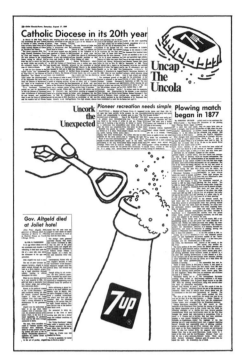

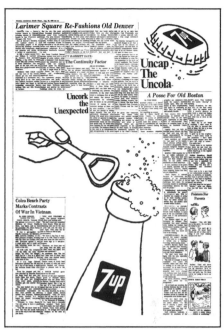

Example G-1. Flex-Form ads. Top two show different handling of news matter around same ad; 7-up devices in red. Color is red in lower specimens, below. Left, it is screened down to pink. Right, only machinery and *i* of sig cut are in color. Top left page is from *Joliet* (Ill.) *Herald-News;* all others from *Peoria* (Ill.) *Journal Star,* originator of Flex-Form.

Front-page Advertising

In America's earliest newspapers there was no typographic distinction between news and advertising. Ads were set in the same text form as news, and the two categories were mixed at random. When display advertising developed, it, too, ran on any page, including the first. Interestingly enough, the front page wasn't considered particularly desirable by the advertiser. In fact, in the 1880's it was definitely the inside pages that he sought for his ad, and often he was prepared to pay a premium for this "preferred" inside position. No one knows why the advertiser reached this interesting conclusion; it apparently was as whimsical and unfounded as today's fallacies about preferred position.

During this century, display ads have gradually been forced off the front page. Occasionally it was done by a courageous publisher who simply marked page one off limits to advertising. More frequently ads were encouraged to move off to avoid constantly raised premium rates or very restrictive rules about their size and typography. Today page-one advertising is seen with some frequency only in New England and California, but there are indications that this undesirable practice is reappearing in other areas.

Front-page advertising is deadly to good page makeup. Usually these ads are pyramided to the right, and so the entire terminal area—second only to the POA in importance—is out of the control of the editor. It is impossible to create a finished page pattern and to get the necessary editorial display in the basement of the page. Type faces in advertising are rarely compatible with that of the news columns, and the mixture creates a typographical hodgepodge.

My greatest antipathy toward front-page advertising is an emotional one; it just doesn't seem appropriate. I recognize and defend the need for advertising revenue. I agree emphatically that there is no ritual uncleanliness about advertising that requires quarantining it to inside pages. I can understand the argument that the front page should be a showcase of all the paper's contents, advertising as well as news. But ads on page one seem to me a distasteful overcommercialization.

Fortunately, no North American newspaper that I have seen has succumbed to a practice common in Latin America and Europe—running ads in the nameplate ears. This position tacitly concedes that the ads there are more important than even the leed story. This must be damaging to editorial self-respect.

Along with display advertising, *reeder ads* ("reader" spelled phonetically to avoid confusion with our major customer) are disappearing from page one. These are small—1- to 4-line—announcements set in body type and in regular, justified measure. They usually don't carry any kind of heads and look like the final paragraph of a news story. Only by an unobtrusive (Adv.) at the end of the widow line is this matter designated as noneditorial. Commonly these are sold on *at-will* or *run-if* basis; they run if there happens to be space. Whenever there is room at the foot of a column, the printer drops in a reeder that happens to fit. The advertiser, of course, is billed only when his reeder appears in print.

I object to this practice because I hate to see readers misled into reading advertising by disguising it as editorial matter. Readers like to read ads; this has been proven beyond doubt. But they hate to be suckered into such reading. Disguising ads is unethical.

One liability of this advertising was discovered by a newspaper I once worked on. A collision of a bus and automobile in our circulation area had brought the greatest number of traffic deaths in a single accident in the state's history. It happened on a holiday and other news was light, so we played it bigger than we might have had the news budget been heftier. More than two columns of body type and many pictures described the scene of horror as bodies were removed from the twisted vehicles. At the bottom of column 8, reading directly out of these descriptions, was the consoling adlet: *Dead carcasses hauled away, call Midstate Rendering Co*. Perhaps it was just coincidence, but that was the last day the paper ran a reeder.

Since editorial fillers have become so rare, these advertising fillers have dwindled, too. One of the advantages that the advertiser saw was that his reeder looked like editorial matter and might get extra readership. If there were no such editorial items, that advantage was lost.

Typographic Regulations for Advertisements

Reeder ads are not the only ones that seek readership by simulating editorial matter. Even more disturbing are larger ones, sold as display advertising, that are made up to look like a news story or picture. The publisher must be alert against this proposed deception of his readers and refuse to be party to such a scheme.

It is difficult, if not impossible, to decree such advertising out of a newspaper, even though the publisher has the right to reject it out of hand without giving a reason. A more effective deterrent is to keep the advertiser from using the same type used by the paper. If the paper uses a Roman head schedule, it can insist that *display reeders* use Sans Serifs. A different body type should be required, especially for the setting of simulated cutlines, and the catchline must be in a different race, too.

The picture that simulates a news photo may be enclosed with a border like a finishing line to make it obviously different.

Display reeders must be labeled as such and are usually identified by a line that repeats the word ADVERTISEMENT clear across the top of the ad. This type should be heavy and conspicuous.

There is always danger of losing revenue and irritating the advertiser who wants to use these devices. There is extra bother for the ad department and comp room in making reeder ads look different from news matter. But the results are worth the trouble. It is more important to keep the goodwill of the newspaper reader than of the advertiser. The publisher need not think that he is abusing his position, often as a monopoly holder, by establishing regulations for advertising. He already has some rules; he obviously wouldn't accept advertising that is obscene or libelous. He wouldn't accept that which, while legal, is in bad taste by community standards. He can, in justice and by law, extend existing restrictions as far as logic or taste requires.

Because the typography of advertising has such an important effect on the overall appearance of the newspaper—and on the reader's acceptance of news matter in the paper—publishers have the duty as well as the right to set certain standards of appearance as well as content. While they fear that the advertiser will be antagonistic to such regulation and that ad linage may suffer, the enforcing of sound typographic rules is actually an advantage to the advertiser. For *borax, schlock,* or *studhorse* ads—overwhelmingly black and brassy ones—may create a false image for the advertiser. They lower the overall quality of the newspaper and therefore every other advertisement is at least a little less effective. For the effectiveness of an individual ad, as we have already noted, is determined to a large degree by the quality of the publication that carries it. Good overall typography—advertising as well as editorial—lends a cachet of quality and authority to every ad in the paper.

Too-black ads require heavy inking on the press, which can result in filling in of halftones in other areas, aggravated set-off and show-through to other pages, and dirty hands for the reader.

Reverse panels, white type on black background, are banned by some papers; others set a maximum on their areas. Still others require that reverses larger than a specified area must be *screened down,* by superimposing a pattern of white dots, to as light as 65% or 70% gray. Type larger tnan designated size must also be screened in some newspapers. That size is determined by the optical weight. A 120-point Caslon might be allowed in full black while a Black Condensed Gothic might have to be screened at 84-point.

Heavy ad borders should be regulated by the publisher. Generally, a refusal will be a favor to the advertiser who wants to use this malfunctional device, as well as to other advertisers in the paper. The first step is to eliminate heavy borders from the newspaper's composing room. There are more than 2,000 different rules and borders that could be used to frame an ad. Even the most lavish type library will offer no more than two or three dozen borders. Thus the principle has already been established: The paper won't furnish all possible ad-border material. After that it's just a question of degree. If the publisher can whittle 2,000 borders down to 30, he can continue the condensation to 20 or 10 or 3. The ones that are eliminated should be the heavy, funereal ones. Only simple, unobtrusive rules should be available to the advertiser.

Of course, ad mat services—those furnished by the paper and those provided by manufacturers—contain much studhorse border material. This should be barred by publisher edict. Rarely does it contribute anything useful to an ad; most of the time it actually detracts from the ad's performance.

Inside News Layout

The functional link between the responsibilities of advertising and editorial departments is the ad dummy. News matter cannot be placed until the ad pyramid has been built.

In a journalistic Utopia, the person who lays the ads would have worked in the news room and the editorial makeup man would have spent time selling ads as well as laying ads, for the more sensitive each is to the other's problems, the more efficiently they can mesh their efforts.

The typical ad dummy given the news room shows only the total area, it does not indicate individual advertisers. But even a dummy that details individual ads doesn't show or suggest all information that is useful to the editor. Often the man who lays the ads doesn't know those facts himself. If he does, he should pass along to the desk the information that an ad has many reverse plates or big areas of black illustration. This will caution the desk against using dark editorial art on that page which might be flooded with ink when the fountain is set to supply the increased amount required by the ad.

Fig. 109. Horizontal ads. Although forbidden in most American papers, horizontal ads are pleasant and functional as shown, left above, in *Frankfurter Allgemeine Zeitung* of Germany. Horizontal half-page ad in *Baltimore News American,* above right, leaves effective area for editorial display. Unusual L-shaped ad, opposite, crosses gutter in center spread in *Seattle* (Wash.) *Post-Intelligencer.*

Ads with large halftone areas or pictures that look like news photos should be signaled so the desk will keep editorial art far removed from it.

As a plus feature, the editor, if he knows about it in time, can use advertising art to enhance his feature material. A news piece about bathing suits, for instance, would be pleasant near a strikingly illustrated ad for such garments. This is best done with stories so strong that they are obviously not mere editorial fluff to curry favor with the advertiser and with stories that have no art of their own. Care must be taken, though, to keep the elements so well separated that the news matter doesn't look like a display reeder.

Certain advertising is unusually sensitive to the news that surrounds it. Airlines don't want a story or jump about an air disaster to be the reading matter next to their ads. Advertisers of liquor, beer, and wine are sensitive to drunk-driving reports. Heat and power companies want their ads far away from reports about gas explosions, especially in homes. The newspaper wouldn't want a story about a Methodist program to run next to an ad for Old Panther Sweat whiskey or obituaries to

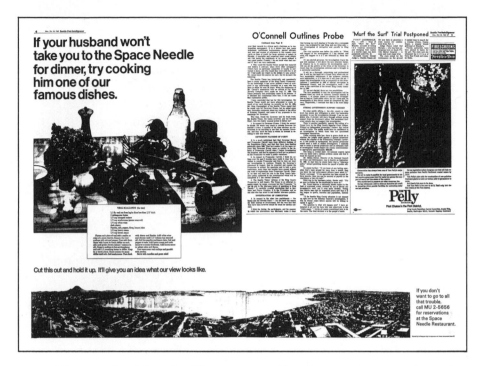
run next to comic-strip ads. The veteran editor learns to spot such stories and develops an almost extrasensory awareness of incipient gaffes.

Some newspapers are experimenting with a series of signals on dummy that will alert the desk to incipient trouble. It is difficult to convey all the relevant information on a dummy, and the incentive to do so is decreased by the fact that it is required only on rare occasions. The publisher must decide whether this signal system is a legitimate insurance against a real risk or whether it's merely a policy against Sputniks dropping on the roof.

The man who draws the ad dummy can give valuable assistance by labeling the individual ad of such sensitive products. A carbon of the original ad dummy would work the same way, of course, in most instances.

But vigilance on the part of the desk is the best insurance. When an editor handles a sensitive story that must run near or next to advertising, he should check with the ad department or metal form to make sure that there is no ad on the proposed page that would create an awkward situation. This alertness can forestall or at least minimize the danger of obvious embarrassments, but it is virtually impossible to note beforehand that a 2-inch story about a disorderly conduct arrest is running alongside the haberdashery ad of the culprit's brother-in-law. Everyone involved can do no more than steel himself against inevitable wrath.

All this discussion assumes that the editorial department dummies all pages and so requires ad dummies. This is essential if inside-page quality is to be maintained. Some newspapers, unfortunately, do not dummy inside pages; others dummy only key pages or those with very little advertising. Some dummy in only one or two leed stories. All these practices put the burden of most of news placement on the printer. Such abdication of editorial responsibility is appalling.

The great variety possible in placing advertising creates innumerable potential page patterns, far too many to attempt to classify. But on all inside pages, with or without advertising, certain principles always apply.

Each inside page must carry a *dominant headline*. This acts as a nucleus around which an obvious page pattern is built. Without such a nucleus, the page does not look made up; it looks accumulated. The dominant head must be obviously the heaviest on the page; it can't be only "a little heavier." A safe, if rough, guideline is that the dominant head should have at least the same number of lines and be at least one column wider and one step in point size larger than the No. 2 head on the page. This recipe can be modified, of course. Three lines of 48-point will obviously outweigh two lines of 24, although both are of the same width. Many a 1-line head is sufficiently heavier than another 2- or 3-liner. But the addition of a kicker will not make a head dominate one of the same size minus kicker. To run two or three heads of identical form and size as the largest on a page is an excellent way of chasing the potential reader away. He just doesn't want to decide which of two or more apparent equals he should read first, so he goes where the decision has been made for him by the editor.

On inside pages there should be a good attention compeller, just as on page one. This need not be the dominant head, but it must be strong enough to grab the entering eye and also to keep the eye from being drawn out of the POA before reading anything there.

Each inside page should have good editorial art. This is most effective at the top of the page. Pictures should be kept as far removed as possible from the ad pyramid. Editorial art that touches advertising, especially if the adjacent ad has strong line illustrations or large halftones, will achieve disappointing readership. Apparently it is mistaken for advertising, and is not read with the same enthusiasm as if it were immediately recognized as a news picture. This, again, does not imply that advertising is anathema to the reader; it merely points out that the reader wants it to be apparent what is advertising and what is news. He apparently dislikes what he cannot readily recognize.

Naked columns, those without a head or picture at the top, should be avoided. To the reader these convey a raw, unfinished appearance. Short folio lines are adequate to dress a naked column.

The biggest danger on inside pages is a tombstone across the top of the page. Breaking the stones is another good reason for keeping editorial art at the top of the page.

A constant danger is that the desk will run headlines too wide and thus exceed the desirable maximum number of characters. But too often the space at the top of the page is so skimpy that the headwriter can't use the normal remedy of going to a larger headletter to reduce the number of letters. In too many instances the ribbon at the top of the page is so shallow that the display type is already deeper than the body type under it.

Some editors run a 1- or 2-column head alongside the ribboned story like a sideline with cutlines. This creates naked columns, of course, but some editors consider this the far lesser of evils. Small pictures, often porkchops, may be run half-up in columns 1 and/or 8 to reduce the width of the ribbon.

The desk should be given permission to fill these impossible areas with house ads. A simple display line extolling the efficacy of classified ads is better than three or four lines of news type. At least it doesn't contribute to the reader's impression that news matter is just packing to keep the ads from rattling around in the page.

Inside-page layout often tempts or requires the desk to use a *Dutch wrap.* A Dutch wrap occurs when a story is run from the last column under its headline into the column at the right. There it runs right under a mass of body type of another story that began higher on the page. In some newspaper shops this is a heinous sin. In others it is given no second thought. Somewhere in between is the practical condition. Dutch wraps should be used most sparingly but not outlawed entirely. There can be rare occasions when such a wrap must be used on inside pages; it should never be tolerated on page one or section pages.

A Dutch wrap must be indicated to the reader by a cutoff rule at the bottom of the first leg of type and at the top of the leg in the next column. (Note that "first leg" refers to the first leg involved in the wrap, not to the first leg in the story. We might have a 3-column head with three legs of type under it, in columns 1 to 3. If we wrap the story into column 4, the cutoff goes at the end of the leg in column 3 and at the top of the wrap in column 4.) These cutoffs act like cushions on a billiard table, making the eye carom into the proper reading channel.

Fig. 110. Inside-page standardization. *Los Angeles* (Calif.) *Times* often carries entire inside page with 2-column head. Lower example adds 1-column head but layout remains consistent.

The two legs of type should overlap a minimum of eight lines, and the second leg should never start lower on the page than the end of the first one. Anything less than this overlap is undesirable, but to separate the two portions entirely is fatal. Sometimes on inside pages when ads are pyramided to the left or in a double pyramid, the first leg of a Dutch wrap may end at an ad and the second leg start alongside the ad but farther down than the foot of the first column. This is particularly bad.

The wrapped, second leg should never begin higher than the headline on the story.

Under no circumstances should more than one Dutch wrap be used on a story. Moreover, one such wrap should be the maximum for any page.

Prepacks

A device especially useful for inside pages, the *prepack,* was invented while the *National Observer* was in the planning stage. This is feature material that can be handled during the lull of a production cycle, "packed" well before using. It is dummied and made up like an ad. It is bordered, and that is the only set part of the layout. Illustrations and body type need not be in regular column increments. Pictures can be handled as silhouettes or with forms other than conventional rectangles. Hand art and line-halftone combinations are pleasant. Heads need not be from the schedule; even hand lettering may be used. All these variations from regular composition and layout are possible because of the additional time possible for prepacking.

Prepacks are made up well in advance of publication. When the desk

Fig. 111. Pre-packs. Examples above are from *National Observer*, originator of technique. Note use of silhouetted halftones, use of signature as headline and combining of line and halftone art. *Fort Lauderdale* (Fla.) *News and Sun-Sentinel* uses 1-column cut with breakbox.

is ready to use such an element, it need only indicate a rectangle of proper size in the dummy, just as the person who lays the ads shows only its area. In neither instance need any detail of the element be shown on the page dummy.

For smaller dailies and weeklies, especially, because their facilities are stretched so thin at deadline time, prepacks can be valuable tools for interesting pages. If subjects are properly chosen, prepacks have a shelf life of several weeks. They can be produced during relatively quiet times in the news and composing rooms and stored for future use. Local features lend themselves well to such treatment. This is exactly the area of news coverage that is usually weakest in smaller papers. By removing the pressure of time from production, prepacks enable the editor to present more of the local features that readers value so highly.

Interestingly, the inventing *National Observer* found that its mechanical facilities were adequate to produce these display elements during the Saturday production cycle. As they didn't have to be prepacked, they could be timely as well as timeless material. No matter when they are produced, though, these features make pleasant additions to the more conventional content of inside pages.

No matter how much effort is required to produce good inside pages, the investment pays handsome dividends. A leading editor who is often asked to judge newspaper excellence contests says, "I always look first at page 9. This is usually a run-of-the-mill inside page. If it's a good one, it's a good indication that the staff hasn't spent all its energy and creativity on front pages. The staff that produces a good page 9 invariably has produced a completely good newspaper."

More important than the plaudits of this judge, though, is the approval of the most important judges, the readers.

chapter **12**

Special Pages

AMERICAN JOURNALISM has recurring flirtations with content departmentalization. News magazines are made up in neatly pigeonholed sections, and application of this technique to newspapers seems inviting in theory. But it wears thin in practice.

In theory, departmentalization is a convenience to the reader. If he is interested in Washington news, he can find all such stories in one familiar place. If he doesn't like economic news, he can skip that entire department.

In practice departmentalization presents many problems. Probably the gravest one is determining the pigeonhole in which to place the story. As government grows constantly larger, a huge percentage of any day's news can be labeled POLITICAL. Is the city budget such a story, or should it come under ECONOMICS? With complex interlocking of events, a single story could just as logically be tabbed LOCAL, STATE, or WASHINGTON. Should all editorials run on their own page, or should one directed to an economic issue run on the business page? (This is not far-fetched; consider how many sports-page columns are really editorials.)

The physical placement of type into departments can be vexatious. Two or three departments appearing on a single page seems inappropriate, yet it is not feasible or even possible to devote a whole page to a single small department. Often the result may be an artificial pruning or expansion of news in a department just to make it fit a predesignated area.

The telling argument against departmentalization may be that it prevents serendipity, finding something interesting while you're looking for something else. It is truly a joy to stumble upon a bright feature, an unexpected story from a familiar place, or a story that throws new light

355

on a familiar or perplexing subject. Many such stories would be hidden from the reader were they identified with some specific department label that the reader found uninteresting.

Remaking pages on the stone would also be difficult. If a new AREA story had to be placed in a later edition, only another AREA story could be displaced. Therefore we might have to bump a good AREA story to make the necessary room and let a weak COUNTY story remain because it wasn't in the proper page.

Departmentalization is sometimes seen as an attraction for potential advertising. TRAVEL and RESORT sections are comparatively new; each was created to offer an attractive package to advertisers. Special editions to support some merchandising event are actually "special sections." Their editorial matter is feature matter, and often its primary nature does not seem to be essential information but only excelsior for packing ads.

There are some departments which are legitimate and functional: the editorial page, the women's, sports, and business pages, and the local, area, or neighborhood sections. In most instances their typography is not unique, but it may be worth looking at.

Often these pages—at least women's, sports, and editorial—have their own headline schedules and sometimes even different cutline type. Those editors who choose to dress special sections in different headletters think that this is the best way to appeal to special audiences. Women's pages are usually dressed in a light headletter to emphasize the supposedly lighter content with particular feminine appeal. For parallel reasons, sports pages often use a heavier headletter weight than news sections. Often these two departments are allowed to make other drastic typographic style changes in body type, picture use, and so on.

It must be granted that these two sections may have well-defined audiences who read only that single section and ignore the rest of the newspaper. But it is doubtful that these audiences exist because of, or are especially attracted by, different head schedules. The sports buff will undoubtedly read the pages devoted to his special interest no matter what headlines are used, and so will the follower of women's news.

The dangers of separate typographical treatment for different departments are obvious and serious. The composing room may be hard put to furnish separate head schedules. It is a rare comp room that will have room on its linecasting machines to keep matrices in position all day long. If this cannot be done, then the operator must *swing magazines,* replace those on the machine with others carrying the desired matrices. This takes time and uncomfortable muscular effort.

The most serious complaint against separate headline schedules is that they tend to fragment a newspaper; this is especially true when different headline styles are used along with different headletters. This fragmentation creates the impression of two or three separate newspapers that just happen to be collected into the same set of pages. The opposite effect should be sought by the editor: Each section should have strong resemblance to every other one. The whole paper should look like a single entity, and any subdivision should look like a subordinate unit, equal but not separate. The more clearly each section is defined by a separate head schedule, the greater the likelihood that the reader of specialized interest is going to stay in that section and not spill over to other pages.

I suggest that the entire newspaper can be dressed in a single head schedule. In addition to the unity created by a single head schedule, this plan is a boon to the composing room. A headline for any section can be set at any time; it need not be deferred until there are enough others to warrant the trouble of swinging a magazine.

The Editorial Page

Editorial pages are enjoying a renaissance after several generations that equated authority with stodginess and dignity with boredom. On this page, more than any other, content is the most important. But good typography is essential too. Unless the reader is exposed to copy by good layout, he won't even know that editorials are treating topics of vital interest to him and doing so in interesting and trenchant style.

Slowly, editors are abandoning the credo that the editorial page must look exactly as it has always looked. Some editors now vary page patterns on this page as much as on the front page.

Proponents of a flexible makeup pattern insist, "The clash of ideas is certainly as exciting as the clash of arms. The world of the mind changes as violently and colorfully as the material world. A good editorial page ought to reflect this vigorous, electric scene."

The editor who subscribes to this theory refuses to be chained down to any standing pattern. One day the editorial column may begin in the primary optical area; the next day a good cartoon or a solid background piece will get the prime position. Editorials may be stretched across the top of the page; they may be boxed in the middle. There may be three or four editorial cartoons one day; the next, a halftone may make the point of an argument. Layout is as flexible as that on page one.

This philosophy requires more work on the part of the editor and of the printer, but the importance of the editorial page is so great—at least

Comment

THE EDMONTON JOURNAL

Published by the proprietor, Southam Press Limited, at the Journal Building, Edmonton, Alberta.
Authorized as second class mail by the Post Office Department, Ottawa, and for payment of postage in cash.

ROSS MUNRO, Publisher — ANDREW SNADDON, Editor

Thursday, November 7, 1968

Why should co-ops have a tax advantage?

THE DECISION of the Trudeau government to tax insurance companies and the dividends and interest earned by their policy-holders appears to have inspired the Equitable Tax Foundation to renew its old fight for the taxing of co-operatives and credit unions in the same way as private business is taxed.

The foundation has asked the Alberta cabinet to help press its fight before the federal government.

The taxing of co-ops is a very hot political potato and, presented with it, many politicians in the past have preferred to start running rather than to discuss it seriously. But there is now a new question that begs an answer: if Ottawa thinks the taxing of insurance companies and policy-holders is necessary as a step toward a fairer sharing of the colossal and growing tax burden, why should not co-ops and their members be similarly taxed on their financial gains?

The foundation is supported by the Alberta Chamber of Commerce and 18 Canadian trade associations representing thousands of small, medium and large businesses who feel they are seriously discriminated against by the tax concessions given to co-ops which are engaged in exactly the same kind of business.

Commercial co-ops and credit unions have grown to big business in Canada. In Alberta alone, the assets of credit unions had reached $87 million by 1967. Commercial co-ops are estimated by the foundation to have captured 7.7 per cent of the Alberta retail food business, 7.9 per cent of the lumber and building materials trade, and 15 per cent of the hardware business.

The foundation has submitted a strong case for:

- *Applying income tax to the net profits of co-ops prior to the deduction of patronage dividends;*
- *Treating patronage dividends in the hands of recipients in the same manner as the dividends paid to shareholders of ordinary corporations;*
- *Abolishing the three-year total tax exemption now given new co-ops and eliminating the other special concessions they enjoy;*
- *Discontinuing the present total tax exemption now enjoyed by credit unions and requiring them to pay income tax on the same basis as competing financial organizations.*

The claim in the past of co-ops and credit unions to tax exemptions has been at least partly ideological. But Canada is not a collectivist society—not yet anyway. It is difficult to see why one kind of business and the private citizens who patronize it should be favored over another kind of business, selling exactly the same kind of goods or services, and the private citizens who patronize or own shares in it.

Dividing research funds

THE FEDERAL government's decision to provide $195,000 for Opposition party research is most commendable. Yet, one must wonder at the allocation of the funds to the three parties on the other side of the House.

As it is at the moment, the government will allow the Conservatives $125,000 in public funds for research purposes; the NDP and the *Creditistes* are to get $35,000 each.

There can be no argument as to the value of some cash being placed at the disposal of the Opposition parties. Hopefully, it will mean a better informed Opposition and a proportionate displacement of unreasoned or unfounded criticism.

But why $125,000 for the Conservatives and $35,000 for both the NDP and the *Creditistes*? That, on the basis of seats won in the June 25 general election, works out to $1,590 per seat for the NDP, $1,736 per seat for the Conservatives and $2,500 per seat for the *Creditistes*.

If one resists the rather obvious temptation to observe that some political parties are in much greater need of research than others, then one must conclude that the allocation of funds by the government has been on a somewhat less than scientific basis, a basis that cannot, surely, be regarded as any guide for the future. In this regard the suggestions put forward by Mr. David Lewis, parliamentary leader of the NDP, are attractive.

Mr. Lewis has suggested that the parties should be given $2,000 per seat, and that the Liberal backbenchers also be provided with funds. Thus, Mr. Lewis would attach a simple formula to the allocation of research funds, in the process removing it from the control of the government party, and at the same time, perhaps take a step toward greater involvement of government backbenchers in their party's governing process.

Notes

SNAKES ARE reported to be a hazard on Canadian relief flights to Biafra—real ones, apparently: nothing to do with all that beer flown in to the troops.

★ ★ ★

AFTER OTTAWA has told the provinces what they must spend money on, Finance Minister Benson says all the provinces "must decide for themselves their own spending and taxing programs." For sheer whimsy, there is nothing like it in all the writings of Lewis Carroll.

"On second thought, it's all yours, fellows!"

How Mayor Daley saw the campaign

by D. J. R. Bruckner
Los Angeles Times Service

CHICAGO

MAYOR RICHARD Daley thinks that "the great wave of emotionalism and hatred" which shattered usual party politics this year subsided in the final weeks before Tuesday's election.

But it left behind it intense division, he says, which will make the problem of governing the nation "undoubtedly one of the biggest and toughest problems the next president will face."

He praised Senator Edmund S. Muskie, the Democratic vice-presidential candidate, "for offering the best possible advice to the American people and to its leaders when he asked us to try to get to know one another and understand each other and to work together. Muskie is right in that approach. If we can get a new commitment among ourselves to live together and work together, we can solve our problems. It is the biggest issue facing this country."

"Politics-as-usual has been torn apart this year by hate campaigns and by an epidemic of fear among the people which grows out of popular unrest over the war in Vietnam," he said in an interview.

Once the unrest and fear stemming from the war spread far enough, he continued, "it came to involve a lot of other things. We have a lot of problems, in the economy and in the cities and throughout the country. The war protest movement simply became a centre for them."

The first victim of the war weariness, Mr. Daley said, was President Johnson. "Just look at the hate campaign that has been conducted against him," he said.

The connection between war weariness and other discontents, Mr. Daley said, showed up most clearly in the law and order issue in the national campaign. As a result of his stiff orders for a police crackdown after ghetto riots here last April and the action of the Chicago police during the Democratic convention, Mr. Daley has become widely identified with the law and order issue. He does not discuss this identification publicly but he is known to be angered by it.

He said the issue is the chief manifestation of the fear he believes has swept over the people, and it is "a very dangerous and confusing one. . . It means different things in different parts of the country. . . It is difficult to know what it means as a national issue. It is not a valid issue.

"I know, and I say to people, that you have to have an orderly society. I know that the constitution gives the people the right of protest and assembly. It is a basic right, and it must be protected. The only emphasis I would add is that the law specifies 'peaceable assembly,' and that is the way it should be.

★ ★ ★

"But you cannot merely have law and order. You have to have social justice along with it. You have to have better housing and schools and jobs and opportunities for everyone."

Furthermore, Mr. Daley added, "Law and order is not in itself a racial issue. It has been made into one by some politicians and other people, but that is very wrong. Disorder is not a racial thing."

George Wallace, he said, was at once the product and centre of the "great wave of emotionalism" in the campaign.

Mr. Daley attributed much of his decline to "the fact that people began to think about the presidency rather than only to feel about the election."

Mr. Daley refuses to criticize the youth who have led many of the protests across the nation — protests, which, he admits, trouble him. Some radical youths have charged that "the establishment" has declared war on them.

Mr. Daley, who acknowledges that he is considered one of the leaders of this establishment, said: "That is nonsense. I know perfectly well that, if there are leaders among the youth, these leaders are establishment of tomorrow. Nobody can prevent that. I know there is an age gap. There was one between me and my father and there is one between me and my sons. But I do not consider that an evil, and I do not consider it a gap in the sense that it is something that cannot be gotten across. We can communicate with one another."

"We do not pay enough attention to the hard-working young people. I talk to some of them sometimes, and they tell me how alienated the establishment is from them. These are young people working hard to get an education or to improve their jobs. . .To me, it looks like they are trying to work to get into the establishment, not to tear it down," Mr. Daley said.

In this respect, he criticizes some of the news media: "Television has a lot to do with the kind of youth leadership you see now. A kid gets on television and says he is the head of some movement, and immediately he is. Then there are imitators springing up all over. I think sometimes the media lose track of the majority of the people, of the young and the old. Not every spokesman has a following, you know."

He believes that a majority of the black people in Chicago "are not ready to follow extremists. I believe that what they want is what everyone else wants—an opportunity to get ahead, and my concern is to see that they get that opportunity. I hear about all these proclamations and movements, but you cannot forget the people and what they want. You have to meet those demands — for homes, jobs, education and equality."

Letters to The Journal

Who's in charge?

I DON'T KNOW why I wasted my time and energy voting and voicing my opinion on store hours. I see by your paper that the city council does just what it pleases anyway.

The majority of the people of Edmonton said they wanted the city to have nothing to do with regulating store hours. Apparently council disagrees.

Are these people elected to do as the people want, or what? Maybe they could answer this without forming a committee to find out what their job is.

109th Street — Average Citizen

Indefensible

THE JOURNAL November 1 carried several letters in defense of the actions of aldermen Evans and Tanner concerning their delay of the third reading of a by-law to get the city out of the regulation of business hours.

I cannot agree at all with the rationalization of their motives.

The delay to give stores an opportunity to reorganize their staffs and plan their operational activities is entirely without foundation. The by-law is not a compulsion; stores do not have to stay open. In effect, the by-law simply says, run your own affairs without city council interference.

Those stores which are not prepared for a change of hours do not *have* to change their hours. They could have made the necessary changes in their own good time.

104th Street — Julian Kinisky

Ode to Peter

CHIEF Commissioner plans "orientation course" at Overlander Lodge for new city council (*Journal news item*).

An ode;

Away up so high in the proud eagle's nest
The Planner looks wide o'er his realm;
"So it isn't as large as an empire to rule!
But c'est Moi - it is me at the helm!
"Of course there will always be flies in the salve
Like those pesky 12 people downstairs.
Now - how do we get them to dance on their strings
Like puppets, but quite unawares?
"We'll wash out their skulls and rinse out their brains
And they'll never feel one twinge of pain.
Our methods are modern and quite up-to-date;
We're no Mao - we're really humane.
"A holiday trip to a lodge in the wilds—
We'll dine them and rock them to rest;
We will seal them off tight from the outside world
Till they lose all their bothersome zest.
"We have lovely ideas hatched out of thin air—
Or inspired right from Heaven, 'tis plain,
We'll adapt them a bit and pour them straight in
To whatever they use for a brain.
"Some brainwashing victims hold out, it is true,
For a week or a month or a year;
But for this motley crew four days is enough—
They'll be docile . . . save for one —and she's queer!
"At the end of four days they will come trooping back
To the tune of the masterly mind—
Like Little Bo-Peep at the head of my sheep—
But they'll leave their heads far behind."

133rd Street — Amused

Laundered language in Prague

by Alfred Friendly
Washington Post Service

PRAGUE

ONE OF THE lesser but still not inconsiderable miseries in communist countries is the never-ending affront to the language.

The jargon and the circumlocutions, their use to cloak and deceive rather than to reveal, the passion for orotund statement, the automatic insertion of the threadbare phrase that has been stripped of all meaning—all this has been long since anatomized by the experts, notably Orwell.

A visitor to a communist country, dropped into the middle of the verbal slough and forced to muck his way through it, can scarcely repress a cry of agony.

The communists, it would seem, have become subscribers to the doctrine that power comes from discovering the secret names of the world's basic objects and forces, but that those names must never be uttered aloud.

It seems significant that almost the first civil regulation ordered by the Soviets was the prohibition of the term "occupation troops" in the Czechoslovak press. They must be referred to as "the troops of the Warsaw Pact countries."

The word "invasion" is itself taboo. The nation's leaders refer to "the August events." Czechoslovakia's consequent state of subjection is euphemized as "this difficult period."

Each day in Prague, the national news agency Ceteka dumps into the swamp two or three score of mimeographed pages from which the news, if any, must be discovered by foreign correspondents in a kind of placer mining process to wash off the sludge.

★ ★ ★

The experts, long experienced in decipherment, know instantly that when President Svoboda refers to "this difficult period" and says: "We must face reality without romanticism, matter of factly and resolutely in harmony with the interests of the further socialist development of our country and the interests and needs of the world's socialist community," he is really saying: "Sorry, friends, but this is how the Russians are making us do it."

The novice often gives up the numbing process in despair, abandoning all hope of ever coming to solid ground.

"The federalization will result in the creation of the qualitatively higher organization prerequisites for the possibility of a new integration of opinions and art based on the profession of common principles," says a resolution of the Central Committee of the Czechoslovak Union of Writers.

The National Trade Union chairman says that "socialism cannot be a matter of strict directives, people cannot be manipulated but must be counted with those who create both contemporeanity and history . . . The present difficulties are just in these distortions resulting from both dogmatic - sectarian and rightist excesses."

The "Big Four" leaders of the country tell its youth: "The legal organs of our party and state are implementing the content of the (Moscow) agreements because they regard them as an open method of solving the given situation, a method corresponding to the realities . . ."

Alexander Dubvek, the Communist Party leader who was to have taken Czechoslovakia into new paths of freedom and "humanism," before the Russians interfered, cuts his speeches from the same dies. A Moscow education is not easily forgotten.

He tells the party faithful in a chemical plant: "The economic party policy of the party will in this connection proceed from the principles of socialist economy: from economic planning linked with the utilization of the objective operation or the law of value and of material interest as well as of correct interaction of the plan and market relations . . .

★ ★ ★

"The implementation of this (federalization) law will involve a great deal of work which will call for great political attentiveness since we must in practice solve very sensitively the practical content of the work and relationships of national and all-state organs so that this may be a contribution to the unity of the state, a contribution to its management and development and a contribution to national development and initiative."

One may only conclude that, owing to immature development of generally valid principles of obfuscation, with respect to creative practice corresponding to scientific realities ridden of all excesses and purged of rigidity in socialist homelands, Czech government statements suffer deformities and imperfections and are, in gobbledegook, mere kindergarten stuff.

Fig. 112. Editorial pages. Strong treatment by *Edmonton* (Alta.) *Journal*. Note prominent label COMMENT, large heads, and generous use of white space.

it should be so great—that any extra effort required to build readership is well worth it.

Editorials and their supporting matter make more difficult reading than the sports page. They pose problems which at best demand that the reader think and at worst disquiet him deeply. Most of us will not willingly plunge into such reading; we must be coaxed.

Editorial-page typography must also distinguish this page of opinion and comment from pages of fact and objectivity. This is not an easy job. The public, it seems, can't distinguish the editorial page and its legitimate subjectivity from the news pages with their studied objectivity. When a reader asks the editor, "Please put this editorial in the paper," he may be referring to a news story, letter to the editor, want ad, or simple announcement—sometimes even an editorial. A distinctly different typographic appearance is a good first step in the attempt to distinguish different pages and their functions. Accurately or not, we do judge a book by its cover.

Historically, the editorial page has carried the masthead. This element includes, among other things, the legally required *indicia* of second-class postal matter. Post Office regulations demand that this matter be carried in the first five pages of a newspaper. The fallacy that a right-hand page was more valuable for advertising meant that the publisher was reluctant to keep an entire odd-numbered page ad-free, as the editorial page customarily is. Thus the last possible left-hand page, page 4, was used for the editorial page and its cargo of indicia. Today the editorial page is still found most frequently near the front of the newspaper, and I have never seen it on an odd-numbered page.

Some papers carry the necessary postal indicia in tiny type in their page-one nameplate area or in an inconspicuous box on the first available inside page. This frees them from a need to keep the whole editorial page near the front of the paper. They can then move it where logic, rather than custom or postal rules, dictates.

In the past decade or so, several newspapers have moved their editorial page to the very last page of the paper. They reason that when the reader has completed the day's news, he is more ready for the mental effort of assaying ideas. They believe, too, that having the editorial page as the very last one assures that the reader will end his visit with that issue on an upbeat.

Whatever the reasons, back-page editorial pages show high readership. This cannot be attributed solely to position, however. Chances are strong that the editor who thinks enough about his editorial page to experiment with its position is also setting high standards for its content.

Another tradition about the editorial page is being set aside. In the past the masthead has always run at the POA with the editorials proper immediately under it. Now the trend is toward using only the nameplate of the paper above the editorials. This is like announcing your name in a public meeting before you state your views; it identifies the editorials as the corporate opinion of the newspaper.

The masthead is run elsewhere, usually at the bottom of the page. This arrangement keeps the leed editorial close to the POA. The masthead itself, because it is usually boxed and may carry ornamentation, gives needed typographic color at the foot of the page.

An interesting bit of trivia: Folio lines traditionally are not used on the editorial page. Date and page number, plus volume and number, are placed in the masthead.

The "volume" of a newspaper is a year's issues. Originally all the issues of the entire year could be bound into a single book, and that is how the term was put into use. Today, of course, the 365 issues of a "volume" of the *Los Angeles Times,* let's say, would make a book of impossible dimensions.

Most weeklies can still get a year's production into a single book. Papers of greater frequency must use several books, often more than one a month. But the volume designation remains the same for an entire year. Almost always that year begins with the first issue of the paper, the historic Vol. I, No. 1, though a few newspapers have adopted the calendar year. A few improperly use two or more volume numbers during a single 12-month span; this isn't illegal, but it is incorrect and confusing. The "number" refers to one entire issue of the paper and is the same for an entire day's production, no matter how many editions there may be.

If possible, editorials should be set in body type larger than that used for straight news. This makes easier reading, physically at least. Headlines on editorials ought to be large too. I am often puzzled by the reasoning of some editors. They put big heads on news stories with great inherent interest, yet they think that editorials—often considerably less interesting—can get enough readership with a small label head.

Editorials proper are set specifically for this page and, usually, for a particular area in the page. They are never bumped off the page by late-breaking copy. They are usually set early in the production cycle. So the line length on editorials can be just about any measure desired. The optimum-format is practical on this page because on most newspapers this is a key, ad-free page. The W-format, also, has advantages for the editorial page. Much material other than the editorials themselves is transmitted as wire tape, and it's efficient to set it by automated line-caster. Some articles on this page might run elsewhere, so it is handy to have some copy on this page set in regular column widths. Much syndicated art is furnished in 11-pica increments, so it helps to have some regular-measure copy to tie in with it.

If the newspaper uses column rules elsewhere, the alleys of open formats help make the page look different from news pages. But if open format is used elsewhere in the paper, alleys alone won't distinguish the opinion page. A few editors use column rules on this page because they want contrast against the open alleys of other pages. But in this case the column rule is centered on a wide strip, often 1 pica wide, instead of the much narrower base of conventional column rule, and so optimum or W-setting is still required.

Some editors label the page OPINION, COMMENT, POINT OF VIEW, or a similar designation. Often the descriptive word is tied around the nameplate.

Sometimes a decorative rule is used as a cutoff at the bottom of every story, with its only function to add some typographic color to set this page apart. Almost any kind of rule or border works here as long as it is not too gaudy, though it must contrast with the rule used for boxes on regular pages.

The most conspicuous element on the typical editorial page is the editorial cartoon. Cartoonists' styles vary, of course, and the tonal weight of their work varies too. All share, however, the distinctive flavor of line work. Many editors like to reinforce this flavor by using other line art on the page. Pen-and-ink sketches of columnists whose pictures are often run with their writings are a favored device. Most syndicates offer sketches of their writers, but if only photographs are available, they can be converted into line art by linear definition.

All column headings on this page should have a strong resemblance. These heads ought to be simple. Here the editor must resist the temptation of busy and cute headings.

Kickered heads work well on columns. If the author's picture is used, it can be placed in the headline area. This obviates the need to set the picture into the type column.

A pleasant problem is that of handling letters to the editor. These letters are the delight of every editor. Whether they are of the Dear-sir-I-concur or the Dear-sir-you-cur variety, they show that the newspaper is being read and that it is performing its major function of comforting the afflicted and afflicting the comfortable. Letters have high readership; it is salutarily humbling for the editor to realize that the epistles of the village idiot will be preferred by the public above his own erudite and scintillating writings.

For many, many years a simple label head on the whole department and 10-point bold labels on individual letters were all that were needed —or at least all that were provided. Today each letter is likely to get a headline, often as large as 4-column 36-point. They aren't necessarily collected under a label LETTERS heading, either; they might run as independent as a column anywhere on the page.

The editor's primary typographic problem is establishing a style that clearly identifies these as letters from readers. Probably the best way is to set the communication as a letter with a formal salutation:

> *Editor, Homeville Gazette*
> *Dear Sir:*

The writer's name is at the end, like the signature on any letter, but without the formal "Yours truly":

> *John H. Smith*
> *1259 East Grandview*
> or
> *Mrs. Richard T. Roe*
> *Hampton Center*

Giving the address lends interest to the letter and may explain the writer's special interest or point of view. This method seems more appropriate than giving a conventional byline, as some newspapers do. This seems to be the mark of the professional writer, and much of the value and interest of these letters are exactly that they are not the work of professionals.

The problems of providing a separate headline schedule for the editorial page, already discussed, are minimized because there are comparatively few heads on this page. For that very reason it may be economically unsound to provide a separate schedule on the Linotype keyboard. For the same reason, it may be feasible to set editorial-page heads in foundry type out of a job case. To many production managers, this sounds like retrogression, but simple hand methods can be more efficient than total mechanization for simple and infrequent jobs.

Choices for an editorial headletter are as many as for any schedule. The letter should be legible and handsome; it should have adequate weight. Often the editorial page is too light. The character count of the letter is of less importance on this page because almost all heads will be in wider measures that take pressure off the headwriter. Unless the face is a variation in weight of the regular headletter, it should be in very marked contrast to it.

Some editors choose an Old Style Roman for this page because of the dignity and authority inherent in these faces. Also because few newspapers use Old Romans for news heads, the contrast is obvious. Square Serifs are excellent for edit-page use, also because so few papers use this race for news heads.

A separate editorial-page head schedule should be rated as a pleasant luxury; it is by no means a necessity.

Some smaller newspapers just can't afford an entire page for editorials. Some must place advertising on this page; some must run news as well as ads. However, this need not destroy the page's identity or value.

If ads must be run, they ought to be typographically quiet and preferably without art. They should be placed in a rectangular area rather than being pyramided and, ideally, should be run clear across the bottom of the page, squared off at the top, of course. The effect is almost as pleasant, though, if full columns at the right of the page carry the ads and a vertical portion of the page is used for editorial purposes.

Advertisers are usually aware of the high readership of the editorial page and look upon this as preferred position. They are usually so pleased to get this position that they will not insist on being next to reading matter. Often they will adopt a more chaste typographical style to be compatible with the tone of the editorial page.

If news matter must run on this page, it too should be segregated into a rectangular area. A conspicuous rule should be used to separate this space from that carrying commentary. The rule used for sideless boxes is effective.

Many editors are concerned whether, how often, and how editorials should be run on the front page. Several years ago, when I was associated with a weekly newspaper, we decided to run an "editorial page"— so labeled—on page one. We had a 9-column format and used the first two columns for the edit section. More often than not, the entire two columns were devoted to this purpose. Along with editorials proper, we ran a from-our-files feature, this-day-in-history for the coming week, and a list of birth, wedding, business, and other significant local anniversaries. This matter has very high readership and had been run on the conventional editorial page when we had one. We used their popularity to attract the reader to the new position for editorials. Later we often ran this feature material elsewhere and cut the "page" down to a small portion of the two columns or left it out entirely. It was regularly moved down the column to allow art or news above it. The technique worked

Fig. 113. Treatment of letters to editor. Editorial page of *Beverly* (Mass.) *Times* devotes most space to letters from readers.

Tampa (Fla.) *Tribune-Times* gives entire Sunday page to letters to editor.

well. With a 9-column page, we found we could provide the needed area on page one with little trouble. Readership of editorials proved high, although I am not convinced it rose only because of the shift to the front page.

If editorials don't run on page one every issue or almost that frequently, they should be carried there only for most exceptional reasons. I hate to place numbers on any editorial judgment, but I'd say that once every two or three years ought to be the maximum for running editorials on page one.

During the past decade, some newspapers have experimentally used halftone art in place of editorial cartoons with very happy results. A photograph can make an editorial point just as effectively as a drawing on many occasions and more effectively on a few. Great care must be taken, however, that the point is made by factual reporting. Camera fakery and distortion to make an argument can quickly destroy the reader's belief in the objectivity of news pictures.

Some editors believe that halftones used as editorials should have some visual differentiation from news-page photos. One way is to include a finishing line around the plate. This is a simple procedure, although it requires a little added care during the guillotining of the individual engraving out of the engraver's *flat*—a group of smaller cuts made as a single piece of metal through the etching process, then cut down into the individual components.

'Perhaps Then I Could Find Some Peace'

TAMPA — On the 25th day of this month it was six months since our son paid the supreme sacrifice in Vietnam.

This has been such a tragic loss to us that there is no way to describe our feelings—the tears that choke us; the sleepless nights; the completely helpless feeling that we could not help our son; could not sit by his bedside and hold his hand as we had done so many times in the past when he was sick or hurt.

We had Thanksgiving dinner early last year so he would not miss the holiday which means so much to the American family. Now he is home, but he does not sleep in his bed any more. Instead I visit him every day in his plot at the cemetery. How many others are tortured the same way we are?

Nobody can help us now. But we might be able to find some consolation if we felt Vietnam was necessary. The Tribune and readers could help by writing your Congressmen. Tell them to let them bomb targets such as railroads, seaports, bridges, hiding places—flush the enemy out. Force them to the peace table instead of asking them.

I was a Marine in WW II. Just as my son was. I was not handicapped by orders not to shoot at shrines. We were not tried for murder for killing the enemy.

Urge Congressmen to let us fight this war like Americans—not like a fighter shadow boxing.

I wish there was a way I could go to Vietnam to see the land and the people my son went to protect.

Perhaps then I could find some peace instead of tearing myself to pieces thinking that my son along with countless other sons, husbands, fathers, sweethearts, and boys next door were deprived of their right to a full and enjoyable life in this wonderful country of ours for no good reason.

ARTHUR A. DENHOFF.

THOMAS DENHOFF

EVERY ONE OF SCHOOL AGE SHOULD LEARN TO SWIM
These Bartow Tots With Safety Equipment Take Lessons

Why A $4,000 Scrapbook Keeper?

TAMPA — As a loyal and devoted city employe, I would like to ask Mayor Greco how he can justify retaining Mrs. Ferlita on his office staff to maintain a scrapbook, at a time when he and his self professed geniuses are crying that the city is so short of moeny and the poor city employes in the lower pay ranges do not earn enough to support their families, and when he is asking his department heads to hold up on filling vacant positions.

At the present time, Mayor Greco has an assistant, a secretary, a receptionist, a second receptionist (scrapbook collector), and a secretary for his assistant on his staff.

If the Mayor needs a scrapbook to remind him of his late appointments and political and friendship appointments to positions that could be handled by existing city personnel, I am sure that one of the girls in the many city departments would be able to keep his scrapbook for him. I for one, would be more than happy to do so, if it would mean saving the city over $4,000 a year in Mrs. Ferlita's salary.

With no money available to buy badly needed vehicles, machinery and equipment for the various city departments, this $4,000 could certainly be put to much better use.

Cut down, cut down is all you get from the Mayor and his assistant. The Mayor should set the example and perhaps then his department heads would follow the lead willingly and city employes would be more patient and understanding.

I love my job dealing with the public and being of service to the citizens of Tampa, but it gets harder to explain to the complaining citizens why things that should be done are not, when they read articles like the one in the July 12 Tampa Tribune.

O.H.

Mrs. Greco's Friend Blames the Press

McGUIRE AIR FORCE BASE — In the July 12 Tribune an article stated that Mayor Greco kept union officials waiting while he talked with "Mrs. Greco and her friend."

When Mrs. Greco and I arrived at the Mayor's office, he was being interviewed by members of the press (the real culprits who kept union officials waiting).

We observed the interview and after the press left, spent less than five minutes alone with Mayor Greco. If the press exaggerates on such a trivial matter, how can the public know what is really fact in the newspapers? — MRS. L. G.

Only Wallace Can Correct Our Mistakes

TAMPA — Yes, we live in the land of the free. Too free and why? Should it be, I ask? It is so much so that the people all over the world as in our own country are taking advantage of it. That is the trouble now.

The Communist, segregationist, free guns and freedom to murderers. Other laws passed by a Supreme Court who thinks up these ungodly laws to be passed as only the higher court can. I can only see that these men instigated much of the recent years of trouble we are having today. Things were not happening so rapidly, if any, until certain laws were passed. It is now getting out of hand. People knew where they stood because they felt fear. You would think the older heads who have lived longer could foretell what passing a law could bring about. There are two ways out of this situation.

First, praying for God to have his way in solving these problems. Then, if it be His will putting a man in as President who can keep do away with some of the trouble and restore things to normal, if possible. Not one who will keep letting new thoughts build up in these men's minds to be passed beyond ever being controlled and he will do something about television shows that encourage crime and sex behavior.

There is only one of the five men running for President who sees these mistakes and might be able to solve some of them. That is George Wallace.

Dick Gregory, the Negro entertainer, made the statement that at least he felt that George Wallace was the most honest man of these men for President. He is not a rich man with money.

We can only help to do our part in trying to better our United States of America by helping support George Wallace financially and always speaking well of him to enlighten people of what he stands for. Too many times people go by what an inexperienced person such as mouthy Claude Kirk might say in his own opinion and fall for it. Let us do our part by helping Mr. Wallace spread his beliefs and issues. Otherwise we can regret not doing so later.

MRS. L. JOHNSON

GEORGE WALLACE
He Sees the Mistakes

Utility Protest

TAMPA — How has the Florida Public Service Commission served the public by palming off the 10 per cent surtax onto the consumers of Tampa Electric Company's electricity?

It positively was not the President's nor the Congress's intent when they passed the 10 per cent surtax on income and corporate taxes for individuals to pay this surtax for corporations.

I protest this action, and doubt if they actually had the authority to do so. How about renaming this derelict Commission the Commission For The Best Interest of the Florida State Uutility Companies?

ANTHONY H. ZILLUISKI

Tax Churches And Club Property Too

TAMPA — The taxpayers of Tampa and Hillsborough County are furnishing, free of charge, to the churches and their apartment houses, etc.; all the clubs and organizations, the streets, police and fire protection. They are leeches on the backs of the taxed people.

You can bet the insurance companies are not giving them free building insurance.

Let's have a referendum and if you own property you can vote for all to pay taxes. — R. E. L. MOBLEY.

'Like Goat Guarding Cabbage Patch'

LAKELAND — By coincidence or otherwise, Claude Kirk seems to have used some understandable political intelligence in aligning himself with Nelson Rockefeller, disregarding the probability of Kirk having badgered Nixon for the GOP's number two spot. In the event of the latter it is indeed conceivable that the clenched teeth conservatism of Nixon slammed the door tight against the flamboyant political amateur with a ravenous appetite for the Vice Presidency.

As a Democrat I would indeed welcome the nomination of Nixon by the GOP, being convinced as I am that Nixon can be easily swamped by any responsible Democrat. Likewise, an ugly paradox seems to be a suicidal political complex on the part of the Republicans to reject any modern minded statesman of the Rockefeller calibre, and it would appear that the dominant minds of the GOP exist in a kind of twilight zone of political never, never. Therefore it seems the GOP is again headed for defeat with two-time loser Nixon.

A dominant reality is that numerous Democrats would cross party lines to vote for Nelson Rockefeller if given an opportunity to do so. That they will be denied this choice is almost a foregone conclusion when the dark lessons of Goldwater and Nixon are brought into focus. Nixon's star is eclipsed and shows only a dim kind of weirdness; sending that man to the White House would be roughly the equivalent of appointing a goat as caretaker of a cabbage patch.

KYZER E. STEWART, SR.

Reimburse Driver For Lost Wages

KEYSVILLE — How about taking a poll on whether car owners should be paid for taking their cars or automobile to the inspection station?

It will cost two to five dollars to take an auto for inspection, depending on loss of wages or time from one's work. — L. B. BROADWELL.

Electoral College Should Reflect Popular Vote

TAMPA — Your very enlightening lead editorial of July 21, contained what I believe to be an inaccuracy (happily, this is a rare occurrence in your newspaper).

You stated that the votes of the electoral college are pledged to the winner(s) of the popular vote in each state. I believe that, technically, although not realistically, a member of the electoral college may vote for a n y o n e of his choosing (though not for two residents of his state). To me, this is the basic weakness of the electoral college. It has the power, in effect, to disfranchise the vast majority of American voters.

The vote of the electoral college should reflect the popular vote, if, indeed, this absurd institution must continue to exist.

CHARLES SHEEHAN

Halt Those Tragic Drownings

PLANT CITY — Since drownings are fast becoming one of the most frequent cause of deaths in the state of Florida, it is obviously apparent that some drastic steps should be taken to reduce same. In order to make such effective laws will have to be legislated, and enforced by all law enforcement officials, with the bulk of them being administered by both fresh and salt water wardens who will be in better contact with such than anyone else.

Listed below are some suggestions which probably should be legislated, in order to prevent these frequent and uncalled for drownings which like auto accidents, are becoming entirely too common, and must be stopped.

It should be made mandatory that everyone at least of school age should know how to swim, and be in possession of a lawful certificate stating such, if they are to boat, bathe, swim, or fish in the waters of the state of Florida, including swimming pools.

Every school in the state should have access to an adequate swimming pool and require every student, under the supervision of the physical education instructor to be taught to swim and rescue.

Every public swimming pool should be required to designate some individual proficient in swimming to teach such on certain days for a nominal sum. Licenses for building private pools should only be issued to those who know how to swim including their families and friends who are to use them.

Boats should never be overloaded nor allowed to be occupied by anyone without a swimming certificate or license, as the case may be.

Owners of boat camps should be held equally responsible for this. A dramatic example of this took place on Lake Easy near Lake Wales in Polk County. A grove man had eight children in a small boat, which capsized, on account of it being overloaded, and all but one child, who clung to the boat, drowned because none of them could swim. In this case two obvious water rules of long standing were flagarantly violated, but no laws prohibiting such were in existence, so far as I know.

Such legal regulations are highly necessary in order to protect people against themselves. For after all is done and said, they are their greatest enemies, and must be protected against themselves.

The Governor should immediately appoint a Legislative Committee to study this situation and offer a solution for improvement. It is a most serious matter and must be intelligently dealt with without further delay.

WILLIAM H. TAYLOR SR.

Letters To The Tribune

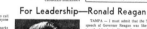

Takes Five Days For Mail To Fort Myers

TAMPA — In reference to the proposal to private industry to take over the Post Office Department, I thoroughly agree.

Unless the Post Office Department can explain, why on the average it takes five days for a letter from our daughter in North Fort Myers to reach us here in Tampa?

Eight days on an average, for a letter from our son in Indianapolis, Ind., to reach Tampa? This also is the case for our mail to reach either place. For example:

We planned on going to Fort Myers for a few days, so we mailed a letter to our daughter three days before we were to leave. We arrived in Fort Myers four days later. Two days after we had arrived in Fort Myers the letter reached our daughter. This happens about every time we write one another.

Yet through Armed Forces Postal System, we can receive a letter from a friend in Thailand in three days.

It is my firm conviction a private concern can do a great deal better job, then than the Post Office is doing.

Also why, when I send a payment, within the city of Tampa, the company calls five days later saying they have not received such. — R. L. K.

Letters must bear the writer's true name (signed in ink or pencil) and street address but, if specifically requested, only initials will be used in publication. The Tribune reserves the right to reject any letter or shorten it to meet space requirements. Normally, a letter may not exceed 500 words and must be written on only one side of the paper. Only original letters, written exclusively to The Tribune, will be considered. Poetry cannot be used.

County Roads Lack White Center Lines

GIBSONTON — There is much talk these days regarding the safety inspection of automobiles, which, supposedly, is to make them safer to drive. That's all fine, but how about Hillsborough County making some of its roads safer to drive on, after the car has passed inspection? I'm referring to white center lines. Here are a few examples:

Gibsonton Drive was black topped at least a year and a half ago, and still has no center line, and there are some bad curves toward its eastern terminus at Highway 301.

A year ago, 78th Street was widened and re-topped south from 22nd Causeway, and still no center line to its terminus at Riverview Drove.

That road, (Riverview Dr.), could also use some paint, as what is there, is very indistinct.

Orient Road from State Road 60, west, no center line.

Bloomingdale Road from 301, east, no line, even at intersections.

These are all through roads, and used by many drivers.

Probably there are many, many more, and this condition should not be allowed to continue. With some of these foggy early mornings we have, it's a wonder that drivers who have to use these roads to get to work, ever get to their destinations without accidents.

I believe the National Safety Council also advocates a solid line along the edges of roads and highways, but at least we should have center lines. — J. F. CAIRNS.

Kirk Should Mind His Own Business

TAMPA — If Gov. Kirk would stay home, attend to his own business and keep his nose out of George Wallace's business I am sure both would be better off.

Yes, I am one of those registered Democrats who voted for Kirk (and have regretted it since). However, we did not have much of a choice at that time.

N. C. MILLER

Suppose Sniper Hit Your Family

BRANDON — Once again it's happened. I refer to the recent incident in New York's Central Park where a sniper, after shooting and killing a young woman, proceeded to fire widly into the park wounding two policemen and an elderly man who later died. Other people could have easily been killed or wounded including many small children.

Events of this nature are no longer rare. Practically every day we hear of someone brandishing a gun, firing into a group of innocent people whether it be in a restaurant, bar, or a public street.

Despite these common occurrences many people still loudly proclaim against stronger firearms control, including gun registration. These people claim: guns don't commit crimes, people do; what we need is stronger law enforcement. I grant you both of those statements may be true but they are weak excuses.

People do commit crimes — and they will continue to do so as long as guns are readily available. I'm not saying tighter gun controls will end crime because this of course is absurd. There are of course other weapons which can be used for criminal purposes but how many so-called criminals would be quite as aggressive if they didn't have a quick firing gun in their hand. As far as stricter law enforcement is concerned this becomes more and more of a problem when anyone — a criminal, or deranged person can very easily obtain a firearm if he has the money to buy it.

In the case of gun registration one very popular cry among the dissenters is, "it will lead to confiscation!" It's amazing but that one statement shows one great weakness. These people are saying, "this is what the Communists want, to unarm America." Don't they realize that by bringing up the question of "confiscation" showing they are losing faith in the Legislative branch of our government, they could really be doing what the Communists want?

Many people will always be violently opposed to stricter gun controls and registration, perhaps there is only one thing that would ever make them change their minds and that is for their loved ones to become the innocent victims of a sniper's fire. That is a horrible thought, but if one opposes tighter gun controls place yourself in that position. It will be hard to imagine for some people, the feeling can never really register until it happens to you — but then it's too late.

Many people who strongly feel we need tighter gun controls make one big mistake, they spend too much time talking and not enough — if any — on action. Don't wait and hope something is done — do something! Not tomorrow or the next day, but today — write to Florida's U.S. Senators and to Congressman Gibbons. Demand as a voter that they work for tighter gun controls. Whatever we do, don't sit back thinking that enough other people will write — maybe they'll be thinking the samething.

I urge those who want stronger gun controls to act now — before it's too late.

C.L.B.

Confiscation Next

BRANDON — Apparently all the demons in hell have been released to confuse good people on the registration of guns and the licensing of their owners. Once this is done it will only take two or three more assassinations to create enough hysteria to bring on the confiscation of all guns by the government.

A. B. McREYNOLDS

POLICE TRY TO FERRET OUT SNIPER
Points Need for Gun Controls

Stop School Vandalism—Report It

TAMPA —Schools cost everyone who pays taxes lots of money and it behooves any one that pays the bill at least to call the Sheriff's Office when they see anyone loitering around any schools.

The County has some real nice parks for children to play in. There is no need for anyone to allow children to play around the schools. Town and Country school does not have one outside light at night. They have been shot with BB's and a great number of windows have holes in them, also put there by BB's.

A junior high has been built there and, while in the process of building, more than $1,800 damage was done and damage is still going on. All fire alarms were pulled in the weekend of July 13-14. People who see this do not report because they don't care to get involved.

Someone should inform the public that schools are built for children to learn to be law-abiding citizens — not hoodlums to tear down and destroy. So, as a taxpayer, please help.

OTTIS B. JONES
Head Custodian,
Webb Jr. High

For Leadership—Ronald Reagan

RONALD REAGAN
'Courage and Wisdom'

TAMPA — I must admit that the TV speech of Governor Reagan was like a breath of fresh air. Here is the man with a keen insight into the ills of our country, and he has the guts to come out and say it. We are desperate for a man in the White House with courage and wisdom.

How I wish this man would get the nomination for President on his party's ticket. I am fed up to my eyebrows with wishy-washy, double-talking, anything-for-a-vote politicians, and I think most of the American people are also.

I am heart-sick and deeply concerned at what is taking place in our country. We cannot survive another four years of "Great Society" insanity. I believe Reagan would give us real leadership, and how I pray for it.

WILLIAM D. ELLIS

A full box around the editorial halftone and its cutlines can help show its distinctive function. The phrase AN EDITORIAL PHOTO, or its equivalent, may be stripped onto the halftone. The corners of the engraving may be rounded off; this takes a little more, but not excessive, time in the engraving department. If the corners are cut off at an angle to make an octagonal, the added effort is minimal.

Among notable campaigns conducted with editorial photography was one in a Southern state where a bond issue earmarked for building a throughway had been approved by voters. The project was delayed inordinately. A series of weekly photos was run with a simple caption: When do we get the Freeway? Among the pictures were those of buildings in the path of the proposed highway that had been condemned and abandoned—and taken off the tax rolls—yet left standing in decrepitude. Another showed a monumental traffic snarl of the variety that the new highway was intended to solve. The cumulative effect was most powerful, and the highway project got under way.

Another great campaign was that of the *Lynchburg* (Virginia) *News*. A new institution for retarded children had been built but couldn't be opened because no budget had been provided for staff and furnishings. A series of photos and a minimum of copy showed the magnificent but empty new facilities and the unspeakable conditions of the dirty, over-crowded, and antiquated building that should have long been replaced. Official action was almost immediate.

In both instances, photography merely presented facts. The truth was so obvious and so powerful that the reader didn't need words to get the point. Nor could the photos be misinterpreted; the bad was so obviously bad that the public indignantly demanded correction for the pictured situation.

The *Miami Herald* has used photographs in an altogether nonfactual manner, as an enticing sugar coating for an editorial message. Typical was a commentary in support of a proposed city ordinance allowing policemen to stop and search suspicious characters. A 36-24-36 damsel, clad in black mesh leotards and a policeman's cap and carrying a night-stick, was presented in a regular pinup pose. If Miami police all looked like this, said the editor in the accompanying compres, there would be no need for a stop-and-frisk law. But . . . and then the serious point was made.

Purists may wince at using beauteous models with sober editorials, but there is no question that the technique draws readers and that unless editorials are read, they are useless. So any device that lures the reader

Fig. 114. *Detroit* (Mich.) *Free Press* devotes whole page to single editorial on Berlin Wall, well-illustrated with staff photos.

Hanoi's tactics will continue

Hanoi's announcement that it considers American fliers shot down over North Viet Nam to be military criminals and that it will try them as such has escalated a shocking and dirty war to a new, shocking and dirty plateau.

It is particularly unsettling because the United States is powerless to reply in kind without resorting to comparably cynical and inhuman tactics. The administration has had to content itself with the strongest language of protest at its command and a plea to the International Red Cross.

In such unhappy circumstances there is only one real hope, and that is that the Communists are bluffing. A slender hope it may be, but the Communists have been known to bark harder than they bite, particularly when barking is the only means available for influencing a more powerful enemy.

For nine months, American airpower has pounded selected targets in North Viet Nam with virtual impunity, and this has hurt. How much it has hurt can be seen by the intensity of the Communist propaganda against the raids.

Yet, talk all it wants, Hanoi has not been able to get the raids stopped. What to do now? Fight a conventional ground war with regular troops? China cannot risk that; so North Viet Nam is left to take the punishment and strike back as best it can.

There is a parallel in the violence of worldwide communism's reaction to any U.S. presence whatsoever in Viet Nam. Why should the Soviet Union and its East European satellites be so insistent in their warnings about a cooling in East-West relations as long as the U.S. follows its current line in Southeast Asia?

Could it be that they see a successful U.S. effort there as a threat to all their plans for triumph in Africa, Asia and Latin America?

Perhaps, for the Communists, the Chinese excel seem to recognize the impossibility of achieving conventional military means; the

—h

Pictured above is Angelica Lake as seen by the camera of Clifford R. Yeich, Times chief photographer. The lake has 24 acres. It is flanked by a grassy expanse, shaded by elms and maples.

It has drinking fountains, picnic tables, lavatories, a parking lot, a concession stand. A pretty picture.

But the lake is still just a picture. Back in 1941, $185,000 in WPA funds was spent to develop the lake into a watering spa for fishing, boating and swimming.

For a time there was bathing

and boating in the area. There is still fishing, a minimal amount. But there is nothing now reminiscent of the late 1920s, when cars with canoes and other small boats made an exodus to the lake site, where there was gaiety, swimming and boating.

Today, the lake is polluted. Until recent years, the water was a border-line type pollution. On clear days when the sun burned off the bacteria, the water was considered safe; on cloudy days, it wasn't. Still, the lake has never been safe for swimming for several years.

Much of the pollution came from the man-made sewage of the 18th Ward. Now, that area has been sewered. But the lake still bears the pollution of storm drainage, and the pollution has been called "staggering."

It can get only worse. It cannot get better under natural conditions.

Within a few weeks, the county will be informed of the results of a feasibility study for the lake site being made by Allyn R. Jennings, a landscape architect.

The findings may not be happy ones as far as bathing is concerned. The shore-line gets steep quickly,

precluding cheap construction of a bathing beach.

But if the costs are enormous, so are the possibilities for an unsurpassable recreation spot in this area. Transferring the storm drainage by a separate sewer line to Fritz's Island and the sewage treatment plant is not an impossibility.

The combined finances and energies of the city, county and Project 70 funds could accomplish wonders at Angelica Lake. The Times urges public officials to examine every one of these possibilities and project them decades beyond, and not just suit them to the deficits of 1965.

PUBLIC FORUM—

Why neighborhood schools?

Editor, The Times:
The present controversy over locations for new schools makes me wonder why we need neighborhood schools.

the right of elderly people to stay in homes they spent a lifetime acquiring is just as important as any other minority rights.

The time has come for us to halt our thinking about

Birch society tactics hit

Editor, The Times:
Your editorial on Oct. 2 dealing with the John Birch Society was both

The utterances of the John Birch Society have a strange parallel with earlier political movements during the '20s and '30s in Germany and Italy.

DREW PEARSON—

Dog thieves use cruelest practices

(Editor's Note: Drew Pearson, on tour of Africa, is in

The purloined pets bring from 10 cents for puppies up to $25 for police dogs.

"... why," said

Fig. 115. *Reading* (Pa.) *Times* uses salon-type photograph to add beauty to editorial page and illustrate local scenic areas.
Miami (Fla.) *Herald* uses incongruous pinup photo to make editorial point.

into body type is legitimate. After all, the editorial cartoonist has long used incongruity to present a serious message; why not incongruous photography?

The hallowed position of the editorial cartoon on the editorial page and in publishers' hearts may become less secure after new information about these drawings becomes better known. Dr. LeRoy Carl, in a doctoral dissertation, analyzed reader reaction to a group of editorial cartoons by some of the leading cartoonists in the country. He asked the artist himself the meaning of his cartoon, then asked the same question of a random sampling of average readers. The results were staggering; well more than half the readers could get no meaning or got a radically wrong one from the cartoon.

Newspapermen long conceded that their erudite editorials might be too difficult for the milkman from Dubuque to understand, but, they hastened to insist, even the lowliest on the educational, social, and economic totem pole could get the meaning of an editorial cartoon. Dr.

Carl's findings show exactly the opposite. Written editorials in his study were well understood. As the writer became more heated in his personal involvement with an issue, his points hit closer to the target of reader comprehension. But the cartoonist's obviously strong feelings added nothing to reader comprehension.

Perhaps the whole question of editorial cartoons requires close examination, more research and discussion, and a series of management decisions.

A comparatively recent practice is using the editorial page as a picture gallery for two pleasant kinds of art: old-time photographs and salon pictures. From-our-files columns have long been a regular and well-read feature on this page. It seems logical that if old words are recalled here, old photos might be presented here too. Whether or not there is philosophical justification for such pictures, the reader loves them. Therefore we might as well use this art as sugar coating for the heavy reading matter on the page.

Salon art probably wound up on the editorial page by default. Every so often, a news cameraman would come across a scene that delighted his eye. He couldn't resist the temptation to put it on film; the picture editor couldn't resist the beauty of the photo. But where to run it? It

Fig. 116. Editorial-page restyling. Original format of editorial page of *Dubuque* (Iowa) *Telegraph-Herald,* top left, was crowded, with large masses of body type. Three other pages shown here are after restyling; note that page pattern varies constantly and drastically. Editorial on volunteer fire departments is reversed on picture of barn blaze. FACE OF AMERICA is continuing feature, using rugged and weathered faces as well as beautiful ones as here.

Fig. 117. Editorial-page restyling. Original format of edit page of *Marion* (Ind.) *Leader-Tribune,* top left, was adequate. But restyling and changing page patterns daily create interest and excitement demonstrated by other three pages here.

Fig. 118. Editorial and op-ed pages of *Dayton* (Ohio) *Daily News* have strong family resemblance.

Op-ed page from *Akron* (Ohio) *Beacon Journal* handles intellectual news as flexibly as it does regular news.

wasn't a news pic, so each editor resisted using up his scarce space with such a cut. Why the editorial-page editor was more amenable is worth pondering. Maybe he saw the charm of the photograph because he wasn't looking for and didn't demand a news angle. Maybe he welcomed the change of pace of halftone art on his pages that were, most of the time, colored exclusively by line art. At any rate, the editorial page more and more frequently is the salon for displaying pictures "just for pretty," as our Pennsylvania Dutch friends would say.

The *opposite-editorial page*—inevitably shortened to *op-ed*—is merely an extension of the editorial page. Its typography has the same functions as those of the editorial page, and it should be in exactly the same style. Thus, the same format and head schedule should be used on both pages, and even the page logo of the editorial page may be repeated on the op-ed.

If the op-ed cannot be entirely ad-free, advertising should be placed in a rectangle clear across the bottom of the page. It should be light in tone and dignified in typography and content. A vertical rectangle, while

Biography In Brief

He Was Talked Into Running-- And Never Quit

By Donn F. Gaynor

A young Akron lawyer stepped off a train one day in 1920, returning from a short business trip to New York, and found that he had been named the Republican Party's nominee for Summit County Prosecuting Attorney, an honor which he thought he had gracefully declined.

So began the political-legal career of Arthur William Doyle, son of a lawyer and judge. Today, after nearly 40 years' continuous service to the bench, he is senior in terms of service to all judges in the State of Ohio, save one.

The exception is Cuyahoga County Common Pleas Judge Sam Silbert, who retires at the end of this year.

ARTHUR W. DOYLE was born Nov. 3, 1893, in West Hill. He still lives there; at 218 Twin Oaks rd.

His father was Dayton A. Doyle, also born in Akron, a member of the old law firm of Dick, Doyle and Bryan, and a judge of Summit County Common Pleas Court for 10 years.

His mother was the former Ida Mae Westfall, who descended from a long line of Pennsylvania Presbyterian ministers.

"I'm related to nearly every Presbyterian minister in Western Pennsylvania today," Judge Doyle said. "I don't dare do anything when I go there."

AFTER GRADUATION from Crosby Elementary School, young Doyle entered Akron High School. He became a member of its baseball team and played fullback on the 1910 state champion football team.

His baseball teammates at Akron High included George Sisler, who later became a star player for the St. Louis Browns, and Joe Thomas, who went on to become vice president, secretary and chief counsel of Firestone.

From Akron High, Doyle went on to Cornell University, graduating with a bachelor of arts degree. He had intended to go East with his Uncle Will Doyle, one of the first professors at Carnegie Tech, to become a teacher. "I was equipped to teach," he said, "but my father became ill and I came home to help him with his properties."

THE ELDER DOYLE later urged his son to continue his education. So Arthur went to Cleveland and Western Reserve University to study law. He received his bachelor of laws degree there shortly after the outbreak of World War I in 1917.

The university held its final exams, and the bar exam, a month earlier than usual in order to let its eager young students — including Doyle — get into the military service.

Three months after enlisting in Cleveland, First Lt. Arthur W. Doyle emerged from the officers' training school at Ft. Benjamin Harrison near Indianapolis. He was sent to Montgomery, Ala., where he joined B battery, 135th Field Artillery of the 37th (Ohio) Division.

IT WAS IN the Argonne Forest in France that Lt. Doyle suffered his only "wound." His unit was firing the famed "French 75" artillery pieces.

"We were firing the No. 1 gun with a lanyard (long rope) because the gun was mired in mud," he recalled. "The lanyard stuck." He walked to the gun, gave the rope a hearty tug, and slipped in the mud just as the piece fired.

The breech block handle, a long piece of metal used to open the breech to load the field piece, whanged him across the nose, smashing it.

"Just that far," he said, indicating about two inches with thumb and forefinger, "and it would have taken my head off."

AFTER THE Armistice in November, 1918, Doyle was sent into Germany where he served in the Army of Occupation. Because of his legal background, he found himself serving on courts-marshal as both a judge and, in several instances, as defense attorney.

He received his discharge in 1919, arriving back in Akron in late Summer. He was given a job with the law firm of Allen, Waters, Young and Andress.

It was in 1920 that he met Jim Corey on the street. Corey was head of the Republican Party here. Corey told him, "You are just the person I'm looking for. We need a candidate for prosecuting attorney and I think you can win."

'It's quite a job to send a man to the electric chair'

"I DECLINED," Doyle said, "but he told me he just had to have some names. He said he probably wouldn't file them anyway." Doyle signed.

"I was just naive enough to believe him," he said. A short time later he found himself the candidate. He was just as surprised when he won the primary, and later won the job — "I went in on the Harding landslide."

Doyle succeeded Cletus Roetzel as prosecutor. W. A. Spencer, assistant to Roetzel, had been Doyle's Democratic opposition in the election.

"He was a swell guy," Doyle said. "I offered him a job as my first assistant. He stayed with me for four years."

DOYLE LATER won a second two-year term but refused to run for a third term. He, Spencer and several of their friends entered the private practice of law. "I was happy and substantially successful for a young guy," he said.

Then, in 1928 he ran for the Common Pleas Court bench. He won that one in the primary. Wendell Willkie, then head of the Democrats in Akron, didn't even run a candidate against Doyle.

In 1936 he ran for Judge of the Ninth District Court of Appeals. He had no primary opposition, but was opposed by Judge George Starn of Wooster. As was his habit by now, Doyle won, replacing the retiring Judge Ross Funk of Wooster on the Appellate Court bench.

HE HAS BEEN in continuous service with the appeals court to this day — it will be 40 years next Jan. 1.

About 10 years ago he was called on for the first time to serve temporarily on the Ohio Supreme Court. He has sat on that bench many times in the intervening years, the last time just last week.

Arthur William Doyle

His fellow lawyers at one time pushed for his appointment to the Federal Court bench in Cleveland. At another time Rep. William Ayres sent Doyle's name to President Dwight D. Eisenhower, recommending him for a seat on the U. S. Supreme Court. Neither job materialized however.

BUT OF ALL the thousands of cases he has heard or presided over during the years, one still stands out in his mind above the others.

He had been on the Common Pleas bench just a few months when he was called upon to sit on a first-degree murder case. The defendant, accused of killing an Akron policeman, was found guilty by a jury which did not recommend mercy.

It became Doyle's duty to sentence the man to the electric chair. He did — "I remember writing out the sentence, just so I could say it properly," —and the man, after exhausting all appeals, died in the electric chair.

"It preyed on my mind for quite a while. It's quite a job to send a man to the electric chair. I remember him standing there in front of me, helpless, surrounded by police — but on the other hand, there was the corpse of that policeman lying in the cemetery."

JUDGE AND MRS. DOYLE have two children, Arthur W. Jr., who has his own real estate brokerage business and three children in Morrisville, Pa.; and daughter Mrs. Roderic C. (Gwynn) Hunsaker in Natick, Mass. Mr. and Mrs. Hunsaker have two sons.

Judge Doyle is a 32nd degree Mason and is or has been a member of a number of lodges and organizations, including the American Legion and VFW. He was elected in 1966 to his current six-year term on the appeals court where he sits with Judges Oscar A. Hunsicker and Myron T. Brenneman.

WHAT WAS PROBABLY his proudest moment came in April, 1967, when Judge Doyle was named by John Schoff Millis, then president of Western Reserve University, as an honorary doctor of law.

The citation that went with the degree reads:

"You have served the Bar with wisdom and dignity. You have given justice a clear and unequivocal reality. You have devoted your keen mind and your humane instincts to the cause of human dignity.

"Because you have served your chosen profession with brilliance for nearly a half century, because you have brought credit to your Alma Mater, we delight to honor you."

The Political Parade

Nye's A Guy With An Eye On The Future

By WILLIAM VANCE
Beacon Journal Politics Writer

In the parlance of politics, 1968, Akron's William B. Nye is what is known as an overdog.

This helps distinguish the 35-year-old Democrat from one who is running against the odds. It also helps explain why Nye is looking beyond the Nov. 5 election to a more difficult campaign.

Vance

Nye is the freshman state senator who represents southeastern Summit County and northern Stark County. He has been doing his homework and is counting on the voters to make him a sophomore.

Neither Nye nor his party elders seems particularly concerned by the strenuous efforts of GOP school teacher Cha les Keller to flunk him out of the class of '69.

Keller's specialty is mathematics, but so far the district's registration figures haven't been adding up for him.

THUS IT IS that young Bill Nye is preparing himself for bigger things.

It isn't generally known around here, but the worst-kept secret in Columbus is that Nye is bidding for the job of Senate minority leader.

The post, which pays an extra $2,000 a year ($14,750 total) will be open before the 108th General Assembly assembles in January. Frank King, Senate Democratic leader since 1959, plans to step down to devote full time to running the Ohio AFL-CIO.

When King's job goes up for grabs, Nye (assuming he's there) and Sen. Charles Carney of Youngstown probably will be the chief grabbers, with Sen. Anthony Novak of Cleveland perhaps groping a bit.

IT WILL BE at this point that Bill Nye will learn, if he hasn't already, the influence labor can exert on the party leadership.

Nye's Summit County colleague, Oliver Ocasek, learned that lesson before the last Senate leadership caucus in 1966.

Ollie had the horses to dethrone King. All he lacked was the killer instinct. While he was waiting for King to bow out gracefully, Frank pulled his rank as AFL-CIO boss.

The word went out that if the party wanted labor's money and muscle to remain behind it, King had to be kept in the saddle.

Exit Ocasek.

MAYBE IT WON'T happen all over again with Nye, but don't bet on it. At any rate, he's no overdog in this one.

Since King will be around to bestow his blessing and vote on a successor, it would appear that Carney, a district director of the United Steelworkers, would have the edge over lawyer Bill Nye and accountant Tony Novak.

Perhaps as interesting as the outcome will be the role Ohio Democratic chairman Eugene "Pete" O'Grady decides to play.

PETE IS ANXIOUS to preserve the labor-party relationship which was strengthened by his predecessor, Mort Neipp, who was instrumental in easing Ocasek out of the leadership in 1966.

But O'Grady is just as anxious to begin grooming a stable of statewide candidates for 1970. Nye has a place in that stable; Carney and Novak do not.

Pete doesn't have to be told that a minority leader gets a lot more statewide notice and is easier to groom than an ordinary state senator.

Could be we'll learn in December who really speaks for the Ohio Democratic Party. Or at least who speaks loudest.

Columbus Report

They'd Like Facts Buried With Bodies

By LACY McCRARY

COLUMBUS — A conspiracy of secrecy has prevailed for about two months about what happened at Ohio Penitentiary on Aug. 21 when five convicts were shot to death.

McCrary

State officials, from mental hygiene and corrections boss Martin Janis on down have taken the position that the public doesn't need to know how the five were killed, why the prisoners rioted in the first place, or anything else about the incident.

The five were shot when Columbus police and Ohio highway patrolmen blasted their way into the pen to rescue nine hostage guards.

SHORTLY AFTER the affair the Highway Patrol was assigned to investigate it and issue a report. In due time the patrol made its report and sent copies to Janis and Franklin County Prosecutor C. Howard Johnson.

There has been much speculation about what the report contains.

Janis has condescended to tell some of us what isn't in the report and to give us some idea of what is covered, but has steadfastly refused to let any newsmen — or the public for that matter — see the report.

Actually Janis has played a stalling game. He first told me I could see it after he had a chance to look it over. That took several days. Then he said he would let me see it when the Franklin County Grand Jury, probing the pen riot, had a chance to look at it.

THEN LAST WEEK he changed his tune and said he couldn't let anyone see it because Prosecutor Johnson told him not to do so.

However, Johnson later told me he didn't tell Janis or anyone else what to do with the report. "I don't give that kind of instructions to anyone," Johnson said.

It is infuriating to meet public officials who almost arrogantly refuse to talk about the most dramatic news event I have ever seen. I was at the pen the day the big blast went off and the policemen went in shooting.

THE FBI, TOO, refuses to talk about its findings.

The Central Ohio Chapter of the American Civil Liberties Union (ACLU) charged that one convict was "summarily executed" in the courtyard after the guards were rescued. And there have been conflicting stories about how the other four were killed, when they were killed and why.

Adjutant Gen. S. T. del Corso shortly afterwards told me highway patrolmen killed about three outside the cells where the guards were held just as they were about to make their threats of burning the guards alive come true.

Columbus police and former Warden Marion Koloski and Corrections Chief Maury Koblentz say they were killed because they refused to obey orders and go inside their cells.

Former Deputy Warden Troy Harris said two were killed in the courtyard. Other officials, including Koloski, said only one was killed in the yard.

IN ADDITION to this conclusion, no one will say if the five who were killed — they include Jesse Wade of Canton — were participants in the riot or if they just happened to get in the way of the police.

I am not saying the five should not have been shot. There may be good reason for it.

But we don't know for sure. Because no one in state government will talk about it. Those five could just as easily have been executed, as the ACLU hints, and the families and friends of these men would have been no wiser because public officials refuse to tell anybody how and why they did.

Now you may ask what difference it makes how they died? Or contend that it isn't really important.

You may be right. Maybe the public which pays for penitentiaries, which pays the salaries of public officials, which in the long run pays the tab for crime and the care and feeding of prisoners, has no right to know what happens inside prison walls.

THAT'S PRECISELY the attitude taken by Janis and his assistants. Ordinarily Janis' department is quick to issue news releases about positive steps taken within the prison system. That's fine. But if you want to be fair and honest, you've got to talk about the other side of the coin.

Janis is unwilling to do that.

Moreover, I've been unable to even find anyone who'll take the responsibility for being in charge of the pen assault.

Del Corso says he was there to assist Koloski. Koloski says when the police went in, they assumed responsibility.

Highway Patrol Supt. Robert Chiaramonte says he was there to assist. Columbus police say it is state property and they were there sort of as guests and the buck hasn't stopped being passed yet.

I say that's a shame.

Behind The Front Page

When The Line's Too Taut

By ROBERT KOTZBAUER

When you stop to think about the increase in prices, wages and everything else during the last decade, it is not surprising that Akron public schools should need new millage this year.

Kotzbauer

This is the only major city in Ohio which has held the line on locally voted school taxes since 1962. Our jump that year was 4.29 mills, and the resulting total for all school purposes — 25.89 — was the highest of all eight large cities in the state.

Since then, however, Dayton's local school tax rate has climbed to 30 mills; Canton is collecting 29.90 mills, Columbus 27.86 and Toledo 26.50. The present Akron school rate is 26.10.

Cincinnati collects 23.60 mills, Cleveland 26 mills and Youngstown 22.90 mills. But like Akron they're seeking increases, Youngstown a whopping 12 mills. Voters here are being asked to approve an eight-mill increase for operating funds.

SINCE 1962, when Akron's schools got their last raise from the voters, the cost of living has gone up about 15 pct.

Only Youngstown among the eight big cities has gained less of an increase in local school taxes than Akron during the last 10 years. Youngstown's local rate since 1958 has climbed only 2.8 mills while Akron's net increase has been 4.18 mills in the same time.

Even at that, Youngstown currently provides more local money to support each pupil — $445 a year — than does Akron — $425.

Columbus' local tax rate for schools has increased by 13.30 mills in 10 years, Cleveland's by 12.10, Canton's by 11.80, Toledo's by 10, Dayton's by 9.10 and Cincinnati's by 8.08 mills.

Vocational Districts

Since the first Ohio joint vocational school districts — Penta-county and Lake County — were organized in 1964, bond issues and operating levies to support these programs have failed more often than they have succeeded. Because of the schools' ability to submit the issues a second time, however, the record is not as bad as it seems.

In all, 34 joint vocational schools have been approved by the State Board of Education, 17 of these have passed the necessary bond issues and levies, and 11 are in operation this Fall.

This year, however, the bottom sort of dropped out of the "new tax" market. Out of nine issues submitted to the voters, including support for a Portage County joint vocational school in September, only one — Montgomery County — was approved.

BYRL SHOEMAKER, director of the division of vocational education, feels it may be necessary to search out new methods of funding because of this emerging "taxpayer resistance."

The schools in operation have been successful, says Shoemaker. Their acceptance in the community is good, and there has been no slow-up in organizing new districts around the state.

Also, says Shoemaker, there's no evidence of any organized opposition to taxes for vocational schools. It's just a tightening-up on the part of individual taxpayers.

★

Pat Paulsen, un-candidate for President on the STAG — Straight Talking American Government — ticket, says the draft should be according to head size. Thin heads would be drafted and the fat heads would be in government. . . .

LeM

Shoemaker

Paulsen

LeMay Passed Up Senate

Sen. Frank J. Lausche recalled the other day that back in 1945, when he was Ohio governor, he offered to appoint Maj. Gen. Curtis LeMay to the U. S. Senate. LeMay declined and Lausche then named his commerce director, James W. Huffman of Columbus, to fill the seat vacated by Harold H. Burton's promotion to the Supreme Court.

Commenting on the appointment, the Beacon Journal at the time expressed unhappiness about Huffman but wasn't too complimentary about LeMay either.

"There is nothing in the record to show what this young military hero knows about legislative work" said the editorial.

★

Who's writing the official government handouts in Columbus?

BJ Columnist Mickey Porter cited a news release from Highway Director Pearl Masheter's office the other day which was confusing, to say the least. But how about this from Gov. Rhodes—

"What is public opinion? It is, among other things, the strongest countervailing influence against the oligarchal tendency which exists in any democracy. (It is) composed of general consensus on range and priority of value preferences.

"A value preference is an emotional response to a set of real or presumed facts, plus the sum total of one's existence."

THE RELEASE, issued to commemorate National Newspaper Week, wound up with this pat on the back (we think) for the press:

"Newspapers strive to present us with facts unfettered by presumption and uncolored by aggrandizement or preference."

We strive, it's true, but sometimes our efforts are jeopardized by printing government handouts.

Fig. 119. Tabloid editorial page. *Skyline*, Chicago neighborhood weekly published by Lerner Newspapers, uses white space generously.

reasonably effective as a fractional editorial "page," is less effective as an op-ed.

If at all possible, another editorial cartoon should be used on this page. This is the most effective way to tie the two pages into a single unit of opinion and comment.

Women's Pages

The weakest pages in the majority of American newspapers are those directed to the most important segment of their readers, the distaff side. The weakness of these pages is demonstrated by the schizophrenia of their titles. This used to be the society section and is still referred to as *soc* (sock) on many papers; then it became the women's department; then family pages or the home department or some "clever," weasel-worded title.

The audience for this department, whatever its name, is important. Women spend more of the family dollars than men. The home demands the major portion of family income, and the director of the home is a most important purchasing agent. Advertisers have to attract the female eye. Women are playing a more important role in every area of human activity, not only social but political, cultural, and economic as well. The newspaperman's dedication to informing especially the influential segment of the citizenry must make the woman reader a primary target for communications.

The staffs of women's departments are good, and they get better all the time. As more and more girls graduate from journalism courses at high school and college levels, there are more qualified "paper dolls" entering the news rooms. Some of them stay city-side but many report to the women's desk. These gals are able and eager.

Why then are women's pages so weak? It's primarily the publisher's fault. Newspaper management is often not really convinced of the value of a real women's section. The publisher doesn't know what he wants this department to do; naturally the staff can't execute a policy that doesn't exist. And when the staff sets its own goal, the publisher rarely gives it the tools to attain the goal.

The first thing the publisher must do is determine how much of his newspaper he wants to devote to the women's department. Then he must decide what kind of material should run in this space. And he must provide the women's staff with usable and adequate typographic resources.

The publisher has every right in the world to be arbitrary in allocating space for women's news. He is justified in pointing out that much news that appears in the rest of the paper is of interest to women. Indeed, most news is. He has the same right to determine whether this is to be a "women's" or a "family" section. The distinction between these two labels may be fine but it is real.

But under any label, these pages become repositories for journalistic flotsam: astrology columns and horoscopes; do-it-yourself psychiatry; advice for ailing love affairs, duodenums, and aspidistras; recipes with such exotic ingredients as humming-bird wings and hearts of orchids; patterns for making maternity dresses or embroidering Dear-Mom pillows.

This material might be justified; after all, a newspaper should entertain its readers. But it should not be confused with legitimate news, and it should not be charged against the news hole of the women's pages. It should go on comics or feature pages.

A continuing headache for the editor of such pages is the increasing number of engagement and wedding stories that must be handled. At the so-called romantic times of the year, these stories squeeze out all others.

An interesting experiment has proven successful for several Canadian metropolitan newspapers: wedding reports are paid for, like classified ads.

This disquiets most editors. News, say they, should be run because it is news, not because someone buys space for it. Converting news into advertising compromises the editorial integrity of a paper.

Fig. 120. Women's page. Section page in *Chicago* (Ill.) *Tribune* is in modular design. Large picture in full process color.

Chicago Tribune
MONDAY, SEPTEMBER 9, 1968

feminique

... followed by classified ads | Section 1C

YOURS EACH MONDAY—FASHIONS FOR: YOUR WEEK • YOUR HOME • YOUR JOB • YOUR SELF

THIS WEEK

Today
SEPTEMBER 9
California became one of the United States on this day in 1850. Considering all the delicious foods and wines they send us, it's a day we all should toast. And, if you're a wine fancier, why not buy a few bottles of your favorite California vintages for the occasion?

Tuesday
SEPTEMBER 10
Music boxes are back in all kinds of guises. Some Peanuts fans will want one with Snoopy sleeping on top of his house, or the Red Baron flying his plane. The family princess will love a jeweled crown to decorate her dressing table, with music as a bonus.

Wednesday
SEPTEMBER 11
If you frequent the theater, concerts, or sporting events, you'll get better seats if you have a copy of "Tickets Please." The book has seating charts for almost every theater, auditorium, stadium, and amphitheater in the area, along with their addresses and box office hours. Price: $3.

Thursday
SEPTEMBER 12
Now's the time to get your fireplace in shape for the winter, order the wood, and get some of those extra-long matches. That first cold day can come along any time now.

Friday
SEPTEMBER 13
Your feet probably took a beating from all that outdoor living this summer. And fall shopping certainly hasn't helped. Why not pamper yourself and have a professional pedicure? You'll think you have two new feet.

Saturday
SEPTEMBER 14
This is a day everyone should fly the American flag. It's the birthday of "The Star-Spangled Banner," written in the early morning 154 years ago. If you don't own a flag, better trot out and get one now.

Sunday
SEPTEMBER 15
There'll be thrills for all when the Medinah Black Horse Troop puts on its "Horsecapades" in Maywood Park today; they'll perform their famous musical drill. You'll also see Roman riding, roping, and other tricks by professionals. Two shows are at 1 and 4 p.m. General admission is $2; box seats are $3 and $4.

Leather, which always before played supporting roles—belts, shoes, handbags, luggage—in the fashion theater, is a full-fledged star now. And these designs by Viola Sylbert for Albert Alfus are in the No. 1 color, brown. Companion to the luggage-colored vest and culotte is an Orlon voile blouse, by Gregory and Goldberg. A coat, in the deepest of mochas, has the important large notched collar—of curly lamb. But even more important in the leather world is "G.M.L." That's genuine milled leather, pulverized and bonded to cloth, dyed and patterned in real leather motifs. The full story on this newer (and less expensive) way to the leather look is inside.

Fig. 121. Inside women's page from *Chicago* (Ill.) *Tribune* is made up in modular rectangles. Note use of rocket head, shown inset in same size.

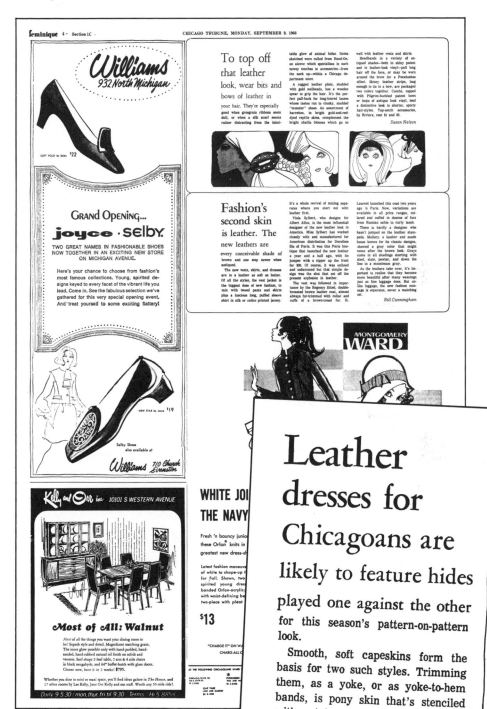

Williams
932 North Michigan

SOFT FOLD by Selby $22

GRAND OPENING...

joyce · selby.

TWO GREAT NAMES IN FASHIONABLE SHOES
NOW TOGETHER IN AN EXCITING NEW STORE
ON MICHIGAN AVENUE.

Here's your chance to choose from fashion's
most famous collections. Young, spirited designs keyed to every facet of the vibrant life you
lead. Come in. See the fabulous selection we've
gathered for this very special opening event.
And treat yourself to some exciting flattery!

NEW STAR by Joyce $19

Selby Shoes
also available at

Williams *710 Church Evanston*

To top off that leather look, wear bits and bows of leather in

your hair. They're especially
good when grosgrain ribbons seem
dull, or when a silk scarf seems
rather distracting from the inimi-

table glow of animal hides. Items
sketched were culled from Head-On,
an alcove which specializes in such
newsy touches in accessories—from
the neck up—within a Chicago department store.

A rugged leather plate, studded
with gold nailheads, has a wooden
spear to grip the hair. It's the perfect pull-back for long-haired lasses
whose tastes run to clunky, studded
"monster" shoes. An assortment of
barrettes, in bright gold-and-red-
dyed reptile skins, complement the
bright challis blouses which go so

well with leather vests and skirts.

Headbands in a variety of antiqued shades—both in shiny patent
and in leather-look vinyl—pull long
hair off the face, or may be worn
around the brow for a Pocahontas
effect. Skinny leather strips, long
enough to tie in a bow, are packaged
two colors together. Combs, topped
with Pilgrim-buckled patent bows
or loops of antique look vinyl, lend
a distinctive look to shorter, sporty
hair-styles. Top-notch accessories,
by Riviera, cost $1 and $2.

Susan Nelson

Fashion's second skin is leather. The

new leathers are
every conceivable shade of
brown and one step newer when
antiqued.

The new vests, skirts, and dresses
are in a leather as soft as butter.
Of all the styles, the vest jacket is
the biggest dose of the new fashion, to
mix with tweed pants and skirts
plus a luscious long, puffed sleeve
shirt in silk or calico printed jersey.

It's a whole revival of mixing separates where you start out with
leather first.

Viola Sylbert, who designs for
Albert Alfus, is the most influential
designer of the new leather look in
America. Miss Sylbert has worked
closely with and manufactured for
American distribution for Dorothee
Bis of Paris. It was this Paris bou-
tique that launched the new leather
a year and a half ago, with its
jumper with a zipper up the front
for $20. Of course, it was unlined
and unhemmed but that simple design was the shot that set off the
present explosion in leather.

The vest was followed in importance by the Regency fitted, double-
breasted brown leather coat, almost
always fur-trimmed with collar and
cuffs of a brown-toned fur. St.

Laurent launched this coat two years
ago in Paris. Now, variations are
lared and cuffed in dozens of furs
from Russian sable to curly lamb.

There is hardly a designer who
hasn't jumped on the leather stam-
pede. Mallory, a leather and suede
house known for its classic designs,
showed a gray color that might
come after the brown look. Grays
come in all shadings starting with
steel, slate, pewter, and down the
line to a moonbean gray.

As the leathers take over, it's important to realize that they become
more beautiful after many wearings
just as fine luggage does. But unlike luggage, the new fashion message is separate, never a matching
set.

Bill Cunningham

MONTGOMERY
WARD

Kelly and Orr inc 10101 S WESTERN AVENUE

Most of All: Walnut

Most of all the things you want your dining room to
be! Superb style and detail. Magnificent matching grain.
The inner glow possible only with hand-padded, hand-
sanded, hand-rubbed natural oil finish on solids and
veneers. Surf-shape 2-leaf table, 2 arm & 4 side chairs
in black naugahyde, and 64" buffet-hutch with glass doors.
Choose now, have it in 2 weeks! $795.

Whether you dine in mini or maxi space, you'll find ideas galore in *The House*, and
17 other rooms by Lee Kelly, Jane Orr Kelly and our staff. Worth any 50 mile ride!

Daily 9 5.30/ mon. thur. fri til 9.30. Terms. HI 5 8865

WHITE JOI
THE NAVY

Fresh 'n bouncy junior
these Orlon® knits in
greatest new dress-sh

Latest fashion maneuve
of white to shape-up f
for Fall. Shown, two
spirited young dress
banded Orlon-acrylic:
with waist-defining be
two-piece with pleat

$13

"CHARGE IT" ON WA
CHARG-ALL C

AT THE FOLLOWING CHICAGOLAND WARD

Leather dresses for Chicagoans are

likely to feature hides

played one against the other
for this season's pattern-on-pattern
look.

Smooth, soft capeskins form the
basis for two such styles. Trimming
them, as a yoke, or as yoke-to-hem
bands, is pony skin that's stenciled
with miniature leopard spots. The
dresses are from El Greco, which

In rebuttal, one involved editor whose integrity is beyond challenge and who is known as a philosopher on journalistic problems made this reply:

Wedding reports are no longer news stories; they are legal notices. Newspapers have run these reports as a public service. This is like the oldtime reading of the banns; it's felt that the public has a right to know when a new family unit is being established through matrimony. And the mother of the bride certainly considers a wedding report as a legal document; if the language varies even a little from the conventional, she is convinced that her daughter is living in sin.

So there is no real difference between this legal notice and one that tells about the probate of a will. If there is unusual news value in either, we can always run a supplementary story. We were forced into this solution by the sheer weight of numbers. In a metropolitan paper we have a hard time justifying the use of space for an occurrence that interests only a tiny fraction of our readers. Still the bride ought to be entitled to have a public record of this event which is so important to her.

Countless other newspapers, large and small, have been selling space for death announcements. No one gets very excited about commercializing this kind of news. The editors had hoped that charging a fee would cut down the number of wedding stories, but the decrease, if any, has been too slight to be noticeable. There are some gains: the stuff is set in agate, the newspapers get some revenue from it, and the announcements aren't charged to the editorial space of the women's pages.

It has grown to a fairly common practice to charge engaged girls and brides for the cost of making engravings of their portraits. This was subjected to the same criticism of commercializing on the news. But the publishers who have adopted the policy have rarely been dissuaded from it by outside critics, and the girls concerned have made little, if any, objection. I oppose charging for editorial space, but I expect that this kind of "news" will eventually be run on a paid basis in most newspapers.

Many newspapers use a separate head schedule for women's pages. Customarily this is a lighter form of the regular news headletter. It is difficult to think of a single news headline face that doesn't offer such a lighter version. For Bodoni Bold, the normal news weight, Bodoni or Bodoni Book, make pleasant women's heads. In Spartan, good women's weights are Light, Book, or Medium in contrast to news Bold, Heavy, or Black. Metromedium and Metrothin make good headletters. The Squares and the Gothics have lighter weights available.

The State
THE COLUMBIA RECORD

Women

Bridal News
Fashions
Social Whirl

News and Features

Section D   Columbia, South Carolina, Sunday, October 20, 1968   Page 1

MRS. JOHN WALTER ROBERTS

Prior to her marriage Saturday in Shandon Methodist Church, Mrs. John Walter Roberts was Miss Doris Jean Knight. She is the daughter of Mr. and Mrs. James C. Knight of Columbia, and the bridegroom is the son of Mr. and Mrs. Oran B. Roberts of Rock Hill.

MARGARET LANDRUM PITTMAN

Mr. and Mrs. Charles Wood Pittman of Columbia announce the engagement of their daughter, Margaret Landrum, and John Dwight Patterson of Phoenix, Ariz., son of Mr. and Mrs. George Daniel Patterson. The wedding will take place in February.

MRS. SCOTT FARLEY WILLIAMSON

Before her wedding Saturday in St. Joseph's Catholic Church, Mrs. Scott Farley Williamson was Miss Mary Ellen Lammers. She is the daughter of Mr. and Mrs. Joseph Henry Lammers of Columbia, and the bridegroom is the son of Mr. and Mrs. Donald Alexander Williamson of Bethesda, Md.

MRS. WISE HENRY BATTEN

Prior to her marriage Saturday in Lawtonville Baptist Church, Estill, Mrs. Wise Henry Batten was Miss Brenda Lee Peeples of Scotia. She is the daughter of Dr. and Mrs. Harrison L. Peeples, and the bridegroom is the son of Mr. and Mrs. D. Wise Batten Jr.

MRS. ROBERT MICHAEL HOOK

Prior to her marriage Saturday in the First Baptist Church of West Columbia, Mrs. Robert Michael Hook was Miss Thresa Roxanne Wooten. She is the daughter of Mr. and Mrs. Tillman Wooten, and the bridegroom is the son of Mr. and Mrs. Perry Hook, all of West Columbia.

MRS. DAVID BELK COKER

Before her wedding Saturday in Salem Methodist Church, Mrs. David Belk Coker was Miss Dianne Monts. She is the daughter of Mr. and Mrs. J. C. Monts of Columbia, and the bridegroom is the son of Mr. and Mrs. Millard Coker, also of Columbia.

MRS. BASIL PARKS MACK

Prior to her marriage Saturday in the First Baptist Church of Cayce, Mrs. Basil Parks Mack was Miss Helene Geneva Sightler. She is the daughter of Mr. and Mrs. J. Woodrow Sightler. The bridegroom is the son of Mrs. W. Leon Mack of Cayce and the late Mr. Mack.

MRS. GEORGE RIVERS

Before her wedding Saturday in Greenlawn Baptist Church, Mrs. George Rivers was Miss Joan Tidwell. She is the daughter of Mr. and Mrs. Willis J. Tidwell, and the bridegroom is the son of Mr. and Mrs. Henry Rivers, all of Columbia.

USC Class Of '43 Plans To Re-Unite For Homecoming

Should Old Acquaintances Be Forgotten?

THIS YEAR it's the University of South Carolina Class of 1943 that will be holding its 25th reunion celebration during festivities planned for Homecoming, Saturday, Oct. 26. Hard at work on details for the reunion party are, left to right, John Dieter, co-chairman, Mrs. Robert Upshur, Mrs. Jere Eggleston, Sam King, chairman, and Mrs. C. C. Ariail. (Staff Photo by Larry Cagle)

By CHRISTIE FANT
Women's Writer

Should old acquaintance be forgot!

Never! says the University of South Carolina Alumni Association.

And the Carolina class of 1943 agrees.

Working hard to pull together the old school ties for a big 25th reunion coincidental with next weekend's Homecoming are a 1943 reunion committee headed by Sam King Jr. as chairman, and Johnny Dieter, co-chairman, along with Charles Knowlton, Libby (Steadman) Ariail, Alva Lumpkin, Sarah (Davies) Gibbes, Betty (Crews) Brandon, Harrell Graham, all of Columbia, and Louis Sossamon of Gaffney.

ALSO HELPING are Lou (Gilland) King, Lillian (Gayle) Douglass, Leone (Strickland) Castles, Doris (Nash) Upshur, Josephine (Stout) Lumpkin, Sarah (Belser) Eggleston.

The committee's hopeful idea of having a reunion party Friday night before Saturday's annual Homecoming institution met with a "terrific response," says chairman King.

Accordingly, plans are being set for a special silver anniversary celebration on the evening of Oct. 25, at Forest Lake Club in Columbia. The social hour will begin at 7:30, dinner is at 8:30 — with roast prime ribs of beef and all the trimmings — and there'll be music and dancing until 11.

Well over 100 reservations are already in, and the reunion committee urges "any who haven't responded, please do so right away so we can count you in."

"And if we've overlooked anybody, please contact Sam King," they also urge, emphasizing the possibility of address and listing errors.

THE IMPACT OF WORLD WAR II on the class of 1943 resulted in some confusion as to who is officially a member of the class, the committee explains.

They propose the following guidelines to help identify members: (1) anyone who graduated in '43, (2) anyone who entered the freshman class in 1939, including those whose schooling was later interrupted, (3) anyone who entered another college as a '39 and later transferred to USC.

Many of the reunion reservations already in are from Columbia's 1943 alumni and their spouses. Many have also been received from out of town.

These include Dean and Mary (Lowry) Davenport, from Panama City, Fla. — Col. Davenport, now retired, flew with the famous Doolittle Raiders in World War II; Sloan (Hungerpiller) Brittain of Newberry; William Harper of Charleston; Dr. Clarence Lyles, Spartanburg; Grover Bowers Jr., Dawson, Ga.; Helen (Anderson) Waring of Summerville; Francis Marion, Greenville; Dr. Robert

Lumpkin, Georgetown.

ALSO COMING are John and Virginia (Braxey) McGowan of Florence — he was senior class president; Sen. John A. Martin of Winnsboro; Lillian (Hanna) Daley, Allendale; Alley (Glominski) Floyd of Conway; J. Herbert Coman of Swansea, N. C.; T. B. and Ann (Cathcart) Forsner of Orangeburg; Mary Faith (Irick) Addy; Capt. (USN) G.E. Lecke, Arlington, Va.; Framphine W. Henderson of Aiken; John D. Clark, Winston Salem.

Joining the Friday festivities, too, will be members of the 1943 law class, and several special guests have been invited — USC President Thomas F. Jones; C. Wallace Martin, vice-president for development; Dick Little, alumni director; and Coaches Paul Dietzel and Frank McGuire.

Memories of the class of 1943 are preserved in the "Garnet and Black," annual yearbook which shared its school colors that year with the red, white and blue.

Significantly, indicating how great was the impact of World War II on the class and the school, the yearbook dedication took the form of a salute to "OUR COUNTRY."

THEIR PRESIDENT in those years was J. Rion McKissick — "The Colonel." Their dream were Childs and Chase and Bradley . . .

"People of Affairs" on campus were McIver Riley, Bob

Quinn, Donald Law, Tom Perrin, Virginia Copeland, Louis Sossamon, Ken Ballenger, Tina Cannon, John McGowan, Millie Zimmerman, Frank Sloan ("Beltmoreless in battle, lean, vibrant, nomadic — has a finger in every University activity"), Art Roberts, Kat Edgerton, Betty Crews, Leone Strickland, Harriet Williams, Dot Derrick, Kat Kathleen Arthur.

Sims Hall was the "new" women's dorm; Preston College was "new" for the men. Melton Field was a drill field for the new Naval ROTC and an exercise field for pre-flight cadets.

Rex Enright was head coach. And Bob McNair, class of '44, was a 1943 initiate of Blue Key.

"Prime plaything of campus society was the dance. Joy came in the wail of a lonesome trumpet."

And the class of 1943 wondered whether — "long after we have sailed away our dreams — will this ancient world we know still be here?"

The Garnet and Black gave an answer — "Just as sure as the stars, just as constant as knowledge, our Alma Mater will flower. The rumble of voices will stay. Bright new faces, Smarter with than ours. Youngsters who will go us one better. They will keep it as we knew it, only more effectively. They will keep the faith."

Now, 25 years later, the class of 1943 will come back. For old acquaintance should not be forgot. And they, too, must keep the faith.

The value of a separate headline schedule for women's pages is challenged by an interesting experiment done by Dr. Jack Haskins for ANPA and for which I helped prepare test materials. We designed a typical women's page around an ad pyramid. Stories and page pattern remained the same, but in one sample all heads were Caslon, another, all Spartan Medium, and so on.

The type faces used for the test schedules were shown separately to the respondents, who were asked to grade the faces on a scale that would indicate the "feminine" qualities of the face. Results were as anticipated: lighter, more graceful faces were selected as feminine ones; heavier and plainer faces were called masculine.

But when those faces were used on the test page, they had no measurable influence on readership. Pages dressed in a masculine hed sked drew as much readership as those with a feminine headletter. Not only page readership but that of individual stories remained without significant differences.

This is not to be interpreted as indicating that there is no value whatsoever in a separate women's-page headletter. The woman reader's acknowledgment of certain faces as having feminine qualities might be subconscious flattery to her; it might contribute a feeling of pleasure or even luxury, comparable to the wearing of lacy lingerie instead of tailored styles. We know that the "image" of an advertiser has a long-range benefit that is not necessarily reflected in immediate increased sales of specific items of merchandise. It may be that an attractive, feminine headletter for women's pages creates an image that attracts the reader in a constant, if unacknowledged, appeal. This factor, if there is one, would establish a high plateau of readership that would not be apparent in the test described. The research does indicate strongly, however, that the women's editor who does not have a separate headline schedule is not facing an acute handicap—or possibly any handicap at all. The same conclusion must be reached for sports, editorial, or other ROP sections that might have separate head schedules.

If the regular news headline schedule is used for women's pages, the desired feminine lightness can still be achieved. Space above and below the head should be doubled; the head should be indented twice as much as for regular news heads. This added white space will dilute the weight of the headletter.

Extra white space can also be achieved by proper handling of pictures. Regular halftones can be indented about twice as much as regular news cuts. Space above and below such cuts should be appropriately enlarged.

Cutlines should, of course, align precisely with the narrower engravings. Catchlines should be one step smaller than on news pages. Silhouettes or modified silhouettes also brighten pages, and because so much art for these pages comes in early, this extra handline need not be an oppressive burden to the engraving department.

Dropping a slug below each paragraph of body type is a good brightening device but it does require extra attention if the operator does it on the Linotype or extra time if the slugs are dropped in on the bank.

Small items that run as a column or in *roundups* are familiar fare on these pages. The masses of body type that result may be leavened by adding a decorative gimcrack between each pair of paragraphs or at less frequent random intervals. There are many appropriate devices and *florets*—stylized floral designs—that seem highly appropriate. The main advantage of such devices is the white space that flanks them. If the ornament is well chosen, it will not give an undesired, fussy look to the page.

Many editors of closed-format newspapers use alleys on women's pages for an airy effect. This is good only if alleys are achieved by some means other than by the usual nut-and-nut indents. The 1-up technique may be used for sub-areas or for the whole page; the W-format may be used for whole pages. Both can also be used on key or advertising pages. The latter require the accommodation of news to ads, as discussed in Chapter 9. Whether the results warrant this extra effort is the editor's decision.

Setting only Italic heads on women's pages is another device which may be used alone or in conjunction with added white space. This is a pleasant technique when used conventionally; it is especially effective when used with the increased amounts of white space just discussed.

A different decorative rule may be used for sideless boxes and to define 1-up areas on women's pages. There are literally scores of such borders in the proper weight and motif, and selection can be based on personal taste.

In an attempt to make their pages look different, many editors of women's sections center headlines or even set them flush right. As we have already noted, any style that fails to bring the eye back to a constant axis of orientation is malfunctional, no matter on what page it is used.

Often body type—especially cutlines—is set with ragged margins, left or right. If such a block is not too long—3 or 4 inches deep—a ragged

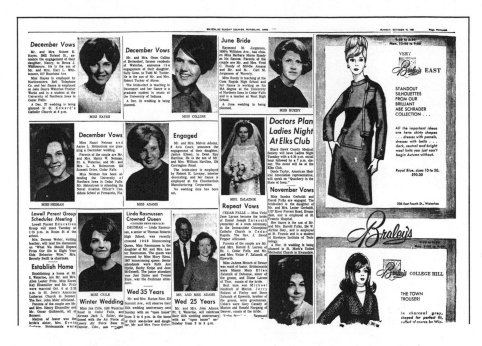

Fig. 123. Checkerboard design is useful in handling large numbers of bridal or engagement pictures. From *Waterloo* (Iowa) *Sunday Courier*.

right margin is acceptable. But body type set flush right or centered is worse than headlines in that style because there are more lines and the irritation of the reader increases with each new line.

There may be some justification for using flush-right cutlines if they are too brief to make an attractive rectangle of justified matter and when they must run against a halftone at its right on a free page. In this case the straight right margin of type fits neatly against the straight left edge of the cut. But this use should be rare.

The abuse of downstyle, by eliminating even capitals on proper nouns, is frequent on women's pages. I've already waxed caustic over this abomination. Sufficient here to point out that the practice is no less reprehensible because it occurs in the women's section. The needs of readability and legibility overshadow the need to be typographically unique.

On feature stories that carry hand-lettered heads, too often the letters are so fancy or so distorted that all legibility is sacrificed. Scripts are beloved by women's editors; this type race has low legibility at best and unless executed by an expert, may lose even that minimum in hand-lettering.

Principles of layout are the same for women's pages as for any other.

WOMEN in the News

8-A THE TAMPA TRIBUNE, Saturday, Aug. 3, 1968

MORNING

Romantic Frills Lure Feminine Hearts

By CAROL NEEF
Tribune Staff Writer

CALL it what you want . . . the romantic look or the Victorian look.

But no matter what you call it, it's a great look. And women who are tired of looking like anything but women will greet this return to femininity with enthusiasm.

Lace and ruffles are emerging in the morning and will be seen on afternoon, cocktail and formal wear.

There is virtually no type of fabric that doesn't look feminine and flattering with the right kind of "lingerie" trim.

Even wool knits that used to be reserved exclusively for suits and tailored dresses have felt the feminizing influence.

One dress in darkest brown double knit is reminiscent of the velvet dresses little girls used to wear for Sunday best. Creamy ivory lace edges the long fitted sleeves and bodice of the slim gown.

A body skimming cotton velvet jacket incorporates two new looks. The muted green, gold and pink print jacket is cut fingertip length with two vents in back. Gold buttons march up the front to the modified Nehru collar. A white lace jabot finishes the neckline.

The jacket can be worn with slim black velvet pants for fall and winter at home wear. It would also look great with a maxi or midi skirt at holiday parties this winter.

After years of sleeveless dresses the year-round, women who possess too fat, too thin or too old arms will hail the return of the sleeve. The lace and ruffles, undoubtedly hastened the sleeve's return. After all who ever saw a ruffle on a sleeveless dress?

And many of fall's prettiest and most alluring cocktail and formal gowns have long sleeves.

One of the most enchanting examples of the Victorian look is a floor length black silk organdy evening gown with extremely full skirt. The long sleeves and bodice are tucked. A wide black patent leather belt accents the high rise waistline. Accordion pleated white ruffles finish the sleeves and fashion the full collar.

Linne Wodnick models three dresses with the modified Victorian influence. Pleated ruffles edge the white cuffs of this dacron and cotton frock and a pleated jabot frames the plastron.

The Good Old Onion Gets Sliced and Pickled

By ANN McDUFFIE
Tribune Food Editor

This month's plentiful foods list features poultry, wheat products, plums, peanuts and peanut butter, watermelons, cantaloups, onions, Bartlett pears and summer vegetables. All are popula: foods and there should be something to please every member o: your family.

Since onion production is expected to break all records this year, now is a good time to put up some pickled onion slices. They make good Christmas gifts. This recipe is one of Mrs. J. Brown Farrior's contributions to The Gasparilla Cookbook.

PICKLED ONION SLICES

5 or 6 large white onions
2 cups iced water
2 cups white vinegar
¼ cup salt
1 heaping tablespoon sugar
1 tablespoon dill weed

Slice onions and soak in iced water to crispen. Boil vinegar, salt, sugar and dill weed and steep ½ hour. Meanwhile, scald jars, and place drained onion rings in them. Strain liquid through cheese cloth and pour over onions. Makes 3 or 4 jars.

Kitchen Corner

You also could prepare—

ONIONS AU GRATIN

12 to 15 medium-sized onions
6 tablespoons butter or margarine
4 tablespoons flour
2 cups milk
½ teaspoon salt
1 cup grated cheese
1 cup flaked bread-crumbs

Peel, wash and cook onions until tender in a large amount of boiling, salted water, uncovered. Mix and cook slowly 4 tablespoons butter or margarine, the flour, milk and salt. When thickened, add cheese. When onions are done, drain and add them to sauce. Pour into a baking dish. Melt the remaining 2 tablespoons butter or margarine in a saucepan and add crumbs, stirring rapidly until all crumbs are well covered. Sprinkle crumbs over the onions and place casserole in a hot oven, 425 degrees F. until crumbs are browned. Yields 4 to 6 servings.

If you are plagued with weeping while peeling, slicing and grating onions, try what Mrs. Herbert McKay does to avoid this nuisance. She ties a sheer white silk chiffon scarf over her head so that it covers her face. That way she can see what she is doing but the onion fumes don't bother her.

NOON

This black rayon and acetate blend fabric has the look of wool. The crisp white ruffles are edged with black and the skirt is gathered.

NIGHT

In the romantic tradition is this ball gown of black silk organdy. The collar is so full it resembles a ruff. The bodice and sleeves are tucked.
—Staff Photos by Dan Fager

The Brides' Book

MRS. MIGUEL CORRAL JR.
. . . Maria Cuervo

Cuervo-Corral

Maria G. Cuervo became the bride of Miguel Corral Jr. yesterday at the home of the bride's mother, Mrs. Estela Ciccarello of 2710 W. Columbus Drive. She is also daughter of Ramon Cuervo of Havana, Cuba.

Mr. Corral is son of Mr. and Mrs. Miguel A. Corral, 687 Geneva Place. The couple will live at 4212 Tacon.

King-Weeks

Nancy Jean King and Bruce Haberlen Weeks were married yesterday at Idlewild Baptist Church. She is daughter of Mr. and Mrs. Charles Lofton King, 315 W. Lambright St. His parents are Mr. and Mrs. Henry T. Weeks Jr. of Silver Spring, Md.

Mrs. Weeks attended St. Petersburg Junior College and is a billing clerk at The Tampa Tribune. Her husband is a sergeant in the U.S. Air Force, MacDill AFB. They will live at 206 E. Virginia Ave.

McElveen-Ross

Kathy McElveen became Mrs. James Earl Ross yesterday at Sarah Spencer Methodist Church. Her parents are Mr. and Mrs. Albert Lee McElveen of 8506 Ola Ave. and he is son of Mrs. Alice E. Ross, 908 W. Orient St., and F. J. Ross, also of Tampa.

Mr. Ross was graduated from Hillsborough High School and served four years with the U.S. Air Force. He is a fireman. His bride, a Leto High School graduate, is employed by [illegible] C. Penney Co. They will be [illegible] home in Tampa.

MRS. R. D. GADDIS
. . . Cheryl Lentz

Lentz-Gaddis

First Baptist Church of Brandon was the setting yesterday for the wedding of Cheryl Gay Lentz and R. Douglas Gaddis. Their parents are Mr. and Mrs. Gary Dean Lentz of Mango and Mr. and Mrs. J. E. Gaddis of Brandon.

Mr. Gaddis is attending St. Petersburg Junior College and his bride is a former student of Florida State University. Their home will be in St. Petersburg.

Schmitt-Kramer

Barbara Ann Schmitt became the bride of Kenneth Ralph Kramer last night at Corpus Christi Catholic Church. Parents of the couple are Mr. and Mrs. Felix J. Schmitt of Temple Terrace and Mr. and Mrs. Regis Kramer of Miami.

The new Mrs. Kramer is a teacher at Robles Elementary School and her husband is employed by St. Regis Paper Co., Forestry Division, in Picayune, Miss., where they will make their home. He is an ex-Marine Corps Sergeant.

MRS. L. A. SWEARENGIN
. . . Melody Barth

Barth-Swearengin

WINTER HAVEN (By Staff Writer) — Melody E. Barth and Larry A. Swearengin were married yesterday in Grace Lutheran Church.

The bride is the daughter of Mr. and Mrs. Bernard J. Barth of Eagle Lake and her husband is the son of Mr. and Mrs. Vernon A. Swearengin.

Mrs. Swearengin was graduated from Winter Haven High School and her husband is attending Polk Junior College. The couple will reside at 153½ Beverly Drive., SE.

Pierce-Bryant

Vivian Carol Pierce and Edward Thomas Bryant were married yesterday at Lake Caroll Baptist Church.

The bride is the daughter of Mrs. Bertha C. Pierce, 1806 Cano Court, and the bridegroom is the son of Mr. and Mrs. William Bryant, 803 April Lane.

The new Mrs. Bryant, a graduate of Thomas Jefferson High School, is secretary for Interprise Corp. Her husband, a Chamberlain High graduate, is employed by the Hillsborough County Parks Department.

The couple will live at 2803 W. Broad St.

MRS. G. R. DANIEL JR.
. . . Linda Beach

Beach-Daniel

The wedding of Linda Susan Beach and Giles Randolph Daniel Jr. took place last night at Nebraska Avenue Church of Christ. The bride is daughter of Mr. and Mrs. Henry L. Beach of 4546 W. Clifton Ave. Parents of the bridegroom are Mr. and Mrs. G. R. Daniel, 1220 E. Curtis St.

The new Mrs. Daniel attended University of South Florida. Her husband is a senior at Lincoln Chiropractic College, Indianapolis, Ind., where the couple will be at home.

Felker-Roberts

Marena Dianne Felker and Earl Richard Roberts Jr. were married yesterday in Good Shepherd Baptist Church.

The bride is the daughter of Mr. and Mrs. Vance R. Felker of Valrico and the bridegroom is the son of Mr. and Mrs. Earl Richard Roberts, 6821 Spencer Circle.

The bride was graduated from Brandon High School and is a clerk-typist at Hillsborough County Hospital. The bridegroom is a student at the University of Tampa.

The couple will reside at 7707 Ola Ave.

Bach-Rigsby

Jeanne Lynn Bach became Mrs. James Allen Rigsby Jr. yesterday at New Orleans Baptist Church. She is daughter of Mrs. Marguerite S. Bach, Apollo Beach, and Arthur E. Bach of Ruskin. The bridegroom is son of Mr. and Mrs. J. A. Rigsby of Tampa.

The new Mrs. Rigsby is a graduate of East Bay High School and is a typist at Florida Department of Agriculture. Her husband, a Hillsborough High School graduate, is a painter at Pricher Truck Service. They will live at 2320 Liberty St.

MRS. B. H. WEEKS
. . . Nancy King

MRS. J. E. ROSS
. . . Kathy McElveen

MRS. K. R. KRAMER
. . . Barbara Schmitt

MRS. E. T. BRYANT
. . . Vivian Pierce

MRS. E. R. ROBERTS JR.
. . . Marena Felker

MRS. J. A. RIGSBY JR.
. . . Jeanne Bach

Women Lawyers Elect Ruth Talley President

PHILADELPHIA (AP) —Ruth Gentry Talley of Bogalusa, La. today assumed the presidency of the National Association of Women Lawyers.

The organization, meeting in conjunction with the annual convention of the American Bar Association, was formed in 1899, 19 years before the ABA admitted women to membership.

Other new officers for the coming year are: Jettie Pierce, Selvig, San Francisco, president-elect; Adele T. Weaver, Miami, Fla., vice president; Jean J. McVeety, Minneapolis, treasurer; Mary Jeann Coyne, Minneapolis, recording secretary; Annie Morton Stout, Memphis, Tenn., corresponding secretary, and Judge Mattie Belle Davis, Miami, Fla. delegate to the ABA.

Ruth Talley, who succeeds Grace D. Cox of New York City, said "women have gained a great deal of statutory equality," and added she hopes that lady lawyers "will continue to prove their ability, interest in and devotion to their profession by greater activity in their professional association."

Mrs. Talley is engaged in the practice of law with four partners in the firm founded by her father.

Executive Board Will Hold Meeting

REDINGTON BEACH (Special) — Mrs. Hazel Talley of St. Petersburg, Democratic national committeewoman-elect of Florida, will be the principal speaker at a 12:30 p.m. luncheon today at the two-day meeting of the executive board of the Florida Democratic Women's Club now in progress at the Tides Hotel and Bath Club.

Mrs. Talley will present the 1968 campaign program of the state Democratic executive committee.

Today's business meeting will be held until the luncheon. Mrs. Walter Boyd of Clearwater, vice president of the 8th Congressional District, assisted by Mrs. Ruth Pearsall of St. Petersburg, are co-hostesses at the quarterly meeting.

Presidents of the three Pinellas County clubs, Mrs. Harold Thompson of Belleair Beach, Mrs. John S. Kennedy of St. Petersburg, and Mrs. Ruth Cheshire of Lealman, will assist.

Other members of the executive board attending include Mrs. Annette Baker Loeser, outgoing national Democratic Committeewoman, Mrs. Fay Owles of Orlando, president of the Democratic Woman's Club of Florida, and Mrs. Christine Maxwell of Tallahassee, who was named "Democratic Woman of the Year."

Anyone interested may attend the luncheon.

Fig. 124. Unusual head schedule of light Gothics and Square Serifs makes attractive women's page in *Tampa* (Fla.) *Tribune*.

Ads should pyramid to the right and be kept as low as possible; there should be a dominant head; naked columns should be avoided; each page must have a picture.

Rarely is it a problem to find a picture for each women's page; often the opposite is true. During the Christmas season, before and after Lent, and in June, the big problem becomes "How do we use all the wedding and engagement pictures that are piling up?" The tone of voice of this query varies from pure inquiry to sheer panic.

An ancient axiom says: "Unrelated art should be widely separated." But in handling great numbers of female portraits, the editor assumes that they are related, at least by common status of betrothal or matrimony. It is much better to gang up as many portraits as possible and handle them as a single large element than to attempt to sprinkle them throughout the section as individual items.

There are several techniques that can relieve the formal checkerboard effect of row after row of same-sized pictures. One or more pictures may be removed from the grid and into the space thus left a headline, a catchline-cutline combination, an appropriate verse set in larger-than-body type, or a line ornament can be set. The ornament may be drawn by the staff artist or taken from the ad-mat service, which generally has many suitable drawings.

A simple device is to run the cutlines of a single portrait above, rather than below, a picture; this break in regularity is pleasant. One picture may be silhouetted. Or a square halftone may be made into a rhomboid by cutting sides at an angle other than 90 degrees. Corners of a single cut may be rounded off or cut in straight lines to make an irregular octagonal.

Any of these devices should be used sparingly. One is enough in any block of pictures.

The size of an engagement or wedding picture is a highly prized status symbol. Old-time society editors dearly enjoyed the power that was theirs to define the 400 of their town. Some were susceptible to subtle bribery. While it sounds ridiculous, it is true that many a girl's life or personality was blighted because her wedding picture was smaller than that of her cousin. Today many editors refuse to be social arbiters; they use only one size for all matrimonial pictures. This takes a lot of pressure off the society desk and probably makes many more happy than disappointed girls.

The wedding of a President's or a mayor's daughter will still demand, and produce, larger pictures. But these are comparatively rare and will not eat into the news hole like the pictures that are made larger because the father of the bride is a potential advertiser or the mother is a member of the same bridge club as the wife of the police reporter.

A bane that ought to be erased by federal legislation is the *sorority drape*. This is the tasteless custom of replacing a conventional dress with black drapery arranged in a deep V at the bosom. This style is dearly beloved of sororities and other female organizations. It prevents, they think, any one girl's overshadowing her sisters by means of a photogenic dress or accessories. But the effect is neither flattering nor pleasant, and sometimes the decolletage seems inappropriate to a nontheatrical young woman.

It is dubious whether the Congress will ever get around to outlawing the sorority drape, so the only applicable law is the one the editor himself lays down. Many newspapers have done just that; they've decreed that all such pictures shall be retouched, that the staff artist paint a dress on the model. This is simple to do, and the effect is an improvement.

If such a policy is put into effect, each young woman who submits such a picture should be told that she will be "dressed" before she appears in print. She should be shown a typical picture which has been so handled. If she feels that she cannot trust the couturial judgment of the artist, she may want to don a dress and have her picture retaken. In all instances, the dress that is painted on should be in unobtrusive style. Often it is only necessary to raise the neckline and perhaps put on short sleeves to convert the drape to an acceptable dress. Addition of very subdued jewelry may help too.

Another plethora on women's pages is the tabular setting of recipes. As the volume of food advertising rises, many publishers commit themselves to packing these ads into food "news." Much of this is about meals and dishes. Some editors set recipes in agate. The reason isn't clear. This is one part of the paper where there should be no need to worry about space. While much food news is just that, news, and many recipes are welcomed by the woman reader (if not her husband), the primary purpose of food news is to fill columns quickly and painlessly. Whether we run two dozen recipes in agate or 15 of them in 8-point really isn't going to stir up appreciable reader reaction, good or bad.

It would seem wiser to begin the long and arduous job of educating the grocer so that he doesn't demand only food news alongside food advertising. Any news of interest to women would serve his purpose just as well and probably even better. The occasional recipe could be dropped in between bridge luncheons and wedding anniversaries, and its tabulation would be a pleasant change in typographic color. Only when there is an accumulation of such tabular matter does it make the page look moth-eaten.

Usually the women's department has a Sunday section page that is ad-free. While the department may have weekday section pages too, these often carry considerable advertising, as this space is considered premium by many advertisers. If the page is a "free" one, it may be made up as discussed later in this chapter. If it is in conventional form, layout principles apply to it as to any front page. Strong attention should always be paid to the basement of the section page.

Sports Pages

The world of sports is a colorful one, filled with all the action and excitement of combat. Contemporary man has few of the outlets for action that his ancestors had. He can't risk his life against a saber-toothed tiger or vent annoyance by bashing a rival over the head with a war club. The mores of our day, as well as the law, prohibit violence, so man must work the adrenalin out of his blood vicariously. When an end makes a vicious tackle on the ball carrier, it's almost as good as punching the boss in the nose. Subconsciously at least, even the most mild-mannered spectator wants to see blood. It is no coincidence that the rougher or more dangerous the sport, the greater its audience. Football packs them in; tiddlywinks has practically no audience appeal.

This, then, is the world that the sports page must reflect.

Thus the whole sports section must speak in a more excited tone of voice. Headlines must be larger than they'd be on a story of the same length on news pages. Hammers are particularly effective on these pages and so are flatout techniques.

Most important is the use of pictures. Every sports page must have at least one large action picture.

Oddly enough, this world of action is enamored of static photographic clichés. Look in the files of your own newspaper and examples will abound. When a baseball player sets a home-run record, do we show him making his climactic hit? Oh, no; we show him holding a baseball with the number of his homers inked on it! The number of ways in which action can be eliminated from sports pictures is testimony to the ingenuity of the cameraman and his editor.

Editors place too much emphasis on immediacy. Even during the summer, athletic action tends to be concentrated in the weekend. If a Tuesday ball game is rained out, the sports writer can always resort to a

Fig. 125. Sports pages. Great number of high school football reports are well handled in inside Saturday page of *Wilmington* (Del.) *Morning News,* left; note large heads. Sunday section page from *Akron* (Ohio) *Beacon Journal* runs important football scores above flag; note index alongside section logo.

"think piece"; he can give a detailed prognostication of the rest of the season. Unfortunately, "think pictures" are concocted for the same reason. The editor ought to prefer an action picture from Sunday over a static, contrived "today" shot. A good picture loses no value because it's a day or two old. It's far better to save a good weekend shot for the dull midweek than it is to play it small and make it compete against other good pictures on Monday.

The editor should steel himself against running "the picture of record." Many an editor will use a poor shot because the cameraman tells him that this is the winning touchdown. A truer record of the game might well be taken on a no-gain line buck if the play resulted in good composition and illustrated the determination of both teams.

Sequence pictures are common on sports pages, primarily because this is one of the few areas where the cameraman can anticipate a sequence. The proper use of sequences has been discussed in Chapter 6, and the principles noted there should be applied to sports-page usage.

Marker art is too often overdone on sports pages. Some newspapers have a practice of labeling every touchdown picture with some flam-

Fig. 126. *Sunday Bulletin* of Philadelphia, Pa., handles overlapping of baseball and football seasons in neat pattern. *Toronto* (Ont.) *Globe and Mail* is quiet in tone; note low-key heads. Panel around nameplate is maroon.

boyant logo. Others will circle the ball on every picture, whether or not such notation is required. Another familiar overuse of marker art is affixing the name to every figure in an athletic picture. Marker art can, of course, increase the usefulness of many sports pictures. The dotted line showing the path of a ball carrier may be significant. It may help the reader to see the label that shows who made a key block or which would-be tackler ended up with his nose in the dirt. But there is no need to identify men who are obviously out of the play; in fact, overidentification may easily become distracting.

Much of the content of sports pages is pure statistics—box scores, team standings, schedules, etc.—and most are set in agate to conserve space and because wire tape is punched for this smaller face. This agate matter makes the page look as if it's in the third day of four-day measles.

Some editors are experimenting with concentrating all such matter on a single page with a simple heading like THE SCOREBOARD. They have been doing that with horse-racing results for many years; large areas are filled entirely with agate track statistics. But opponents contend that a box score should be right with its story and that huge concentration—a whole page or two—of agate type might discourage reading. Research

Fig. 127. Participant sports, often played down, get full treatment on lively pages from *Deseret News* of Salt Lake City, Utah.

indicates, though, that there are two kinds of readers of sports news. One of them is engrossed by statistics; he doesn't really want to read an account of a game, he just wants to know that ol' Stretch Culligan maintained his average of 31.2 points per game. The other reader is bored by statistics; he wants a verbal account of the contest and no more. Concentrating tabular material in one area should serve the needs of both groups. Eliminating agate from the typical page will make for more attractive typography.

Such an all-agate page should carry at least one large and strong action picture. This is required to stop the reader who is not particularly interested in statistical matter.

Generally, the reader will not buy a newspaper to find out the result of a game. Radio or television brings that almost instantaneously. The only possible exception is on Sunday morning, especially when seasons overlap. With a dozen big-league baseball games and scores of football contests at the same time, the reader just can't remember all the scores he has heard on the air. On Sunday morning, he wants to know who beat whom and by how much. So the simple presentation of many scores is a useful newspaper service.

Usually these are final scores alone, set in 14- or 18-point and pre-

Bosox win; stay alive

Chop Cards' margin to 3-2 with 3-1 win; idle today

ST. LOUIS (UPI)—Stopper Jim Lonborg stuck his s t u r d y right arm in the dike and prevented the Boston Red Sox from being drowned Monday, pitching the American League champions to a dramatic three-hit, 3-1 victory over the St. Louis Cardinals in the fifth game of the World Series.

Lonborg's tense triumph l e f t the battling Red Sox down three games to two and force the Series to shift back to Boston's Fenway Park for a sixth game on Wednesday.

The do-or-die victory was considerably more difficult for Lonborg than his o n e - h i t, 5-0 triumph in the second game because the Sox m a n a g e d to scrape only one unearned run in the first eight i n n i n g s before a.lding two more t a l l i e s, one also tallied, in the ninth.

The 6-foot-5, 24-year-old Californian lost a bid for a second consecutive World Series shutout with two out in the ninth inning when Roger Maris whacked his sixth Series homer over the right field wall.

Ken Harrelson and E l s t o n Howard, both late-season acqui-

s i t i o n s, singled across a run a p i e c e and another tallied on Maris's throwing error. Third baseman Mike Shannon's error in the third inning set up the first Boston score.

The rest was all Lonborg, just as it had been all season during which the towering right-hander won 22 games. He won the pennant clincher in Boston a week ago Sunday and now has been the winning pitcher in all of the last three Red Sox victories.

In setting a record for the fewest hits allowed by a pitcher in two consecutive complete Series games, Lonborg was superb. He showed no effects of a slight cold he had caught in the unseasonable cold St. Louis weather.

Only Maris hit the ball sharply against Lonborg, singling sharply to right in the fourth inning

after Dal Maxvill had legged an infield hit in the third. Following Maris's single, Lonborg retired 12 men in a row before shortstop Rico Petrocelli booted Julian Javier's grounder with one out in the eighth.

He pitched out of that jam, however, by retiring pinch hitter Dave Ricketts on a grounder to first and g e t t i n g pinch hitter Phil Gagliano on a pop-up. He rolled through the first two hitters in the ninth before Maris b a s e d an 0-1 pitch down the right field line. The poised Lonborg, however, then nailed Orlando Cepeda for the final out on a grounder to third.

Youthful southpaw Steve Carlton dueled Lonborg through two scoreless innings before Joe Foy singled for the first Boston hit with one out in the third. He went to second as Mike Andrews dropped a sacrifice bunt

down the third base line and reached first safely when Shannon bobbled the ball.

After Carlton got Carl Yastrzemski looking at a third strike, Harrelson, signed by the Sox in late August for a $75,000 two-year contract a f t e r being fired by K a n s a s City owner Charles Finley, bounced a single into left field for his first Series hit, scoring Foy.

Carlton steadied and set the Sox down in the next three innings before being lifted for a pinch-hitter. Andrews' single in the fifth and Yastrzemski's double in the eighth were the only other Boston hits until the fatal ninth.

"We're going home now," said Boston Manager Dick Williams, "and that makes all the difference in the world."

St. Louis M a n a g e r Red Schoendienst had only one pleas-

ant moment during the crisp fall afternoon—and that came before the start of the game when his wife sang the National Anthem.

Williams nominated r o o k i e Gary W a s l e w s k i, another string-bean righthander w h o pitched three perfect innings of relief on Saturday, to start the sixth game .on Wednesday. He will be opposed by another rookie, bespectacled Dick Hughes, who lost the s e c o n d game to Lonborg.

	ab r h bi		ab r h bi
Boston		**St. Louis**	
Foy 3b	5 1 1 0	Brock lf	4 0 0 0
Andrews 2b	3 0 1 0	Flood cf	4 0 0 0
Ystrzmsk lf	3 0 1 0	Maris rf	4 1 2 1
Harrelson rf	3 0 1 1	Cepeda 1b	4 0 0 0
Tartabull rf	0 0 0 0	McCarver c	3 0 0 0
Scott 1b	4 1 1 0	Shannon 3b	3 0 0 0
Smith cf	4 1 1 0	Javier 2b	3 0 0 0
Petrocelli ss	3 0 0 0	Maxvill ss	2 0 1 0
Howard c	4 0 1 1	Ricketts ph	1 0 0 0
Lonborg p	4 0 0 0	Willis p	0 0 0 0
		Lamabe p	0 0 0 0
		Carlton p	1 0 0 0
		Tolan ph	1 0 0 0
		Washburn p	0 0 0 0
		Gagliano ph	1 0 0 0
		Bressoud ss	0 0 0 0
Totals	33 3 6 2	**Totals**	31 1 3 1

BOSTON .... 001 000 001—3
ST. LOUIS .... 000 000 001—1
E—Shannon, Petrocelli, Maris. DP— St. Louis 2. LOB—Boston 7, St. Louis 3. 2B—Yastrzemski, Smith, HR—Maris. S— Andrews.

	ip h r er bb so
Lonborg (W)	9 3 1 1 0 4
Carlton (L)	6 3 2 1 1 4
Washburn	2 1 0 0 0 2
Willis	0 1 2 1 3 0
Lamabe	1 1 0 0 0 2

Schoendienst: Howard's hit decided game

FALLEN ST. LOUIS CARD SS JULIAN JAVIER MAKES GREAT STOP
. . . and relays to second baseman Dal Maxvill for start of double play.

SUN-BULLETIN—UPI

Blooper the key —not Lonborg

ST. LOUIS (UPI)—Jim Lonborg didn't decide the ball game; Elston Howard did.

That's the view of Red Schoendienst, manager of the beaten St. Louis Cardials.

"That ball Howard hit in the ninth," grumbled Schoendienst. "If we could have gotten out of that inning, I thought we would tie it and go on to win."

Howard's bloop single to right drove home George Scott and Reggie Smith scored the third Boston Red Sox run of the game on Roger Maris's high throw to the plate.

Cardinal reliever Jack Lamabe, who served the pitch to Howard, said he threw "a fast ball which Howard hit off his hands.

"It was a 2-1 pitch," Lamabe said, "and I was hoping it would go foul."

Howard's game-breaking blow came near the end of a three-hit performance by Lonborg, who had beaten the Cards on a one-hitter in the second game of the World Series in Boston.

"Lonborg just didn't give us much," Schoendienst said. "We swung at a lot of bad pitches."

Cardinal centerfielder Curt Flood said, "Lonborg did a heck of a job. He stepped in with the chips down and won big."

Flood said, "Lonborg seemed to be throwing harder to me than in the second game, but some of the guys didn't think so. Maybe he was just throwing harder to me because I'm a little guy."

Without Howard's run-scoring single in the ninth, the Cards could have tied the game on Maris's homer in the bottom half of the inning. Maris nailed one of Lonborg's pitches and sent it over the wall in right field.

Utah heavyweight Doyle plans major upset of Joe Frazier

NEW YORK (UPI)—In boxing parlance, Tony Doyle, a have collected 13, seven of them in swimming.

Heats were held in eight of the nine events on Friday's swimming program. Because of a small entry list, no heats were conducted in the women's

But Doyle, who faces heralded Joe Frazier in a scheduled 10-Calif., took three of the four heats in the women's 400-meter freestyle. Miss Meyer set a Mexican all-comers record by winning her heat in 4:53.2. She already has won a gold medal in the pre-Olympics.

The good-looking Irishman from Draper, Utah, isn't given a chance against Frazier, a former Olympic heavyweight champ and one of the most promising youngsters in the fight business.

However, the Westerner and his manager, Angelo Curley, have other opinions. "Doyle decisioned Frazier once before when the two were amateurs again," said Curley as Doyle woun.l _.. workouts at Clancy's Gym in New York before leaving for Philadelphia.

"Tony has the style to beat Frazier. It's true he doesn't have the knockout record of Frazier but Tony is a better fighter. He will outbox Frazier," said Curley.

"We wouldn't have taken the fight unless we thought Tony could take Frazier," said Curley, who feels his fighter will pull the upset of the year.

Frazier, who is unbeaten in 17 pro fights, tangles with Doyle in the first bout ever staged in the $12 million Spectrum Arena in Philadelphia.

Frazier took the Doyle bout "to even the score" with the Utah boxer. Doyle and Buster Mathis are the only fighters with wins over Frazier and both won while they were campaigning as amateurs.

"Mathis is going to have to wait," said Frazier, who said Doyle was his immediate concern. Frazier doesn't consider the bout a gamble. "I feel I can take any man that steps into the ring with me."

Central beats SV in STAC by 24-6
STORY PAGE 38

Fig. 128. Sports page in compact layout. *Sun-Bulletin* of Binghamton, N.Y., designs page in horizontal units. This is last page of paper; note reefer, cols. 1-2, inviting reader inside.

sented in some checkerboard design at the top of the sports section page.

Such "glut of occurrences" tempts the sports editor to use layercake or shotgun heads. This temptation should be resisted stoutheartedly. It may be difficult to decide whether the Army victory over Notre Dame is more important than a 3-game tie of the World Series or the successful defense of his title by the local golf champion. Although the editor may slough off making such decisions by using shotgun heads, the reader must still make them. He can't read two stories at once. If the editor's choice doesn't suit all his readers, at least it won't scare them away. Leaving decisions for the reader, however, tends to send him hustling to another page, and the editor cannot afford this loss.

Ganging stories and identifying them by a label kicker or logo can add to the pleasure and convenience of the reader. The kicker might say NATIONAL LEAGUE and the main head carry the late developments; all the individual stories would be carried with only a score—*CUBS* 5, *CINCY* 4—in 24-point as subheads. Or a BIG 10 logo could be dropped into each story from that conference, no matter where the story happened to run.

Business Pages

For many years, business pages consisted of practically nothing but market reports. Any other news from this important segment of American life was carried as a small item under a standing head. But as readers showed a growing interest in business stories, newspapers expanded coverage to meet that demand. Today, business pages carry real news, not just public-relations puffs.

Market reports still account for the greatest portion of news space. There is little opportunity for creativity in these listings. For economic reason as well as the pressure of deadlines, this matter is set by wire tape in all but a few newspaper plants. Even metropolitans that use no other tape find that automation for this voluminous setting is almost essential for carrying closing markets in afternoon editions. This is particularly true in the Eastern time zone, where the closing time of the market coincides with that of final editions.

About the only local editorial decision is that of the agate face in which the markets will be set. Most papers set markets in Sans Serifs because of their high legibility, but there are some excellent agates in

Roman. All the popular news body types are cut in 5½-point. In either race, the face must meet requirements discussed in Chapter 3.

Index letters, those showing the start of each alphabetical division, should be conspicuous. At least an 18-point is required, and a 24-point is often desirable. With the extra weight of a Poster Bodoni or Spartan Extra Black, a 14-point may be adequate. It gives effective contrast to carry the general roundup story, set in normal body type and carrying a large head, on the markets page or pages.

Business-page editors like to maintain dignified page makeup in most instances, although there are a few that make up these pages exactly as they would regular news sections.

Using the *billboarding* technique for heads—surrounding them with unusual amounts of white space—gives a distinctive flavor to business pages. They look interesting and newsy yet maintain a pleasing aura of authority. A billboarded 14-point head occupies the same amount of space as that normally taken by a 24-point of the same number of lines. The unusually large amount of space above and below the head should be complemented by a generous indent, left and right. The left indent would be 1 or 2 picas wide, even though it sets up an axis of orientation to the right of the start of the story.

Every page, including the ones that carry market reports, should have a strong picture. For many years the only available business photos were portraits of executives or catalog shots of new products. Slowly public-relations departments began releasing pictures that resembled news shots. As these pictures were eagerly accepted by newspapers, PR men were encouraged to break even farther from convention. Today their photo releases are often excellent in ingenuity of content as well as technically. But the alert business-page editor should create his own pictures whenever possible. Company public-relations offices will usually be more than glad to take the picture according to directions of the editor.

Business pages often carry personal columns by the editor. The heading should be appropriate to the page and to other column headings throughout the paper. An excellent technique is to set matter about 15 picas wide (the regular 1½-column setting is convenient) and alternate in placing items flush left and flush right in a 2-column hole. This may take a little extra work of dropping spacing material along the items, but some composing rooms report that they can get lockup sufficient for stereotyping without such spacing.

Amusement Pages

Legitimate theaters and cinemas, restaurants and night clubs, and radio and television are often given pages of their own. They require no special typography.

Theater pages are usually black with advertising. Movie ads are challenged only by those for used cars as the "worst in the paper." So editorial matter must build in maximum amounts of fresh air.

Because there are so many small ads on the typical movie and restaurant pages, it is often necessary to use a double pyramid. But the POA should be left open, even though a short pyramid must be built up on the left of the page. Magazine-style ad placement, where narrow pillars of advertising run high on the page with news matter at either side, can be effective on these pages or any others with many small ads.

Comic Pages

Although movie and television screens have widened consistently over the past two decades, their newspaper equivalent, the comic strip, has shrunk. Comic strips, even in the days of 12- and 13-pica columns, used to be in full-page width. The need to save paper during World War II narrowed the strips, and the proliferation of such features since then has maintained the pressure for space. The typical newspaper uses strips in 4-column widths today. When an occasional paper uses a 5- or 6-column strip, it seems gigantic. The fine draftsmanship of such strips as *Steve Canyon, Terry and the Pirates, Gil Thorpe,* and *On Stage* deserves to be seen in larger sizes, though.

Almost all newspapers gang the comics—*strips* and *panels*—on one or two pages. Only a rare few still scatter strips at random throughout the paper, a practice that was widespread before World War II. All surveys show that readers prefer to find their regular funnies on a page or pages that are always in the same position. For no good reason, the comic page has most frequently been the second to last one in the paper. But this pattern is slowly being changed. *Today* and the *St. Louis Post-Dispatch,* which dress up their comics with spot color, place them on the back page of a section to make it most convenient for the press room and thus make editorial color available for the front page too.

Panel comics, especially those that do not have much continuity, can be run wild through the paper. Specialized panels are now drawn for almost every newspaper section—sports, women's, outdoors, teens, and even stock markets. Many of them are in 1-column size and so are convenient for providing art on tight pages.

The practice grows to use comic panels on classified-ad pages to relieve the deadly gray. The hope is that the reader attracted by the comic will be added to the readership of the advertising too.

Placement of comic strips has no measurable effect on their popularity. Some editors prefer to alternate dark strips (those with large masses of black, such as *Rex Morgan, M.D.* or *Buzz Sawyer*) with light ones (such as *Peanuts* or *Andy Capp*). Some say that this makes it easier to control ink on the press, but most admit that they do it only because it pleases their own eye.

Because strips are sized to the narrowest possible column widths, they are less than full columns wide in matted form. This extra space may be used for running the title of the comic sideways at its left. True, this is contrary to an axiom of typography that says, "Type should never be run sideways." In this case, however, the type probably will not be read, no matter which way it runs. The reader rarely recognizes a strip by its name, anyway; he identifies it with the name of the leading character.

If the titles run at the sides, a pica of white space ought to be placed between individual comics for the most pleasant effect though many papers reduce this separation. Other editors run the titles above the strip just to provide horizontal separation.

If the white area at the sides of comics is large enough, it may be sold for advertising. By its size, it will accept only a single line of type, which must, of course, run sideways. But the high readership of such pages and the fact that advertising is rarely placed on them make this a truly premium position. For advertisers whose main job is only to keep their name before the public instead of presenting sales copy for specific merchandise, these narrow ribbons can be most effective. Drive-ins, record shops, amusement parks, and similar businesses are natural prospects for such space.

If comics don't fill the whole page, other news matter should be light and amusing. Crossword puzzles, horoscopes, and perhaps radio-TV listings seem appropriate. Type and pictorial features for children are often run here, too, although it might be wiser to run them on other inside pages to accustom the child to moving throughout the entire newspaper.

This technique will work, of course, only if the children's feature has high readership. Many surveys indicate, however, that this readership is low and that it comes as a rub-off from the comics. Should this feature be moved to another page then, most of its current readership may be lost. So the editor must go back to his basic need: Find or produce good copy for the kids.

Teen Pages

Newspapers are slowly becoming aware that they must fight much more vigorously for younger readers than they have in the past. Except for the comics and an occasional innocuous bedtime story or encyclopedia feature, there is little in the typical American paper for children. So they turn to television. Then, by some overnight magic, the child is supposed to become an inveterate newspaper reader. It just doesn't work out that way.

To lure this huge audience and to sell advertising directed at their multimillion-dollar market, teen pages are becoming fairly common as a weekly feature and occasionally on a daily basis. Most began as school-news pages, usually carrying "correspondence" from each area school. Gradually the scope expanded to wider subject matter, and more capable people were placed in charge—or given more time to do the job.

Teen pages need not be dramatically different from regular pages. Their typographic tone of voice should be higher pitched, about like that of the sports page. More teaser heads may be used, and pictures should be as gay and informal as possible.

Now we ought to hope that the needs of younger children be met. This means more than an added Peter Rabbit episode or instructions for making a small atom bomb from household supplies. Children of tender years are interested in news events; they hear reports on the air. Like adults, the youngsters want to learn more about the event in printed form. But we fail to give it to them.

I believe that each of the top six to a dozen stories each day ought to be condensed into a brief paragraph written in a child's vocabulary. Indeed, there should probably be two such versions, one for children of six to nine, another for those from ten to thirteen or fourteen. After that, the youngsters are perfectly capable of adult reading. Weekly news magazines for children have tremendous circulation. The obvious interest and need of the younger generation ought to be served by newspapers instead. Then we wouldn't have the formidable task of converting a young adult, thoroughly acclimatized to electronic media, to an ardent user of print media.

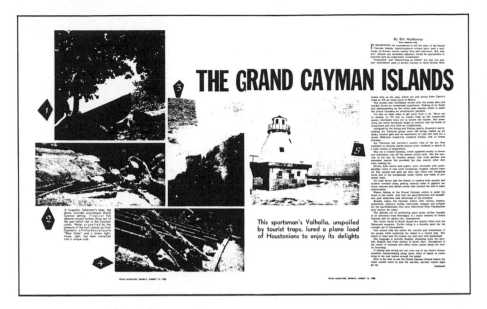

By Bill McMurray

THE GRAND CAYMAN ISLANDS

This sportsman's Valhalla, unspoiled
by tourist traps, lured a plane load
of Houstonians to enjoy its delights

Fig. 129. Oriented layout. Spread of *Texas Magazine* of *Houston* (Texas) *Chronicle* shows tightly woven pages. Right margins align in *1* and *2*. Bottoms of *2, 3* and *5* align. Top of *4* lines up with caption for *3*; right margin of *5* aligns with blurb. Note how slight misalignment on folder hides part of G in head.

Magazine Pages

There are two kinds of magazine pages that a newspaper editor may have to work with. One is the obvious one, that in the Sunday magazine section of the paper or in a special merchandising section in tabloid format. The other is on a normal full page.

Many editors find that long stories, conveniently designated "magazine length," have high readership. Such a story, with its attendant art, may fill a whole 8-column page or even a column or so more. Subject matter may be anything from shoes and ships to sealing wax, and while these features are usually run on section pages, they may begin almost any department of the Sunday paper. This is the favorite day to run such material; space is usually more plentiful, and the composing room needs copy that can be set well before the weekend rush.

Often these features are presented in a *free page*. This is one where type is not confined to regular column divisions and where generous amounts of white space are used to help create pleasing or striking page patterns. A free page need not be a solid rectangle of type; often whole or parts of columns are deliberately left blank. Free pages allow maximum creativity to the editor, but he must maintain strict personal discipline to assure the controlled layout that is necessary for greatest readership.

An excellent technique for free pages is the *oriented layout*. By this system, also called the *buddy system* or *no-orphan technique,* every element in a layout is oriented along an obvious axis. Most of these are vertical, although horizontal axes are also used whenever possible. At least two elements must align on each vertical axis; these are obviously the buddies who give this system its nickname. No element may stand alone, as an "orphan"; each must have at least one buddy sharing an axis. (In conventional newspaper pages, column rules or alleys are the constant vertical axes, and the top and bottom of the page are the horizontal ones. The page is strongly oriented in both directions.)

The orienting technique was developed for advertising layouts. It is the only pattern that can be produced "by the numbers" and thus has proved popular among advertising men, who don't have the talent, interest, or time required to do a creative layout for the many accounts they must service. Making an oriented layout proceeds in a well-defined sequence.

The first element to be placed on the page is centered or positioned flush left or flush right. The next element may be centered, too, or it must align vertically with at least one edge of the first one.

As each element is placed, lines drawn downward from its edges create new axes on which succeeding elements may be placed. The latter elements may be aligned on the axes on either their own right or left margins, depending on whether there is space and whether it will then relate logically with earlier elements. Elements may align not only on the edges of engravings but on strong elements or lines within a picture.

When an element is centered, it must be very obvious where the center line is and what area it bisects. If one side of an area is defined by the side of a halftone but the other runs into a margin, an element mathematically centered in the area will not appear to be so because the eye will include the margin as part of the basic area.

Pictures and cutlines are combined into a single unit for the purposes of doing an oriented layout.

Wherever possible, elements should be aligned on common horizontal axes too.

The layout man must remember the ancient axioms as he creates an oriented layout. "Pictures above type" is an important one. There must be a strong attention compeller in the POA. There should be a minimum of distance—and no distracting pictorial elements—between the end of

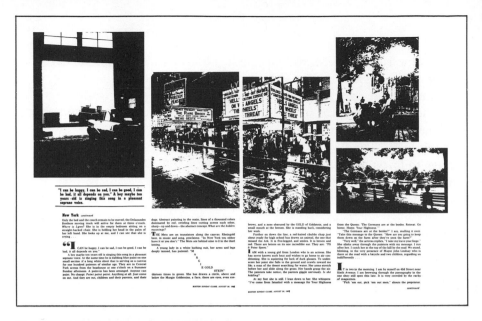

Fig. 130. Misalignment during folding becomes apparent in position of two center pictures and folio lines at page bottom.

the head and the start of body type. Never should the eye be forced into "reverse gear" in order to read an element farther to the left or above the axis of orientation for any given unit or mass of type.

Display elements should bridge across alleys. If any part of a headline aligns at its left on an alley, it may look as if it is a separate head carrying only that body type in the column directly below it.

After an oriented layout has been created by following mechanical alignments, the editor may shift some of the elements a little. This may be to make a pattern that is more pleasing to his eye, or it may be to effect an optical alignment which is not apparent when the lining up was done mechanically.

If the first letter in a headline is *A*, for instance, the head cannot be aligned on the left serif of the *A*. The axis of this letter is about halfway between the serif and the apex. Letters with a vertical stroke at their left—*B, D, E, F, H,* etc.—will align on that stroke. But letters with curves on the left side—*C, O, G,* etc.—and with diagonals—*V, X,* and *W* and some *M*'s and *N*'s—must be aligned on their mass rather than on their left-most component.

Tight orientation, one in which several elements align on conspicuous axes, is usually pleasing to the reader because it assures him that a firm hand has placed the elements in the page.

When the orienting technique is used on tab-sized magazine pages, a new factor is added. Magazine pages are usually designed in pairs of facing pages, *spreads*. The exception is, of course, when an editorial page faces a full-page ad.

If the editor has a choice, he should start a story with a 2-page spread and then go to a single page or pages. This is far more effective than starting with a single page and then progressing to a spread. We ought always to lure the reader with the choicest bait; there seems little logic in starting with a single page, then presenting the spread either when it's too late to catch the reader or after he is already in the story.

Working with facing pages, the editor has a new problem—he must *jump the gutter,* the center margins, to tie the two pages together in a single, well-knit unit.

The most obvious way to bridge the gutter is to run a picture or a headline across it. This can tie the two pages together very strongly. But the danger of misalignment is grave. By the very nature of the folder and cutter on the newspaper press, it is easy for the paper to be misaligned a pica or more during these operations. If this misalignment is horizontal, a headline will break at the gutter in an unpleasant way. If it is vertical, there may be a strip of white down the gutter, where the two halves of a photo are supposed to meet snugly. Or a strip of the halftone may be folded over too far so that it is visible on a page well removed from the spread.

Such misalignment, always annoying to the reader, becomes more frequent because pages of newspaper magazines rarely are stapled together. So, during normal reading, facing pages may slide up and down or sideways to misalign elements even though they were handled perfectly on the press. Only on *center spreads,* where facing pages are on the same sheet of paper, is there no problem of alignment at the gutter.

The editor will seek other methods of bridging the gutter. If the head must run across the center margin, he will never break it within a word; misalignment then is gross. He will try to avoid a break even at the end of a word. If possible, he will set the portion of a head on one page in a size, and perhaps even form, of type different from that on the other page. Wickets and tripods are useful. Then possible misalignments are not as conspicuous. In these cases, the content of the head must be such that the visual break is logical.

If a picture must run across the gutter, the editor will take great pains that no important detail is at the break, for if the sheet is improperly folded, that detail may be hidden on the reverse page.

Well-defined margins are good devices for tying together opposite pages. Elements at obviously the same distance from the top of the page will look aligned even if the pages themselves slip considerably out of alignment during reading.

The editor should avoid *trapped space,* white areas completely or almost surrounded by typographic elements. This hole-in-the-doughnut effect is unpleasant to the reader. It is better to place this white at the outside of the layout and so create an irregular silhouette for the whole page. The more irregular that silhouette, the more pleasing it can be to the reading eye.

An interesting technique is to use conventional columns on the magazine page and align them all at the top margin. But the bottom of the page is kept irregular by varying the depth of the columns. Depth variations should be in a minimum of eight lines of body type. It doesn't matter which columns are the deepest on insides or margins of pages. At least one leg of type should be completely filled, running down to the lower margin.

For no matter how irregular any page silhouette, each margin of the page should be defined by at least one element that touches that margin. This may be a picture or a mass of body or display type.

Free pages are most effective when they carry no advertising. They are more pleasing to the typical reader in tabloid or compact format than in full pages. This is undoubtedly because the reader associates such makeup with the smaller page of the typical magazine.

Inside pages have far more similarity than disparity of makeup. Although there are minor differences that stem from the kind of editorial material they must carry, all inside pages should be made up according to the same principles.

Even if the economic pressure for high inside quality were less, the editor's own pride in his product should be sufficient to focus attention and effort on these important areas.

chapter 13

Pasteup for Offset

AT EVERY WORKSHOP or clinic on newspaper design, an inevitable question is: "How do you lay out a good page for offset?" The answer is, of course: "The same way you do for letterpress."

This answer rarely satisfies, at least not until further explanation is tendered. It goes something like this:

Layout is the presentation of visual communication. The reader is concerned only with what he sees on a piece of paper. He doesn't care how that image is placed there, be it by offset, letterpress, rotogravure, silk screen—or hand-lettered by elves deep in Transylvania. Even the expert finds it hard to distinguish, merely by looking at a printed piece, by what printing process it was produced. This page of the book you're reading right now was printed by offset; it would be difficult to tell it from the same form printed by relief.

The typographer, too, is concerned primarily with the image. He gets involved with the mechanics of printing only as they produce the image efficiently—or don't. He must be familiar with the techniques of setting relief type so he can keep the results of space-band operation within certain limits and so he can avoid the nuisance of butted slugs. He must be aware of stereotype shrinkage so he can build in protection against distortion. He must know the principles of offset so he can best use them to put a good image on paper. He must know the processes of setting type for platemakers' use in order to ensure against undisciplined workmanship that might result in a poor printed image. But he is not interested in mechanics for themselves; he is interested in them only as the means for placing an image on paper.

The methods of printing the image—especially in the preliminaries of preparing the forms—can influence the appearance of the image to a slight extent. The 90-degree-angled rigidity of the metal used in letter-press almost automatically presents type in strictly horizontal lines. The ability of offset to use fine halftone screens on coarse paper influences the editor to use more photographs. He must learn these influences and use—or resist—them as best transmits communication.

Offset is a *planographic* printing process. Instead of the printing image being raised from the bearing surface as in relief, letterpress, the image for offset is on the same plane as the bearer. Offset is an abbreviation for *offset lithography,* also called *photo lithography* or *photo offset.* Unlike letterpress, which was the result of many men's experiments, labor, and innovation, lithography was invented by a single man, Alois Senefelder. His patent is dated 1799, which makes lithography the newest of the three major printing processes.

Senefelder based his invention on the simple fact that not only will oil not mix with water, the two repel each other. He drew an image on a piece of limestone with a greasy, oily crayon. Then he sloshed water across the stone. The water wetted the stone but was repelled by the oily surfaces. The reverse occurred when he ran an ink roller across the stone. The water on the stone repelled the oily ink, but the ink was held by the greasy substance on the stone. Thus there was a layer of ink lying precisely on the crayon image. When a sheet of paper was pressed on the stone, that layer of ink was lifted off and became the image on the paper.

Offset lithography adds one step to Senefelder's process and changes one ingredient. Instead of a piece of stone, the bearer of the printing image is a thin sheet of aluminum. The printing image need no longer be written or drawn by hand; it is put on the plate by photography. The thin metal plate is wrapped around a cylinder. It is wetted, then inked, as in the original process, but the layer of ink is then "lithographed" onto a rubber blanket, wrapped around a contacting cylinder. The blanket, in turn, is pressed against a sheet of paper wrapped around a third cylinder. The layer of ink is *set off,* or offset, to the paper as the printed image.

Lithography reached its heyday in the latter 1800's; the beloved Currier & Ives prints, for instance, were lithographs. The rapid rise of photography during the same era made a marriage between the two processes inevitable and fruitful. Offset was invented, for all practical purposes, in 1904, although experiments had been going on for the preceding quarter century. By the 1930's, offset had grown to a major division of commercial printing, but it had little application to newspaper production until after World War II. Since that time it has grown steadily. The development of web-fed offset presses made the process practical for daily newspapers as well as for the weeklies that had been using sheet-fed presses. Quicker methods of platemaking were powerful incentives to the growth of offset. We have already noted the use of offset for preprinted advertising in Chapter 8, and in the late 60's the *St. Louis Post-Dispatch* installed huge offset presses in its own plant.

Newspapers also use a third printing method, *rotogravure,* or *roto.* Gravure—the "roto" merely refers to the use of rotary presses—is an *intaglio,* or *incised,* printing process. Here the printing image is below the bearing surface. The simplest form of gravure printing is the etching of the fine artist. He scratches, or burns by acid, an image into a copper plate. Then he rolls ink across the plate; it's a thin fluid, and it fills all the incisions. With a rag or the heel of his hand, he wipes the ink off the face of the plate, leaving only that in the depressions. As the paper is pressed on the plate, the ink is lifted out of the grooves and makes the image on the paper. In commercial use, the gravure printing plate is a copper cylinder completely covered with tiny, regular ink wells. It turns through an ink trough; the wiping is done mechanically by a *doctor blade.* The printing is onto paper fed off an endless roll—the characteristic of all rotary presses.

Rotogravure gives even higher fidelity to halftone reproductions on rough newsprint than offset does. Its process color is the most brilliant of any printing, mostly because roto ink is transparent, and light, reflecting off the paper, comes through the ink. This becomes projected, rather than reflected, color, which is always more sparkling. Sunday magazine sections are excellent demonstrations of the high quality of rotogravure. A few newspapers print Sunday comics by roto, and even this garden-variety flat color is strikingly brilliant.

The production of roto cylinders is expensive in time and money and is feasible only for magazines or other sections that can be prepared far in advance and that can attract the necessary advertising revenues to compensate for the high manufacturing cost. Offset plates, by means of relatively new methods and materials, can be made in a matter of minutes and are relatively inexpensive, little or no more costly than curved stereotype plates.

Gravure and offset share an important characteristic; they are printed by photographically made plates, not with type and photoengravings. The plates are simply photographs of the type, printed not on paper as an ordinary picture is, but on a metal plate, after which chemical reactions create the ink-attractive water-repellent characteristics of the offset plate and the incised images of the gravure cylinder.

Photographically made plates—large-area photoengravings—are also used for letterpress. Made on thin metal, they become *wraparound plates,* providing the same curved surface for rotary presses that stereotype plates do. This technique is still used primarily for commercial printing, but newspapers make whole advertisements in the form of photoengravings, locking them up into the flatform along with other typographic relief elements.

For making photo plates, it is not necessary to have relief type and engravings; all that is needed is to have images that can be photographed. *Reproduction type, phototype,* or strikeon type is adequate—in fact, ideal—for this purpose. These elements are assembled into pages by pasting them in proper positions on large sheets of paper rather than locking up metal elements.

The result is a *pasteup,* or mechanical, copy ready for the platemaker's camera. The word is also an adjective, describing a newspaper or form prepared in this manner. As a verb, the word is split in two; we "paste up" a "pasteup."

Photographs are converted into screened negatives, but the following step, photoengraving, is eliminated, for the platemaking negative is merely combined with line negatives of the type of the page.

A sad situation is that the general quality of pasteup newspapers printed by offset is distinctly below that of pasted-up gravure papers or those printed by letterpress. This is not a blanket indictment of pasteup, of course, nor is it a blanket indictment of offset newspapers. The consistently fine quality of rotogravure absolves the pasteup technique, and there are enough excellent offset newspapers to prove that this printing process is a good one. Only newspapers that find the shoe of adverse criticism fits them should put on the footwear.

It must constantly be emphasized that offset and pasteup are not synonymous. Nor are they indissoluble partners. (Just as pasteup is used for other printing methods, so hot-metal type can be used for offset platemaking. Several excellent newspapers make up and lock up in hot metal, make plates from the resultant page proofs, and print by offset.) Yet the distinction is often overlooked, even among newspapermen.

As a result, critics have been falsely labeled as antioffset because they have criticized the poor typography of pasteup papers. Fortunately they have not been accused of being antiletterpress, even though they might have been as outspoken against poor typography in relief-printed newspapers.

It is an easily demonstrable fact that many pasteup-offset newspapers are of regrettably poor quality, in both typography and printing. And it is no coincidence, to me, that in many instances that same low quality is

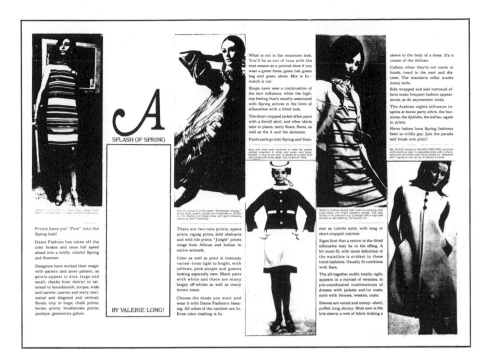

Fig. 131. Modular layout. Page in *Skyline,* Chicago weekly, is built up of tall rectangles. Panel in second column is blank but border creates harmonious shape.

apparent in the reporting, writing, photographing, and editing of the news. The management that tolerates low quality in one area will rarely set high standards in any others.

Some of the trouble can be traced to the overselling of offset. In the 1950's especially, offset was submitted as the panacea for all journalistic and printing ills. Unfortunately it wasn't; no single process can solve all problems. But many publishers ran away from their letterpress mechanical problems and converted to offset. As a result they no longer had inefficient letterpress plants; now they had inefficient offset plants. The lack of craftsmanship and pride that produced poor letterpress reproductions was just as obvious in the poor offset images.

In many cases offset not only failed to meet acceptable standards of printing; it also failed to effect substantial savings. Actually, it sometimes cost considerably more than letterpress. Paper wastage was a major factor. The pressman must keep a constant balance between two fluctuating variables, ink and water, but the press operates at such high speed that by the time he has made necessary adjustments, a great number of spoiled copies may have been printed. Photographic materials and presensitized metal plates are expensive; darkroom employees can waste staggering amounts of money by carelessness or ineptness.

Proofing of advertising is a problem for offset newspapers. In letterpress operations, it is simple to pull a proof or several proofs from the made-up ad form. This is a matter of a few minutes in time and a few cents of cost. But the only way to duplicate a pasteup ad is by a photocopier. Photocopying machines capable of meeting the comp room's needs are expensive hardware, and the paper on which the copy is made is many times more expensive than the copy newsprint on which letterpress proofs are pulled.

The publisher of a fine and thriving weekly newspaper confessed that the change from letterpress to offset almost bankrupted him, and a great many months went past before he could get his operation out of the red. He was an able executive and his crew had produced a superior relief-printed newspaper, but he and they found the switch to a new process difficult to make if they insisted on maintaining high standards.

This is not to undervalue offset. It is merely to suggest that the publisher change processes only after hard thought. When new printing equipment is needed, offset seems highly desirable. But when letterpress equipment is in the shop, especially if it has been amortized, it is often advisable to retain and improve it. In many instances the replacement of worn blankets, a switch to better-quality news ink, and the adjustment of linecasters so that all typographic material is absolutely type-high will improve print quality dramatically. This requires only a small fraction of the cost of conversion to offset. A publisher ought to exploit his present equipment and method processes to the utmost before considering a change.

The greatest overselling, though, was of pre-presstime jobs—strikeon composition and pasting up. The publisher was promised that these processes could permanently rid him of the headaches of the composing room. He could replace the expensive linecaster with a cheap typewriter. Even more significant, he could replace graphic arts craftsmen—with their skills and the salaries they warrant—with high school girls, housewives, and others who are eager to work at minimum rates.

There were flies in this ointment. Strikeon equipment, because of its relatively short life and low trade-in value, is not nearly as inexpensive as at first glance it seems. Low-priced help didn't have the necessary skills to produce a good newspaper. It takes more than mere typing ability to achieve good strikeon composition; it takes the talent and interest of a graphic arts worker to create good pasteup pages.

But this has been the dark side of the picture. There is a brighter one. The *Dubuque Telegraph-Herald* in Iowa, the *Worthington Globe* in Minnesota, and the *Hornell Tribune* and the *Ithaca Journal* in New

York are among the many newspapers that prove that pasteup and offset can produce superlative newspapers.

Many newspapers are in existence today only because they could use strikeon and pasteup. It is infinitely better to have a living newspaper with lower typographic standards than a dead one of impeccable quality. The ideal, of course, is to have it both alive and healthy and with high standards in every area of journalism and communication.

To utilize new techniques of newspaper production, we must first analyze the problems involved. We must recognize the strengths so we can exploit them; we must recognize the weaknesses so we can correct them.

Strikeon Composition

In this and previous chapters, reference has been made to the machines that produce strikeon composition as "typewriters." This is an oversimplification; the typical strikeon machine is far more sophisticated than the writing machine at the reporter's desk. (It also costs 20 times as much—or even more.)

There are strong similarities between them. On all these machines, simple or elaborate, paper is held against a cylindrical platen. A raised character, much like a piece of metal type, is struck against an inked or carbon-paper ribbon, and the image of the character placed on the paper. Their keyboards are much alike; on the sophisticated machines there are extra keys for special functions, but the placement of the alphabet is identical on all.

A conventional typewriter can produce strikeon composition; many a Ladies Aid or Chamber of Commerce bulletin is set in this way. The typographical weakness of the ordinary typewriter is that each character is given exactly the same width. So the *M* and *W* must be crowded, the *g, e, a,* etc., are normal; the *l* and *i* look like telephone poles in the middle of a prairie.

Popularity of electric typewriters brought along popularity of *proportional spacing* for office correspondence. Characters were divided into three widths for typewriters and five for strikeon machines, and each letter was given approximately the space required for its normal design. This is still a far cry from the 18 different widths of the Linofilm or the unlimited ones of the linecasters, but it is a striking improvement.

There still remains the problem of justification, though.

To justify a line on an office typewriter, the typist must first produce an ordinary line of typing. (Usually she will do a whole letter or story.)

She notes how far each line falls short of or exceeds the desired length. Then she retypes the line, inserting extra space between words or crowding two letters into a single space. This is tedious work, and the result is neither handsome nor readable.

The *Varityper* makes the job easier. After the trial line has been typed, the operator makes a simple setting and retypes the line on the same paper, a little farther to the right on the platen. Spacing between words is automatically adjusted to effect a justified line. (The Varityper gives another advantage. Instead of carrying each character on a permanent key lever, all the characters are on a single curved metal bar. When the keyboard strike is made, the bar moves so that the desired character is in position and then a tiny hammer hits it against the ribbon. This bar can be changed easily and quickly, and so the operator can use different fonts in the same composition. The *IBM Selectric* gives the same advantage; all its characters are placed on a metal sphere, a little smaller than a golf ball. Its paper remains stationary; the ball moves across it rather than having the paper move past the striking point.)

The most effective justification is done automatically. The Justowriter and the *Flexowriter* produce perforated tape by manual typing; this then actuates a second machine that does the justified strikeon composition.

The Associated Press has recently introduced its *Offsetter*. This machine is actuated by telegraphic impulses. Instead of producing perforated tape and typewritten hard copy, it makes only the latter but in variably spaced characters in justified lines on glossy paper. It is good strikeon material, ready for pasteup. By eliminating all extra composition work in the newspaper plant, the Offsetter saves substantial time and expense. Editing of this material is so difficult, though, that few editors have the time or temerity to take on the task. Thus the material is customarily used just as it comes from the wire. The editor has abdicated his rights and responsibility of deciding how news should be reported in his paper.

The rebuttal is, of course, that much wire news is of routine reports that wouldn't be changed by the local desk, no matter how simple that operation. It is also pointed out that the AP copy desk is manned by excellent editors and that their work doesn't need extra polishing by the local desk. All this is true, but the point remains that editing is being done by a distant newsman, unknown to and not responsible to the newspaper editor.

Quality of strikeon composition has been consistently improved in the past decade. Two weaknesses remain, however. It is difficult to produce a character of proper typographic color by striking an image through a

Fig. 132. One-theme magazine. *Topics,* magazine section of *Don Mills* (Ont.) *Mirror,* devotes six full stories to single topic. Cover shows cancer cell in red-black duotone. Distinctive heading identifies theme stories. Regular news runs in back of magazine, below left.

ribbon. It is difficult to design a tightly knitting typeface within the limitations of assigned widths. More improvements may be expected, but each one raises the price of the machine. If all weaknesses were corrected, the strikeon machine would probably cost as much as a linecaster.

Other Composition for Pasteup

All offset or pasteup newspapers do not use strikeon composition. A great many use genuine cold type, that produced by highly sophisticated phototypesetting machines—the Photon, Linofilm, Fotosetter, and ATF Typesetter. These machines produce composition of the highest typographic standards. In some instances it is even better than that of hot metal.

These machines have great capacity, more than can economically be used by any but large newspapers. Their cost is commensurate; that, too, restricts their use to larger papers.

Composition for pasteup can also be produced from hot metal. We have noted that a few newspapers make up entire pages using conventional metal type and methods, then pulling a reproduction proof of the whole page. More commonly, repros are made from galleys, and individual components are assembled by pasteup. Either of these methods is economical if linecasters are in condition too good to warrant replacement and when skilled craftsmen cannot, or will not, change to new methods.

Hot-metal repros are more frequently used for display type, editorial and advertising. Some publishers insist that it is at least as economical to set heads in hot metal and then pull repro proofs. The true cost of this hot metal versus phototype depends on many factors, among them the availability and condition of linecasters and the personnel to man them. But there are many good machines for the photographic setting of headlines, and their use grows.

Evaluation of Pasteup

An obvious advantage of pasteup is its lightweight materials. A galley of linecaster slugs weighs several pounds; a "galley" of strikeon or photo composition weighs an ounce. Furniture and spacing necessary to create white space in a letterpress form weigh several pounds; the white space in a pasteup weighs nothing. Lightweight materials can be handled more quickly and precisely than type metal. Although he lifts only a little at a time, the printer working on the stone may handle over a quarter ton of metal in a day. As he becomes fatigued, his efficiency drops sharply.

Pasteup makes pictures, halftone and line, inexpensive and easy to use.

Pasteup is clean; it's a white-collar job. In a constantly tight labor market, this makes it easier to recruit good people for the newspaper composing and news rooms.

Small newspapers customarily provided quarters that were colorful and perhaps even romantic but were also crowded and inconvenient and verged on grimy. Today's pasteup-offset operations have changed this picture dramatically. Such a transformation took place at the plant of the *Hudson* (New York) *Register-Star* when it converted from letterpress, and it is typical of many similar newspapers. It is unusual only in that two afternoon papers are printed in the same plant. Morning-afternoon combinations are frequent, of course; however, at the time the *R-S* plant began producing the *Catskill Mail,* it was the only plant that did two papers almost simultaneously.

Hudson has a population of 10,000, and the *Register-Star* has almost that large a circulation. Catskill, just across the Hudson River on the west bank, is a town of 5,900 with circulation of 4,500. The towns are linked by a bridge.

A handsome carpeted and air-conditioned room is news room and composing room combined. The news staff is at the front of the area. At the far end is the photo unit of a phototypesetting machine. Tape is punched in a small adjoining room—light, airy, and soundproofed. Along the left of the room are the pasteup tables.

Photo composition is carried the few steps to the tables; other photographic materials come via a pass-through from the darkroom. The editors have instant access to page pasteup; the craftsmen can easily query the desk when occasion demands. Ads can be made up beforehand and adhered to the page forms or can be done right at the final pasteup.

It is a pleasant and efficient place to work, and the quality of staff and crew is high. Details vary, but the general description of the Hudson office applies to many American and Canadian plants.

The advantages of pasteup are substantial. Though there are thorns with every rose, the disadvantages of pasting up can be completely overcome if the editor feels it is worth the effort. It is!

The major disadvantage of pasteup is the direct result of one of its advantages. Pasteup allows great freedom to the typographic designer. No longer is he under the stern discipline of unyielding type metal and steel chases. Unfortunately, freedom often becomes license, and the results are anything but good. Irresponsible application of the new flexibility can create abominable readability and legibility.

In the enthusiasm of the new freedom, many makeup men forgot two ancient axioms: "Anything that's difficult to set in hot metal is difficult to read." The reverse is also true: "Matter that is easy to prepare in hot metal is easy to read."

One of the hot-metal restrictions that irks the inexperienced layout man is that type must run in straight and horizontal lines. He chafes under it. Once freed by the beneficence of pasteup, he swirls type lines in flowing curves and places straight lines at sharp angles. He fails to realize that typographers have eschewed such handling of type not only because it is physically difficult; they would have done so even if it were easy, because they know that type is read most efficiently in straight, horizontal lines.

So, to the good typographer, the allegedly harsh discipline of rigid metal is not that at all. It is merely a reminder of standards which the facts of readability have already imposed.

The external discipline of metal helps police the self-discipline of art and craftsmanship. To run metal type in wavy lines is a difficult task that usually requires Rube Goldberg devices. To cock a headline at a 45-degree angle means cutting all kinds of bastard spacing material. To steal a little white space to facilitate justifying a column means that the printer must actually pilfer a piece of metal. To overlap metal elements is impossible in the confines of a chase. Yet any of these typographic crimes can be committed in pasteup with no effort at all.

So in pasteup the typographer must impose mental discipline to take the place of metal discipline.

As with all layout, the pasteup job begins on the copy desk. The editor should be more precise in the preparation of his offset dummy than he has been with letterpress dummies, for it is a weakness of pasteup that precise manipulation in small increments is far more difficult than it is in hot metal with its solid three dimensions.

The desk—and everyone else involved—may find it advantageous to use a new system of measurement. Instead of points and picas, the pasteup craftsman often finds it more advantageous to measure in *lines of body type* (abbreviated to *BL,* for body lines, or just plain *L*). Advertising people have been doing this with agate lines for a long time, and the change is neither difficult nor unprecedented.

The headline schedule shows the depth of each head in lines; conversion charts make it easy to translate agate lines or inches of advertising and picas or inches of photos to BL's.

It is standard operating procedure to paste up on sheets of paper gridded by camera-invisible blue ink in 1-pica squares. It is worth the effort for a paper to produce its own sheets in the 8- or 9-point increments of its own body-type size. Note that a BL is the equivalent of the Linotype slug—type height plus ledding.

The page dummy is most efficient if it is at least twice as long as the customary 8½ x 11 inches used by most editors. The width is inconsequential; the dummy must be precise primarily in depths. While a longer dummy is less convenient on a crowded news desk, if it is kept narrow it can be handled with minimal inconvenience.

The entire page should be dummied as close as possible to the last line. While this admonition applies to hot-metal makeup too, it is always possible to make final, small adjustments in the chase. This is not nearly as easy in pasteup. The ledding which the hot-metal compositor does so casually to justify a column is a major task in cold type. A metal line can be shifted from one column to another without a second thought; in pasteup this requires careful cutting and pasting that eats up time.

The need for precise dummies demands equally precise copy control. Wire material can readily be converted to BL's by measuring the physical length of the manuscript and applying a conversion ratio. The hard copy produced by a wire-service reperforator is already broken down into lines, the equivalent of BL's. All that's necessary is to count them.

Local copy should be typewritten at specified and unvarying line lengths so it, too, can readily be converted to BL's.

A convenient ratio is 2 or 2½ BL's per typewritten line. Any typewritten line of less than 2 BL's is inefficient and slows down the writer as he does his copy.

Unforeseeable widows or unbreakable words can easily change the length of a story by a line or two. So the pasteup man should note on the dummy how much space has been allotted. Suppose a story has been dummied in for 65 lines, but the cold type actually makes only 62. The pasteup man determines where he is going to place his equivalent of ledding. This spacing is done between paragraphs; in pasteup he can't work with increments as thin as ledds; he must use spacing in the size of slug. In this case he will probably decide to use a BL at the end of each of the first three grafs.

In case a story must be squared in two or more legs, it will save time to premeasure the cold type to determine whether and how much ledding is needed.

Once it is determined where extra spacing is to go, it becomes simple to cut the phototype into proper segments and paste them into position.

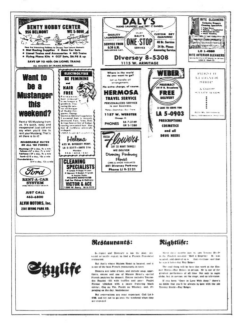

Fig. 133. Free columns. Makeup of *Skyline* of Chicago is simplified by ability to leave columns unfilled. Top left, display ads hang from page top in free columns; editorial matter is squared off at bottom. Top right, sinkage—area for headline—varies to accommodate length of stories.

Opposite, *Sun,* Sunday magazine section of Baltimore, Md., Sunpapers, uses free columns on right page of spread. Note that at least one column—here col. 2—must touch bottom margin.

In case the finished strikeon is longer than has been dummied, the pasteup man should check on other stories in the column to see if he can gain the needed space. This should be done only by removing the equivalent of ledding elsewhere in the column, never by stealing spacing. If he can't find the needed extra space, he should notify the desk at once. The earlier the desk is notified of the need to cut copy, the more flexibility it has, because it can cut other stories in the column or reduce the length of stories still to be dummied in.

Some penny pinchers begrudge the time of the technician and the editor and cry that this negates too much of the savings of pasteup. But there is no real saving if the quality of the product is deteriorated by haste.

The ability to vary spacing in pasteup is a much-abused freedom. To underline the necessary discipline, the pasteup man should be provided with at least two aluminum gauges. The most efficient, in my opinion, is a metal bar attached at right angles to a small pencil-like handle. In use,

ADULTS·IN·RESIDENCE AT GOUCHER

non-academic families move onto campus to help bridge the gap between town and gown

Story by HELEN HENRY
Photos by ELLIS MALASHUK

the handle is parallel to column rules with the metal gauge parallel to lines of type. The craftsman holds the gauge in his left hand and positions the material with his right.

These gauges should be in 1-BL and 1-pica sizes, although the exact dimension will depend on the particular spacing used by the paper. If a pica is designated as the space between a story and the next head, the pasteup man should be required to place the gauge on the grid sheet before he lays down the following head. It can be argued—and is, loud and vigorously—that a good craftsman can estimate the required distance, especially when helped by the printed grid. This is true, but the use of a physical device eliminates any chance of error and also reiterates the need for maintaining the minimum spacing. The little extra time it takes to use the gauge is well repaid in higher standards.

These increments of spacing may be scribed into transparent T-squares or triangles, but then the psychological effect of the tangible gauge is lost. It may seem to be belaboring a triviality, but it should be pointed out that this psychological discipline is a real and important one.

A T-square is the indispensable tool of the pasteup man. This seems too obvious to require noting, yet it is appalling to observe how frequently the craftsman neglects to use this tool. He prides himself on his keen eye, steady nerves, trained muscles, and other red-blooded virtues. He can lay down a perfectly horizontal line with only the printed grid to guide him—he says. It isn't so. Meticulous checking of such claims proves that even the most capable pasteup man will be out of alignment more than half the time. Sure, this misalignment is slight. But a line off horizontal as little as four or five degrees is annoying to the reader.

Overlapping of pasted material is absolutely inexcusable. There is just no explaining away this lack of craftsmanship and standards. The publisher who allows such sloppiness depreciates his own stature as a journalist, for surely a reader will not attribute very high standards of accuracy to a news story that doesn't show even minimal standards in its typography.

Accidents happen, and it is possible that an improperly waxed piece of copy may shift on the grid or a sliver of waste paper may adhere to the face of typographic material, all unnoticed by the craftsman. So a second person should be given the responsibility of checking each pasteup before it goes to the camera. This may be a fairly detailed proofreading to determine that the proper head runs with a story or the proper cutlines with a picture. It may even include the proofreading of body type. Or the inspection may be only for the most glaring of physical errors—shifted, dropped-off, overlapping, or misaligned type elements.

If platemaking is done by *reflex* process without the conventional negative, this is the final opportunity for proofreading the page proof, as it were. By this process the image of the pasteup is captured on a *photographic matrix*. This is all-black photopaper with the image visible only because of a difference in reflection. It is possible to identify the image but not easily enough to use for proofreading.

The normal page proof for an offset job is a blueprint or similar photocopy made from the negative which will be used for actually making the plate. The preparation of such a proof costs more time and money than for proof of a letterpress page. For this reason some pound-foolish publishers just skip this proofing operation, thus scorning even the most elementary standards of craftsmanship and accuracy.

If a letterpress edition is railroaded with minimal or even no proofreading, errors can be detected in the first press run and changes made with comparative ease. But corrections in offset will require a complete new plate, so here the ounce of prevention certainly outweighs the cure.

Art for Pasteup

Whether to use *Veloxes* or to *strip in* screened negatives is the topic of a vigorous debate.

In conventional platemaking, areas where halftones are to go are left blank on the pasteup. Then the line negative is made. Meanwhile photographs have been converted into screened negatives, which are later stripped into the line neg. A Velox is a photoprint made up of a halftone dot pattern instead of in continuous tone. It is line copy, of course. Thus it can be pasted up with the other line elements and then only a single negative need be made. With the reflex process, there are no negatives so Veloxes must be used.

My preference is for Veloxes. There is no extra work involved. Somewhere before press time a continuous-tone original must be converted into a halftone screen pattern; it doesn't matter whether this is in negative form or on photopaper. Veloxes may be retouched far more simply than the original glossy. Pasting in the Velox allows a last-minute checkup to assure proper positioning and cropping of the picture. Quality of printed reproduction from the Velox is as high as from stripped-in negatives. The difference in cost between stripping in and using Veloxes is negligible.

All other pictorial materials should be originals. An incomprehensible tactic is to clip recurring material from a copy of the newspaper. Then we have the paradox of "worn" material. In letterpress the printing surface actually wears down so it prints poorly; in offset the wear of the printing surface is so slight during normal newspaper runs that it can be disregarded. But using reproduced, instead of original, camera copy results in the same dirty printing that worn relief elements produce.

Even when an image has been printed with great care on fine paper, there is some loss of fidelity from the original during each reproductive step. On newsprint and by common newspaper printing methods, the loss is greater. If such flawed material is used for pasting up, the percentage of loss rises. If printed materials are consecutively used for pasteups, the printed image may be a dozen steps from the original, with accumulated loss of fidelity at each step.

Material which is commonly clipped for pasting up includes the nameplate and masthead, standing headings, and signatures from ads. The irony is that this practice doesn't save anyone any time; it takes no more time or effort to paste in the original than one clipped from the last issue of the paper. It is necessary, of course, to retrieve original matter from the pasteups for each issue and to file them for easy access. It is usually a good investment to have several Photostats made of original artwork that is going to be reused. These should be in various sizes if they vary in common use.

Laziness and shiftlessness of hired help cannot always be eliminated and therefore the publisher may find his offset operation hampered by some of the disadvantages of letterpress. This is regrettable but understandable. What is difficult to comprehend, though, is that some offset publishers are not only willing to accept another handicap of letterpress, they pay substantially to become a victim.

A trade-journal advertisement of late 1968 hailed "a compressing lens . . . a practical means of squeezing your page so it can print a 32" page on a 30" roll."

Yes, this is exactly what it sounds like: imposition of stereotype distortion on pasteup pages!

It is true that a minute photographic reduction of a page can beneficially sharpen strikeon composition. But this is a total reduction, up and down as well as sideways, that maintains the letterform, not the single horizontal distortion of the anamorphic lens. This therapeutic reduction is slight, certainly not a whole inch—about 7%—across the page as the distorting lens boasts about.

There is a philosophical difference, too. When the publisher reduces a whole page, he contributes as much of his vertical—and chargeable—column as he asks the advertiser to donate of his purchased column width.

If there is magic in a 30-inch roll, the pasteup ought to be to that dimension. To impose artificial shrinkage is not only of dubious value but of debatable propriety. Thousands of good letterpress weekly newspapers were handicapped over decades because the undiscerning national space buyer lumped all weeklies under the unpalatable label of the poorly printed one. Are all offset papers to be tarred with the brush of the photographically distorted ones?

Advertisers in letterpress papers have long been aware of stereotype shrinkage as an inevitable concomitant of the process. It has never been hidden from them and it is acknowledged in the published "trade practices" of the industry. But photographic shrinkage has not been announced to the customer, just the contrary. If his hackles rise by this artificial and unnecessary device, it would seem inevitable.

No newspaper organization can police against this practice. But we might hope that press associations would at least go on record with their disapproval.

There is only one factor that offset may add to the problem of page layout: the abundance of pictures. The cost of reproducing halftones by offset is so low that it has no inhibiting effect on the number of pictures in an issue. On the contrary, the beautiful halftone reproduction by offset printing and the greater reader attraction of local pictures combine to create pressures for using many pictures.

Often it is impossible to isolate unrelated art adequately. Then the editor turns his course 180 degrees and deliberately gangs unrelated art. He may use his combinations as a whole picture page or he may use them in less-than-page areas. Stacking pictures in a chimney is an excellent device that gives the typographical impact of a large halftone area yet allows the reader to inspect each individual picture with minimal competition from the ones above and below.

If there is more than one picture on a single topic, all related art should be run together. It is not a good technique to run pictures of a single event on several or many pages.

Except for the greater number of pictures economically available to tempt the editor, offset has zero effect on layout. It does have some on typography, however.

Type for Pasteup

Offset has a tendency to lighten body type and darken headletters. Therefore the publisher must choose a body type with adequate typographic color and avoid heavy display faces.

If he is setting by a phototype machine, his choice of body type is wide. Because the typographic quality of the sophisticated phototype-setting machine is so high, the publisher might well choose a face which hasn't been associated with newspaper use. Caledonia is such a one. It has excellent color that reproduces handsomely by offset. Its fitting is excellent, and the character-per-line count is fine. There is no stereotype shrinkage in offset, so we don't require letterforms with built-in corrections to such distortion.

The deepest-colored body type available should be chosen without going to a regular boldface. Sans Serifs and Gothics should be avoided for body type; this admonition applies for offset exactly as for letterpress.

Tape punchers should be instructed, "Set lines as tightly as possible." This may reduce their production somewhat and this is a difficult lesson to teach, but it is false economy to increase production by lowering standards.

If at all possible, there should be some shooting down from page copy to plate. This reduction must usually be slight because there may be distortion at the outer portions of the lens in great size variances. But even a slight reduction tends to sharpen the strikeon image. Body type must be chosen so that it will provide an image of comfortable reading size even after such reduction. Interlineal spacing should be the same as with hot metal.

The choice of a headletter for offset printing should be based on the same criteria as that of one for letterpress printing and discussed in Chapter 5.

It is a persistent and aggravating puzzle to the observer of American and Canadian newspapers that so many publishers, as they go to photo-type and offset, should choose ugly, black Gothics for headlines. Although some newspapers that went to strikeon composition retained hot metal for larger headlines, most of them at least augmented metal with one of the many photo headline machines. Others discarded all metal type. Suddenly they were freed from the handicap of a poor library of hot metal.

Typographic materials, especially in display sizes, do not wear out rapidly. Unless an editor is of Social Security age, he undoubtedly has inherited many fonts of type and matrices that were bought by someone else. Often they are ugly or dated faces; almost always the library has just accumulated instead of being planned.

It is easy to say that a font has long been amortized and that it should be disposed of because it doesn't fit into the typographic needs of the newspaper any more—if it ever did. But it takes a kind of courage to throw away a still perfectly usable tool and spend good money for a replacement. So most newspaper plants have at least some material which is being used just because it's there, not because it pleases anyone on the staff.

But when the newspaper goes to an entirely new process, old material becomes useless and new materials must be purchased. This is the rare opportunity of creating a "perfect" typographic library. But what does the publisher do now? Does he plan a type library on current and projected needs? Does he enlist the advice of his staff members, layout men, or typographers? Does he study all the available faces? In too many instances the answer is an obvious No!

In a random but wide examination of American newspapers in 1967, it was noted that almost 40% of the papers that had adopted phototype during the previous two years had chosen Gothics for headlines. Incidentally, each one of these was the heavy, cramped Gothic that the Europeans so appropriately call Grotesk; none was the attractive Modeled Gothic of recent design.

Gothic block letterforms are never handsome. Their weight is heavy, and offset reproduction tends to increase the weight of display letters. When contrasted against the light strikeon body type, often washed out even more in offset, the Gothic reminds us strongly of the Rhineland savage for whom it was named. It is bad enough to have to use an unhandsome letter because the publisher has little real choice; to use it of his own free will, chosen over handsome and effective headletters, is a perplexing anomaly.

The publisher must also set some basic rules about the art in his offset newspaper. He must insist on good pictures and good photographs. Even the fine-screen reproduction of offset is not going to improve a poor glossy. And the finest technical excellence will not hide lack of communication in a picture.

The publisher must insist on highest technical standards for Velox, screening, or platemaking camera. Operators should constantly check their work against a *gray scale,* a gauge that shows the values of gray in 10% steps. The darkroom technician compares the tones of his negative or print visually against the scale to determine that there is adequate gradation in value. Yet many darkrooms don't even have this basic gauge.

Too often the sky on an outdoor shot is bleached out so it looks like a silhouetted halftone. Equally often, skin tones become chalky and eyes cavernous as middle values are lost. This inferior craftsmanship should not be tolerated.

Establishing and vigorously policing high standards does not lessen the place of offset in the American newspaper world. Just the opposite; the finest compliment that we can pay to any art or craft is to insist that it reach its highest level of excellence. Offset printing and pasting up of forms are going to be with us for a long, long time. They are good tools for communication. Good tools deserve to be used with pride and skill.

chapter **14**

Restyling the Newspaper

"SHALL I MAKE TYPOGRAPHIC CHANGES gradually, or shall I make a drastically complete restyling?" This question is constantly asked by editors.

Of course, there is another question: "Shall I make any changes at all?" The answer to this one is relatively easy. You can't win the 1970 Indianapolis 500 with a 1940 racing car. You can't compete in the communications market of the 1970's with a newspaper of the 1940's. Some changes are always required.

It is interesting to examine drastic changes that were made in the summer of 1968 by *Newsday,* on Long Island, New York, the paper with the seventh-largest evening circulation in the United States. For its whole lifetime of more than 27 years, this successful paper had been battling against the image of sensationalism that its tabloid format conveyed. This impression was probably intensified because most *Newsday* readers are familiar with the *New York Daily News,* which originally gave "tabloid" its connotation of siren-and-bell journalism.

Newsday attempted to make its image more conservative and also more attractive by switching from sans serifs headletters to Century, a Transitional Roman. Page one was changed from the classical poster-page pattern of the tabloid to a more magazinish style. The paper was left in three sections, identified by thumb tabs, as discussed in Chapter 9. But their contents were more tightly departmentalized. All general news goes in the main section; women's news is in the second section, and sports in the third. By this method the editor, Harry F. Guggenheim, and the publisher, Bill Moyers, hope that family members can read that section which most interests them without having to wait for someone else.

But our first two questions, posed after a decision for change has been made, are perplexing, for there are no pat answers. The competitive situation has a major bearing on the method in which change is made. I worked with a newspaper that had approved a completely new typographic style manual which called for changes all the way from the nameplate to the arrangement of the comics page. But the top editors couldn't agree on the piecemeal or the one-fell-swoop technique. Nothing happened for months while the debate continued. Meanwhile the paper's major competitor was erecting a new building and installing new presses. Then it leaked out that it was going to do some major typographic rebuilding too; a completely restyled newspaper would be presented to the public when the new building was opened.

This was all the stimulus my clients required. Their changes were made, swiftly and completely. The detailed planning that had gone on made it possible to effect the changeover in only a short time and so beat the competitor to the punch.

The corporate personality of the newspaper is a factor; the more conservative the paper, the slower it moves into change. The ability of the staff and mechanical crews must be taken into account. An inexperienced staff or an overtaxed back shop, especially if its equipment is inadequate, may find it far more practical to make many small changes than one big one. Typographic changes can be a spring tonic to the staff. One eminent editor says that the increase of morale and interest of all personnel makes a change worthwhile even if no other benefits accrue.

The publisher's own feelings are a valid influence on changes. It's his newspaper, and he has the right to make decisions on any basis he chooses.

When a new newspaper begins, naturally all typographic decisions must be made at one time. (This occurs far more frequently than most people, even newspapermen, realize. Deaths of newspapers get top play in all mass media, but journalistic birth announcements get little attention. Yet there are new papers being born each year, not only weeklies but dailies as well.)

Another time when a complete restyling seems logical is when a newspaper changes frequency of publication—weekly to daily, weekly to semiweekly, five days to six, or adding a Sunday edition. When new equipment, especially a new press, removes mechanical handicaps, a totally new product may be desirable.

On the other hand, many newspapers think that a long-existing appearance is an asset that should be cherished. Within reason, that is a

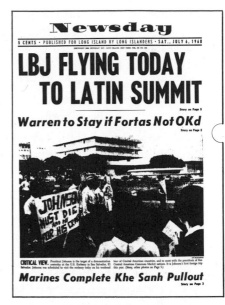

Fig. 134. Overnight restyling. Last edition of week was in familiar format for *Newsday* of Garden City, Long Island, N.Y. Restyling over weekend resulted in new look, opposite, using Century Bold hed sked. (Copyright © *Newsday*; used by permission.)

valid conclusion. Certainly no one would suggest that the *New York Times* overnight adopt the typography of the *National Enquirer* or even the *National Observer*. But even the most conservative of papers can—and should—make minor changes if they are true improvements. Usually an individual change will not affect the overall appearance and personality of a newspaper. The changes can be made over a long period so that the reader is never aware, from day to day, they have been made. He can see the total change only by referring to newspaper files, which the typical reader seldom if ever has occasion to do.

Some editors hesitate to make changes because they think that they will lose face, that they will thereby admit that their product has been inferior in the past. This attitude is incongruous. An important part of the gross national product comes from the automobile industry, which exists almost on change alone. When Detroit introduces a new transmission, it certainly makes no apology for that which had been used in the past. And no physician refuses to use a new miracle drug because he hadn't used it 25 years ago.

The technique of the automotive industry in introducing innovations should be used by newspaper publishers too.

We are all interested in the new. "Be the first kid in your block . . ." is an appeal that also affects adults. But all of us are creatures of habit and may be irritated when a familiar routine like our newspaper's style is

Newsday

THE LONG ISLAND NEWSPAPER

5 CENTS
MONDAY
JULY 8, 1968

Cong: May Ask Outside Aid

National Liberation Front spokesman warns that the Viet Cong may ask for the aid of international 'volunteers' if the U.S. does not withdraw its troops from South Vietnam. Story on Page 3.

SOUTHERN HOSPITALITY. An elderly woman greets President Johnson as he leaves a cathedral in San Salvador yesterday. At Johnson's side is his daughter, Mrs. Luci Nugent. The President was to leave El Salvador today on the return leg of his trip to Central America, stopping briefly in four countries to drop off their presidents, who attended joint meetings. Story, other photos on Page 2.

AP Radiophoto

LBJ to Visit 4 More Latin Countries

The President says that he desires a 'new road of hope' for western countries. Story on Page 2.

HHH: Study Delegates

Vice president asks look at New York group's ethnic basis. Story on Page 5.

CORE Is Split On Black Power

Parley closes as 'rebels' quit. Story on Page 7.

Fig. 135. "The Widget," short-lived but exciting *World Journal Tribune* of New York City, began life in Sans Serifs dress, here. Overnight it changed to Bodoni, opposite, to achieve "more elegant and legible appearance."

changed without warning. Therefore major changes should be promoted well in advance.

Promotion

The reader should be told that something is brewing. He should be assured that the new product will be an improvement. His curiosity and desire should both be whetted.

When the *Christian Science Monitor* made a very drastic change in appearance, the woe-sayers really had something to wag their heads about. The *Monitor*'s readership was undoubtedly conservative in taste, and the percentage of older readers, whose habits had longer periods for solidifying, was high. But the staff did a masterful job of advance promotion. Not only was this done by house ads, well ahead of the change-over, but a personal letter was sent to every subscriber, explaining why changes were to be made but not dampening anticipation by giving specifics.

The *Louisville* (Kentucky) *Courier-Journal* used different tactics. In January of 1965 it ran an experimental issue in six columns. Reader reaction was solicited, and it came in by the barrel. It was overwhelmingly favorable, for the reader was not being handed a *fait accompli*. No

Wall St. Broker Mysteriously Missing

By ERWIN SAVELSON
World Jou...al Tribune Staff

Wealthe broker Edward T. Shean, a general partner in the Wall St. firm of Lazard Freres, disappeared March 10 while en route to Columbia Presbyterian Medical Center for a checkup, it was learned today.

A spokesman for Lazard Freres said there was "no problem" at the firm regard-

ing the 43-year-old Shean, whose retirement as a partner was announced over the last weekend.

However, it became known that a 17-State police missing persons alarm has been issued for Shean, who lives with his second wife at 1 Gracie Square and was formerly married to Caroline Wainwright, granddaughter of George Jay Gould.

The police alarm was broad-

cast at 7:40 a.m. on March 12. Shean's wife said she last saw her husband at 9 a.m. on March 10.

The spokesman for Lazard Freres said other partners and associates of Shean were as much puzzled by his disappearance as his family and that he still has a large credit balance as the firm.

"He called to say that he was first coming to our office

as 44 Wall St. and then was going to Presbyterian Hospital for a checkup," the spokesman added. "Other than that, we don't know what happened and we haven't heard from him."

Shean, whose father, Edward J. Shean, retired recently as a member of the New York Stock Exchange, was graduated from Taft School and interrupted his education at Princeton University to serve

as a lieutenant in the Naval Reserve from 1944 to 1946.

In 1945, he was married to Caroline Brereton Wainwright, daughter of Carroll Livingston Wainwright and of the late Lady Hector Macneal, who was Edith Kingdon Gould.

She is a great-granddaughter of the first Jay Gould, founder of the Gould fortune. Her father was a cousin of Gen. Jonathan M. Wainwright, hero

of the battle for Corregidor.

In 1948, Shean was graduated from Princeton with a bachelor of arts degree and joined Lee Higginson, a Stock Exchange member firm, where he was assistant to the manager of the syndicate department.

Shean joined his father's firm, E. J. Shean & Co., in February 1950, and stayed with that company until 1953.

He became associated with Lazard Freres as manager of its bond department in 1954 and was elevated to a partner in January 1961.

He lived with his first wife and their five children in Greenwich. They were divorced in 1963 and he married the grand-daughter of M. J. (Mike) Meehan, who had a spectacular career as a Stock Exchange member in 1929.

The Weather

Fair and cool tonight, low 35 to 40. Tomorrow fair and milder. Outlook: Thursday fair and cool.

(Weather Map on P. 43.)

World Journal Tribune
©1967 World Journal Tribune Inc.

VOL. 1, NO. 202   NEW YORK, TUESDAY, APRIL 4, 1967   10 CENTS

SPORTS
FINAL

Latest Markets

Plus Bklyn, Queens, L.I.

HORSEMEN VOTE STRIKE

No Big A Racing Tomorrow

By PAT LYNCH
World Journal Tribune Staff

Aqueduct today called off tomorrow's racing as the result of the horsemen's strike. Today's racing was not affected.

Cliff McCartney of the racing secretary's office confirmed that not one entry for tomorrow had been received. Normally at 9 a.m., the racing secretary's office has what it calls the "first rundown" which usually accounts for 25 per cent of a card, or about 30 entries.

A spokesman for Gov. Rockefeller indicated that the governor did not plan to call any special session of the Legislature to deal the impasse.

Asked when Rockefeller planned to do about the threatening situation, the spokesman replied, "nothing."

Assembly Speaker Anthony J. Travia said through his counsel, Harold Fisher, that he did not plan to ask for any special session.

"The problem is the governor's," Fisher said.

The shutdown will result in the stake being an estimated $548,000 a day in taxi revenues.

About 600 employees and milkmen members of the New York division of the powerful Horsemen's Benevolent and Protective Assn. voted all Aqueduct last night not to enter horses at 10:30 a.m. this morning for tomorrow's program. The racing stoppage would continue, they waved, until their demands for purse raises, which were billed in committee in the recently concluded session of the State Legislature, are granted.

CALLED UNFAIR

In fact, the horsemen upped the ante. Instead of asking the state to yield one-half of one per cent of its legalized parimutuel cut of 10 per cent, the HBPA subcommittee on purses, led by threadbare Jack Dreyfus Jr., owner of the Hobeau Farm, was instructed to fight for an original request of one per cent. This figure would give New York horsemen a $7,000,000 purse raise which would merely bring Aqueduct owners even with purse percentages throughout the rest of the country.

The THRBA membership was thoroughly aroused by what it regarded as cavalier and unfair treatment in the dying minutes of the Legislature.

Rockefeller recognized the pleas of New York horsemen this winter. A compromise on the original one per cent was reached. The governor agreed to one-half of one per cent for thoroughbred owners, 95 per cent of whom lose money at Aqueduct and Saratoga, where the State's 10 per cent of the play is the largest in the land.

Turn to Page 41, 4th Section

FBI Arrests 14 in Draft Fraud Ring

By PAUL MESKIL
World Journal Tribune Staff

The Federal Bureau of Investigation today announced arrest of 14 men on charges of obtaining draft deferments through the use of fraudulent documents.

Assistant Director John F. Malone, in charge of the New York FBI office, ordered the roundup after the 14 were indicted by a federal grand jury in Brooklyn.

Six of those arrested are fathers who allegedly arranged draft deferments for their sons.

Among those indicted was Jay Pontana, 28, a booking agent for rock-'n-roll groups and other entertainers. Malone described Pontana, of 3198 Nostrand Ave., Bklyn. as a middleman who conducted negotiations between prospective draft-dodgers and the local that supplied the fake documents.

The indictments resulted from investigation of a draft-dodging ring masterminded by Solomon Gottfried, 57, a per-

sonnel technician for the Nassau County Civil Service Commission, and Paul George Miller, 28, an Army veteran.

USED RESERVE FORMS

When this ring was smashed by the FBI in March of 1966, 18 men were arrested. The new roundup brings the arrest total to 32. Gottfried, of 2 Elves Lane, Levittown, L. I., and Miller, of 86-23 57th Ave., Flushing, Queens, pleaded guilty to Selective Service violations and are awaiting sentencing.

They allegedly obtained hundreds of Defense Department forms used to notify Selective Service boards that po-

---

Turn to Page 2

Jets Rip N. Viet In Record Raids

SAIGON, April 4 (AP)—U.S. warplanes hammered North Viet Nam today with the heaviest raids in five months as a spokesman disclosed the loss of the 500th American plane over the Communist North in two years and two months of bombing.

Air Force, Navy and Marine aircraft flying under the best weather conditions in weeks blasted storage areas, bridges, trucks and cargo barges in 147 missions. It was the heaviest

attack since Nov. 4, when 155 missions were flown.

[United Press International estimated than 500 planes took part in the 147 missions.

[In the central highlands of South Viet Nam, U.S. Marine pilots used a new weapon—"burrowing blockbusters"—against underground fortifications that have resisted conventional bombs. The one-ton bomb, designed specifically for the purpose, is capable of penetrating 30 feet underground and is equipped for delayed-action explosions over a 12-hour period.]

[The 500th plane lost over the North was downed Sunday, and the pilot was listed as missing in action. So far, about 250

Stocks Rally, Head Higher

Stocks rallied this afternoon to cancel out early losses and head higher.

The market averages turned topside after a morning of decline. Advances took the lead over losses after trailing by as much as two to one in weak early trading.

Details on Page 40   Turn to Page 2

Aqueduct Results

FIRST	1—Eccentrical (Turcotte)	11.80	5.20	2.80
	2—Ted's Day (Feliciano)		10.60	4.40
	3—Right Reason (Shoemaker)			2.40
SECOND	1—Eskimo Princess (Rossello)	14.20	6.40	3.80
	3—King's Valentine (DMiJuch)		3.30	4.00
	2—Two Onthe Aisle (Cordero)			3.80

Daily Double—(1-8)—paid $76.00

GUESS WHO . . . Today's mystery couple lives in a mansion and the husband works downtown. He used to walk to work regularly, but then so did everybody else. And he has his own radio program. Check your answers on the first page of the third section. You are probably right.

World Journal Tribune Photo by Mel Finkelstein

Did Politics Kill Race Bill?

Was the bill whose legislative death set off a strike at Aqueduct killed by political jockeying?

This was the big question being asked today by politicians, thoroughbred horsemen and racing fans as Aqueduct officials cancelled racing as the track tomorrow.

In Albany and New York, observers raised the names of Gov. Rockefeller, Assembly Speaker Anthony J. Travia, Yonkers Raceway owner Martin Tananbaum and former Assembly Speaker Joseph Carlino in discussing the dilemma at Aqueduct.

Senate Minority Leader Joseph Zaretzki said the bill which would have reduced the state's take on racing at the flat tracks by some $3.5 million was defeated in its dying—

Under the bill, which had Rockefeller's blessing, the state's 10 per cent share of the—

ANTHONY J. TRAVIA
As convention opened

Turn to Page 41, 4th Section

Carson Quits TV In Strike Dispute

By AL SALERNO
World Journal Tribune Columnist

Johnny Carson quit the NBC-TV "Tonight" show today in a dispute with the network growing out of the strike by the American Federation of Television and Radio Artists.

The performer said he was taking the action, effective immediately, because the network had violated his contract by broadcasting repeat programs of the "Tonight" show since the start of the television strike last week.

There was no immediate comment from NBC.

Another casualty of the strike may be the movieland's Oscar awards program.

Comedian Bob Hope an-

nounced that he would not serve as master of ceremonies for any strike-defying telecast of the Academy Awards presentations scheduled for Monday.

Hope's statement came as a paralyzing sympathy walkout by television craft unions was threatened against the nation's

---

Turn to Page 2

'Battle of the Book' Goes On

Manchester's Wife 'Sorry' For Jackie

By DOROTHY McCARDLE
World Journal Tribune Special

MIDDLETOWN, Conn., April 4—Mrs. William Manchester, wife of the author of the controversial account of the assassination of President Kennedy, has never met Mrs. John F. Kennedy.

"And I don't want to, either," she said during an interview at her home in this quiet college town.

Judy Manchester, the former Julia Marshall of Baltimore, spread her hands in a "so what?" gesture and

Turn to Page 13

Salinger Blames It All On Himself

By ANTHONY COWDY
World Journal Tribune Special

LONDON, April 4 — "My judgment wasn't very good," said Pierre Salinger, once press secretary for John F. Kennedy, explaining that he —not Jacqueline Kennedy—picked William Manchester to write "The Death of a President."

"That was a time when you went home and you got drunk and you cried.

"I chose a man who has precipitated a world-wide battle. He's done more harm

Turn to Page 12

Today's World Journal Tribune

one said to him, "Your familiar old daily visitor is being supplanted by a new one." Instead, he was told that this was an experiment for only a day and not a sharp break in familiar, comfortable habit. Now, whether he approved or not, he could relax for that single day and enjoy the break in routine. The change was made permanent seven months later in the *Courier-Journal* and its sister *Times*. The reader had the feeling that he had been a participant in the transition and he welcomed it.

These tactics may not be feasible for most newspapers. But all of them can and should do a studied job of advance promotion. House ads will be the major medium to readers; but direct mail and, certainly, face-to-face explanations are essential with advertisers, local and national.

First announcements should be teasers. The reader should be told that on a given day his newspaper will present innovations designed for his comfort, ease, and pleasure. In the issue just before the change, specifics should be given in as large an ad as possible. Billboards, transit advertising, and radio and television can be used effectively in larger cities.

On the day of the change, a front-page story should herald the change from a prominent position. Many publishers use their leed editorial to expand on the announcement. It is good tactics to use any occasion to polish the "image" of the newspaper.

Too often the paper is taken for granted by its community; usually this is the fault of the paper. When a department store opens a new shoe department, it gets a news story, but when the newspaper expands its facilities, the story is often played down or not printed at all.

Community leaders should be quoted on the change. If there have been dry runs, the dignitaries should be shown the changes so their comments can appear in the first edition in the new look. If comments must be made on the first actual edition, these should run, prominently displayed, in the very next issue. Political, business, and cultural leaders should include oculists and optometrists, teachers and educators, artists and printers, as well as advertisers in varied lines. Leading questions can elicit the comments sought without distorting the honest views of the subject.

Advertisers should be given a preview of the changes if at all possible. After all, they are, in a sense, partners in the newspaper; they, as we all do, enjoy having inside and advance information. Your message to them is, "We are improving the quality of our newspaper to build the readership that allows your advertising to work more effectively." This, incidentally, is the absolute truth and not just a facile sales pitch.

It is a happy fact that well-promoted typographic improvements result in increased advertising linage. Some of this is due to the new interest and attention that the advertiser gives to the newspaper which he has probably taken for granted. Some is due to the direct promotion which is aimed at the advertiser. Much is due to the extra pulling power that advertising derives from heightened reader interest.

Preparation of promotional material is a pleasure. There is the constant stimulus of working on a campaign uniquely your own. And there is the added excitement that comes from a comparatively rare promotion. Most daily newspaper staffs prefer to prepare their own campaign. But manufacturers and suppliers of typographic materials have plenty of promotional material which they furnish to smaller papers that can't spare the manpower to create their own promotions or as idea-starters for larger newspapers.

It should be emphasized that every newspaper that does restyling should promote it; the size of the publication is a factor in determining only the extent of the campaign.

A typical promotion schedule might be this one which the *News-Press* of Santa Barbara, California, used when it adopted a 9-point Corona as its new body type. *T-day* is the day the new type went into use.

T-minus-9 days:
A contest with cash prizes for newspaper carrier boys was begun to determine the best sales pitch in each district.
T-minus-8:
The first teaser ad began running in the paper. This was made up in three sizes and as many as space permitted were run in each edition. Radio teasers, as short spot announcements, were begun.
T-minus-7:
The first teaser house ad was rerun, again in three sizes and as many places as space allowed.
T-minus-6:
The second teaser ad was run.
T-minus-5:
The third teaser ad ran. Especial care was taken to run this in all the sections of the paper. All employees were informed of the change by a note in their payroll envelope.
T-minus-4:
Fourth teaser ad ran, again scattered as widely as possible throughout the paper. Letters went to all advertisers, civic leaders, physicians and optometrists, educators, and officials.
T-minus-3:
Fifth teaser ad.

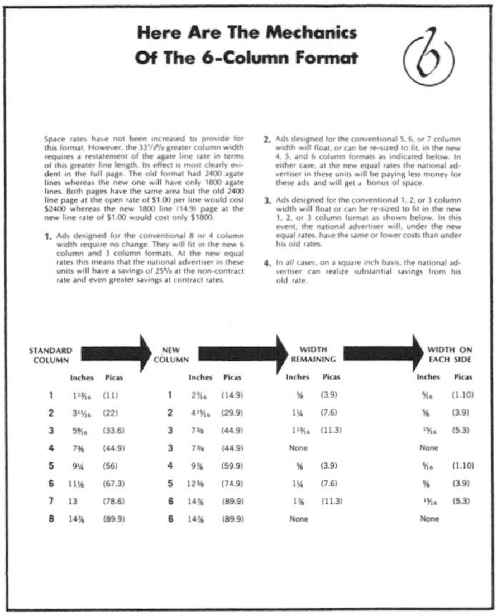

Here Are The Mechanics Of The 6-Column Format

(b)

Space rates have not been increased to provide for this format. However, the 33 1/3% greater column width requires a restatement of the agate line rate in terms of this greater line length. Its effect is most clearly evident in the full page. The old format had 2400 agate lines whereas the new one will have only 1800 agate lines. Both pages have the same area but the old 2400 line page at the open rate of $1.00 per line would cost $2400 whereas the new 1800 line (14.9) page at the new line rate of $1.00 would cost only $1800.

1. Ads designed for the conventional 8 or 4 column width require no change. They will fit in the new 6 column and 3 column formats. At the new equal rates this means that the national advertiser in these units will have a savings of 25% at the non-contract rate and even greater savings at contract rates.

2. Ads designed for the conventional 5, 6, or 7 column width will float, or can be re-sized to fit, in the new 4, 5, and 6 column formats as indicated below. In either case, at the new equal rates the national advertiser in these units will be paying less money for these ads and will get a bonus of space.

3. Ads designed for the conventional 1, 2, or 3 column width will float or can be re-sized to fit in the new 1, 2, or 3 column format as shown below. In this event, the national advertiser will, under the new equal rates, have the same or lower costs than under his old rates.

4. In *all* cases, on a square inch basis, the national advertiser can realize substantial savings from his old rate.

STANDARD COLUMN			NEW COLUMN			WIDTH REMAINING		WIDTH ON EACH SIDE	
	Inches	Picas		Inches	Picas	Inches	Picas	Inches	Picas
1	1 13/16	(11)	1	2 7/16	(14.9)	5/8	(3.9)	5/16	(1.10)
2	3 11/16	(22)	2	4 15/16	(29.9)	1 1/4	(7.6)	5/8	(3.9)
3	5 9/16	(33.6)	3	7 3/8	(44.9)	1 13/16	(11.3)	15/16	(5.3)
4	7 3/8	(44.9)	3	7 3/8	(44.9)	None		None	
5	9 1/4	(56)	4	9 7/8	(59.9)	5/8	(3.9)	5/16	(1.10)
6	11 1/8	(67.3)	5	12 3/8	(74.9)	1 1/4	(7.6)	5/8	(3.9)
7	13	(78.6)	6	14 7/8	(89.9)	1 7/8	(11.3)	15/16	(5.3)
8	14 7/8	(89.9)	6	14 7/8	(89.9)	None		None	

Fig. 136. Typographic promotion. Change to optimum format by Louisville, Ky., newspapers was well promoted. Among tools was comprehensive book of 9 x 11 inches with cover (*a*) in black and brick red. On page *b* is shown relation of old and new ad sizes; spot colors are sand and brick. Page *c* shows how 11-pica ads can be placed in new, wider columns. Page *d* shows uses of ROP spot color; rectangles are in sand color, beer ad in red.

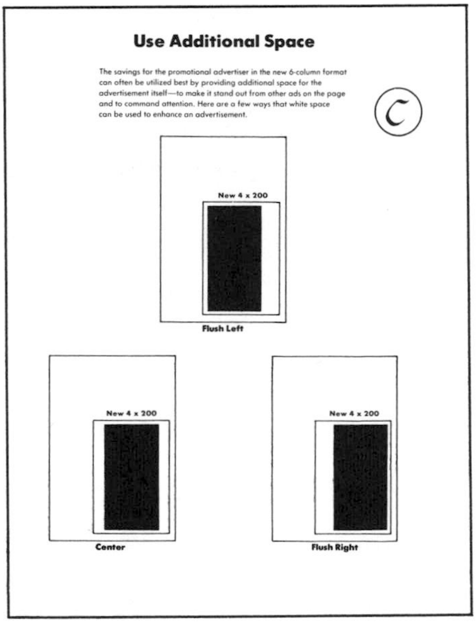

Use Additional Space

(c)

The savings for the promotional advertiser in the new 6-column format can often be utilized best by providing additional space for the advertisement itself—to make it stand out from other ads on the page and to command attention. Here are a few ways that white space can be used to enhance an advertisement.

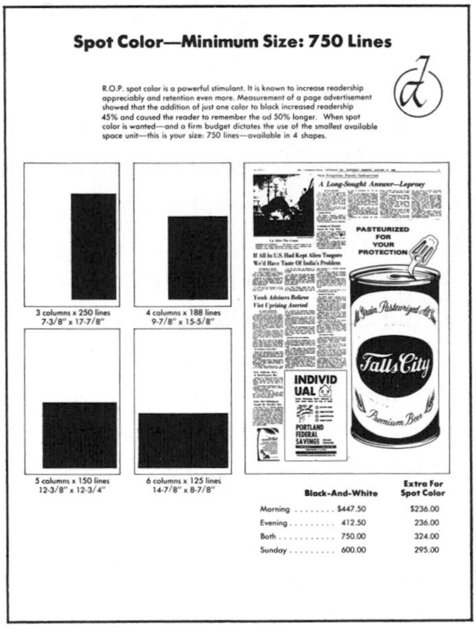

Spot Color—Minimum Size: 750 Lines

(d)

R.O.P. spot color is a powerful stimulant. It is known to increase readership appreciably and retention even more. Measurement of a page advertisement showed that the addition of just one color to black increased readership 45% and caused the reader to remember the ad 50% longer. When spot color is wanted—and a firm budget dictates the use of the smallest available space unit—this is your size: 750 lines—available in 4 shapes.

	Black-And-White	Extra For Spot Color
Morning	$447.50	$236.00
Evening	412.50	236.00
Both	750.00	324.00
Sunday	600.00	295.00

T-minus-2:
Sixth teaser ad ran in color. This appeared wherever color and space were available as well as on the back page of the radio-TV log section.

T-minus-1:
Full page in color announced the type change. Feature story with art showed process of changing over and composing-room men looking over sample settings.

T-Day:
Full-page ad in color announced "Today!" Seven hundred extra single sheets were run for circulation-department use. Page one story ran, well displayed. There was editorial comment on the change. Rack poster cards went up. Bumper strips were attached by the circulation department to every car in the newspaper parking lot. A series of radio announcements began; these used the voices of *News-Press* employees from all departments.

T-plus-1:
A reaction story, with plenty of art, ran on the front page. This carried comments from local and state dignitaries. A series of plugger ads, in small and medium sizes, began on a definite schedule instead of the previous "when available" system. Radio spots by employees continued and were augmented by interviews with leading citizens, doctors, and educators. This phase of the program continued for two weeks.

For daily newspapers this is a practical schedule. Concentrating the advance campaign into eight days maintains a brisk tempo, and continuing the post-change series for two weeks seems about long enough to exploit the "new" angle. Naturally, typography is one of the features of a newspaper that should be mentioned in continuing self-promotion.

When a newspaper wins an award, typographic or otherwise, it should be occasion for strong promotion. When activities of the newspaper are reported in trade journals, the article should be reprinted, either as a straight editorial feature or in a house ad.

Whenever typographic changes are made, minor or complete, the publisher should invest in dry runs. Many proposed changes can be evaluated only by seeing how they will look in the finished product. The appearance of body type, for instance, will not be identical in every newspaper. Variations in newsprint, ink, stereotyping, and press capabilities will be reflected in the finished product. The average tonal values of local advertising varies from one newspaper to another, and editorial typography will be affected by its surroundings.

Dry runs offer news and composing-room personnel a chance to become familiar with new procedures while free from the pressure of actual production deadlines. Minor but important modifications of proposed style are often suggested during dry runs.

Fig. 137. Typographic promotion. *Newsday* promoted new appearance aggressively. Advance news story, above left, ran three days before restyling. Ads of various sizes and shapes, above and opposite, ran daily for two weeks after changeover.

Read Today's Newsday

Newsday / 5 CENTS THURSDAY JULY 1968
THE LONG ISLAND NEWSPAPER

Reds Free Jet With 231 Aboard

Swift release comes after U.S. apologizes to Soviet about navigational error. Story on Page 3.

Return of Ray To U.S. Seen Within Weeks

Appeal to a high British court is the next step for accused slayer of Martin Luther King Jr. Story on Page 5.

Paris Sees Little Change	Bonn Sees Much Hope
Story Page 2.	Story Page 2.

ARMS CURBS are supported by President Johnson in speech. Story on Page 4.

Newsday has a new look. The entire paper, including the front page, has been redesigned in an improved, easy-to-read format. Headlines in new, more graceful Century type have replaced the old black banners on the front page and other headlines throughout the paper.

Our new format contains more news than ever. Whether it is news about the nation or your neighbors, sports or world events, Newsday concentrates on the news that makes a difference to you.

Our innovations include a completely new business and financial section, the Earlybird Weekend Stock Review which lists weekly comparative data on 750 stocks one full day before any other publication, and the section called

The Family, which cente... bers of your family.

Then there's the new... the most provocative co... The emphasis is on idea... with every columnist in... and we hope you'll use o... tell us what you think.

Other attractions a... the regular weekly ma... that comes with the pap... in Today's Newsday for...

MORE NEWS AND A NEW LOOK i...

Newsday

The Long Island Newspaper ● Still 5...

Get Today's Newsday

MORE NEWS AND A NEW LOOK

Newsday / STILL 5 CENTS
THE LONG ISLAND NEWSPAPER

U.S. Aircraft Lost in

Tuesday, July 9, 1968

Fig. 137-B. Doorknob cards (inset) were used extensively and posters of same design were widely distributed at newsstands and elsewhere.

The number of dry runs will depend on circumstances, of course. When a new newspaper begins, it is necessary for all members of the team to learn procedures, style, and inter- and intra-departmental liaison. Before *Today* began publication in Cocoa, Florida, seven complete editions, including a fat Sunday one, were dry-run. Even before this, reporters were covering beats and writing stories and the desk and composing-room supervisors were processing them up to the point of actually setting type.

Increasing the frequency of an existing publication probably requires no dry runs to sharpen mechanical techniques. Nor does a minor change in body or head type. In the latter case, sample runs are necessary only for the purpose of determining how the type works in a specific manufacturing situation.

Typographic Experimentation

On an existing newspaper, it is practical to keep two pages standing for experimenting. These should be a front page and a typical inside one. To determine a new head dress, the page need not be remade; new headlines merely replace original ones. Page patterns may be drastically changed—from vertical to horizontal, for instance—without resetting body type. The sample page should be *tailgated,* actually stereotyped and run through the press. This assures the editor that he is seeing the changes just as his readers will.

It is wise to maintain a modicum of secrecy on all dry runs. Then the effect of a change will not be diluted by premature and perhaps piecemeal disclosure. It contributes to the enthusiasm of the staff to work under security; we all like a little cloak-and-dagger to spice daily routines.

For preliminary sampling the *paste-and-Stat* technique is adequate. If a new head dress or page patterning is being considered, the editor uses a printed page of his paper. From another newspaper using the proposed headletter he cuts appropriately sized heads and pastes them over the existing ones. He aligns them properly, horizontally and vertically, but doesn't worry about covering all the old type. Nor does he have to cut out the new heads in precise rectangles.

The typographer should not concern himself with the content of typographic material at this stage. There need be no connection in copy between head and body type. Fragments of words are adequate. This seems obvious, of course, but too often unnecessary work is created in

Fig. 138. Typographic Promotion. *Nashville* (Tenn.) *Banner* uses skyline head in magenta and 3-color promotional box, cols. 4-5, to announce new body type. Note large nameplate, with period; newspaper name is cyan, eagle is black, flag in natural colors.

pasting up because of the needless preoccupation with copy when tonal values are all that should interest us now.

After the page has been pasted up, a negative, same-size Photostat is shot. On this neg all necessary retouching is done. Because the tonal values are reversed, black India ink is used instead of the white tempera paint that would be required to retouch the original pasteup. Ink is far more convenient than paint and is completely opaque; there is no danger of blotting of the pigment on the slick photopaper as there would be with highly absorbent newsprint.

Often there will be a shadow around the edges of the pasted-on material; this is easily inked out. Portions of the original heads that might not have been pasted over are eliminated the same way. If more space is required above and below heads, this is easily achieved by blacking out some body type. If heads are to be shorter than the clipped ones, unwanted letters are inked out.

Body type can be manipulated too. If shorter paragraphs are desired, blacking out can create widow lines and indentions. Extra space between paragraphs is added with a stroke of the pen. Alleys are created or widened in the same way.

When retouching is complete, a positive Photostat is made. This will be a close facsimile of a printed page, especially if dull-finish photopaper is used. The Stat should be trimmed to the same margins as those of the printed page. Wide margins change the appearance of a page to a great extent, and for the better. There can be disappointment when the final printed page appears with margins far skimpier than those of the Stat.

When new page patterns are under study, two techniques may be used. A previously printed page may be the basic ingredient. On it headlines clipped from other pages are pasted where desired. Unwanted heads are covered with blocks of body type clipped from other pages. For the neatest appearance, these clips should be from the same general area of the printed page as that where they will be pasted. This is especially necessary for stereotyped papers, for mat shrinkage is not uniform throughout a page and the clipping may be wider or narrower than the column it is supposed to cover.

When a radically different column width of body type is contemplated or when a new newspaper is being built, it is convenient to make up a page completely with body type. Proofs of this form are used for pasting up, and heads and display elements can be positioned anywhere without the need of filling in areas of body type.

When the *National Observer* was in the planning stage, such pages were proofed with an interesting variation. The body-type area was the

THE CHRISTIAN SCIENCE MONITOR

— An International Daily Newspaper —

New England Edition

VOL. 56 · NO. 384 · 10 CENTS

BOSTON, SUNDAY, APRIL 30, 1965

THE CHRISTIAN SCIENCE MONITOR

An International Daily Newspaper

New England Edition

VOL. 68 ·NO. 203 · 10 CENTS

BOSTON, FRIDAY, JANUARY 23, 1965

Fig. 139. Meticulous attention to detail is demonstrated by steps in creation of new nameplate for Christian Science Monitor. Top sketch brought decision to use cap-and-small-cap style and wheat motif. Second sketch led to swashing of first R.

First proof of actual metal elements permitted fine changes in position, above, to final form of nameplate, below.

THE CHRISTIAN SCIENCE MONITOR

An International Daily Newspaper

VOL. 57, NO.82

Use Melior FOCUS

on science

BOSTON, JANUARY 7, 1965

Set in 12 pt Garamond Bold

Move pics to right →

Congo crisis

Washington wants

EASTERN EDITION · 10c

TWO SECTIONS

28 picas

THE CHRISTIAN SCIENCE MONITOR

An International Daily Newspaper

VOL. 57, NO. 82
TWO SECTIONS

EASTERN EDITION ★ 10c

BOSTON, WEDNESDAY, JANUARY 7, 1965

Fig. 140. Typographic style manual. Typical page of elaborate typo manual of *Chicago* (Ill.) *Sun-Times*. In same size as newspaper page, book pages, then, can demonstrate newspaper pages.

Fig. 141. Typographic style manual. Cover and typical pages, 8½ x 11 inches, from typo manual of *Newark* (N.J.) *News.*

size of the printed page, and the nameplate was printed above this area. When a front page was to be pasted up, the bottom of the proof was trimmed to the proper page depth. When inside pages were experimented with, the nameplate was sliced off.

Typographic Style Manual

Before the actual changeover takes place, a *typographic style manual* should be prepared. In fact, every newspaper should have one. Even if no changes are contemplated, it is a good investment of time and effort to prepare such a manual.

A good typo manual serves several functions. It maintains necessary consistency in typographic usage that is possible only when specifications have been committed to writing; no dilutions in style will come from spontaneous experimenting by an individual deskman. Everything that has been committed to writing frees human memory of the need to remember that material, and so more mental energies can be diverted to the creative process.

Written specifications prevent misunderstandings between the desk and the composing room and simplify communication between them. They also spare the deskman from making top-of-the-head decisions, usually demanded under extreme pressure of deadlines.

A good manual should include every specification that will possibly be used in the newspaper, not only the routine ones but those that will occur only with walking-on-water stories. Sensational stories have a habit of breaking close to deadline and can be handled most efficiently when preplanned guidelines are used.

No good editor would want to use another's typo manual. It is the individual modification that demonstrates creativity and gives the paper a unique appearance and personality. Editorial style books can be identical among newspapers. They almost have to be, for local copy must be compatible with wire-service style when wire tape is used. There must be some uniformity in typography in the use of wire tape, of course, but this usually involves only inconspicuous elements.

The typographic manual may be as simple as a few typewritten sheets in a folder or looseleaf binder. Or it may be an elaborately printed one. Among notable printed manuals are those of the *Boston Globe* and the *Toronto Star*. For large newspapers this is an excellent investment. Their personnel changes on the desk are fairly frequent as assignments are shifted or new staffers added. A complete typo manual cuts training or acclimatizing time to a minimum.

One classic manual is that of the *Chicago Sun-Times*. Prepared by the late Quentin Gore, its managing editor and one of the best newspaper typographers in America, it is a fascinating book that is used by many journalism teachers. It is the same size as the *Sun-Times* page and each page, in addition to carrying verbal instructions, is a demonstration of techniques.

An adjunct to this manual is another booklet which is used by both the *Sun-Times* and *Chicago Daily News* staffs. It was done by Edwin H. Muehsler and is provocatively titled *It Takes Two To Tango*. The "Two" refers to the two newspapers which are produced in the same plant. Each has its own headletter, but they share the same body type, a practical necessity. This, however, is as far as mutuality goes. Not only does each have its own headline library and typographic style; the formats differ just as much as could be possible. The *Sun-Times* is a 6-column compact, the *Daily News* is a conventional 8-columner. The manual tells each staff how to use composing-room facilities most effectively while maintaining the unique identity of its own paper.

Some editors begrudge the time and effort of preparing a typographic manual. Some belittle the need; they enjoy challenge of flying by instinct instead of by radio beams. Others fear that a manual will restrict the creativity of the staff. But a good manual has an escape hatch. A familiar phrase is: "Exception to the style specified by this manual will be made only with the express permission of the (managing) editor."

This has provided workable flexibility for creativity. If a deskman has a minor flash of inspiration, he probably won't think it important enough to seek permission for its use. So minor variations in style are kept out of the print. Any one of these variations may be sound and pleasant in itself, but their random use will dilute the consistency which is essential to good readership, efficient production, and typographic harmony. The larger the desk staff, the greater the danger of individual "inspiration."

Yet when the deskman feels an exception is important enough to ask for editorial permission, chances are good that the exception is warranted. Even if the editor decides against its use at that time, he can assess its value at leisure and perhaps later amend the manual to incorporate it.

Good typography results from painstaking attention to detail. Thought or effort devoted to even the most minute detail is rarely a waste. And the guideposts of functionalism are useful in every phase of planning, executing, and merchandising typographic changes.

chapter 15

The Newspaper of the Future

THE BROADWAY STAGE has been called "the fabulous invalid" because it always manages to outlive those who remark on its delicate health and would consign it to the coffin. The newspaper industry is also the frequent subject of premature obituaries. But its collective health remains robust.

The number of newspapers in the United States has not declined since World War II, and the total circulation of all newspapers has increased annually. Much growth is necessary, of course, just to stand still; as a country's population grows, its newspaper circulation must also grow just to maintain its percentage of coverage. American newspapers are more than holding their own in the population-circulation ratio.

People will always want news. As technology shrinks the world, it expands the appetite for news, for people are always most interested in local news. "Local" used to mean an area no larger than a county or even much less. But today the intimate involvement of reader with newsmaker, thanks to instantaneous communication, makes an astronaut a "neighbor" and the daily doings of a first lady as "local" as that of the housewife next door.

Of course, we wonder whether mass-circulated news will be carried primarily by print or electronic media. For several decades, soothsayers have predicted electronic devices that would produce a newspaper right in the reader's home. Technically this is possible right now. The *Wall Street Journal,* for instance, has perfected the *facsimile* process and uses it routinely on the Pacific Coast. After a page has been made up in hot metal in San Francisco, it is used to make both a stereo matrix and a repro proof. The mat makes the plates used for printing in San Francisco. The repro proof is transmitted 392 miles by radio microwave to Riverside, near Los Angeles. There a full-page line engraving is made on thin zinc. This original plate is curved to fit the rotary press cylinder and is actually used to print the paper. This wraparound technique eliminates the need for stereotyping. John H. Perry, Jr., head of a thriving group of newspapers in Florida, has also utilized facsimile and micro transmission with outstanding success.

The technique has developed extremely rapidly. It was first tried by *Asahi Shimbun* in Japan in 1959. It took a half hour to transmit a newspaper page, and the proof was scanned at 350 lines per inch. Three years later, when the *WSJ* began using the system on a daily basis, it took only five minutes to transmit a page and scanning was at 1,000 lines per inch.

The cost of necessary equipment for such transmissions is not exorbitant by standards of industrial installations, but for the typical newspaper reader to receive such pages in his home is as yet entirely unrealistic on a cost basis.

Less ambitious projections place a Teletype printer in the living room and foresee the householder tearing off a story as the copyboy does now, then sinking into his easy chair to read it. While the cost of such transmission is lower than facsimile, it still requires a capital investment far too steep for any circulation department to assume, and it is certainly one most readers would refuse to make.

Equally deleterious is the low typographic quality of such machines, be they Teletype, tickers, or computer printouts. The Navy found this out dramatically when it invented a machine that would "read" Russian printing and translate it into English. American scientists would read the translations—which, by machine, are pretty clumsy—and decide which were worth human—and readable—translation. But the typography of the computer printout was so poor that the human reader's capacity was severely limited by eye fatigue. The Pentagon found it well worth the substantial investment required to produce the machine's output in the top-quality typography of the Linofilm phototypesetter.

It is possible to raise the quality of hard copy as the Associated Press has done with its Offsetter. But each higher level of quality requires a correspondingly higher price, which makes it even less feasible for home use.

It is not realistic to expect the reader to assume the editorial function as he must when he handles such wire copy. The editor is paid to read

Fig. 142. Contemporary page patterns. *Chicago* (Ill.) *Daily News* creates always-lively pages. Above left, typical front page. Above right, "second front page," technique invented by *News;* its top portion is in Chicago format. Opposite, front page with large full-color photo.

the whole huge product of a news service wire and to weed out those stories which, in his judgment, will not interest his reader. Those which he passes on to the reader are graded and labeled by headlines, to make the reader's further choice to read or discard as easy as possible.

We would assume that there would be weeding out before material was placed on the transmitter to the home. But we would also assume that the reader will get at least as much news, in Teletyped form, as he now gets in printed pages. That makes reams and reams of copy, and the reader just isn't going to wade through all that to find those items that interest him. To expect him to do so would push him into the audience for electronic rip-and-read news coverage.

The basic advantages of the newspaper remain constant no matter what technological advances this medium or its competitors evolve.

The greatest advantage of a written or printed medium is the convenience of time and place. You can read a newspaper when and where you want to, not receive news only when a broadcaster decides to transmit it. or where a receiver is available. You can read at your own speed, skimming the nonessential, pondering and rereading the difficult. You can store the newspaper—casually, as by a clipping in wallet or scrap-

Seize James Earl Ray

Story below in Column 5

Hot

Tonight — Partly cloudy; low in the lower 70s. Sunday—Continued hot, with a chance of evening thundershowers, high in lower 90s.

Map and chart on Page 39.

CHICAGO DAILY NEWS

An Independent Newspaper

©1968 by Field Enterprises Inc.

Red Streak

Weekend Edition

93d Year, Number 136   158 Pages in 10 Sections   Saturday, June 8, 1968   20 Cents   ☆   Phone 321-2000

A nation's farewell to RFK

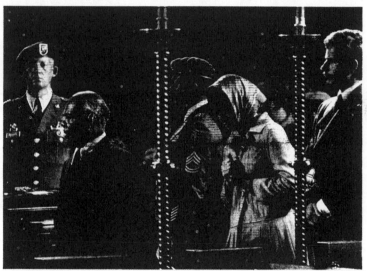

Daily News photo by Henry Gill

These millions believed in Bobby because he best symbolized their own thoughts and hopes and dreams--because he was young, yes, but because he cared enough to be involved in their struggle with a bewildering world.

2,300 at funeral mass

Teddy, archbishop offer eulogies in St. Patrick's

By Robert Gruenberg and Richard Christiansen
Staff Writers

NEW YORK — Sen. Robert F. Kennedy, America's slain young lion of politics who tried to move the world, was placed to rest in solemn requiem mass Saturday.

Some 2,300 mourners, led by President Johnson and Vice President Humphrey, attended the ceremony in towering St. Patrick's Cathedral.

The nation's elite were inside the church, while untold millions joinedthem in prayer and meditation throughout the world.

DESPITE the tears and grief visible on the faces of the mourners, it was markedly a time of joy as well as sorrow. According to Roman Catholic doctrine, the mass marked the beginning of Sen. Kennedy's eternal life with God.

And his fight for a better life for all Americans was emphasized — and re-emphasized—during the two-hour funeral mass. In the most

In The News today

Beeline	13	Fischetti	16
Bridge	41	Freudenheim	16
Business	47-49	Horoscope	41
Carmichael	43	Knight	16
Comics	40	Lisagor	3
Crossword	36	Obituaries	33
Deaths	33	People	13
Editorials	14	Religion	18
		Ross	13
		Rowan	16
		Sports	43-46
		Suburbia	17
		Travel	21-30
		Want Ads	34-42
		Wilson	13
		Women	31,32

solemn terms, the torch was taken up.

"He had a dream." Archbishop Terence J. Cooke said "the dream of an America purged of prejudice, assuring freedom for all her citizens, a land of truly equal opportunity.

"He pursued that dream with even greater courage and enthusiasm than when he climbed mountains and forded streams."

THE SERVICE began with a tremendously moving meditation reading by Sen. Edward M. Kennedy, the last son of a family that gave three sons to its nation.

His voice breaking at times, he described his brother as a man who "gave us strength in time of trouble" and "will always be at our side."

"My brother need not be idealized or enlarged in death beyond what he was in life," Sen. Kennedy said.

"He is to be remembered simply as a good and decent man who saw wrong and tried to right it, saw suffering and

Turn to Page 9, Column J

James Ray seized in London

WASHINGTON (AP)—James Earl Ray, chief suspect in the slaying of the Rev. Dr. Martin Luther King Jr., has been arrested in London, Atty. Gen. Ramsey Clark announced Saturday.

Ray, object of an intensive manhunt for two months, was arrested by Scotland Yard detectives as he passed through British immigration offices for a flight to Brussels, Clark said.

FBI Director J. Edgar Hoover said Ray is being held under maximum security conditions on a passport violation.

RAY WAS ARMED with a fully loaded pistol when taken into custody at 11:15 a.m.,

Turn to Page 2, Column 1

Family bravely bears burden of public grief

By Lynn Langway
Staff Writer

NEW YORK—When the members of Robert Kennedy's family last walked among New York City crowds, they walked in hope and happiness, and the people said how young and almost gay they often seemed.

"She looks just like a little girl," one old man said last month, marveling at the slen-

Memorial section

The Daily News on Monday will publish a special keepsake section in memoriam to Robert F. Kennedy. It will be titled "RFK: He Carried the Torch" and will include full color photos and a narrative account of the New York senator's remarkable life, tragic death and his place in history.

A notice to our readers

Because of the unusual demand for today's Daily News, some readers may receive copies without the usual Saturday supplements. The Daily News will mail these supplements next week to any reader missing them who calls our circulation department at 321-3858.

der, pearl-haired Ethel Kennedy, who came cheerful and hair-ribboned and miniskirted, with her husband while he campaigned in city settlement houses.

"He can't be any older than my teen-age son," a local politician's wife exclaimed about Senator Edward Kennedy, as she scrambled for his autograph at a victory party for a New York Senate hopeful when the Kennedys had backed.

Wherever they went, quipping at each other, handshaking along the streets, or like Jacqueline Kennedy, simply out walking with their shiny-haired, well-mannered children, the Kennedys pulled crowds who wondered at their energy and glamor.

NOW, when they see the Kennedys walk in sadness,

Turn to Page 7, Column 1

445

Fig. 143. Advanced layout techniques. Weekend edition of *Daily Ryersonian* is produced by journalism students at Ryerson Institute of Technology in Toronto, Ont. Regular tabloid pages, above, become one-theme section with pages printed sideways, opposite. Although these look like single full-format page, they are facing tab pages and not on same sheet. Note use of rocket heads. Note, too, folio lines on wide pages. Section is called *TGIF*, "Thank God It's Friday!"

book; formally, as in bound files or microfilm. It is difficult to envision a person searching tapes of news broadcasts as he now scans newspaper files in a library.

Highly important, too, is the authenticity that printing lends to communication. "I know it's so; I read it in the newspaper" is a powerful rebuttal to anyone who doubts the veracity of a report. Newspapers are going to have to work, though, to maintain that attitude. Occasional polls show that there are some instances where the credibility of radio or television has been rated higher than that of newspapers. But these have been somewhat tainted by slanted or ambiguous questions. Overall, newspapers are still chosen by Americans as the most trustworthy medium, though newspaper people certainly cannot afford to rest on their laurels and ignore even the slight gains of competitors.

It is, then, reasonable to suppose that printing will be the major conveyor of news, at least for the foreseeable future. And whether that printing is by relief, intaglio, planographic, or electronic means, the

reader must still be wooed by good layout and typography. And the principles of those arts will not materially change.

John E. Allen, the first editor of *Linotype News,* was also the first man to write and talk about newspaper design as a true art. He never received the acclaim to which he was entitled, but his significant first book—*Newspaper Makeup,* in 1936—still makes good reading and good sense today. Although applications have changed, principles that he promulgated then are perfectly valid today. The few newspaper-design specialists who practice today all acknowledge their indebtedness to Allen and their conviction that the principles used today will be valid tomorrow.

Competition for reader's time will increase. Already, television is finding that it is not sufficient just to be on the scene of an event or to be able to give immediate news flashes. A better educated and more sophisticated audience is demanding higher standards of news coverage in all media. Because standards maintained by newspapers have been so markedly higher than those of radio and television, it means that newspapers must work much harder to continue improvement. It's much easier to gain yardage at the middle of a football field than within the last feet before the opponent's goal line.

Improvement in newspapers must come in all areas. We must improve our techniques of reporting. We must reexamine our fealty to "objective reporting," for we have found that old criterion of "nothing but the

Delaware State News

THE DOWNSTATE DAILY   10c Copy   DOVER, DEL., TUESDAY, APRIL 11, 1967   674-3600   VOL. - 66   NO. - 71

Around the World

Await LBJ; Hope For U.S. $

PUNTA DEL ESTE, Uruguay — Latin-American foreign ministers awaited the arrival of President Johnson today for the inter-American summit conference with hopes he was bringing some concession giving their economies a bigger share of U. S. markets or a freer hand with U. S. aid dollars.

Powell Seen Reelected Today

NEW YORK — Adam Clayton Powell is the overwhelming favorite in today's special election to fill his old House seat.

S. Koreans Kill 4 Invaders

SEOUL, Korea — The South Korean Army killed four North Koreans from two groups that invaded the southern part of the demilitarized zone north of Seoul Monday, an Army spokesman reported.

Liberal Sees Demo Dissent

WASHINGTON — A leader of liberal House Democrats, Rep. James G. O'Hara of Michigan, recently elected chairman of the increasingly influential House Democratic Study Group, predicted today his party soon will propose changes in major administration programs, in hopes of heading off Republican innovations.

Viet Malaria Brought To U.S.

ATLANTA, Ga. — An alarming increase of malaria in the United States has been traced to a Vietnamese parasite which causes a delayed infection in American servicemen, a federal health official said today.

British Deny UN Complaint

LONDON — Foreign Secretary George Brown today rejected complaints of three United Nations peacemakers that the British had failed to help their mission in South Arabia.

High Court Hears Appeals

WASHINGTON — The Supreme Court was asked Monday to declare invalid the Virginia law forbidding the marriage of whites and Negroes.

In another case, the court announced Monday in a rare action that it will keep indefinitely on its docket the case of convicted slayer Melvin Davis Rees Jr., under death sentence in the 1959 slaying of Carroll Vernon Jackson of Louisa County, Va. He was ruled mentally ill last January.

Moslem To Run In India

NEW DELHI, India — Vice President Zakir Husain, a Moslem, was chosen by the ruling Congress party Monday to run for president in mostly Hindu India. He was favored by Prime Minister Indira Gandhi.

Feds Tackle ITT, ABC Case

WASHINGTON — The Justice Department tried to prove today that the American Broadcasting Company, seeking to merge with International Telephone & Telegraph Corp., is not in as weak a competitive position as ITT says it is. ITT contends the merger would make ABC more able to compete with the other two major television networks, CBS and NBC.

And Furthermore...

Samuel J. Fox, executive secretary of the Shell Fisheries Commission, charges that the state auditor is conducting "an investigation, not an audit." Jack Russell reports the details on Page 3. (State News Photo by Dave Smith).

'Camp-In' Tomorrow!

Other towns have their sit-ins, pray-ins, love-ins, and be-ins, but Dover is to see a "camp-in" tomorrow. Area campers — with their rigs — plan to gather at Legislative Hall for the public hearing on state beachland development. Page 7.

Remap Left To Court

The reapportionment of the state will probably fall in the lap of the federal courts since, last night, the General Assembly's Legislative Council threw up its arms in despair at reaching agreement on the problem. Page 3.

Strike Could Pinch You

A coast-to-coast trucking shutdown pinched the supply lifeline of the country's merchants and manufacturers today, amid predictions that consumers soon will feel the squeeze. Page 9.

It Was 'Oscar' Night

The Academy of Motion Pictures Arts and Sciences gave its awards last night . . . . Its "Oscars." A British picture walked away with the greatest number of awards. Only one of the top winners was present to receive his "Oscar." Page 20.

Action Line
674-3600

QUESTION: Is a mailman supposed to stop and pick up mail in a mailbox when the red flag is up, even though he does not have mail to leave? (A. B.)

ANSWER: On rural routes the mailman is supposed to stop when the flag is up. But in the city they are not. (SOURCE: J Clements Bowdle, Dover postmaster.)

AN ACTION LINE FOLLOWUP: On Feb. 1, Action Line answered G. P. of Briar Park, who wanted to know if a mail box at the corner of Voshell Road and Park Lane would be replaced (it was removed because the lock was jammed.) Charles Clemastine, supervisor of mails, reports that the box was replaced shortly after the Action Line appeared in the DSN.

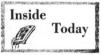

Inside Today

RIOTING STUDENTS and Nashville, Tenn. officials made their first moves toward the conference table today, after three nights of racial violence around the city's Negro college campuses. Page 9.

DOVER'S TRAFFIC problem won't be solved by designating more streets "one-way". The Safety Advisory Committee reported against that idea at last night's council meeting. Acceptance of the report wasn't unanimous, however. Page 7.

SMYRNA'S TOWN CHARTER meeting last night was the scene of a stormy debate on the right to run for office. Page 3.

U. S. WARPLANES delivered heavy attacks against North Viet Nam yesterday, as ground fighting in the south was generally slack. Page 7.

FEATURE	PAGE
Ask Judy	15
Astro-Guide	4
Comics	16
Coming Events	16
Daily Record	17
Dear Abby	4
Doctor Brady	4
Editorial Page	4
Golf Gossip	15
Grist from the Miller	4
Obituaries	17
People Pages	10,11
Rustling Around	4
Sports Pages	13-15
Swing!	4
Television Listings	2
Theatres	4

Cold

Mostly sunny and cooler today with high temperatures 58 to 62. Clear and rather cold with frost likely tonight and lowest 30 to 38. Tomorrow fair with highs in the upper 50s and low 60s. Northerly winds 10 to 20 mph and gusty today becoming variable less than 10 mph tonight. Small craft warnings remain displayed.

Five Day Forecast

Temperatures for the period Tuesday through Saturday will average near normal along the coast and above normal in the interior in the Maryland-Delaware area. Highs will average in the upper 50s and low 60s except near 60 on the coast. Lows will average in the 40s. Cooler Tuesday and Wednesday. Warmer Thursday and Friday. Little or no precipitation.

Fig. 144. *Delaware State News* of Dover, Del., uses imaginative front-page patterns. Paper is printed offset; composition is strikeon.

truth" is often inadequate for conveying "the truth, the whole truth." We must improve photojournalism. We must improve typesetting and printing, especially of process color. And there must be some feasible news ink that won't rub off and make newspaper reading a dirtier job than digging bituminous coal.

There will be improvement in typography and layout too, if only because research in this area is increasing. Much research up to now has been testing principles that earlier printers articulated from instinct or trial and error. A typical example of such research is reported in a Ph.D. dissertation by Richard O. Martin. Dr. Martin reduced type elements to simple rectangles of gray in order to eliminate any subconscious influence that the verbal content might have on the respondent, for he had determined that when the copy consisted of "good" words or conjured up pleasant connotations, the reader liked the typography, too. He tested the completely nonverbal layouts and determined that the long-accepted principles of balance, unity, rhythm, and the like were perfectly valid.

When the art of typography has a completely validated body of principles and references, research can move into entirely new and unexplored areas.

It is worth note that interest in the graphic arts develops in recurring cycles. A period of intense attention to typography and layout is followed by one in which the mechanics of composing and press rooms take paramount interest. The two cycles overlap, of course, just as the esthetics and practicalities of the graphic arts overlap.

John Allen did his significant missionary work in the 1930's. During this period the Ayer Awards were established, another indication of the great interest which his work focused upon newspaper typography. These awards were discontinued in 1968 on the ground that there was no longer a need for them, that they had fulfilled their purpose of spurring interest in newspaper typography and layout. They certainly did do that. Occasionally an absolute typographic aberration won the coveted silver cup, but over the years, Ayer winners were consistently the best-designed papers in the United States and became examples that many editors followed in raising the quality of their newspapers.

Most state newspaper associations give awards for outstanding typography and layout, but there is still a need for a prestigious national prize. The Inland Press Association's annual prizes are the most sought today and have the highest and most valid standards for judging. The name of the group is misleading; although it began as an organization of newspapers from the heartland of the nation, its membership today includes

8 THE GLOBE AND MAIL, SATURDAY, OCT. 26, 1968

CANADA background on events and issues from across the nation

BRITISH COLUMBIA

TEAM pulls itself and the NPA into a Vancouver political confrontation

By JOHN CLARKE

VANCOUVER — The new civic organization known as TEAM for short, or The Electors Action Movement, has been unable to avoid what it fervently hoped for—a confrontation with the ruling Non-Partisan Association, which two months ago was not even sure whether it would be around come election time in December. The NPA will field a full slate and campaign vigorously in opposition to TEAM.

The single issue which has led to revitalization of the NPA is the TEAM proposal for a return to a modified form of the ward system.

The word "ward" has been a dirty word in Vancouver since 1935 when the system of area representation was thrown out by referendum ballot. It had become synonymous with corruption.

Of course, the NPA, whose name signifies its policy of non-involvement in party politics, has tried very hard not to say anything about TEAM's proposal. It can't very well become embroiled in a public controversy on a policy issue since its activity is confined to picking, as candidates, the best people who are free to act without the constraint of any specific political platform.

But a sudden surge of interest followed the TEAM announcement. NPA president Arthur Ross told a press conference: "The NPA will continue to be an effective force in civic affairs and will welcome the opportunity to support any candidate . . . who is dedicated to the principle of good government and not bound by special interests of any self-appointed group."

The NPA has not said flatly it is opposed to the ward system but the inference is clear from Mr. Ross' statement that it was dumped because of the abuses it produced and "there has been no corruption at city hall since the NPA came on the scene 30 years ago."

The introduction of this issue makes the December election more than a simple clash for control. The voters will, in essence, be deciding whether they want a return to area representation because, for TEAM, it is a central theme.

Vancouver is the only major city in Canada without area representation. Its system of the past 33 years has been to elect aldermen at large, each of whom is responsible to the electorate as a whole rather than to geographic sections of it.

In TEAM's view this has led to one of the weakest city governments in Canada, and it has proposed what it calls a modified form of area representation.

Says TEAM president Arthur Phillips: "In the Thirties, all the aldermen were elected from wards but they also had power to spend some of the city's money in their ward and to hand out city jobs. That sort of political patronage was normal in those days but it is unacceptable now. TEAM does not advocate a return to that system."

Instead, it proposed that some aldermen should be elected at large and some from districts. In this way, it hopes to create a balance, with a council capable of taking a broad view while at the same time preserving a more intimate contact with the people. It believes that the people have become so alienated that it is no longer possible for them to make an intelligent choice from 40 or 50 names running for the 10 aldermanic seats.

By making it an issue, TEAM wants the Vancouver taxpayers to think the old problem through again. Vancouver was not alone in suffering from city corruption in the Nineteen Thirties, including one of the most obnoxious practices of the time—"log rolling." One alderman needing support for a project in his ward would get a commitment from others in return for a similar pledge from him when they needed something done.

Now the question is being asked whether replacement of that system by at-large representation was the only answer.

The NPA is in an awkward corner on the issue. It can hardly favor the TEAM idea. But by getting even a negative commitment from its candidates, it could be accused of dictating a policy, something it has sworn never to do.

It looks like a lively election.

NOVA SCOTIA

A most definite no to school integration

By DULCIE CONRAD

HALIFAX — The Halifax Board of School Commissioners decided to extend its 100-year-old "separate school" system into the surrounding suburbs which are destined to become part of the large metropolis through annexation Jan. 1.

In doing so, board members ignored the wishes of thousands of Catholic and non-Catholic petitioners who wanted to see the county's existing "integrated" school system maintained and eventually introduced into the inner-city—mainly for "education, social and economic" reasons.

It was of little consolation to them that the Nineteenth Century dual system would be "phased" in over several years and that no new schools would be built until needed.

This has been the hottest issue before local residents in recent years. Even 500 students attending a fully integrated high school in one of the communities that will be affected pleaded with school board members not to force separate schools into their area.

"It would be morally wrong to do ." they argued.

But they, and the more than 8,000 people who signed petitions, were up against the full weight of the archdiocesan committee on education representing the Roman Catholic laity; the Catholic Women's League, the Knights of Columbus and Archbishop James M. Hayes himself.

Ironically, individual members of the Knights took around one petition that was signed by 7,937 residents of the existing city and the areas to be annexed opposing the separate school system. These petitioners plan to appeal the board's decision to Education Minister Gerald Doucet. And a number of suburban associations have already gone on record to continue their opposition to the extension of the separate school system after annexation, or any time in the future.

Doucet: an appeal by the petitioners.

For the most part, those who reside in the five mushrooming suburban communities affected are young, articulate professionals whose children have always attended integrated schools. Halifax County school administrators have also kept an open policy toward religious education.

In Halifax, where Roman Catholics constitute about 53 per cent of the population, schools have been built for Catholic students and others have been built, in the same district, for non-Catholic students. Although every parent has the right to send a child to any school within his district, last year only 98 children out of a student population of 18,000 enrolled on this basis.

In Halifax, Catholic students attend one centrally located senior high school where the boys are segregated from the girls. A senior high school for non-Catholics is nearby. In Halifax County, all the high schools are integrated.

Last year, when a high school was needed for north-end students, school commissioners were forced to add on to each of the two existing schools because "politically aware" city fathers dilly-dallied too long on where to build the "integrated" high school. Their excuse was that they could not find an appropriate site.

Most taxpayers are quick to point out that this type of thinking is "too expensive" to maintain at a time when education costs are spiralling.

As soon as annexation became a reality, the school board (comprised of seven aldermen and six Government-appointed members) knew the issue would have to be resolved. Last May, it appointed from among its members a special six-man committee to make a comprehensive study and to see what was done elsewhere in Canada. During the intervening months, the committee met in secret. But leaks to the press indicated four of its members favored extending the separate school system into country areas to be annexed, which was recommended to the full school board early this week.

Before a hushed, packed public gallery at city hall, board members voted 9-3 to extend the separate school system.

Ratepayers, who were not permitted to speak, were incensed after the meeting because the "undemocratic" decision was made by a board on which there was no representation from the areas to be annexed.

They also complained bitterly that board members had placed "too much emphasis" on the religious aspect instead of "investigating all the financial and social implications."

But there were only three members of the school board who agreed with them. Board chairman Robert McQuinn, a Government-appointed member and local druggist, did not vote. Of the nine others, seven are known Catholics.

Some residents feel the issue could have been avoided if the three-man Government-appointed Board of Public Utilities, which ordered the annexation, had also ruled on this contentious problem.

ONTARIO

Brunelle: a helping (Tory) hand for the North

Brunelle: a plan for developing North.

By DONALD NEWMAN

By tradition, Conservatives stand for private enterprise—dedicated to the proposition that a good government is one which does not get in the way of the private sector of the economy.

But since Confederation the realities of developing a huge country with a miniscule population have frequently forced the Conservatives to assess that doctrine. And, when they have found it wanting, they have shown a willingness to bend it to fit the situation.

Sir John A. Macdonald realized that to develop and populate the western frontier, he would have to commit the resources of his Government behind the Canadian Pacific Railway. Now, Lands and Forests Minister Rene Brunelle has become the latest Conservative to publicly endorse government participation in developing Canada's last frontier; the North.

Speaking this month to the Canadian Council of Resources Ministers, meeting in Halifax, Mr. Brunelle reviewed the efforts of private capital in developing the North—and found them wanting.

With the exception of cities like Sudbury, Sault Ste. Marie and the Lakehead, Mr. Brunelle said private development in Northern Ontario has generally been limited to small communities based on only one, primary resource industry.

"While regional endowment in natural resources can be a positive asset leading to growth, total dependence on such resources can also lead to narrow, and often precariously based, regional economies . . ."

In addition to the economic uncertainties, Mr. Brunelle said that the present system of developing Northern Canada has created "small, scattered, and in many cases isolated" communities, often lacking sewer and water facilities, medical and dental services and limited secondary educational opportunities.

To further complicate matters, he pointed out that processing of the natural resources into some form of manufactured, finished product is generally uneconomic because of the distance between the course of the resource and the heavily populated southern areas where the goods are marketed.

Mr. Brunelle's conclusion: "This hit and miss, unplanned development based solely on the discovery of isolated resources is not the answer to northern development . . .

"The answer lies in planned political and administrative decisions aimed at determining the form and character northern development should take."

He proposed that provincial governments undertake a long-term planning program for northern development, starting with a stock-taking of known resources in their northern environs.

This should be followed by an assessment of the "socio-economic potential" of each resource to determine a priority scale for development of them.

And, he added: "The plan should also include a schedule for providing accessories to development, namely access, transportation, population centres with adequate educational and health facilities and adequate local government."

QUEBEC

Getting the word on de Gaulle's France

By FRANK HOWARD

QUEBEC — Some time before the end of next month the first contingent of French-speaking journalists will be boarding a trans-Atlantic jet for a six-month stay in France at the expense of the governments of France and Quebec.

The first 13, all employed by Quebec news media, were chosen earlier this week by a seven-man jury made up of Government officials from the two governments and representatives of the Quebec press.

The program includes travel throughout France, courses in news-handling, practical work with agencies like Agence-France-Presse and the state-owned broadcasting system (ORTF).

The return fare is paid by France, as are travelling expenses in France. Paris also gives an allowance of $330 a month for living expenses.

To this amount will be added a $250 grant from the Quebec Government.

Marcel Thivierge, second in command of the Quebec Government Information Service and a member of the jury which selected the first contingent, said that if the program works out, groups of 13 will be sent to France every six months.

The first group was made up only of members of the press.

The program is available to other French-speaking former colonies of France. Also French-speaking journalists from outside Quebec may apply. But their applications will be handled outside the Quebec-France program.

For example, on the first trip there will be a 14th Canadian, an employee of the Ottawa daily Le Droit. His application was handled by the French Embassy in the federal capital.

The date for the departure has not yet been set, but it is expected before the end of November, Mr. Thivierge said.

Other members of the jury were A. F. Mercier, general manager of the Quebec daily Le Soleil and a representative of the Daily Newspaper Publishers' Association of the province; Mrs. Therese Bergeron, a representative of the Union Canadienne des Journalistes de Langue Francaise; Gilles Gariepy, a representative of L'Alliance Canadienne des Syndicaliste Journalistes and a reporter for the Montreal daily Le Devoir; Jacques de Rome, representing the Quebec Department of Inter-Governmental Affairs; Philippe Bey, information officer at the French Consulate-General here (a second member of the consulate staff has been assigned to the jury, but he did not participate in the first batch of selections) and a representative of the Quebec Weekly Newspapers Association.

The list of those selected for the first trip includes Jean-Paul de Lagrave, Gilles Pratte and Andre Trudelle, all of the Montreail daily La Presse, Andre Dionne, Jean-Claude Rivard and Anne-Marie Voisard of Quebec's Le Soleil, Guy Deshaies and Nicole Gladu of Montreal-Matin, Normand Lassonde of L'Action (Quebec), Roch Poisson of Photo-Journal (Montreal), Virginie Boulanger, La Patrie (Montreal), Patrice Julien (Channel 10, Montreal), Real Pelletiere, CBC Montreal.

Manning: Social Credit with him is one thing, and without him it is another.

ALBERTA

Mr. Manning leaves a taxing question

By BERNARD TIERNEY

EDMONTON — It's just possible that when Premier E. C. Manning announced his decision to retire last month he saved Albertans from the imposition of a sales tax.

Last spring, after handing the Alberta Legislature its third consecutive deficit budget, Provincial Treasurer A. O. Aalborg gloomily suggested that the introduction of a sales tax was "something to think about" in the immediate future.

Since then things have gone from bad to worse. It was learned last week, for example, that the 1967-68 fiscal year deficit, orginally estimated at $67-million, had in fact turned out to be more than $99-million.

That, Provincial Auditor Keith Huckvale pointed out, meant that the province had gone into the red $180-million in just two years; it meant that the province's treasury surplus, accumulated over the years, was down to $512-million, $355-million of which is tied up in non-liquid investment; which in turn meant that with liquid reserves of just $157-million, and with an anticipated deficit of at least $70-million in the 1968-69 fiscal year, the province must, very soon, think in terms of either balanced budgets (and hence higher taxes, or reduced expenditures) or a return to direct borrowing.

Since Alberta's Social Credit Government is not noted for its enthusiasm for direct borrowing, it might easily have been supposed that higher taxation lay in the future for Albertans. And, in view of Mr. Aalborg's gloomy warning seven months ago, it might easily have been supposed that this higher taxation might come in the form of a sales tax.

But no. Mr. Aalbourg just last month, when he must have been aware of the larger-than-expected deficit for the 1967-68 fiscal year, announced that a sales tax would be "deferred indefinitely" if he had anything to do with it.

What changed the gloomy warning to a promise to fight sales tax?

The Manning resignation comes easily to mind. And, in the process, it poses an interesting question: why should Alberta's Socreds, with a 47-seat majority in the Legislature, and with up to three years before they must call an election, be concerned about imposing a sales tax, even though Mr. Manning is retiring?

The obvious answer, of course, is that Social Credit with Mr. Manning is one thing to Alberta's voters, and Social Credit without Mr. Manning yet another, and the introduction of a sales tax would only emphasize that difference in the mind of the voter.

It is possible that the Socreds Mr. Manning leaves behind do not intend to wait three years before going to the voters. It could be that they have decided the advantages of waiting and allowing a new leader to establish himself are outweighed by the advantages of going quickly to the electorate for a fresh mandate while Mr. Manning and Social Credit are still, in the mind of the Alberta voter, synonymous.

With an election in the offing, who needs a sales tax?

MANITOBA

Will the city slickers equal the country boys?

By ELLEN SIMMONS

WINNIPEG — Perhaps nowhere in Canada is urban-country rivalry more pronounced than in Manitoba. More than half of the province's 974,000 people live in one urban area—Metropolitan Winnipeg. Yet, in spite of this, and in spite of the modest influx of industry into the province, Manitoba remains, politically at least, rural and farm oriented.

There are 57 seats in the Manitoba Legislature. Of these, only 20 are allotted to the 500,000 urban voters in Metro Winnipeg. The weighting in favor of country over city is such that, by statute, it takes seven city votes to match four rural votes. And the disparity was even greater 10 years ago.

Last week, however, the Manitoba Electoral Divisions Boundaries Commission unveiled a new political map, which, if adopted, will bring the province much closer to representation by population. The commission recommends that Metro Winnipeg be given seven additional seats, bringing representation in the urban area to 27 of the 57 seats. Rural and Northern Manitoba together would have 30 seats, with one new seat to be created in the north around the nickel mining town of Thompson.

The commission which proposed the redistribution is politically independent. It consists of Chief Justice C. Rhodes Smith of the Manitoba Court of Appeal, Dr. H. H. Saunderson, president of the University of Manitoba, and Charland Prud'homme, chief electoral officer for the province. It is claimed to be the first politically independent electoral boundaries commission in Canada, and possibly in the Commonwealth.

The formula used by the commission to determine representation in the redistribution was essentially simple: it divided the number of people by the number of seats and allowed a tolerance of 25 per cent to permit the drawing of more viable boundaries. The result of this redraft is that the largest riding, Transcona in Greater Winnipeg, will have 19,700 people; the smallest, the proposed new constituency of Thompson in Northern Manitoba, will have 12,600.

The commission intends to hold five public hearings throughout the province to audit comments and complaints. After that, the proposals must go to the Legislature for approval.

Some opposition can be expected. Most of it will probably come from rural electors, who want the tradition of rural domination of the Legislature maintained.

At a two-day caucus of Government MLAs after the report was released several Conservatives were reported to favor limiting the number of new urban seats to five. So far, there has been no official pronouncement from either the Liberals or the New Democrats. But Liberal strength now lies almost entirely in rural areas and the official Opposition can hardly be happy over the prospect of seeing so many of its long-captive ridings disappear. The NDP, on the other hand, draws most of its strength from the city. The party now has 11 members to the Liberals' 13. Should the proposed redistribution be enacted, the next provincial election should produce exciting battles throughout the Metropolitan area.

Fig. 145. Modular makeup. ***Toronto*** **(Ont.)** ***Globe and Mail*** **emphasizes rectangular elements on inside page by use of borders.**

Saigon Insisting on 'Guarantee' of N. Viet Lull

Both Vietnams Said Blocking Bomb Halt

WASHINGTON (AP) — President Johnson apparently has run into difficulties in both Hanoi and Saigon in his efforts to arrange final terms for an end to the U.S. bombing of North Vietnam.

Before ordering a bombing halt, U.S. officials said, Johnson is determined to receive North Vietnamese assurances his action will move forward the deadlocked Paris peace talks and freeze the level of combat in South Vietnam.

There still has been no word here of those assurances.

South Vietnamese leaders are reported meanwhile to have refused to sign a joint declaration proposed by the United States on halting the bombing.

President Nguyen Van Thieu is said to have several objections, among them that there should be no end to the bombing of the North unless Hanoi gives firm guarantees it will not escalate the war.

U.S. Ambassador Ellsworth Bunker, who met with Thieu three times Wednesday, met again with the South Vietnamese president today, presumably in an effort to iron out the difficulties.

White House press secretary George Christian said today, "I have nothing to report to you beyond what was said yesterday" when he issued a statement saying there was no basic change in the Vietnam situation and "no breakthrough."

Christian would not comment on the meetings between Bunker and Thieu, nor would he discuss a statement by Australian Prime Minister John Gordon that Johnson had been in touch with him concerning a possible bombing halt.

Johnson administration leaders generally sought to keep bombing-halt negotiations secret. But information available in official quarters here is focused on the problems with North Vietnam.

Officials said privately they must know in advance what would happen in the field if the United States ended the bombing.

Johnson is believed seeking assurances from Hanoi that the lull in the fighting, the decline in troop infiltrations from the North to the South and the withdrawal of economy units from around South Vietnamese cities would not be reversed following an end of the bombing.

South Vietnamese leaders appear to object to Johnson accepting whatever North Vietnamese "assurance he might get." They are insisting on "guarantees" that North Vietnam will not escalate the war.

An end to the bombing has been the essential North Vietnamese condition for moving the Paris peace talks into a new, second phase in which specific issues involved in ending the war would be negotiated.

The United States has committed itself to include the South Vietnamese government in the phase and North Vietnam says the South Vietnamese National Liberation Front must be a participant.

Resolution of this problem by including both would be a measure of North Vietnam's seriousness in the view of U.S. officials.

Another concern is restoring the zone dividing North and South Vietnam as a demilitarized buffer. The United States frequently has demanded this in the Paris talks as an important step in de-escalating the war.

Various other steps, such as ending infiltration through Laos and Cambodia also have been demanded by the United States.

Air strikes, restricted to North Vietnam's southern panhandle since March 31, are continuing meanwhile and more are planned for today. At the sane time Pentagon figures show that bad weather has reduced sorties over the North by 30 per cent since midsummer.

The weather could be expected to drop the level even further in the next six months, a factor that likely would be considered in weighing the risks of a full halt.

In Paris, U.S. and North Vietnamese peace negotiators met for the 26th time, and the American spokesman said afterward there had been movement but "I cannot characterize it as progress."

Initially U.S. spokesmen refused either to confirm or deny Wednesday the possibility of a break. But in midmorning the White House issued a statement that U.S. policy was unchanged and there had been "no breakthrough" on the bombing issue.

Vice - President Hubert H. Humphrey said in a speech to suburban St. Louis housewives that the matter at the moment was "very sensitive," and added, "for me at this stage to say anything further would add only to the confusion which you already have."

Stock Market In Peace Rally

NEW YORK (AP) — The stock market embarked on a "peace rally" in record-breaking trading today, making a big gain at the start but trimming it in early afternoon.

The Dow Jones industrial average at noon was up 5.28 at 960.59, having backpedaled from a rise of 7.46 in the first half hour.

Rumors that a Vietnam bombing halt was imminent accounted for a big buildup of orders, many of them when the market was closed Wednesday. This was added to the normal pent-up demand on a mid-week closing.

Even though President Johnson denied that a bombing halt was near, Wall Street continued to act as if it were a fact and many traders climbed aboard the band-wagon.

First-hour volume was a record 7.66 million shares, topping the previous record of 6.74 million made on Oct. 3.

Stocks likely to be helped by peace were among the gainers, such as savings-and-loan and building issues. The most-active of the S-&-Ls was Great Western Financial, up a fraction, Among building materials, U.S. Gypsum gained more than 2 and Johns-Manville 1.

Demand among mutual funds, pension funds and other big institutions accounted for much of the increased trading and was reflected by the transfer of huge blocks. Among these were 510,000 shares of Bristol-Myers, unchanged at 75½, and 304,200 shares of National Dairy, up 1⅜ at 45.

Turnover for the first two hours was 11.43 million shares compared with 5.87 million for the like period Tuesday.

Wall Streeters thought it possible the day's total might top the historic record of 21.35 million shares of June 13.

The Associated Press average of 60 stocks at noon was up 1.6 at 356.6 with industrials up 2.9, rails up .4 and utilities up .5.

Gains outnumbered losses by something more than 2 to 1, paring the early ratio of 3 to 1.

Among volume leaders, General Electric gained more than 3, Magnavox, United Utilities preferred, Montgomery Ward, Chrysler, General Motors and Metromedia a point or better.

(Associated Press Wirephoto)

Retired Gen. Curtis E. LeMay (right), candidate for vice president with George Wallace, shakes hands with U.S. commander in Vietnam Gen. Creighton Abrams after a briefing session in Vietnam. LeMay is on a fact finding tour. A hawk who has suggested bombing North Vietnam "back to the Stone Age," LeMay's visit coincides with U.S. efforts to achieve a bombing halt as a preliminary step toward peace.

Thursday, October 17, 1968

WAUKESHA FREEMAN

The Articulate Voice of Waukesha County

Single Copy 10c • Home Delivery 50c

109th Year—No. 171 | Two Sections, 20 Pages

Michael Wilson

Sussex Marine Killed in Vietnam

SUSSEX — A 20 year old Sussex man has died of wounds he suffered while on patrol with the Marines in Vietnam.

Marine Pfc. Michael J. Wilson, son of Mr. and Mrs. Orden R. Wilson, 211 W. Main St., Sussex, had been wounded Sept. 27 in the Quang Nam province. He died Monday, according to his father.

Wilson entered the Marine Corps in June, 1967. He had been in Vietnam since December 1.

He was a 1966 Hamilton High school graduate and had worked for the A. O. Smith Corp.

Besides his parents, he is survived by brother Robert, at home.

Funeral arrangements are pending at the A. A. Schmidt Funeral home, Menomonee Falls.

Sen. Benson Is M.C.

Taylor Benson, Democratic candidate for lieutenant governor of Wisconsin, will be master of ceremonies at the Waukesha County Democratic party fund-raising dinner Saturday.

The dinner will be held at Clifford's Supper Club on Hy. 24 in Muskego. Among those expected to attend is Dr. Carol Baumann, ninth congressional district candidate.

Czech Sendoff for Russ Premier Is Cool One

PRAGUE (AP) — Soviet Premier Alexei N. Kosygin was given a correct but cool sendoff today before he returned to Moscow after signing a treaty permitting some Soviet troops to remain in Czechoslovakia.

Kosygin said Wednesday most of the occupation troops, including all from Poland, East Germany, Hungary and Bulgaria, would be withdrawn soon. But he gave no indication of how many Soviet troops will stay. Estimates of the occupation force range from 250,000 to 500,000.

Details of the agreement, signed by Kosygin and Czechoslovakia's premier, Oldrich Cernik, may be made public Friday when it comes up for ratification in the National Assembly.

Kosygin, Foreign Minister Andrei A. Gromyko and Defense Minister Marshal Andrei A. Grechko were seen off at Prague Airport by Cernik and other government officials. But the leave taking was as cool as was the Russians' reception on arrival 24 hours earlier.

Some of the Soviet troops, who entered Czechoslovakia Aug. 20-21 with Warsaw Pact allies to reverse the country's liberalization drive, already were settling into permanent installations.

At Mlada Boleslav, an automobile manufacturing town north of Prague, Soviet troops moved into vacated Czechoslovak barracks that will become one of their major installations.

The Soviet command was quoted by a Prague newspaper, Svoboda—Freedom—as saying that rank-and-file soldiers will be allowed in town only in organized groups and only officers and cadre will have free movement.

Astronauts Take Audience on Tour

SPACE CENTER, HOUSTON (AP) — Blinking like a star, Apollo 7 provided a sparkling predawn show for early-rising Californians today, minutes before the astronauts took television viewers on a matter-of-fact tour of their smooth-running spaceship.

Numerous residents in the Los Angeles area gathered in small groups and stepped from their cars to view Apollo 7 as it streaked from horizon to horizon in just two minutes at 17,500 miles an hour.

"It was just a big, blinking star—that's all it looked like to me," said one observer. "And it was really easy to distinguish because it was the only thing up there except the moon."

Navy Capt. Walter M. Schirra Jr., Air Force Maj. Donn F. Eisele and civilian astronaut Walter Cunningham were unaware that they were observed as they sped on the downhill leg of their marathon mission.

With more than half the planned 11-day flight behind them, they reported they were eager to hurry home.

They took time from the demanding chore of checking the many complex systems of their space chariot this morning to beam episode No. 4 of the Wally, Walt and Donn television show as Apollo 7 zipped south of the southern United States.

It was a routine 12-minute tour of the space cabin.

Mrs. Eisele and two of her children, Melinda, 14, and Donn H., 12, missed the telecast because they were outside hoping to glimpse the spaceship as it zipped over Houston.

Apollo 7 is expected to be visible in the Houston area at dawn Friday, with the sighting zone moving farther east with each progressive day.

Public Works Budget Of $1.1 Million OK'd

ALTHOUGH Waukesha's budget committee Wednesday cut more than $372,000 from the improvement projects and equipment budget of the public works department, the committee approved expenditures of $1,163,357 for 1969.

The approved figure represents a 30 per cent increase over the 1969 budget figure of $812,905.

The largest increase in expenditures was approved for sanitary sewer and drain projects. The total tentatively approved for 1969 is $383,000, an increase of 71 per cent over the 1968 figure.

The committee approved an $80,000 project to install an interceptor sewer from White Rock Ave. to Jefferson Ave. (An interceptor sewer is one that collects sewage for a large area and carries it to a point of disposal.)

Other projects included $60,000 for a Hy. A pumping station to the Kings Park subdivision and $46,000 for a force main at the Greenmeadow pump station.

The approved roadway of streets budget totaled $314,500, a 24 per cent increase over 1968. The budget committee approved $180,000 for street paving projects totaling 5.7 miles. This included the following paving work: Lowell Heights and Waldale subdivisions; Grandview Blvd. from Summit Ave. to Northview Rd.; the remaining unpaved half of Greenway Terr.; Hine Ave. from Madison St. to Summit Ave. and Madison St. from Moreland Blvd. to Washington Ave.

A sum of $50,000 was approved for the right-of-way purchase for the Barstow St. project, but sewer, drainage and paving funds for the project were not approved this year. City Engineer Rodney VandenNoven explained the approved money would be used to purchase land to widen the street. He said the Parking Utility might purchase the remaining part of the land.

The committee approved $377,500 for storm sewer projects, a 7 per cent increase, after slashing $115,900 from the department's request.

Storm sewer projects were approved for the following areas: Merrill Crest subdivision, $25,000; Gascoigne subdivision, $5,500; Sunset Heights subdivision, $13,000; a 50 per cent reduction in the request to $12,500 for a drainage ditch from the Fox River to Center Rd.; sewers on Progress Ave. from Sentry Dr. to Prairie Ave., $26,000; Sunset Dr. to West Ave., $30,000; University Dr. from Summit Ave. north, $25,000; Pebble Valley subdivision, $25,000; South Park Estates II, $25,000; Kings Park subdivision, $25,000; Center Rd. from Burr Oak Blvd. north, $46,000; the Borlen property from Racine Ave. south, $35,000; Morey St. from Pewaukee Rd. to Morey Lane, $11,500; Greenway Terrace subdivision, $25,000.

The committee approved expenditures of $19,000 for street signs and guides. This includes work on the Moreland Blvd., White Rock Ave. intersection and $9,000 to upgrade school crossing signals. The 1968 budget figure was $26,500.

The committee cut the total street lighting requests of $4,500 from the budget. Last year $23,000 was allocated.

An equipment budget of $69,857, representing a 7 per cent increase, was approved by the committee. Two items, a new air compressor and a back hoe costing a total of $17,000, were deleted from the budget request.

Rain and Cooler

WISCONSIN — Showers likely and cooler tonight and Friday. Lows tonight in the 40s extreme northwest to around 60 extreme southeast. Highs Friday in the 40s northwest, in the 50s southeast.

Minimum temperature: 63.
Mean temperature: 70.
Temperature range here yesterday: high, 80; low, 60.
Temperature range here a year ago: high, 51; low, 41.
Precipitation in 24 hours ending at noon: None.

Local Hourly Temperature

Hour	7	8	9	10	11	12
Temp	65	66	67	68	70	70

Tosa Man Dies During Exercise

A Wauwatosa man, who was told to lose weight, died of a heart attack at 6:15 p.m. Wednesday while exercising in the YMCA gymnasium.

The victim was Allan Barry, 35, of 9239 W. Mt. Vernon Ave. He was pronounced dead at Waukesha Memorial Hospital.

Coroner James Welch said Barry had seen a physician a week earlier and was told he had high blood pressure and a high chloresterol count in the blood.

A prospective employer had reportedly told Barry to lose weight if he wanted to be hired in an apprenticeship program.

Barry was on the basketball court shooting baskets with a group of other men when he collapsed and died, Welch said.

N.Y. High Court Takes McCarthy Off Ballot

ALBANY, N. Y. (AP) — U.S. Sen. Eugene F. McCarthy was ruled off the presidential ballot today in New York State by the state's highest court, which held that his name should not be listed against his will.

The unanimous decision by the Court of Appeals, overturning a lower-court decision, came as good news to supporters of Vice President Hubert H. Humphrey, who had feared that McCarthy's presence on the ballot would undermine Humphrey's chances of winning New York's 43 electoral votes.

McCarthy himself had formally declined the nomination to be the presidential candidate of the newly formed Coalition party, a Vietnam peace group, but the party insisted anyway that its 43 electors, pledged to him, had a right to appear on the ballot.

The Court of Appeals agreed with the original decision of New York's secretary of state that McCarthy should not have to appear on the ballot against his will. The secretary of state's finding was overruled by the Appellate Division of State Supreme Court. The Court of Appeals reversed the Appellate Division.

Medicaid Request Lowered to $4 Million

Welfare Budget Cut by 8 Per Cent

THE COUNTY Board's Finance Committee Wednesday recommended cuts totalling $578,905 in the Social Service Department's 1969 budget.

The 8 per cent cut, a recommendation to the County Board, reduces the department's total budget to about $6,374,000.

The recommended total budget represents an increase of 23 per cent over the department's 1968 budget of $4.9 million.

The county's share of the $6,374,000 budget is approximately $1,852,000 with state and federal aids supplying the remaining $4,522,000.

Funds for three programs were cut by the committee. Medical assistance funds were reduced from $4.4 million to $4 million, a cut of nine per cent. The county's share of the recommended budget is about $950,000. Director Joseph Himden once said as much as $5.5 million might be needed for the program.

General relief which is totally supported by county funds, was cut from $110,000 to $105,000.

Aid to Dependent Children (ADC) funds were cut by 12 per cent from $1,473,905 to $1.3 million. The department has asked for $1,573,053.

The county's share of the ADC expenditures is about $416,000 with the remainder to come from state and federal funds.

Speaking of the ADC program Sup. Herbert J. Gross, Menomonee Falls said he was told Social Services had more discretionary powers in that item than in any other. He thought the department should try to live within the budget ultimately set by the County Board.

Sup. Howard Halaska, Elm Grove, chairman of the Social Services board, said the board's requests were as low as he thought they could be and added that if any items were cut, he was sure a request would have to be made later in the year for additional funds.

According to the budget procedure, the department initially makes a budget request which is then reviewed by the Social Services board. The Finance Committee then reviews the total budget request.

All cuts in the budget were made from the Social Services Board requests, which in all cases were lower than the requests from the department.

For 1968 the county budgeted $600,000 for its share of medical assistance (medicaid) expenditures. The sum will be insufficient by at least $240,000.

The County Board last month refused to appropriate the additional funds. A declaratory judgement from a Circuit Court is to be sought to determine the legality of the board's refusal.

Not included in the 1969 budget request is any sum which may be needed for additional personnel and for anticipated — but not yet negotiated — pay increases for present employes.

Himden has said that 17 new employes will be needed in 1969. The department now has about 90.

Fig. 146. Modular makeup. While less obvious than page opposite, makeup of *Waukesha* (Wis.) *Freeman* is also modular. Only ASTRONAUT story in cols. 2-3 is not rectangular. Note use of inset 2-line initials on most stories.

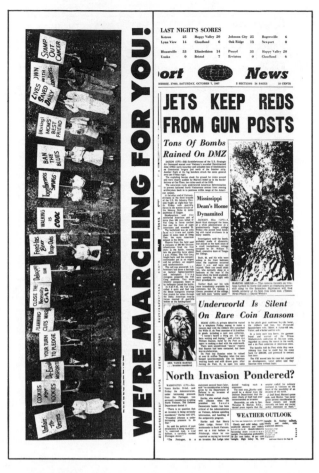

Fig. 147. Half-page format. Cooperation between *Kingsport* (Tenn.) *News* and Mead Paper Co. resulted in unique half-page flap over front page. Closed flap, above, has large picture, running sideways, of Community Chest volunteers. Headline in red. Reverse of flap, opposite, is institutional advertisement for charity drive.

newspapers from California to New Jersey. A more descriptive name for its awards might extend their appeal.

The ferment of typographic change bubbled merrily through the Thirties, even though the Great Depression had stifled mechanical research and development. World War II halted both cycles. Printing manufacturers made armament; newspapers, patching together makeshift staffs to replace the men in uniform, had no time to experiment with typography.

With the end of the war, the cycle of mechanical improvement was resumed. The publishers' concern was directed to their composing rooms especially, for during the war years worn linecasters could not be re-

placed and could be repaired only with makeshift expedients. Now manufacturers resumed building graphic arts machines and business was brisk. The Comet Linotype, which speeded linecasting to 12 lines per minute, was a product of this era. Corporate skills developed during military manufacturing were put to good use too. Mergenthaler, for instance, had made telescopic gunnery equipment for the Navy. Its work in optics and electronics was the base on which its Linofilm was invented and developed.

The mid-1950's saw another period of keen interest in newspaper typography and fruitful experiment. This was followed by the mushrooming of phototypesetting and the introduction of the computer into the composing room. Now typography has become Topic A again.

It's interesting to note that most of the significant typographic innovations of the current cycle have been developed by the daily press. This is the exact opposite of what took place in previous cycles. In the earlier periods it was the weekly editor who was the creator and innovator. The

THE Spectator

WEST FRANKLIN
RURAL-URBAN

OHIO'S LARGEST WEEKLY NEWSPAPER

Vol. XI, No. 35   Total No. 555   Columbus, Ohio, Thursday, November 18, 1966   Second Class Postage Paid at Columbus, Ohio   10 Cents

Lawsuit Is Filed In
Mineral Rights Feud

Columbus Attorney John Dunkle has filed a $110,000 lawsuit in Franklin County Common Pleas Court that is expected to legally clear up the question of mineral rights in a Darbydale sand and gravel "mine." The suit, filed on behalf of Warren A. Creamer, 8326 Harrisburg-pk, Orient, names Edward A. Tonti, Skyview Sand and Gravel, Inc. and Karl L. Trinkle as defendants. Dunkle claims Creamer still retains mineral rights to the mine even though Tonti is the owner of the Darbydale property. The suit, for damages, a detailed accounting of minerals extracted and a possible restraining order from "further depleting minerals from the field," was filed Tuesday.

New Church Is Eyed
In Ridgewood Area

The Methodist Church will organize a new congregation in the Ridgewood area of Norwich Township, east of Hilliard. Rev. Donald C. Dixon, 27, now serving the Carroll Methodist charge in Fairfield County, has been appointed pastor. The first service of the new congregation is expected to be held after the first of the year. The exact site of the church has not yet been determined. It will be located within the area bounded by the Scioto River on the east, Dublin on the north and the proposed outerbelt east of Hilliard. The southern boundary is about five miles south of Dublin. Methodist officials say they've decided a church is needed in that area based upon present building activity and an expected six-fold increase in population within the next 25 years. Arrangements have been made to rent the facilities of Ridgewood Elementary School, 4199 Dublin-rd, for services until a church can be built.

REV. DONALD DIXON

Davis Resigns State
Appraisal Position

A State Highway administrator has resigned his post to go into business for himself at more money. Hugh M. B. Davis, administrator for the state's right-of-way department, says his resignation is effective Dec. 15. He says he's found his job of appraising for the state can be more lucrative doing appraisals on his own. The state job pays $10,900. No successor has been named. Next in line is Daniel Billingsley, Davis' assistant. Davie, 55, resides at 2940 Neil-av. He has been in the state appraisal bureau since January, 1956.

Hilliard Post Plans
Decorating Contest

American Legion Memorial Post 614, Hilliard, will sponsor a "Christmas Greetings" home decoration contest for residents in that municipality. Judging will take place Wednesday, Dec. 29. Plaques will be awarded for the most attractive homes in three classes: (1) Door and entrance, (2) Window, and (3) Overall. All homes in Hilliard are eligible. No registration is necessary.

Deadlines Moved Up

The Spectator will be delivered the day before Thanksgiving — one day earlier than usual.

Advertising and publicity deadlines for the Thanksgiving edition have been moved forward.

Display ad copy for all paper combinations must be at The Spectator office by 5 p.m. Thursday, Nov. 18; individual papers must have material by 5 p.m. Friday, Nov. 19.

Classified ad copy will be accepted until noon Monday, Nov. 22. For the convenience of advertisers, the switchboard will be open until 3:30 p.m. Saturday, Nov. 20. Society and church news will not be accepted after 3 p.m. Friday, Nov. 19. All other items must be in the office by 10 a.m. Monday, Nov. 22.

Inside   The Spectator

BURLY-Q? In dear ole' innocent Columbus? Mercy! — Editorial Page.

FREEDOM-RINGERS are not too free with information on themselves. See Page 7.

TRIBUTES to John F. Kennedy — Read "Still Reason To Weep" (Editorial Page) and "A Man's Truest Monument (Metro Page 3).

Not Every Hero Wears A Medal

It was a clear day. Frederick Richard Bebb, 73, 4941 Beacon Hill-rd, was helping Prairie Norton School children across busy W. Broad-st where he works for $25 a week as a safety patrolman. A car sped east . . . showed no signs of stopping for the red light at that Buena Vista intersection in New Rome. Bebb heard the kids scream . . . he instinctively leaped in front of the automobile. The motorist saw him and skidded his car to the side of the road . . . missing Bebb by inches. There's no medal on Bebb's chest for his deed, no letter of citation. Men like him don't need them.

West Jefferson Is Going Broke;
Streetlights, Salary Cuts Seen

A Time For Nature . . .

It's Fall in Ohio . . . a time to get close to nature before everything green and alive dies for the winter. Kathy Harp, 17, 306 Powder Mill-ln, pauses to appreciate the plight of the squirrel as he stores his supply of winter food.

Levy Defeat Is
The Prime Factor

By JOHN AUBLE, JR.

West Jefferson Mayor-elect Gene Graves was sullen. His dark eyes searched for an answer. His village is going broke . . . dead broke.

Solicitor William Culp tried to be of comfort.

★

TUESDAY'S W-J RECOUNT RESULTS:

D. Gene Graves — 481
Luther Forbis — 471
Richard Ater — 301

★

"This happened one other time," Culp said. "Back in the early Fifties."

But things were cheaper then. The village ran up an electric bill of $2800 to keep street lights on. It would cost almost too much to ask for credit again.

(Continued on Page 7)

★ ★ ★

.25-Caliber Pistol
Is Found In W-J

By JOHN AUBLE, JR.

A quick-thinking West Jefferson woman put a .25-caliber pistol in the hands of Madison County Sheriff authorities Monday night — the same type of gun used to kill service station attendants Joseph Scowden on Oct. 2 and Claude Quesenberry on Nov. 11.

Sheriff's deputies say that preliminary ballistics checks indicate that the pistol is not the same weapon used in the two killings but they have not finished investigating the case.

Two Georgesville teenagers, who claimed they found the pistol, tried to sell it Monday in Ada's Market on W. Town-st in West Jefferson at about

(Continued on Page 7)

Cosmetology Trade Taught South-Western Girls

Grove City, Pleasant View and Franklin Heights seniors are going at it with powder 'n paint as the South-Western School District tests the values of technical training.

One of the most unusual vocational fields to be taught at the Grove City Technical High on Park-st is cosmetology — the scientific study and practice of beauty culture.

The students spend four-and-a-half hours per day at the study which will make them eligible to take the State Cosmetology Board examination upon graduation qualifying them for immediate employment.

For nominal fees, they beautify women customers in the Grove City area. The students must, however, practice for 300 hours on mannequins before testing their talents on the patrons.

The course — in addition to regular high school studies — is taught by Patricia Rutherford, a registered cosmetologist hired by the South-Western district to instruct the young hairsetters.

Under her leadership the girls learn the fine art of shampooing, hair cutting, facials, manicures and other facets of the trade.

There's also instruction in skin diseases, anatomy, chemistry and electricity — all subjects pertinent to the field.

The school system says that "cosmetology, as a professional career, offers many opportunities and rewards. Both are available to those students who receive a thorough training, who have developed an attractive appearance and a charming personality, and who observe professional ethics."

COSMETOLOGY IS NOT ALL GLAMOR FOR GALS
. . . Cleaning Brushes Is Part of Course

explanation was that the daily represented such a huge capital invest-ment that its managers were reluctant to jeopardize it even slightly by using untried techniques. So the pattern was for the weekly to invent and perfect a technique and then for the daily to adopt it. The larger the daily, the later it adopted the new ideas.

But today's creativity is frequently displayed by the metropolitans. The smaller dailies, tied so closely to wire-tape transmission, find that the tape is not only a supporting hammock but a trapping net. They can no longer innovate as they once could; they must follow the dictates—benevolent as they may be—of distant wire-service editors.

These wire-service news editors are able, dedicated men, but their experience and responsibilities have not involved them in typography. Their tools are words; as long as those words are committed to paper in form adequate for the typesetter, the wire services had no need to con-cern themselves with typographical display. Thus the service editor has been reluctant to encourage the fuss and bother he thinks will surround his office with any change of transmission specifications. He thinks, today, that the desires of some of his clients for wire tape that will set optimum line lengths is just a passing whim that should be discouraged. The more these wire-service men have to do with specifying typesetting, the less opportunity the local publisher has to produce a newspaper that reflects his own judgment and creativity.

It is difficult, though, to explain the demise of the weekly editor as a typographic innovator. True, many a weekly man is producing a visually exciting newspaper and is using the most modern of techniques. But as a whole, the weekly press has not been blazing any typographic trails.

Some editors have been eased out of this activity by their adoption of pasteup. In the past, most weekly editors have possessed at least the basic skills of the printer. They have operated Linotypes, sometimes writing their columns and editorials right at the keyboard. They have worked on the stone; making up their own front page in type gave many of them great satisfaction. The editor was familiar with the problems and proce-dures of the composing room. If he were struck by inspiration, he could readily transform his brainstorm into tangible form.

But to convert an idea into print now, he must instruct some techni-cian who actually does the work. It's hard to be an inventor when someone else must use the hammer and saw; much inspiration is lost if its owner cannot also supply the perspiration.

The editor faces pasteup procedures with which he has little famil-iarity and for which his technical skills have little usefulness. As he attempts to instruct the person doing the actual pasting up, the editor finds he has no common vocabulary with the employee and the allusions to hot metal that sprinkle the editor's instructions are so much gibberish to the worker. So the editor tends to withdraw from the final makeup process, and the unsupervised employees have no personal standards of typographic quality to guide their work.

The people who do pasteup in smaller shops usually have no background in the printer's craft. They are most often women who have no compelling interest in the job. They do not have the pride of craftsmanship as the hot-metal printer does; they have little interest in typographic creativity. Perhaps we misjudge them; maybe it's just that they have no opportunity to display pride or interest. Or maybe their training has been so brief and sketchy, so concentrated on the mechanics, that they have mastered no principles on which creativity may build. Having such people as intermediates between the creative editor and his printed page must certainly inhibit his experimenting. (An effective way to instill pride of craftsmanship is the technique used by the *Athens* [Georgia] *Banner-Herald*. Each pasteup man—actually they are all girls—is given a byline: "Page composed by Jane Wills." This rewards good work, and it makes the craftsman highly conscious of quality. Each of us will work more painstakingly when we know we will be publicly identified with the results.)

Another factor about pasteup that is usually overlooked is that it is more difficult to experiment with it than with hot metal in the chase. Pasteup seems easy, far easier than manipulating type slugs. And it may be when a regular, conventional style is followed. But the difficulties of ledding body type or dividing it equally into legs and the pesky handling of tiny slivers of paper thus created have a dampening effect on innovations. Without the metallic discipline of well-defined columns in a chase, it is difficult to create fresh techniques without losing the newspaper appearance that the reader demands. These difficulties are complicated by pressures of time, of course. Pressures of this kind may be lifted, and creativity be given a little more elbow room as new techniques and materials speed the mechanical processes.

But no matter who the creator is, it's good for the whole newspaper industry to have the experiments and the successes of new typography.

An interesting development is the appearance in newspaper tables of organization of a new title: graphic arts director. There are only a handful, literally to be counted on the fingers, of men who now hold this job. But their number will grow.

I anticipate that the experience of graphic arts directors will parallel that of picture editors 25 years ago. They, too, were a rare breed in the

Fig. 149. Pertinent quotations are strongly displayed in unconventional treatments by *Boston* (Mass.) *Globe*, *Chicago* (Ill.) *Daily News*, and *Yonkers* (N.Y.) *Herald Statesman.*

late 1940's. But as a few newspapers created such jobs and reported the successes of these new picture editors, other papers followed the example and established their own photo desk.

Before the duties of the picture editor were consolidated into one person's responsibility, most of them had been performed in one way or another. Similarly many of the duties of a graphic arts director are being carried out in newspaper plants where no such individual exists. But increasing demands and increasing knowledge in the field require more knowledge, experience, time, and effort than can be provided by persons who perform duties on a part-time basis.

The graphic arts director must be a specialist, but his responsibilities are anything but narrow. He must not only provide liaison among editorial, advertising, circulation, promotion, and mechanical departments. He must also have knowledge and skill in each of these disparate fields. His area of responsibility is the only one that overlaps each of the others and that links their efforts.

Journalism schools are already getting demands for young people trained in newspaper typography and its attendant arts and crafts. New courses of study appear in college catalogs. But just as journalism schools cannot now train enough editorial and advertising personnel, so they won't be able to train enough potential graphic arts directors. The industry itself is going to have to train most of these people.

Whatever the title of the newspaper typographer, his job remains a vital one. Certainly in this age a citizen of a free country constantly needs more information about the grave decisions his nation faces; he will get most of it by reading his newspaper. Yet the task of reading becomes more oppressive every day.

Within the lifetime of half of the Americans alive today, the total knowledge of mankind has doubled. Well within the lifetime of the rest of the population, that knowledge will double again—and maybe even once more. All of this knowledge is committed to writing and printing. No wonder, then, that the typical American feels like Noah in the rain of printer's ink. He must read frantically to keep abreast of developments in his own field; if we expect him to read further, we must make it not only easy and convenient but also pleasurable and rewarding. This responsibility the typographer shares with the writer and editor.

A further responsibility which the typographer shares with every educated person, is that of fighting illiteracy. By his work he is not only a user, but also a custodian of the alphabet and should see that it is kept rustfree and sharp, not dulled by misuse. Affirmatively, the typographer

Fig. 150. *Lowell* (Mass.) *Sun* has three separate head schedules. News pages are dressed in Spartan Bold, above; last page of paper is "second front page." Women's pages are dressed in Bodoni and sports in Square Serifs. Page-one picture is full process color; top two on back page are green-black duotones. Tint block under SPORTS WIRE is lettuce green.

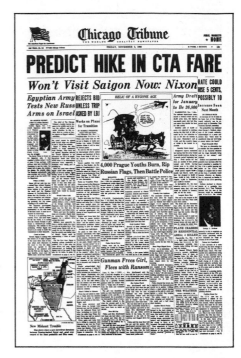

Fig. 151. Gradual restyling. *Chicago (Ill.) Tribune* maintains traditional front page but uses contemporary formats inside. Opposite is split-run neighborhood page in op format. Note Century Bold head schedule and arrow pointing to promotional story.

by means of his special skills can help establish programs to aid reading training.

Probably no one has taught more people to read than Dr. Frank Laubach and his volunteers. Most of this work was done in foreign fields; now the Laubach Literacy Program—along with others—is using its each-one-teach-one techniques in the United States.

The Laubach Foundation recognized that a grown man who is learning to read is not content to sharpen his abilities on the doings of Dick and Jane and the run-run-running of their dog Spot. Yet the things he is interested in—from instruction manuals on his job to the report of his favorite sport—are written in a vocabulary he hasn't yet mastered. The answer to this problem was a newspaper. *News For You* is a weekly, written for two levels of reading skills, third and fourth grade for one edition, a grade higher for the next. It covers all the regular news of the week, from politics to prizefighting. It also carries articles about road signs, the way to endorse a check, the meaning of the Fourth of July— all homely things that we take for granted but which can be awesomely confusing to the illiterate. As he reads more fluently and expands his reading vocabulary, progression into a regular newspaper is a logical step.

The need to wipe out illiteracy is particularly challenging to the typographer and the newspaperman. For here is a great reservoir of

Our Town

You, Too, Can Sway City Hall

BY JERRY SHNAY

IN THESE perilous times, it isn't often when a citizen wants to shoot off a couple of firecrackers in the direction of City hall.

Usually, the more irate want to shoot off the top of City hall.

But Mrs. Fred Trupke, a resident of the Logan Square area, praises the powers that are for safeguarding children in the neighborhood.

A construction firm working on the Milwaukee avenue subway has been storing steel girders in the open. They became a magnet for the scrambling, curious feet of children.

In dumping the girders, work crews had torn up trees and left them piled near the girders. The tangle of limbs and trunks was another potential hazard.

Complaints to the construction company seemed to do little.

City hall was next. There, Henry Zalewski, Chicago's assistant chief engineer, had the right attitude and the answer.

He showed the residents a letter giving the company permission to use two blocks for storage but requiring it to replace any trees and grass destroyed. In addition, the steel girders would have to be fenced.

Wouldn't you know it. Three days later the area was fenced. And Mrs. Trupke says "We're glad we made the trip."

WALTER CONLEY, 75, of 5411 Oketo av., will be back on the job in September.

That makes it nice for the 50 or so school children he shepherds across the busy intersection of Potter road and Northwest highway in Park Ridge each day.

It also makes things pleasant for the motorists he greets there.

Someone asked what happened to the jolly old crossing guard. The Park Ridge police department answered that the ards are hired only during the school year.

Conley is twice a great-grandfather and has been a crossing guard for the last five years.

"I like to say hello to the motorists," he says. "This is a busy intersection, you know."

EVANSTON HAS been saved again from the evils of demon rum, with the aid of you-know-who.

The city council last week killed a proposal for the sale of liquor in dry Evanston.

Credit for this turndown, says Mrs. Frederick J. Tooze, should go to the Women's Christian Temperance union.

Mrs. Tooze should know. She is president of the Evanston-based organization.

"We are happy over the results. We have worked diligently for such an outcome."

Keeping Evanston dry is the W. C. T. U.'s thing, so to speak. "Of course, Evanston was dry long before we moved here in 1900," said Mrs. Tooze.

"Mrs. Frances Willard called Evanston a classic city," Mrs. Tooze added. "That's because there were no bars or liquor establishments then. It was free of any tai[illegible]

Keeping [illegible] any taint has been a [illegible]

"Every fe[illegible] a proposal comes up, b[illegible]ink Evanston will ever go [illegible]id. "We work hard to keep [illegible]

It must be [illegible]he W. C. T. U. claims a me[illegible]of 250,000 teetotalers, worki[illegible] a program of education.

With Evanston [illegible]ry, all those 21-year-olds from [illegible]estern university will have to co[illegible] to frequent the establishments al[illegible]the south side of Howard street if [illegible] want to imbibe.

Format Changes

The Sunday Neighborhood News sections make their appearance today in a new place and with several improvements of content and makeup. Radio and television pages, with which Neighborhood News has shared this section for several years, have moved up front for the convenience of readers. The Our Town column has turned over its function of answering the queries of readers to the Action Express, which appears on the first page of the second news section daily and Sunday. It will now turn the eye of its new conductor, Jerry Shnay, on bright and interesting people and happenings in the communities and suburbs of Chicago. Jerry has been sports editor of the Northwest Indiana-Calumet section of the Neighborhood News department. He will be glad to hear from readers on 222-3101. The Thursday Neighborhood News will share the new makeup but will continue to appear in its own section.

[TRIBUNE Staff Photo by Harold Revoir]

BE SEATED, PLEASE—This 4½-story all Fun Sky Slide, which opened last week at 7100 S. Cicero av., promises to be fun for those who enjoy toboggan-like rides. But 35 m. p. h. hardly qualifies it as a sedate sport. And watch that second hill. It's a thriller.

Chicago Tribune
SUNDAY, AUGUST 4, 1968
Section 10 5

SOUTH
NEIGHBORHOOD NEWS

Altgeld Asks CTA Service

BY ANN McFEATTERS

Altgeld Gardens residents want better bus service and they think it should be provided by the transit authority.

Twice last week members of the Altgeld-Murray Community council, led by Mrs. Bessie Lowe, chairman of the group's transportation committee, met with Kermit B. Coleman, an American Civil Liberties union lawyer.

They discussed bus serice in the area and how to get CTA routes into the project.

Now Served by Safeway

Altgeld Gardens, a housing authority project at 133d street and Ellis avenue, now is served by the South Suburban Safeway Lines, Inc., which provides transportation from various communities south of 83d street to the Loop.

Safeway runs buses in Ellis avenue and 133d street. Fare from Altgeld to the Loop is now 40 cents—it was raised from 35 cents in June.

The nearest CTA route, in Indiana avenue, requires a walk of about a mile—in a 45 m. p. h., sidewalkless street—for most of the area's estimated 4,000 bus riders.

Several years ago the possibility of CTA service to the Gardens was discussed. It was decided then that the South Suburban Lines provided adequate service. Now the residents aren't so sure.

Protest Fare Increase

The community council, representing 17 block clubs, bitterly protested the last fare increase, also opposed by a petition filed with the Illinois Commerce commission by the city of Chicago.

One of the strongest objections was and is a reduction in the number of runs at night.

"When I moved here two years ago," Mrs. Lowe said, "the buses ran every half hour all night long. A lot of people here work late or have to get to work very early so we need all night service."

Ray Johnson, bus line vice president, said the last bus arrives in Altgeld at 2:20 a. m. and the first one leaves at 4:40 a. m. "We didn't really cut much out."

Bus Service Expensive

Another major objection is cost. "It's just too expensive," Mrs. Lowe said. "The South Suburban fare is 40 cents but many have to switch onto the CTA before reaching their destination.

"This is one of the poorest areas of the city and that's a lot of money for us."

It was alleged at the council meeting that Safeway had "arbitrarily" cut off service five or six times this year in reprisal for acts of vandalism.

Johnson also denied this saying that the company had cut down on service "only after the King incident."

Police, Guards Inadequate

Residents also said that police and guard protection were inadequate and had been cut "after the area became Negro."

The transportation problem was brought into focus during the recent 26-day strike against Safeway by its drivers and mechanics. Service began only recently.

Coleman said, "The transportation problem is major. South Suburban just alleviates it to some extent."

He said he would try to arrange meetings with George De Ment, CTA board chairman, "to see whether it is possible to get him to recognize the need for CTA service to Altgeld."

Housing Law Passed

BY RICHARD PHILLIPS

The village of Homewood has joined the list of five south suburban communities with open housing laws.

The Homewood village board unanimously passed an open housing law last week. About 25 people attended the village board meeting, some of whom asked the board to delay a vote in favor of more study or to hold a referendum on the issue.

Board members said that the issue has been pending for several months and that two public hearings were held.

Write Composite Ordinance

The new ordinance is a composite of open housing laws passed in Park Forest and Champaign and contains elements of a model ordinance proposed by the Illinois Human Relations commission.

The Homewood law prohibits discrimination in all buying or selling except in the renting of an owner-occupied apartment house of four or less units.

Fines up to $500 are provided, along with the revocation or suspension of a real estate broker's license.

The village community relations commission would conduct investigations in alleged cases of discrimination based on race, creed, color, or national origin. Authority to file suit, however, would rest with the village board.

Other Laws

Other south suburbs with similar open housing ordinances are Park Forest, Harvey, Flossmoor, and Joliet. Markham has a de facto open housing law in which real estate brokers must show all house listings to prospective clients or forfeit a $1,000 bond posted with the city.

Open housing ordinances are being considered in Dolton, Olympia Fields, Riverdale, South Holland, Chicago Heights, and East Chicago Heights.

Unless communities pass open housing laws as least as strong as the national housing law by Jan. 1, 1970—when all provisions of the national law go into effect—a person's first recourse in a discrimination case will be with the federal government.

Plan Steger Carnival

Steger fire department's 29th annual homecoming carnival, an event that means four days of fun for visitors, and wet competition for 15 other fire departments, will begin this week.

Starting at 6:30 p. m. Thursday thru next Sunday, the carnival will be located at Kiwanis park in Steger, 35th street and Phillips avenue. Admission will be free each night, and rides will be free Thursday night, said Harold Hecht, fire chief.

Rides to Entertain

In addition to games and nine varieties of rides, teams from 16 metropolitan fire departments will engage in a water fight. In a series of elimination bouts two fire departments will attempt to force a ball hung high on a cable stretched between two poles across to the opponents using only water pressure.

The final matches between the surviving teams will be held at 6:30 p.m. Sunday.

At 1:30 p. m. Saturday, the Steger fire department auxiliary will start a "kiddie parade" at the fire station, 33d place and Emerald avenue. Prizes will be given to the children with best costumes. Pets will not be allowed, Chief Hecht requested.

Parade Starts Sunday

At 1:30 p. m. next Sunday the grand parade will start at 30th street and Chicago road, going south on Chicago road to 34th street, and then east to Florence avenue and on to Kiwanis park. Sponsoring the parade will be the Veterans of Foreign Wars.

It will include floats, drum and bugle corps, several bands and fire trucks from 25 metropolitan fire departments including Harvey, Hazel Crest, Chicago Heights, Park Forest, Crete, and Riverdale.

Proceeds from the carnival, which drew 30,000 persons last year, will be used to purchase equipment for the 35-man volunteer fire department of Steger, Hecht said.

DUR Offers Study of 67th Street Area

BY ANN PLUNKETT

The department of urban renewal [DUR] has completed a preliminary land use study for the 67th street-Stony Island avenue urban renewal area.

The area is bounded by 66th and 67th streets on the north, Cornell avenue and the alley east of East End avenue on the east, 71st street on the south and Blackstone avenue and the alley west of Stony Island avenue on the west.

The study makes proposals for residential development, shopping facilities, a service district, a park-playground and for traffic circulation. Copies of the study have been sent to the South Shore commission and The Woodlawn organization, said Frank Siudzinski, information officer for the DUR.

Propose New Housing

New housing is proposed along the west side of Stony Island avenue between 68th, 69th, and 71st streets. Scattered deteriorated structures east of the alley east of Stony Island avenue also may be replaced with new housing.

The study advocated retention of large, sound residential structures which contain first floor retail shops and are located on the west side of Stony Island avenue between 66th place and 68th street.

A shopping center with adjoining parking spaces is proposed for west of Stony Island avenue in the vicinity of 67th street.

Design School Greenway

Parkside elementary school, 6938 East End av., is scheduled for a park-playground to be built on one-half block east or west of the school. A pedestrian greenway, designed as an extension of the playground, will be built from the school along 69th street west to Stony Island avenue. The greenway also will run north along the east side of Stony Island avenue to 67th street.

The study proposed the widening of Stony Island avenue between east 67th street and 69th place to meet the long-range improvement goals for the city, Siudzinski said.

The final land use plan for the area will be determined after meetings with community organizations, he said.

Community Groups Respond to Plans

The department of urban renewal proposal to rehabilitate the Stony Island avenue-67th street area met with approval and some questions from the South Shore commission and the Woodlawn organization.

Julian Klugman, commission director, said his organization was primarily interested in clearing out the "badly deteriorated business district" on the east side of Stony Island avenue from 67th to 69th streets.

"The businessmen have been informed thru public meetings, and they gave no objections," Klugman said. "However they would like to know when renewal is coming. Several are caught in the choice of not knowing whether to make improvements now, do nothing, or move out."

Klugman said the commission favors widening Stoney Island avenue to safely accommodate traffic and building a narrow park walk way. "But we don't know if a median strip should be included," he said.

Klugman said the roadways hould be bridged by an extension of Jackson park. The organization also approvesan enlargement of park area surrounding Parkside elementary school, 6938 S. East End av.

"The biggest question we have," he said, "is whether the shopping center will be built. This would significantly change the number of homes to be destroyed."

The Rev. Arthur Brazier of the Woodlawn organization, the other group to be affected, said that altho amall committees have discussed the proposal for the last year, no large gathering of residents in the Parkside school area has met on the issue.

"The urban planners finished the study on their own, and we have not had a chance to work it out," he said.

Chicago Hts. Passes Controversial Laws

The Chicago Heights city council has passed two controversial ordinances, one aimed at eliminating home-operated beauty shops, and the other to impose censorship on movies and all printed matter.

The home beauty shop ordinance was passed by a 4-to-1 council vote, with Councilman William Schramm dissenting

The ordinance allows an estimated 25 beauty shops that operate in violation of zoning codes—half of the city's total number of beauty shops—to continue operation as "nonconforming" to the code. The ordinance, provides for immediate closing of these shops if the council chooses to enforce all provisions of the ordinance, Schramm said.

New Censorship Law

The council pased the censorship law Monday by a 3- to 2 vote, with Schramm and Councilman George Bonick voting against the measure. Both questioned the legal basis of any form of censorship.

Schramm also said the new law does not differ substantially from a censorship ordinance passed by the council in 1954.

Sponsoring the new code was Mayor Maurino Richton, who said he was prompted by parents' complaints of children seeing the movie, "The Graduate," at one of Chicago Heights' two movie theaters.

Abandon Earlier Proposal

Richton abandoned an earlier censorship proposal in favor of the new law. He originally had proposed a Chicago Heights motion picture review board to screen movies meant for general circulation. The board would have been empowered to place an "adults only" label on selected movie advertising and to force the theater owner to prohibit people under 18 years of age from seeing the movie.

[TRIBUNE Staff Photo]

SANDS OF TIME—Examining a sand model of the herbiverous Triceratops, which roamed Montana, Wyoming, and Colorado thousands of years ago, are members of the West Pullman park sand-modeling team, 123d street and Stewart avenue. The youngsters, guided by Mrs. Ralph Koch (left), art craft instructor, plan to shape a perfected model in competition with other sandy creations from 50 parks Friday at Jackson park, 6401 Stony Island av. The event is the park district's "bucket brigade" sand-modeling contest; youngsters are allowed 15 minutes to produce a finished product.

Fig. 152. Modular layout was well handled in Sunday format of *New York Herald-Tribune*. Note large picture at right.

potential newspaper circulation, not to mention the economic and social strength that is largely untapped.

The typographer can help reach these handicapped people by means outside his newspaper, as well. The typographer, for instance, is becoming important in other mass media. The so-called "graphics" of television and the movies is growing in importance. "Visual" is an important part of "audio-visual" communication. In every area, the typographer is experimenting, learning and creating things that aid his counterpart in other specialties. The whole audience for visual, nonverbal communication grows more sophisticated. There are no more hicks, no more rubes. With few exceptions, the rural and isolated family reads the same magazines, sees the same TV graphics, attends the same movies as the family in Manhattan. Their taste is conditioned by the same factors just as their reading procedures are conditioned by the same left-to-right, top-to-bottom writing and printing. Newspaper typography must combine good taste with physical functionalism.

The tools of the typographer may change. Already, a version of the Linofilm makes intricate mechanical drawings from instructions tapped on a keyboard. Another machine arranges elements of an advertisement and puts a border around the whole according to computer specifications. There are machines that will display reporter's copy in a desk-top screen where copyreaders make conventional corrections by "writing" on it with "pencils" that project a sharp beam of light.

Photographers in the darkroom display a negative to a closed-circuit TV camera that converts it to a positive image at an editor's desk. He makes his selection from the screen and designates cropping by using indicators on the side of the screen like the coordinates on the margins of road maps. Magazines that must remake many regional editions call on the computer, which will tell the editor where the changing ads are supposed to go and what editorial content in storage will fit the new areas available to him.

These are fascinating new aids to the typographer. But they are only the means, never the end. The end is communication. And communication demands the decoder as well as the encoder.

The decoder, the receiver, will read a printed page in A.D. 2100 along the same paths as he does today. For that is a condition set by the Latin alphabet. And despite the efforts of many experimenters, the alphabet is not going to change.

The great formalizer of the alphabet was printing and the tremendous volume of books that the presses produced. Suppose Congress tried to change the alphabet. It just wouldn't work. What would we do with our bulging libraries if the alphabet changed? Reprint every worthwhile book? How would an old-alphabet parent teach his children the new one? Would youngsters have to learn both forms? Would the middle-aged man have to learn the second alphabet? Could he keep his job if he couldn't learn about new developments now printed in an alphabet foreign to him? The sheer volume of printed matter now in existence has frozen the shape and use of the alphabet even more rigidly than legislation could.

Thus the typographer's art and skill are in no danger of obsolescence. The portrait artist today may use acrylic paint instead of oils, but he must still capture the likeness of his subject. The landscape painter no longer has to squeeze little sea beasts to give him purple pigments or grind up dried insects to get a red. But he must compose his picture by the same principles that have been valid for centuries. Similarly the tools of the typographer may—will—change. But his principles will not. As long as communication remains his goal and his audience is human beings, the principles he masters today will remain valid. And within those principles is always opportunity for innovation and creativity. The newspaper typographer is not going to be replaced by a computer. And he is not going to run out of responsibility or challenge.

Glossary

A

a, Greek, letterform like d with ascender cut off, as in italic form of face in this setting.

a, Roman, letterform in which short stem bends to left over bowl, as in face used in this setting.

absorption, process of drying ink by soaking into paper fibers.

accent face, letterform of exaggerated weight or radically different form used to enliven headline schedule.

achromatic, noncolor; black, white, and gray.

ad alley, that part of composing room that produces display advertising.

admonitory head, one with omitted subject which is thus peremptory phrase.

AdPro, special inks for process color printing by newspapers.

agate, 5½-point type. Also, any face used to set tabular matter in newspapers. Also, that copy itself.

agate line, measurement of area used in billing display advertising, $\frac{1}{14}$ inch deep and 1 column wide.

A head, largest 1-column head in schedule.

air, fresh, white space.

alley, strip of white space separating columns of type in newspaper page.

American Square Serifs, ethnic division of type race, in monotonal form with serifs heavier than regular strokes. *See also* Egyptian.

anchor, to place strong display elements in corners of newspaper.

angle, basic modification of letterform. Tilting to right creates Italic or Oblique; to left, Backslant.

ANPA, American Newspaper Publishers Association.

ANR, American Newspaper Representatives, advertising sales and service organization serving weekly and small daily newspapers.

apex, sharp angle at top of letter such as A.

arm, horizontal stroke on *T*, top diagonal projection of *K*, diagonal lines of *Y*.

armpit, to place narrow headline immediately under wider one. Also, combination of headlines so created.

art, all pictorial matter in newspaper. Also, original copy for platemaker.

ascender, that portion of lowercase letter projecting above meanline. Also, letter itself that has such projection.

asterisk, bug, special sign used to refer to footnote. In newspapers, used as decorative device between paragraphs of body type.

ATF Typesetter, phototypesetting machine in which negatives of letterforms are on turning disk.

attention compeller, typographic element with strong visual attraction.

at-will, advertisements, usually small, that are run only when there is room for them. Advertiser gives newspapers right to decide when.

author's alteration, AA, any change in type not required to correct error of typesetter.

axis of orientation, A/O, vertical line at left of series of lines of type to which reading eye automatically returns to begin successive lines.

B

back down, to begin section of newspaper, especially classified, at its last page and working toward front.

back shop, mechanical departments of newspaper, especially composing and engraving.

backslant, letterform that tilts to left.

ball, circular element at beginning of curved stroke on Roman a.

bank, one line of head. Also that area in composing room where typographic material is stored prior to use.

banner, large multicolumn head on front page, usually at least 4 columns wide.

bar, horizontal stroke on *e* and *A*.

barker, hammer head (*which see*).

baseline, that on which bottom of primary letters align.

basement, lower half of newspaper page, especially front or section.

bay mortise, rectangle cut out of halftone so picture surrounds three sides of opening.

beak, serif on arm of *K*.

beard, horizontal serif on vertical stroke of *G*.

beaten proof, rough print made by pressing paper on inked form by pounding on covering block of wood.

Ben Day, system of adding dot or line pattern to line drawings by imprinting on negative or engraver's metal, named after inventor.

b.f., boldface.

billboarded, headline surrounded by

(*billboarded cont'd*)
exaggerated amount of white space.

BL, body line, increment of measurement—height of one line of strikeon body type—for dummying pasteups.

Black Letter, race of type made of straight thick and thin lines meeting at sharp angles. Erroneously called Old English, which is one of its families.

blocked ads, those laid so they form rectangle.

block letter, Gothic letterform.

blueprint, photocopy on which image appears in distinctive blue.

body, type of comparatively small size used in blocks of copy, as contrasted to display such headlines. Also, metal block carrying type character.

boldface, letter of normal form and width but of heavier strokes.

bold graf, paragraph of news matter set in boldface to relieve large masses of type.

boldline, first line of occasional paragraph set in boldface, usually capping first words.

book, two pieces of copy paper sandwiching one of carbon paper. Measurement for reporter's writing; first book is about 200 words because space is left for headline, succeeding books average 300 words.

borax, dark, jumbled advertising.

border, plain or ornamental frame around advertising, etc. Border material is usually wider or more ornate than rules used for similar purpose.

Bourges sheets, plastic materials used to lighten areas of photo or add color to artwork.

bowl, circle or major part thereof in

(*bowl cont'd*)

letterform, especially that which meets stem, as in *b* and *d*. Letters such as *a, e, g, c,* and *o* also have bowls.

box, typographic element surrounded on four sides, or top and bottom only, with border or rule.

brace, page pattern in which series of multicolumn heads meet side of picture or box. Also, typographic device like large decorative parenthesis.

bracketed serif, one which joins main stroke of letter in curve, characteristic of Old Style Romans.

brayer, roller with attached handle used to ink type form by hand.

break-box, rule around three or four sides of headline with gap in center of top rule into which is set smaller head.

breaker head, divider, large subhead usually at least 14-point.

breakline, centered headline with rule at each end filling all of column width.

break page, first page of any section beyond first. *See* section page.

bright, short, interesting, often humorous editorial feature. Also, artist's paint brush formed with sharp point.

brilliant, name used to designate 3½-point type.

broken rule, coin-edge, border of small, parallel lines.

buddy system, oriented layout (*which see*).

bug, asterisk. Also, label of printers' union.

bullet, large period used as typographic ornament.

bump, to tombstone heads (*which see*).

buried ad, one which does not touch editorial reading matter.

burn, to expose photosensitive metal to light through negative to create printing plate.

burn in, to provide dark areas artificially in photograph, especially to provide plain background for white surprinted type.

butted slugs, those which combine two or more sections to make single line of type.

byline, that at beginning of article that identifies writer.

C

c&lc, u&lc, style of composition in which each word is capped.

c&sc, capitals and small capitals, style of composition all in caps with each word starting with larger letter.

California job case, receptacle for storing font of foundry type.

calligraphy, beautiful writing, technically all hand-lettering but commonly that in Script or Cursive form, usually with many swashes and ligatures.

Canadian wrap, system of subdividing longer story into series of 2-leg units under 2-column subheads.

canopy, to run headline across picture and horizontally adjacent story.

capitals, caps, majuscules, big letters. Original form of Latin letters.

caps-and-down, upper-and-lowercase composition.

captions, explanatory matter accompanying pictures. Most commonly used for magazines; in newspapers usually called cutlines.

catchline, line of display type between picture and cutlines.

center spread, two facing pages at center of section of newspaper. *See* double truck.

channel, narrow section in Linotype magazine that holds all matrices of one character or spacing of one size.

chapel, local group of printers' union.

chase, rectangle of steel in which are gathered elements of printing form, for newspaper use usually a page.

Chicago format, Detroit format, page of four columns of 1½-column measure and one of double-column measure.

chimney, series of heads and/or pictures of same width stacked to fill entire page depth.

chopped head, one of two or more lines of varying column width.

chroma, characteristic of color that indicates brightness.

circus makeup, flamboyant page patterns.

classified, want ads, adlets, liners, agate; that advertising set in identical body type and with small or no headlines, then grouped by subjects.

claw, element protruding from top loop of *g.*

closed format, one using rules to separate columns of type.

coin-edge, broken rule, border composed of small, parallel lines.

cold type, type matter produced by phototypesetting, although commonly used to include strikeon and pasteon matter too.

collect run, issue of a newspaper produced by having each press unit print only one of several sections.

color, apparent tone or density of type page. Also, typographic devices to alter such tone. Also, hues used in printing newspaper; *see* process, ROP, and spot.

Columbian, name once used to designate 16-point type. Also, famed model of platen press used for

(*Columbian cont'd*)
printing small newspapers in eighteenth century.

column-inch, area 1 inch deep and 1 column wide, used for measuring newspaper contents, especially advertising.

column rule, thin vertical division line on newspaper page.

combination, combo, two or more related pictures grouped as single element.

combination engraving, one including halftone and line work in single printing plate.

common diagonal, system of scaling pictures that uses principle that all rectangles of same proportions have diagonal at the same angle to horizon.

compact, newspaper format using page of 4 to 6 columns approximately 15 inches deep and of more conservative makeup than tabloid which uses same size sheet.

composing stick, shallow 3-sided metal box in which type or Ludlow matrices are composed by hand.

composition, material set on linecaster or by hand. Also, setting and arranging type.

compositor, printer who sets type or assembles typographic elements into printing forms.

comprehensives, *comprees* (*compreez*), cutlines so detailed that no additional story is required. Also, as comp, detailed dummy for advertising.

concentric circles, special engraver's screen creating halftone image by varying widths of circles on common axis.

Condensed, letterform in which weight of strokes and height of letters remains normal but width is reduced.

connotative head, teaser headline, (*which see*).

constants, those typographic elements which are same in all issues of newspaper, i.e., nameplate, masthead, folio lines, etc.

continuation line, one which indicates story is continued on later page.

continuous tone, photographic or hand art such as oil painting, watercolor, etc., in which gradations of gray or hues are produced by adding white or gray pigment.

copy, all original material to be converted to type or engravings, but especially news content.

copy cutter, back-shop supervisor who separates copy into groups for setting by properly equipped linecasters.

copy factor, numerical designation of ratio to determine length of type column produced by given amount of typewritten copy.

copy fit, to determine by mathematics area which given amount of typewritten copy will occupy as type.

copyholder, assistant to proofreader.

copy log, record of all copy sent to Linotype and platemaker.

copy marker, back-shop supervisor who gives specific instructions for setting of unmarked advertising copy.

correction line, new Linotype slug set to correct an error in previous setting.

counter, white space enclosed by, and surrounding, a type character.

cpp, characters per pica, copy-fitting method.

credit line, that which identifies person who has made photo appearing in newspaper, especially if not staff member.

crop, to eliminate unwanted areas in

(*crop cont'd*)

photograph by actually cutting or, most frequently, by indicating them with marginal marks.

crossline, headline of single, full line.

cross stroke, horizontal in *t* and *f*.

Cursive, ethnic division of Written type race in which letters are not joined.

cut, photoengraving.

cutlines, explanatory matter accompanying picture. In magazines usually called captions.

cutoff rule, thin, horizontal dividing lines in newspaper page. Also, printing element that places such image on paper. Often "rule" is omitted.

cyan, vivid blue used for filtering and printing process color.

cylinder, impression, that which presses paper on inked form.

cylinder press, flatbed, one in which paper is pressed on flat form by impression cylinder.

D

dash, punctuation mark. Also small horizontal rule used as decoration on newspaper page, commonly 3 ems long and called jim-dash.

dateline, opening of news, usually wire, story, showing origin and date of filing. Erroneously used for folio lines (*which see*).

deck, portion of headline set in single type style and size.

decoder, in communications theory, receiver of message.

decorative rule, printing elements that produce horizontal lines in form more ornate than simple monotone.

definitive head, summary head, (*which see*).

demo art, marker art, hand art added to photograph to emphasize cer-

(*demo art cont'd*)

tain elements, such as X marking spot of auto crash.

department logo, display device, often combining miniature of newspaper flag, which identifies department on page.

descender, portion of lowercase letter projecting below baseline. Also, letter which has such projection.

desk, administrative center and personnel of an editorial department of newspaper, especially city desk, which directs local staff. Also, copy desk, where verbal content of newspaper is prepared for typesetting and page display.

Detroit format, Chicago format (*which see*).

display, arrangement of typographic elements to make them conspicuous and appealing to the reader. Also, advertising that uses large type, pictures, and masses of white space. Also, size of type used for headlines.

display reeders, advertising designed to look like news stories or pictures.

divider, breaker, large subhead usually at least 14-point.

division label, letters designating subgroups within tabulation such as market reports or classified ads.

doctor blade, device on rotogravure press which scrapes ink off face of printing cylinder, allowing only that within incised image to remain.

dodge, to manipulate printing of photograph to create artificially light area, especially for a plain background for black surprinted type.

dominant head, heaviest one on inside page, which acts as nucleus for page pattern.

double pyramid, placement of advertisements in two half-pyramidal masses which form a V opening at center of page.

double spread, two facing newspaper pages, especially at center of section, thus on same sheet of paper.

double truck, advertisement on center spread, made up as a single 2-page unit and so using space customarily in gutter. Also chase large enough for 2-page unit.

downstairs, lower half of newspaper page, especially of front and section pages.

downstyle, capping only first word and proper nouns in headlines.

draftsman's tape, narrow, rolled, gummed material used to place lines, rules, and borders on pasteup for platemaking.

dragon's blood, resin acid resist used in photoengraving process.

drop, secondary deck of headline.

dual kickers, two small, short heads above main head, one flush left, other flush right.

dummy, drawn guide that printer follows to produce page pattern designed by editor. Also, to draw such guide.

duplex, second typeface available on linecaster matrix, customarily boldface although it may be italic or even totally different face.

duotone, color-printing technique which creates single image from two impressions, one in dark ink, usually black, other in light hue. Both plates are made from single black-and-white photograph, unlike 2-color process plates.

duplicate plates, replicas of printing plates made by stereotyping, electrotyping, or (for offset) step-and-repeat process.

Dutch, Transitional Roman letterform.

Dutch wrap, continuation of body type to column at right not covered by headline.

dynamic balance, informal yet studied page pattern.

E

ear, editorial matter at top corners of front page alongside flag.

edition, all copies of newspaper printed at one time without typographic changes. Erroneously used for issue (*which see*).

editorial, article of comment that represents newspaper's corporate opinion. Also, all matter in newspaper not advertising. Also, department responsible for producing such matter.

Egyptian Square Serifs, ethnic division of type race in monotonal form with serifs same weight as main strokes. *See also* American.

electrotype, duplicate relief printing plate made by copper-plating process.

Elgrama, mechanical engraving machine which makes zinc relief printing plates in line or parallel-line halftones.

ellipsis, three periods indicating connection between physically separated units of type.

Elrod, stripcasting machine that produces rules, borders, spacing, etc.

em, blank space in square of size of type. Called mutton or mut to avoid confusion with en. Erroneously, synonym for pica.

en, vertical half of em. Called nut to avoid confusion with em.

encoder, in communications theory, sender of message.

English, name formerly used to designate 14-point.

English line-fall, style of setting ragged-right body type with no hyphenation at end of line.

engraver, photoengraver.

engraving, photoengraving, a relief printing plate made by action of acid on metal plate which is partially protected by resistant substance, produced by action of light.

error line, Linotype slug in which correction must be made.

ethnic, secondary division of type races, such as Modern and Old Style in Romans.

eutectic, quality which makes liquid expand as it hardens. In graphic arts most frequently used to describe type metal.

evergreen, editorial feature material without compelling time factor to dictate when it can be used.

excelsior, editorial matter used to fill space around advertising rather than for information. Also, name used to designate 3-point type. Also (capitalized), family of body type.

expo art (for expository), charts, graphs, diagrams, etc.

expo line, brief description under name that identifies portrait.

exposure, reader, number or percentage of people who pause to observe any element on newspaper page.

Extended, variation of normal letterform with same weight and height but broadened width.

eyebrow, kicker head (*which see*).

F

face, style or cut of type. Also, that portion of slug or type which meets paper in printing.

facsimile, method of transmitting images by wire or radio waves.

fallow corner, top right and lower left of page.

family, major division of typefaces, after race or ethnic group.

feathering, irregular edges of paint on smooth surface.

finial, curved finishing stroke replacing serifs in some Italics.

finishing line, thin black border around halftone.

first impression, that side of paper printed first, less desirable because it is subject to smudging when reverse is printed.

first revise, proof after first corrections have been made.

flag, nameplate, name of newspaper in display form on page one. Erroneously called masthead (*which see*).

flat, group of engraver's negatives placed on one sheet of glass for single exposure to sensitized metal plate. Also, group of smaller photoengravings made on single sheet of metal and handled as single unit until cut apart at end of manufacture. Also, wide but shallow brush similar to, but smaller than, those used by house painters.

flatbed, cylinder press.

flat color, spot color, any used in printing except for process color (*which see*).

flatout, 1-up technique (*which see*).

Flex-Form, (also FlexForm) style of display advertising in very irregular form and floating alone in page of editorial matter.

Flexowriter, trademarked name for strikeon composing machine.

floating flag, nameplate narrower than full width of page, displayed in positions other than at top of page.

flong, blank piece of laminated paper

(*flong cont'd*)
from which stereotype matrix is made.

floor man, printer who makes up newspaper pages or advertisements on stone.

flopping, process of turning platemaker's negative upside down to create mirror image of printed matter.

floret, decorative typographic element usually in form of stylized flower.

flush left, type set so lines are even at left margin.

flush right, type set so lines are even at right margin.

folio lines, technically page numbers but in common usage includes volume and number, date, and name of newspaper in small type on inside pages. Erroneously, dateline.

font, collection of type and spacing materials required to set copy in one size and face.

foot, bottom margin of page.

form, all typographic elements arranged for printing, especially as full page. Also, to curve stereotype flong prior to casting.

format, general appearance of newspaper, especially page size and number of columns.

Fototronic, trademarked name of phototypesetting machine using cathode-ray tube.

foundry type, bars of metal from which protrude relief printing characters.

4-across-5, flatout technique in which four columns of type are spread across a 5-column area.

frame makeup, page pattern in which single stories occupy all of first and last columns of front page.

free line-fall, ragged-right setting of

(*free line-fall cont'd*)
body type. English line-fall uses no hyphenation at end of line.

free page, one in which type and pictures are not arranged in conventional columns.

French spacing, system in which no more than 3-em space is placed between words.

fresh air, white space on printed page.

front, used as noun to designate first page of any section after first. *See* section page.

front squirt, accidental discharge of molten type metal through unfilled line of linecaster matrices.

full box, border around four sides of type block.

full format, newspaper page of about 15 x 21 inches using seven to nine columns.

functionalism, philosophy of typography that requires all printing elements do necessary job efficiently.

furniture, rectangles of wood or metal used to fill blank spaces in printing form.

G

galley, shallow 3-sided tray in which type is stored after setting and before being placed in form.

galley proof, first impression of type, made to detect errors.

ghost, to lighten background of photo without obliterating entirely.

gimcrack, typographic ornament.

golden rectangle, area in proportion of about 3 x 5, considered by ancient Greeks as most pleasant of such shapes.

Gothic, ethnic division of Monotone type race, with letterforms in all equal strokes, cramped curves, and no serifs.

go up, use one more column of space than of type, use flatout technique.

graf, abbreviation for paragraph.

gray scale, series of rectangles in varying values of gray for measuring proper tonal values in photographic negatives and prints.

Greek a, *see* a, Greek.

Grotesk, European name for Gothic type.

gutter, margins between facing pages.

H

Hadego, trademarked name of photographic machine for setting headlines.

hairline, thinnest rule used in newspapers, thinnest stroke in letterform.

hairline-on-6-point, thin printing rule, about 2 points wide, carried on metal bar 6 points wide. Formerly standard specification for column rules which in recent years has been narrowed to 3 or 4 points.

half-round, stereotype plate of one regular newspaper page or two tabloid pages in semi-cylindrical form.

halftone, technique for reproducing continuous-tone originals by pattern of dots or lines of various sizes and proximity. Also, any picture so reproduced.

half-up, technique flatout in which one half-column of space is used in addition to that occupied by legs of type.

hammer, reverse kicker, short one-line head, twice as large as the main head which is below and to right.

hand art, any nonphotographic illustrative material.

hanging indent, style of setting type so second and each succeeding line are indented same amount at left.

hang the elevator, to operate keyboard of linecasting machine more rapidly than casting and distribution of matrices is occurring.

hard copy, strikeon matter produced simultaneously with photocomposition as guide for operator or for proofreading.

head, abbreviation for headline. Also, margin at top of page.

heading, label heads, often ornamented.

headletter, typeface used for headlines.

headline, display type that seeks to attract the reader into body type usually by summarizing story. Also, largest type elements in advertisements.

Headliner, trademarked name of photographic machine for setting headlines.

headline schedule, hed sked, all headline forms used by a publication, usually grouped by column-widths.

hellbox, receptacle in composing room for waste metal. Also figurative place to consign all unwanted editorial matter.

hen-and-chicks, layout principle in which definitely larger picture is nucleus of pattern of smaller ones around it.

Hi-Fi, preprinted advertisement in wallpaper design without head or foot margins.

hood, 3-sided box around headline.

horizontal makeup, layout technique that disposes most body type in flat, shallow areas.

horse, hasten reading of proofs by eliminating copyholder.

hot metal, all metallic printing elements. Also, composition in metal especially in contrast to photographic material used in pasteup.

hue, that characteristic which identifies colors to human eye.

I

i&e, identification-and-exposition lines (*which see*).

IBM Selectric, trademarked name for strikeon composing machine.

identification-and-exposition lines, ident-and-expo, picture identification in which first (ident) line gives name of subject and second (expo) gives terse explanation of news interest.

ident line, name of person under photo, usually portrait.

idiot tape, raw tape, that which is perforated in unjustified style for automated typesetting.

impression cylinder, that which presses paper upon inked form to make printed reproduction.

incised, intaglio (*which see*).

index, table of contents for newspaper.

index letters, those which indicate alphabetical subdivisions of tabulated material such as stock market quotations.

indicia, legal data indicating newspaper's qualifications for second-class mailing privileges.

initial, first letter in word set in larger or more decorative face. *See* inset and rising initial.

inline, style of type in which white line runs down center of main strokes of letter.

in-reading cutlines, those in series in which copy continues uninterrupted from one set to next. Also, headlines in such style.

insert, sandwich (*which see*).

inset initial, large letter occupying area cut out of top left corner of mass of body type.

inside spread, two facing pages at middle of a newspaper section.

intaglio, method of printing in which image consists of lines incised into

(*intaglio cont'd*)
metal plate. Commercial form is gravure.

interlocking mortise, combination of two halftone plates, each with a corner removed and with two notches in juxtaposition.

internal mortise, completely surrounded opening, usually rectangular, cut out of halftone plate, into which is inserted type or another picture.

Intertype, trademarked name of keyboarded linecaster.

inverted pyramid, headline style of centered lines each narrower than one above it.

island, style of laying newspaper advertising so it is completely surrounded by editorial matter.

issue, all copies of newspapers printed in one day, consisting of one or more editions (*which see*).

Italic, form of Roman type race which slants to right. Used erroneously to indicate all slanted type, which in other races correctly is Oblique.

Italx, *Itlx, Ital, X,* abbreviations for Italics.

J

jam, to place headlines so they touch each other. *See* tombstone and armpit.

jaw in, to place blank metal pieces at each end of area where linecaster matrices are assembled to make line of type shorter than slug on which it is cast.

jim-dash, small, usually 3-em, rule used to separate decks of head.

jump, to continue story from one page, usually the front, to another. Also, story so continued.

jump head, headline on continued portion of a story.

jump line, line in body type that indicates story has been continued from earlier page.

jump the gutter, layout technique to tie facing pages into single oriented composition.

Justape, trademarked name of computer whose sole function is to convert raw tape into justified form.

justify, to set type so left and right margins are straight. Also, to make all columns in page same length.

Justowriter, trademarked name of typewriter that operates by tape and produces justified lines of strikeon composition.

K

keyline drawing, simple outline drawing of forms in accompanying halftone for purposes of identification.

key page, one without advertising or, in op format, on which ads are squared off in half- or full-page masses.

key plate, basic printing plate, usually for black, upon which is registered areas of spot color. Also, drawing from which such plate is made.

kicker, small head, usually underscored, above and slightly to left of main head.

Klischograph, trademarked name for mechanical engraving machine that makes relief printing plates of typemetal slabs by mechanically gouging out unwanted areas.

L

L, BL, line (of body type), height of line of type plus ledding, increment for vertical measurement for dummying pasteup pages.

label, unchanging headline without art, usually consisting only of word

(*label cont'd*)
or phrase, used to identify regular, recurring features.

lay the ads, to create dummy which shows placement of display advertising.

layercake, placement of two or more page-wide headlines so that upper ones are separated from their stories.

layout, pattern of elements in printing form. Also, written diagram which instructs printer how to produce such form. Also, as two words, act of producing such patterns.

layout man, nonprinter who plans arrangement of newspaper page or advertisement and prepares dummies or orally instructs printer or makeup man.

lc, lowercase.

lca, lowercase-alphabet length, length, in points, of line of type including all minuscules of font.

leader (leeder), row of dots or dashes connecting two or more elements in tabulations, such as name of stock and its price.

ledd (phonetic spelling for lead), piece of metal that creates 6 points of blank space. Also, to add interlineal spacing to affect readability or to justify column.

ledded, body type set with additional interlineal spacing.

leed (phonetic spelling for lead), first part of news story which usually gives all major information in summary form. Also, main story or editorial in issue or on page.

leg, vertical subdivision of mass of body type arranged in several columns. Also, lower diagonal strokes of *R* and *K*.

legibility, that quality which makes it easy for reader to see and compre-

(*legibility cont'd*)
hend comparatively few printed characters as in headline.

Legibility Group, trademarked name for series of Linotype faces, the first specifically designed for newspaper body use.

letterpress, relief printing in which raised image captures ink and deposits it on paper. That kind of printing referred to when no adjective accompanies word.

letterspacing, additional spacing between letters in word.

library, all typefaces available in newspaper printing plant.

ligature, two or more characters on single piece of type or matrix, which join or overlap.

Linasec, trademarked name of machine that converts raw tape into justified tape with human decisions on hyphenation.

line, single horizontal unit of a headline. Also, banner (*which see*). Also, art or plates that are not continuous tone.

linear definition, line cut made from continuous-tone art.

linecaster, machine that produces line of type as single metal bar.

line cut, photoengraving in simple masses of black and white, as opposed to halftone (*which see*).

lines, abbreviation for cutlines (*which see*).

lines of force, arrangements of elements within picture that tend to direct eye in certain directions.

link, connecting element between two loops of *g*.

Linofilm, trademarked name of sophisticated phototypesetting machine.

Linotron, trademarked name for cathode-ray tube phototypesetting machine.

Linotype, trademarked name of key-boarded linecaster. Because this was first of such machines, it is often erroneously used generically to describe all linecasters.

linked heads, in-reading headlines (*which see*).

list index, table of contents that merely gives name of feature.

local, typesetting tape produced in newspaper plant as contrasted to that punched elsewhere and transmitted by wire.

lock up, to arrange all elements in complete newspaper page, then wedge them tightly into chase by use of quoins.

logo, abbreviation of logotype. Also, newspaper nameplate. Also, signature cut in advertisement. Also, identification of page or section in newspaper, i.e., women's or sports.

logotype, two or more characters on single piece of type or matrix (*see* ligature).

loose register, design of elements in color that does not require precise placement.

lowercase, lc, small letters of alphabet.

lowercase-alphabet length, lca, measurement in points of line containing all small letters of font.

Ludlow, trademarked name of linecaster for which matrices are gathered and distributed by hand, used mostly for display sizes.

M

magazine, container from which matrices are drawn for setting on keyboarded linecaster. Also, layout style in which elements are often not in regular column increments and in which large areas of white space are used for display effect.

magazine placement, arrangement of

(*magazine placement cont'd*) editorial copy in vertical areas along which advertising runs on one or two sides.

magenta, red hue used for filtering and printing process color.

mailers, employees who count and package newspapers for delivery.

majuscule, capital letters of alphabet.

makeup, general style in which elements are arranged on newspaper page. Also, as two words, to produce forms from which newspaper is printed.

makeup man, printer who arranges newspaper pages or advertisements according to direction of dummy or editorial layout man.

marker art, halftones to which have been added hand art to point out elements in picture, e.g., X marking spot of event.

masthead, collection of information including name of publisher of newspaper, time and place of publication, etc., usually found on editorial page. Erroneously used to refer to nameplate.

mat, abbreviation of matrix.

matrix, mold from which type characters, newspaper pages, illustrations, etc., are cast. For casting type, singly or in lines, the matrix is of brass; for casting printing plates, stereotype molds (flongs) are of heavy laminated paper.

matrices, plural of matrix.

maximum format, max format, newspaper page made up with greatest number of columns possible on paper sheet.

meanline, that which marks top of primary letters.

measure, length of line of type.

mechanical, pasteup, cold type arranged as copy for platemaker.

mechanical engraving machine, one

(*mechanical engraving cont'd*)
that makes printing plate by scanning original copy, then burning, gouging, or incising away unwanted material, leaving printing image in relief.

message, information transmitted in communications process.

metal pasteup, mechanical system in which type and other elements, cut down to shallow pieces, are fixed to metal base by double-faced adhering tape.

mezzotint, special engraver's screen which gives effect of crayon drawing.

minimum line length, shortest measure in which type can be set for effective reading.

minuscule, small letters of alphabet.

miter, to cut rules at 45-degree angle so they will make snug corner of box.

model's release, formal permission given by subject of photograph for use of picture, especially in advertising.

Modern, ethnic division of Roman type race; face with thicks and thins, swelling of curved strokes and thin, straight, unbracketed serifs.

modified silhouette, halftone plate on which subject is partially outlined and with one or more straight edges.

mold, small box on linecaster which determines size of slug that carries line of relief type.

Monotone, race of type including Gothic and Sans Serifs made up of strokes of equal weight and without serifs.

Morisawa, trademarked name for phototypesetting machine used especially for display sizes.

mortise, to cut area out of halftone

(*mortise cont'd*)
plate so that type or another picture may be inserted. Such opening cut out of the corner of rectangular plate is notch or external mortise. Opening completely surrounded by plate is internal mortise; that surrounded on three sides is bay.

mouthpiece, orifice through which molten type metal is forced against row of linecaster matrices.

multiface perforator, one that produces perforated tape for actuating linecaster not using unit matrices (*which see*).

N

naked column, one without a headline or art at its top.

nameplate, flag, logo, name of newspaper in display form as it appears on page one. Erroneously called masthead.

neck, link, connecting element between bowls of *g*.

negative, film material in which image is transparent against black background. Also, any reproduction in which black-on-white image has been transformed to white-on-black. Also, white area around or within black or dark images.

news row, that section of composing room primarily concerned with compositing and making up editorial material.

N-matter, type set at regular 1-column measure when used with wider measures to make page in W-format (*which see*), or to accommodate advertising to optimum format (*which see*).

noise, static, extraneous and distracting matter, visual or audible, injected into communications system.

nonpareil, 6-point spacing slug. Also,

(*nonpareil cont'd*)
name once used to designate 6-point type.

no-orphan technique, oriented layout (*which see*).

notch, mortise that removes rectangle from one corner of halftone plate.

Novelty, subdivision of Ornamented type race in which letter form is changed drastically.

NRM, next to reading matter, instructions given by most advertisers for the placement of their ad.

number, issue of newspaper, all versions of newspaper produced on one day consisting of one or more editions (*which see*).

nut-and-nut, style of indenting body type 1 en at each end of line.

O

Oblique, letterform which slants to right. In Roman race only this form is Italic.

offset, abbreviation for offset lithography.

Offsetter, trademarked name for machine that produces strikeon composition by telegraphic impulses rather than customary readout of Teletypesetter.

offset lithography, planographic printing process in which image is transferred from printing plate to rubber blanket, then set off to paper.

Old English, family in Text race, often used incorrectly to designate race itself.

Old Style, subdivision of Roman type race in which serifs are bracketed and difference between thin and thick strokes is minimized.

1½-up, flatout technique in which 1½ columns of space is added to that occupied by type set 1½ columns wide.

1-up, layout technique which uses one more column of space than of type; also called flatout.

on the hook, typewritten copy awaiting conversion into set type.

opaque, to remove from negative unwanted flaws such as shadows of pasted-on material, dust specks, etc.

op-ed, opposite editorial, page of comment facing editorial page.

open format, one in which column rules are replaced by alleys.

operator, printer who mans Linotype or any keyboard used in typesetting.

optical center, point 10% above mathematical center of page.

optical magnets, typographic elements of strong interest to readers.

optimum format, one which uses body type in measure at or near optimum line length.

optimum line length, that which is easiest to read, at higher speed, with lower fatigue and with maximum comprehension.

oriented layout, buddy system, no-orphan technique, one in which all elements are studiedly aligned on common vertical and horizontal axes.

Ornamented, type race in which decorative additions are made to face, or letterform is drastically changed.

overlay, sheet of transparent plastic placed over drawing and on which is drawn those areas to be printed in color or are written instructions to platemaker.

overline, display type above picture.

overset, type in excess of what can be used for given issue and too timely to be held for future use.

over-the-roof, skyline banner.

Oxford rule, border consisting of heavy and light rule in parallel pairs.

oxidation, process of ink drying as solvent unites with oxygen in air.

P

page proof, first impression of whole form.

panel, cartoon consisting of single rectangle, in contrast to strip which is made up of several sections in horizontal arrangement.

parallel line, special engraver's screen which creates halftone effect by parallel lines of varying thickness.

paste-and-Stat, method of producing experimental newspaper pages by pasting new elements over undesired ones, then making photocopy.

pasteon, disposable cold-type characters arranged and affixed to a mechanical (*which see*).

pasteup, mechanical (*which see*). Also, in two words, to prepare mechanical.

Perpendicular, conventional, upright letterform. Used only when emphasizing contrast to oblique form.

phonogram, picture of sound, a character of the alphabet.

photocopy, reproduction of advertisement or page made by reflected light and chemical development.

photoengraver, craftsman who produces relief printing plates by action of light and acid.

photoengraving, cut, relief printing plate made by actions of light on sensitized metal and acid on unexposed portions. Also, process of manufacturing such plates.

photographic matrix, photographic image of mechanical from which is made offset plate without use of negative.

Photo-Lathe, trademarked name for mechanical engraving machine that makes parallel-line halftones and line cuts in zinc.

photo lithography, offset printing (*which see*).

Photon, trademarked name for sophisticated phototypesetting machine.

photo offset, offset printing (*which see*).

Photostat, trademarked name for photocopying machine. Also, photocopy so made. Also, misused as generic term for all photocopies.

phototype, images of letterforms placed photographically on film or paper, cold type.

pica, unit of printer's measurement, 12 points. Also, name formerly used to designate 12-point type.

picture, photographic communication, used in contrast to photograph, which may be solely ornamental.

pinched, stroke of Gothic letterform narrowed as it meets stem to allow adequate void.

planographic, printing process, such as lithography, in which image in neither raised nor recessed from plate surface.

platemaker, craftsman who produces photoengravings or offset or gravure printing plates.

platen, flat surface which impresses paper against inked type in simple printing press. Also, roll holding paper on typewriter.

platen press, clamshell, clapper, simple machine in which paper, held on flat surface is pressed against type form.

POA, primary optical area (*which see*).

point, printer's unit of measurement, approximately $\frac{1}{72}$ inch, actually

(*point cont'd*)

.01384. Also, any punctuation mark.

porkchop, thumbnail, half-column portrait.

positive, reproduction in which image appears black on white or transparent background.

poster makeup, that commonly used for page one by tabloid newspapers; consists of large photo and few headlines, without body type.

pot, receptacle for molten type metal in linecaster.

precede (accent on first syllable), explanatory matter that runs before news story. Also spelled phonetically, preseed.

prepack, technique of making up editorial matter as advertising is, free from normal column increments, and well in advance of use.

preprint, advertising printed on rolls of paper which are then rewound and shipped to newspapers to thread into their own press. Most frequently printing is by gravure, although offset is also used. *See* Hi-Fi and Spectacolor.

preseed, precede (*which see*).

pressman, printer who mans machinery that imprints image on paper.

press plate, stereotype from which actual printing is done.

primary letter, minuscules without ascenders or descenders.

primary optical area, POA, top left corner of page or subdivision thereof, where reading eye first enters.

printer, technically craftsman who makes up forms or operates presses but expanded to compositors and, often, proofreaders, on newspaper. Also, machine such as Teletype that produces typewritten

(*printer cont'd*)

copy from instructions sent by wire or radio.

printer's devil, young apprentice believed, in early days of printing, to be emissary of Satan.

printing element, any relief or incised metal object or chemical plate that places an ink image on paper.

process color, system of printing three primary colors to reproduce full spectrum of nature.

progression, general arrangement of contents in newspaper.

proof, rough print of type or plate used to detect errors. Also, relatively hastily made photoprint to show content of negative. *See also* repro and galley.

proofpress, simple machine for producing impressions used to detect errors in type form.

proofreader, person who examines rough impressions to detect and instruct correction of typographic errors.

proportional spacing, typewriter that allots different widths to different characters.

ProType, trademarked name for simple machine for producing phototype, especially in display sizes.

prove (often perverted to proof), to make rough impression of type form to detect errors.

pull-out, independently numbered portion of tabloid newspaper designed to be removed and thus become second section.

punch, mirror image of character made in high relief of hard metal used to impress, in softer metal, matrix from which type is cast.

pyramid, advertising on newspaper page. Also, pattern for arranging advertising roughly as one or two triangles on page. Also, abbrevia-

(*pyramid cont'd*)
tion for inverted pyramid, headline form.

Q

quad, quadrat, piece of metal less than type-high used for spacing.

quadrant makeup, technique in which newspaper page is divided into quarters, each of which is made up as relatively independent area.

quadrat, quad, blank printing element for spacing.

quoin, metal wedge, used in pairs, to hold page of type firmly in chase.

R

race, primary division of type faces.

radial leaders (pronounced leeders), those made with rounded printing surface to avoid damage to press blankets.

ragged right, unjustified type.

rail, on the, setting type from duplexes of matrices.

raw tape, that perforated without division into lines.

razzle-dazzle, circus makeup, flamboyant page patterns.

readability, characteristic which makes it easy to read large masses of body type.

readability range, extent of line lengths easy and pleasant to read.

reader, tape, mechanism that converts code in perforated tape to linecaster operations.

reader ads, also reeders, short sales messages set in body type and mixed in columns with editorial matter.

reader exposure, number or percentage of people who pause to observe any material on newspaper page.

reader traffic, movement of reader through all pages of newspaper.

read-in, style of cutlines in which display type is part of sentence continued in body size.

reading diagonal, broadly defined path of eye from top left to lower right during reading of page.

readout, smaller headline between banner and story.

read-through, style of cutlines in which opening phrase is set in boldface and/or all-caps.

receiver, in communications theory, person who sees or hears, then comprehends, message.

reeder, reader ad.

reefer, line or two of type, set into news story, that refers reader to associated material elsewhere in paper.

reflex, system of making photocopies or offset plates by light reflected from original art rather than through negative.

reglet, strip of wood, usually 1 pica wide, used for spacing in type form, especially to create alleys.

relief, printing method in which raised characters or elements capture and deposit ink.

reperforator, mechanism attached to Teletype which produces perforated type as well as hard copy.

repro, reproduction proof, impression printed with great care and used as copy for platemaking.

reproduction type, that used to make repro (*which see*).

retouch, to correct errors or strengthen weaknesses in photograph.

reverse, printing plate or area with black background on which type appears in white. Also, photographic or chemical process that converts black-on-white image to white-on-black.

reverse kicker, hammer (*which see*).

ribbon, shallow horizontal area, especially that no deeper than 2 inches, above ad not quite full page deep.

rim, group of copyreaders who sit around desk (often horseshoe-shaped) who prepare copy for composing room according to instructions of supervising editor sitting within opening, in the slot.

ring machine, Linotype used primarily for setting correction lines.

rising initial, first letter of word in large size and/or ornamental form that aligns with first line of body type and projects above type block.

river, unwanted strips of white space within blocks of body type resulting from excessive spacing between words.

rolling a mat, making stereotype flong (*which see*).

Roman, type race characterized by thinning and swelling of curved strokes and with serifs. Also, perpendicular form of this race. Used erroneously instead of Perpendicular for other type races.

Roman a, see a, Roman.

ROP, run of press, color printed on ordinary newspaper press. Also, that matter in newspaper not given and not requiring special position.

rotary, printing press in which image on curved surface prints on continuous roll of paper.

rotogravure, process of intaglio printing (*which see*) on endless roll of paper.

rough, rough dummy, sketchy same-size drawing showing placement of typographic elements in form.

roundups, collection of small items on similar topic combined into single story or running under single headline.

rule, element that prints line or lines simpler than those of border.

runaround, body type set at various measures so it forms opening into which picture or display type can be inserted.

run-if, at-will; advertisements, usually small, that run only when there is room for them.

run-in, technique in which catchline becomes part of sentence continuing in cutlines.

running dummy, rough plan for arranging newspaper page prepared before all available material is on hand and consequently often revised.

runover, Dutch wrap (*which see*).

S

saddle, style of gathering and binding pages in which once-folded sheets are successively inserted into similarly folded ones.

sandwich, interpolated notice in column of body type calling reader's attention to associated material on other pages. Usually enclosed with decorative rules top and bottom.

Sans Serifs, ethnic division of Monotone type race (*which see*), usually with curves more graceful than those of Gothic.

scale, to determine size of plate to be made from artwork of specified size.

Scan-A-Graver, trademarked name for mechanical engraver that produces plastic halftone relief plates by burning away unwanted areas with heated stylus.

schedule, headline, all headlines used in newspaper.

schlock, heavy, unattractive advertising.

scorch, to drive excess moisture from flong prior to casting. This process

(*scorch cont'd*)
combines with forming, curving flong into semicylinder.

screamer, banner head (*which see*).

screen, device used to reduce continuous-tone original art to halftone plate. Also, designation for fineness of halftone so produced, e.g., 85-line screen indicates plate with 85 rows of halftone dots per linear inch. Also, to reduce tone of black areas of art or type by superimposing pattern of white dots on printing surface.

Script, subdivision of Written type race in which characters are connected.

second-impression page, that on back of previously printed sheet of paper and which often permits better reproduction of halftones.

second-strike, those pages of newspapers which are printed after reverse side is printed, and which usually create better reproduction of halftones.

section logo, display device, usually combining miniature of newspaper flag, which identifies section.

section page, break, split, front, Z, first page of any section beyond first.

self-contained picture, that which runs in newspaper without accompanying story.

sender, in communications theory, originator of message.

separation, color, method of making plate by means of chromatic filters for each of primary colors for process printing. Also, negative or photoprint that shows only one of the primary colors in exact strengths as it appears in full-color original.

sequence, series of pictures showing

(*sequence cont'd*)
consecutive action at short intervals.

series, subdivision of family of type.

serif, small finishing stroke at end of main strokes of letter.

set, width, in thousandths of inch, of *M* in font of unit matrices (*which see*).

set off, transfer, often undesirable, of ink from printed to facing sheet of paper. In offset lithography, deliberate transfer of image from rubber blanket to printed sheet.

set tight, instructions to compositor to minimize space between words.

7-format, 1-up technique for whole newspaper page in which seven normal newspaper columns are placed on area normally occupied by eight.

sexn, abbreviation for section page.

shade, value of hue obtained by adding black to color.

Shaded, Ornamented typeface with alterations made on printing surface of character.

shading line, thin white line near one side of strokes of type character.

shading sheet, transparent plastic with regular pattern of lines or dots, in black or white, for adding gray tones to line drawings.

Shadowed, subdivision of Ornamented type race with additions outside strokes of character.

sheet-fed, gravure printing produced on single pieces of paper as compared to endless roll used in rotogravure.

shoot down, to make printing plate smaller than original art.

shotgun head, single headline carrying two decks, each with its own story.

shoulder, space at sides of piece of type.

shrinkage, narrowing of stereotype flong during scorching process.

sidebar, closely related story subordinate to main one.

side heads, wickets and tripods (*which see*).

sideless box, decorative rule or border at top and bottom only of type block.

sideline, line of display type under picture and immediately at left of cutlines.

signature, group of pages printed on single sheet of paper prior to folding and cutting to create individual pages.

silhouette, halftone plate from which entire background has been removed.

single-character matrices, Linotype mats, usually in display sizes, that do not carry a duplex.

skyline, headline, usually without accompanying body type, at top of page one.

slot, chief copy editor who occupies seat inside horseshoe-shaped desk and directs work of copyreaders who sit around outside, the rim.

slug, piece of spacing material 6 points thick. Also, line of type from linecaster. Also, usually as "slug line," word or phrase used to identify story in composing room.

slug line, significant word or two that identifies story throughout its processing.

small cap, a letter in the form of a capital but about two-thirds its size.

soc (pronounced sock), society, women's pages or section.

solid, type set without additional interlineal spacing.

sorority drape, costume consisting of plain black fabric over shoulders and forming deep V neckline, used

(*sorority drape cont'd*)
to maintain conformity among portraits of women.

space, advertising areas in newspaper, especially in sense of salable commodity.

spaceband, device of two interacting wedges which produces equal space between words in linecaster composition and thus lines of equal measure.

specialized decks, hammers, kickers, wickets, and tripods (*which see*).

special screen, one used by platemakers to create halftone effect by means other than regular pattern of dots.

special taper, spaceband for Linotype that produces maximum range of spaces between words.

Spectacolor, preprinted advertising, usually by rotogravure, with precise top and bottom margins.

split page, front page of any section beyond first.

spot, ornamental typographic element or small drawing.

spot color, flat color, any other than process.

spread, double spread, two facing pages, especially in magazine or book. Center spread is one at center of publication so both pages are printed on same sheet.

spur, sharp projection at bottom of vertical stroke of G.

squared off, blocked, advertisements placed so the top line of the mass is straight.

Square Serifs, type race of monotonal strokes and heavy serifs. Egyptian Squares have serifs as heavy as main strokes; American Squares have serifs heavier than main strokes.

S/S, same size, instruction to platemaker.

standing heads, those which are re-used without change.

Stat, abbreviation for Photostat (*which see*).

static, noise, extraneous and distracting oral or visual material in communications system.

stem, vertical stroke in letterform, especially that which meets bowl or arms.

stepped head, one in which, with lines of approximately equal length, first is flush left, last flush right, and middle, if any, centered.

stereo, abbreviation for stereotype, used to describe matrices, casts and process.

stereotype, process in which printing plate is cast from mold, flong, of paper made from original type form. Also, printing plate, curved or flat, so cast.

stereotyper, craftsman who makes flat or curved printing plates by casting typemetal into mold of laminated paper.

stereotype matrix, mold of typographic elements made of paper in laminated layers and used to cast stereotype plate.

stick, metal receptacle in which type is gathered during composing.

stickful, rough measure for composition, about 2 column-inches.

stick-on, alphabet characters printed in white or black on paper or self-adhesive plastic sheets for arrangement into cold-type composition.

stickup initial, rising initial (*which see*).

stone, working surface—once slate or marble, now steel—on which printing forms are made up.

straight matter, body composition as contrasted to display matter. Also, editorial matter as contrasted to advertising.

straight run, method of printing several copies of newspaper simultaneously. *See* collect run.

streamer, banner headline (*which see*).

strikeon, composition produced by typewriter or similar machine.

stripcaster, machine that casts rules, borders, spacing material, etc., in long, narrow form.

strip comics, those in horizontal area made up of several smaller rectangles.

strip in, to combine headline so it surprints on halftone. Also, to combine line and halftone negatives prior to making offset plates.

studhorse, large, dark type and advertising using it with heavy rules and borders.

style, consistent literary or typographic usage as established for a specific publication.

subhead, short line of centered boldface capitals used to break up large masses of body type.

summary, copy, usually on page one, that combines condensed versions of news stories with index.

summary head, headline form that gives brief condensation of news story.

sunken initial, inset initial (*which see*).

swash, decorative, elongated stroke of letter. Also, letter so decorated.

swing magazine, to replace whole magazine of matrices on linecaster with one used only occasionally.

symmetrical, page pattern in which each element is balanced exactly by another of same size.

system, in communications theory, physical area or equipment through which message moves from sender to receiver.

T

tabloid, tab, newspaper format with page approximately 11 x 15 inches. Also, journalistic approach concentrating on frothy content and flashy display.

tail, tiny straight stroke on *Q* and curved portion of *g* below baseline.

tailgate, to run experimental pages at end of regular press run.

take, smaller amount of copy, type, paper, etc., into which large job is divided for convenience and efficiency for one or more workers.

tape, narrow ribbons of paper with perforations in code that actuate linecasters.

tape puncher, printer who produces coded tape by actuating keyboard.

teaser head, one which piques interest of reader by only hinting at content of story.

Teletype, trademarked name for machine that produces typewritten copy from code carried by telegraph or radio.

tempera, poster paint used to retouch photographs.

terminal area, lower right portion of printed page.

Text, Black Letter, race of type. Erroneously called Old English. Also, body type. Also, verbatim reprint of speech or official document.

30-dash, typographic device indicating end of story in typewritten or typeset form.

3-em dash, thin horizontal line three times as wide as height of typeface it is used with.

3-em space, material to create blank area one-third as wide as height of type face it is used with.

thumbnail, small, hastily drawn dummy for advertisement. Also,

(*thumbnail cont'd*)
half-column portraits. Also, single quotation mark or apostrophe.

time matter (short for anytime), that feature copy which does not demand immediate use.

tint, value of color created by mixing white with hue.

tint block, printing element that lays down simple mass of color, with no detail, over which is printed type or art.

title page, first page of any section after first. *See* section page.

tombstone, bumped, headlines side by side.

tone, value, relative darkness of page or block of type or photograph.

tower, chimney, vertical arrangement of horizontal elements in newspaper page.

Transitional, subdivision of Roman type race with characteristics of both Old Style and Modern forms.

trapped space, area of white space completely surrounded by typographic elements.

tripod, headline form of a single line of large type at immediate left of two lines of smaller type.

TTS, Teletypesetter, trademarked name for machine that actuates linecaster from code in perforated tape.

turning the rules, recently revived practice of showing mourning by reversing column rules so broad irregular base prints.

turtle, steel table, usually just large enough to hold single page, on which printing form is made up.

2-digit code, system of designating headlines in which first digit indicates column width and second, relative weight.

type, rectangular block of metal from which protrudes character, or line

(*type cont'd*)
of characters, in relief. Also, such blocks collectively. Also, similar pieces on a typewriter. Also, printed characters. Also, negatives of such characters used to produce photographic images.

typeface, reference to type stressing style or design.

type high, .918 inches, standard distance from bed of press or stone to printing surface of all relief elements.

type library, all type faces and rules, borders, and ornaments available for use in one printing establishment.

type metal, eutectic alloy of lead, tin, and antimony.

typo, abbreviation of typographic error.

typographic color, density of gray effected by mass of type.

typographic error, error in setting made by typesetter.

typographic style manual, codification of all approved uses of type elements in newspaper.

typography, basic philosophy regarding use of printing elements.

Typosetter, trademarked name for machine that produces display sizes of photographic type.

typositor, craftsman who sets type and arranges it in page form.

U

u&lc, upper-and-lowercase, style of setting type which capitalizes each word.

underpinning, metal blocks used to support printing surface of Ludlow type slugs.

underscored, typographic elements, especially headlines, which are given added weight by a rule immediately beneath them.

unit matrices, those for keyboarded linecaster designed with constant ratio of widths of letters, required for setting type by wire tape.

uppercase, capital letters.

V

value, tone, weight of color, type masses or photographs measured by comparison to gray.

Varityper, trademarked name for strikeon machine for producing justified columns. All type characters are on single bar, which makes possible quick and easy changing of face.

Velox, trademarked name for photoprint with image in halftone-dot pattern rather than continuous tones.

Venetian, Transitional Roman letterform.

vertex, junction of two diagonal strokes at bottom of letter such as *V.*

vertical makeup, page pattern in which no element crosses column rule or alley between columns 4 and 5.

void, blank areas around and within type character.

volume, all issues of newspaper published within one year. Volume of newspaper thus indicates its age.

W

W-format, that which uses several normal columns with wider one, usually 1½-column, to allow room for alleys.

W-matter, that set wider than 1 column for use in W-format.

wave rule, one which prints undulating line.

web, wide strip of paper feeding off roll and winding through rotary printing press.

weight, relative thickness of strokes comprising type character.

well, deep, narrow opening for editorial matter between two steep ad pyramids, especially when clear to bottom of page.

wicket, headline with two short lines of small type immediately at left of single larger line.

widow, type line shorter than full measure, usually 50% or less.

width, basic variation of letterform that results in Condensed or Extended forms.

wire copy, editorial matter supplied by outside sources, especially that transmitted by telegraph or Teletype from news services.

wire tape, that perforated by impulses transmitted by telegraph and used to actuate linecasters.

wraparound, thin relief printing plate

(*wraparound cont'd*) wrapped around a cylinder to utilize principles of rotary-press.

wrapper page, first page of any section after first. *See* section page.

Written, type race resembling form of casual writing.

X

x-height, distance between baseline and meanline of type.

Z

zinc, common synonym for all photo-engravings, even those of copper or magnesium.

Zip-A-Tone, trademarked name for shading sheets (*which see*).

zombie, style of setting body type with hyphenation at any point, not only between syllables.

Z-page, first page of any section after first. *See* section page.

Index